Your Companion Site — Even more help for studying!

bedfordstmartins.com/mckaywest

FREE Online Study Guide—Improve your performance!
Get immediate feedback on your progress with

- Quizzing
- Key terms review
- Map and visual activities
- Timeline activities
- Note-taking outlines

FREE History Research and Writing Help
Refine your research skills, evaluate sources, and organize your findings with

- *Make History* maps, documents, images, and Web sites
- History Research and Reference Sources
- More Sources and How to Format a History Paper
- Build a Bibliography
- Tips on Avoiding Plagiarism

A History of Western Society

■ Henry Lamb, *A Soldier of Free France*, 1941.

A History of Western Society

VOLUME C
From the Revolutionary Era to the Present

Tenth Edition

John P. McKay
University of Illinois at Urbana-Champaign

Bennett D. Hill
Late of Georgetown University

John Buckler
University of Illinois at Urbana-Champaign

Clare Haru Crowston
University of Illinois at Urbana-Champaign

Merry E. Wiesner-Hanks
University of Wisconsin–Milwaukee

Joe Perry
Georgia State University

BEDFORD/ST. MARTIN'S

Boston • New York

FOR BEDFORD/ST. MARTIN'S

Publisher for History: Mary Dougherty
Director of Development for History: Jane Knetzger
Executive Editor for History: Traci Mueller Crowell
Senior Developmental Editor for History: Laura Arcari
Senior Production Editor: Christina Horn
Senior Production Supervisor: Nancy Myers
Executive Marketing Manager: Jenna Bookin Barry
Associate Editor: Lynn Sternberger
Production Assistant: Alexis Biasell
Senior Art Director: Anna Palchik
Text Design: Brian Salisbury
Copyeditor: Sybil Sosin
Map Editor: Charlotte Miller
Indexer: Leoni Z. McVey
Page Layout: Boynton Hue Studio
Photo Research: Carole Frohlich and Elisa Gallagher, The Visual
Connection Image Research, Inc.

Cover Design: Billy Boardman
Cover Art: Henry Lamb (English, 1885–1960), *A Soldier of Free France*, 1941. Oil on canvas. Photo: The Art Archive/Imperial War Museum.
Cartography: Mapping Specialists, Ltd.
Composition: NK Graphics
Printing and Binding: RR Donnelley and Sons

President: Joan E. Feinberg
Editorial Director: Denise B. Wydra
Director of Marketing: Karen R. Soeltz
Director of Editing, Design, and Production: Susan W. Brown
Assistant Director of Editing, Design, and Production: Elise S. Kaiser
Managing Editor: Elizabeth M. Schaaf

Library of Congress Control Number: 2010920486

Manufactured in the United States of America.

1 2 3 4 5 6   14 13 12 11 10

For information, write: Bedford/St. Martin's, 75 Arlington Street, Boston, MA 02116 (617-399-4000)

ISBN-10: 0-312-68773-7   ISBN-13: 978-0-312-68773-1 (combined edition)
ISBN-10: 0-312-64059-5   ISBN-13: 978-0-312-64059-0 (Vol. 1)
ISBN-10: 0-312-64060-9   ISBN-13: 978-0-312-64060-6 (Vol. 2)
ISBN-10: 0-312-64061-7   ISBN-13: 978-0-312-64061-3 (Vol. A)
ISBN-10: 0-312-64062-5   ISBN-13: 978-0-312-64062-0 (Vol. B)
ISBN-10: 0-312-64063-3   ISBN-13: 978-0-312-64063-7 (Vol. C)
ISBN-10: 0-312-63827-2   ISBN-13: 978-0-312-63827-6 (Since 1300)
ISBN-10: 0-312-64058-7   ISBN-13: 978-0-312-64058-3 (Since 1300 for Advanced Placement)

▪ Brief Contents

■ Contents

20 The Revolution in Politics
1775–1815   618

21 The Revolution in Energy and Industry
ca. 1780–1850   654

22 Ideologies and Upheavals
1815–1850   684

23 Life in the Emerging Urban Society
1840–1900 716

24 The Age of Nationalism
1850–1914 748

25 The West and the World
1815–1914   780

26 War and Revolution
1914–1919   814

27 The Age of Anxiety
ca. 1900–1940   852

28 Dictatorships and the Second World War
1919–1945   886

29 Cold War Conflict and Consensus
1945–1965   922

30 Challenging the Postwar Order
1960–1991   958

31 Europe in an Age of Globalization
1990 to the Present   994

Maps, Figures, and Tables

Maps

Figures and Tables

▪ Special Features

Living in the Past

Listening to the Past

Individuals in Society

▪ Preface

With this, the tenth edition of *A History of Western Society*, we invite our colleagues and current and past adopters to join us in seeing the book as if for the first time. For us, this edition—undertaken at a new publishing house—has been an opportunity to revisit our original vision and to thereby realize the most thorough reconsideration of our text since we first began. *A History of Western Society* grew out of the initial three authors' desire to infuse new life into the study of Western Civilization. We knew that historians were using imaginative questions and innovative research to open up vast new areas of historical interest and knowledge. At that point, social history was dramatically changing the ways we understood the past, and we decided to create a book that would re-create the lives of ordinary people in appealing human terms, while also giving major economic, political, cultural, and intellectual developments the attention they unquestionably deserve. The three new authors who have joined the original author team—and who first used the book as students or teachers—remain committed to advancing this vision for today's classroom. With its new look, line-by-line edits aimed at increasing the book's readability and accessibility, reinvigorated scholarship, and broader definition of social history that reflects where instructors and students are now, we've rethought every element of the book to bring the original vision into the twenty-first century and make the past memorable for a new generation of students and instructors.

History as a discipline never stands still, and over the last several decades cultural history has joined social history as a source of dynamism. Because of its emphasis on the ways people made sense of their lives, *A History of Western Society* has always included a large amount of cultural history, ranging from foundational works of philosophy and literature to popular songs and stories. The focus on cultural history has been heightened in this tenth edition in a way that highlights the interplay between men's and women's lived experiences and the ways men and women reflect on these experiences to create meaning. The joint social and cultural perspective requires—fortunately, in our opinion—the inclusion of objects as well as texts as important sources for studying history, which has allowed us to incorporate the growing emphasis on material culture in the work of many historians.

These new directions have not changed the central mission of the book, which is to introduce students to the broad sweep of Western Civilization in a fresh yet balanced manner. Every edition has incorporated new research to keep the book up-to-date and respond to the changing needs of readers and instructors, and we have continued to do this in the tenth edition. As we have made these changes, large and small, we have sought to give students and teachers an integrated perspective so that they could pursue—on their own or in the classroom—the historical questions that they find particularly exciting and significant.

Textual Changes

For the tenth edition we took the time to revisit, reconsider, and revise every paragraph of the book. We paid painstaking attention to the writing, and we're proud of the results. Informed by recent scholarship, every chapter was revised with an aim toward readability and accessibility. Several main lines of revision have guided our many changes. In particular, as noted above, we have broadened the book's focus on social history to include a greater emphasis on cultural history. This increased emphasis is supported in every chapter by the use of artifacts that make history tangible and by the new Living in the Past visual feature, described below, that demonstrates the intersection between society and culture. In addition, the social and cultural context of Western Civilization has been integrated throughout the narrative, including expanded and new sections on Egyptian life, common people in Charlemagne's empire, artistic patronage during the Renaissance, identities and communities of the Atlantic world, eighteenth-century education, nineteenth-century family life, consumer society between the two world wars, life under Nazi occupation, and state and society in the East Bloc, among others.

The tenth edition continues to reflect Europe's interactions with the rest of the world and the role of gender in shaping human experience. The global context of European history is reflected in new scholarship on the steppe peoples of Central Asia, Muslim views of the Crusades, the Atlantic world, decolonization, and globalization. New scholarship on gender is woven throughout the book and is included in sections on Frankish queens, medieval prostitution, female humanists, politics and gender during the French Revolution, and gender roles during industrialization.

These major aspects of revision are accompanied by the incorporation of a wealth of new scholarship and subject areas. Additions, among others, include material on Paleolithic and Neolithic life (Chapter 1); the Neo-Babylonians (Chapter 2); the later period of the Roman Empire in the West (Chapter 7); the bubonic plague in eastern Europe (Chapter 12); the Jesuits (Chapter 14); the limits of enlightened absolutism (Chapter 17); eighteenth-century beliefs and practices (Chapter 19); expanded coverage of the peasant revolt (Chapter 20); sections on the Battle of the Somme, waging total war, and the human costs of World War I (Chapter 26); popular support for National Socialism (Chapter 27); the affluent society (Chapter 30); and up-to-date coverage of the economic downturn in Europe, the Iraq War, and the global recession (Chapter 31).

Organizational Changes

To meet the demands of the evolving course, we took a close and critical look at the book's organization, and have made several major changes in the organization of chapters to reflect the way the course is taught today. Chapter 7 now begins in 250 with the reforms of Diocletian and Constantine, and includes material on the debate over the decline of the Roman Empire in the West as well as a more comprehensive discussion of the barbarian migrations. To increase clarity, we've combined the separate chapters on absolutism in western and eastern Europe into a single chapter on absolutism and constitutionalism. Volume 2 also features a completely revised and updated post-1945 section featuring a third, new, postwar chapter, "Europe in an Age of Globalization, 1990 to the Present." In response to the growth in new and exciting scholarship for this period, the postwar chapters have been completely rewritten by new author Joe Perry with new scholarship on decolonization, consumerism as an aspect of the Cold War, new patterns of immigration and guest worker programs, the growth and decline of the welfare state in eastern and western Europe, and Europe's place in an era of increasing globalization, including the challenges to liberalism mounted by new social movements.

Features

We are proud of the diverse special features that expand upon the narrative and offer opportunities for classroom discussion and assignments, and in the new edition we have expanded our offerings to include a brand new feature created in response to current research trends that is sure to get students and instructors talking. This **NEW** visual feature, **Living in the Past**, uses social and cultural history to show how life in the past was both similar to and different from our lives today. Focusing on relatively narrow aspects of social and cultural history to write compelling stories that would encourage students to think about the way the past informs the present was both a challenge and a pleasure. The resulting thirty-one essays—one in each chapter—introduce students to the study of material culture, encourage critical analysis, and engage and inform with fascinating details about life in the past. Richly illustrated with images and artifacts, each feature includes a short essay and questions for analysis.

We use these features to explore the deeper ramifications of things students might otherwise take for granted, such as consumer goods, factories, and even currency. Students connect to the people of the past through a diverse range of topics such as "Assyrian Palace Life and Power," "Roman Table Manners," "Foods of the Columbian Exchange," "Coffeehouse Culture," "The Immigrant Experience," "A Model Socialist Steel Town," and "The Supermarket Revolution."

In our years of teaching Western Civilization, we have often noted that students come alive when they encounter stories about real people in the past. To give students a chance to see the past through ordinary people's lives, each chapter includes one of the popular **Individuals in Society** biographical essays that offer brief studies of individuals or groups, informing students about the societies in which they lived. This feature grew out of our long-standing focus on people's lives and the varieties of historical experience, and we believe that readers will empathize with these human beings as they themselves seek to define their own identities. The spotlighting of individuals, both famous and obscure, perpetuates the book's continued attention to cultural and intellectual developments, highlights human agency, and reflects changing interests within the historical profession as well as the development of "micro-history." **NEW** features include essays on Cyrus the Great; Queen Cleopatra; the Venerable Bede; Meister Eckhart; Rose Bertin, "Minister of Fashion"; Josiah Wedgwood; Germaine de Staël; and Armando Rodrigues, West Germany's "One-Millionth Guest Worker."

Each chapter also continues to include a primary source feature titled **Listening to the Past**, chosen to extend and illuminate a major historical issue through the presentation of a single original source or several voices. Each opens with an introduction and closes with questions for analysis that invite students to evaluate the evidence as historians would. Selected for their interest and importance and carefully fitted into their historical context, these sources allow students to hear the past and to observe how history has been shaped by individuals. **NEW** topics include "Cicero and the Plot to Kill Caesar," "Augustus's *Res Gestae*," "Eirik's Saga," "Perspectives on Humanist Learning and Women," "Denis Diderot's 'Supplement to Bougainville's Voyage,'" "Contrasting Views on the Effects of Rural Industry," "Abbé de Sieyès, 'What Is the Third Estate?,'" "Herder and Mazzini on the Development of Nationalism," "Lin Zexu and Yamagata Aritomo, Confronting Western Imperialism," and "The Nixon-Khrushchev 'Kitchen Debate.'" In addition to using documents as part of our special feature program, we have quoted extensively from a wide variety of primary sources in the narrative, demonstrating that such quotations are the "stuff" of history. We believe that our extensive program of using primary sources as an integral part of the narrative as well as in extended form in the "Listening to the Past" chapter feature will help readers learn to interpret and think critically.

With the goal of making this the most student-centered edition yet, we paid renewed attention to the book's pedagogy. To help guide students, each chapter opens with a **chapter preview with focus questions** keyed to the main chapter headings. These questions are repeated within the chapter and again in **NEW chapter reviews**. Many of the questions have been reframed for this edition, and new summary answers have been added to the chapter review. Each chapter review concludes with a carefully selected list of annotated **suggestions for further reading**, revised and updated to keep them current with the vast amount of new work being done in many fields.

To help students understand the material and prepare for exams, each chapter includes **NEW Looking Back, Looking Ahead** conclusions. Replacing the former chapter summaries, each conclusion provides an insightful synthesis of the chapter's main developments, while connecting to events that students will encounter in the chapters to come. In this way students are introduced to history as an ongoing process of interrelated events.

To promote clarity and comprehension, boldface **key terms** in the text are defined in the margins and listed in the chapter review. **NEW phonetic spellings** are located directly after terms that readers are likely to find hard to pronounce. The **chapter chronologies**, which review major developments discussed in each chapter, have been improved to more closely mirror the key events of the chapter, and the number of topic-specific **thematic chronologies** has been expanded, with new chronologies on "Art and Philosophy in the Hellenic Period" and "Major Figures of the Enlightenment," among others. Once again we also provide a **unified timeline** at the end of the text. Comprehensive and easy to locate, this useful timeline allows students to compare developments over the centuries.

The high-quality art and map program has been thoroughly revised and expanded. The new edition features more than **600 contemporaneous illustrations**. To make the past tangible, and as an extension of our enhanced attention to cultural history, we include over **100 artifacts**—from swords and fans to playing cards and record players. As in earlier editions, all illustrations have been carefully selected to complement the text, and all include captions that inform students while encouraging them to read the text more deeply. Completely redesigned and reconceptualized for the new edition, **87 full-size maps** illustrate major developments in the narrative. In addition, **61 NEW spot maps** are embedded in the narrative to show areas under discussion. **NEW** maps in the tenth edition highlight such topics as the Persian wars, the Hanseatic League, the Russian civil war, the Holocaust, Cold War Europe, pollution in Europe, and the Soviet war in Afghanistan, among others.

We recognize students' difficulties with geography and visual analysis, and the new edition includes the popular **Mapping the Past map activities** and **NEW Picturing the Past visual activities**. Included in each chapter, these activities give students valuable skills in reading and interpreting maps and images by asking them to analyze the maps or visuals and make connections to the larger processes discussed in the narrative. All these activities can be completed online and submitted directly to instructors at the free online study guide.

To showcase the book's rich art program and to signal our commitment to this thorough and deep revision, the book has been completely redesigned. The dynamic new contemporary design engages and assists students with its clear, easy-to-use pedagogy.

Acknowledgments

It is a pleasure to thank the many instructors who read and critiqued the manuscript through its development:

Georgia Bonny Bazemore, Eastern Washington University
John Beeler, University of Alabama
Dudley R. Belcher, Tri-County Technical College
Stephen A. Beluris, Moorpark College
Nancy B. Bjorklund, Fullerton College
Paul Bookbinder, University of Massachusetts, Boston
Edward A. Boyden, Nassau Community College
Harry T. Burgess, St. Clair County Community College
Jacqueline de Vries, Augsburg College
Daniel Finn, Valencia Community College
Jennifer Foray, Purdue University
Gary Forsythe, Texas Tech University
Lucille M. Fortunato, Bridgewater State College
Robert Genter, Nassau Community College
Stephen Gibson, Allegany College of Maryland
Andrew L. Goldman, Gonzaga University
Anthony Heideman, Front Range Community College
Jason M. Kelly, Indiana University
Keith Knutson, Viterbo University
Lynn Lubamersky, Boise State University
Susan A. Maurer, Nassau Community College
Greg Mauriocourt, Technical College of the Lowcountry
Jennifer McNabb, Western Illinois University
Elisa Miller, Rhode Island College
James M. Mini, Montgomery County Community College
Mary Lou Mosley, Paradise Valley Community College
Lisa Ossian, Des Moines Area Community College
Scott W. Palmer, Western Illinois University
Dennis Ricci, Community College of Rhode Island and Quinsigamond Community College
James Robertson, Montgomery County Community College
Daniel Robison, Troy University
Jahan Salehi, Guilford Tech Community College
Carol Longenecker Schmidt, Tri-County Technical College
Robert Shipley, Widener University
Karen Sonnelitter, Purdue University
Donathan Taylor, Hardin-Simmons University
Norman R. West, SUNY at Suffolk
Shelley Wolbrink, Drury University
Robert Zajkowski, Hudson Valley Community College

It is also a pleasure to thank the many editors who have assisted us over the years, first at Houghton Mifflin and now at Bedford/St. Martin's. At Bedford/St. Martin's, these include senior development editor Laura Arcari, with assistance from Beth Welch, for developing the new "Living in the Past" features; freelance development editor Michelle McSweeney; associate editors Lynn Sternberger and Jack Cashman; executive editor Traci Mueller Crowell; director of development Jane Knetzger; publisher for history Mary Dougherty; map editor Charlotte Miller; photo researcher Carole Frohlich; text permissions editor Sandy Schechter; and Christina Horn, senior production editor, with the assistance of Alexis Biasell and the guidance of managing editor Elizabeth Schaaf and assistant managing editor John Amburg. Other key contributors were designer Brian Salisbury, page makeup artist Cia Boynton, copyeditor Sybil Sosin, proofreaders Andrea Martin and Angela Hoover Morrison, indexer Leoni McVey, and cover designer Billy Boardman. We would also like to thank editorial director Denise Wydra and president Joan E. Feinberg.

Many of our colleagues at the University of Illinois, the University of Wisconsin–Milwaukee, and Georgia State University continue to provide information and stimulation, often without even knowing it. We thank them for it. We also thank the many students over the years with whom we have used earlier editions of this book. Their reactions and opinions helped shape the revisions to this edition, and we hope it remains worthy of the ultimate praise that they bestowed on it, that it's "not boring like most textbooks." Merry Wiesner-Hanks would, as always, also like to thank her husband Neil, without whom work on this project would not be possible. Clare Haru Crowston thanks her husband Ali and her children Lili, Reza, and Kian, who are a joyous reminder of the vitality of life that we try to showcase in this book. John McKay expresses his deep appreciation to JoAnn McKay for her keen insights and unfailing encouragement. Joe Perry thanks Andrzej S. Kaminski and the expert team assembled at Lazarski University for their insightful comments and is most grateful to Joyce de Vries for her unstinting support and encouragement.

Each of us has benefited from the criticism of our coauthors, although each of us assumes responsibility for what he or she has written. John Buckler has written the first six chapters; building on text originally written by Bennett Hill, Merry Wiesner-Hanks has assumed primary responsibility for Chapters 7 through 14; building on text originally written by Bennett Hill and John McKay, Clare Crowston has assumed primary responsibility for Chapters 15 through 20; John McKay has written and revised Chapters 21 through 25; and Joe Perry has written and revised Chapters 26 through 31, building on text originally written by John McKay.

▪ Versions and Supplements

A History of Western Society is supported by numerous resources—study tools for students, materials for instructors, and many options for packaging the book with documents readers, trade books, atlases, and other guides—that are free or available at a substantial discount. Descriptions follow; for more information, visit the book's catalog site at **bedfordstmartins.com/mckaywest/catalog**, or contact your local Bedford/St. Martin's sales representative.

Available Versions of This Book

To accommodate different course lengths and course budgets, *A History of Western Society* is available in several different formats, including three-hole punched loose-leaf Budget Books versions and e-books, which are available at a substantial discount.

- Combined edition (Chapters 1–31): available in hardcover, loose-leaf, and e-book formats
- Volume 1, From Antiquity to the Enlightenment (Chapters 1–17): available in paperback, loose-leaf, and e-book formats
- Volume 2, From the Age of Exploration to the Present (Chapters 15–31): available in paperback, loose-leaf, and e-book formats
- Volume A, From Antiquity to 1500 (Chapters 1–13): available in paperback
- Volume B, From the Later Middle Ages to 1815 (Chapters 12–20): available in paperback
- Volume C, From the Revolutionary Era to the Present (Chapters 20–31): available in paperback
- Since 1300 (Chapters 12–31): available in paperback and e-book formats
- Since 1300 for Advanced Placement (Chapters 12–31): available in hardcover and e-book formats

Our innovative e-books give your students the content you want in a convenient format at about half the cost of a print book. **Bedford/St. Martin's e-Books** have been optimized for reading and studying online. **CourseSmart e-Books** can be downloaded or used online, whichever is more convenient for your students.

Companion Site

Our new companion site at **bedfordstmartins.com/mckaywest** gathers free and premium resources, giving students a way to extend *A History of Western Society* online. This book-specific site provides a single destination that students can use to practice, read, write, and study, and to find and access quizzes and activities, study aids, and history research and writing help.

FREE Online Study Guide. Available at the companion site, this popular resource provides students with self-review quizzes and activities for each chapter, including a multiple-choice self-test that focuses on important concepts; an identification quiz that helps students remember key people, places, and events; a flash-card activity that tests students' knowledge of key terms; and map activities to strengthen students' geography skills. Instructors can monitor students' progress through an online Quiz Gradebook or receive e-mail updates.

FREE History Research and Writing Help. Also available at the companion site, this resource includes **History Research and Reference Sources**, with links to history-related databases, indexes, and journals; **More Sources and How to Format a History Paper**, with clear advice on how to integrate primary and secondary sources into research papers and how to cite and format sources correctly; **Build a Bibliography**, a simple Web-based tool that generates bibliographies in four commonly used documentation styles; and **Tips on Avoiding Plagiarism**, an online tutorial that reviews the consequences of plagiarism and features exercises to help students practice integrating sources and recognize acceptable summaries.

Instructor Resources

Bedford/St. Martin's has developed a wide range of teaching resources for this book and for this course. They range from lecture and presentation materials and assessment tools to course management options. Most can be downloaded or ordered at **bedfordstmartins.com/mckaywest/catalog**.

HistoryClass for *A History of Western Society*. HistoryClass, a Bedford/St. Martin's Online Course Space, puts the online resources available with this textbook in one convenient and completely customizable course space. There you can access an interactive e-book and primary sources reader; maps, images, documents, and links; chapter review quizzes; interactive multimedia exercises; and research and writing help. In HistoryClass you can get all our premium content and tools and assign, rearrange, and mix them with your own resources. For more information, visit **yourhistoryclass.com**.

Bedford/St. Martin's Course Cartridges. Whether you use Blackboard, WebCT, Desire2Learn, Angel, Sakai, or Moodle, we have free content and support available to help you plug our content into your course management system. Registered instructors can download cartridges with no hassle and no strings attached. Content includes our most popular free resources and book-specific content for *A History of Western Society*. Visit **bedfordstmartins.com/cms** to see a demo, find your version, or download your cartridge.

Instructor's Resource Manual. The instructor's manual offers both experienced and first-time instructors tools for presenting textbook material in engaging ways. It includes chapter review material, teaching strategies, and a guide to chapter-specific supplements available for the text.

Guide to Changing Editions. Designed to facilitate an instructor's transition from the previous edition of *A History of Western Society* to the current edition, this guide presents an overview of major changes as well as of changes in each chapter.

Computerized Test Bank. The test bank includes a mix of fresh, carefully crafted multiple-choice, definition, short-answer, and essay questions for each chapter. The questions appear in Microsoft Word format and in easy-to-use test bank software that allows instructors to easily add, edit, re-sequence, and print questions and answers. Instructors can also export questions into a variety of formats, including WebCT and Blackboard.

PowerPoint Maps, Images, Lecture Outlines, and i>clicker Content. These presentation materials are downloadable individually from the Media and Supplements tab at **bedfordstmartins.com/mckaywest/catalog** and are available on *The Bedford Lecture Kit Instructor's Resource CD-ROM*. They include ready-made and fully customizable PowerPoint multimedia presentations built around lecture outlines with embedded maps, figures, and selected images from the textbook and with detailed instructor notes on key points. Also available are maps and selected images in JPEG and Power-Point formats; content for i>clicker, a classroom response system, in Microsoft Word and PowerPoint formats; the Instructor's Resource Manual in Microsoft Word format; and outline maps in PDF format for quizzing or handing out. All files are suitable for copying onto transparency acetates.

Overhead Map Transparencies. This set of full-color acetate transparencies includes 130 maps for the Western Civilization course.

Make History: Free Documents, Maps, Images, and Web Sites. Finding the source material you need is simple with Make History. Here the best Web resources are combined with hundreds of carefully chosen maps and images and helpfully annotated. Browse the collection of thousands of resources by course or by topic, date, and type. Available at **bedfordstmartins.com/makehistory**.

Videos and Multimedia. A wide assortment of videos and multimedia CD-ROMs on various topics in Western Civilization is available to qualified adopters through your Bedford/St. Martin's sales representative.

Packaging Opportunities

Save your students money and package your favorite text with more! For information on free packages and discounts of up to 50 percent, visit **bedfordstmartins.com/mckaywest/**

catalog, or contact your local Bedford/St. Martin's sales representative.

e-Book. The e-book for this title can be packaged with the print text at no additional cost.

Sources of Western Society, **Second Edition**. This primary-source collection—available in Volume 1, Volume 2, and Since 1300 versions—provides a revised and expanded selection of sources to accompany *A History of Western Society*, Tenth Edition. Each chapter features five or six written and visual sources by well-known figures and ordinary individuals alike. Now including nineteen visual sources and 30 percent more documents, this edition offers both breadth and depth. A new Viewpoints feature highlights two or three sources that address the same topic from different perspectives. Document headnotes and reading and discussion questions promote student understanding. Available free when packaged with the text.

Sources of Western Society **e-Book**. The reader is also available as an e-book. When packaged with the print or electronic version of the textbook, it is free.

Rand McNally Atlas of Western Civilization. This collection of over fifty full-color maps highlights social, political, and cross-cultural change and interaction from classical Greece and Rome to the postindustrial Western world. Each map is thoroughly indexed for fast reference. Available for $3.00 when packaged with the text.

The Bedford Glossary for European History. This handy supplement for the survey course gives students historically contextualized definitions for hundreds of terms—from *Abbasids* to *Zionism*—that they will encounter in lectures, reading, and exams. Available free when packaged with the text.

The Bedford Series in History and Culture. More than one hundred titles in this highly praised series combine first-rate scholarship, historical narrative, and important primary documents for undergraduate courses. Each book is brief, inexpensive, and focused on a specific topic or period. For a complete list of titles, visit **bedfordstmartins.com/bshc**. Package discounts are available.

Trade Books. Titles published by sister companies Hill and Wang; Farrar, Strauss and Giroux; Henry Holt and Company; St. Martin's Press; Picador; and Palgrave Macmillan are available at a 50 percent discount when packaged with Bedford/St. Martin's textbooks. For more information, visit **bedfordstmartins.com/tradeup**.

The Social Dimension of Western Civilization. Combining current scholarship with classic pieces, this reader's forty-eight secondary sources, compiled by Richard M. Golden, hook students with the fascinating and often surprising details of how everyday Western people worked, ate, played, celebrated, worshiped, married, procreated, fought, persecuted, and died. Package discounts are available.

The West in the Wider World: Sources and Perspectives. Edited by Richard Lim and David Kammerling Smith, the first college reader to focus on the central historical question "How did the West become the West?" offers a wealth of written and visual source materials that reveal the influence of non-European regions on the origins and development of Western Civilization. Package discounts are available.

A Pocket Guide to Writing in History. This portable and affordable reference tool by Mary Lynn Rampolla provides reading, writing, and research advice useful to students in all history courses. Concise yet comprehensive advice on approaching typical history assignments, developing critical reading skills, writing effective history papers, conducting research, using and documenting sources, and avoiding plagiarism—enhanced by practical tips and examples throughout—have made this slim reference a bestseller. Package discounts are available.

A Student's Guide to History. This complete guide provides the practical help students need to be successful in any history course. In addition to introducing students to the nature of the discipline, author Jules Benjamin teaches a wide range of skills from preparing for exams to approaching common writing assignments, and explains the research and documentation process with plentiful examples. Package discounts are available.

20
The Revolution in Politics

1775–1815

The last years of the eighteenth century were a time of great upheaval as a series of revolutions and wars challenged the old order of monarchs and aristocrats. The ideas of freedom and equality, ideas that have not stopped shaping the world since that era, flourished and spread. The revolutionary era began in North America in 1775. Then in 1789 France, the most populous country in western Europe and a center of culture and intellectual life, became the leading revolutionary nation. It established first a constitutional monarchy, then a radical republic, and finally a new empire under Napoleon that would last until 1815. During this period of constant domestic turmoil, French armies violently exported revolution beyond the nation's borders, eager to establish new governments throughout much of Europe. Inspired both by the ideals of the Revolution on the continent and by internal colonial conditions, the slaves of Saint-Domingue rose up in 1791. Their rebellion would eventually lead to the creation of the new independent nation of Haiti in 1804. In Europe and its colonies abroad, the world of modern politics was born. ■

Life in Revolutionary France. On the eve of the French Revolution, angry crowds like this one gathered in Paris to protest the high-handed actions of the royal government. Throughout the Revolution, decisive events took place in the street as much as in the chambers of the National Assembly.

CHAPTER PREVIEW

Background to Revolution
■ What social, political, and economic factors formed the background to the French Revolution?

Politics and the People, 1789–1791
■ How did the events of 1789 result in a constitutional monarchy in France, and how did the new constitution affect the various members of French society at home and in the colony of Saint-Domingue?

World War and Republican France, 1791–1799
■ How and why did the Revolution take a radical turn at home and in the colonies?

The Napoleonic Era, 1799–1815
■ Why did Napoleon Bonaparte assume control of France, and what factors led to his downfall? How did the new republic of Haiti gain independence from France?

Background to Revolution

What social, political, and economic factors formed the background to the French Revolution? ◼

The origin of the French Revolution has been one of the most debated topics in history. In order to understand the path to revolution, numerous interrelated factors must be taken into account. These include deep social changes in France, a long-term political crisis that eroded monarchical legitimacy, the practical and ideological effects of the American Revolution, the impact of new political ideas derived from the Enlightenment, and, perhaps most important, a financial crisis created by France's participation in expensive overseas wars.

estates The three legal categories, or orders, of France's inhabitants: the clergy, the nobility, and everyone else.

Legal Orders and Social Reality

As in the Middle Ages, France's 25 million inhabitants were still legally divided into three orders, or **estates**—the clergy, the nobility, and everyone else. As the nation's first estate, the clergy numbered about one hundred thousand and had important privileges. It owned about 10 percent of the land and paid only a "voluntary gift," rather than regular taxes, to the government every five years. Moreover, the church levied a property tax (tithe) on landowners.

The second estate consisted of some four hundred thousand nobles, the descendants of "those who fought" in the Middle Ages. Nobles owned about 25 percent of the land in France outright, and they too were lightly taxed. Moreover, nobles continued to enjoy certain manorial rights, or privileges of lordship, that dated back to medieval times. These included exclusive rights to hunt and fish, village monopolies on baking bread and pressing grapes for wine, fees for justice, and a host of other entitlements. In addition, nobles had "honorific privileges" such as the right to precedence on public occasions and the right to wear swords. These rights conspicuously proclaimed the nobility's legal superiority and exalted social position.

Everyone else—nearly 98 percent of the population—was a commoner, legally a member of the third estate. A few commoners—prosperous merchants, lawyers, and officials—were well educated and rich, and they might have purchased manorial rights as a way of obtaining profit and social honor. Yet the vast majority of the third estate consisted of peasants, rural agricultural workers, urban artisans, and unskilled day laborers. Thus the third estate was a conglomeration of very different social groups united only by their shared legal status.

In discussing the origins of the French Revolution, historians long focused on growing tensions between the nobility and the comfortable members of the third estate, the bourgeoisie (boorzh-wah-ZEE), or upper middle class. Increasing in size, wealth, culture, and self-confidence, this rising bourgeoisie became progressively exasperated by feudal laws restraining the economy and by the pretensions of a nobility that was closing ranks against middle-class aspirations. As a result, the French bourgeoisie eventually rose up to lead the entire third estate in a great social revolution that destroyed feudal privileges and established a capitalist order based on individualism and a market economy.

A FAUT ESPERER Q'EU JEU LA FINIRA BEN TOT.

l'étuleur en Campagne Ap. 1789.

The Three Estates In this political cartoon from 1789 a peasant of the third estate struggles under the weight of a happy clergyman and a plumed nobleman. The caption—"Let's hope this game ends soon"—sets forth a program of reform that any peasant could understand. (Réunion des Musées Nationaux/Art Resource, NY)

In the last thirty years, the French Revolution's origins have been subject to what historians refer to as revisionism, or new interpretations. A flood of research uncovered in the late twentieth century challenged the long-accepted view and led to revised theories. Above all, revisionist historians have questioned the existence of growing social conflict between a progressive capitalistic bourgeoisie and a reactionary feudal nobility in eighteenth-century France. Instead, they see both bourgeoisie and nobility as highly fragmented, riddled with internal rivalries. The ancient sword nobility, for example, made up of people who descended from the oldest noble families, was separated by differences in wealth, education, and worldview from the newer robe nobility, people who acquired noble titles through service in the royal administration and judiciary. Differences within the bourgeoisie—between wealthy financiers and local lawyers, for example—were no less profound. Rather than standing as unified blocs against each other, nobility and bourgeoisie formed two parallel social ladders increasingly linked together at the top by wealth, marriage, and Enlightenment culture.

Revisionist historians note that the nobility and the bourgeoisie were not really at odds in the economic sphere. Investment in land and government service were the preferred activities of both groups, and the ideal of the merchant capitalist was to gain enough wealth to retire from trade, purchase an estate, and live nobly as a large landowner. Wealthy members of the third estate could even move into the second estate by serving the government and purchasing noble positions. At the same time, wealthy nobles often acted as aggressive capitalists, investing especially in mining, metallurgy, and foreign trade. In addition, until the Revolution actually began, key sections of the nobility were liberal and generally joined the bourgeoisie in opposition to the government.

Revisionists have clearly shaken the belief that the bourgeoisie and the nobility were inevitably locked in growing conflict before the Revolution. Yet they also make clear that the Old Regime had ceased to correspond with social reality by the 1780s. Legally, society was still based on rigid orders inherited from the Middle Ages, but in reality those distinctions were often blurred.

An upper echelon of aristocratic and bourgeois notables saw itself as an educated elite that stood well above the common masses. Although wealthy and influential, society's upper crust was frustrated by a bureaucratic monarchy that continued to claim the right to absolute power. Meanwhile, for France's laboring poor—the vast majority of the population—traditions remained strong and life itself remained a struggle.

The Crisis of Political Legitimacy

Overlying these social changes was a structural deadlock in France's tax system and the century-long political and fiscal struggle between the monarchy and its opponents sparked by the expenses of a series of foreign wars. When the Sun King, Louis XIV, finally died in 1715 and was succeeded by his five-year-old great-grandson, Louis XV (r. 1715–1774), the system of absolutist rule was challenged. Under the young monarch's regent, the duke of Orléans (1674–1723), a number of institutions retrieved powers they had lost under the Sun King. Most important, the high courts of France—the parlements—regained their ancient right to evaluate royal decrees publicly in writing before they were registered and given the force of law. The restoration of this right, which had been suspended under Louis XIV, was a fateful step. The magistrates of the parlements were leaders of the robe nobility who passed their judicial offices from father to son. By allowing a well-entrenched and highly articulate branch of the

Chronology

1773	Boston Tea Party
1775–1783	American Revolution
1786–1789	Height of French monarchy's financial crisis
1789	Feudalism abolished in France; ratification of U.S. Constitution; storming of the Bastille
1789–1799	French Revolution
1790	Burke, *Reflections on the Revolution in France*
1791	Slave insurrection in Saint-Domingue
1792	Wollstonecraft, *A Vindication of the Rights of Woman*
1793	Execution of Louis XVI
1793–1794	Robespierre's Reign of Terror
1794	Robespierre deposed and executed; France abolishes slavery in all territories
1794–1799	Thermidorian reaction
1799–1815	Napoleonic era
1804	Haitian republic declares independence
1812	Napoleon invades Russia
1814–1815	Napoleon defeated and exiled

nobility to evaluate the king's decrees before they became law, the duke of Orléans sanctioned a counterweight to absolute power.

These implications became clear when the heavy expenses of war in the eighteenth century proved unbearable for the state treasury. Because many privileged groups escaped direct taxes and indirect taxes were relatively low, revenue from taxation could not meet the costs of war. The War of the Austrian Succession (see Chapter 17) plunged France into financial crisis and pushed the state to attempt a reform of the tax system. In 1748 Louis XV's finance minister decreed a 5 percent income tax on every individual regardless of social status. The result was a vigorous protest from those previously exempt from taxation—the nobility, the clergy, towns, and some wealthy bourgeoisie—led by the influential Parlement of Paris. The monarchy retreated; the new tax was dropped.

Following the disastrously expensive Seven Years' War (see Chapter 18), the conflict re-emerged. The government tried to maintain emergency taxes after the war ended; the Parlement of Paris protested and even challenged the basis of royal authority, claiming that the king's power had to be limited to protect liberty. Once again the government caved in and withdrew the taxes. The judicial opposition then asserted that the king could not levy taxes without the consent of the Parlement of Paris.

After years of attempted compromise, Louis XV finally roused himself to defend his absolutist inheritance. "The magistrates," he angrily told the Parlement of Paris in a famous face-to-face confrontation, "are my officers. . . . In my person only does the sovereign power rest."[1] In 1768 Louis appointed a tough career official named René de Maupeou (moh-POO) as chancellor and ordered him to crush the judicial opposition. Maupeou abolished the existing parlements and exiled the vociferous members of the Parlement of Paris to the provinces. He created new and docile parlements of royal officials, known as the Maupeou parlements, and he began once again to tax the privileged groups. Public opinion as a whole sided with the old parlements, however, and there was widespread criticism of "royal despotism."

Learned dissent was accompanied by scandalous libels. Known as Louis *le bien-aimé* (beloved Louis) in his youth, the king found his people turning against him for moral as well as political reasons. Kings had always maintained mistresses, who were invariably chosen from the court nobility. Louis XV broke that pattern with Madame de Pompadour, daughter of a disgraced bourgeois financier. As the king's favorite mistress from 1745 to 1750, Pompadour exercised tremendous influence over literature, art, and the decorative arts, using her patronage to support Voltaire and promote the rococo style (see Chapter 17). Even after their love affair ended,

Pompadour wielded considerable influence over the king, helping bring about the alliance with Austria that resulted in the Seven Years' War. Pompadour's low birth and hidden political influence generated a stream of resentful and illegal pamphleteering.

After Pompadour, the king appeared to sink ever lower in immorality, and the stream of scandalmongering became a torrent. Lurid and pornographic depictions of the court ate away at the foundations of royal authority, especially among the common people. The king was being stripped of the sacred aura of God's anointed on earth (a process called *desacralization*) and was being reinvented in the popular imagination as a degenerate.

Despite the progressive desacralization (dee-SAY-kruh-ligh-ZAY-shun) of the monarchy, its power was still great enough to overcome opposition; Louis XV would probably have prevailed had he lived to a ripe old age, but he died in 1774. The new king, Louis XVI (r. 1774–1792), was a shy twenty-year-old with good intentions. Taking the throne, he is reported to have said, "What I should like most is to be loved."[2] The eager-to-please monarch yielded in the face of vehement opposition from France's educated elite. He dismissed chancellor Maupeou and repudiated the strong-willed minister's work. Louis also waffled on the economy, dismissing controller-general Turgot when his attempts to liberalize the economy drew fire (see Chapter 18). A weakened but unreformed monarchy now faced a judicial opposition that claimed to speak for the entire French nation.

The American Revolution and Its Impact

Coinciding with the first years of Louis XVI's reign, the American Revolution had an enormous impact on France in both practical and ideological terms. French expenses to support the colonists bankrupted the Crown, while the ideals of liberty and equality provided heady inspiration for political reform.

Like the French Revolution, the American Revolution had its immediate origin in struggles over increased taxes. The high cost of the Seven Years' War—fought with little financial contribution from the colonies—doubled the British national debt. When the government tried to recoup some of the losses by increasing taxes in the colonies in 1765, the colonists reacted with anger. The key questions were political rather than economic. To what extent could the home government assert its power while limiting the authority of colonial legislatures and their elected representatives? Accordingly, who should represent the colonies, and who had the right to make laws for Americans? The British government replied that Americans were represented in Parliament, albeit indirectly (like most British people themselves), and that the absolute supremacy of Parliament throughout the empire could not be questioned. Many Americans felt otherwise.

In 1773 the dispute over taxes and representation flared up again after the British government awarded a monopoly on Chinese tea to the East India Company, suddenly excluding colonial merchants from a lucrative business. In response, Boston men disguised as Indians held a rowdy "tea party" and threw the company's tea into the harbor. This led to extreme measures. The so-called Coercive Acts closed the port of Boston, curtailed local elections, and greatly expanded the royal governor's power. County conventions in Massachusetts protested vehemently and urged that the acts be "rejected as the attempts of a wicked administration to enslave America."

Other colonial assemblies joined in the denunciations. In September 1774 the First Continental Congress met in Philadelphia, where the more radical members argued successfully against concessions to the Crown. Compromise was also rejected by the British Parliament, and in April 1775 fighting began at Lexington and Concord. The uncompromising attitude of the British government and its use of German mercenaries dissolved long-standing loyalties to the home country and rivalries among the separate colonies. Some colonists remained loyal to the Crown; large numbers of these Loyalists emigrated to the northern colonies of Canada.

On July 4, 1776, the Second Continental Congress adopted the Declaration of Independence. Written by Thomas Jefferson, it boldly listed the tyrannical acts committed by George III (r. 1760–1820) and confidently proclaimed the natural rights of mankind and the sovereignty of the American states. The Declaration of Independence in effect universalized the traditional rights of English people and made them the rights of all mankind. It stated that "all men are created equal. . . . They are endowed by their Creator with certain unalienable rights. . . . Among these are life, liberty, and the pursuit of happiness."

The European powers closely followed the course of the American Revolution. The French wanted revenge

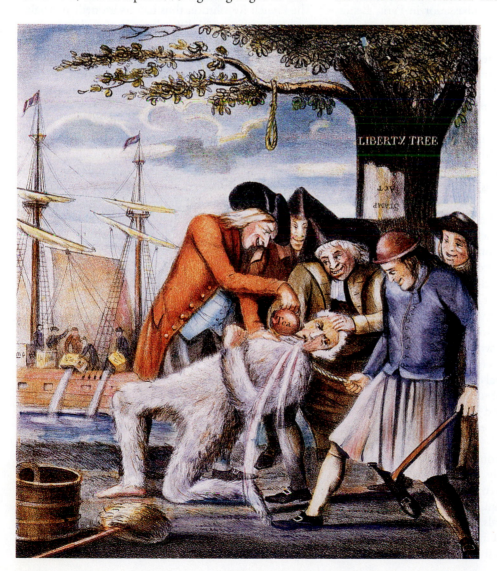

Toward Revolution in Boston
The Boston Tea Party was only one of many angry confrontations between British officials and Boston patriots. On January 27, 1774, an angry crowd seized a British customs collector and tarred and feathered him. This English cartoon from 1774 satirizes the event. What does the noose in the "liberty tree" suggest about the cartoonist's view of these events? (The Granger Collection, New York)

LIBERTY TREE

Commemorative Teapot
Manufacturers were quick to bring products to the market celebrating weighty political events, like this British teapot heralding "Stamp Act Repeal'd." By purchasing such items, ordinary people could champion political causes of the day and bring public affairs into their private lives. (Peabody Essex Museum, Salem, Massachusetts)

for the humiliating defeats of the Seven Years' War. They sympathized with the rebels and supplied guns and gunpowder. By 1777 French volunteers were arriving in Virginia, and a dashing young nobleman, the marquis de Lafayette (1757–1834), quickly became one of George Washington's most trusted generals. In 1778 the French government offered a formal alliance to the American ambassador in Paris, Benjamin Franklin, and in 1779 and 1780 the Spanish and Dutch declared war on Britain, their rival in transatlantic trade. Catherine the Great of Russia helped organize the League of Armed Neutrality in order to protect neutral shipping rights, which Britain refused to recognize.

Thus by 1780 Great Britain was engaged in an imperial war against most of Europe as well as against the thirteen colonies. In these circumstances, and in the face of severe reverses, a new British government decided to cut its losses and offered peace on extremely generous terms. By the Treaty of Paris in 1783, Britain recognized the independence of the thirteen colonies and ceded all its territory between the Allegheny Mountains and the Mississippi River to the Americans. Out of the bitter rivalries of the Old World, the Americans snatched dominion over a vast territory.

Europeans who dreamed of a new era were fascinated by the political lessons of the American Revolution. The Americans had begun with a revolutionary defense against tyrannical oppression, and they had been victorious. They had then shown how rational beings could assemble to exercise sovereignty and write a permanent constitution—a new social contract. All this gave greater reality to the concepts of individual liberty and representative government and reinforced one of the primary ideas of the Enlightenment: that a better world was possible.

No country felt the consequences of the American Revolution more directly than France. Hundreds of French officers served in America and were inspired by the experience, the marquis de Lafayette chief among them. French intellectuals and publicists engaged in passionate analysis of the new federal Constitution—ratified in 1789—as well as the constitutions of the

various states of the new United States.

Perhaps more important, the expenses of supporting America's revolutionary forces provided the last nail in the coffin for the French treasury.

Financial Crisis

The French Revolution thus had its immediate origins in the king's financial difficulties. Thwarted by the Parlement of Paris in its efforts to raise revenues by reforming the tax system, the government was forced to finance all of its enormous expenditures during the American war with borrowed money. As a result, the national debt and the annual budget deficit soared.

By the 1780s fully 50 percent of France's annual budget went for interest payments on the debt. Another 25 percent went to maintain the military, while 6 percent was absorbed by the king and his court at Versailles. Less than 20 percent of the entire national budget was available for the productive functions of the state, such as transportation and general administration. This was an impossible financial situation.

The king was too weak to take the drastic measure of declaring partial bankruptcy and forcing his creditors to accept greatly reduced payments, as previous monarchs had done. Nor could the king and his ministers print money and create inflation to cover their deficits. Unlike England and Holland, which had far larger national debts relative to their populations, France had no central bank, no paper currency, and no means of creating credit. Faced with imminent financial disaster in 1786, the royal government had no alternative but to try to increase taxes. Since France's tax system was unfair and out-of-date, increased revenues were possible only through fundamental reform.

In 1787 Louis XVI's minister of finance revived old proposals to impose a general tax on all landed property as well as to form provincial assemblies to help administer the tax, and he convinced the king to call an Assembly of Notables to gain support for the idea. The notables, who were mainly important noblemen and high-ranking clergy, insisted that such sweeping tax changes required the approval of the **Estates General**, the representative body of all three estates, which had not met since 1614.

In an attempt to reassert his authority, the king dismissed the notables and established new taxes by decree. In stirring language, the judges of the Parlement of Paris promptly declared the royal initiative null and void. When the king tried to exile the judges, a tremendous wave of protest swept the country. Frightened investors also refused to advance more loans to the state. Finally, in July 1788, Louis XVI bowed to public opinion and called for a spring session of the Estates General.

Politics and the People, 1789–1791

How did the events of 1789 result in a constitutional monarchy in France, and how did the new constitution affect the various members of French society at home and in the colony of Saint-Domingue? ■

The calling of the Estates General opened a Pandora's box of social and political demands across the country. The process of electing delegates and formulating grievances politicized the French as no event in their prior history had done. As delegates at Versailles struggled over who truly represented the nation, the common people of France took matters into their own hands, rising up against noble lords and even reaching out to the royal family in their demands for change. Meanwhile, the complex slave society of colonial Saint-Domingue was rocked by conflicting political aspirations inspired by events in Paris.

The Formation of the National Assembly

Once Louis had agreed to hold the Estates General, the three orders—clergy, nobility, and commoners—separately elected delegates in each electoral district and prepared their own lists of grievances. The process of drafting their complaints unleashed a flood of debate and discussion across France, helping to galvanize public opinion and demands for reform.

Results of the elections reveal the political loyalties and mindsets of each estate on the eve of the Revolution. The local assemblies of the clergy elected mostly parish priests rather than church leaders, demonstrating their dissatisfaction with the church hierarchy. The nobility voted in a majority of conservatives, primarily from the provinces, where nobles were less wealthy and more numerous. Despite this conservative showing, fully one-third of noble representatives were liberals committed to major changes. The third estate experienced great popular participation in the elections. Almost all male commoners over age twenty-four had the right to vote, and they elected primarily lawyers and government officials to represent them, with few delegates representing business or the poor.

Although the elected representatives displayed a range of differing political viewpoints, the petitions for change coming from the three estates showed a surprising degree of consensus about the issues at stake. There was general agreement that royal absolutism should give way to a constitutional monarchy in which laws and taxes would require the consent of the Estates General in regular meetings. All agreed that individual liberties would have to be guaranteed by law and that economic regulations should be loosened. The striking similarities in the grievance petitions of the clergy, nobility, and third estate reflected a shared commitment to a basic reform platform among the educated elite.

On May 5, 1789, the twelve hundred delegates of the three estates paraded in medieval pageantry through the streets of Versailles to an opening session resplendent with feudal magnificence. Hopes were high throughout France for serious reform of state finance and politics in cooperation with the king. For the moment, there was no talk of revolution, only reform, and cries of "long live the king" interrupted his opening speech to the Estates General.

Despite these high hopes, the Estates General was almost immediately deadlocked due to arguments about voting procedures. Controversy had begun during the electoral process, when the government confirmed that, following precedent, each estate should meet and vote separately. During the lead-up to the Estates General, critics denounced this situation and demanded a single assembly dominated by the third estate to ensure fundamental reforms. In his famous pamphlet "What Is the Third Estate?" the abbé Emmanuel Joseph Sieyès (himself a member of the first estate) argued that the nobility was a tiny overprivileged minority and that the neglected third estate constituted the true strength of the French nation. (See "Listening to the Past: Abbé de Sieyès, 'What Is the Third Estate?'" page 626.) The government conceded that the third estate should have as many delegates as the clergy and the nobility combined, but then rendered this act meaningless by upholding voting by separate order. Reform-minded critics saw fresh evidence of an aristocratic conspiracy.

The issue came to a head in June 1789 when the delegates of the third estate refused to transact any business until the king ordered the clergy and nobility

Estates General
A legislative body in prerevolutionary France made up of representatives of each of the three classes, or estates; it was called into session in 1789 for the first time since 1614.

Abbé de Sieyès, "What Is the Third Estate?"

LISTENING TO THE PAST

In the flood of pamphlets that appeared after Louis XVI's call for a meeting of the Estates General, the most influential was written in 1789 by a Catholic priest named Emmanuel Joseph Sieyès. In "What is the Third Estate?" the abbé Sieyès vigorously condemned the system of privilege that lay at the heart of French society. The term "privilege" combined the Latin words for "private" and "law." In Old Regime France, no one set of laws applied to all; over time, the monarchy had issued a series of particular laws, or privileges, that enshrined special rights and entitlements for select individuals and groups. Noble privileges were among the weightiest.

Sieyès rejected this entire system of legal and social inequality. Deriding the nobility as a foreign parasite, he argued that the common people of the third estate, who did most of the work and paid most of the taxes, constituted the true nation. His pamphlet galvanized public opinion and played an important role in convincing representatives of the third estate to proclaim themselves a "National Assembly" in June 1789. Sieyès later helped bring Napoleon Bonaparte to power, abandoning the radicalism of 1789 for an authoritarian regime.

❝ 1. What is the Third Estate? Everything.
2. What has it been until now in the political order? Nothing.
3. What does it want? To become something.

. . . What is a Nation? A body of associates living under a *common* law and represented by the same *legislature*.

Is it not more than certain that the noble order has privileges, exemptions, and even rights that are distinct from the rights of the great body of citizens? Because of this, it [the noble order] does not belong to the common order, it is not covered by the law common to the rest. Thus its civil rights already make it a people apart inside the great Nation. It is truly *imperium in imperio* [a law unto itself].

As for its *political* rights, the nobility also exercises them separately. It has its own representatives who have no mandate from the people. Its deputies sit separately, and even when they assemble in the same room with the deputies of the ordinary citizens, the nobility's representation still remains essentially distinct and separate: it is foreign to the Nation by its very principle, for its mission does not emanate from the people, and by its purpose, since it consists in defending, not the general interest, but the private interests of the nobility.

The Third Estate therefore contains everything that pertains to the Nation and nobody outside of the Third Estate can claim to be part of the Nation. What is the Third Estate? EVERYTHING. . . .

By Third Estate is meant the collectivity of citizens who belong to the common order. Anybody who holds a legal privilege of any kind leaves that common order, stands as an exception to the common law, and in consequence does not belong to the Third Estate. . . . It is certain that the moment a citizen acquires privileges contrary to common law, he no longer belongs to the common order. His new interest is opposed to the general interest; he has no right to vote in the name of the people. . . .

In vain can anyone's eyes be closed to the revolution that time and the force of things have brought to pass; it is none the less real. Once

This bust, by the sculptor Pierre Jean David d'Angers, shows an aged and contemplative Sieyès reflecting, perhaps, on his key role in the outbreak and unfolding of the Revolution.
(Erich Lessing/Art Resource, NY)

upon a time the Third Estate was in bondage and the noble order was everything that mattered. Today the Third is everything and nobility but a word. Yet under the cover of this word a new and intolerable aristocracy has slipped in, and the people has every reason to no longer want aristocrats. . . .

What is the will of a Nation? It is the result of individual wills, just as the Nation is the aggregate of the individuals who compose it. It is impossible to conceive of a legitimate association that does not have for its goal the common security, the common liberty, in short, the public good. No doubt each individual also has his own personal aims. He says to himself, "protected by the common security, I will be able to peacefully pursue my own personal projects, I will seek my happiness where I will, assured of encountering only those legal obstacles that society will prescribe for the common interest, in which I have a part, and with which my own personal interest is so usefully allied." . . .

Advantages which differentiate citizens from one another lie outside the purview of citizenship. Inequalities of wealth or ability are like the inequalities of age, sex, size, etc. In no way do they detract from the *equality* of citizenship. These individual advantages no doubt benefit from the protection of the law; but it is not the legislator's task to create them, to give privileges to some and refuse them to others. The law grants nothing; it protects what already exists until such time that what exists begins to harm the common interest. These are the only limits on individual freedom. I imagine the law as being at the center of a large globe; we the citizens without exception, stand equidistant from it on the surface and occupy equal places; all are equally dependent on the law, all present it with their liberty and their property to be protected; and this is what I call the *common rights* of citizens, by which they are all alike. All these individuals communicate with each other, enter into contracts, negotiate, always under the common guarantee of the law. If in this general activity somebody wishes to get control over the person of his neighbor or usurp his property, the common law goes into action to repress this criminal attempt and puts everyone back in their place at the same distance from the law. . . .

It is impossible to say what place the two privileged orders [the clergy and the nobility] ought to occupy in the social order: this is the equivalent of asking what place one wishes to assign to a malignant tumor that torments and undermines the strength of the body of a sick person. It must be *neutralized*. We must re-establish the health and working of all organs so thoroughly that they are no longer susceptible to these fatal schemes that are capable of sapping the most essential principles of vitality. **”**

Source: Excerpt from pp. 65–70 in *The French Revolution and Human Rights: A Brief Documentary History*, edited, translated and with an introduction by Lynn Hunt. Copyright © 1996 by Bedford Books of St. Martin's Press. Used by permission of Bedford/St. Martin's.

QUESTIONS FOR ANALYSIS

1. What criticism of noble privileges does Sieyès offer? Why does he believe nobles are "foreign" to the nation?

2. How does Sieyès define the nation, and why does he believe that the third estate constitutes the nation?

3. What relationship between citizens and the law does Sieyès envision? What limitations on the law does he propose?

to sit with them in a single body. Finally, after a six-week war of nerves, a few parish priests began to go over to the third estate, which on June 17 voted to call itself the **National Assembly**. On June 20 the delegates of the third estate, excluded from their hall because of "repairs," moved to a large indoor tennis court where they swore the famous Oath of the Tennis Court, declaring:

> *The National Assembly, considering that it has been called to establish the constitution of the realm, to bring about the regeneration of public order, and to maintain the true principles of the monarchy, nothing may prevent it from continuing its deliberations in any place it is forced to establish itself and, finally, the National Assembly exists wherever its members are gathered.*

Taking the first step toward revolution, the members of the National Assembly pledged not to disband until they had written a new constitution.

The king's response to this crucial challenge to his authority was disastrously ambivalent. On June 23 he made a conciliatory speech to a joint session in which he urged reforms, and four days later he ordered the three estates to meet together. At the same time, the vacillating and indecisive monarch apparently followed the advice of relatives and court nobles who urged him to dissolve the National Assembly by force. Belatedly asserting his divine right to rule, the king called an army of eighteen thousand troops toward the capital, and on July 11 he dismissed his finance minister and other more liberal ministers. It appeared that the monarchy was prepared to renege on its promises for reform and to use violence to restore its control.

National Assembly The first French revolutionary legislature, made up primarily of representatives of the third estate and a few from the nobility and clergy, in session from 1789 to 1791.

The Storming of the Bastille

While delegates at Versailles were pressing for political rights, economic hardship gripped the common people. A poor grain harvest in 1788 had caused the price of bread to soar, unleashing a classic economic depression of the preindustrial age. With food so expensive and with so much uncertainty, the demand for manufactured goods collapsed. Thousands of artisans and small traders were thrown out of work. Bread riots broke out in Paris and the surrounding area in late April and May. In Paris perhaps 150,000 of the city's 600,000 people were without work by July 1789.

Against this background of poverty and ongoing political crisis, the people of Paris entered decisively onto the revolutionary stage. They believed that they should

The Tennis Court Oath, June 20, 1789 Painted two years after the event shown, this dramatic painting by Jacques-Louis David depicts a crucial turning point in the early days of the Revolution. On June 20 delegates of the third estate arrived at their meeting hall in the Versailles palace to find the doors closed and guarded. Fearing the king was about to dissolve their meeting by force, the deputies reassembled at a nearby indoor tennis court and swore a solemn oath not to disperse until they had been recognized as the National Assembly. (Musée de la Ville de Paris, Musée Carnavalet, Paris/Lauros/Giraudon, The Bridgeman Art Library)

have steady work and enough bread at fair prices to survive. They also feared that the dismissal of the king's moderate finance minister would put them at the mercy of aristocratic landowners and grain speculators. At the beginning of July, knowledge spread of the massing of troops near Paris, and it seemed that the royal government was prepared to use violence to impose order. Angry crowds formed, and passionate voices urged action. On July 13, 1789, the people began to seize arms for the defense of the city, and on July 14 several hundred people marched to the Bastille (in English ba-STEEL) to search for weapons and gunpowder.

The Bastille, once a medieval fortress, was a royal prison guarded by eighty retired soldiers and thirty Swiss mercenaries. The governor of the fortress-prison refused to hand over the powder, panicked, and ordered his men to resist; the guards killed ninety-eight people attempting to enter. Cannon were brought to batter the main gate, and fighting continued until the prison surrendered. The

governor of the prison was later hacked to death, and his head was stuck on a pike and paraded through the streets. The next day a committee of citizens appointed the marquis de Lafayette commander of the city's armed forces.

The popular uprising forestalled the king's attempt to reassert his authority. On July 17 Louis announced the reinstatement of his liberal finance minister and the withdrawal of troops from Paris. The National Assembly was now free to continue its work without the threat of royal military intervention.

Peasant Revolt and the Rights of Man

Just as the laboring poor of Paris had been roused to a revolutionary fervor, the struggling French peasantry had also reached its boiling point, and in the summer of 1789 the countryside sent the delegates at

> Free expression of thoughts and opinions is one of the most precious rights of mankind: every citizen may therefore speak, write, and publish freely.
>
> —**Declaration of the Rights of Man and of the Citizen**

The Figure of Liberty In this painting, the figure of Liberty bears a copy of the Declaration of the Rights of Man and of the Citizen in one hand and a pike to defend them in the other. The painting, by female artist and ardent revolutionary Nanine Vallain, hung in the Jacobin club until its fall from power. (Musée de la Revolution Française, Vizille/The Bridgeman Art Library)

Versailles a radical and unmistakable message. Throughout France peasants began to rise in insurrection against their lords, ransacking manor houses and burning feudal documents that recorded their obligations. In some areas peasants reinstated traditional village practices, undoing recent enclosures and reoccupying old common lands. They seized forests, and taxes went unpaid. Fear of marauders and vagabonds hired by vengeful landlords—called the **Great Fear** by contemporaries—seized the rural poor and fanned the flames of rebellion.

Faced with chaos, yet afraid to call on the king to restore order, some liberal nobles and middle-class delegates at Versailles responded to peasant demands with a surprise maneuver on the night of August 4, 1789. The duke of Aiguillon, a powerful noble landowner, declared that the peasantry was seeking "to throw off at last a yoke that has for many centuries weighted it down."[3] He urged equality in taxation and the elimination of feudal dues. In the end, all the old noble privileges—peasant serfdom where it still existed, exclusive hunting rights, fees for justice, village monopolies, the right to make peasants work on the roads, and a host of other dues—were abolished along with the tithes paid to the church. Thus the French peasantry achieved an unprecedented victory in the early days of revolutionary upheaval. Henceforth, French peasants would seek mainly to protect and consolidate their triumph.

Having granted new rights to the peasantry, the National Assembly moved forward with its mission of reform. On August 27, 1789, it issued the Declaration of the Rights of Man and of the Citizen, which stated, "Men are born and remain free and equal in rights." The declaration also maintained that mankind's natural rights are "liberty, property, security, and resistance to oppression" and that "every man is presumed innocent until he is proven guilty." As for law, "it is an expression of the general will; all citizens have the right to concur personally or through their representatives in its formation. . . . Free expression of thoughts and opinions is one of the most precious rights of mankind: every citizen may therefore speak, write, and publish freely." In short, this call of the liberal revolutionary ideal guaranteed equality before the law, representative government for a sovereign people, and individual freedom. This revolutionary credo, only two pages long, was disseminated throughout France and Europe and around the world.

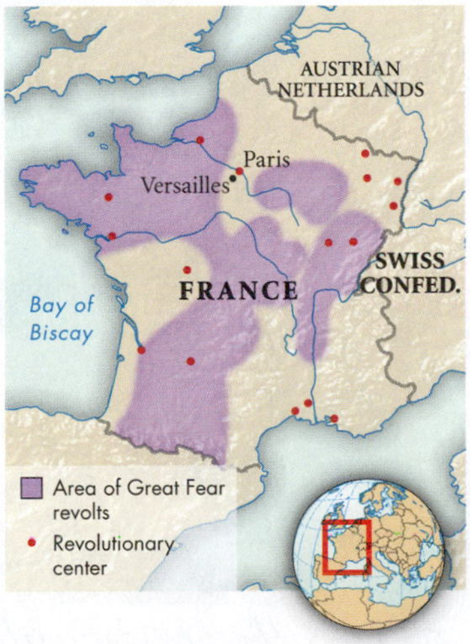

AUSTRIAN NETHERLANDS
Paris
Versailles
FRANCE
SWISS CONFED.
Bay of Biscay
Area of Great Fear revolts
Revolutionary center

The Great Fear, 1789

Great Fear The fear of noble reprisals against peasant uprisings that seized the French countryside and led to further revolt.

Parisian Women March on Versailles

While high-minded in principle, the National Assembly's declaration had little practical effect for the poor and hungry people of Paris, where a revolutionary spirit continued to smolder. The economic crisis in the city worsened after the fall of the Bastille, as aristocrats fled the country and the luxury market collapsed. Foreign markets also shrank in the aftermath of the crisis, and unemployment among the urban working class grew. In addition, women—the traditional managers of food and resources in poor homes—could no longer look to the church, which had been stripped of its tithes, for aid.

On October 5 some seven thousand desperate women marched the twelve miles from Paris to Versailles to demand action. This great crowd, "armed with scythes, sticks and pikes," invaded the National Assembly. Interrupting a delegate's speech, a tough old woman defiantly shouted into the debate, "Who's that talking down there? Make the chatterbox shut up. That's not the point: the point is that we want bread."[4] Hers was the genuine voice of the people, essential to any understanding of the French Revolution.

constitutional monarchy
A form of government in which the king retains his position as head of state, while the authority to tax and make new laws resides in an elected body.

The women invaded the royal apartments, killed some of the royal bodyguards, and furiously searched for the queen, Marie Antoinette, who was widely despised for her frivolous and supposedly immoral behavior. "We are going to cut off her head, tear out her heart, fry her liver, and that won't be the end of it," they shouted, surging through the palace. It seems likely that only the intervention of Lafayette and the National Guard saved the royal family. But the only way to calm the disorder was for the king to live closer to his people in Paris, as the crowd demanded.

A Constitutional Monarchy and Its Challenges

The day after the women's march on Versailles, the National Assembly followed the king to Paris, and the next two years, until September 1791, saw the consolidation of the liberal revolution. Under middle-class leadership, the National Assembly abolished the French nobility as a legal order and pushed forward with the creation of a **constitutional monarchy**, which Louis XVI reluctantly agreed to accept in July 1790. In the final constitution, the king remained the head of state, but all lawmaking power now resided in the National Assembly, elected by the wealthiest half of French males. New laws broadened women's rights to seek divorce, to inherit

The Women of Paris March to Versailles On October 5, 1789, a large group of poor Parisian women marched to Versailles to protest the price of bread. For the people of Paris, the king was the baker of last resort, responsible for feeding his people during times of scarcity. The angry women forced the royal family to return with them and to live in Paris, rather than remain isolated from their subjects at court. (Erich Lessing/Art Resource, NY)

Village Festival in Honor of Old Age, 1795 The French Revolution inaugurated many new civic festivals in an attempt to erase memories of the Catholic holidays and feast days of the prerevolutionary era. As in bygone days, the new festivals, like this one honoring village elders, included dancing, drinking, and courting among the young couples of the village. Many people, however, especially in rural France, missed the religious tenor of prerevolutionary holidays. (Bibliothèque nationale de France/Archives Charmet/The Bridgeman Art Library)

property, and to obtain financial support for illegitimate children from fathers, but women were not allowed to hold political office or even vote.

This decision was attacked by a small number of men and women who believed that the rights of man should be extended to all French citizens. The liberal marquis de Condorcet accused the legislators of having "violated the principle of equality of rights by quietly depriving half of mankind of the right to participate in the formation of the laws."[5] Olympe de Gouges (1748–1793), a self-taught writer and woman of the people, took up her pen to protest the evils of slavery as well as the injustices done to women. In September 1791 she published her "Declaration of the Rights of Woman," a direct challenge to revolutionaries to respect the ideals of the great 1789 declaration. De Gouges's pamphlet echoed its famous predecessor, proclaiming, "Woman is born free and remains equal to man in rights." She further demanded that both sexes be "equally admissible to all public dignities, offices, and employments, according to their ability, and with no other distinction than their virtues and talents."

Such arguments found little sympathy among leaders of the Revolution. The editor of one revolutionary journal offered a public response to complaints he had received from women about their exclusion from politics. He agreed that they should be allowed to speak in assemblies, but not to vote or serve as representatives. As he explained, "a household should never remain deserted for a single instant. When the father of a family leaves to defend or lay claim to the rights of property, security, equality, or liberty in a public assembly, the mother of the family, focused on her domestic duties, must make order and cleanliness, ease and peace reign at home."[6] His sentiments represented the opinions of the vast majority of legislators and ordinary Frenchmen.

In addition to ruling on women's rights, the National Assembly replaced the complicated patchwork of historic provinces with eighty-three departments of approximately equal size. Monopolies, guilds, and workers' associations were prohibited, and barriers to trade within France were abolished in the name of economic liberty.

631

Thus the National Assembly applied the spirit of the Enlightenment in a thorough reform of France's laws and institutions.

The National Assembly also imposed a radical reorganization on the country's religious life. It granted religious freedom to the small minority of French Jews and Protestants. In November 1789 it nationalized the Catholic Church's property and abolished monasteries as useless relics of a distant past. The government used all former church property as collateral to guarantee a new paper currency, the assignats (A-sihg-nat), and then sold the property in an attempt to put the state's finances on a solid footing. Although the land was sold in large blocks, peasants eventually purchased much when it was subdivided. These purchases strengthened their attachment to the new revolutionary order in the countryside.

Imbued with the rationalism and skepticism of the eighteenth-century philosophes (see Chapter 17), many delegates distrusted popular piety and "superstitious religion." Thus in July 1790, with the Civil Constitution of the Clergy, they established a national church with priests chosen by voters. The National Assembly then forced the Catholic clergy to take a loyalty oath to the new government. The pope formally condemned this attempt to subjugate the church, and only half the priests of France swore the oath. Many sincere Christians, especially those in the countryside, were upset by these changes in the religious order. The attempt to remake the Catholic Church, like the abolition of guilds and workers' associations, sharpened the conflict between the educated classes and the common people that had been emerging in the eighteenth century.

Revolutionary Aspirations in Saint-Domingue

The French Revolution radically transformed not only the territorial nation of France but its overseas colonies as well. On the eve of the Revolution, Saint-Domingue—the most profitable of all Caribbean colonies—was even more rife with social tensions than France itself. The island was inhabited by a variety of social groups who resented and mistrusted one another. The European population included French colonial officials, wealthy plantation owners and merchants, and poor immigrants. Greatly outnumbering the white population were the

Saint-Domingue Slave Life Although the brutal conditions of plantation slavery left little time or energy for leisure, slaves on Saint-Domingue took advantage of their day of rest on Sunday to engage in social and religious activities. The law officially prohibited slaves of different masters from mingling together, but such gatherings were often tolerated if they remained peaceful. This image depicts a fight between two slaves, precisely the type of unrest and violence feared by authorities. (Musée du Nouveau Monde, La Rochelle/Photos12.com — ARJ)

colony's five hundred thousand slaves, along with a sizable population of free people of African and mixed African and European descent. Members of this last group referred to themselves as "free coloreds" or free people of color.

The 1685 *Code Noir* (Black Code) that set the parameters of slavery had granted free people of color the same legal status as whites: they could own property, live where they wished, and pursue any education or career they desired. From the 1760s on, however, colonial administrators began rescinding these rights, and by the time of the Revolution, myriad aspects of free coloreds' lives—from the professions they could practice, to the names they could adopt, to the clothes they could wear—were ruled by discriminatory laws. White planters eagerly welcomed these laws, convinced that the best defense of slavery was a rigid color line.

The political and intellectual turmoil of the 1780s, with its growing rhetoric of liberty, equality, and fraternity, raised new challenges and possibilities for each of these groups. For slaves, news of abolitionist movements in France and the royal government's own attempts to rein in the worst abuses of slavery led to hopes that the mother country might grant them freedom. Free people of color found in such rhetoric the principles on which to shore up their eroded legal and political rights. They looked to reforms in Paris as a means of gaining political enfranchisement and reasserting equal status with whites. The white elite, not surprisingly, saw matters very differently. Infuriated by talk of abolition and determined to protect their way of life, they looked to revolutionary ideals of representative government for the chance to gain control of their own affairs, as had the American colonists before them. The meeting of the Estates General and the Declaration of the Rights of Man and of the Citizen raised these conflicting colonial aspirations to new levels.

The National Assembly frustrated the hopes of all these groups. Cowed by colonial representatives who claimed that support for free people of color would result in slave insurrection and independence, the Assembly refused to extend French constitutional safeguards to the colonies. Instead, it ruled that each colony would draft its own constitution, with free rein over decisions on slavery and the enfranchisement of free people of color. After dealing this blow to the aspirations of slaves and free coloreds, the committee also reaffirmed French monopolies over colonial trade, thereby angering planters as well.

In July 1790 Vincent Ogé (aw-ZHAY), a free man of color, returned to Saint-Domingue from Paris determined to redress these issues. He raised an army of several hundred and sent letters to the new Provincial Assembly of Saint-Domingue demanding political rights for all free citizens, a statute already passed in France. After initial victories, his army was defeated, and Ogé

himself was tortured and executed by colonial officials. In May 1791, in an attempt to respond to what it perceived as partly justified grievances, the National Assembly granted political rights to free people of color born to two free parents who possessed sufficient property. When news of this legislation arrived in Saint-Domingue, the white elite was furious, and the colonial governor refused to enact it. Violence now erupted between groups of whites and free coloreds in parts of the colony. The liberal revolution had failed to satisfy the contradictory ambitions in the colonies.

World War and Republican France, 1791–1799

How and why did the Revolution take a radical turn at home and in the colonies? ■

When Louis XVI accepted the final version of the National Assembly's constitution in September 1791, a young and still obscure provincial lawyer and delegate named Maximilien Robespierre (1758–1794) concluded that "The Revolution is over." Robespierre (ROHBZ-pee-air) was right in the sense that the most constructive and lasting reforms were in place; no substantial reforms in the way of liberty would be gained in the next generation. Yet he was wrong in the sense that a much more radical stage lay ahead. New heroes and new ideologies were to emerge in revolutionary wars and international conflict in which Robespierre himself would play a central role.

Foreign Reactions to the Revolution

The outbreak and progress of revolution in France produced great excitement and a sharp division of opinion in Europe and the United States. Liberals and radicals saw a mighty triumph of liberty over despotism. In Great Britain, especially, they hoped that the French example would lead to a fundamental reordering of Parliament, which was in the hands of the aristocracy and a few wealthy merchants. On the other hand, conservative leaders such as British statesman Edmund Burke (1729–1797) were deeply troubled by the aroused spirit of reform. In 1790 Burke published *Reflections on the Revolution in France*, in which he defended inherited privileges in general and those of the English monarchy and aristocracy in particular. He glorified the unrepresentative Parliament and predicted that reform like that occurring in France would lead only to chaos and tyranny. Burke's work sparked much debate.

One passionate rebuttal came from a young writer in London, Mary Wollstonecraft (1759–1797). Determined to be independent in a society that expected women of her class to become obedient wives, Wollstonecraft (WOOL-stuhn-kraft) struggled for years to earn her living as a governess and a teacher—practically the only acceptable careers for single educated women—before attaining success as a translator and author. Incensed by Burke's book, she immediately wrote a blistering, widely read attack, *A Vindication of the Rights of Man* (1790). Two years later, she published her masterpiece, *A Vindication of the Rights of Woman* (1792). Like de Gouges one year before her, Wollstonecraft demanded equal rights for women. She advocated rigorous coeducation, which would make women better wives and mothers, good citizens, and economically independent. Women could manage businesses and enter politics if only men would give them the chance. Wollstonecraft's analysis testifies to the power of the Revolution to excite and inspire outside of France. The controversial book was quickly reissued in French and American editions. It became a classic of the early feminist movement.

> **Jacobin club** A political club in revolutionary France whose members were well-educated radical republicans.

The kings and nobles of continental Europe, who had at first welcomed the revolution in France as weakening a competing power, began to feel as threatened by its message, as did conservatives such as Burke. In June 1791 Louis XVI and Marie Antoinette were arrested and returned to Paris after trying unsuccessfully to slip out of France. For supporters of the Revolution, the attempted flight was proof that the king's professed acceptance of the constitution was a sham and that he was a traitor intent on procuring foreign support for an invasion of France. The shock of the arrest of a crowned head of state led the monarchs of Austria and Prussia to issue the Declaration of Pillnitz two months later. The Declaration professed the rulers' willingness to intervene in France to restore Louis XVI's monarchical rule if necessary. It was expected to have a sobering effect on revolutionary France without causing war.

But the crowned heads of Europe misjudged the revolutionary spirit in France. The new representative body that convened in Paris in October 1791, called the Legislative Assembly, had completely new delegates and a different character. The great majority of the legislators were still prosperous, well-educated middle-class men, but they were younger and less cautious than their predecessors. Many of the deputies belonged to the political **Jacobin club**, named after the former monastery in which they held their meetings. Such clubs had proliferated in Parisian neighborhoods since the beginning of the Revolution, drawing men and women to debate the burning political questions of the day.

The Outbreak of War

The new representatives to the Assembly whipped themselves into a patriotic fury against the Declaration of

The Capture of Louis XVI, June 1791
This painting commemorates the midnight arrest of Louis XVI and the royal family as they tried to flee France in disguise and reach counter-revolutionaries in the Austrian Netherlands. Recognized and stopped at Varennes, just forty miles from the border, the king still nearly succeeded, telling municipal officers that dangerous mobs controlled Paris and securing promises of safe passage. But within hours the local leaders reversed themselves, and by morning Louis XVI was headed back to Paris. (Bibliothèque nationale de France)

Pillnitz. If the kings of Europe were attempting to incite war against France, then "we will incite a war of people against kings. . . . Ten million Frenchmen, kindled by the fire of liberty, armed with the sword, with reason, with eloquence would be able to change the face of the world and make the tyrants tremble on their thrones."[7] Only Robespierre and a very few others argued that people would not welcome liberation at the point of a gun. Such warnings were brushed aside. France would "rise to the full height of her mission," as one deputy urged. In April 1792 France declared war on Francis II, the Habsburg monarch.

France's crusade against tyranny went poorly at first. Prussian forces joined Austria against the French, who broke and fled at their first military encounter with this First Coalition. The road to Paris lay open, and it is possible that only conflict between the Eastern monarchs over the division of Poland (see Chapter 17) saved France from an early and total defeat.

The Assembly declared the country in danger, and volunteers rallied to the capital. In this supercharged wartime atmosphere, rumors of treason by the king and queen spread in Paris. On August 10, 1792, a revolutionary crowd attacked the royal palace at the Tuileries (TWEE-luh-reez), while the king and his family fled for their lives to the nearby Legislative Assembly. Rather than offering refuge, the Assembly suspended the king from all his functions, imprisoned him, and called for a new National Convention to be elected by universal male suffrage. Monarchy in France was on its deathbed, mortally wounded by war and popular upheaval.

The Second Revolution

The fall of the monarchy marked a rapid radicalization of the Revolution, a phase that historians often call the **second revolution**. Louis's imprisonment was followed by the September Massacres. Wild stories that imprisoned counter-revolutionary aristocrats and priests were plotting with the allied invaders seized the city. As a result, angry crowds invaded the prisons of Paris and slaughtered half the men and women they found. In late September 1792 the new, popularly elected National Convention proclaimed France a republic, a nation in which the people, instead of a monarch, held sovereign power.

All the members of the National Convention were republicans, and at the beginning almost all belonged to the Jacobin (JA-kuh-bihn) club of Paris. But the Jacobins themselves were increasingly divided into two bitterly competitive groups—the **Girondists** (juh-RAHN-dihsts), named after a department in southwestern France that was home to several of their leaders, and **the Mountain**, led by Robespierre and another young lawyer, Georges Jacques Danton. The Mountain was so called because its members sat on the uppermost benches on the left side of the assembly hall. A majority of the indecisive Convention members, seated in the "Plain" below, floated back and forth between the rival factions.

This division emerged clearly after the National Convention overwhelmingly convicted Louis XVI of treason. The Girondists accepted his guilt but did not wish to put the king to death. By a narrow majority, the Mountain carried the day, and Louis was executed on January 21, 1793, on the newly invented guillotine. One of his last statements was "I am innocent and shall die without fear. I would that my death might bring happiness to the French, and ward off the dangers which I foresee."[8] But both the Girondists and the Mountain were determined to continue the "war against tyranny." The Prussians had been stopped at the Battle of Valmy on September 20, 1792, one day before the republic was proclaimed. French armies then invaded Savoy and captured Nice, moved into the German Rhineland, and by November 1792 were occupying the entire Austrian Netherlands (modern Belgium).

Everywhere they went, French armies of occupation chased the princes, abolished feudalism, and found support among some peasants and middle-class people. But the French armies also lived off the land, requisitioning food and supplies and plundering local treasures. The liberators looked increasingly like foreign invaders. International tensions mounted. In February 1793 the National Convention, at war with Austria and Prussia, declared war on Britain, Holland, and Spain as well. Republican France was now at war with almost all of Europe, a great war that would last almost without interruption until 1815.

Groups within France added to the turmoil. Peasants in western France revolted against being drafted into the army, with the Vendée region of Brittany emerging as the epicenter of revolt. Devout Catholics, royalists, and foreign agents encouraged their rebellion, and the counter-revolutionaries recruited veritable armies to fight for their cause.

In March 1793 the National Convention was locked in a life-and-death political

> **second revolution** From 1792 to 1795, the second phase of the French Revolution, during which the fall of the French monarchy introduced a rapid radicalization of politics.
>
> **Girondists** A moderate group that fought for control of the French National Convention in 1793.
>
> **the Mountain** Led by Robespierre, the French National Convention's radical faction, which seized legislative power in 1793.

Areas of Insurrection, 1793

- ◼ Vendée Rebellion
- ◼ Counter-revolutionary insurrections

struggle between members of the Mountain and the more moderate Girondists, with the radicals accusing the Girondists of inciting sedition in the provinces. With the middle-class delegates so bitterly divided, the laboring poor of Paris once again emerged as the decisive political factor. The laboring poor and the petty traders were often known as the **sans-culottes** (sanz-koo-LAHT, "without breeches") because their men wore trousers instead of the knee breeches of the aristocracy and the solid middle class. They demanded radical political action to guarantee them their daily bread. The Mountain, sensing an opportunity to outma-

neuver the Girondists, joined with sans-culottes activists in the city government to engineer a popular uprising. On June 2, 1793, armed sans-culottes invaded the Convention and forced deputies to arrest twenty-nine Girondist deputies for treason. All power passed to the Mountain.

The Convention also formed the Committee of Public Safety in April 1793 to deal with the threats from within and outside France. The committee, which Robespierre led, was given dictatorial power to deal with the national emergency. Moderates in the leading provincial cities of Caen, Bordeaux, Lyon, and Marseilles revolted against the committee's power and demanded a decentralized government. Counter-revolutionary forces in the Vendée won significant victories, and the repub-

sans-culottes The laboring poor of Paris, so called because the men wore trousers instead of the knee breeches of the aristocracy and middle class; the word came to refer to the militant radicals of the city.

Des Tetes! _du Sang! _ la Mort! _à la Lanterne! _à la Guillotine. _point de Reine! _Je suis la Déesse de la Liberté! _l'egalité! _que Londres soit brûlé! _que Paris soit Libre! _Vive la Guillotine! _

Mrs Mary Stokes delt

A PARIS BELLE.

Picturing the Past

Contrasting Visions of the Sans-Culottes These two images offer profoundly different representations of a sans-culotte woman. The image on the left was created by a French artist, while the image on the right is English. The French words above the image on the right read in part, "Heads! Blood! Death! . . . I am the Goddess of Liberty! . . . Long Live the Guillotine!" (Bibliothèque nationale de France)

ANALYZING THE IMAGE How would you describe the woman on the left? What qualities does the artist seem to ascribe to her, and how do you think these qualities relate to the sans-culottes and the Revolution? How would you characterize the facial expression and attire of the woman on the right? How does the inclusion of the text contribute to your impressions of her?

CONNECTIONS What does the contrast between these two images suggest about differences between French and English perceptions of the sans-culottes and of the French Revolution? Why do you think the artists have chosen to depict women?

To complete this activity online, go to the Online Study Guide at bedfordstmartins.com/mckaywest.

lic's armies were driven back on all fronts. By July 1793 only the areas around Paris and on the eastern frontier were firmly held by the central government. Defeat seemed imminent.

Total War and the Terror

A year later, in July 1794, the central government had reasserted control over the provinces. In addition, the Austrian Netherlands and the Rhineland were once again in the hands of conquering French armies, and the First Coalition was falling apart. This remarkable change of fortune was due to the revolutionary government's success in harnessing, for perhaps the first time in history, the explosive forces of a planned economy, revolutionary terror, and modern nationalism in a total war effort.

Robespierre and the Committee of Public Safety advanced with implacable resolution on several fronts in 1793 and 1794. Claiming they alone could speak for the "general will" of the French people, they sought to impose republican unity across the nation, on pain of death if necessary. First, they collaborated with the fiercely patriotic and democratic sans-culottes, who retained the common people's faith in fair prices and a moral economic order and who distrusted most wealthy capitalists and all aristocrats. Thus in September 1793 Robespierre and his coworkers established, as best they could, a planned economy with egalitarian social overtones. Rather than let supply and demand determine prices, the government set maximum allowable prices for key products. Though the state was too weak to enforce all its price regulations, it did fix the price of bread in Paris at levels the poor could afford. Rationing was introduced, and bakers were permitted to make only the "bread of equality"—a brown bread made of a mixture of all available flours. White bread and pastries were outlawed as luxuries. The poor of Paris may not have eaten well, but at least they ate.

The people also worked, mainly to produce arms and munitions for the war effort. The government told craftsmen what to produce, nationalized many small workshops, and requisitioned raw materials and grain. The second

revolution and the ascendancy of the sans-culottes had produced an embryonic emergency socialism, which thoroughly frightened Europe's propertied classes and greatly influenced the subsequent development of socialist ideology.

Second, while radical economic measures supplied the poor with bread and the armies with weapons, the **Reign of Terror** (1793–1794) solidified the home front. Special revolutionary courts responsible only to Robespierre's Committee of Public Safety tried "enemies of the nation" for political crimes. Some forty thousand French men and women were executed or died in prison. Another three hundred thousand suspects were arrested. Robespierre's Reign of Terror is one of the most controversial phases of the French Revolution. Presented as a necessary measure to save the republic, the Terror was a political weapon directed against all suspected of opposing the revolutionary government. As Robespierre himself put it, "Terror is nothing more than prompt, severe inflexible justice."[9] For many Europeans of the time, however, the Reign of Terror represented a frightening perversion of the generous ideals of 1789, strengthening the belief that France

Reign of Terror The period from 1793 to 1794 during which Robespierre's Committee of Public Safety tried and executed thousands suspected of treason and a new revolutionary culture was imposed.

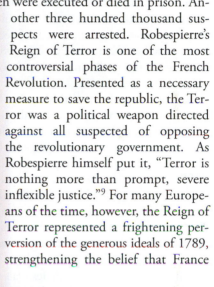

❝ Terror is nothing more than prompt, severe inflexible justice. ❞

—ROBESPIERRE

The Guillotine Prior to the French Revolution, methods of execution included hanging and being broken at the wheel. Only nobles enjoyed the privilege of a relatively swift and painless death by decapitation, delivered by an executioner's ax. The guillotine, a model of which is shown here, was devised by French revolutionaries as a humane and egalitarian form of execution. Ironically, due to the mass executions under the Terror, it is now seen instead as a symbol of revolutionary cruelty. (Musée de la Ville de Paris, Musée Carnavalet, Paris/Lauros/Giraudon, The Bridgeman Art Library)

had foolishly replaced a weak king with a bloody dictatorship.

In their efforts to impose unity, the Jacobins took actions to suppress women's participation in political debate, which they perceived as disorderly and a distraction from women's proper place in the home. On October 30, 1793, the National Convention declared that "The clubs and popular societies of women, under whatever denomination are prohibited." Included in the ban were such groups as the Society of Revolutionary Republican Women, a club of militant women that had called for the creation of female armies to combat counter-revolution.[10] Among those convicted of sedition was writer Olympe de Gouges, who was sent to the guillotine in November 1793.

Beyond imposing political unity by force, the program of the Terror also included efforts to transform French citizens into true republican patriots by bringing the Revolution into all aspects of everyday life. The government sponsored revolutionary art and songs as well as a new series of secular holidays and open-air festivals to celebrate republican virtue and a love of nation. They attempted to rationalize French daily life by adopting the decimal system for weights and measures and a new calendar based on ten-day weeks. (See "Living in the Past: A Revolution of Culture and Daily Life," page 640.) An important element of this cultural revolution was the campaign of **dechristianization**, which aimed to eliminate Catholic symbols and beliefs. Many churches were sold, clerics were humiliated and persecuted, and religious images and statues were destroyed. Fearful of the hostility aroused in rural France, Robespierre called for a halt to dechristianization measures in mid-1794.

The third and perhaps most decisive element in the French republic's victory over the First Coalition was its ability to draw on the explosive power of patriotic dedication to a national state and a national mission. An essential part of modern nationalism, which would fully emerge

dechristianization
Campaign to eliminate Christian faith and practice in France undertaken by the revolutionary government.

The French Revolution

■ National Assembly (1789–1791)

May 5, 1789	Estates General meets at Versailles
June 17, 1789	Third estate declares itself the National Assembly
June 20, 1789	Oath of the Tennis Court
July 14, 1789	Storming of the Bastille
July–August 1789	Great Fear
August 4, 1789	Abolishment of feudal privileges
August 27, 1789	Declaration of the Rights of Man and of the Citizen
October 5, 1789	Women march on Versailles; royal family returns to Paris
November 1789	National Assembly confiscates church land
July 1790	Civil Constitution of the Clergy establishes a national church; Louis XVI agrees to constitutional monarchy
June 1791	Royal family arrested while fleeing France
August 1791	Declaration of Pillnitz; slave insurrections in Saint-Domingue

■ Legislative Assembly (1791–1792)

April 1792	France declares war on Austria; enfranchisement of free people of color
August 1792	Mob attacks the palace, and Legislative Assembly takes Louis XVI prisoner

■ National Convention (1792–1795)

September 1792	September Massacres; National Convention abolishes monarchy and declares France a republic
January 1793	Louis XVI executed
February 1793	France declares war on Britain, Holland, and Spain; revolts take place in some provinces
March 1793	Struggle between Girondists and the Mountain
April 1793	Creation of the Committee of Public Safety
June 1793	Arrest of Girondist leaders
September 1793	Price controls instituted; British troops invade Saint-Domingue
October 1793	National Convention bans women's political societies
1793–1794	Reign of Terror
February 1794	Abolishment of slavery in all French territories
Spring 1794	French armies victorious on all fronts
July 1794	Robespierre executed; Thermidorian reaction begins

■ The Directory (1795–1799)

1795	Economic controls abolished; suppression of the sans-culottes begins
1796	France regains control of Saint-Domingue under Toussaint L'Ouverture
1799	Napoleon seizes power

throughout Europe in the nineteenth century, this commitment was something new in history. With a common language and a common tradition newly reinforced by the ideas of popular sovereignty and democracy, large numbers of French people were stirred by a common loyalty. They developed an intense emotional commitment to the defense of the nation, and they saw the war as a life-and-death struggle between good and evil.

Everyone had to participate in the national effort. According to a famous decree of August 23, 1793:

> *The young men shall go to battle and the married men shall forge arms. The women shall make tents and clothes, and shall serve in the hospitals; children shall tear rags into lint. The old men will be guided to the public places of the cities to kindle the courage of the young warriors and to preach the unity of the Republic and the hatred of kings.*

The all-out mobilization of French resources under the Terror combined with the fervor of modern nationalism to create an awesome fighting machine. After August 1793 all unmarried young men were subject to the draft, and by January 1794 the French had about eight hundred thousand soldiers on active duty in fourteen armies. A force of this size was unprecedented in the history of European warfare; French armed forces outnumbered their enemies almost four to one.[11] The revolutionary government deployed this awesome force to combat internal as well as external enemies. Bitter resistance from the Vendée rebels could not withstand the ruthless forces of the republic, resulting in some one hundred thousand deaths among the opposition forces.

Well-trained, well-equipped, and constantly indoctrinated, the enormous armies of the republic were led by young, impetuous generals. These generals often had risen from the ranks, and they personified the opportunities the Revolution offered gifted sons of the people. Following orders from Paris to attack relentlessly, French generals used mass assaults at bayonet point to overwhelm the enemy. "No maneuvering, nothing elaborate," declared the fearless General Hoche. "Just cold steel, passion and patriotism."[12] By spring 1794 French armies were victorious on all fronts. The republic was saved.

Revolution in Saint-Domingue

Just as the sans-culottes had been instrumental in pushing forward more radical reforms in France, the second stage of revolution in Saint-Domingue also resulted from decisive action from below. In August 1791 slaves, who had been witnesses to the confrontation between whites and free coloreds for over a year, took events into their own hands. Groups of slaves held a series of nighttime meetings to plan a mass insurrection. These meetings reportedly included religious ceremonies in which participants made ritual offerings and swore a sacred oath

Slave Revolt on Saint-Domingue Starting in August 1791 the slaves of Saint-Domingue rose in revolt, an event captured vividly by this engraving. (Giraudon/Art Resource, NY)

A Revolution of Culture and Daily Life

LIVING IN THE PAST

THE FRENCH REVOLUTION BROUGHT SWEEPING POLITICAL AND SOCIAL CHANGE to France, removing one of the oldest monarchies in Europe in favor of broad-based representative government and eliminating age-old distinctions between nobles and commoners. Revolutionaries feared, however, that these measures were not enough to transform the nation. They therefore undertook a parallel

revolution of culture intended to purify and regenerate the French people and turn former royal subjects into patriotic citizens capable of realizing the dream of liberty, equality, and fraternity.

To bring about cultural revolution, officials of the new republic targeted the most fundamental elements of daily life: the experience of space and time. Prior to the Revolution, regions of France had their own systems of measurement, meaning that the length of an inch or the weight of a pound differed substantially across the realm. Disgusted with the inefficiency of this state of affairs and determined to impose national unity, the government adopted the decimal-based metric system first proposed in 1670. The length of the meter was scientifically set at one ten-millionth of the distance from the pole to the equator. Henceforth, all French citizens would inhabit spaces that were measured and divided in the same way.

The government attempted a similar rationalization of the calendar. Instead of twelve months of varying lengths, each of the twelve months on the new revolutionary calendar was made up of three ten-day weeks, with a five- or six-day interval at the end of each year. To mark the total rebirth of time, the new calendar began at Year 1 on the day of the foundation of the French Republic (September 22, 1792). A series of festivals with patriotic themes replaced the traditional Catholic feast days. There was even a short-lived attempt to put the clock on a decimal system.

Cultural revolution also took on more concrete forms. Every citizen was required to wear a cockade on his or her hat, like the one shown on this plate celebrating the festival of the Supreme Being (a form of deism promoted by Robespierre as the state religion), to symbolize loyalty to the republic. Enterprising merchants sold a plethora of everyday goods with revolutionary themes. One could eat from revolutionary plates, drink from revolutionary mugs, waft revolutionary fans, and even decorate the home with revolutionary wallpaper. Living the French Revolution meant entering a whole new world of sense and experience.

Plate showing a festival of the Cult of the Supreme Being. (Erich Lessing/Art Resource, NY)

Revolutionary calendar. (Snark/Art Resource, NY)

QUESTIONS FOR ANALYSIS

1. How easy do you think it would have been to follow the new revolutionary calendar? Why did revolutionaries believe it was necessary to create a new calendar?

2. How would you describe the festival of the Supreme Being as it is shown on the plate? What values of the Revolution does it seem to emphasize?

3. Why were ordinary objects, like plates and playing cards, decorated with symbols of the Revolution? What does this tell you about the ways everyday life was drawn into the experience of revolution?

Revolutionary playing card. (Musée de la Ville de Paris, Musée Carnavalet, Paris/Lauros/Giraudon, The Bridgeman Art Library)

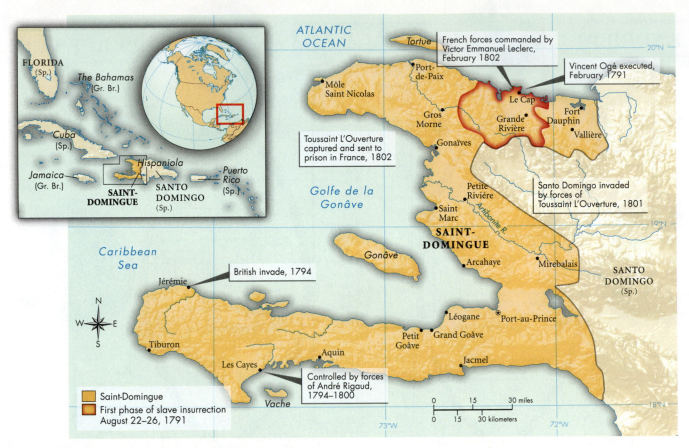

Map 20.1 **The War of Haitian Independence, 1791–1804** Neighbored by the Spanish colony of Santo Domingo, Saint-Domingue was the most profitable European colony in the Caribbean. In 1770 the French transferred the capital from Le Cap to Port-au-Prince. Slave revolts erupted in the north near Le Cap in 1791. Port-au-Prince became capital of the newly independent Haiti in 1804.

of secrecy and revenge. The rituals belonged to the religious practices, later known as "voodoo," that slaves had created on Saint-Domingue plantations from a combination of Catholicism and African cults. French soldiers later reported that religious incantations and African songs accompanied rebel slaves into combat. African culture thus played an important role in the Saint-Domingue revolution, alongside Enlightenment ideals of freedom and equality.

Revolts began on a few plantations on the night of August 22. Within a few days the uprising had swept much of the northern plain, creating a slave army estimated at around 2,000 individuals. By August 27 it was described by one observer as "10,000 strong, divided into 3 armies, of whom 700 or 800 are on horseback, and tolerably well-armed."[13] During the next month slaves attacked and destroyed hundreds of sugar and coffee plantations.

On April 4, 1792, as war loomed with the European states, the National Assembly issued a decree enfranchising all free blacks and free people of color. The Assembly hoped this measure would win the loyalty of free blacks and their aid in defeating the slave rebellion.

Warfare in Europe soon spread to Saint-Domingue

(Map 20.1), adding another complicating factor to its domestic conflicts. Since the beginning of the slave insurrection, the Spanish in neighboring Santo Domingo had supported rebel slaves, and in early 1793 they began to bring slave leaders and their soldiers into the Spanish army. Toussaint L'Ouverture (TOO-sahn LOO-vairtoor) (1743–1803), a freed slave who had joined the revolt, was named a Spanish officer. In September the British navy also blockaded the colony, and invading British troops captured French territory on the island. For the Spanish and British, revolutionary chaos provided a tempting opportunity to capture a profitable colony.

Desperate for forces to oppose France's enemies, the commissioners sent by the newly elected National Convention promised freedom to slaves who fought for France. By October 1793 they had abolished slavery throughout the colony. On February 4, 1794, the Convention ratified the abolition of slavery and extended it to all French territories, including the Caribbean colonies of Martinique and Guadeloupe. In just four years insurgent slaves had ended centuries of bondage in the French Caribbean and won full political rights.

For the future, the problem loomed of how these rights would be applied. The most immediate question, however, was whether France would be able to retain the colony, which was still under attack by Spanish and British forces. The tide began to turn when Toussaint L'Ouverture switched sides, bringing his military and political skills, along with four thousand well-trained soldiers, to support the French war effort.

By 1796 the French had gradually regained control of the colony, and L'Ouverture had emerged as the key leader of the combined slave and free colored forces. In May 1796 he was named commander of the western province of Saint-Domingue (see Map 20.1). The increasingly conservative nature of the French government during the Thermidorian reaction, however, threatened to undo the gains made by former slaves and free people of color. As exiled planters gained a stronger voice in French policymaking, L'Ouverture and other local leaders grew ever more wary of what the future might hold.

The Thermidorian Reaction and the Directory

The success of the French armies led Robespierre and the Committee of Public Safety to relax the emergency economic controls, but they extended the political Reign of Terror. In March 1794, to the horror of many sans-culottes, Robespierre's Terror wiped out many of his critics. Two weeks later, Robespierre sent long-standing collaborators, including the famous orator Danton, up the steps to the guillotine. A group of radicals and moderates in the Convention, knowing that they might be next, organized a conspiracy. They howled down Robespierre when he tried to speak to the National Convention on July 27, 1794—a date known as "9 Thermidor" according to France's newly adopted republican calendar. The next day it was Robespierre's turn to be shaved by the revolutionary razor.

As Robespierre's closest supporters followed their leader to the guillotine, France unexpectedly experienced a thorough reaction to the despotism of the Reign of Terror. In a general way, this **Thermidorian reaction** recalled the early days of the Revolution. The respectable middle-class lawyers and professionals who had led the liberal Revolution of 1789 reasserted their authority, drawing support from their own class,

the provincial cities, and the better-off peasants. In 1795 the National Convention abolished many economic controls, let prices rise sharply, and severely restricted the local political organizations in which the sans-culottes had their strength.

The collapse of economic controls, coupled with runaway inflation, hit the working poor very hard. After the Convention used the army to suppress the sans-culottes' protests, the urban poor lost their revolutionary fervor. Excluded and disillusioned, they would have little interest in and influence on politics until 1830. The poor of the countryside turned toward religion as a relief from earthly cares. Rural women, especially, brought back the Catholic Church and the open worship of God as the government began to soften its antireligious revolutionary stance.

As for the middle-class members of the National Convention, in 1795 they wrote yet another constitution that they believed would guarantee their economic position and political supremacy. As in previous elections, the mass of the population voted only

> **Thermidorian reaction** A reaction to the violence of the Reign of Terror in 1794, resulting in the execution of Robespierre and the loosening of economic controls.

The Execution of Robespierre Completely wooden except for the heavy iron blade, the guillotine was painted red for Robespierre's execution, a detail not captured in this black-and-white engraving of the 1794 event. Large crowds witnessed the execution in a majestic public square in central Paris, then known as the Place de la Revolution and now called the Place de la Concorde (Harmony Square). (Snark/Art Resource, NY)

for electors, whose number was cut back to men of substantial means. Electors then elected the members of a reorganized legislative assembly as well as key officials throughout France. The new assembly also chose a five-man executive called the Directory.

The Directory continued to support French military expansion abroad. War was no longer so much a crusade as a means to meet ever-present, ever-unsolved economic problems. Large, victorious French armies reduced unemployment at home and were able to live off the territories they conquered and plundered. Yet the French people felt a widespread disgust with war and food rationing, and they quickly grew weary of the unprincipled actions of the Directory. This general dissatisfaction revealed itself clearly in the national elections of 1797, which returned a large number of conservative and even monarchist deputies who favored peace at almost any price. The members of the Directory, fearing for their skins, used the army to nullify the elections and began to govern dictatorially. Two years later Napoleon Bonaparte ended the Directory in a coup d'état (koo day-TAH) and substituted a strong dictatorship for a weak one. The effort to establish stable representative government had failed.

The Napoleonic Era, 1799–1815

Why did Napoleon Bonaparte assume control of France, and what factors led to his downfall? How did the new republic of Haiti gain independence from France? ■

For almost fifteen years, from 1799 to 1814, France was in the hands of a keen-minded military dictator of exceptional ability. One of history's most fascinating leaders, Napoleon Bonaparte (1769–1821) realized the need to put an end to civil strife in France in order to create unity and consolidate his rule. And he did. But Napoleon saw himself as a man of destiny, and the glory of war and the dream of universal empire proved irresistible. For years he spiraled from victory to victory, but in the end he was destroyed by a mighty coalition united in fear of his restless ambition.

Napoleonic Code French civil code promulgated in 1804 that reasserted the 1789 principles of the equality of all male citizens before the law and the absolute security of wealth and private property as well as restricting rights accorded to women by previous revolutionary laws.

Napoleon's Rule of France

Born in Corsica into an impoverished noble family in 1769, Napoleon left home and became a lieutenant in the French artillery in 1785. After a brief and unsuc-

> **❝ May they learn from you that the God of peace is also the God of armies, and that He fights alongside those who defend the independence and liberty of France. ❞**
>
> **—NAPOLEON BONAPARTE**

cessful adventure fighting for Corsican independence in 1789, he returned to France as a French patriot and a dedicated revolutionary. Rising rapidly in the new army, Napoleon was placed in command of French forces in Italy and won brilliant victories there in 1796 and 1797. His next campaign, in Egypt, was a failure, but Napoleon returned to France before the fiasco was generally known, and his reputation remained intact.

Napoleon soon learned that some prominent members of the legislature were plotting against the Directory. The dissatisfaction of these plotters stemmed not so much from the fact that the Directory was a dictatorship as from the fact that it was a weak dictatorship. Ten years of upheaval and uncertainty had made firm rule much more appealing than liberty and popular politics to these disillusioned revolutionaries. The abbé Sieyès personified this evolution in thinking. In 1789 he had written that the nobility was grossly overprivileged and that the entire people should rule the French nation. Now Sieyès's motto was "Confidence from below, authority from above."

Like the other members of his group, Sieyès wanted a strong military ruler. The flamboyant thirty-year-old Napoleon, nationally revered for his heroism, was ideal. Thus the conspirators and Napoleon organized a takeover. On November 9, 1799, they ousted the Directors, and the following day soldiers disbanded the legislature at bayonet point. Napoleon was named first consul of the republic, and a new constitution consolidating his position was overwhelmingly approved in a plebiscite in December 1799. Republican appearances were maintained, but Napoleon became the real ruler of France.

The essence of Napoleon's domestic policy was to use his popularity and charisma to maintain order and end civil strife. He did so by working out unwritten agreements with powerful groups in France whereby the groups received favors in return for loyal service. Napoleon's bargain with the solid middle class was codified in the famous Civil Code of March 1804, also known as the **Napoleonic Code**, which reasserted two

The Coronation of Napoleon, 1804 In this detail from a grandiose painting by Jacques-Louis David, Napoleon, instead of the pope, prepares to crown his wife, Josephine, in an elaborate ceremony in Notre Dame Cathedral. Napoleon, the ultimate upstart, also crowned himself. Pope Pius VII, seated glumly behind the emperor, is reduced to being a spectator. (Louvre/Réunion des Musées Nationaux/Art Resource, NY)

of the fundamental principles of the Revolution of 1789: equality of all male citizens before the law, and absolute security of wealth and private property. Napoleon and the leading bankers of Paris established the privately owned Bank of France in 1800, which loyally served the interests of both the state and the financial oligarchy. Peasants were appeased when Napoleon defended the gains in land and status they had claimed during the Revolution.

At the same time, Napoleon built on the bureaucracy inherited from the Revolution and the Old Regime to create a thoroughly centralized state. He consolidated his rule by recruiting disillusioned revolutionaries for the network of ministers, prefects, and centrally appointed mayors that depended on him and came to serve him well. Only former revolutionaries who leaned too far to the left or to the right were pushed to the sidelines.[14] Nor were members of the old nobility slighted. In 1800 and again in 1802 Napoleon granted amnesty to one hundred thousand émigrés on the condition that they return to France and take a loyalty oath. Members of this returning elite soon ably occupied many high posts in the expanding centralized state. Napoleon also created a new imperial nobility in order to reward his most talented generals and officials.

Napoleon applied his diplomatic skills to healing the Catholic Church in France so that it could serve as a bulwark of social stability. After arduous negotiations, Napoleon and Pope Pius VII (pontificate 1800–1823) signed the Concordat (kuhn-KOHR-dat) of 1801. The pope gained the precious right for French Catholics to practice their religion freely, but Napoleon gained political power: his government now nominated bishops, paid the clergy, and exerted great influence over the church in France. In an 1802 proclamation, he called on priests to help instill patriotism for the "fatherland":

> *Exert for it all the force and ascendancy of spirit that your ministry gives you; that your lessons and examples may form in young citizens the love of our institutions, respect for and attachment to the tutelary authorities which have been created to protect them; may they learn from you that the God of peace is also the God of armies, and that He fights alongside those who defend the independence and liberty of France.*

The domestic reforms of Napoleon's early years were his greatest achievement. Much of his legal and administrative reorganization has survived in France to this day. More generally, Napoleon's domestic initiatives gave the great majority of French people a welcome sense of stability and national unity.

Order and unity had a price: authoritarian rule. Women, who had often participated in revolutionary politics without having legal equality, lost many of the gains they made in the 1790s. Under the new Napoleonic Code, women were dependents of either their fathers or their husbands, and they could not make contracts or have bank accounts in their own names. Napoleon and his advisers aimed at re-establishing a family monarchy, where the power of the husband and father was as absolute over the wife and the children as that of Napoleon was over his subjects.

Free speech and freedom of the press were continually violated. By 1811 only four newspapers were left, and they were little more than organs of government propaganda. The occasional elections were a farce. Later laws prescribed harsh penalties for political offenses, and people were watched carefully under an efficient spy system. People suspected of subversive activities were arbitrarily detained, placed under house arrest, or consigned to insane asylums. After 1810 political suspects were held in state prisons, as they had been during the Terror. There were about twenty-five hundred such political prisoners in 1814.

Napoleon's Expansion in Europe

Napoleon was above all a great military man. After coming to power in 1799 he sent peace feelers to Austria and Great Britain, the two remaining members of the Second Coalition that had been formed against France in 1798. When these overtures were rejected, French armies led by Napoleon decisively defeated the Austrians. In the Treaty of Lunéville (1801), Austria accepted the loss of almost all its Italian possessions, and German territory on the west bank of the Rhine was incorporated into France. The British agreed to the Treaty of Amiens in 1802, allowing France to remain in control of Holland, the Austrian Netherlands, the west bank of the Rhine, and most of the Italian peninsula. The Treaty of Amiens was clearly a diplomatic triumph for Napoleon, and peace with honor and profit increased his popularity at home.

In 1802 Napoleon was secure but driven to expand his power. Aggressively redrawing the map of Germany so as to weaken Austria and encourage the secondary states of southwestern Germany to side with France, Napoleon tried to restrict British trade with all of Eu-

German Confederation of the Rhine, 1806

rope. He then plotted to attack Great Britain, but his Mediterranean fleet was destroyed by Lord Nelson at the Battle of Trafalgar on October 21, 1805. Invasion of England was henceforth impossible. Renewed fighting had its advantages, however, for the first consul used the wartime atmosphere to have himself proclaimed emperor in late 1804.

Austria, Russia, and Sweden joined with Britain to form the Third Coalition against France shortly before the Battle of Trafalgar. Actions such as Napoleon's assumption of the Italian crown had convinced both Alexander I of Russia and Francis II of Austria that Napoleon was a threat to their interests and to the European balance of power. Yet the Austrians and the Russians were no match for Napoleon, who scored a brilliant victory over them at the Battle of Austerlitz in December 1805. Alexander I decided to pull back, and Austria accepted large territorial losses in return for peace as the Third Coalition collapsed.

Napoleon then proceeded to reorganize the German states to his liking. In 1806 he abolished many of the tiny German states as well as the ancient Holy Roman Empire and established by decree the German Confederation of the Rhine, a union of fifteen German states minus Austria, Prussia, and Saxony. Naming himself "protector" of the confederation, Napoleon firmly controlled western Germany.

Napoleon's intervention in German affairs alarmed the Prussians, who mobilized their armies after more than a decade of peace with France. Napoleon attacked and won two more brilliant victories in October 1806 at Jena and Auerstädt, where the Prussians were outnumbered two to one. The war with Prussia, now joined by Russia, continued into the following spring. After Napoleon's larger armies won another victory, Alexander I of Russia was ready to negotiate the peace. In the subsequent treaties of Tilsit in 1807, Prussia lost half of its population, while Russia accepted Napoleon's reorganization of western and central Europe and promised to enforce Napoleon's economic blockade against British goods.

The War of Haitian Independence

In the midst of these victories, Napoleon was forced to accept defeat overseas. With Toussaint L'Ouverture acting increasingly as an independent ruler of the western province of Saint-Domingue, another general, André

Rigaud, set up his own government in the southern peninsula, which had long been more isolated from France than the rest of the colony. Both leaders maintained policies, initially established by the French, of requiring former slaves to continue to work on their plantations. They believed that reconstructing the plantation economy was crucial to maintaining their military and political victories, and thus harshly suppressed resistance from former slaves.

Tensions mounted, however, between L'Ouverture and Rigaud. While L'Ouverture was a freed slave of African descent, Rigaud belonged to the free colored elite. This elite resented the growing power of former slaves like L'Ouverture, who in turn accused them of adopting the racism of white settlers. Civil war broke out between the two sides in 1799 when L'Ouverture's forces, led by his lieutenant Jean Jacques Dessalines (deh-suh-LEEN), invaded the south. Victory over Rigaud gave L'Ouverture control of the entire colony. (See "Individuals in Society: Toussaint L'Ouverture," page 648.)

This victory was soon challenged by Napoleon, who had his own plans for using profits from Caribbean plantations as a basis for expanding French power. His new constitution of 1799 opened the way for a re-establishment of slavery much feared in the colony. When the colonial assembly of Saint-Domingue, under L'Ouverture's direction, drafted its own constitution — which reaffirmed the abolition of slavery and granted L'Ouverture governorship for life — Napoleon viewed it as a seditious act. He ordered his brother-in-law, General Charles-Victor-Emmanuel Leclerc, to lead an expedition to the island to crush the new regime. Napoleon placed a high premium on bringing the colony to heel, writing to Leclerc: "Once the blacks have been disarmed and the principal generals sent to France, you will have done more for the commerce and civilization of Europe than we have done in our most brilliant campaigns." An officer sent to serve in the colony had a more cynical interpretation, writing that he was being sent to "fight with the Negroes for their own sugar."[15]

In 1802 Leclerc landed in Saint-Domingue. Although Toussaint L'Ouverture cooperated with the French and turned his army over to them, he was arrested and deported to France, along with his family, where he died in 1803. Jean Jacques Dessalines united the resistance under his command and led it to a crushing victory over the French forces. Of the fifty-eight thousand French soldiers, fifty thousand were lost in combat and to disease. On January 1, 1804, Dessalines formally declared the independence of Saint-Domingue and the creation of the new sovereign nation of Haiti, the name used by the pre-Columbian inhabitants of the island. The Haitian constitution was ratified in 1805.

Haiti, the second independent state in the Americas and the first in Latin America, was thus born from the first successful large-scale slave revolt in history. Fearing the spread of slave rebellion to the United States, President Thomas Jefferson refused to recognize Haiti. Both the American and the French Revolutions thus exposed their limits by acting to protect economic interests at the expense of revolutionary ideals of freedom and equality. Yet Haitian independence had fundamental repercussions for world history, helping spread the idea that liberty, equality, and fraternity must apply to all people.

The Napoleonic Era

November 1799	Napoleon overthrows the Directory
December 1799	Napoleon's new constitution approved
1800	Foundation of the Bank of France
1801	France defeats Austria and acquires Italian and German territories in the Treaty of Lunéville; Napoleon signs papal Concordat
1802	Treaty of Amiens
1803	Death of Toussaint L'Ouverture in France
January 1804	Declaration of Haitian independence
March 1804	Napoleonic Code
December 1804	Napoleon crowned emperor
May 1805	First Haitian constitution
October 1805	Britain defeats the French fleet at the Battle of Trafalgar
December 1805	Napoleon defeats Austria and Russia at the Battle of Austerlitz
1807	Napoleon redraws map of Europe in the treaties of Tilsit
1808	Spanish revolt against French occupation
1810	Height of the Grand Empire
June 1812	Napoleon invades Russia
Fall–Winter 1812	Napoleon makes a disastrous retreat from Russia
March 1814	Russia, Prussia, Austria, and Britain sign the Treaty of Chaumont, pledging alliance to defeat Napoleon
April 1814	Napoleon abdicates and is exiled to Elba; Louis XVIII restored to constitutional monarchy
February–June 1815	Napoleon escapes from Elba but is defeated at the Battle of Waterloo; Louis XVIII restored to throne for second time

Toussaint L'Ouverture

INDIVIDUALS IN SOCIETY

LITTLE IS KNOWN OF THE EARLY LIFE of Saint-Domingue's brilliant military and political leader Toussaint L'Ouverture. He was born in 1743 on a plantation outside Le Cap owned by the Count de Bréda. According to tradition, L'Ouverture was the eldest son of a captured African prince from modern-day Benin. Toussaint Bréda, as he was then called, occupied a privileged position among slaves. Instead of performing backbreaking labor

in the fields, he served his master as a coachman and livestock keeper. He also learned to read and write French and some Latin, but he was always more comfortable with the Creole dialect.

During the 1770s the plantation manager emancipated L'Ouverture, who subsequently leased his own small coffee plantation, worked by slaves. He married Suzanne Simone, who already had one son, and the couple had another son during their marriage. In 1791 he joined the slave uprisings that swept Saint-Domingue, and he took on the *nom de guerre* ("war name") "L'Ouverture," meaning "the opening." L'Ouverture rose to prominence among rebel slaves allied with Spain and by early 1794 controlled his own army. A devout Catholic who led a frugal and ascetic life, L'Ouverture impressed others with his enormous physical energy, intellectual acumen, and air of mystery. In 1794 he defected to the French side and led his troops to a series of victories against the Spanish. In 1795 the National Convention promoted L'Ouverture to brigadier general.

Over the next three years L'Ouverture successively eliminated rivals for authority on the island. First he freed himself of the French commissioners sent to govern the colony. With a firm grip on power in the northern province, L'Ouverture defeated General André Rigaud in 1800 to gain control in the south. His army then marched on the capital of Spanish Santo Domingo on the eastern half of the island, meeting little resistance. The entire island of Hispaniola was now under his command.

With control of Saint-Domingue in his hands, L'Ouverture was confronted with the challenge of building a post-emancipation society, the first of its kind. The task was made even more difficult by the chaos wreaked by war, the destruction of plantations, and bitter social and racial tensions. For L'Ouverture the most pressing concern was to re-establish the plantation economy. Without revenue to pay his army, the gains of the rebellion could be lost. He therefore encouraged white planters to return and reclaim their property. He also adopted harsh policies toward former slaves, forcing them back to their plantations and restricting their ability to acquire land. When they resisted, he sent troops across the island to enforce submission. L'Ouverture's 1801 constitution reaffirmed his draconian labor

policies and named L'Ouverture governor for life, leaving Saint-Domingue as a colony in name alone. In June 1802 French forces arrested L'Ouverture and jailed him at Fort de Joux in France's Jura Mountains near the Swiss border. L'Ouverture died of pneumonia on April 7, 1803. It was left to his lieutenant, Jean Jacques Dessalines, to win independence for the new Haitian nation.

QUESTIONS FOR ANALYSIS

1. Toussaint L'Ouverture was both slave and slave owner. How did each experience shape his life and actions?
2. What did Toussaint L'Ouverture and Napoleon Bonaparte have in common? How did they differ?

Equestrian portrait of Toussaint L'Ouverture. (Réunion des Musées Nationaux/Art Resource, NY)

648

The Grand Empire and Its End

Napoleon resigned himself to the loss of Saint-Domingue, but he still maintained imperial ambitions in Europe. Increasingly, he saw himself as the emperor of Europe, not just of France. The so-called **Grand Empire** he built had three parts. The core, or first part, was an ever-expanding France, which by 1810 included Belgium, Holland, parts of northern Italy, and much German territory on the east bank of the Rhine. The second part consisted of a number of dependent satellite kingdoms, on the thrones of which Napoleon placed (and replaced) the members of his large family. The third part comprised the independent but allied states of Austria, Prussia, and Russia. After 1806 both satellites and allies were expected to support Napoleon's **Continental System**, a blockade in which no ship coming from Britain or her colonies was allowed to dock at any port controlled by the French. It was intended to halt all trade between Britain and continental Europe, thereby destroying the British economy and its military force.

The impact of the Grand Empire on the peoples of Europe was considerable. In the areas incorporated into France and in the satellites (Map 20.2), Napoleon abolished feudal dues and serfdom. Some of the peasants and middle class benefited from these reforms. Yet Napoleon had to put the prosperity and special interests of France first in order to safeguard his power base. Levying heavy taxes in money and men for his armies, he came to be regarded more as a conquering tyrant than as an enlightened liberator. Thus French rule sparked patriotic upheavals and encouraged the growth of reactive nationalism, for individuals in different lands learned to identify emotionally with their own embattled national families as the French had done earlier.

The first great revolt occurred in Spain. In 1808 a coalition of Catholics, monarchists, and patriots rebelled against Napoleon's attempts to make Spain a French satellite. French armies occupied Madrid, but the foes of Napoleon fled to the hills and waged uncompromising guerrilla warfare. Spain was a clear warning: resistance to French imperialism was growing.

Yet Napoleon pushed on, determined to hold his complex and far-flung empire together. In 1810, when

Grand Empire The empire over which Napoleon and his allies ruled, encompassing virtually all of Europe except Great Britain and Russia.

Continental System A blockade imposed by Napoleon to halt all trade between continental Europe and Britain, thereby weakening the British economy and military.

Francisco Goya, *The Third of May 1808* Spanish master Francisco Goya created a passionate and moving indictment of the brutality of war in this painting from 1814, which depicts the close-range execution of Spanish rebels by Napoleon's forces in May 1808. Goya's painting evoked the bitterness and despair of many Europeans who suffered through Napoleon's invasions. (Erich Lessing/Art Resource, NY)

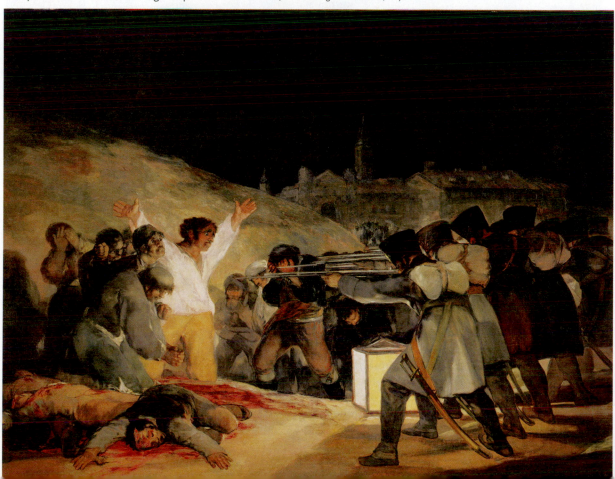

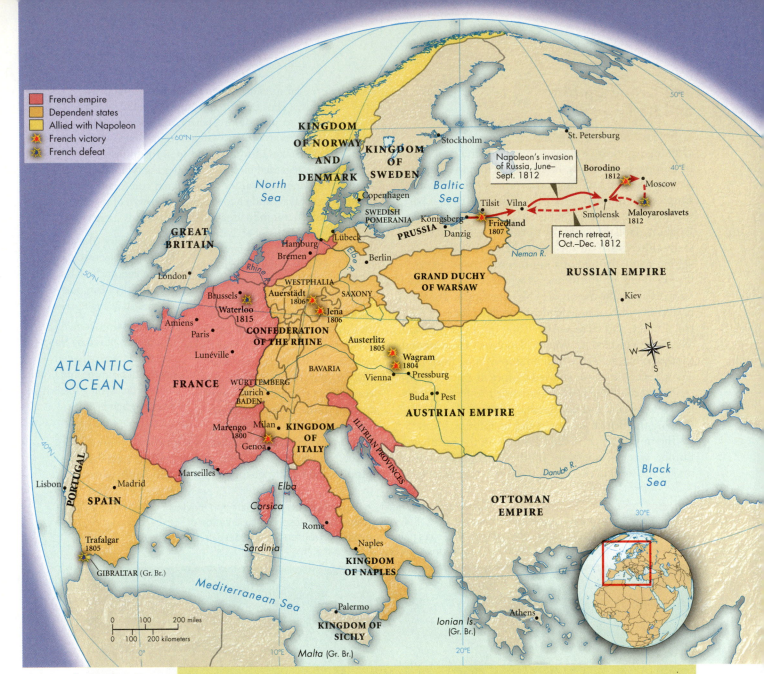

French empire
Dependent states
Allied with Napoleon
French victory
French defeat

KINGDOM OF NORWAY AND DENMARK
KINGDOM OF SWEDEN
North Sea
Stockholm
St. Petersburg
Copenhagen
Baltic Sea
SWEDISH POMERANIA
Königsberg
Tilsit Vilna
Borodino 1812 Moscow
Napoleon's invasion of Russia, June–Sept. 1812
GREAT BRITAIN
Hamburg
Lübeck
PRUSSIA
Danzig
Friedland 1807
Neman R.
Smolensk
Maloyaroslavets 1812
French retreat, Oct.–Dec. 1812
London
Bremen
Berlin
RUSSIAN EMPIRE
Rhine
WESTPHALIA
SAXONY
GRAND DUCHY OF WARSAW
Brussels
Auerstädt 1806
Kiev
Waterloo 1815
Jena 1806
Amiens
Paris
CONFEDERATION OF THE RHINE
Austerlitz 1805
Luneville
BAVARIA
Wagram 1804
Vienna
Pressburg
ATLANTIC OCEAN
FRANCE
WÜRTTEMBERG
Zurich
BADEN
Buda Pest
AUSTRIAN EMPIRE
Marengo 1800 Milan
KINGDOM OF ITALY
Genoa
ILLYRIAN PROVINCES
Danube R.
Black Sea
Marseilles
Elba
Lisbon
Madrid
PORTUGAL
SPAIN
Corsica
Rome
OTTOMAN EMPIRE
Trafalgar 1805
Sardinia
Naples
GIBRALTAR (Gr. Br.)
Mediterranean Sea
KINGDOM OF NAPLES
Palermo
Ionian Is. (Gr. Br.)
Athens
KINGDOM OF SICILY
Malta (Gr. Br.)

0   100   200 miles
0   100   200 kilometers

Mapping the Past

Map 20.2 Napoleonic Europe in 1812 Only Great Britain remained at war with Napoleon at the height of the Grand Empire. Many British goods were smuggled through Helgoland, a tiny but strategic British possession off the German coast. Compare this map with Map 16.2 (page 493), which shows the division of Europe in 1715.

ANALYZING THE MAP How had the balance of power shifted in Europe from 1715 to 1812? What changed, and what remained the same? What was the impact of Napoleon's wars on Germany and the Italian peninsula?

CONNECTIONS Why did Napoleon succeed in achieving vast territorial gains where Louis XIV did not?

To complete this activity online, go to the Online Study Guide at bedfordstmartins.com/mckaywest.

the Grand Empire was at its height, Britain still remained at war with France, helping the guerrillas in Spain and Portugal. The Continental System, expected to force the British "nation of shopkeepers" to its knees, was a failure. Instead, it was France that suffered from Britain's counter-blockade, which created hard times for French artisans and the middle class. Perhaps looking for a scapegoat, Napoleon turned on Alexander I of Russia, who in

1811 openly repudiated Napoleon's war of prohibitions against British goods.

Napoleon's invasion of Russia began in June 1812 with a force that eventually numbered 600,000, probably the largest force yet assembled in a single army. Only one-third of this Great Army was French, however; nationals of all the satellites and allies were drafted into the operation. Originally planning to winter in the Russian city of Smolensk if Alexander did not sue for peace, Napoleon reached Smolensk and recklessly pressed on toward Moscow. The great Battle of Borodino that followed was a draw, and the Russians retreated in good order. Alexander ordered the evacuation of Moscow, which the Russians then burned in part, and he refused to negotiate. Finally, after five weeks in the scorched and abandoned city, Napoleon ordered a retreat. That retreat was one of the greatest military disasters in history. The Russian army, the Russian winter, and starvation cut Napoleon's army to pieces. When the frozen remnants staggered into Poland and Prussia in December, 370,000 men had died and another 200,000 had been taken prisoner.[16]

Leaving his troops to their fate, Napoleon raced to Paris to raise yet another army. Possibly he might still have saved his throne if he had been willing to accept a France reduced to its historical size—the proposal offered by Austria's foreign minister, Prince Klemens von Metternich. But Napoleon refused. Austria and Prussia deserted Napoleon and joined Russia and Great Britain in the Treaty of Chaumont in March 1814, by which the four powers pledged allegiance to defeat the French emperor.

All across Europe patriots called for a "war of liberation" against Napoleon's oppression. Less than a month later, on April 4, 1814, a defeated Napoleon abdicated his throne. After this unconditional abdication, the victorious allies granted Napoleon the island of Elba off the coast of Italy as his own tiny state. Napoleon was allowed to keep his imperial title, and France was required to pay him a yearly income of 2 million francs.

The allies also agreed to the restoration of the Bourbon dynasty under Louis XVIII (r. 1814–1824) and promised to treat France with leniency in a peace settlement. The new monarch tried to consolidate support among the people by issuing the Constitutional Charter, which accepted many of France's revolutionary changes and guaranteed civil liberties.

Yet Louis XVIII—old, ugly, and crippled by gout— lacked the magnetism of Napoleon. Hearing of political unrest in France and diplomatic tensions in Vienna, Napoleon staged a daring escape from Elba in February 1815. Landing in France, he issued appeals for support and marched on Paris with a small band of followers. French officers and soldiers who had fought so long for their emperor responded to the call. Louis XVIII fled, and once more Napoleon took command. But Napoleon's gamble was a desperate long shot, for the allies were united against him. At the end of a frantic period known as the Hundred Days, they crushed his forces at Waterloo on June 18, 1815, and imprisoned him on the rocky island of St. Helena, far off the western coast of Africa. Louis XVIII returned to the throne, and the allies dealt more harshly with the apparently incorrigible French. As for Napoleon, he took revenge by writing his memoirs, nurturing the myth that he had been Europe's revolutionary liberator, a romantic hero whose lofty work had been undone by oppressive reactionaries.

LOOKING BACK LOOKING AHEAD

UNTIL 1789 the medieval ordering of French society into three estates remained in force, and the king, claiming to embody the nation in his person by the grace of God, continued to rule absolutely. Yet monumental changes had occurred over the eighteenth century as population grew, urbanization spread, and literacy increased. Enlightenment ideals influenced members of all three estates, who increasingly questioned the power of the monarchy and the rigid structure of society. As the sacred aura of the monarchy diminished, the royal government became increasingly incapable of resolving the urgent financial and political crises of the Old Regime. Exactly who should have the power, however, and how France should be governed, were questions that had many conflicting answers and resulted in decades of war and instability.

The age of revolution both drew on and affected European colonies in the Americas. The high stakes of colonial empire had heightened competition among European states, leading to a series of wars that generated crushing costs for overburdened treasuries. As was the case for the British in their North American colonies, the desperate need for new taxes weakened the French state and opened the door to revolution. In turn, the ideals of the French Revolution inspired slaves and free people of color in Saint-Domingue, thus opening the promise of liberty, equality, and fraternity to people of all races.

As complex as its origins are the long legacies of this period of revolution. Nineteenth- and early-twentieth-century Europe experienced periodic convulsions of revolution as successive generations struggled over political rights first proclaimed by the generation of 1789. Meanwhile, as dramatic events unfolded in France, a parallel revolution had gathered steam across the Channel. This was the British Industrial Revolution, originating around 1750 and accelerating through the end of the eighteenth century. After 1815 the twin forces of industrialization and democratization would combine to create the modern nation-states of Europe.

CHAPTER REVIEW

■ What social, political, and economic factors formed the background to the French Revolution? (p. 620)

An earlier generation of historians believed that the origins of the French Revolution lay in a single cause: class struggle between the nobility and the rising bourgeoisie. It is now clear that there were multiple causes of the Revolution. One was the growing ties — rather than conflict — between nobles and the wealthy bourgeoisie, who had grown economically and culturally closer over the course of the eighteenth century. The upper echelon's frustration with absolute rule emerged in political struggles between the monarchy and its officers, particularly in the high law courts. Public opinion turned against the monarchy as a rising torrent of political theory, cheap pamphlets, and gossip offered scathing and even pornographic depictions of the king and his court. With their sacred royal aura severely tarnished, Louis XV and his successor Louis XVI were unable to respond to the financial crises generated by French involvement in the Seven Years' War and the American Revolution. French support of the American colonists' fight for independence from Britain, moreover, inspired many to embrace the real possibility of political freedom. Louis XVI's half-hearted efforts to redress the situation were quickly overwhelmed by elite and popular demands for fundamental reform.

■ How did the events of 1789 result in a constitutional monarchy in France, and how did the new constitution affect the various members of French society at home and in the colony of Saint-Domingue? (p. 625)

When the Estates General gathered in 1789, delegates from the third estate refused to accept the old system of one vote per estate. Instead, they proclaimed that they alone constituted a "National Assembly" and refused to disband. Popular revolts prevented the king from intervening, and he was forced to accept the situation. Pushed forward by calls for freedom and equality from the streets of Paris to the faraway countryside, the National Assembly established a constitutional monarchy in 1791. The new constitution abolished the second estate and ended feudalism, thereby eliminating Old Regime privileges. Only men were given the right to vote for the new Assembly, however, and even among men, those in the lower economic stratum were disenfranchised. In the spirit of economic freedom, guilds and workers' associations were outlawed, which benefited merchants but threatened the livelihoods of master artisans and prevented workers from defending their rights. To the horror of the pope and devout French Catholics, the government seized church property and imposed an oath of loyalty on priests. The new constitution waffled in regard to the French colony of Saint-Domingue. By allowing the colonies to make their own laws regarding slavery and voting rights, it disheartened the slaves and free coloreds. And by reaffirming French trade monopolies, it angered the white planters.

■ How and why did the Revolution take a radical turn at home and in the colonies? (p. 633)

Support for constitutional monarchy ended with the royal family's attempted flight in June 1791. The new Legislative Assembly, comprising younger and more radical delegates led by members of the Jacobin club, declared war on Austria and proclaimed France a republic. With the execution of the royal couple and the declaration of terror as the order of the day, the French Revolution took an increasingly radical turn from the end of 1792.

After initial military defeats, France was largely victorious, mostly because of the total war effort undertaken by the Jacobin leadership. To defend the Revolution against its perceived internal enemies, Jacobins eliminated political opponents and then factions within their own party. They also attempted to bring about a cultural revolution, in part by attacking Christianity and substituting secular republican festivals. The Directory government that took power after the fall of Robespierre restored political equilibrium at the cost of the radical platform of social equality he had pursued. In Saint-Domingue, Spain and England profited from revolutionary conflict to invade the colony. To gain military support, the National Assembly agreed to enfranchise free people of color and to free any slave who fought on their side.

■ Why did Napoleon Bonaparte assume control of France, and what factors led to his downfall? How did the new republic of Haiti gain independence from France? (p. 644)

Wearied by the weaknesses of the Directory, a group of conspirators gave Napoleon Bonaparte control of France. His reputation as a brilliant military leader and his charisma and determination made him seem ideal to lead France to victory over its enemies. However, Napoleon's relentless ambitions ultimately led to his downfall. Not satisfied with his successes throughout Europe, and struggling to maintain his hold on Spain and Portugal, Napoleon made the fatal mistake of attempting to invade Russia in the summer of 1812. After a disastrous retreat from Moscow, he was eventually forced to abdicate the throne in 1814. His story is paralleled by that of Toussaint L'Ouverture, another soldier who emerged into the political limelight from the chaos of revolution, only to endure exile and defeat. Unlike Napoleon, L'Ouverture's cause ultimately prevailed. After his exile, war between the French forces and the armies he had led and inspired resulted in French defeat and independence for Saint-Domingue.

Suggested Reading

Bell, David A. *The Cult of the Nation in France: Inventing Nationalism, 1680–1800*. 2001. Traces early French nationalism through its revolutionary culmination.

Blanning, T. C. W. *The French Revolutionary Wars (1787–1802)*. 1996. A masterful account of the revolutionary wars that also places the French Revolution in its European context.

Broers, Michael. *Europe Under Napoleon*. 2002. Probes Napoleon's impact on the territories he conquered.

Connelly, Owen. *The French Revolution and Napoleonic Era*. 1991. An excellent introduction to the French Revolution and Napoleon.

Desan, Suzanne. *The Family on Trial in Revolutionary France*. 2004. Studies the effects of revolutionary law on the family, including the legalization of divorce.

Dubois, Laurent. *Avengers of the New World: The Story of the Haitian Revolution*. 2004. An excellent and highly readable account of the revolution that transformed the French colony of Saint-Domingue into the independent state of Haiti.

Englund, Steven. *Napoleon: A Political Life*. 2004. A good biography of the French emperor.

Hunt, Lynn. *Politics, Culture and Class in the French Revolution*, 2d ed. 2004. A pioneering examination of the French Revolution as a cultural phenomenon that generated new festivals, clothing, and songs, and even a new calendar.

Landes, John B. *Visualizing the Nation: Gender, Representation, and Revolution in Eighteenth-Century France*. 2001. Analyzes images of gender and the body in revolutionary politics.

Schechter, Ronald. *Obstinate Hebrews: Representations of Jews in France, 1715–1815*. 2003. An illuminating study of Jews and attitudes toward them in France from Enlightenment to emancipation.

Sutherland, Donald. *France, 1789–1815*. 1986. An overview of the French Revolution that emphasizes its many opponents, as well as its supporters.

Tackett, Timothy. *When the King Took Flight*. 2003. An exciting re-creation of the royal family's doomed effort to escape from Paris.

Notes

1. Quoted in R. R. Palmer, *The Age of Democratic Revolution*, vol. 1 (Princeton, N.J.: Princeton University Press, 1959), pp. 95–96.
2. Quoted in G. Wright, *France in Modern Times*, 4th ed. (New York: W. W. Norton, 1987), p. 34.
3. P. H. Beik, ed., *The French Revolution* (New York: Walker, 1970), p. 89.
4. G. Pernoud and S. Flaisser, eds., *The French Revolution* (Greenwich, Conn.: Fawcett, 1960), p. 61.
5. Quoted in Lynn Hunt, ed., *The French Revolution and Human Rights: A Brief Documentary History* (Boston/New York: Bedford/St. Martin's, 1996), p. 119.
6. Louis-Marie Prudhomme, *Revolutions of Paris*, quoted in Hunt, *The French Revolution and Human Rights*, p. 130.
7. Quoted in L. Gershoy, *The Era of the French Revolution, 1789–1799* (New York: Van Nostrand, 1957), p. 150.
8. Pernoud and Flaisser, *The French Revolution*, pp. 193–194.
9. Cited in Wim Klooster, *Revolutions in the Atlantic World: A Comprehensive History* (New York and London: New York University Press, 2009), p. 74.
10. Quotation from Hunt, *The French Revolution and Human Rights*, p. 138.
11. T. Blanning, *The French Revolutionary Wars, 1787–1802* (London: Arnold, 1996), pp. 116–128.
12. Quoted ibid., p. 123.
13. Quoted in Laurent Dubois, *Avengers of the New World: The Story of the Haitian Revolution* (Cambridge, Mass.: Harvard University Press, 2004), p. 97.
14. I. Woloch, *Napoleon and His Collaborators: The Making of a Dictatorship* (New York: W. W. Norton, 2001), pp. 36–65.
15. Quoted in Dubois, *Avengers of the New World*, pp. 255–256.
16. D. Sutherland, *France, 1789–1815: Revolution and Counterrevolution* (New York: Oxford University Press, 1986), p. 420.

Key Terms

estates (p. 620)
Estates General (p. 625)
National Assembly (p. 627)
Great Fear (p. 629)
constitutional monarchy (p. 630)
Jacobin club (p. 634)
second revolution (p. 635)
Girondists (p. 635)
the Mountain (p. 635)
sans-culottes (p. 636)
Reign of Terror (p. 637)
dechristianization (p. 638)
Thermidorian reaction (p. 643)
Napoleonic Code (p. 644)
Grand Empire (p. 649)
Continental System (p. 649)

For practice quizzes and other study tools, visit the Online Study Guide at **bedfordstmartins.com/mckaywest**.

For primary sources from this period, see ***Sources of Western Society*, Second Edition**.

For Web sites, images, and documents related to topics in this chapter, visit Make History at **bedfordstmartins.com/mckaywest**.

21

The Revolution in Energy and Industry

ca. 1780–1850

While the revolution in France was opening a new political era, another revolution was beginning to transform economic and social life. The Industrial Revolution began in Great Britain around the 1780s and started to influence continental Europe after 1815. Some historians see industrial development as basically moderate and evolutionary, but it was rapid and brought about numerous radical changes. Quite possibly only the development of agriculture during Neolithic times had a comparable impact and significance.

The Industrial Revolution profoundly modified much of human experience. It changed patterns of work, transformed the social class structure and the way people thought about class, and eventually altered the international balance of political power. The Industrial Revolution also helped ordinary people gain a higher standard of living as the widespread poverty of the preindustrial world was gradually reduced.

Unfortunately, the improvement in the European standard of living was limited until about 1850 for at least two reasons. First, even in Britain, only a few key industries experienced a technological revolution. Many more industries continued to use old methods, especially on the continent, and this held down the increase in total production. Second, the increase in total population, which began in the eighteenth century (see Chapter 18), continued across Europe as the era of the Industrial Revolution unfolded. The rapid growth in population threatened to eat up the growth in production and to leave most individuals poorer than ever. As a consequence, rapid population growth provided a somber background for European industrialization and made the wrenching transformation all the more difficult. ■

© Manchester Art Gallery, U.K./The Bridgeman Art Library

Life in the Industrial Revolution. This realistic painting from mid-nineteenth-century northern England shows women textile workers as they relax and socialize on their lunch break. Most of the workers are young and probably unmarried.

CHAPTER PREVIEW

The Industrial Revolution in Britain
■ What were the origins of the Industrial Revolution in Britain, and how did it develop between 1780 and 1850?

Industrialization in Continental Europe
■ How after 1815 did continental countries respond to the challenge of industrialization?

Relations Between Capital and Labor
■ How did the Industrial Revolution affect people of all social classes, and what measures were taken to improve the conditions of workers?

The Industrial Revolution in Britain

What were the origins of the Industrial Revolution in Britain, and how did it develop between 1780 and 1850? ■

The Industrial Revolution began in Great Britain, that historic union of Scotland and Wales with England—the wealthiest and the dominant part of the country. The transformation in industry was something new in history, and it was quite unplanned. With no models to copy and no idea of what to expect, Britain had to pioneer not only in industrial technology but also in social relations and urban living. Between 1793 and 1815, these formidable tasks were complicated by almost constant war with France. Just as France was the trailblazer in political change, Britain was the leader in economic development, and it must therefore command special attention.

Eighteenth-Century Origins

Although many aspects of the British Industrial Revolution are still matters for scholarly debate, it is generally agreed that the industrial changes that did occur grew out of a long process of development. Without a doubt, the expanding Atlantic economy of the eighteenth century served mercantilist Britain remarkably well. The colonial empire that Britain aggressively built, augmented by a strong position in Latin America and in the African slave trade, provided a growing market for British manufactured goods.

Agriculture also played a central role in bringing about the Industrial Revolution in Britain. English farmers were second only to the Dutch in productivity in 1700, and they were continually adopting new methods of farming as the century went on. The result, especially before 1760, was a period of bountiful crops and low food prices. The ordinary English family did not have to spend almost everything it earned just to buy bread. Thus the family could spend more on manufactured goods—a razor for the man or a shawl for the woman. Moreover, in the eighteenth century the members

Cottage Industry and Transportation in Eighteenth-Century England

Map legend:
Industrial areas
- Coal deposit
- Metal goods
- Woolen cloth
- Canals, 1800
- Navigable rivers

of the average British family were redirecting their labor away from unpaid work for household consumption toward work for wages that they could spend on goods, a trend reflecting the increasing commercialization of the entire European economy (see Chapter 18).

As manufacturing expanded to supply both foreign and British customers, the domestic market for raw materials was well-positioned to meet the growing demands of manufacturers. In an age when it was much cheaper to ship goods by water than by land, no part of England was more than fifty miles from navigable water. Beginning in the 1770s, a canal-building boom greatly enhanced this natural advantage. Rivers and canals provided easy movement of England's and Wales's enormous deposits of iron and coal, resources that would be critical raw materials in Europe's early industrial age. Nor were there any tariffs within the country to hinder trade, as there were in France before 1789 and in politically fragmented Germany.

Britain had a host of other assets that helped give rise to its industrial leadership. Unlike eighteenth-century France, Britain had an effective central bank and well-developed credit markets. The monarchy and the aristocratic oligarchy, which had jointly ruled the country since 1688, spent lavishly on stylish luxuries and provided stable and predictable government. At the same time, the government let the domestic economy operate with few controls, encouraging personal initiative, technical change, and a free market. Finally, Britain had long had a large class of hired agricultural laborers, rural proletarians whose numbers were further increased by the second great round of enclosures (the division of common lands into privately held and managed properties) in the late eighteenth century. These rural wage earners were relatively mobile—compared to village-bound peasants in France and western Germany, for example—and along with cottage workers they formed a potential industrial labor force for capitalist entrepreneurs.

All these factors combined to initiate the **Industrial Revolution**, a term first coined by awed contemporaries in the 1830s to describe the burst of major inventions and technical changes they had witnessed in certain industries. This technical revolution went hand in hand with an impressive quickening in the annual rate of industrial growth in Britain. Whereas industry had grown at only 0.7 percent between 1700 and 1760

Industrial Revolution

A term first coined in the 1830s to describe the burst of major inventions and economic expansion that took place in certain industries, such as cotton textiles and iron.

(before the Industrial Revolution), it grew at the much higher rate of 3 percent between 1801 and 1831 (when industrial transformation was in full swing).[1] The decisive quickening of growth probably came in the 1780s, after the American War of Independence (1775–1783) and just before the French Revolution (1789–1799).

Therefore, the great economic and political revolutions that shaped the modern world occurred almost simultaneously, though they began in different countries. The Industrial Revolution was, however, a longer process than the political upheavals. It was not complete in Britain until 1850 at the earliest, and it had no real impact on continental countries until after the end of the Napoleonic wars in 1815.

Chronology

ca. 1765	Hargreaves invents spinning jenny; Arkwright creates water frame
1769	Watt patents modern steam engine
1775–1783	American Revolution
ca. 1780–1850	Industrial Revolution; population boom in Great Britain
1789–1799	French Revolution
1799	Combination Acts passed
1810	Strike of Manchester cotton spinners
1824	Combination Acts repealed
1830	Stephenson's *Rocket*; first important railroad
1830s	Industrial banks in Belgium
1833	Factory Act
1842	Mines Act
1851	Great Exhibition held at Crystal Palace

The First Factories

The pressure to produce more goods for a growing market was directly related to the first decisive breakthrough of the Industrial Revolution—the creation of the world's first large factories in the British cotton textile industry. Technological innovations in the manufacture of cotton cloth led to a new system of production and social relationships. Since no other industry experienced such a rapid or complete transformation before 1830, these trailblazing developments deserve special consideration. Although the putting-out system of merchant capitalism (see Chapter 18) was expanding all across Europe in the eighteenth century, this pattern of rural industry was most fully developed in Britain. There, under the pressure of growing demand, the system's limitations began to outweigh its advantages for the first time. This was especially true in the British textile industry after about 1760.

A constant shortage of thread in the textile industry focused attention on ways of improving spinning. Many a tinkering worker knew that a better spinning wheel promised rich rewards. It proved hard to spin the traditional raw materials—wool and flax—with improved machines, but cotton was different. Cotton textiles had first been imported into Britain from India by the East India Company as a rare and delicate luxury for the upper classes, and by 1760 a tiny domestic cotton industry had emerged in northern England. After many experiments over a generation, a gifted carpenter and jack-of-all-trades, James Hargreaves, invented his cotton-spinning jenny about 1765. At almost the same moment, a barber-turned-manufacturer named Richard Arkwright invented (or possibly pirated) another kind of spinning machine, the water frame. These break-

throughs produced an explosion in the infant cotton textile industry in the 1780s, when it was increasing the value of its output at an unprecedented rate of about 13 percent each year. By 1790 the new machines were producing ten times as much cotton yarn as had been made in 1770.

Hargreaves's **spinning jenny** was simple, inexpensive, and powered by hand. Arkwright's **water frame**, however, quickly acquired a capacity of several hundred spindles and demanded much more power—waterpower. The water frame thus required large specialized mills, factories that employed as many as one thousand workers from the very beginning. The water frame could spin only a coarse, strong thread, which was then put out for respinning on hand-powered cottage jennies. Around 1790, an alternative technique invented by Samuel Crompton also began to require more power than the human arm could supply. After that time, all cotton spinning was gradually concentrated in factories.

The first consequences of these revolutionary developments in the textile industry were more beneficial than is generally believed. Cotton goods became much cheaper, and they were increasingly bought and treasured by all classes. In the past, only the wealthy could afford the comfort and cleanliness of underwear, which was called body linen because it was made from expensive linen cloth. Now millions of poor people, who had earlier worn nothing underneath their coarse, filthy

spinning jenny A simple, inexpensive, hand-powered spinning machine created by James Hargreaves in 1765.

water frame A spinning machine created by Richard Arkwright that had a capacity of several hundred spindles and used waterpower; it therefore required a larger and more specialized mill—a factory.

Woman Working a Spinning Jenny The loose cotton strands on the slanted bobbins shown in this illustration of Hargreaves's spinning jenny passed up to the sliding carriage and then on to the spindles (inset) in back for fine spinning. The worker, almost always a woman, regulated the sliding carriage with one hand, and with the other she turned the crank on the wheel to supply power. By 1783 one woman could spin by hand a hundred threads at a time. (spinning jenny: Mary Evans Picture Library/The Image Works; spindle: Picture Research Consultants & Archives)

outer garments, could afford to wear cotton slips and underpants as well as cotton dresses and shirts. Families using cotton in cottage industry were freed from their constant search for adequate yarn from scattered part-time spinners, since all the thread needed could be spun in the cottage on the jenny or obtained from a nearby factory. The wages of weavers, now hard-pressed to keep up with the spinners, rose markedly until about 1792. Weavers were among the best-paid workers in England. As a result, large numbers of agricultural laborers became hand-loom weavers, while mechanics and capitalists sought to invent a power loom to save on labor costs. This Edmund Cartwright achieved in 1785. But the power looms of the factories worked poorly at first, and hand-loom weavers continued to receive good wages until at least 1800.

Unfortunately, working conditions in the early cotton factories were less satisfactory than those of cottage weavers and spinners, and adult workers were reluctant to work in them. Therefore, factory owners often turned to young children who had been abandoned by their parents and put in the care of local parishes. Parish officers often "apprenticed" such unfortunate foundlings to factory owners. The parish thus saved money, and the factory owners gained workers over whom they exercised almost the authority of slave owners.

Apprenticed as young as five or six years of age, boy and girl workers were forced by law to labor for their "masters" for as many as fourteen years. Housed, fed, and locked up nightly in factory dormitories, the young workers received little or no pay. Hours were appalling—commonly thirteen or fourteen hours a day, six days a week. Harsh physical punishment maintained brutal discipline. To be sure, poor children typically worked long hours and frequently outside the home for brutal masters, but the wholesale coercion of orphans as factory apprentices constituted exploitation on a truly unprecedented scale. This exploitation ultimately piqued the conscience of reformers, reinforced more humanitarian attitudes toward children and their labor in the early nineteenth century, and resulted in laws to protect young workers (see page 678).

A Pioneering Silk Mill In the 1600s Italians invented a machine to spin the thread for the silk that rich people loved. Their carefully guarded secret was stolen in 1717 by John Lombe, who then built this enormous silk mill in England. But the factory production of textiles only took off when the spinning of cotton — a fabric for all classes — was mechanized in the later eighteenth century. (© The Art Gallery Collection/Alamy)

The creation of the world's first modern factories in the British cotton textile industry in the 1770s and 1780s, which grew out of the putting-out system of cottage production, was a major historical development. Both symbolically and substantially, the big new cotton mills marked the beginning of the Industrial Revolution in Britain. By 1831 the largely mechanized cotton textile industry towered above all others, accounting for fully 22 percent of the country's entire industrial production.

The Problem of Energy

The growth of the cotton textile industry might have been stunted or cut short if water from rivers and streams had remained the primary source of power for the new factories, but this did not occur. Instead, an epoch-making solution was found to the age-old problem of energy and power.

Human beings have long used their toolmaking abilities to construct machines that convert one form of energy into another for their own benefit. In the medi-

eval period, people began to develop water mills to grind their grain and windmills to pump water and drain swamps. More efficient use of water and wind in the sixteenth and seventeenth centuries enabled human beings to accomplish more; intercontinental sailing ships were a prime example. Nevertheless, even into the eighteenth century, society continued to rely mainly on wood for energy, and human beings and animals continued to perform most work. This dependence meant that Western civilization remained poor in energy and power. No matter how hard people worked, they could not produce very much.

The shortage of energy had become particularly severe in Britain by the eighteenth century. Wood was in ever-shorter supply, yet it remained tremendously important. It served as the primary source of heat for all homes and industries and as a basic raw material. Processed wood (charcoal) was the fuel that was mixed with iron ore in the blast furnace to produce pig iron. The iron industry's appetite for wood was enormous, and by 1740 the British iron industry was stagnating.

The Steam Engine Breakthrough

As this early energy crisis grew worse, Britain looked toward its abundant and widely scattered reserves of coal as an alternative to its vanishing wood. Coal was first used in Britain in the late Middle Ages as a source of heat. By 1640 most homes in London were heated with coal, and it was also used in industry to provide heat for making beer, glass, soap, and other products. The breakthrough came when industrialists began to use coal to produce mechanical energy and to power machinery.

As more coal was produced, mines were dug deeper and deeper and were constantly filling with water. Mechanical pumps, usually powered by animals walking in circles at the surface, had to be installed. At one mine, fully five hundred horses were used in pumping. Such power was expensive and bothersome. In an attempt to overcome these disadvantages, Thomas Savery in 1698 and Thomas Newcomen in 1705 invented the first primitive **steam engines**. Both engines burned coal to produce steam, which was then used to operate a pump. Although both models were extremely inefficient, by the early 1770s many of the Savery engines and hundreds of the Newcomen engines were operating successfully in English and Scottish mines.

In the early 1760s, a gifted young Scot named James Watt (1736–1819) was drawn to a critical study of the steam engine. Watt was employed at the time by the University of Glasgow as a skilled craftsman making scientific instruments. The Scottish universities were pioneers in practical technical education, and in 1763 Watt was called on to repair a Newcomen engine being used in a physics course. After a series of observations, Watt saw

steam engines A breakthrough invention by Thomas Savery in 1698 and Thomas Newcomen in 1705 that burned coal to produce steam, which was then used to operate a pump; the early models were superseded by James Watt's more efficient steam engine, patented in 1769.

James Nasmyth's Mighty Steam Hammer Nasmyth's invention was the forerunner of the modern pile driver, and its successful introduction in 1832 epitomized the rapid development of steam power technology in Britain. In this painting by the inventor himself, workers manipulate a massive iron shaft being hammered into shape at Nasmyth's foundry near Manchester. (Science & Society Picture Library, London)

that the Newcomen engine's waste of energy could be reduced by adding a separate condenser. This splendid invention, patented in 1769, greatly increased the efficiency of the steam engine.

To invent something in a laboratory is one thing; to make it a practical success is quite another. Watt needed skilled workers, precision parts, and capital, and the relatively advanced nature of the British economy proved essential. A partnership in 1775 with Matthew Boulton, a wealthy English industrialist, provided Watt with adequate capital and exceptional skills in salesmanship that equaled those of the renowned pottery king, Josiah Wedgwood. (See "Individuals in Society: Josiah Wedgwood," page 662.) In the craft tradition of locksmiths, tinsmiths, and millwrights, Watt found skilled mechanics who could install, regulate, and repair his sophisticated engines. From ingenious manufacturers such as the cannonmaker John Wilkinson, Watt was gradually able to purchase precision parts. This support allowed him to create an effective vacuum and regulate a complex engine. In more than twenty years of constant effort, Watt made many further improvements. By the late 1780s, the firm of Boulton and Watt had made the steam engine a practical and commercial success in Britain.

The steam engine of Watt and his followers was the Industrial Revolution's most fundamental advance in technology. For the first time in history, humanity had, at least for a few generations, almost unlimited power at its disposal. For the first time, inventors and engineers could devise and implement all kinds of power equipment to aid people in their work. For the first time, abundance was at least a possibility for ordinary men and women.

The steam engine was quickly put to use in several industries in Britain. It drained mines and made possible the production of ever more coal to feed steam engines elsewhere. Steam power began to replace waterpower in the cotton-spinning mills during the 1780s, contributing greatly to that industry's phenomenal rise. Steam also took the place of waterpower in flour mills, in the malt mills used in breweries, in the flint mills supplying the pottery industry, and in the

mills exported by Britain to the West Indies to crush sugar cane.

Steam power promoted important breakthroughs in other industries. The British iron industry was radically transformed. The use of powerful steam-driven bellows in blast furnaces helped ironmakers switch over rapidly from limited charcoal to unlimited coke (which is made from coal) in the smelting of pig iron after 1770. In the 1780s, Henry Cort developed the puddling furnace, which allowed pig iron to be refined in turn with coke.

Strong, skilled ironworkers—the puddlers— "cooked" molten pig iron in a great vat, raking off globs of refined iron for further processing. Cort also developed heavy-duty steam-powered rolling mills, which were capable of spewing out finished iron in every shape and form. The economic consequence of these technical innovations was a great boom in the British iron industry. In 1740 annual British iron production was only 17,000 tons. With the spread of coke smelting and the impact of Cort's inventions, production had reached 260,000 tons by 1806. In 1844 Britain produced 3 million tons of iron. This was a truly amazing expansion. Once scarce and expensive, iron became the cheap, basic, indispensable building block of the economy.

The Coming of the Railroads

The second half of the eighteenth century saw extensive construction of hard and relatively smooth roads, particularly in France before the Revolution. Yet it was passenger traffic that benefited most from this construction. Overland shipment of freight, relying solely on horsepower, was still quite limited and frightfully expensive; shippers used rivers and canals for heavy freight

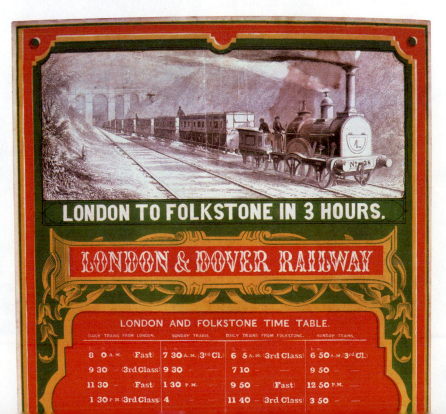

The New World of Speed A colorful timetable poster lists the trains from London to Folkstone, the English Channel's gateway port to the European continent, and proudly proclaims a speedy journey. Tunneling through hills and spanning rivers with bridges, railroad construction presented innumerable challenges and required enormous amounts of capital and labor. (Private Collection/The Bridgeman Art Library)

LONDON TO FOLKSTONE IN 3 HOURS.

LONDON & DOVER RAILWAY

LONDON AND FOLKSTONE TIME TABLE.

DAILY TRAINS FROM LONDON.		SUNDAY TRAINS.		DAILY TRAINS FROM FOLKSTONE.		SUNDAY TRAINS.	
8 0 A.M.	Fast	7 30 A.M.	3rd Cl.	6 5 A.M.	3rd Class	6 50 A.M.	3rd Cl.
9 30	3rd Class	9 30		7 10		9 50	
11 30	Fast	1 30 P.M.		9 50	Fast	12 50 P.M.	
1 30 P.M	3rd Class	4		11 40	3rd Class	3 50	

INDIVIDUALS IN SOCIETY

AS THE MAKING OF CLOTH AND IRON WAS REVOLUTIONIZED by technical change and factory organization, so too were the production and consumption of pottery. Acquiring beautiful tableware became a craze for eighteenth-century consumers, and continental monarchs often sought prestige in building royal china works. But the grand prize went to Josiah Wedgwood, who wanted to "astonish the world."

The twelfth child of a poor potter, Josiah Wedgwood (1730–1795) grew up in the pottery district of Staffordshire in the English Midlands, where many tiny potteries made simple earthenware utensils for sale in local markets. Growing up as an apprentice in the family business inherited by his oldest brother, Wedgwood struck off on his own in 1752. Soon manager of a small pottery, Wedgwood learned that new products recharged lagging sales. Studying chemistry and determined to succeed, Wedgwood spent his evenings experimenting with different chemicals and firing conditions.

In 1759, after five years of tireless efforts, Wedgwood perfected a beautiful new green glaze. Now established as a master potter, he opened his own factory and began manufacturing teapots and tableware finished in his green and other unique glazes, or adorned with printed scenes far superior to those being produced by competitors. Wedgwood's products caused a sensation among consumers, and his business quickly earned substantial profits. Subsequent breakthroughs, including ornamental vases imitating classical Greek models and jasperware for jewelry, contributed greatly to Wedgwood's success.

Competitors were quick to copy Wedgwood's new products and sell them at lower prices. Thus Wedgwood and his partner Thomas Bentley sought to cultivate an image of superior fashion, taste, and quality in order to develop and maintain a dominant market position. They did this by first capturing the business of the trend-setting elite. In one brilliant coup the partners first sold a very large cream-colored dinner set to Britain's queen, which they quickly christened "Queen's ware" and sold as a very expensive, must-have luxury to English aristocrats. Equally brilliant was Bentley's suave expertise in the elegant London showroom selling Wedgwood's imitation Greek vases, which became the rage after the rediscovery of the Roman towns Pompeii and Herculaneum in the mid-eighteenth century.

Above all, once Wedgwood had secured his position as the luxury market leader, he was able to successfully extend his famous brand to the growing middle class, capturing an enormous mass market for his "useful ware." Thus when sales of a luxury good grew "stale," Wedgwood made tasteful modifications and sold it to the middling classes for twice the price his competitors could charge. This unbeatable combination of mass appeal and high prices all across Europe brought Wedgwood great fame and enormous wealth.

A workaholic with an authoritarian streak, Wedgwood contributed substantially to the development of the factory system. In 1769, he opened a model factory on a new canal he had promoted. With two hun-

Typical Wedgwood jasperware, this elegant cylindrical vase, decorated in the form of a miniature Roman household altar, was destined for the luxury market. (Image copyright © The Metropolitan Museum of Art/Art Resource, NY)

Josiah Wedgwood perfected jasperware, a fine-grained pottery usually made in "Wedgwood blue" with white decoration. (Down House, Kent, Darwin Heirlooms Trust)

dred workers in several departments, Wedgwood exercised tremendous control over his workforce, imposing fines for many infractions, such as being late, drinking on the job, or wasting material. He wanted, he said, to create men who would be like "machines" that "cannot err." Yet Wedgwood also recognized the value in treating workers well. He championed a division of labor that made most workers specialists who received ongoing training. He also encouraged employment of family groups, who were housed in company row houses with long narrow backyards suitable for raising vegetables and chickens. Paying relatively high wages and providing pensions and some benefits, Wedgwood developed a high-quality labor force that learned to accept his rigorous discipline and carried out his ambitious plans.

QUESTIONS FOR ANALYSIS

1. How and why did Wedgwood succeed?
2. Was Wedgwood a good boss or a bad one? Why?
3. How did Wedgwood exemplify the new class of factory owners?

whenever possible. It was logical, therefore, that inventors would try to use steam power.

As early as 1800, an American drove a "steamer on wheels" through city streets. Other experiments followed. In the 1820s, English engineers created steam cars capable of carrying fourteen passengers at ten miles an hour — as fast as the mail coach. But the noisy, heavy steam automobiles frightened passing horses and damaged themselves as well as the roads with their vibrations. For the rest of the century, horses continued to reign on highways and city streets.

The coal industry had long been using plank roads and rails to move coal wagons within mines and at the surface. Rails reduced friction and allowed a horse or a human being to pull a heavier load. Thus once a rail capable of supporting a heavy locomotive was developed in 1816, all sorts of experiments with steam engines on rails went forward. In 1825 after ten years of work, George Stephenson built an effective locomotive. In 1830 his *Rocket* sped down the track of the just-completed Liverpool and Manchester Railway at sixteen miles per hour. This was the world's first important railroad, fittingly steaming in the heart of industrial England. The line from Liverpool to Manchester was a financial as well as a technical success, and many private companies were quickly organized to build more rail lines. Within twenty years, they had completed the main trunk lines of Great Britain (Map 21.1). Other countries were quick to follow.

Rocket The name given to George Stephenson's effective locomotive that was first tested in 1830 on the Liverpool and Manchester Railway at 16 miles per hour.

The significance of the railroad was tremendous. It dramatically reduced the cost and uncertainty of shipping freight over land. This advance had many economic consequences. Previously, markets had tended to be small and local; as the barrier of high transportation costs was lowered, markets became larger and even nationwide. Larger markets encouraged larger factories with more sophisticated machinery in a growing number of industries. Such factories could make goods more cheaply and gradually subjected most cottage workers and many urban artisans to severe competitive pressures.

In all countries, the construction of railroads created a strong demand for unskilled labor and contributed to the growth of a class of urban workers. Hard work on construction gangs was done in the open air with animals and hand tools. Many landless farm laborers and poor peasants, long accustomed to leaving their villages for temporary employment, went to build railroads. By the time the work was finished, life back home in the village often seemed dull and unappealing, and many men drifted to towns in search of work. By the time they sent for their wives and sweethearts to join them, they had become urban workers.

The railroad changed the outlook and values of the entire society. The last and culminating invention of the Industrial Revolution, the railroad dramatically revealed the power and increased the speed of the new age. Racing down a track at sixteen miles per hour or, by 1850, at a phenomenal fifty miles per hour was a new and awesome experience. As a French economist put it after a ride on the Liverpool and Manchester in 1833, "There are certain impressions that one cannot put into words!" Some great painters, notably Joseph M. W. Turner (1775–1851) and Claude Monet (moh-NAY) (1840–1926), succeeded in expressing this sense of power and awe. So did the massive new train stations, the cathedrals of the industrial age. Leading railway engineers such as Isambard Kingdom Brunel and Thomas Brassey, whose tunnels pierced mountains and whose bridges spanned valleys, became public idols—the astronauts of their day. Everyday speech absorbed the images of railroading. After you got up a "full head of steam," you "highballed" along. And if you didn't "go off the track," you might "toot your own whistle." The railroad fired the imagination.

Crystal Palace The location of the Great Exhibition in 1851 in London, an architectural masterpiece made entirely of glass and iron.

Industry and Population

In 1851 London hosted a famous industrial fair called the Great Exhibition in the newly built **Crystal Palace**, an architectural masterpiece that helped draw millions of visitors. (See "Living in the Past: Visiting the Crystal Palace Exhibition," page 666.) For the visiting multitude, one fact stood out: the little island of Britain was the "workshop of the world." Britain alone produced two-thirds of the world's coal and more than one-half of its iron and cotton cloth. More generally, it has been carefully estimated that in 1860 Britain produced a truly remarkable 20 percent of the entire world's output of industrial goods, whereas it had produced only about 2 percent of the world total in 1750.[2] Experiencing revolutionary industrial change, Britain became the first industrial nation (see Map 21.1).

As the British economy significantly increased its production of manufactured goods, the gross national product (GNP) rose roughly fourfold at constant prices between 1780 and 1851. In other words, the British people as a whole increased their wealth and their national income dramatically. At the same time, the population of Britain boomed, growing from about 9 million in 1780 to almost 21 million in 1851. Thus growing numbers consumed much of the increase in total production. According to one important study, average consumption per person increased by only 75 percent between 1780 and 1851, as the growth in the total population ate up a large part of the fourfold increase in GNP in those years.[3]

Although the question is still debated, many economic historians now believe that rapid population growth in Great Britain was not harmful because it facilitated industrial expansion. More people meant a more mobile labor force, with a wealth of young workers in need of employment and ready to go where the jobs were.

Contemporaries were much less optimistic. In his famous and influential *Essay on the Principle of Population* (1798), Thomas Malthus (1766–1834) examined the dynamics of human populations. He argued that "there are few states in which there is not a constant effort in the population to increase beyond the means of subsistence. This constant effort as constantly tends to subject the lower classes of society to distress, and to prevent any great permanent melioration of these conditions."[4]

Map 21.1 The Industrial Revolution in England, ca. 1850 Industry concentrated in the rapidly growing cities of the north and the center of England, where rich coal and iron deposits were close to one another.

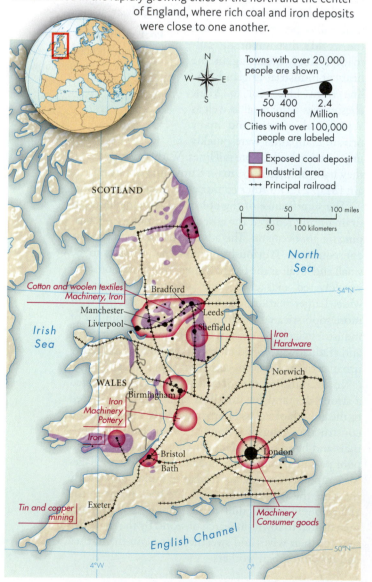

" There are few states in which there is not a constant effort in the population to increase beyond the means of subsistence. "

—THOMAS MALTHUS

Since, in his opinion, population would always tend to grow faster than the food supply, Malthus concluded that the only hope of warding off such "positive checks" to population growth as war, famine, and disease was "prudential restraint." That is, young men and women had to limit the growth of population by the old tried-and-true means of marrying late in life. But Malthus was not optimistic about this possibility. The powerful attraction of the sexes would cause most people to marry early and have many children.

Wealthy English stockbroker and leading economist David Ricardo (1772–1823) coldly spelled out the pessimistic implications of Malthus's thought. Ricardo's depressing **iron law of wages** posited that because of the pressure of population growth, wages would always sink to subsistence level. That is, wages would be just high enough to keep workers from starving. With Malthus and Ricardo setting the tone, economics was soon dubbed "the dismal science."

Malthus, Ricardo, and their many followers were proved wrong—in the long run. However, until the 1820s, or even the 1840s, contemporary observers might reasonably have concluded that the economy and the total population were racing neck and neck, with the outcome very much in doubt. The closeness of the race added to the difficulties inherent in the journey toward industrial civilization. There was another problem as well. Perhaps workers, farmers, and ordinary people did not get their rightful share of the new wealth. Perhaps only the rich got richer, while the poor got poorer or made no progress. We will turn to this great issue after looking at the process of industrialization in continental countries.

Industrialization in Continental Europe

How after 1815 did continental countries respond to the challenge of industrialization? ■

The new technologies developed in the British Industrial Revolution were adopted rather slowly by businesses in continental Europe. Yet by the end of the nineteenth century, several European countries as well as the United States had also industrialized their economies to a con-

siderable but variable degree. This meant that the process of Western industrialization proceeded gradually, with uneven jerks and national and regional variations. Scholars are still struggling to explain these variations, especially since good answers may offer valuable lessons in our own time for poor countries seeking to improve their material condition through industrialization and economic development. The latest findings on the Western experience are encouraging. They suggest that there were alternative paths to the industrial world in the nineteenth century and that, today as then, there was no need to follow a rigid, predetermined British model.

National Variations

European industrialization, like most economic developments, requires some statistical analysis as part of the effort to understand it. Comparative data on industrial production in different countries over time help give us an overview of what happened. One set of data, the work of a Swiss scholar, compares the level of industrialization on a per capita basis in several countries from 1750 to 1913. These data are far from perfect because there are gaps in the underlying records. But they reflect basic trends and are presented in Table 21.1 for closer study.

As the heading of Table 21.1 makes clear, this is a per capita comparison of levels of industrialization—a comparison of how much industrial product was produced, on average, for each person in a given country in a given year. Therefore, all the numbers in Table 21.1 are expressed in terms of a single index number of 100, which equals the per capita level of industrial goods in Great Britain (and Ireland) in 1900. Every number in the table is thus a percentage of the 1900 level in Britain and is directly comparable with other numbers. The countries are listed in roughly the order that they began to use large-scale, power-driven technology.

What does this overview of European industrialization tell us? First, and very significantly, one sees in the first column that in 1750 all countries were fairly close together and that Britain was only slightly ahead of its archenemy, France. Second, the column headed 1800 shows that Britain had opened up a noticeable lead over all continental countries by 1800, and that gap progressively widened as the British Industrial Revolution accelerated to 1830 and reached full maturity by 1860. The British level of per capita industrialization was twice

> **iron law of wages**
> Theory proposed by English economist David Ricardo suggesting that the pressure of population growth prevents wages from rising above the subsistence level.

LIVING IN THE PAST

IN 1851 BRITAIN HOSTED A SPECTACULAR EVENT, the Great Exhibition of the Works of Industry of All the Nations, popularly known as the Crystal Palace Exhibition. The more than 6 million visitors from all over Europe marveled at the gigantic new exhibition hall set in the middle of a large, centrally located park. The building was made entirely of glass and iron, both of which were now cheap and abundant in Great Britain. Little wonder that people bought millions of souvenirs picturing the Crystal Palace. The handsome depiction shown here brightened the lid of a ceramic pot.

Entering the 1,800-foot-long domed hall — five times the length of an American football field — visitors could peruse an astonishing 1,500 exhibits arranged by country of origin. Many other exhibits featured machines and industrial products, for the Crystal Palace was the grandest and most recent staging of the industrial fair, which was designed to promote prosperity and the diffusion of technical knowledge. Half of the exhibits were British, and many proudly demonstrated the country's dominant position in machine tools and factory production.

Other countries' displays showed that industrial progress was spreading. For example, the small American exhibit featured a few sophisticated industrial products, such as Samuel Colt's prizewinning six-shot revolver.

This great industrial fair was also a consumer's paradise. In many ways the exhibits foretold the creation of big department stores in the 1860s and 1870s, and even the coming of mass consumption and enclosed shopping malls. While the British dominated in industrial goods, other countries led in the

Lid to a souvenir pot showing the Crystal Palace.
(Fitzwilliam Museum, Cambridge University, UK/Bridgeman Giraudon/The Bridgeman Art Library)

View of the French furniture exhibit. (Private Collection/The Stapleton Collection/The Bridgeman Art Library)

luxury products that greatly appealed to aspiring members of the middle class. The luxury products of French artisans stood out, and France won more prizes in the furniture category than any other nation. Many other handmade luxuries came from Persia, China, and India. Last but not least, the Crystal Palace was equipped with some of the very first public toilets, where a small fee purchased a clean seat, a towel, a comb, and a shoeshine.

QUESTIONS FOR ANALYSIS

1. Describe the Crystal Palace. In what ways was it a revolutionary building?

2. Compare the products that Britain and France presented. How do you explain the differences?

3. The Crystal Palace Exhibition exceeded all expectations. How do you account for its success?

Samuel Colt's six-shot revolver. (Visual Connection Archive)

Table 21.1
Per Capita Levels of Industrialization, 1750–1913

	1750	1800	1830	1860	1880	1900	1913
Great Britain	10	16	25	64	87	100	115
Belgium	9	10	14	28	43	56	88
United States	4	9	14	21	38	69	126
France	9	9	12	20	28	39	59
Germany	8	8	9	15	25	52	85
Austria-Hungary	7	7	8	11	15	23	32
Italy	8	8	8	10	12	17	26
Russia	6	6	7	8	10	15	20
China	8	6	6	4	4	3	3
India	7	6	6	3	2	1	2

Note: All entries are based on an index value of 100, equal to the per capita level of industrialization in Great Britain in 1900. Data for Great Britain includes Ireland, England, Wales, and Scotland.

Source: P. Bairoch, "International Industrialization Levels from 1750 to 1980," *Journal of European Economic History* 11 (Spring 1982): 294, U.S. Journals at Cambridge University Press.

the French level in 1830, for example, and more than three times the French level in 1860. All other large countries (except the United States) had fallen even further behind Britain than France had at both dates.

Third, variations in the timing and in the extent of industrialization in the continental powers and the United States are also apparent. Belgium, achieving independence from the Netherlands in 1831 and rich in iron and coal, led in adopting Britain's new technology, and it experienced a truly revolutionary surge between 1830 and 1860. France developed factory production more gradually, and most historians now detect no burst in French mechanization and no acceleration in the growth of overall industrial output that may accurately be called revolutionary. They stress instead France's relatively good pattern of early industrial growth, which was unjustly tarnished by the spectacular rise of Germany and the United States after 1860. In general, eastern and southern Europe began the process of modern industrialization later than northwestern and central Europe. Nevertheless, these regions made real progress in the late nineteenth century, as growth after 1880 in Austria-Hungary, Italy, and Russia suggests.

Finally, the late but substantial industrialization in eastern and southern Europe meant that all European states (as well as the United States, Canada, and Japan) managed to raise per capita industrial levels in the nineteenth century. These continent-wide increases stood in stark contrast to the large and tragic decreases that occurred at the same time in many non-Western countries, most notably in China and India, as Table 21.1 clearly shows. European countries industrialized to a greater or lesser extent even as most of the non-Western world

deindustrialized. Thus differential rates of wealth- and power-creating industrial development, which heightened disparities within Europe, also greatly magnified existing inequalities between Europe and the rest of the world. We shall return to this momentous change in world economic relationships in Chapter 25.

The Challenge of Industrialization

The different patterns of industrial development suggest that the process of industrialization was far from automatic. Indeed, building modern industry was an awesome challenge. To be sure, throughout Europe the eighteenth century was an era of agricultural improvement, population increase, expanding foreign trade, and growing cottage industry. Thus when the pace of British industry began to accelerate in the 1780s, continental businesses began to adopt the new methods as they proved their profitability. British industry enjoyed clear superiority, but at first the continent was close behind.

By 1815, however, the situation was quite different. No wars in the early industrial period had been fought on British soil, so Britain did not experience nearly as much physical destruction or economic dislocation as the continent did. Rather, despite the wartime challenges that it did face, British industry maintained the momentum of the 1780s and continued to grow and improve between 1789 and 1815. On the continent, by contrast, the upheavals that began with the French Revolution disrupted trade, created runaway inflation, and fostered social anxiety. War severed normal communications between Britain and the continent, severely handicapping continental efforts to use new British machinery and technology. Moreover, the years from 1789 to 1815 were, even for the privileged French economy receiving special favors from Napoleon, a time of "national catastrophe"—in the graphic words of a famous French scholar.[5] Thus France and the rest of Europe were further behind Britain in 1815 than in 1789.

This widening gap made it more difficult, if not impossible, for other countries to follow the British pattern in energy and industry after peace was restored in 1815. Above all, in the newly mechanized industries, British goods were being produced very economically, and these goods had come to dominate world markets completely while the continental states were absorbed in war between 1792 and 1815. In addition, British technology had become so advanced and complicated that very few engineers or skilled technicians outside England understood it. Moreover, the technology of steam power had grown much more expensive. It involved large investments in the iron and coal industries and, after 1830, required the existence of railroads, which were very costly. Continental business people had great difficulty finding the large sums of money the new methods demanded, and there was a shortage of laborers accus-

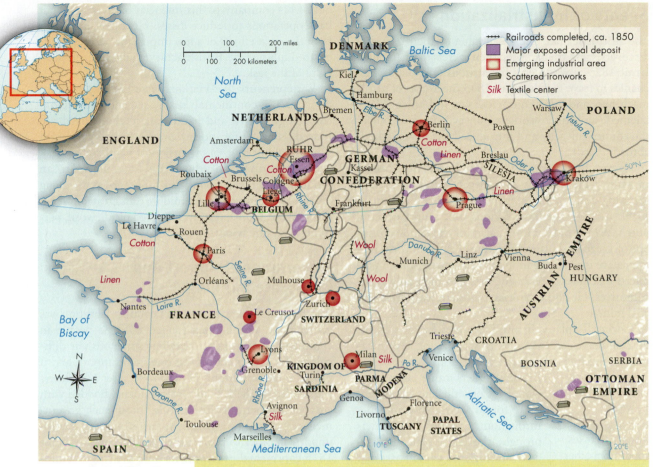

Mapping the Past

Map 21.2 **Continental Industrialization, ca. 1850** Although continental countries were beginning to make progress by 1850, they still lagged far behind Britain. For example, continental railroad building was still in an early stage, whereas the British rail system was essentially complete (see Map 21.1). Coal played a critical role in nineteenth-century industrialization both as a power source for steam engines and as a raw material for making iron and steel.

ANALYZING THE MAP Locate the major exposed (that is, known) coal deposits in 1850. Which countries and areas appear rich in coal resources, and which appear poor? Is there a difference between northern and southern Europe?

CONNECTIONS What is the relationship between known coal deposits and emerging industrial areas in continental Europe? In England (see Map 21.1)?

To complete this activity online, go to the Online Study Guide at **bedfordstmartins.com/mckaywest**.

tomed to working in factories. All these disadvantages slowed the spread of modern industry (Map 21.2).

After 1815, however, when continental countries began to face up to the British challenge, they had at least three important advantages. First, most continental countries had a rich tradition of putting-out enterprise, merchant capitalists, and skilled urban artisans (see Chapter 18). Such a tradition gave continental firms the ability to adapt and survive in the face of new market conditions. Second, continental capitalists did not need to develop their own advanced technology. Instead,

they could simply "borrow" the new methods developed in Great Britain, as well as engineers and some of the financial resources these countries lacked. European countries such as France and Russia also had a third asset that many non-Western areas lacked in the nineteenth century. They had strong independent governments that did not fall under foreign political control. These governments could fashion economic policies to serve their own interests, as they proceeded to do. They would eventually use the power of the state to promote industry and catch up with Britain.

Agents of Industrialization

The British realized the great value of their technical discoveries and tried to keep their secrets to themselves. Until 1825 it was illegal for artisans and skilled mechanics to leave Britain; until 1843 the export of textile machinery and other equipment was forbidden. Many talented, ambitious workers, however, slipped out of the country illegally and introduced the new methods abroad.

One such man was William Cockerill, a Lancashire carpenter. He and his sons began building cotton-spinning equipment in French-occupied Belgium in 1799. In 1817 the most famous son, John Cockerill, purchased the old summer palace of the deposed bishops of Liège in southern Belgium. Cockerill converted the palace into a large industrial enterprise, which produced machinery, steam engines, and then railway locomotives. He also established modern ironworks and coal mines.

Cockerill's plants in the Liège area became an industrial nerve center, continually gathering new information and transmitting it across Europe. Many skilled British workers came illegally to work for Cockerill, and some went on to found their own companies throughout Europe. Newcomers brought the latest plans and secrets, so Cockerill could boast that ten days after an industrial advance occurred in Britain, he knew all about it in Belgium.

Thus British technicians and skilled workers were a powerful force in the spread of early industrialization. A second agent of industrialization were talented entrepreneurs such as Fritz Harkort, a business pioneer in the German machinery industry. Serving in England as a Prussian army officer during the Napoleonic wars, Harkort was impressed and enchanted with what he saw. He concluded that Germany had to match all these English achievements as quickly as possible. Setting up shop in an abandoned castle in the still-tranquil Ruhr Valley, Harkort felt an almost religious calling to build steam engines and become the "Watt of Germany."

Harkort's basic idea was simple, but it was enormously difficult to carry out. Lacking skilled laborers to do the job, Harkort turned to England for experienced, though expensive, mechanics. Getting materials also posed a great problem. He had to import the thick iron boilers that he needed from England at great cost. In spite of all these problems, Harkort built and sold engines, winning fame and praise. His ambitious efforts over sixteen years also resulted in large financial losses for himself and his partners, and in 1832 he was forced

tariff protection

A government's way of supporting and aiding its own economy by laying high taxes on imported goods from other countries, as when the French responded to cheaper British goods flooding their country by imposing high tariffs on some imported products.

out of his company by his financial backers, who cut back operations to reduce losses. His career illustrates both the great efforts of a few important business leaders to duplicate the British achievement and the difficulty of the task.

Entrepreneurs like Harkort were obviously exceptional. Most continental businesses adopted factory technology slowly, and handicraft methods lived on. Indeed, continental industrialization usually brought substantial but uneven expansion of handicraft industry in both rural and urban areas for a time. Artisan production of luxury items grew in France as the rising income of the international middle class created foreign demand for silk scarves, embroidered needlework, perfumes, and fine wines.

Government Support and Corporate Banking

Another major force in continental industrialization was government, which often helped business people in continental countries to overcome some of their difficulties. **Tariff protection** was one such support, and it proved quite important. For example, after Napoleon's wars ended in 1815, France was suddenly flooded with cheaper and better British goods. The French government responded by laying high tariffs on many British imports in order to protect the French economy. After 1815 continental governments bore the cost of building roads and canals to improve transportation. They also bore to a significant extent the cost of building railroads. Belgium led the way in the 1830s and 1840s. In an effort to tie the newly independent nation together, the Belgian government decided to construct a state-owned system. Built rapidly as a unified network, Belgium's state-owned railroads stimulated the development of heavy industry and made the country an early industrial leader. Several of the smaller German states also built state systems.

The Prussian government provided another kind of invaluable support. It guaranteed that the state treasury would pay the interest and principal on railroad bonds if the closely regulated private companies in Prussia were unable to do so. Thus railroad investors in Prussia ran little risk, and capital was quickly raised. In France the state shouldered all the expense of acquiring and laying roadbed, including bridges and tunnels. Finished roadbed was leased to a carefully supervised private company, which usually benefited from a state guarantee of its debts. In short, governments helped pay for railroads, the all-important leading sector in continental industrialization.

The career of German journalist and thinker Friedrich List (1789–1846) reflects government's greater role in industrialization on the continent than in England. List considered the growth of modern industry of the utmost importance because manufacturing was a primary means of increasing people's well-being and relieving their poverty. Moreover, List was a dedicated nationalist. He wrote that the "wider the gap between the backward and advanced nations becomes, the more dangerous it is to remain behind." A backward, agricultural nation was not only poor but also weak, increasingly unable to defend itself and maintain its political independence. To promote industry was to defend the nation.

The practical policies that List focused on in articles and in his influential *National System of Political Economy* (1841) were railroad building and the tariff. List supported the formation of a customs union, or *Zollverein* (TSOL-feh-rign), among the separate German states. Such a tariff union came into being in 1834, allowing goods to move between the German member states without tariffs, while erecting a single uniform tariff against other nations. List wanted a high protective tariff, which would encourage infant industries, allowing them to de-

❝ The wider the gap between the backward and advanced nations becomes, the more dangerous it is to remain behind. ❞

—**FRIEDRICH LIST**

velop and eventually hold their own against their more advanced British counterparts. He denounced the British doctrine of free trade as part of Britain's attempt to dominate the entire world.

At no other epoch has the world seen a manufacturing and commercial power possessing such immense resources as those in the hands of the power which now holds sway [Britain] pursuing a system that is so consistently selfish. It is absorbing with untiring energy the manufacturing and commercial industries of the world and the important colonies, and it is making the rest of the world, like the Hindus, its serfs in all industrial and commercial relations.[6]

A German Ironworks, 1845 The Borsig ironworks in Berlin mastered the new British method of smelting iron ore with coke. Germany, and especially the state of Prussia, was well endowed with both iron and coal, and the rapid exploitation of these resources after 1840 transformed a poor agricultural country into an industrial powerhouse. (akg-images)

By the 1840s List's **economic nationalism**, designed to protect and develop the national economy, had become increasingly popular in Germany and elsewhere.

Finally, banks, like governments, also played a larger and more creative role on the continent than in Britain. Previously, almost all banks in Europe had been private, organized as secretive partnerships. Because of the possibility of unlimited financial loss, the partners of private banks tended to be quite conservative and were content to deal with a few rich clients and a few big merchants. They generally avoided industrial investment as being too risky.

In the 1830s, two important Belgian banks pioneered in a new direction. They received permission from the growth-oriented government to establish themselves as corporations enjoying limited liability. That is, stockholders could now lose only their original investments in the bank's common stock, and they could not be forced by the courts to pay for any additional losses out of other property they owned if the bank went bankrupt. Publicizing the risk-reducing advantage of limited liability for investors, these Belgian banks were able to attract many shareholders, large and small. They mobilized impressive resources for investment in big companies, became industrial banks, and successfully promoted industrial development.

Similar corporate banks became important in France and Germany in the 1850s and 1860s. Usually working in collaboration with governments, corporate banks established and developed many railroads and many companies working in heavy industry, which were also increasingly organized as limited liability corporations. The most famous such bank was the Crédit Mobilier of Paris, founded by Isaac and Emile Pereire, two young Jewish journalists from Bordeaux. The Crédit Mobilier advertised extensively. It used the savings of thousands of small investors as well as the resources of big ones. The activities of the bank were far-reaching; it built railroads all over France and Europe. As Emile Pereire had said in 1835, "It is not enough to outline gigantic programs on paper. I must write my ideas on the earth."

The combined efforts of skilled workers, entrepreneurs, governments, and industrial banks meshed successfully between 1850 and the financial crash of 1873. This was a period of unprecedentedly rapid economic growth on the continent. In Belgium, Germany, and France, key indicators of modern industrial development—such as railway mileage, iron and coal production, and steam-engine capacity—increased at average annual rates of 5 to 10 percent. As a result, rail networks were completed in western and much of central Europe, and the leading continental countries mas-

tered the industrial technologies that had first been developed in Great Britain. In the early 1870s, Britain was still Europe's most industrial nation, but a select handful of countries were closing the gap that had been opened up by the Industrial Revolution.

economic nationalism Policies aimed at protecting and developing a country's economy.

class-consciousness An individual's sense of class differentiation.

Relations Between Capital and Labor

How did the Industrial Revolution affect people of all social classes, and what measures were taken to improve the conditions of workers? ■

Industrial development brought new social relations and intensified long-standing problems between capital and labor in both urban workshops and cottage industry (see Chapter 18). A new group of factory owners and industrial capitalists arose. These men and women and their families strengthened the wealth and size of the middle class, which had previously been made up mainly of merchants and professional people. The nineteenth century became the golden age of the middle class. Modern industry also created a much larger group, the factory workers. For the first time, large numbers of men, women, and children came together under one roof to work with complicated machinery for a single owner or a few partners in large companies.

The growth of new occupational groups in industry stimulated new thinking about social relations. Often combined with reflections on the French Revolution, this thinking led to the development of a new overarching interpretation—a new paradigm—regarding social relationships. Briefly, this paradigm argued, with considerable success, that individuals were members of economically determined classes that had conflicting interests. Accordingly, the comfortable, well-educated "public" of the eighteenth century came increasingly to see itself as the backbone of the middle class (or the middle classes), and the "people" gradually transformed themselves into the modern working class (or working classes). And if the new class interpretation was more of a deceptive simplification than a fundamental truth for some critics, it appealed to many because it seemed to explain what was happening. Therefore, conflicting classes existed, in part, because many individuals came to believe they existed and developed an appropriate sense of class feeling—what Marxists call **class-consciousness**.

The New Class of Factory Owners

Early industrialists operated in a highly competitive economic system. As the careers of Watt and Harkort illustrate, there were countless production problems, and

Picturing the Past

Ford Maddox Brown, *Work* This midcentury painting provides a rich and realistic visual representation of the new concepts of social class that became common by 1850. (Birmingham Museums and Art Gallery/The Bridgeman Art Library)

ANALYZING THE IMAGE Describe the different types of work shown. What different social classes are depicted, and what kinds of work (or leisure) are the members of the different social classes engaged in?

CONNECTIONS What does this painting and Ford's title for it (*Work*) suggest about the artist's opinion of the work of common laborers?

To complete this activity online, go to the Online Study Guide at **bedfordstmartins.com/mckaywest.**

success and large profits were by no means certain. Manufacturers therefore waged a constant battle to cut their production costs and stay afloat. Much of the profit had to go back into the business for new and better machinery. "Dragged on by the frenzy of this terrible life," according to one of the dismayed critics, the struggling manufacturer had "no time for niceties. He must conquer or die, make a fortune or drown himself."[7]

Most early industrialists drew upon their families and friends for labor and capital, but they came from a variety of backgrounds. Many, such as Harkort, were from well-established merchant families with a rich network of contacts and support. Others, such as Watt, Wedgwood, and Cockerill, were of modest means, especially in the early days. Artisans and skilled workers of exceptional ability had unparalleled opportunities.

Members of ethnic and religious groups who had been discriminated against in the traditional occupations controlled by the landed aristocracy jumped at the new chances and often helped one another. Scots, Quakers, and other Protestant dissenters were tremendously important in Britain; Protestants and Jews dominated banking in Catholic France. Many of the industrialists were newly rich, and, not surprisingly, they were very proud and self-satisfied.

As factories and firms grew larger, opportunities declined, at least in well-developed industries. It became considerably harder for a gifted but poor young mechanic to start a small enterprise and end up as a wealthy manufacturer. Formal education (for sons and males) became more important as a means of success and advancement, and formal education at the advanced level was expensive. In Britain by 1830 and in France and Germany by 1860, leading industrialists were more likely to have inherited their well-established enterprises, and they were financially much more secure than their struggling fathers and mothers had been. They also had a greater sense of class-consciousness; they were fully aware that ongoing industrial development had widened the gap between themselves and their workers.

The wives and daughters of successful businessmen also found fewer opportunities for active participation in Europe's increasingly complex business world. Rather than contributing as vital partners in a family-owned enterprise, as so many middle-class women had done, these women were increasingly valued for their ladylike gentility. By 1850 some influential women writers and most businessmen assumed that middle-class wives and daughters should steer clear of undignified work in offices and factories. Rather, a middle-class lady should protect and enhance her femininity. She should concentrate on her proper role as wife and mother, preferably in an elegant residential area far removed from ruthless commerce and the volatile working class.

The New Factory Workers

The social consequences of the Industrial Revolution have long been hotly debated. The condition of British workers during the transformation has always generated the most controversy among historians because Britain was the first country to industrialize and because the social consequences seemed harshest there. Before 1850 other countries had not proceeded very far with industrialization, and almost everyone agrees that the economic conditions of European workers improved after 1850. Thus the experience of British workers to about 1850 deserves special attention. (Industrial growth also promoted rapid urbanization, with its own awesome problems, as will be shown in Chapter 23.)

From the beginning, the Industrial Revolution in Britain had its critics. Among the first were the romantic poets. William Blake (1757–1827) called the early factories "satanic mills" and protested against the hard life of the London poor. William Wordsworth (1770–1850) lamented the destruction of the rural way of life and the pollution of the land and water. Some handicraft workers—notably the **Luddites**, who attacked whole factories in northern England in 1812 and after—smashed the new machines, which they believed were putting them out of work. Doctors and reformers wrote eloquently of problems in the factories and new towns, while Malthus and Ricardo concluded that workers would earn only enough to stay alive.

Luddites Group of handicraft workers who attacked whole factories in northern England in 1812 and after, smashing the new machines that they believed were putting them out of work.

This pessimistic view was accepted and reinforced by Friedrich Engels (1820–1895), the future revolutionary and colleague of Karl Marx. After studying conditions in northern England, this young middle-class German published in 1844 *The Condition of the Working Class in England*, a blistering indictment of the middle classes. "At the bar of world opinion," he wrote, "I charge the English middle classes with mass murder, wholesale robbery, and all the other crimes in the calendar." The new poverty of industrial workers was worse than the old poverty of cottage workers and agricultural laborers, according to Engels. The culprit was industrial capitalism, with its relentless competition and constant technical change. Engels's extremely influential charge of middle-class exploitation and increasing worker poverty was embellished by Marx and later socialists.

Meanwhile, other observers believed that conditions were improving for the working people. Andrew Ure (yoo-RAY) wrote in 1835 in his study of the cotton industry that conditions in most factories were not harsh and were even quite good. Edwin Chadwick, a great and conscientious government official well acquainted with the problems of the working population, concluded that the "whole mass of the laboring community" was increasingly able "to buy more of the necessities and minor luxuries of life."[8] Nevertheless, those who thought conditions were getting worse for working people were probably in the majority.

In an attempt to go beyond the contradictory judgments of contemporaries, some historians have looked at different kinds of sources. Statistical evidence is one such source. If working people suffered a great economic decline, as Engels and later socialists asserted, then the purchasing power of the working person's wages must have declined drastically.

Scholarly statistical studies have weakened the idea that the condition of the working class got much worse with industrialization. But the most recent scholarship also confirms the view that the early years of the Industrial Revolution were hard ones for British workers. There was little or no increase in the purchasing power of the average British worker from about 1780 to about 1820. The years from 1792 to 1815, a period of almost constant warfare with France, were particularly difficult. Food prices rose faster than wages, and the living conditions of the laboring poor declined. Only after 1820, and especially after 1840, did real wages rise substantially, so that the average worker earned and consumed roughly 50 percent more in real terms in 1850 than in 1770.[9] In short, there was considerable economic improvement for workers throughout Great Britain by 1850, but that improvement was hard won and slow in coming.

This important conclusion must be qualified, however. First, the hours in the average workweek increased, as some economic historians now believe it had been increasing in parts of northern Europe since the late seventeenth century. Thus, to a large extent, workers earned more simply because they worked more. Indeed, in England nonagricultural workers labored about 250 days per year in 1760 as compared to 300 days per year in 1830, while the normal workday remained an exhausting eleven hours throughout the entire period. In 1760 nonagricultural workers still observed many religious and public holidays by not working, and Monday was popularly known as "Saint Monday" because so many workers took the day off. These days of leisure and relaxation declined rapidly after 1760, and by 1830 nonagricultural workers had joined landless agricultural laborers in toiling six rather than five days a week.[10]

Second, the wartime decline in the average worker's real wages and standard of living from 1792 to 1815 had a powerful negative impact on workers. These difficult war years, with more unemployment and sharply higher prices for bread, were formative years for the new factory labor force, and they colored the early experience of modern industrial life in somber tones.

Another way to consider the workers' standard of living is to look at the goods that they purchased. Again the evidence is somewhat contradictory. Speaking generally, workers ate somewhat more food of higher nutritional quality as the Industrial Revolution progressed, except during wartime. Diets became more varied; people ate more potatoes, dairy products, fruits, and vegetables. Clothing improved, but housing for working people probably deteriorated somewhat. In short, per capita use of specific goods supports the position that the standard of living of the working classes rose, at least moderately, after the long wars with France.

Work in Early Factories

What about working conditions? Did workers eventually earn more only at the cost of working longer and harder? Were workers exploited harshly by the new factory owners?

The first factories were cotton mills, which began functioning in the 1770s along fast-running rivers and streams and were often located in sparsely populated areas. Cottage workers in the vicinity, accustomed to the putting-out system, were reluctant to work in the new factories even when they received relatively good wages because factory work was unappealing. In the

Workers at a Large Cotton Mill This 1833 engraving shows adult women operating power looms under the supervision of a male foreman, and it accurately reflects both the decline of family employment and the emergence of a gender-based division of labor in many English factories. The jungle of belts and shafts connecting the noisy looms to the giant steam engine on the ground floor created a constant din. (Time Life Pictures/Getty Images)

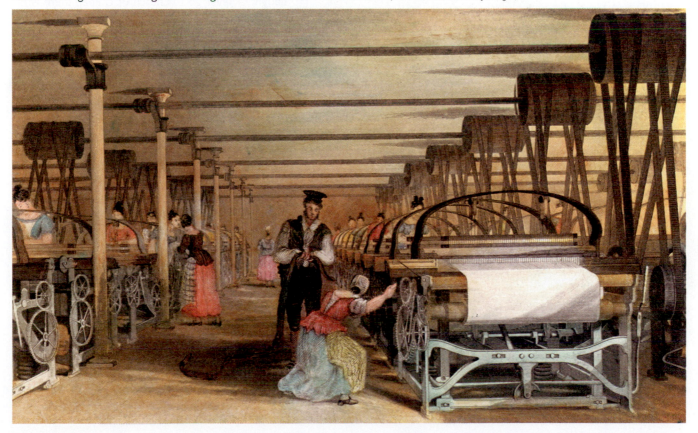

LISTENING TO THE PAST

The use of child labor in British industrialization quickly attracted the attention of humanitarians and social reformers. This interest led to investigations by parliamentary commissions, which resulted in laws limiting the hours and the ages of children working in large factories. Designed to build a case for remedial legislation, parliamentary inquiries gave large numbers of workers a rare chance to speak directly to contemporaries and to historians.

The moving passages that follow are taken from testimony gathered in 1841 and 1842 by the Ashley Mines Commission. Interviewing employers and many male and female workers, the commissioners focused on the physical condition of the youth and on the sexual behavior of workers far underground. The subsequent Mines Act of 1842 sought to reduce immoral behavior and sexual bullying by prohibiting underground work for all women and girls (and for boys younger than ten).

Mr. Payne, coal master

❝ That children are employed generally at nine years old in the coal pits and sometimes at eight. In fact, the smaller the vein of coal is in height, the younger and smaller are the children required; the work occupies from six to seven hours per day in the pits; they are not ill-used or worked beyond their strength; a good deal of depravity exists but they are certainly not worse in morals than in other branches of the Sheffield trade, but upon the whole superior; the morals of this district are materially improving; Mr. Bruce, the clergyman, has been zealous and active in endeavoring to ameliorate their moral and religious education. . . . ❞

Ann Eggley, hurrier, 18 years old

❝ I'm sure I don't know how to spell my name. We go at four in the morning, and sometimes at half-past four. We begin to work as soon as we get down. We get out after four, sometimes at five, in the evening. We work the whole time except an hour for dinner, and sometimes we haven't time to eat. I hurry [move coal wagons underground] by myself, and have done so for long. I know the corves [small coal wagons] are very heavy, they are the biggest corves anywhere about. The work is far too hard for me; the sweat runs off me all over sometimes. I am very tired at night. Sometimes when we get home at night we have not power to wash us, and then we go to bed. Sometimes we fall asleep in the chair. Father said last night it was both a shame and a disgrace for girls to work as we do, but there was naught else for us to do. I began to hurry when I was seven and I have been hurrying ever since. I have been 11 years in the pits. The girls are always tired. I was poorly twice this winter; it was with headache. I hurry for Robert Wiggins; he is not akin to me. . . . We don't always get enough to eat and drink, but we get a good supper. I have known my father go at two in the morning to work . . . and he didn't come out till four. I am quite sure that we work constantly 12 hours except on Saturdays. We wear trousers and our shifts in the pit and great big shoes clinkered and nailed. The girls never work naked to the waist in our pit. The men don't insult us in the pit. The conduct of the girls in the pit is good enough sometimes and sometimes bad enough. I never went to a day-school. I went a little to a Sunday-school, but I soon gave it over. I thought it too bad to be confined both Sundays and week-days. I walk about and get the fresh air on Sundays. I have not learnt to read. I don't know my letters. I never learnt naught. I never go to church or chapel; there is no church or chapel at Gawber, there is none nearer than a mile. . . . I have never heard that a good man came into the world who was God's son to save sinners. I never heard of Christ at all. Nobody has ever told me about him, nor have my father and mother ever taught me to pray. I know no prayer; I never pray. ❞

Patience Kershaw, aged 17

❝ My father has been dead about a year; my mother is living and has ten children, five lads and five lasses; the oldest is about thirty, the youngest is four; three lasses go to mill; all the lads are colliers, two getters and three hurriers; one lives at home and does nothing; mother does nought but look after home.

factory, workers had to keep up with the machine and follow its relentless tempo. Moreover, they had to show up every day, on time, and work long, monotonous hours under the constant supervision of demanding overseers, and they were punished systematically if they broke the work rules. For example, if a worker was late to work, or accidentally spoiled material, or nodded off late in the day, the employer imposed fines that were deducted from the weekly pay. Children and adolescents were often beaten for their infractions.

Cottage workers were not used to that kind of life and discipline. All members of the family worked hard and long, but in spurts, setting their own pace. They could interrupt their work when they wanted to. Women

This illustration of a girl dragging a coal wagon was one of several that shocked public opinion and contributed to the Mines Act of 1842. (© British Library Board)

All my sisters have been hurriers, but three went to the mill. Alice went because her legs swelled from hurrying in cold water when she was hot. I never went to day-school; I go to Sunday-school, but I cannot read or write; I go to pit at five o'clock in the morning and come out at five in the evening; I get my breakfast of porridge and milk first; I take my dinner with me, a cake, and eat it as I go; I do not stop or rest any time for the purpose; I get nothing else until I get home, and then have potatoes and meat, not every day meat. I hurry in the clothes I have now got on, trousers and ragged jacket; the bald place upon my head is made by thrusting the corves; my legs have never swelled, but sisters' did when they went to mill; I hurry the corves a mile and more under ground and back; they weigh 300 cwt.;* I hurry 11 a day; I wear a belt and chain at the workings to get the corves out; the putters [miners] that I work for are *naked* except their caps; they pull off all their clothes; I see them at work when I go up; sometimes they beat me, if I am not quick enough, with their hands; they strike me upon my back; the boys take liberties with me, sometimes, they pull me about; I am the only girl in the pit; there are about 20 boys and 15 men; all the men are naked; I would rather work in mill than in coal-pit. **"**

*An old English unit of weight equaling 112 pounds.

Isabel Wilson, 38 years old, coal putter

" When women have children thick [fast] they are compelled to take them down early. I have been married 19 years and have had 10 bairns [children]; seven are in life. When on Sir John's work was a carrier of coals, which caused me to miscarry five times from the strains, and was gai [very] ill after each. Putting is no so oppressive; last child was born on Saturday morning, and I was at work on the Friday night.

Once met with an accident; a coal brake my cheek-bone, which kept me idle some weeks. I have wrought below 30 years, and so has the guid man; he is getting touched in the breath now.

None of the children read, as the work is no regular. I did read once, but no able to attend to it now; when I go below lassie 10 years of age keeps house and makes the broth or stir-about. **"**

Source: *Voices of the Industrial Revolution: Selected Readings from the Liberal Economists and Their Critics*, pp. 87–90, edited by J. Bowditch and C. Ramsland (Ann Arbor: The University of Michigan Press, 1961). Reprinted by permission of the publisher.

QUESTIONS FOR ANALYSIS

1. How does Payne's testimony compare with that of Ann Eggley and Patience Kershaw?

2. Describe the work of Eggley, Kershaw, and Wilson. What strikes you most about the testimonies of these workers?

3. The witnesses were responding to questions from middle-class commissioners. What did the commissioners seem interested in? Why?

and children could break up their long hours of spinning with other tasks. On Saturday afternoon the head of the family delivered the week's work to the merchant manufacturer and got paid. Saturday night was a time of relaxation and drinking, especially for the men. Recovering from his hangover on Tuesday, the weaver bent to his task on Wednesday and then worked frantically to meet his deadline on Saturday. Like some students today, he might "pull an all-nighter" on Thursday or Friday in order to get his work in.

Also, early factories resembled English poorhouses, where totally destitute people went to live at public expense. Some poorhouses were industrial prisons, where the inmates had to work in order to receive their food and lodging. The similarity between large brick factories and large stone poorhouses increased the cottage workers' fear of factories and their hatred of factory discipline. It was cottage workers' reluctance to work in factories that prompted the early cotton mill owners to turn to abandoned and pauper children for their labor. As we have seen, these owners contracted with local officials to employ large numbers of these children, who had no say in the matter. Pauper children were often badly treated and terribly overworked in the mills, as they were when they were apprenticed as chimney sweeps, market girls, shoemakers, and so forth. In the eighteenth century, semi-forced child labor seemed necessary and was socially accepted. From our modern point of view, it was cruel exploitation and a blot on the record of the new industrial system.

Working Families and Children

By the 1790s the early pattern was rapidly changing. The use of pauper apprentices was in decline, and in 1802 it was forbidden by Parliament. Many more textile factories were being built, mainly in urban areas, where they could use steam power rather than waterpower and attract a workforce more easily than in the countryside. The need for workers was great. As a result, people came from near and far to work in the cities, both as factory workers and as laborers, builders, and domestic servants. Yet as they took these new jobs, working people did not simply give in and accept the highly disciplined system of labor that had formerly repelled them. Rather, they helped modify the system by carrying over old, familiar working traditions.

For one thing, workers often came to the mills and the mines as family units. This was how they had worked on farms and in the putting-out system. The mill or mine owner bargained with the head of the family and paid him or her for the work of the whole family. In the cotton mills, children worked for their mothers or fathers, collecting scraps and "piecing" broken threads together. In the mines, children sorted coal and worked the ventilation equipment. Their mothers hauled coal in the tunnels below the surface, while their fathers hewed with pick and shovel at the face of the seam.

The preservation of the family as an economic unit in the factories from the 1790s on made the new surroundings more tolerable, both in Great Britain and in other countries, during the early stages of industrialization. Parents disciplined their children, making firm measures socially acceptable, and directed their upbringing. The presence of the whole family meant that children and adults worked the same long hours (twelve-hour shifts were normal in cotton mills in 1800). In the early years, some very young children were employed solely to keep the family together. For example, the early industrialist Jedediah Strutt believed that children should be at least ten years old to work in his textile mills, but he reluctantly employed seven-year-olds to satisfy their parents. Adult workers were not particularly interested in limiting the minimum working age or hours of their children as long as family members worked side by side. Only when technical changes threatened to place control and discipline in the hands of impersonal managers and overseers did adult workers protest against inhuman conditions in the name of their children.

Some enlightened employers and social reformers in Parliament definitely felt otherwise. They argued that more humane standards were necessary, and they used widely circulated parliamentary reports to influence public opinion. For example, Robert Owen (1771–1858), a very successful manufacturer in Scotland, testified in 1816 before an investigating committee on the basis of his experience. He stated that "very strong facts" demonstrated that employing children under ten years of age as factory workers was "injurious to the children, and not beneficial to the proprietors."[11] Workers also provided graphic testimony at such hearings as the reformers pressed Parliament to pass corrective laws. They scored some important successes.

Their most significant early accomplishment was the **Factory Act of 1833**. It limited the factory workday for children between nine and thirteen to eight hours and that of adolescents between fourteen and eighteen to twelve hours, although the act made no effort to regulate the hours of work for children at home or in small businesses. Children under nine were to be enrolled in the elementary schools that factory owners were required to establish. The employment of children declined rapidly. Thus the Factory Act broke the pattern of whole families working together in the factory because efficiency required standardized shifts for all workers.

Ties of blood and kinship were important in other ways in Great Britain in the formative years between about 1790 and 1840. Many manufacturers and builders hired workers through subcontractors. They paid the subcontractors on the basis of what the subcontractors and their crews produced—for smelting so many tons of pig iron or moving so much dirt or gravel for a canal or roadbed. Subcontractors in turn hired and fired their own workers, many of whom were friends and relations. The subcontractor might be as harsh as the greediest capitalist, but the relationship between subcontractor and work crew was close and personal. This kind of personal relationship had traditionally existed in cottage industry and in urban crafts, and it was more acceptable to many workers than impersonal factory discipline. This system also provided people with an easy way to find a job. Even today, a friend or relative who is

Factory Act of 1833 English law that led to a sharp decline in the employment of children by limiting the hours that children over age nine could work and requiring younger children to attend factory-run elementary schools.

a supervisor is frequently worth a host of formal application forms.

Ties of kinship were particularly important for newcomers, who often traveled great distances to find work. Many urban workers in Great Britain were from Ireland. Forced out of rural Ireland by population growth and deteriorating economic conditions from 1817 on, Irish in search of jobs took what they could get. As early as 1824, most of the workers in the Glasgow cotton mills were Irish; in 1851 one-sixth of the population of Liverpool was Irish. Like many other immigrant groups held together by ethnic and religious ties, the Irish worked together, formed their own neighborhoods, and not only survived but also thrived.

The Sexual Division of Labor

The era of the Industrial Revolution witnessed major changes in the sexual division of labor. In preindustrial Europe most people generally worked in family units. By tradition, certain jobs were defined by gender—women and girls for milking and spinning, men and boys for plowing and weaving—but many tasks might go to either sex. Family employment carried over into early factories and subcontracting, but by the 1830s it was collapsing as child labor was restricted and new attitudes emerged. A different sexual division of labor gradually arose to take its place. By 1850 the man was emerging as the family's primary wage earner, while the married woman found only limited job opportunities. Generally denied good jobs at good wages in the growing urban economy, women were expected to concentrate on housework, raising the children, and some craftwork at home.

This new pattern of **separate spheres**, which will be considered further in Chapter 23, had several aspects. First, all studies agree that married women from the working classes were much less likely to work full-time for wages outside the house after the first child arrived, although they often earned small amounts doing putting-out handicrafts at home and taking in boarders. Second, when married women did work for wages outside the house, they usually came from the poorest families, where the husbands were poorly paid, sick, unemployed, or missing. Third, these poor married or widowed women were joined by legions of young unmarried women, who worked full-time but only in certain jobs, of which textile factory work, laundering, and domestic service were particularly important. Fourth, all women were generally confined to low-paying, dead-end jobs. Virtually no occupation open to women paid a wage sufficient for a person to live independently. Men predominated in the better-paying, more promising employments. Evolving gradually, but largely in place by 1850, the new sexual division of labor in Britain constituted a major development in the history of women and of the family.

If the reorganization of paid work along gender lines is widely recognized, there is no agreement on its causes. One school of scholars sees little connection with industrialization and finds the answer in the deeply ingrained sexist attitudes of a "patriarchal tradition," which predated the economic transformation. These scholars stress the role of male-dominated craft unions in denying working women access to good jobs and relegating them to unpaid housework. Other scholars, stressing that the gender roles of women and men can vary enormously with time and culture, look more to a combination of economic and biological factors in order to explain the emergence of a sex-segregated division of labor.

Three ideas stand out in this more recent interpretation. First, the new and unfamiliar discipline of the clock and the machine was especially hard on married women of the laboring classes. Above all, relentless factory discipline conflicted with child care in a way that labor on the farm or in the cottage had not. A woman operating earsplitting spinning machinery could mind a child of seven or eight working beside her (until such work was outlawed), but she could no longer pace herself through pregnancy or breast-feed her baby on the job. Thus a working-class woman had strong incentives to concentrate on child care within her home if her family could afford it.

Second, running a household in conditions of primitive urban poverty was an extremely demanding job in its own right. There were no supermarkets or public transportation. Everything had to be done on foot. Shopping and feeding the family constituted a never-ending challenge. The wife marched from one tiny shop to another, dragging her tired children (for who was to watch them?) and struggling valiantly with heavy sacks and tricky shopkeepers. Yet another brutal job outside the house—a "second shift"—had limited appeal for the average married woman from the working class. Thus many women might well have accepted the emerging division of labor as the best available strategy for family survival in the industrializing society.[12]

> **separate spheres** A gender division of labor with the wife at home as mother and homemaker and the husband as wage earner.

Third, why were the young, generally unmarried women who did work for wages outside the home segregated and confined to certain "women's jobs"? No doubt the desire of males to monopolize the best opportunities and hold women down provides part of the answer. Yet as some feminist scholars have argued, sex-segregated employment was also a collective response to the new industrial system. Previously, at least in theory, young people worked under a watchful parental eye. The growth of factories and mines brought unheard-of opportunities for girls and boys to mix on the job, free of familial supervision. Continuing to mix after work, they were "more likely to form liaisons, initiate courtships, and respond to advances."[13] Such intimacy also led to more unplanned pregnancies and fueled the illegitimacy explosion that had begun in the late eighteenth century and that gathered force until at least 1850 (see Chapter 19). Thus segregation of jobs by gender was partly an effort by older people to help control the sexuality of working-class youths.

Investigations into the British coal industry before 1842 provide a graphic example of this concern. (See "Listening to the Past: The Testimony of Young Mine Workers," page 676.) The middle-class men leading the inquiry, who expected their daughters and wives to pursue ladylike activities, often failed to appreciate the physical effort of the girls and women who dragged with belt and chain the heavy carts of coal along narrow underground passages. But they professed horror at the sight of girls and women working without shirts, which was a common practice because of the heat, and they quickly assumed the prevalence of licentious sex with the male miners, who also wore very little clothing. In fact, most girls and married women worked for related males in a family unit that provided considerable protection and restraint. Yet many witnesses from the working class also believed that "blackguardism and debauchery" were common and that "they are best out of the pits, the lasses." Some miners stressed particularly the danger of sexual aggression for girls working past puberty. As one explained: "I consider it a scandal for girls to work in the pits. Till they are 12 or 14 they may work very well but after that it's an abomination. . . . The work of the pit does not hurt them, it is the effect on their morals that I complain of."[14]

Mines Act of 1842 English law prohibiting underground work for all women and girls as well as for boys under ten.

The **Mines Act of 1842** prohibited underground work for all women and girls as well as for boys under ten.

Some women who had to support themselves protested against being excluded from coal mining, which paid higher wages than most other jobs open to working-class women. But provided they were part of families that could manage economically, the girls and the women who had worked underground were generally pleased with the law. In explaining her satisfaction in 1844, one mother of four provided real insight into why many married working women accepted the emerging sexual division of labor:

> While working in the pit I was worth to my [miner] husband seven shillings a week, out of which we had to pay 2½ shillings to a woman for looking after the younger children. I used to take them to her house at 4 o'clock in the morning, out of their own beds, to put them into hers. Then there was one shilling a week for washing; besides, there was mending to pay for, and other things. The house was not guided. The other children broke things; they did not go to school when they were sent; they would be playing

> about, and get ill-used by other children, and their clothes torn. Then when I came home in the evening, everything was to do after the day's labor, and I was so tired I had no heart for it; no fire lit, nothing cooked, no water fetched, the house dirty, and nothing comfortable for my husband. It is all far better now, and I wouldn't go down again.[15]

The Early Labor Movement in Britain

Many kinds of employment changed slowly during and after the Industrial Revolution in Great Britain. In 1850 more British people still worked on farms than in any other occupation. The second-largest occupation was domestic service, with more than one million household servants, 90 percent of whom were women. Thus many old, familiar jobs outside industry lived on and provided alternatives for individual workers. This helped ease the transition to industrial civilization.

Within industry itself, the pattern of artisans working with hand tools in small shops remained unchanged in many trades, even as others were revolutionized by technological change. For example, as in the case of cotton and coal, the British iron industry was completely dominated by large-scale capitalist firms by 1850. Many large ironworks had more than one thousand people on their payrolls. Yet the firms that fashioned iron into small metal goods, such as tools, tableware, and toys, employed on average fewer than ten wage workers who used time-honored handicraft skills. Only gradually after 1850 did some owners find ways to reorganize some handicraft industries with new machines and new patterns of work. The survival of small workshops gave many workers an alternative to factory employment.

Working-class solidarity and class-consciousness developed in small workshops as well as in large factories. In the northern factory districts, where thousands of "hired hands" looked across at a tiny minority of managers and owners, anticapitalist sentiments were frequent by the 1820s. Commenting in 1825 on a strike in the woolen center of Bradford and the support it had gathered from other regions, one paper claimed with pride that "it is all the workers of England against a few masters of Bradford."[16] Modern technology and factory organization had created a few versus the many.

The transformation of some traditional trades by organizational changes, rather than technological innovations, could by themselves also create ill will and class feeling. The classical liberal concept of economic freedom and laissez faire emerged in the late eighteenth century, and it continued to gather strength in the early nineteenth century (see Chapter 22). As in France during the French Revolution, the British government attacked monopolies, guilds, and workers combinations in the name of individual liberty. In 1799 Parliament passed the **Combination Acts**, which outlawed unions and strikes. In 1813 and 1814, Parliament repealed the old and often disregarded law of 1563 regulating the wages of artisans and the conditions of apprenticeship. As a result of these and other measures, certain skilled artisan workers, such as bootmakers and high-quality tailors, found aggressive capitalists ignoring traditional work rules and trying to flood their trades with unorganized women workers and children to beat down wages.

The capitalist attack on artisan guilds and work rules was bitterly resented by many craftworkers, who subsequently played an important part in Great Britain and in other countries in gradually building a modern labor movement to improve working conditions and to serve worker needs. The Combination Acts were widely disregarded by workers. Printers, papermakers, carpenters, tailors, and other such craftsmen continued to take collective action, and societies of skilled factory workers also organized unions. Unions sought to control the number of skilled workers, limit apprenticeship to members' own children, and bargain with owners over wages.

They were not afraid to strike; there was, for example, a general strike of adult cotton spinners in Manchester in 1810. In the face of widespread union activity, Parliament repealed the Combination Acts in 1824, and unions were tolerated, though not fully accepted, after 1825. The next stage in the development of the British trade-union movement was the attempt to create a single large national union. This effort was led not so much by working people as by social reformers such as Robert Owen. Owen, a self-made cotton manufacturer (see page 678), had pioneered in industrial relations by combining firm discipline with concern for the health, safety, and hours of his workers. After 1815 he experimented with cooperative and socialist communities, including one at New Harmony, Indiana. Then in 1834 Owen organized one of the largest and most visionary of the early national unions, the Grand National Consolidated Trades Union.

When Owen's and other grandiose schemes collapsed, the British labor movement moved once again after 1851 in the direction of craft unions. The most famous of these "new model unions" was the Amalgamated Society of Engineers, which represented skilled machinists. These unions won real benefits for members by

fairly conservative means and thus became an accepted part of the industrial scene.

British workers also engaged in direct political activity in defense of their own interests. After the collapse of Owen's national trade union, many working people went into the Chartist movement, which sought political democracy. The key Chartist demand—that all men be given the right to vote—became the great hope of millions of aroused people. Workers were also active in campaigns to limit the workday in factories to ten hours and to permit duty-free importation of wheat into Great Britain to secure cheap bread. Thus working people developed a sense of their own identity and played an active role in shaping the new industrial system. They were neither helpless victims nor passive beneficiaries.

Combination Acts English laws passed in 1799 that outlawed unions and strikes, favoring capitalist business people over skilled artisans. Bitterly resented and widely disregarded by many craft guilds, the acts were repealed by Parliament in 1824.

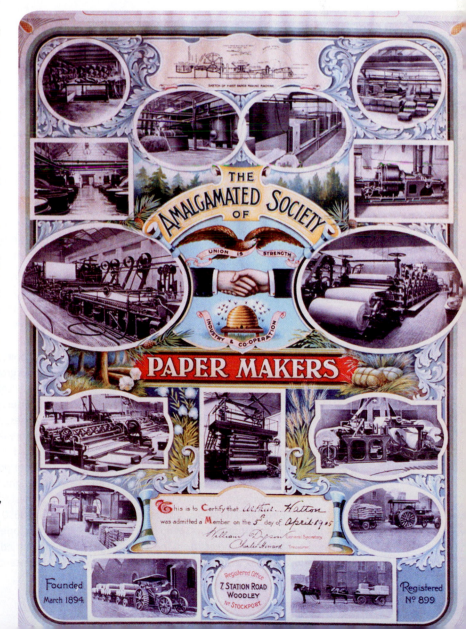

Union Membership Certificate This handsome membership certificate belonged to Arthur Watton, a properly trained and certified papermaker of Kings Norton in Birmingham, England. Members of such unions proudly framed their certificates and displayed them in their homes, showing that they were skilled workers. (Courtesy, Sylvia Waddell)

LOOKING BACK LOOKING AHEAD

ONE POPULAR IDEA in the 1830s, first developed by a French economist, was that Britain had experienced an "industrial revolution" at the same time that France had experienced the French Revolution. One revolution was economic, while the other was political; one was ongoing and successful, while the other had failed and come to a definite end in 1815, when Europe's conservative monarchs defeated Napoleon and restored the French kings of the Old Regime.

In fact, in 1815 the French Revolution, like the Industrial Revolution, was an unfinished revolution. Just as Britain was in the midst of its economic transformation and the states of northwestern Europe would begin rapid industrialization only in the 1850s, so too after 1815 were the political conflicts and ideologies of revolutionary France still very much alive. The French Revolution had opened the era of modern political life in Europe. It had brought into existence many of the political forces and ideologies that would interact with industrialization to refashion Europe and create a new urban society. Moreover, in 1815 the unfinished French Revolution carried the very real possibility of renewed political upheaval. This possibility, which conservatives feared and radicals longed for, would become dramatic reality in 1848, when political revolutions swept across Europe like a whirlwind.

CHAPTER REVIEW

■ What were the origins of the Industrial Revolution in Britain, and how did it develop between 1780 and 1850? (p. 656)

As markets for manufactured goods increased both domestically and overseas, Britain was able to respond with increased production, largely because of its stable government, abundant natural resources, and flexible labor force. The first factories arose as a result of technical innovations in spinning cotton, thereby revolutionizing the textile industry. The widespread availability and affordability of cotton provided benefits for many, but also resulted in the brutal forced labor of orphaned children on a large scale. The demand for improvements in energy led to innovations and improvements in the steam engine, which transformed the iron industry among others. In the early nineteenth century, transportation of goods was greatly enhanced when railroads were built, largely by unskilled farm workers who subsequently often left their villages for a more exciting life in towns.

■ How after 1815 did continental countries respond to the challenge of industrialization? (p. 665)

For reasons including warfare on home soil and barriers to trade, continental Europe lagged behind England in industrialization in 1815. But after 1815, some continental countries, especially France, Belgium, and Germany, gradually built on England's technical breakthroughs, such as textile machinery and steam engines. Entrepreneurs set up their own factories and hired skilled urban workers from the area along with English immigrants experienced in the new technologies.

England tried to limit the spread of trade secrets, and financing was difficult for early continental capitalists, but government intervention, such as tariff protection and infrastructure, was a great boon to industrialization on the continent. In addition, newly established corporate banks worked in conjunction with governments to invest heavily in railroads and other industries.

■ How did the Industrial Revolution affect people of all social classes, and what measures were taken to improve the conditions of workers? (p. 672)

The rise of modern industry had a profound impact on people and their lives, beginning in Britain in the late eighteenth century. Industrialization led to the growing size and wealth of the middle class, as factory owners took their place beside successful merchants and professional people. These early entrepreneurs at first came from diverse backgrounds, providing economic opportunities for religious and ethnic minorities, but by the middle of the nineteenth century, wealthy industrial families controlled large enterprises, and it was difficult for the poor but talented person to break in. The modern industrial working class also developed during this time, filling the need for vast quantities of labor power. Rigid rules, stern discipline, and long hours weighed heavily on factory workers, and improvements in the standard of living came slowly, but they were substantial by 1850. Family members often worked together in early factories, but as restrictions were placed on child labor, married women withdrew increasingly from wage work and concentrated on child care and household responsibilities.

At the same time many young women worked before they were married, and jobs for young workers were often separated by gender in an attempt to control sexual behavior. The era of industrialization also fostered new attitudes toward child labor, encouraged protective factory legislation, and called forth a new sense of class feeling and an assertive labor movement.

Suggested Reading

Cameron, Rondo, and Larry Neal. *A Concise Economic History of the World*, 4th ed. 2003. Provides an introduction to key issues related to the Industrial Revolution and has a carefully annotated bibliography.

Davidoff, Leonore, and Catherine Hall. *Family Fortunes: Men and Women of the English Middle Class, 1750–1850*, rev. ed. 2003. Examines both economic activities and cultural beliefs with great skill.

Dolan, Brian. *Wedgwood: The First Tycoon*. 2004. A comprehensive study of the famous entrepreneur.

Fuchs, Rachel G. *Gender and Poverty in Nineteenth-Century Europe*. 2005. Provides a broad comparative perspective.

Gaskell, Elizabeth. *Mary Barton*. 1848. Gaskell's famous novel offers a realistic portrayal of the new industrial society.

Goodman, Jordan, and Katrina Honeyman. *Gainful Pursuits: The Making of Industrial Europe, 1600–1914*. 1988. An excellent general treatment of European industrial growth.

Horn, Jeff. *Understanding the Industrial Revolution: Milestones in Business History*. 2007. Clear, concise, and engaging, this is an excellent work for students.

Kemp, Tom. *Industrialization in Europe*, 2d ed. 1985. A useful overview.

Landes, David. *Dynasties: Fortunes and Misfortunes of the World's Great Family Businesses*. 2006. A collection offering fascinating and insightful histories of famous enterprises and leading capitalists.

Pomeranz, Kenneth. *The Great Divergence: China, Europe, and the Making of the Modern World Economy*. 2000. A sophisticated reconsideration of why western Europe underwent industrialization and China did not.

Stearns, Peter N. *The Industrial Revolution in World History*, 3d ed. 2007. A useful brief survey.

Thompson, E. P. *The Making of the English Working Class*. 1963. A fascinating book in the Marxian tradition that is rich in detail and early working-class lore.

Valenze, Deborah. *The First Industrial Woman*. 1995. A gender study that reinvigorates the debate between optimists and pessimists about the consequences of industrialization in Britain.

Walton, Whitney. *France and the Crystal Palace: Bourgeois Taste and Artisan Manufacture in the 19th Century*. 1992. Examines the gradual transformation of handicraft techniques and their persistent importance in the international economy.

Notes

1. N. F. R. Crafts, *British Economic Growth During the Industrial Revolution* (Oxford: Oxford University Press, 1985), p. 32.
2. P. Bairoch, "International Industrialization Levels from 1750 to 1980," *Journal of European Economic History* 11 (Spring 1982): 269–333.
3. Crafts, *British Economic Growth*, pp. 45, 95–102.
4. Quoted by J. Bowditch and C. Ramsland, eds., *Voices of the Industrial Revolution* (Ann Arbor: University of Michigan Press, 1961), p. 55, from the fourth edition of Thomas Malthus, *Essay on the Principle of Population* (1807).
5. M. Lévy-Leboyer, *Les banques européennes et l'industrialisation dans la première moitié du XIXe siècle* (Paris: Presses Universitaires de France, 1964), p. 29.
6. Friedrich List, *The National System of Political Economy*, trans. G. A. Matile (Philadelphia: J. B. Lippincott, 1856), p. 61; edited slightly.
7. J. Michelet, *The People*, trans. with an introduction by J. P. McKay (Urbana: University of Illinois Press, 1973; original publication, 1846), p. 64.
8. Quoted in W. A. Hayek, ed., *Capitalism and the Historians* (Chicago: University of Chicago Press, 1954), p. 126.
9. Crafts, *British Economic Growth*, p. 95.
10. H-J. Voth, *Time and Work in England, 1750–1830* (Oxford: Oxford University Press, 2000), pp. 268–270; also pp. 118–133.
11. Quoted in E. R. Pike, *"Hard Times": Human Documents of the Industrial Revolution* (New York: Praeger, 1966), p. 109.
12. See especially J. Brenner and M. Rama, "Rethinking Women's Oppression," *New Left Review* 144 (March–April 1984): 33–71, and sources cited there.
13. J. Humphries, "...'The Most Free from Objection'...: The Sexual Division of Labor and Women's Work in Nineteenth-Century England," *Journal of Economic History* 47 (December 1987): 948.
14. Ibid., p. 941; Pike, *"Hard Times,"* p. 266.
15. Pike, *"Hard Times,"* p. 208.
16. Quoted in D. Geary, ed., *Labour and Socialist Movements in Europe Before 1914* (Oxford: Berg, 1989), p. 29.

Key Terms

Industrial Revolution (p. 656)

spinning jenny (p. 657)

water frame (p. 657)

steam engines (p. 660)

Rocket (p. 663)

Crystal Palace (p. 664)

iron law of wages (p. 665)

tariff protection (p. 670)

economic nationalism (p. 672)

class-consciousness (p. 672)

Luddites (p. 674)

Factory Act of 1833 (p. 678)

separate spheres (p. 679)

Mines Act of 1842 (p. 680)

Combination Acts (p. 680)

For practice quizzes and other study tools, visit the Online Study Guide at **bedfordstmartins.com/mckaywest**.

For primary sources from this period, see ***Sources of Western Society*, Second Edition**.

For Web sites, images, and documents related to topics in this chapter, visit Make History at **bedfordstmartins.com/mckaywest**.

22

Ideologies and Upheavals

1815–1850

The momentous economic and political transformation of modern times began in the late eighteenth century with the Industrial Revolution in England and then the French Revolution. Until about 1815, these economic and political revolutions were separate, involving different countries and activities and proceeding at very different paces. After peace returned in 1815, economic and political changes tended to fuse, reinforcing each other and bringing about what historian Eric Hobsbawm has incisively called the dual revolution. For instance, the growth of the industrial middle class encouraged the drive for representative government, and the demands of the French sans-culottes (laboring poor) in 1793 and 1794 inspired many socialist thinkers. Radical change was eventually a constant, but the particular results varied enormously. In central and eastern Europe especially, the traditional elites—the monarchs, noble landowners, and bureaucrats—proved capable of defending their privileges and eventually used nationalism to respond to the dual revolution and to serve their interests, as we shall see in Chapter 24.

The dual revolution also posed a tremendous intellectual challenge. The meanings of the economic, political, and social changes that were occurring, as well as the ways they would be shaped by human action, were anything but clear. In literature, art, and music, the uncertainty of the era was reflected in the exuberance of the romantic movement. In politics, powerful new ideological forces emerged: a revitalized conservatism and three ideologies of change—liberalism, nationalism, and socialism. All played critical roles in the political and social battles of the era and the great popular upheaval that eventually swept across Europe in the revolutions of 1848. ■

Life in the Revolutionary Era. The sight of revolutionaries storming public areas was widespread in many parts of Europe between 1830 and 1848. Here Louis Philippe, the new French king, leaves in 1830 for the Paris city hall to greet the people. The three-colored Republican flag he has just accepted goes before him.

CHAPTER PREVIEW

The Aftermath of the Napoleonic Wars

■ How did the victorious allies fashion a general peace settlement, and how did Metternich uphold a conservative European order?

The Spread of Radical Ideas

■ What were the basic tenets of liberalism, nationalism, and socialism, and what groups were most attracted to these ideologies?

The Romantic Movement

■ What were the characteristics of the romantic movement, and who were some of the great romantic artists?

Reforms and Revolutions Before 1848

■ How after 1815 did liberal, national, and socialist forces challenge conservatism in Greece, Great Britain, and France?

The Revolutions of 1848

■ Why in 1848 did revolution triumph briefly throughout most of Europe, and why did it fail almost completely?

The Aftermath of the Napoleonic Wars

How did the victorious allies fashion a general peace settlement, and how did Metternich uphold a conservative European order? ■

The eventual triumph of revolutionary economic and political forces was by no means certain as the Napoleonic era ended. Quite the contrary. The conservative, aristocratic monarchies of Russia, Prussia, Austria, and Great Britain — known as the Quadruple Alliance — had finally defeated France and reaffirmed their determination to hold France in line. But many other international questions were outstanding, and the allies agreed to meet at the **Congress of Vienna** to fashion a general peace settlement.

Congress of Vienna A meeting of the Quadruple Alliance — Russia, Prussia, Austria, and Great Britain — and restoration France to fashion a general peace settlement that began after the defeat of Napoleon's France in 1814.

Most people felt a profound longing for peace. The great challenge for political leaders in 1814 was to construct a settlement that would last and not sow the seeds of another war. Their efforts were largely successful and contributed to a century unmarred by destructive generalized war (Map 22.1).

The European Balance of Power

The allied powers were concerned first and foremost with the defeated enemy, France. Agreeing to the restoration of the Bourbon dynasty (see Chapter 20), the allies were lenient toward France after Napoleon's abdication. The first Peace of Paris gave France the boundaries it possessed in 1792, which were larger than those of 1789, and France did not have to pay any war repa-

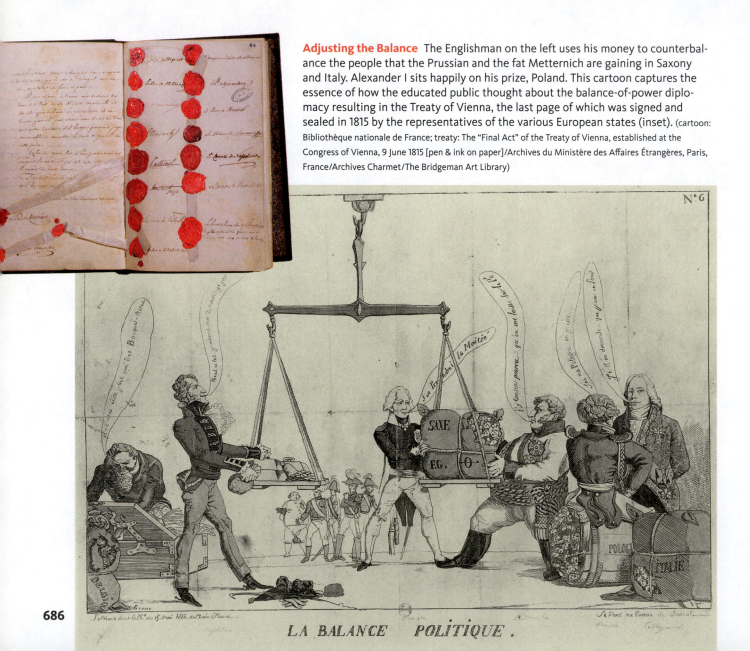

Adjusting the Balance The Englishman on the left uses his money to counterbalance the people that the Prussian and the fat Metternich are gaining in Saxony and Italy. Alexander I sits happily on his prize, Poland. This cartoon captures the essence of how the educated public thought about the balance-of-power diplomacy resulting in the Treaty of Vienna, the last page of which was signed and sealed in 1815 by the representatives of the various European states (inset). (cartoon: Bibliothèque nationale de France; treaty: The "Final Act" of the Treaty of Vienna, established at the Congress of Vienna, 9 June 1815 [pen & ink on paper]/Archives du Ministère des Affaires Étrangères, Paris, France/Archives Charmet/The Bridgeman Art Library)

LA BALANCE POLITIQUE.

rations. Thus the victorious powers did not foment a spirit of injustice and revenge in the defeated country.

When the four allies of the Quadruple Alliance (plus a representative of the restored Bourbon monarch in France) met together at the Congress of Vienna, assisted in a minor way by a host of delegates from the smaller European states, they also agreed to raise a number of formidable barriers against renewed French aggression. The Low Countries—Belgium and Holland—were united under an enlarged Dutch monarchy capable of opposing France more effectively. Above all, Prussia received considerably more territory on France's eastern border so as to stand as the "sentinel on the Rhine" against France. In these ways, the Quadruple Alliance combined leniency toward France with strong defensive measures.

In their moderation toward France, the allies were motivated by self-interest and traditional ideas about the balance of power. To Klemens von Metternich (MEH-tuhr-nihk) and Robert Castlereagh (KA-suhl-ray), the foreign ministers of Austria and Great Britain, respectively, as well as their French counterpart, Charles Talleyrand, the balance of power meant an international equilibrium of political and military forces that would discourage aggression by any combination of states or, worse, the domination of Europe by any single state.

The Great Powers—Austria, Britain, Prussia, Russia, and France—used the balance of power to settle their own dangerous disputes at the Congress of Vienna. There was general agreement among the victors that each of them should receive compensation in the form of territory for their successful struggle against the French. Great Britain had already won colonies and strategic outposts during the long wars. Metternich's Austria gave up territories in Belgium and southern Germany but expanded greatly elsewhere, taking the rich provinces of Venetia and Lombardy in northern Italy as well as former Polish possessions and new lands on the eastern coast of the Adriatic. More contentious was the push for greater territory by Russia and Prussia. When France, Austria, and Great Britain allied against these powers, Russia accepted a small Polish kingdom and Prussia took only part of Saxony (see Map 22.1). This compromise was very much within the framework of balance-of-power ideology.

Unfortunately for France, Napoleon suddenly escaped from his "comic kingdom" on the island of Elba and reignited his wars of expansion for a brief time (see Chapter 20). Yet the second Peace of Paris, concluded after Napoleon's final defeat at Waterloo in 1815, was still

1790s–1840s	Romantic movement in literature and the arts
1809–1848	Metternich serves as Austrian foreign minister
1810	Staël, *On Germany*
1815	Holy Alliance formed; revision of Corn Laws in Britain
1819	Carlsbad Decrees issued by German Confederation
1830	Greece wins independence from Turks
1832	Reform Bill in Britain
1845–1851	Great Famine in Ireland
1847	Ten Hours Act in Britain
1848	Revolutions in France, Austria, and Prussia; Marx and Engels, *The Communist Manifesto*

relatively moderate toward France. Fat old Louis XVIII was restored to his throne for a second time. France lost only a little territory, had to pay an indemnity of 700 million francs, and had to support a large army of occupation for five years. The rest of the settlement already concluded at the Congress of Vienna was left intact. The members of the Quadruple Alliance, however, did agree to meet periodically to discuss their common interests and to consider appropriate measures for the maintenance of peace in Europe. This agreement marked the beginning of the European "congress system," which lasted long into the nineteenth century and settled many international crises through international conferences and balance-of-power diplomacy.

Repressing the Revolutionary Spirit

There was also a domestic political side to the reestablishment of peace. Within their own countries, the leaders of the victorious states were much less flexible. In 1815 under Metternich's leadership, Austria, Prussia, and Russia embarked on a crusade against the ideas and politics of the **dual revolution**. This crusade lasted until 1848. The first step was the **Holy Alliance**, formed by Austria, Prussia, and Russia in September 1815. First proposed by Russia's Alexander I, the alliance soon became a symbol of the repression of liberal and revolutionary movements all over Europe.

In 1820 revolutionaries succeeded in forcing the monarchs of Spain and the southern Italian kingdom of the Two Sicilies to grant liberal constitutions against their wills. Metternich was horrified: revolution was rising once

dual revolution A term that historian Eric Hobsbawm used for the economic and political changes that tended to fuse and reinforce each other after 1815.

Holy Alliance An alliance formed by the conservative rulers of Austria, Russia, and Prussia in September 1815 that became a symbol of the repression of liberal and revolutionary movements all over Europe.

Great Powers
- Great Britain
- France
- Kingdom of Prussia
- Austrian Empire
- Russian Empire
- Boundary of the German Confederation

Mapping the Past

Map 22.1 Europe in 1815 In 1815 Europe contained many different states, but after the defeat of Napoleon international politics was dominated by the five Great Powers: Russia, Prussia, Austria, Great Britain, and France. (The number rises to six if one includes the Ottoman Empire.)

ANALYZING THE MAP Trace the political boundaries of each Great Power, and compare their geographical strengths and weaknesses. What territories did Prussia and Austria gain as a result of the war with Napoleon?

CONNECTIONS How did Prussia's and Austria's territorial gains contribute to the balance of power established at the Congress of Vienna? What other factors enabled the Great Powers to achieve such a long-lasting peace?

To complete this activity online, go to the Online Study Guide at bedfordstmartins.com/mckaywest.

again. Calling a conference at Troppau in Austria under the provisions of the Quadruple Alliance, he and Alexander I proclaimed the principle of active intervention to maintain all autocratic regimes whenever they were threatened. Austrian forces then marched into Naples in 1821 and restored Ferdinand I to the throne of the Two Sicilies, while French armies in 1823 likewise restored the Spanish regime.

In the following years, Metternich continued to battle against liberal political change. Sometimes he could do

little, as in the case of the new Latin American republics that broke away from Spain. Nor could he undo the dynastic change of 1830 in France or Belgium's achieving independence from the Netherlands in 1831. Nonetheless, until 1848 Metternich's system proved quite effective in central Europe, where his power was the greatest.

Metternich's policies dominated not only Austria and the Italian peninsula but also the entire German Confederation, which the peace settlement of Vienna

1820 Revolts in Spain and Italy

one of Europe's most ancient institutions, and conservatives regarded tradition as the basic source of human institutions.

Metternich firmly believed that liberalism, as embodied in revolutionary America and France, had been responsible for a generation of war with untold bloodshed and suffering. Like many other conservatives then and since, Metternich blamed liberal middle-class revolutionaries for stirring up the lower classes, which he believed desired nothing more than peace and quiet.

The threat of liberalism appeared doubly dangerous to Metternich because it generally went with national aspirations. Liberals believed that each people, each national group, had a right to establish its own independent government and seek to fulfill its own destiny. The idea of national self-determination was repellent to Metternich because it threatened to destroy the Austrian Empire and revolutionize central Europe.

The vast Austrian Empire of the Habsburgs was a great dynastic state. Formed over centuries by war, marriage, and luck, it was made up of many peoples (Map 22.2). The Germans had long

> **Carlsbad Decrees** Issued in 1819, these decrees were designed to uphold Metternich's conservatism, requiring the German states to root out subversive ideas and squelch any liberal organizations.

had called into being. The confederation comprised thirty-eight independent German states, including Prussia and Austria (see Map 22.1). These states met in complicated assemblies dominated by Austria, with Prussia a willing junior partner in the execution of repressive measures. It was through the German Confederation that Metternich had the infamous **Carlsbad Decrees** issued in 1819. These decrees required the thirty-eight German member states to root out subversive ideas in their universities and newspapers. The decrees also established a permanent committee with spies and informers to investigate and punish any liberal or radical organizations.

Metternich and Conservatism

Metternich's determined defense of the status quo made him a villain in the eyes of most progressive, optimistic historians of the nineteenth century. Yet rather than denounce the man, we can try to understand him and the general conservatism he represented. Born into the middle ranks of the landed nobility of the Rhineland, Prince Klemens von Metternich (1773–1859) was an internationally oriented aristocrat who made a brilliant diplomatic career in Austria. Austrian foreign minister from 1809 to 1848, the cosmopolitan and conservative Metternich had a pessimistic view of human nature, which he believed was ever prone to error, excess, and self-serving behavior. Thus Metternich concluded that strong governments were necessary as a bulwark to protect society from the baser elements of human behavior. Metternich also defended his class and its rights and privileges with a clear conscience. The nobility was

Prince Klemens von Metternich This portrait by Sir Thomas Lawrence reveals much about Metternich the man. Handsome, refined, and intelligent, Metternich was a great aristocrat who was passionately devoted to the defense of his class and its interests. (The Royal Collection © 2010 Her Majesty Queen Elizabeth II)

Map 22.2 Peoples of the Habsburg Monarchy, 1815 The old dynastic state was a patchwork of nationalities. Note the widely scattered pockets of Germans and Hungarians.

dominated the empire, yet they accounted for only one-fourth of the population. The Magyars (Hungarians), a substantially smaller group, dominated the kingdom of Hungary, though they did not account for a majority of the population in that part of the Austrian Empire.

The Czechs, the third major group, were concentrated in Bohemia and Moravia. There were also large numbers of Italians, Poles, and Ukrainians as well as smaller groups of Slovenes, Croats, Serbs, and Romanians. The various Slavic peoples, together with the Italians and the Romanians, represented a widely scattered and completely divided majority in an empire politically dominated by Germans and Hungarians. Different ethnic groups often lived in the same provinces and even in the same villages. Thus the different parts and provinces of the empire differed in languages, customs, and institutions.

The multiethnic state Metternich served was both strong and weak. It was strong because of its large population and vast territories; it was weak because of its

many and potentially dissatisfied nationalities. In these circumstances, Metternich virtually had to oppose liberalism and nationalism, for Austria was simply unable to accommodate these ideologies of the dual revolution.

In his efforts to hold back liberalism and nationalism Metternich was supported by Russia and, to a lesser extent, by the Ottoman Empire. Bitter enemies, these far-flung empires were both absolutist states with powerful armies and long traditions of expansion and conquest. Both were multinational empires made up of many peoples, languages, and religions, but in each case most of the ruling elite came from the dominant ethnic group — the Orthodox Christian Russians centered in central and northern Russia, and the Muslim Ottoman Turks of Anatolia (much of modern Turkey). After 1815, both of these multinational absolutist states worked to preserve their respective traditional conservative orders. Only after 1850 did each in turn experience a profound crisis and embark on a program of fundamental reform and modernization, as we shall see in Chapter 24.

The Spread of Radical Ideas

What were the basic tenets of liberalism, nationalism, and socialism, and what groups were most attracted to these ideologies? ■

In the years following the peace settlement of 1815 intellectuals and social observers sought to understand the revolutionary changes that had occurred and were still taking place. Almost all of these basic ideas were radical. In one way or another, the new ideas rejected conservatism, with its stress on tradition, a hereditary monarchy, a strong and privileged landowning aristocracy, and an official church. Radical thinkers developed and refined alternative visions—alternative ideologies—and tried to convince society to act on them. In contrast to Metternich and conservatism, these new philosophies of liberalism, nationalism, and socialism started with an optimistic premise about human nature. Although they reached very different conclusions about how best to achieve progress, or how far progress should extend, with time, each of the new movements was very successful.

Liberalism and the Middle Class

The principal ideas of **liberalism**—liberty and equality—were by no means defeated in 1815. First realized successfully in the American Revolution and then achieved in part in the French Revolution, liberalism demanded representative government as opposed to autocratic monarchy, and equality before the law as opposed to legally separate classes. The idea of liberty also meant specific individual freedoms: freedom of the press, freedom of speech, freedom of assembly, and freedom from arbitrary arrest. In Europe only France with Louis XVIII's Constitutional Charter and Great Britain with its Parliament and historic rights of English men and women had realized much of the liberal program in 1815. Even in those countries, liberalism had not fully succeeded.

Although liberalism retained its cutting edge, it was seen by many as being a somewhat duller tool than it had been. The reasons for this were that liberalism faced more radical ideological competitors in the early nineteenth century. Opponents of liberalism especially criticized its economic principles, which called for unrestricted private enterprise and no government interference in the economy. This philosophy was popularly known as the doctrine of **laissez faire** (lay-say FEHR). (This form of liberalism is often called "classical" liberalism in the United States in order to distinguish it sharply from modern American liberalism, which usually favors more government programs to meet social needs and to regulate the economy.)

As we saw in Chapter 18 Adam Smith posited the idea of a free economy in 1776 in opposition to mercantilism and its attempt to regulate trade. Smith argued that freely competitive private enterprise would give all citizens a fair and equal opportunity to do what they did best and would result in greater income for everyone, not just the rich. In early-nineteenth-century Britain this economic liberalism was embraced most enthusiastically by business groups and thus became a doctrine associated with business interests. Businessmen used the doctrine to defend their right to do as they wished in their factories. Labor unions were outlawed because they supposedly restricted free competition and the individual's "right to work."

In the early nineteenth century liberal political ideals also became more closely associated with narrow class interests. Early-nineteenth-century liberals favored representative government, but they generally wanted property qualifications attached to the right to vote. In practice, this meant limiting the vote to the well-to-do. Workers and peasants, as well as the lower middle class of shopkeepers, clerks, and artisans, did not own the necessary property and thus could not vote.

As liberalism became increasingly identified with the middle class after 1815, some intellectuals and foes of conservatism felt that liberalism did not go nearly far enough. Inspired by memories of the French Revolution and the example of Jacksonian democracy in the young American republic, they called for universal voting rights, at least for males, and for democracy. These democrats and republicans were more radical than the liberals, and they were more willing than most liberals to endorse violent upheaval to achieve goals. All of this meant that liberals and radical democratic republicans could join forces against conservatives only up to a point.

liberalism The principal ideas of this movement were equality and liberty; liberals demanded representative government and equality before the law as well as individual freedoms such as freedom of the press, freedom of speech, freedom of assembly, and freedom from arbitrary arrest.

laissez faire A doctrine of economic liberalism that believes in unrestricted private enterprise and no government interference in the economy.

nationalism The idea that each people had its own genius and its own specific unity, which manifested itself especially in a common language and history, and often led to the desire for an independent political state.

The Growing Appeal of Nationalism

Nationalism was a second radical idea in the years after 1815—an idea destined to have an enormous influence in the modern world. Nationalism had its immediate origins in the French Revolution and the Napoleonic wars, and there were already hints of its remarkable ability to spread and develop.

Early advocates of the "national idea," or nationalism, were strongly influenced by Johann Gottfried von Herder, an eighteenth-century philosopher and historian who argued that each people had its own genius and its own cultural unity. (See "Listening to the Past: Herder and Mazzini on the Development of Nationalism," page 694.) For nationalists coming after Herder this cultural unity was basically self-evident, manifesting itself especially in a common language, history, and territory. In fact, in the early nineteenth century such cultural unity was more a dream than a reality as far as most nationalities were concerned. Local dialects abounded, and peasants from nearby villages often failed to understand each other. As for historical memory, it divided the inhabitants of the different German or Italian states as much as it unified them. Moreover, a variety of ethnic groups shared the territory of most states.

Despite these basic realities, sooner or later European nationalists usually sought to turn the cultural unity that they perceived into political reality. They sought to make the territory of each people coincide with well-defined boundaries in an independent nation-state. It was this political goal that made nationalism so explosive in central and eastern Europe after 1815, when there were either too few states (Austria, Russia, and the Otto-

man Empire) or too many (the Italian peninsula and the German Confederation), and when different peoples overlapped and intermingled.

In recent years scholars have been trying to understand how the nationalist vision, often fitting so poorly with existing conditions and promising so much upheaval, was so successful in the long run. Of fundamental importance in the rise of nationalism was the development of complex industrial and urban society, which required much better communication between individuals and groups.[1] These communication needs promoted the use of a standardized national language within many countries, creating at least a superficial cultural unity as a standard tongue spread through mass education. When a minority population was large and concentrated, the nationalist campaign for a standardized language often led the minority group to push for a separate nation-state.

Many scholars also argue that nations are recent creations, the product of the new, self-conscious nationalist ideology. Thus nation-states emerged in the nineteenth century as "imagined communities" that sought to bind millions of strangers together around the abstract concept of an all-embracing national identity. This meant bringing citizens together with emotionally charged symbols and ceremonies, such as independence holidays and patriotic parades. On these occasions the imagined nation of spiritual equals might celebrate its most hallowed traditions, which were often recent inventions.[2]

Historians also stress the dynamic, ever-changing character of nationalism. Industrialism and mass education, so important in the later nineteenth century, played only a minor role before 1850. In those years the faith in nationhood was fresh, idealistic, and progressive.

Between 1815 and 1850 most people who believed in nationalism also believed in either liberalism or radical democratic republicanism. A common faith in the creativity and nobility of the people was perhaps the single most important reason for the linking of these two concepts. Liberals and especially democrats saw the people as the ultimate source of all government. Yet liberals and nationalists agreed that the benefits of self-government would be possible only if the people were united by common traditions that transcended local interests and even class differences.

Building German Nationalism As popular upheaval in France spread to central Europe in March 1848, Germans from the solid middle classes came together in Frankfurt to draft a constitution for a new united Germany. This woodcut commemorates the solemn procession of delegates entering Saint Paul's Cathedral in Frankfurt, where the delegates would hold their deliberations. Festivals, celebrations, and parades helped create a feeling of belonging to a large unseen community, a nation binding millions of strangers together. (akg-images)

" In laboring according to the true principles of our country we are laboring for Humanity. "

—GUISEPPE MAZZINI

Early nationalists usually believed that every nation, like every citizen, had the right to exist in freedom and to develop its character and spirit. They were confident that a symphony of nations would promote the harmony and ultimate unity of all peoples. As the French historian Jules Michelet (zhool meesh-LAY) put it in *The People* in 1846, each citizen "learns to recognize his country . . . as a note in the grand concert; through it he himself participates and loves the world." Similarly, the great Italian patriot Guiseppe Mazzini (1805–1872) believed that "in laboring according to the true principles of our country we are laboring for Humanity." (See "Listening to the Past: Herder and Mazzini on the Development of Nationalism," page 694.) Thus the liberty of the individual and the love of a free nation overlapped greatly in the early nineteenth century.

Yet early nationalists also stressed the differences among peoples. Even early nationalism developed a strong sense of "we" and "they." To this "we-they" outlook, it was all too easy for nationalists to add two highly volatile ingredients: a sense of national mission and a sense of national superiority. Even Michelet, so alive to the national aspirations of other peoples, could not help speaking in 1846 of the "superiority of France"; the principles espoused in the French Revolution had made France the "salvation of mankind."

Russian and German nationalists had a very different opinion of France. In the narratives they constructed, the French often seemed oppressive, as the Russians did to the Poles and as the Germans did to the Czechs. Thus "they" often emerged as the enemy, and underlying ideas of national superiority and national mission would eventually lead to aggression and conflict.

French Utopian Socialism

Socialism, the new radical doctrine after 1815, began in France, although France lagged far behind Great Britain in developing modern industry and experiencing the industrial conflicts that arose between a few factory owners and a multitude of factory workers. Early French socialist thinkers were acutely aware that the political revolution in France, the rise of laissez faire, and the emergence of modern industry in Britain were transforming society. They were disturbed because they saw these developments as fomenting selfish individualism and splitting the community into isolated fragments.

There was, they believed, an urgent need for a further reorganization of society to establish cooperation and a new sense of community.

Early French socialists believed in economic planning. Inspired by the emergency measures of 1793 and 1794 in France, they argued that the government should rationally organize the economy and not depend on destructive competition to do the job. Early socialists also shared an intense desire to help the poor, and they preached that the rich and the poor should be more nearly equal economically. Finally, socialists believed that private property should be strictly regulated by the government or that it should be abolished and replaced by state or community ownership. Planning, greater economic equality, and state regulation of property—these were the key ideas of early French socialism and of all socialism since.

One of the most influential early socialist thinkers was a nobleman, Count Henri de Saint-Simon (awn-REE duh san-see-MOHN) (1760–1825). Saint-Simon optimistically proclaimed the tremendous possibilities of industrial development: "The age of gold is before us!" The key to progress was proper social organization that required the "parasites"—the court, the aristocracy, lawyers, and churchmen—to give way, once and for all, to the "doers"—the leading scientists, engineers, and industrialists. The doers would carefully plan the economy and guide it forward by undertaking vast public works projects and establishing investment banks. Saint-Simon also stressed in highly moralistic terms that every social institution ought to have as its main goal improved conditions for the poor.

After 1830 the socialist critique of capitalism became sharper. Charles Fourier (sharl FOR-ee-ay) (1772–1837), a lonely, saintly man, envisaged a socialist utopia of mathematically precise, self-sufficient communities, each made up of 1,620 people. Fourier was also an early proponent of the total emancipation of women. According to Fourier, young single women were shamelessly "sold" to their future husbands for dowries and other financial considerations. Therefore, Fourier called for the abolition of marriage, free unions based only on love, and sexual freedom. Many middle-class men and women found these ideas, which were shared and even practiced by some followers of Saint-Simon, shocking and immoral.

Louis Blanc (1811–1882), a sharp-eyed, intelligent journalist, focused on practical improvements. In his *Organization of Work* (1839), he urged workers to agitate for universal voting rights and to take control of the state peacefully. Blanc believed that the state should set up

socialism A backlash against the emergence of individualism and the fragmentation of society, and a move toward cooperation and a sense of community; the key ideas were economic planning, greater economic equality, and state regulation of property.

LISTENING TO THE PAST

The German historian and philosopher Johann Gottfried von Herder (1744–1803) established the foundations of cultural nationalism. Writing shortly before the French Revolution, Herder's multivolume Ideas for the Philosophy of History of Humanity *(1784–1791) focused on the long, unconscious evolution of human communities. This process had produced national communities, each of which was joined together by a common language*

and by popular traditions, such as legends, proverbs, and folk songs. Herder believed that each language and each people was equally valid and equally worthy of respect.

A German born in Prussia, Herder hated Prussian militarism and was in no way partial to the Germans in his study. For example, he lauded the peaceful character of the Slavs and often decried the barbaric behavior of the warrior Germans. Stressing the cultural genius of each nationality, Herder advocated the preservation of traditions but not the creation of political entities or nation-states. The following passage is taken from Herder's concluding section on the different peoples of northern Europe.

Johann Gottfried von Herder, "Ideas for the Philosophy of History of Humanity"

❝ This is more or less a picture of the peoples of Europe. What a multicolored and composite picture! . . . Sea voyages and long migrations of people finally produced on the small continent of Europe the conditions for a great league of nations. Unwittingly the Romans had prepared it by their conquests. Such a league of nations was unthinkable outside of Europe. Nowhere else have people intermingled so much, nowhere else have they changed so often and so much their habitats and thereby their customs and ways of life. In many European countries it would be difficult today for the inhabitants, especially for single families and individuals, to say, from which people they descend, whether from Goths, Moors, Jews, Carthaginians or Romans, whether from Gauls, Burgundians, Franks, Normans, Saxons, Slavs, Finns or Illyrians, or how in the long line of their ancestors their blood had been mixed. Hundreds of causes have tempered and changed the old tribal composition of the European nations in the course of the centuries; without such an intermingling the common spirit of Europe could hardly have been awakened.

. . . Like the geological layers of our soil, the European peoples have been superimposed on each other and intermingled with each other, and yet can still be discerned in their original character. The scholars who study their customs and languages must hurry and do

so while these peoples are still distinguishable: for everything in Europe tends towards the slow extinction of national character. But the historian of mankind should beware lest he exclusively favors one nationality and thereby slights others who were deprived by circumstances of chance and glory. . . .

No European people has become cultured and educated by itself. Each one has tended to keep its old barbarian customs as long as it could, supported therein by the roughness of the climate and the need of primitive warfare. No European people for instance has invented its own alphabet; the whole civilization of northern, eastern and western Europe has grown out of seeds sown by Romans, Greeks and Arabs. It took a long time before this could grow in the hard soil and could produce its own fruit, which at first lacked sweetness and ripeness. A strange vehicle, an

Johann Gottfried von Herder, renowned eighteenth-century philosopher and historian (left), and Guiseppe Mazzini, Italian patriot in later life after years in exile (far right). (Herder: akg-images; Mazzini: Hulton Archive/Getty Images)

alien religion [Christianity], was necessary to accomplish by spiritual means that which the Romans had not been able to do through conquest. Thus we must consider above all this new means of human education, which had no lesser aim than to educate all peoples to become one people, in this world and for a future world, and which was nowhere more effective than in Europe. "

Like Herder, Giuseppe Mazzini (1805–1872) believed that language determined nationality and that each people had its particular genius. But unlike Herder, Mazzini and many other nationalists of the pre-1848 era also believed that each nationality required a politically independent nation-state. Only a Europe of nation-states would provide the proper framework for securing freedom, democracy, social justice, and even international peace.

The leading prophet of Italian nationalism and unification before 1848, Mazzini founded a secret society called Young Italy to fight for the unification of the Italian states in a democratic republic. Mazzini's group inspired numerous local insurrections and led Italy's radicals in the unsuccessful revolutions of 1848. Mazzini's best-known work was The Duties of Man, *a collection of essays. The following selection from this work was written in 1858 and addressed to Italian workingmen.*

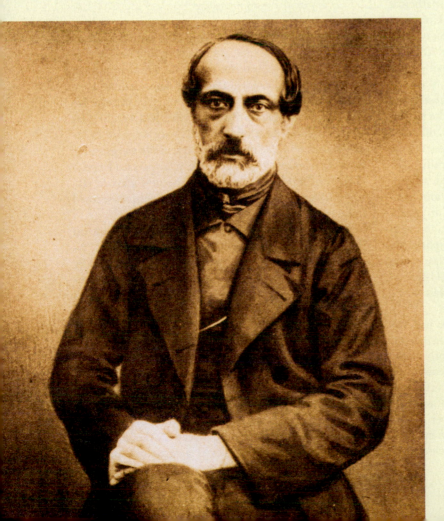

Giuseppe Mazzini, "Duties Towards Your Country"

" Your first Duties . . . are to Humanity. . . . But what can each of you, with his isolated powers, do for the moral improvement, for the progress of Humanity? . . .

God gave you the means of multiplying your forces and your powers of action indefinitely when he gave you a Country, when, like a wise overseer of labor, who distributes the different parts of the work according to the capacity of the workmen, he divided Humanity into distinct groups upon the face of our globe, and thus planted the seeds of nations. Evil governments have disfigured the design of God, which you may see clearly marked out, as far, at least, as regards Europe, by the courses of the great rivers, by the lines of the lofty mountains, and by other geographical conditions; they have disfigured it by conquest, by greed, by jealousy of the just sovereignty of others; disfigured it so much that today there is perhaps no nation except England and France whose confines correspond to this design.

[These evil governments] did not, and they do not, recognize any country except their own families and dynasties, the egoism of caste. But the divine design will infallibly be fulfilled. Natural divisions, the innate spontaneous tendencies of the peoples will replace the arbitrary divisions sanctioned by evil governments. The map of Europe will be remade. The Countries of the People will rise, defined by the voice of the free, upon the ruins of the Countries of Kings and privileged castes. Between these Countries there will be harmony and brotherhood. And then the work of Humanity for the general amelioration, for the discovery and application of the real law of life, carried on in association and distributed according to local capacities, will be accomplished by peaceful and progressive development.

Then each of you, strong in the affections and in the aid of many millions of men speaking the same language, endowed with the same tendencies, and educated by the same historic tradition, may hope by your personal effort to benefit the whole of Humanity.

Without Country you have neither name, voice, nor rights, no admission as brothers into the fellowship of the Peoples. You are the bastards of Humanity. Soldiers without a banner, . . . you will find neither faith nor protection. . . . Do not beguile yourselves with the hope of emancipation from unjust social conditions if you do not first conquer a Country for yourselves; where there is no Country there is no common agreement to which you can appeal; the egoism of self-interest rules alone, and he who has the upper hand keeps it, since there is no common safeguard for the interests of all. "

Sources: Hans Kohn, *Nationalism: Its Idea and History* (Princeton, N.J.: D. Van Nostrand Company Inc., 1955), pp. 108–110; G. Mazzini, *The Duties of Man and Other Essays* (London: J. M. Dent and Sons, 1907), pp. 51–54.

QUESTIONS FOR ANALYSIS

1. How, according to Herder, did European nationalities evolve to create "the common spirit of Europe"?
2. Why, according to Mazzini, should Italian workers support Italian unification?
3. How are Herder's and Mazzini's views similar? How do they differ?

government-backed workshops and factories to guarantee full employment. The right to work had to become as sacred as any other right.

Finally, there was Pierre Joseph Proudhon (1809–1865), a self-educated printer who wrote a pamphlet *What Is Property?* in 1840. His answer was that it was nothing but theft. Property was profit that was stolen from the worker, who was the source of all wealth.

Of great importance, the message of French utopian socialists interacted with the experiences of French urban workers. Workers cherished the memory of the radical phase of the French Revolution, and they became violently opposed to laissez-faire laws that denied workers the right to organize in guilds and unions. Developing a sense of class in the process, workers favored collective action and government intervention in economic life. Thus the aspirations of workers and utopian theorists reinforced each other, and a genuine socialist movement emerged in Paris in the 1830s and 1840s. To Karl Marx was left the task of establishing firm foundations for modern socialism.

The Birth of Marxian Socialism

In 1848 Karl Marx (1818–1883) and Friedrich Engels (see Chapter 21) published *The Communist Manifesto*, which became the bible of socialism. The son of a Jewish lawyer who had converted to Christianity, the atheistic young Marx had studied philosophy at the University of Berlin before turning to journalism and economics. He read widely in French socialist thought, and like Fourier he looked forward to the emancipation of women and the abolition of the family. By the time Marx was twenty-five, he was developing his own socialist ideas.

Early French socialists often appealed to the middle class and the state to help the poor. Marx ridiculed such appeals as naive. He argued that the interests of the middle class and those of the industrial working class were inevitably opposed to each other. Indeed, according to the *Manifesto*, the "history of all previously existing society is the history of class struggles." In Marx's view, one class had always exploited the other, and with the advent of modern industry, society was split more clearly than ever before: between the middle class—the **bourgeoisie** (boor-ZHWAH-zee)—and the modern working class—the **proletariat**.

Just as the bourgeoisie had triumphed over the feudal aristocracy, Marx predicted that the proletariat would conquer the bourgeoisie in a violent revolution. While a tiny minority owned the means of production and grew richer, the ever-poorer proletariat was constantly growing in size and in class-consciousness.

bourgeoisie The middle-class minority who owned the means of production and, according to Marx, exploited the working-class proletariat.

proletariat The industrial working class who, according to Marx, were unfairly exploited by the profit-seeking bourgeoisie.

❝ The history of all previously existing society is the history of class struggles. ❞
—KARL MARX

In this process, the proletariat was aided, according to Marx, by a portion of the bourgeoisie who had gone over to the proletariat and who (like Marx and Engels) "had raised themselves to the level of comprehending theoretically the historical moment." The critical moment, Marx thought, was very near, as the last lines of *The Communist Manifesto* make very clear.

> Germany . . . is on the eve of a bourgeois revolution, that is bound to be . . . the prelude to an immediately following proletarian revolution. . . .
>
> The Communists disdain to conceal their views and aims. They openly declare that their ends can be attained only by the forcible overthrow of all existing social conditions. Let the ruling classes tremble at a Communist revolution. The proletarians have nothing to lose but their chains. They have a world to win. WORKING MEN OF ALL COUNTRIES, UNITE!

Marx's ideas united sociology, economics, and all human history in a vast and imposing edifice. He synthesized in his socialism not only French utopian schemes but also English classical economics and German philosophy—the major intellectual currents of his day. Following David Ricardo, who had taught that labor was the source of all value, Marx went on to argue Proudhon's case that profits were really wages stolen from the workers. Moreover, Marx incorporated Engels's charges of terrible oppression of the new class of factory workers in England. Thus Marx's doctrines seemed to be based on hard facts.

Marx's theory of historical evolution was built on the philosophy of the German Georg Hegel (1770–1831). Hegel believed that each age is characterized by dominant ideas that produce opposing ideas and eventually a new synthesis. The idea of being had been dominant initially, for example, and it had produced its antithesis, the idea of nonbeing. This idea in turn had resulted in the synthesis of becoming. Thus history has pattern and purpose.

Marx retained Hegel's view of history as a dialectic process of change but made economic relationships between classes the driving force. This dialectic explained the decline of agrarian feudalism and the rise of industrial capitalism. Marx stressed repeatedly that the "bourgeoisie, historically, has played a most revolutionary

Mr. and Mrs. Karl Marx Active in the revolution of 1848, Marx fled from Germany in 1849 and settled in London. There Marx and his young wife lived a respectable middle-class life while he wrote *Capital*, the weighty exposition of his socialist theories. Marx also worked to organize the working class, and he earned a modest income as a journalist and received financial support from his coauthor, Friedrich Engels. (Time Life Pictures/ Mansell/Getty Images)

part. . . . During its rule of scarcely one hundred years the bourgeoisie has created more massive and more colossal productive forces than have all preceding generations together."

Marx's next idea, that it was now the bourgeoisie's turn to give way to the socialism of revolutionary workers, appeared to many the irrefutable capstone of a brilliant interpretation of humanity's long development. Thus Marx pulled together powerful ideas and insights to create one of the great secular religions out of the intellectual ferment of the early nineteenth century.

The Romantic Movement

What were the characteristics of the romantic movement, and who were some of the great romantic artists? ■

The early nineteenth century was a time of change in literature and the other arts as well as politics. Known as the romantic movement, this artistic change was in part a revolt against the emphasis on rationality, order, and restraint that characterized the Enlightenment and the controlled style of classicism.

Forerunners of the romantic movement appeared from about 1750 on. Of these, Rousseau (see Chapter 17)—the passionate advocate of feeling, freedom, and natural goodness—was the most influential. Romanticism then crystallized fully in the 1790s, primarily in England and Germany. The French Revolution kindled the belief that radical reconstruction was also possible in cultural and artistic life (even though many early English and German romantics became disillusioned with events in France and turned from liberalism to conservatism in politics). Romanticism gained strength until the 1840s, when it gradually gave way to realism (see Chapter 23).

Romanticism's Tenets

Romanticism was characterized by a belief in emotional exuberance, unrestrained imagination, and spontaneity in both art and personal life. In Germany early romantics of the 1770s and 1780s called themselves the Sturm und Drang (storm and stress), and many romantic artists of the early nineteenth century lived lives of tremendous emotional intensity. Suicide, duels to the death, madness, and strange illnesses were not uncommon among leading romantics. Romantic artists typically led bohemian lives, wearing their hair long and uncombed in preference to powdered wigs, and rejecting the materialism of refined society. Great individualists, the romantics believed the full development of one's unique human potential to be the supreme purpose in life.

Nowhere was the break with classicism more apparent than in romanticism's general conception of nature. Classicism was not particularly interested in nature. In the words of the eighteenth-century English author Samuel Johnson, "A blade of grass is always a blade of grass; men and women are my subjects of inquiry." The romantics, in contrast, were enchanted by nature. For some it was awesome and tempestuous, while others saw nature as a source of spiritual inspiration. As the great

> **romanticism** A movement at its height from about 1790 to the 1840s that was in part a revolt against classicism and the Enlightenment, characterized by a belief in emotional exuberance, unrestrained imagination, and spontaneity in both art and personal life.

English landscape artist John Constable declared, "Nature is Spirit visible."

Most romantics saw the growth of modern industry as an ugly, brutal attack on their beloved nature and on the human personality. They sought escape—in the unspoiled Lake District of northern England, in exotic North Africa, in an imaginary idealized Middle Ages.

Diverse, exciting, and important, the study of history became a romantic passion. History was the key to a universe that was now perceived to be organic and dynamic, not mechanical and static as the Enlightenment thinkers had believed. Nor was it restricted to the biographies of great men or the work of divine providence. Historians such as Jules Michelet, who focused on the development of societies and human institutions, promoted the growth of national aspirations, fanning the embers of memory and encouraging entire peoples to seek in the past their special destinies.

Literature

Romanticism found its distinctive voice in poetry, as the Enlightenment had in prose. Its first great poets were British: Wordsworth, Coleridge, and Scott were all active by 1800, to be followed shortly by Byron, Shelley, and Keats.

A towering leader of English romanticism, William Wordsworth (1770–1850) was deeply influenced by Rousseau and the spirit of the early French Revolution. Wordsworth settled in the rural Lake District of England with his sister, Dorothy, and Samuel Taylor Coleridge (1772–1834). In 1798 Wordsworth and Coleridge published their *Lyrical Ballads*, which abandoned flowery classical conventions for the language of ordinary speech and endowed simple subjects with the loftiest majesty. One of the best examples of Wordsworth's romantic credo and genius is "Daffodils." After describing the joyful experience of wandering into a field of flowers, the writer reflects on the power of that single experience in the last stanza of the poem:

> *For oft, when on my couch I lie*
> *In vacant or in pensive mood,*
> *They flash upon that inward eye*
> *Which is the bliss of solitude;*
> *And then my heart with pleasure fills,*
> *And dances with the daffodils.*

Here indeed are simplicity and love of nature in commonplace forms that could be appreciated by everyone. Wordsworth's conception of poetry as the "spontaneous overflow of powerful feeling recollected in tranquility" is well illustrated by this stanza.

Classicism remained strong in France under Napoleon and inhibited the growth of romanticism there. In 1813 Germaine de Staël (duh STAHL) (1766–1817), a Franco-Swiss writer living in exile, urged the French to throw away their worn-out classical models. Her study *On Germany* (1810) extolled the spontaneity and enthusiasm of German writers and thinkers, and it had a powerful impact on the post-1815 generation in France. (See "Individuals in Society: Germaine de Staël," at right.) Between 1820 and 1850, the romantic impulse broke through in the poetry and prose of Lamartine, de Vigny, Hugo, Dumas, and Sand. Of these, Victor Hugo (1802–1885) became the most well known in both poetry and prose.

Son of a Napoleonic general, Hugo achieved an amazing range of rhythm, language, and image in his lyric poetry. His powerful novels exemplified the romantic fascination with fantastic characters, exotic historical settings, and human emotions. The hero of Hugo's famous *The Hunchback of Notre Dame* (1831) is the great cathedral's deformed bell-ringer, a "human gargoyle" overlooking the teeming life of fifteenth-century Paris. Renouncing his early conservatism, Hugo equated freedom in literature with liberty in politics and society. Hugo's political evolution was thus exactly the opposite of Wordsworth's, in whom youthful radicalism gave way to middle-aged caution. As the contrast between the two artists suggests, romanticism was a cultural movement compatible with many political beliefs.

Amandine Aurore Lucie Dupin (1804–1876), generally known by her pen name, George Sand, defied the narrow conventions of her time in an unending search for self-fulfillment. After eight years of unhappy marriage she abandoned her husband and took her two children to Paris to pursue a career as a writer. There Sand soon achieved fame and wealth, eventually writing over eighty novels on a variety of romantic and social themes. George Sand's striking individualism went far beyond her flamboyant preference for men's clothing and her notorious affairs. Her semi-autobiographical novel *Lélia* was shockingly modern, delving deeply into her tortuous quest for sexual and personal freedom.

In central and eastern Europe, literary romanticism and early nationalism often reinforced each other. Seeking a unique greatness in every people, well-educated romantics plumbed their own histories and cultures. Like modern anthropologists, they turned their attention to peasant life and transcribed the folk songs, tales, and proverbs that the cosmopolitan Enlightenment had disdained. The brothers Jacob and Wilhelm Grimm were particularly successful at rescuing German fairy tales from oblivion. In the Slavic lands, romantics played a decisive role in converting spoken peasant languages into modern written languages. The most influential of all Russian poets, Aleksander Pushkin (1799–1837), rejecting eighteenth-century attempts to force Russian poetry into a classical straitjacket, used his lyric genius to mold the modern literary language.

INDIVIDUALS IN SOCIETY

RICH, INTELLECTUAL, PASSIONATE, AND ASSERTIVE, Germaine Necker de Staël (1766–1817) astonished contemporaries and still fascinates historians. She was strongly influenced by her parents, poor Swiss Protestants who soared to the top of prerevolutionary Parisian society. Her brilliant but rigid mother filled Germaine's head with knowledge, and each week the precocious child listened, wide-eyed and attentive, to illustrious writers and philosophers performing at her mother's salon. At age twelve, she suffered a physical and mental breakdown. Only then was she allowed to have a playmate and romp and run on the family estate. Her adoring father was Jacques Necker, a banker who made an enormous fortune and became France's reform-minded minister of finance before the Revolution. Worshiping her father in adolescence, Germaine also came to love politics.

Accepting at nineteen an arranged marriage with Baron de Staël-Holstein, a womanizing Swedish diplomat bewitched by her dowry, Germaine began her life's work. She opened an intellectual salon and began to write and publish. Her wit and exuberance attracted foreigners and liberal French aristocrats, one of whom became the first of many lovers as her marriage soured and she searched unsuccessfully for the happiness of her parents' union. Fleeing Paris in 1792 and returning after the Thermidorian reaction (see page 643), she subsequently angered Napoleon by criticizing his dictatorial rule. In 1803 he permanently banished her from Paris.

Retiring again to her isolated estate in Switzerland and skillfully managing her inherited wealth, Staël fought insomnia with opium and boredom with parties that attracted luminaries from all over Europe. Always seeking stimulation for her restless mind, she traveled widely in Italy and Germany and drew upon these experiences in her novel *Corinne* (1807) and her study *On Germany* (1810). Both works summed up her romantic faith and enjoyed enormous success.

Staël urged creative individuals to abandon traditional rules and classical models. She encouraged them to embrace experimentation, emotion, and enthusiasm. Enthusiasm, which she had in abundance, was the key, the royal road to creativity, personal fulfillment, and human improvement. Thrilling to music, for example, she felt that only an enthusiastic person could really appreciate this gift of God, this wordless message that "unifies our dual nature and blends senses and spirit in a common rapture."*

Yet a profound sadness runs through her writing. This sadness, so characteristic of the romantic temperament, grew in part out of disappointments in love and prolonged exile. But it also grew out of the insoluble predicament of being an enormously gifted woman in an age of intense male chauvinism. Little wonder that uneasy male competitors and literary critics took delight in ridiculing and defaming her as a neurotic and masculine woman, a mediocre and unnatural talent who had foolishly dared to enter the male world of serious thought and action. Even her supporters could not accept her for what she was. The admiring poet Lord Byron recognized her genius and called her "the most eminent woman author of this, or perhaps of any century." But he quickly added that "she should have been born a man."†

*Quoted in G. R. Besser, *Germaine de Staël Revisited* (New York: Twayne Publishers, 1994), p. 106. Enhanced by a feminist perspective, this fine study is highly recommended.

†Quoted ibid., p. 139.

Germaine de Staël. (Erich Lessing/Art Resource, NY)

Buffeted and saddened by scorn and condescension because of her gender, Staël advocated equal rights for women throughout her life. Only with equal rights and duties — in education and careers, in love and marital relations — could an exceptional woman like herself, or indeed any woman, ever hope to realize her intellectual and emotional potential. Practicing what she preached as best she could, Germaine de Staël was a trailblazer in the struggle for women's rights.

QUESTIONS FOR ANALYSIS

1. In what ways did Germaine de Staël's life and thought reflect basic elements of the romantic movement?
2. Why did male critics often attack Staël? What do these criticisms tell us about gender relations in the early nineteenth century?

John Constable, *The Hay Wain* Constable's love of a spiritualized and poetic nature radiates from this masterpiece of romantic art. Exhibited in Paris in 1829, *The Hay Wain* created a sensation and made a profound impression on the young Delacroix. The cottage on the left still stands, open to the public as a small museum devoted to Constable and his paintings. (National Gallery, London, U.K./The Bridgeman Art Library)

Art and Music

One of the greatest and most moving romantic painters in France was Eugène Delacroix (oe-ZHEHN deh-luh-KWAH) (1798–1863), probably the illegitimate son of French foreign minister Talleyrand (see page 687). Delacroix was a master of dramatic, colorful scenes that stirred the emotions. He was fascinated with remote and exotic subjects, whether lion hunts in Morocco or dreams of languishing, sensuous women in a sultan's harem. Yet he was also a passionate spokesman for freedom.

In England the most notable romantic painters were Joseph M. W. Turner (1775–1851) and John Constable (1776–1837). Both were fascinated by nature, but their interpretations of it contrasted sharply, aptly symbolizing the tremendous emotional range of the romantic movement. Turner depicted nature's power and terror; wild storms and sinking ships were favorite subjects. Constable painted gentle Wordsworthian landscapes in which human beings were at one with their environment, the comforting countryside of unspoiled rural England.

It was in music that romanticism realized most fully and permanently its goals of free expression and emo-

tional intensity. Abandoning well-defined structures, the great romantic composers used a wide range of forms to create a thousand musical landscapes and evoke a host of powerful emotions. Romantic composers also transformed the small classical orchestra, tripling its size by adding wind instruments, percussion, and more brass and strings. The crashing chords evoking the surge of the masses in Chopin's Revolutionary Etude, and the bottomless despair of the funeral march in Beethoven's Third Symphony—such were the modern orchestra's musical paintings that plumbed the depths of human feeling.

This range and intensity gave music and musicians much greater prestige than in the past. Music no longer simply complemented a church service or helped a nobleman digest his dinner. It became a sublime end in itself, most perfectly realizing the endless yearning of the soul. The unbelievable one-in-a-million performer—the great virtuoso who could transport the listener to ecstasy and hysteria—became a cultural hero. People swooned for Franz Liszt (1811–1886), the greatest pianist of his age, as they scream for rock stars today.

The first great romantic composer is also the most famous today. Ludwig van Beethoven (BAY-toh-vuhn)

(1770–1827) used contrasting themes and tones to produce dramatic conflict and inspiring resolutions. As one contemporary admirer wrote, "Beethoven's music sets in motion the lever of fear, of awe, of horror, of suffering, and awakens just that infinite longing which is the essence of Romanticism." Beethoven's range and output were tremendous. At the peak of his fame, he began to lose his hearing. He considered suicide but eventually overcame despair: "I will take fate by the throat; it will not bend me completely to its will."[3] Beethoven continued to pour out immortal music, although his last years were silent, spent in total deafness.

Reforms and Revolutions Before 1848

How after 1815 did liberal, national, and socialist forces challenge conservatism in Greece, Great Britain, and France? ■

While the romantic movement was developing, liberal, national, and socialist forces battered against the conservatism of 1815. In some countries, change occurred gradually and peacefully. Elsewhere, pressure built up like steam in a pressure cooker without a safety valve and eventually caused an explosion in 1848. Three important countries—Greece, Great Britain, and France—experienced variations on this basic theme between 1815 and 1848.

National Liberation in Greece

National, liberal revolution, frustrated in Italy and Spain by conservative statesmen, succeeded first after 1815 in Greece. Since the fifteenth century, the Greeks had been living under the domination of the Ottoman Turks. In spite of centuries of foreign rule, the Greeks had survived as a people, united by their language and the Greek Orthodox religion. It was natural that the general growth of national aspirations and a desire for independence would inspire some Greeks in the early nineteenth century. This rising national movement led to the formation of secret societies and then to revolt in 1821, led by Alexander Ypsilanti (ip-suh-LAN-tee), a Greek patriot and a general in the Russian army.

At first, the Great Powers, particularly Metternich, were opposed to all revolution, even revolution against the Islamic Turks. They refused to back Ypsilanti and supported the Ottoman Empire. Yet for many Europeans, the Greek cause became a holy one. Educated Americans and Europeans were in love with the culture of classical Greece; Russians were stirred by the piety of their Orthodox brethren. Writers and artists, moved by the romantic impulse, responded enthusiastically to the Greek national struggle. The famous English romantic poet Lord Byron even joined the Greeks to fight "that Greece may yet be free."

The Greeks, though often quarreling among themselves, battled on against the Turks and hoped for the eventual support of European governments. In 1827 Great Britain, France, and Russia yielded to popular demands at home and directed Turkey to accept an

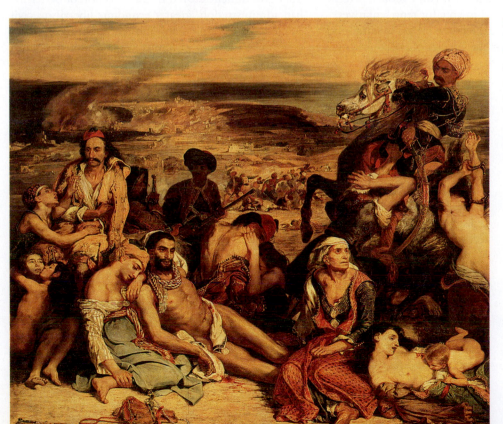

Delacroix, *Massacre at Chios*
The Greek struggle for freedom and independence won the enthusiastic support of liberals, nationalists, and romantics. The Ottoman Turks were portrayed as cruel oppressors who were holding back the course of history, as in this moving masterpiece by Delacroix. (Réunion des Musées Nationaux/Art Resource, NY)

Greek Independence, 1830

armistice. When the Turks refused, the navies of these three powers trapped the Turkish fleet at Navarino and destroyed it. Russia then declared another of its periodic wars of expansion against the Turks. This led to the establishment of a Russian protectorate over much of present-day Romania, which had also been under Turkish rule. Great Britain, France, and Russia finally declared Greece independent in 1830 and installed a German prince as king of the new country in 1832. In the end, the Greeks had won: a small nation had gained its independence in a heroic war of liberation against a foreign empire.

Liberal Reform in Great Britain

Eighteenth-century British society had been both flexible and remarkably stable. It was dominated by the landowning aristocracy, but that class was neither closed nor rigidly defined. Successful business and professional people could buy land and become gentlefolk, while the common people had more than the usual opportunities of the preindustrial world. Basic civil rights for all were balanced by a tradition of deference to one's social superiors. Parliament was manipulated by the king and was thoroughly undemocratic, with only about 8 percent of the population allowed to vote for representatives.

By the 1780s there was growing interest in some kind of political reform, but the French Revolution threw the British aristocracy into a panic for a generation, making it extremely hostile to any attempts to change the status quo. Conflicts between the ruling class and laborers were sparked in 1815 with revision of the **Corn Laws**. Britain had been unable to import cheap grain from eastern Europe during the war years, leading to high prices and large profits for the landed aristocracy. With the war over, grain could be imported again, allowing the price of wheat and bread to go down and benefiting almost everyone except the aristocracy. The aristocracy, however, rammed far-reaching changes in the Corn Laws

Corn Laws British laws, revised in 1815, that prohibited the importation of foreign grain unless the price at home rose to improbable levels, thus benefiting the aristocracy but making food prices high for working people.

Battle of Peterloo A protest that took place at Saint Peter's Fields in Manchester in reaction to the revision of the Corn Laws; it was broken up by armed cavalry.

Reform Bill of 1832 A major British political reform that increased the number of male voters by about 50 percent and gave political representation to new industrial areas.

through Parliament. The new regulation prohibited the importation of foreign grain unless the price at home rose to improbable levels. Seldom has a class legislated more selfishly for its own narrow economic advantage or done more to promote a class-based view of political action.

The change in the Corn Laws, coming as it did at a time of widespread unemployment and postwar economic distress, triggered protests and demonstrations by urban laborers, who were supported by radical intellectuals. In 1817 the Tory government, which was completely controlled by the landed aristocracy, responded by temporarily suspending the traditional rights of peaceable assembly and habeas corpus. Two years later, Parliament passed the infamous Six Acts, which, among other things, placed controls on a heavily taxed press and practically eliminated all mass meetings. These acts followed an enormous but orderly protest, at Saint Peter's Fields in Manchester, that had been savagely broken up by armed cavalry. Nicknamed the **Battle of Peterloo**, in scornful reference to the British victory at Waterloo, this incident demonstrated the government's determination to repress dissenters.

Strengthened by ongoing industrial development, the new manufacturing and commercial groups insisted on a place for their new wealth alongside the landed wealth of the aristocracy in the framework of political power and social prestige. They called for many kinds of liberal reform: reform of town government, organization of a new police force, more rights for Catholics and dissenters, and reform of the Poor Laws that provided aid to some low-paid workers. In the 1820s, a less frightened Tory government moved in the direction of better urban administration, greater economic liberalism, civil equality for Catholics, and limited imports of foreign grain. These actions encouraged the middle classes to press on for reform of Parliament so they could have a larger say in government.

The Whig Party, though led like the Tories by great aristocrats, had by tradition been more responsive to middle-class commercial and manufacturing interests. In 1830 a Whig ministry introduced "an act to amend the representation of the people of England and Wales." After a series of setbacks, the Whigs' **Reform Bill of 1832** was propelled into law by a mighty surge of popular support. Significantly, the bill moved British politics in a democratic direction and allowed the House of Commons to emerge as the all-important legislative body. The new industrial areas of the country gained representation in the Commons, and many old "rotten boroughs"—electoral districts that had very few voters and that the landed aristocracy had bought and sold—were eliminated. The number of voters increased by about 50 percent, giving about 12 percent of adult men in Britain and Ireland the right to vote. Comfortable middle-class groups in the urban population, as well as

The Anti–Corn Law Movement in Action This contemporary illustration focuses on the Anti–Corn Law League's remarkable ability to mobilize a broad urban coalition that was dedicated to free trade and the end of tariffs on imported grain (or "corn"). Each League supporter was encouraged to join the national organization and receive a membership card like the one shown here, attend meetings and lectures, and demonstrate in the streets. (cartoon: The Granger Collection, New York; card: © Museum of London, U.K./The Bridgeman Art Library)

some substantial farmers who leased their land, received the vote. Thus the pressures building in Great Britain were successfully—though only temporarily—released. A major reform had been achieved peacefully. Continued fundamental reform within the system appeared difficult but not impossible.

The principal radical program for continued reform was embodied in the "People's Charter" of 1838 and the Chartist movement (see Chapter 21). Partly inspired by the economic distress of the working class in the 1830s and 1840s, the Chartists' core demand was universal male (but not female) suffrage. They saw complete political democracy and rule by the common people—the great majority of the population—as the means to a good and just society. Hundreds of thousands of people signed gigantic petitions calling on Parliament to grant all men the right to vote, first and most seriously in 1839, again in 1842, and yet again in 1848. Parliament rejected all three petitions. In the short run, the working poor failed with their Chartist demands, but they learned a valuable lesson in mass politics.

While calling for universal male suffrage, many working-class people joined with middle-class manufac-

turers in the Anti–Corn Law League, founded in Manchester in 1839. Mass participation made possible a popular crusade led by fighting liberals, who argued that lower food prices and more jobs in industry depended on repeal of the Corn Laws. Much of the working class agreed. When Ireland's potato crop failed in 1845 (see page 705) and famine prices for food seemed likely in England, Tory prime minister Robert Peel joined with the Whigs and a minority of his own party to repeal the Corn Laws in 1846 and allow free imports of grain. England escaped famine. Thereafter the liberal doctrine of free trade became almost sacred dogma in Great Britain.

The following year, the Tories passed a bill designed to help the working classes, but in a different way. The Ten Hours Act of 1847 limited the workday for women and young people in factories to ten hours. Tory aristocrats continued to champion legislation regulating factory conditions. They were competing vigorously with the middle class for the support of the working class. This healthy competition between a still-vigorous aristocracy and a strong middle class was a crucial factor in Great Britain's peaceful evolution. The working classes could make temporary alliances with either competitor to better their own conditions.

Ireland and the Great Famine

The people of Ireland did not benefit from the political competition in Britain. The great mass of the population (outside of the northern counties of Ulster, which were partly Presbyterian) were Irish Catholics, who rented their land from a tiny minority of Church of England Protestants. These landlords were content to use their power to grab as much as possible.

The result was that the condition of the Irish peasantry around 1800 was abominable. The typical peasant lived in a wretched cottage and could afford neither shoes nor stockings. Hundreds of shocking accounts describe hopeless poverty. The novelist Sir Walter Scott wrote:

> *The poverty of the Irish peasantry is on the extreme verge of human misery; their cottages would scarce serve for pig styes even in Scotland; and their rags seem the very refuse of a sheep, and are spread over their bodies with such an ingenious variety of wretchedness that you would think nothing but some sort of perverted taste could have assembled so many shreds together.*[4]

A compassionate French traveler agreed, writing that Ireland was "pure misery, naked and hungry. . . . I saw the American Indian in his forests and the black slave in his chains, and I believed that I was seeing the most extreme form of human misery; but that was before I knew the lot of poor Ireland."[5]

Yet in spite of terrible conditions, population growth sped onward. The 3 million of 1725 reached 4 million in 1780 and doubled to 8 million by 1840. In addition, between 1780 and 1840, another 1.75 million people left Ireland for Britain and America in search of better living conditions.

Ireland's population explosion, part of Europe's general population growth since the early eighteenth century (see Chapter 18), was caused in part by the extensive cultivation of the potato. A single acre of land spaded and planted with potatoes could feed an Irish family of six for a year, and the potato also could thrive on boggy wastelands. Needing only a big potato patch to survive, Irish men and women married early. To be sure, the young couple was embracing a life of extreme poverty. They would literally live on potatoes—ten pounds a day for an average male—moistened at best with a cup of milk.

Yet the decision to marry and have large families made sense. Landlords leased land for short periods only.

The Discovery of the Potato Blight Although the leaves usually shriveled and died, they could also look deceptively healthy. In this painting by Daniel McDonald an Irish family has dug up its potato harvest and just discovered to its horror that the blight has rotted the crop. Like thousands of Irish families, the family now faces the starvation and mass epidemics of the Great Famine. (Department of Irish Folklore, University College, Dublin)

Peasants had no incentive to make permanent improvements because anything beyond what was needed for survival would quickly be taken by higher rent. Rural poverty was inescapable and better shared with a spouse, while a dutiful son or a loving daughter was an old person's best hope of escaping destitution.

As population and potato dependency grew, conditions became more precarious. From 1820 onward deficiencies and diseases in the potato crop became more common. In 1845 and 1846, and again in 1848 and 1851, the potato crop failed in Ireland. The result was unmitigated disaster—the **Great Famine**. Blight attacked the young plants, and the tubers rotted. Widespread starvation and mass fever epidemics followed. Yet the British government, committed to rigid laissez-faire ideology, was slow to act. When it did, its relief efforts were tragically inadequate. Moreover, the government continued to collect taxes, landlords demanded their rents, and tenants who could not pay were evicted and their homes destroyed. Famine or no, Ireland remained the conquered jewel of foreign landowners.

The Great Famine shattered the pattern of Irish population growth. Fully 1 million emigrants fled the famine between 1845 and 1851, and at least 1.5 million died or went unborn because of the disaster. Alone among the countries of Europe, Ireland experienced a declining population in the second half of the nineteenth century, as it became a land of continuous out-migration, late marriage, early death, and widespread celibacy.

The Great Famine also intensified anti-British feeling and promoted Irish nationalism, for the bitter memory of starvation, exile, and British inaction was burned deeply into the popular consciousness. Patriots could call on powerful collective emotions in their campaigns for land reform, home rule, and, eventually, Irish independence.

The Revolution of 1830 in France

Louis XVIII's Constitutional Charter of 1814—theoretically a gift from the king but actually a response to political pressures—was basically a liberal constitution (see Chapter 20). The economic and social gains made by sections of the middle class and the peasantry in the French Revolution were fully protected, great

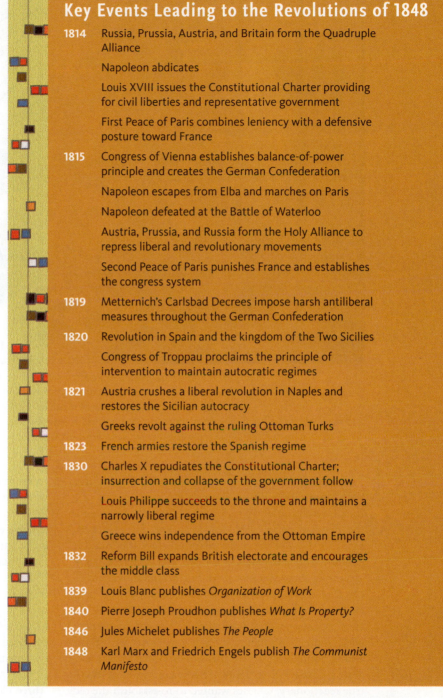

Key Events Leading to the Revolutions of 1848

1814	Russia, Prussia, Austria, and Britain form the Quadruple Alliance
	Napoleon abdicates
	Louis XVIII issues the Constitutional Charter providing for civil liberties and representative government
	First Peace of Paris combines leniency with a defensive posture toward France
1815	Congress of Vienna establishes balance-of-power principle and creates the German Confederation
	Napoleon escapes from Elba and marches on Paris
	Napoleon defeated at the Battle of Waterloo
	Austria, Prussia, and Russia form the Holy Alliance to repress liberal and revolutionary movements
	Second Peace of Paris punishes France and establishes the congress system
1819	Metternich's Carlsbad Decrees impose harsh antiliberal measures throughout the German Confederation
1820	Revolution in Spain and the kingdom of the Two Sicilies
	Congress of Troppau proclaims the principle of intervention to maintain autocratic regimes
1821	Austria crushes a liberal revolution in Naples and restores the Sicilian autocracy
	Greeks revolt against the ruling Ottoman Turks
1823	French armies restore the Spanish regime
1830	Charles X repudiates the Constitutional Charter; insurrection and collapse of the government follow
	Louis Philippe succeeds to the throne and maintains a narrowly liberal regime
	Greece wins independence from the Ottoman Empire
1832	Reform Bill expands British electorate and encourages the middle class
1839	Louis Blanc publishes *Organization of Work*
1840	Pierre Joseph Proudhon publishes *What Is Property?*
1846	Jules Michelet publishes *The People*
1848	Karl Marx and Friedrich Engels publish *The Communist Manifesto*

intellectual and artistic freedom was permitted, and a parliament with upper and lower houses was created. Immediately after Napoleon's abortive Hundred Days, the moderate, worldly king refused to bow to the wishes of die-hard aristocrats who wanted to sweep away all the revolutionary changes. Instead, Louis appointed as his ministers moderate royalists, who sought and obtained the support of a majority of the representatives elected to the lower Chamber of Deputies between 1816 and Louis's death in 1824.

Great Famine The result of four years of potato crop failure in Ireland, a country that had grown dependent on potatoes as a dietary staple.

The Fall of Algiers In July 1830 France assembled more than six hundred ships and attacked the Ottoman dependency of Algeria. The ferocious naval bombardment shown in this engraving destroyed the capital's fortifications. After the surrender French soldiers rampaged through the city, and news of this brutal behavior encouraged Muslims in the interior to revolt and fight on until 1847. (Musée de la Ville de Paris, Musée Carnavalet, Paris, France/Lauros/Giraudon/The Bridgeman Art Library)

Louis XVIII's charter was anything but democratic. Only about 100,000 of the wealthiest males out of a total population of 30 million had the right to vote for the deputies who, with the king and his ministers, made the laws of the nation. Nonetheless, the "notable people" who did vote came from very different backgrounds. There were wealthy businessmen, war profiteers, successful professionals, ex-revolutionaries, large landowners from the old aristocracy and the middle class, Bourbons, and Bonapartists. The old aristocracy, with its pre-1789 mentality, was a minority within the voting population. It was this situation that Louis's successor, Charles X (r. 1824–1830), could not abide. A true reactionary, Charles wanted to re-establish the old order in France. Increasingly blocked by the opposition of the deputies, Charles's government turned in 1830 to military adventure in an effort to rally French nationalism and gain popular support. A long-standing economic and diplomatic dispute with Muslim Algeria, a vassal state of the Ottoman Empire, provided the opportunity.

In June 1830, a French force of thirty-seven thousand crossed the Mediterranean, landed to the west of Algiers, and took the capital city in three short weeks. Victory seemed complete, but in 1831 tribes in the interior revolted and waged a fearsome war until 1847, when French armies finally subdued the country. Bringing French, Spanish, and Italian settlers to Algeria and leading to the expropriation of large tracts of Muslim land, the conquest of Algeria marked the rebirth of French colonial expansion.

Emboldened by the good news from Algeria, Charles repudiated the Constitutional Charter in an attempted coup in July 1830. He issued decrees stripping much of the wealthy middle class of its voting rights, and he censored the press. The immediate reaction, encouraged by journalists and lawyers, was an insurrection in the capital by printers, other artisans, and small traders. In "three glorious days," the government collapsed. Paris boiled with revolutionary excitement, and Charles fled. Then the upper middle class, which had fomented the revolt, skillfully seated Charles's cousin, Louis Philippe, duke of Orléans, on the vacant throne.

Louis Philippe (r. 1830–1848) accepted the Constitutional Charter of 1814; adopted the red, white, and blue flag of the French Revolution; and admitted that he was merely the "king of the French people." In spite of such symbolic actions, the situation in France remained fundamentally unchanged. The vote was extended only from 100,000 to 170,000 citizens. For the upper middle class, there had been a change in dynasty in order to protect the status quo and the narrowly liberal institutions of 1815. Republicans, democrats, social reformers, and the poor of Paris were bitterly disappointed. They had made a revolution, but it seemed for naught.

The Revolutions of 1848

Why in 1848 did revolution triumph briefly throughout most of Europe, and why did it fail almost completely? ■

The late 1840s in Europe were hard economically and tense politically. The potato famine in Ireland in 1845 and 1846 had many echoes on the continent. Bad harvests jacked up food prices and caused misery and unemployment in the cities and in the countryside. A profound economic crisis, caused in the final analysis by a combination of rapid population growth and industrialization efforts that were only beginning to provide more jobs and income, gripped continental Europe.

The political and social response to the economic crisis was unrest and protest. (See "Living in the Past: Revolutionary Experiences in 1848," page 710.) "Prerevolutionary" outbreaks occurred all across Europe: in the northern part of Austria in 1846, a civil war in Switzerland in 1847, and an uprising in Naples, Italy, in January 1848. Only the most advanced and the most backward major countries—reforming Great Britain and immobile Russia—escaped untouched. Governments toppled; monarchs and ministers bowed or fled. National independence, liberal democratic constitutions, and social reform: the lofty aspirations of a generation seemed at hand. Yet in the end, the revolutions failed.

A Democratic Republic in France

By the late 1840s, revolution in Europe was almost universally expected, but it took revolution in Paris—once again—to turn expectations into realities. For eighteen years Louis Philippe's "bourgeois monarchy" had been characterized by stubborn inaction and complacency. There was a glaring lack of social legislation, and politics was dominated by corruption and selfish special interests. With only the rich voting for deputies, many of the deputies were docile government bureaucrats.

The government's stubborn refusal to consider electoral reform heightened a sense of class injustice among middle-class shopkeepers, skilled artisans, and unskilled working people, and it eventually touched off a popular revolt in Paris. Workers joined by some students began tearing up the cobblestones and building barri-cades in the narrow streets of Paris on the night of February 22, 1848. Armed with guns and dug in behind their makeshift fortresses, the workers and students demanded a new government. By February 24, as the National Guard broke ranks and joined the revolutionaries, Louis Philippe had refused to order a full-scale attack by the regular army and had abdicated in favor of his grandson. But the common people in arms would tolerate no more monarchy. This refusal led to the proclamation of a provisional republic, headed by a ten-man executive committee and certified by cries of approval from the revolutionary crowd.

The revolutionaries immediately set about drafting a constitution for France's Second Republic. Moreover, they wanted a truly popular and democratic republic so that the common people—the peasants, the artisans, and the unskilled workers—could participate in reforming society. In practice, building such a republic meant giving the right to vote to every adult male, and this was quickly done. Revolutionary compassion and sympathy for freedom were expressed in the freeing of all slaves in French colonies, the abolition of the death penalty, and the establishment of a ten-hour workday for Paris.

Yet there were profound differences within the revolutionary coalition in Paris. On the one hand, there were the moderate liberal republicans of the middle class. They viewed universal male suffrage as the ultimate concession to be made to popular forces, and they strongly opposed any further radical social measures. On the other hand, there were radical republicans and hard-pressed artisans. Influenced by a generation of utopian socialists, and appalled by the poverty and misery of the urban poor, the radical republicans were committed to some kind of socialism. So were many artisans, who hated the unrestrained competition of cutthroat capitalism and advocated a combination of strong craft unions and worker-owned businesses.

Worsening depression and rising unemployment brought these conflicting goals to the fore in 1848. Louis Blanc (see page 693), who along with a worker named Albert represented the republican socialists in the provisional government, pressed for recognition of a socialist right to work. Blanc asserted that permanent government-sponsored cooperative workshops should be established for workers. Such workshops would be an alternative to capitalist employment and a decisive step toward a new, noncompetitive social order.

The moderate republicans wanted no such thing. They were willing to provide only temporary relief. The resulting compromise set up national workshops—soon to become little more than a vast program of pick-and-shovel public works—and established a special commission under Blanc to "study the question." This satisfied no one. The national workshops were, however,

Picturing the Past

The Triumph of Democratic Republics This French illustration offers an opinion of the initial revolutionary breakthrough in 1848. The peoples of Europe, joined together around their respective national banners, are achieving republican freedom, which is symbolized by the Statue of Liberty and the discarded crowns. The woman wearing pants at the base of the statue — very radical attire — represents feminist hopes for liberation. (Musée de la Ville, Paris/Giraudon/The Bridgeman Art Library)

ANALYZING THE IMAGE How many different flags can you count and/or identify? How would you characterize the types of people marching and the mood of the crowd?

CONNECTIONS What do the angels, Statue of Liberty, and discarded crowns suggest about the artist's view of the events of 1848? Do you think this illustration was created before or after the collapse of the revolution in France? Why?

To complete this activity online, go to the Online Study Guide at bedfordstmartins.com/mckaywest.

better than nothing. An army of desperate poor from the French provinces and even from foreign countries streamed into Paris to sign up. As the economic crisis worsened, the number enrolled in the workshops soared from 10,000 in March to 120,000 by June, and another 80,000 were trying unsuccessfully to join.

While the workshops in Paris grew, the French masses went to the election polls in late April. Voting in most cases for the first time, the people of France elected to the new Constituent Assembly about five hundred moderate republicans, three hundred monarchists, and one hundred radicals who professed various brands of social-

ism. One of the moderate republicans was the author of *Democracy in America*, Alexis de Tocqueville (TOHK-vihl) (1805–1859), who had predicted the overthrow of Louis Philippe's government.

Tocqueville observed that the socialist movement in Paris aroused the fierce hostility of France's peasants as well as the middle and upper classes. The French peasants owned land, and according to Tocqueville, "private property had become with all those who owned it a sort of bond of fraternity."[6] Returning from Normandy to take his seat in the new Constituent Assembly, Tocqueville saw that a majority of the members were firmly committed to the republic and strongly opposed to the socialists and their artisan allies, and he shared their sentiments.

This clash of ideologies—of liberal capitalism and socialism—became a clash of classes and arms after the elections. The new government's executive committee dropped Blanc and thereafter included no representative of the Parisian working class. Fearing that their socialist hopes were about to be dashed, artisans and unskilled workers invaded the Constituent Assembly on May 15 and tried to proclaim a new revolutionary state. But the government was ready and used the middle-class National Guard to squelch this uprising. As the workshops continued to fill and grow more radical, the fearful but powerful propertied classes in the Assembly took the offensive. On June 22, the government dissolved the national workshops in Paris, giving the workers the choice of joining the army or going to workshops in the provinces.

The result was a spontaneous and violent uprising. Frustrated in attempts to create a socialist society, masses of desperate people were now losing even their life-sustaining relief. A voice from the crowd cried out when the famous astronomer François Arago counseled patience, "Ah, Monsieur Arago, you have never been hungry!"[7] Barricades sprang up again in the narrow streets of Paris, and a terrible class war began. Working people fought with the courage of utter desperation, but this time the government had the army and the support of peasant France. After three terrible "June Days" of street fighting and the death or injury of more than ten thousand people, the republican army under General Louis Cavaignac stood triumphant in a sea of working-class blood and hatred.

The revolution in France thus ended in spectacular failure. The February coalition of the middle and working classes had in four short months become locked in mortal combat. In place of a generous democratic republic, the Constituent Assembly completed a constitution featuring a strong executive. This allowed Louis Napoleon, nephew of Napoleon Bonaparte, to win a landslide victory in the election of December 1848. The appeal of his great name as well as the desire of the propertied classes for order at any cost had produced a semi-authoritarian regime.

The Austrian Empire in 1848

Throughout central Europe, the first news of the upheaval in France evoked feverish excitement and eventually revolution. Liberals demanded written constitutions, representative government, and greater civil liberties from authoritarian regimes. When governments hesitated, popular revolts followed. Urban workers and students served as the shock troops, but they were allied with middle-class liberals and peasants. In the face of this

united front, monarchs collapsed and granted almost everything. The popular revolutionary coalition, having secured great and easy victories, then broke down as it had in France. The traditional forces—the monarchy, the aristocracy, the regular army—recovered their nerve, reasserted their authority, and took back many, though not all, of the concessions. Reaction was everywhere victorious.

The revolution in the Austrian Empire began in Hungary in 1848, where nationalistic Hungarians demanded national autonomy, full civil liberties, and universal suffrage. When the monarchy in Vienna hesitated, Viennese students and workers took to the streets and raised the barricades in defiance of the government, while peasant disorders broke out in parts of the empire. The Habsburg emperor Ferdinand I (r. 1835–1848) capitulated and promised reforms and a liberal constitution. Metternich fled in disguise toward London. The old absolutist order seemed to be collapsing with unbelievable rapidity.

The coalition of revolutionaries was not stable, however. When the monarchy abolished serfdom, with its degrading forced labor and feudal services, the newly free peasants lost interest in the political and social questions agitating the cities. Meanwhile, the coalition of urban revolutionaries also broke down along class lines over the issue of socialist workshops and universal voting rights for men.

The revolutionary coalition was also weakened, and ultimately destroyed, by conflicting national aspirations. In March the Hungarian revolutionary leaders pushed through an extremely liberal, almost democratic, constitution. But the Hungarian revolutionaries also sought to transform the mosaic of provinces and peoples that was the kingdom of Hungary into a unified, centralized, Hungarian nation. To the minority groups that formed half of the population—the Croats, Serbs, and Romanians—such unification was completely unacceptable. Each felt entitled to political autonomy and cultural independence. In a somewhat similar way, Czech nationalists based in Bohemia and the city of Prague came into conflict with German nationalists. Thus conflicting national aspirations within the Austrian Empire enabled the monarchy to play off one ethnic group against the other.

Finally, the conservative aristocratic forces regained their nerve under the rallying call of the archduchess Sophia, a Bavarian princess married to the emperor's brother. Deeply ashamed of the emperor's collapse before a "mess of students," she insisted that Ferdinand, who had no heir, abdicate in favor of her son, Francis Joseph.[8] Powerful nobles organized around Sophia in a secret conspiracy to reverse and crush the revolution.

Their first breakthrough came when the army bombarded Prague and savagely crushed a working-class revolt there on June 17. Other Austrian officials and

LIVING IN THE PAST

THE STRIKING SIMILARITIES between the different national revolutions in 1848 suggest that Europeans lived through common revolutionary experiences that shaped a generation, and this was indeed true. The first such experience was raising the barricades, fighting in the streets, and overthrowing rulers or forcing major concessions. The result of this astonishing triumph was a tremendous surge in political participation and civic activity throughout most of Europe. This unprecedented "mass politics" took many forms. Politics in the streets—demonstrations, protests, open-air meetings—played an ongoing role as large crowds pressured kings and legislatures. Newspaper publishing exploded as censorship ended and interest in public affairs soared. In Paris, where many new papers like *Le Salut Public* (The Public Safety) appeared, daily newspaper production increased eightfold in three months. In the Austrian Empire peasants freed from serfdom listened to newspapers read aloud in taverns and followed developments. Intense political activity led to a multitude of political clubs and associations based on occupation. Women also formed organizations for the welfare of children and families, although few women as yet pushed for equal rights.

Newly politicized and increasingly divided into competing groups, the peoples of Europe then shared the onslaught of reaction and the trauma of defeat and civil war. In Prague and in Paris, almost simultaneously, army commanders found a deadly response to urban uprisings. First they used cannon and field artillery to bombard and destroy the fighters behind their makeshift fortifications. Only then did obedient infantrymen attack and take the barricades in hand-to-hand combat, as Prussian soldiers did later in Frankfurt. Fleeing insurgents were hunted down and often shot. Thus the remembered experiences of 1848 included a tragic finale of grief and mourning. This is captured in the painting *Memory of the Civil War* by Ernest Meissonier, an artillery captain in the French National Guard who viewed at close range the carnage of the June Days in Paris.

Front page of *Le Salut Public* (akg-images)

Street fighting in Frankfurt, 1848 (The Granger Collection, New York)

QUESTIONS FOR ANALYSIS

1. Examine the French newspaper. What does it reveal about the rise of mass politics in 1848?

2. The 1848 revolutions increased political activity, yet they were crushed. How does the scene of fighting in Frankfurt help to explain this outcome?

3. Consider Meissonier's *Memory of the Civil War*. In what ways do societies transmit and revise their historical memories?

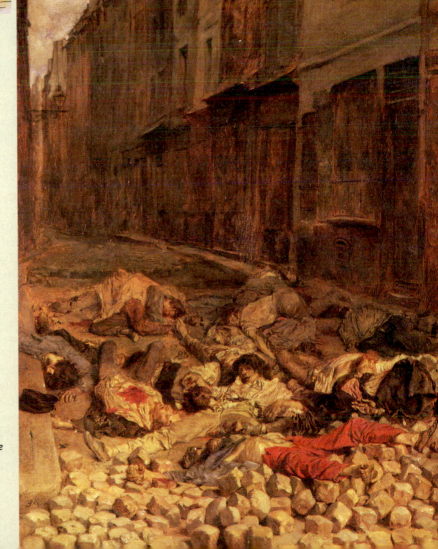

Ernest Meissonier, *Memory of the Civil War* (Louvre/Lauros/Giraudon/ The Bridgeman Art Library)

Guarding the Barricades in Vienna Workers and students took full control of Vienna in May 1848, when they raised the barricades and dug in. In this painting a number of men and women eat, relax, and discuss the situation. Women were active in supportive roles during the revolution. (Wien Museum Karlsplatz, Vienna/The Bridgeman Art Library)

nobles began to lead the minority nationalities of Hungary against the revolutionary government. At the end of October, the well-equipped, predominately peasant troops of the regular Austrian army used heavy cannon to attack the student and working-class radicals dug in behind barricades in Vienna and retook the city at the cost of more than four thousand casualties. Thus the determination of the Austrian aristocracy and the loyalty of its army were the final ingredients in the triumph of reaction and the defeat of revolution.

When Francis Joseph (r. 1848–1916) was crowned emperor of Austria immediately after his eighteenth birthday in December 1848, only Hungary had yet to be brought under control. Another determined conservative, Nicholas I of Russia (r. 1825–1855), obligingly lent his iron hand. On June 6, 1849, 130,000 Russian troops poured into Hungary and subdued the country after bitter fighting. For a number of years, the Habsburgs ruled Hungary as a conquered territory.

Prussia and the Frankfurt Assembly

After Austria, Prussia was the largest and most influential German kingdom. Prior to 1848, the goal of middle-class Prussian liberals had been to transform absolutist Prussia into a liberal constitutional monarchy, which would lead the thirty-eight states of the German Confederation into the liberal, unified nation desired by liberals throughout the German states. The agitation following the fall of Louis Philippe encouraged Prussian liberals to press their demands. When the artisans and factory workers in Berlin exploded in March 1848 and joined temporarily with the middle-class liberals in the struggle against the monarchy, the autocratic yet compassionate Frederick William IV (r. 1840–1861) vacillated and finally caved in. On March 21, he promised to grant Prussia a liberal constitution and to merge Prussia into a new national German state that was to be created.

But urban workers wanted much more and the Prussian aristocracy wanted much less than the moderate constitutional liberalism the king conceded. The workers issued a series of democratic and vaguely socialist demands that troubled their middle-class allies, and the conservative clique gathered around the king to urge counter-revolution.

As an elected Prussian Constituent Assembly met in Berlin to write a constitution for the Prussian state, a self-appointed committee of liberals from various German states began organizing for the creation of a unified German state. Meeting in Frankfurt in May, a National Assembly composed of lawyers, professors, doctors, officials, and businessmen convened to write a German federal constitution. However, their attention shifted from drafting a constitution to deciding how to respond to Denmark's claims on the provinces of Schleswig (SHLEHS-wihg) and Holstein, which were inhabited primarily by Germans. Debating ponderously, the National Assembly at Frankfurt finally called on the Prussian army to oppose Denmark in the name of the German nation. Prussia responded and began war with Denmark. As the Schleswig-Holstein issue demonstrated, the national ideal was a crucial factor motivating the German middle classes in 1848.

In March 1849, the National Assembly finally completed its drafting of a liberal constitution and elected King Frederick William of Prussia emperor of the new German national state (minus Austria and Schleswig-Holstein). By early 1849, however, reaction had been successful almost everywhere. Frederick William had reasserted his royal authority, disbanded the Prussian Constituent Assembly, and granted his subjects a limited, essentially conservative constitution. Reasserting that he ruled by divine right, Frederick William contemptuously refused to accept the "crown from the gutter." Bogged down by their preoccupation with nationalist issues, the reluctant revolutionaries in Frankfurt had waited too long and acted too timidly.

When Frederick William, who really wanted to be emperor but only on his own authoritarian terms, tried to get the small monarchs of Germany to elect him emperor, Austria balked. Supported by Russia, Austria forced Prussia to renounce all its schemes of unification in late 1850. The German Confederation was re-established. Attempts to unite the Germans—first in a liberal national state and then in a conservative Prussian empire—had failed completely.

LOOKING BACK LOOKING AHEAD
VIEWED FROM A BROAD historical perspective, Europe's economic and social foundations in 1750 remained agricultural and rural. Peasants living in villages tilled the land, while landlords and the ruling classes collected rents and taxes. Political life was dominated by the authoritarian styles associated with absolutism, although the critical thinking of the Enlightenment was beginning to affect the intellectual and cultural elites, who began to challenge and question the status quo. By the 1790s, the British Industrial Revolution and the French Revolution were bringing fundamental changes to economic and political life in parts of Europe. In Great Britain new technologies and factory organization turned the focus away from agriculture and the land and toward industry and cities. In revolutionary France liberal ideals of representative government and legal equality were being realized, if only briefly. After 1815, the dual revolution provided Europe with new visions of political and social life. Liberalism intermingled with nationalism and socialism to challenge the restoration of the conservative order.

Much of world history in the past two centuries can be seen as the progressive unfolding of the dual revolution. In Europe in the nineteenth century, as in Asia and Africa in more recent times, the interrelated economic and political transformation was built on complicated histories, strong traditions, and highly diverse cultures. Although defeated in 1848, the new political ideologies associated with the French Revolution were destined to triumph after 1850. Above all, nationalism, with its commitment to the nation-state and the imagined community of a great national family, would become the dominant political force, responding to national problems and guiding European imperial expansion after 1875. At the same time, industrialization and new relationships between classes would privilege cities and promote a new urban society, as agriculture and rural life gradually declined. Diverse, complicated, and fascinating, this new urban society was emerging by 1850. By 1900, it dominated northwestern Europe and was making steady inroads to the east and south.

CHAPTER REVIEW

■ **How did the victorious allies fashion a general peace settlement, and how did Metternich uphold a conservative European order? (p. 686)**

In 1814 the victorious allied powers sought to restore peace and stability in Europe. The Quadruple Alliance — Russia, Prussia, Austria, and Great Britain — dealt moderately with France by giving it the boundaries it had possessed in 1792 and by not assigning war reparations. The peace settlement also included strong defensive measures, resolved the various disputes among the Great Powers, and laid the foundations for beneficial international cooperation throughout much of the nineteenth century. Led by Metternich, the conservative powers used intervention and repression as they sought to prevent the spread of subversive ideas and radical changes in domestic politics. The formation of the Holy Alliance was the first step in this crusade against the ideas and politics of the dual revolution.

■ **What were the basic tenets of liberalism, nationalism, and socialism, and what groups were most attracted to these ideologies? (p. 691)**

After 1815 the ideologies of liberalism, nationalism, and socialism all developed to challenge the existing order in this period of early industrialization and rapid population growth. The principal ideas of the liberalism movement were equality and liberty, which were expressed in representative government, civil rights, and limited government regulation of the economy. Nationalism was based on the notion that each people had its own genius and cultural unity; to this was then added the idea that each people also deserved its own political entity and its own government. The key ideas of socialism were economic planning, greater economic equality, and the state regulation of property. All of these basic tenets in one way or another rejected conservatism, with its stress on tradition, hereditary monarchy and aristocracy, and an official church. Business groups and the middle class were attracted to liberalism; liberals and democrats were attracted to nationalism; and workers and utopian theorists were drawn to socialism.

■ **What were the characteristics of the romantic movement, and who were some of the great romantic artists? (p. 697)**

The romantic movement, breaking decisively with the dictates of classicism, reinforced the spirit of change and revolutionary anticipation. The movement was characterized by a belief in self-expression, imagination, and spontaneity in art as well as in personal life. Among the most notable poets and writers, Wordsworth, Hugo, and Pushkin stand out. So do two brilliant Frenchwomen, Germaine de Staël and Amandine Dupin, known by her pen name of George Sand. Famous romantic artists included Turner with his turbulent seascapes, Constable with his peaceful English countryside, and Delacroix with his exotic scenes. In music romantic composers, led by Beethoven, Liszt, and Chopin, plumbed the depths of human emotions, and virtuoso performers became cultural heroes.

■ **How after 1815 did liberal, national, and socialist forces challenge conservatism in Greece, Great Britain, and France? (p. 701)**

Inspired by modern nationalism, Greek patriots rebelled against their Turkish rulers, and with the help of the European powers they won their national independence after a long struggle. In Great Britain the liberal challenge to the conservative order eventually led to fundamental reforms, as high tariffs on imported grain were reduced and then abolished, more men gained the right to vote with the Reform Act of 1832, and the factory workday for women and children was reduced to ten hours in 1847. In France, a three-day revolution in 1832 replaced the reactionary Charles X with the more moderate Louis Philippe, but little else changed.

■ **Why in 1848 did revolution triumph briefly throughout most of Europe, and why did it fail almost completely? (p. 707)**

In 1848 the increasing pressures of bad harvests, unemployment, rapid population growth, and a severe economic crisis exploded dramatically across Europe as they culminated in liberal and nationalistic revolutions. Monarchies panicked and crumbled in the face of popular uprisings and widespread opposition that cut across class lines, and the revolutionaries triumphed, first in France and then all across the continent. Yet very few revolutionary goals were realized. The moderate, nationalistic middle classes were unable to consolidate their initial victories. Instead, they drew back when artisans, factory workers, and radical socialists rose up to present their own much more revolutionary demands. This retreat facilitated the efforts of dedicated aristocrats in central Europe to reassert their power. And it made possible the crushing of Parisian workers by a coalition of solid bourgeoisie and landowning peasantry in France. Thus the lofty ideals of a generation drowned in a sea of blood and disillusion.

Suggested Reading

Berger, Stefan, ed. *A Companion to Nineteenth-Century Europe, 1789–1914.* 2006. A useful study with an up-to-date bibliography.

Chadwick, Owen. *The Secularization of the European Mind in the Nineteenth Century.* 1976. Considers the important place of religion in nineteenth-century thought.

Gildea, Robert. *Barricades and Borders: Europe, 1800–1914,* 2d ed. 1996. A recommended general study.

Greene, Abigail. *Fatherlands: State-Building and Nationhood in Nineteenth-Century Germany.* 2001. A brilliant discussion of the smaller German states.

Lindemann, Albert S. *A History of European Socialism.* 1983. A stimulating survey of early socialism and Marxism.

Malia, Martin, and Terence Emmons. *History's Locomotives: Revolutions and the Making of the Modern World.* 2006. An ambitious comparative work of high quality.

Mann, Thomas. *Buddenbrooks.* 1901. A wonderful historical novel that traces the rise and fall of a prosperous German family over three generations.

Merriman, John. *Police Stories: Building the French State, 1815–1851.* 2006. An outstanding and innovative compendium.

Pilbeam, Pamela. *French Socialists Before Marx: Workers, Women, and the Social Question.* 2000. Shows the significant role of women in utopian socialism.

Rapport, Mike. *1848: Year of Revolution.* 2008. A stimulating, well-written account that examines all of Europe.

Rubinstein, W. D. *Britain's Century: A Political and Social History, 1815–1905.* 1998. An excellent English history.

Sheehan, James J. *German History, 1770–1866.* 1993. A stimulating general history.

Shelley, Mary. *Frankenstein.* 1818. A great nineteenth-century romantic novel that draws an almost lovable picture of the famous monster and is highly recommended.

Sperber, Jonathan. *The European Revolutions, 1848–1851.* 1993. A solid synthesis of the great revolutionary upheaval.

Notes

1. E. Gellner, *Nations and Nationalism* (Oxford: Basil Blackwell, 1983), especially pp. 19–39.
2. This paragraph draws on the influential views of B. Anderson, *Imagined Communities: Reflections on the Origins and Spread of Nationalism,* rev. ed. (London/New York: Verso, 1991), and E. J. Hobsbawm and T. Ranger, eds., *The Invention of Tradition* (Cambridge, U.K.: Cambridge University Press, 1983).
3. Quoted in F. B. Artz, *From the Renaissance to Romanticism: Trends in Style in Art, Literature, and Music, 1300–1830* (Chicago: University of Chicago Press, 1962), pp. 276, 278.
4. Quoted by G. O'Brien, *The Economic History of Ireland from the Union to the Famine* (London: Longmans, Green, 1921), p. 21.
5. Ibid., pp. 23–24.
6. A. de Tocqueville, *Recollections* (New York: Columbia University Press, 1949), p. 94.
7. M. Agulhon, *1848* (Paris: Éditions du Seuil, 1973), pp. 68–69.
8. W. L. Langer, *Political and Social Upheaval, 1832–1852* (New York: Harper & Row, 1969), p. 361.

Key Terms

Congress of Vienna (p. 686)
dual revolution (p. 687)
Holy Alliance (p. 687)
Carlsbad Decrees (p. 689)
liberalism (p. 691)
laissez faire (p. 691)
nationalism (p. 691)
socialism (p. 693)
bourgeoisie (p. 696)
proletariat (p. 696)
romanticism (p. 697)
Corn Laws (p. 702)
Battle of Peterloo (p. 702)
Reform Bill of 1832 (p. 702)
Great Famine (p. 705)

For practice quizzes and other study tools, visit the Online Study Guide at **bedfordstmartins.com/mckaywest**.

For primary sources from this period, see *Sources of Western Society,* **Second Edition**.

For Web sites, images, and documents related to topics in this chapter, visit Make History at **bedfordstmartins.com/mckaywest**.

23

Life in the Emerging Urban Society

1840–1900

The era of intellectual and political upheaval that culminated in the revolutions of 1848 was also an era of rapid industrialization and urbanization. Industrial growth posed enormous challenges for all elements of Western society, from young factory workers confronting relentless discipline to aristocratic elites maneuvering to retain political power. After 1848, as Western political development veered off in an uncharted direction, the growth of towns and cities rushed forward with undiminished force. Thus Western society was urban and industrial in 1900 as surely as it had been rural and agrarian in 1800. Progress, in the form of new industries and big businesses, better living conditions for the masses, growing secularism, and a budding feminist movement, was the order of the day.

This emerging urban society benefited city dwellers, through improvements in health and the urban environment, but living conditions varied greatly according to one's status. While average people experienced wage increases, poverty was not eliminated and the gap between rich and poor remained as great as ever. The size of the middle classes grew in this period, and as middle-class people reaped the benefits of industrialization and scientific progress, they fragmented into an upper middle class that often mimicked the lives of the aristocracy, a solid "middle middle" class defined by the professions and business owners, and a lower middle class made up of shopkeepers and officeworkers. Despite this growing middle class, most urban dwellers continued to belong to the working classes. ■

Urban Life in the Nineteenth Century. The excitement and variety of urban life sparkle in this detail from a depiction of an entertainment gala given for the public by London's Royal Dramatic College.

CHAPTER PREVIEW

Taming the City
■ What was life like in the cities, and how did urban life change in the nineteenth century?

Rich and Poor and Those in Between
■ What did the emergence of urban industrial society mean for rich and poor and those in between?

The Changing Family
■ How did working-class and middle-class families change as they coped with the challenges and the opportunities of the developing urban civilization?

Science and Thought
■ What major changes in science and thought reflected and influenced the new urban society?

Taming the City

What was life like in the cities, and how did urban life change in the nineteenth century? ■

Since the Middle Ages, European cities had been centers of government, culture, and large-scale commerce. They had also been congested, dirty, and unhealthy. Beginning in the early nineteenth century, the Industrial Revolution took these unfortunate realities of urban life to unprecedented levels. While historians may debate whether the over-all societal impact of industrialization was generally positive or negative, there is little doubt that rapid urban growth worsened long-standing overcrowding and unhealthy living conditions and posed a frightening challenge for society. It would require the full-scale efforts of government leaders, city planners, reformers, scientists, and reform-minded citizens to tame the ferocious savagery of the traditional city.

Industry and the Growth of Cities

The main causes of such a poor quality of urban life—pervasive poverty, lack of medical knowledge, and deadly overcrowding—had existed for centuries. Because the typical city had always been a "walking city" with no public transportation, masses of people needed to live in close proximity to the shops and markets, resulting in dreadfully dense housing conditions. Packed together almost as tightly as possible, people in cities were always more likely to die from the spread of infectious disease than were their rural counterparts. In the larger towns, more people died each year than were born, on average, and urban populations were able to maintain their numbers only because newcomers were continually arriving from rural areas. Transplanted farm workers fatalistically viewed the grim realities of city life, and death, as the urban equivalents of bad weather and poor crops.

Deplorable urban conditions did not originate with the Industrial Revolution, but the Industrial Revolution did reveal those conditions more nakedly than ever before. The steam engine freed industrialists from dependence on the energy of fast-flowing streams and rivers so that by 1800 there was every incentive to build new factories in urban areas. Cities had better shipping facilities than the countryside and thus better supplies of coal and raw materials. There were also many hands wanting work in the cities, for

Mapping the Past

Map 23.1 **European Cities of 100,000 or More, 1800–1900** There were more large cities in Great Britain in 1900 than in all of Europe in 1800.

ANALYZING THE MAP Compare the spatial distribution of cities in 1800 with the distribution in 1900. Where in 1900 are large cities concentrated in clusters?

CONNECTIONS In 1800, what common characteristics were shared by many large European cities? (For example, how many big cities were capitals and/or leading ports?) Were any common characteristics shared by the large cities in 1900? What does this suggest about the reasons behind this dramatic growth?

To complete this activity online, go to the Online Study Guide at bedfordstmartins.com/mckaywest.

cities drew people like a magnet. And it was a great advantage for a manufacturer to have other factories nearby to supply the business's needs and buy its products. Therefore, as industry grew, there was also a rapid expansion of already overcrowded and unhealthy cities.

The challenge of the urban environment was felt first and most acutely in Great Britain. In the 1820s and 1830s, the populations of a number of British cities were increasing by 40 to 70 percent each decade. The number of people living in cities of 20,000 or more in England and Wales jumped from 1.5 million in 1801 to 6.3 million in 1851 and reached 15.6 million in 1891. Such cities accounted for 17 percent of the total English population in 1801, 35 percent as early as 1851, and fully 54 percent in 1891. Other countries duplicated the English pattern as they industrialized (Map 23.1).

Except on the outskirts, early-nineteenth-century cities in Britain were using every scrap of land to the fullest extent. Parks and open areas were almost nonexistent. Buildings were erected on the smallest possible lots in order to pack the maximum number of people into a given space. Narrow houses were built wall to wall in long rows. These row houses had neither front nor back yards, and only a narrow alley in back separated one row from the next. Other buildings were built around tiny courtyards completely enclosed on all four sides. Many people lived in extremely small, often overcrowded cellars or attics. "Six, eight, and even ten occupying one room is anything but uncommon," wrote a Scottish doctor for a government investigation in 1842.

These highly concentrated urban populations lived in extremely unsanitary and unhealthy conditions. Open drains and sewers flowed alongside or down the middle of unpaved streets. Toilet facilities were primitive in the extreme. In parts of Manchester, as many as two hundred people shared a single outhouse. Such privies filled up rapidly, and since they were infrequently emptied, sewage often overflowed and seeped into cellar dwellings. Moreover, some courtyards in poorer neighborhoods became dunghills, collecting excrement that was sometimes sold as fertilizer. By the 1840s there was among the better-off classes a growing, shocking "realization that," as one scholar put it, "millions of English men, women, and children were living in shit."[1]

Who or what was responsible for these awful conditions? The crucial factors were the tremendous pressure of more people and the total absence of public transportation. People simply had to jam themselves together if they were to be able to walk to shops and factories. Another factor was that government in Great Britain,

both local and national, was slow to provide sanitary facilities and establish adequate building codes. This slow pace was probably attributable more to a need to explore and identify what precisely should be done than to rigid middle-class opposition to government action. Certainly, Great Britain had no monopoly on overcrowded and unhealthy urban conditions; many continental cities were every bit as bad.

Most responsible of all was the sad legacy of rural housing conditions in preindustrial society combined with appalling ignorance. Housing was far down on the newcomer's list of priorities, and many people carried the filth of the mud floor and the dung of the barnyard with them to the city. Moreover, ordinary people generally took dirt for granted. One English miner told an investigator, "I do not think it usual for the lasses [in the coal mines] to wash their bodies; my sisters never wash themselves." As for the men, "their legs and bodies are as black as your hat."[2]

The Advent of the Public Health Movement

Toward the middle of the nineteenth century, people's fatalistic acceptance of their overcrowded, unsanitary surroundings began to give way to a growing interest in reform and improvement. The most famous early reformer was Edwin Chadwick, one of the commissioners charged with the administration of relief to paupers under Britain's revised Poor Law of 1834. Chadwick was a follower of radical philosopher Jeremy Bentham (1748–1832), whose approach to social issues, called **utilitarianism**, had taught that public problems ought to be dealt with on a rational, scientific

utilitarianism The idea of Jeremy Bentham that social policies should promote the "greatest good for the greatest number."

719

basis and according to the "greatest good for the greatest number." Applying these principles, Chadwick soon became convinced that disease and death actually caused poverty, because a sick worker was an unemployed worker and orphaned children were poor children. Most important, Chadwick believed that disease could be prevented by cleaning up the urban environment. That was his "sanitary idea."

Chadwick collected detailed reports from local Poor Law officials on the "sanitary conditions of the laboring population" and published his hard-hitting findings in 1842. This mass of widely publicized evidence proved that disease was related to filthy environmental conditions, which were in turn caused largely by lack of drainage, sewers, and garbage collection.

Chadwick correctly believed that the stinking excrement of communal outhouses could be dependably carried off by water through sewers at less than one-twentieth the cost of removing it by hand. The cheap iron pipes and tile drains of the industrial age would provide running water and sewerage for all sections of town, not just the wealthy ones. In 1848, with the cause strengthened by the cholera epidemic of 1846, Chadwick's report became the basis of Great Britain's first public health law, which created a national health board and gave cities broad authority to build modern sanitary systems.

The public health movement won dedicated supporters in the United States, France, and Germany from the 1840s on. Governments accepted at least limited responsibility for the health of all citizens, and their programs broke decisively with the age-old fatalism of urban populations. By the 1860s and 1870s, European cities were making real progress toward adequate water supplies and sewerage systems, city dwellers were beginning to reap the reward of better health, and death rates began to decline (Figure 23.1).

The Bacterial Revolution

Although improved sanitation in cities promoted a better quality of life and some improvements in health care, effective control of communicable disease required a great leap forward in medical knowledge and biological

King Cholera This 1852 drawing from *Punch* tells volumes about the unhealthy living conditions of the urban poor. In the foreground children play with a dead rat and a woman scavenges a dung heap. Cheap rooming houses provide shelter for the frightfully overcrowded population. Such conditions and contaminated water spread deadly cholera epidemics from India throughout Europe in the 1800s. The doctor's medicine chest seen here could only provide patients with opium mixtures to relieve pain and reduce intestinal swelling. (drawing: The British Library; chest: Science & Society Picture Library)

theory. Early reformers such as Chadwick were seriously handicapped by the prevailing miasmatic theory of disease—the belief that people contract disease when they breathe the bad odors of decay and putrefying excrement. In the 1840s and 1850s keen observation by doctors and public health officials pinpointed the role of bad drinking water in the transmission of disease and suggested that contagion was spread through filth and not caused by it, thus weakening the miasmatic idea.

The breakthrough was the development of the **germ theory** of disease by Louis Pasteur (pas-TUHR) (1822–1895), a French chemist who began studying fermentation for brewers in 1854. Using his microscope to develop a simple test that brewers could use to monitor the fermentation process and avoid spoilage, Pasteur found that fermentation depended on the growth of living organisms and that the activity of these organisms could be suppressed by heating the beverage—by pasteurization. The breathtaking implication was that specific diseases were caused by specific living organisms—germs—and that those organisms could be controlled in people as well as in beer, wine, and milk.

By 1870 the work of Pasteur and others had demonstrated the general connection between germs and disease. When, in the middle of the 1870s, German country doctor Robert Koch (kawkh) and his coworkers developed pure cultures of harmful bacteria and described their life cycles, the dam broke. Over the next twenty years, researchers—mainly Germans—identified the organisms responsible for disease after disease. These discoveries led to the development of a number of effective vaccines.

Acceptance of the germ theory brought about dramatic improvements in the deadly environment of hospitals and surgery (see Chapter 19). In 1865, when Pasteur showed that the air was full of bacteria, English surgeon Joseph Lister (1827–1912) immediately grasped the connection between aerial bacteria and the problem of wound infection. He reasoned that a chemical disinfectant applied to a wound dressing would "destroy the life of the floating particles." Lister's antiseptic principle worked wonders. In the 1880s, German surgeons developed the more sophisticated practice of sterilizing not only the wound but also everything—hands, instruments, clothing—that entered the operating room.

The achievements of the bacterial revolution coupled with the public health movement saved millions of lives, particularly after about 1880. Mortality rates began to decline dramatically in European countries (see Figure 23.1) as the awful death sentences of the past—diphtheria, typhoid, typhus, cholera, yellow fever—became vanishing diseases. City dwellers benefited especially from these developments. By 1910 a great silent revolution had occurred: the death rates for people of all ages in urban areas were generally no greater than those for people in rural areas, and sometimes they were lower.

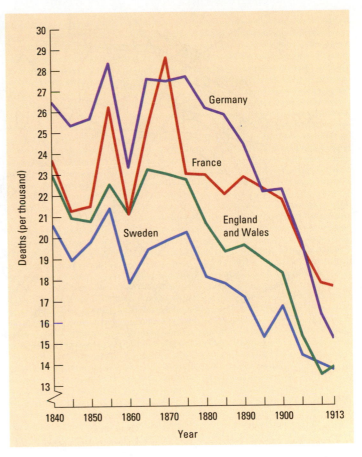

Figure 23.1 **The Decline of Death Rates in England and Wales, Germany, France, and Sweden, 1840–1913** A rising standard of living, improvements in public health, and better medical knowledge all contributed to the dramatic decline of death rates in the nineteenth century.

Improvements in Urban Planning

In addition to public health improvements in nineteenth-century cities, more effective urban planning was a major key to a better quality of urban life. France took the lead during the rule of Napoleon III (r. 1848–1870), who sought to promote the welfare of all his subjects through government action. He believed that rebuilding much of Paris would provide employment, improve living conditions, and testify to the power and glory of his empire. In the baron Georges Haussmann (HOWS-muhn) (1809–1884), an aggressive, impatient Alsatian whom he placed in charge of Paris, Napoleon III found an authoritarian planner capable of bulldozing both buildings and opposition. In twenty years, Paris was completely transformed (Map 23.2).

The Paris of 1850 was a labyrinth of narrow, dark streets, the results of desperate overcrowding and a lack of effective planning. In a central city not twice the size

germ theory The idea that disease was caused by the spread of living organisms that could be controlled.

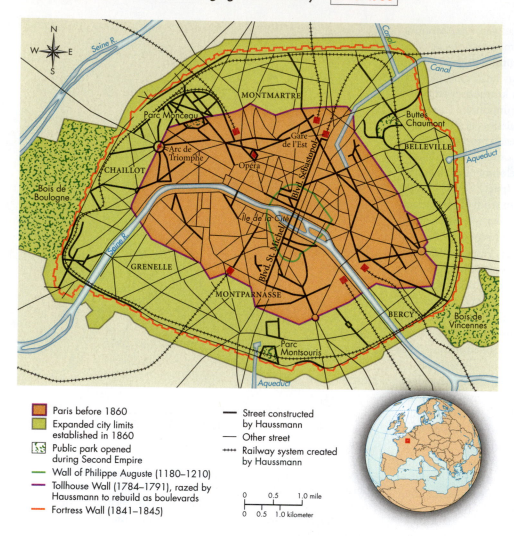

Map 23.2 The Modernization of Paris, ca. 1850–1870 The addition of broad boulevards, large parks, and grandiose train stations transformed Paris. The cutting of the new north-south axis—known as the Boulevard Saint-Michel—was one of Haussmann's most controversial projects. It razed much of Paris's medieval core and filled the Île de la Cité with massive government buildings.

tion of better housing, especially for the middle classes. Small neighborhood parks and open spaces were created throughout the city, and two very large parks suitable for all kinds of holiday activities were developed—one on the affluent west side and one on the poor east side of the city. The city also improved its sewers, and a system of aqueducts more than doubled the city's supply of clean, fresh water.

Rebuilding Paris provided a new model for urban planning and stimulated modern urbanism throughout Europe, particularly after 1870. In city after city, public authorities mounted a coordinated attack on many of the interrelated problems of the urban environment. As in Paris, improvements in public health through better water supply and waste disposal often went hand in hand with new boulevard construction. Cities such as Vienna and Cologne followed the Parisian example of tearing down old walled fortifications and replacing them with broad, circular boulevards on which office buildings, town halls, theaters, opera houses, and museums were erected. These ring roads and the new boulevards that radiated outward eased movement and encouraged urban expansion (see Map 23.2). Zoning expropriation laws, which allowed a majority of the owners of land in a given quarter of the city to impose major street or sanitation improvements on a reluctant minority, were an important mechanism of the new urbanism.

of New York's Central Park lived more than one-third of the city's 1 million inhabitants. Terrible slum conditions and extremely high death rates were facts of life. There were few open spaces and only two public parks for the entire metropolis.

For two decades Haussmann and his fellow planners proceeded on many interrelated fronts. With a bold energy that often shocked their contemporaries, they razed old buildings in order to cut broad, straight, tree-lined boulevards through the center of the city as well as in new quarters on the outskirts (see Map 23.2). These boulevards, designed in part to prevent the easy construction and defense of barricades by revolutionary crowds, permitted traffic to flow freely and afforded impressive vistas. Their creation also demolished some of the worst slums. New streets stimulated the construc-

Public Transportation

The development of mass public transportation often accompanied urban planning, greatly enhancing urban living conditions toward the end of the nineteenth century. In the 1870s, many European cities authorized private companies to operate horse-drawn streetcars, which had been developed in the United States, to carry riders along the growing number of major thoroughfares. Then in the 1890s, the real revolution occurred: European countries adopted another American transit innovation, a streetcar that ran on the newly harnessed power of electricity (see page 741).

Electric streetcars were cheaper, faster, more dependable, cleaner, and more comfortable than their horse-drawn counterparts. Millions of Europeans—workers, shoppers, schoolchildren—hopped on board during the workweek. On weekends and holidays, streetcars carried millions on happy outings to parks and the countryside, to racetracks and music halls. In 1886 the horse-drawn streetcars of Austria-Hungary, France, Germany, and Great Britain were carrying about 900 million riders. By 1910 electric streetcar systems in the four countries were carrying 6.7 billion riders.[3] Each man, woman, and child was using public transportation four times as often in 1910 as in 1886.

Good mass transit helped greatly in the struggle for decent housing. The new boulevards and horse-drawn streetcars had facilitated a middle-class move to better and more spacious housing in the 1860s and 1870s; after 1890 electric streetcars meant people of even modest means could access new, improved housing. Though still crowded, the city was able to expand and become less congested. In England in 1901, only 9 percent of the urban population was "overcrowded" in terms of the official definition of more than two persons per room. On the continent, many city governments in the early twentieth century were building electric streetcar systems that provided transportation to new public and private housing developments for the working classes beyond the city limits. Suburban commuting was born.

Rich and Poor and Those in Between

What did the emergence of urban industrial society mean for rich and poor and those in between? ■

As the quality of urban life was improving across Europe, the class structure was becoming more complex and diverse. Urban society featured many distinct social groups, all of which existed in a state of constant flux and competition. The gap between rich and poor remained enormous and quite traditional, but there were countless gradations between the extremes.

The Distribution of Income

By 1850 at the latest, working conditions were improving. Moreover, real wages—that is, wages received by

workers adjusted for changes in the prices they paid—were rising for the mass of the population, and they continued to do so until 1914. The real wages of British workers, for example, almost doubled between 1850 and 1906. Similar increases occurred in continental countries as industrial development quickened after 1850. Ordinary people took a major step forward in the centuries-old battle against poverty, reinforcing efforts to improve many aspects of human existence.

There is another side to the income coin, however. Greater economic rewards for the average person did not eliminate hardship and poverty, nor did they make the wealth and income of the rich and the poor significantly more equal, as economic historians have clearly demonstrated. In almost every advanced country around 1900, the richest 5 percent of all households in the population received about a third of all national income, and the richest 20 percent of households received from 50 to 60 percent of all national income. At the other end, the entire bottom 80 percent received only 40 to 50 percent of all income. Moreover, the bottom 30 percent of all households received 10 percent or less of all income.

To understand the full significance of these statistics, one must realize that the middle classes were smaller than they are today. In the nineteenth century, they accounted for less than 20 percent of the population. In short, this meant that the upper and middle classes alone received more than half of all income, while the poorest 80 percent—the working classes, including peasants and agricultural laborers—received less altogether than the two richest classes. Moreover, in the nineteenth century income taxes on the wealthy were light or nonexistent. Thus the gap between rich and poor remained enormous at the beginning of the twentieth century. Indeed, it was probably almost as great as it had been in the late eighteenth century, in the age of agriculture and aristocracy.

The great gap between rich and poor endured, in part, because industrial and urban development made society more diverse and less unified. Society had not split into two sharply defined opposing classes, as Karl Marx had predicted (see Chapter 22). Instead, economic specialization enabled society to produce more effectively and in the process created more new social groups than it destroyed. There developed an almost unlimited range of jobs, skills, and earnings; one group or subclass blended into another in a complex, confusing hierarchy. Thus the tiny elite of the very rich and the sizable mass of the dreadfully poor were separated by a range of subclasses, each filled with individuals struggling to rise or at least to hold their own in the social order. In this atmosphere of competition and hierarchy, neither the middle classes nor the working classes acted as a unified force. This social and occupational hierarchy developed enormous

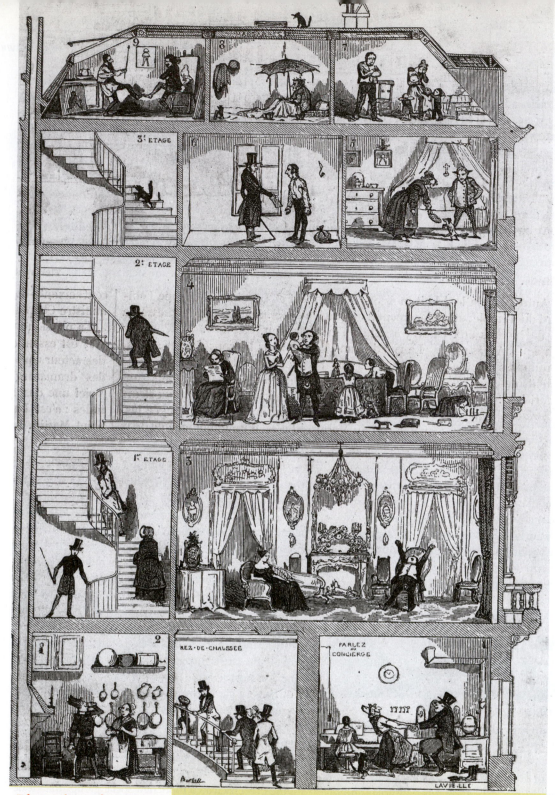

Picturing the Past

Apartment Living in Paris This drawing shows a typical layout for a European city apartment building in about 1850. (Bibliothèque nationale de France)

ANALYZING THE IMAGE Describe the inhabitants of each floor. How does the economic condition of the tenants differ from the 1st Étage (American second floor) to the garret apartments on the top floor?

CONNECTIONS What does this drawing suggest about urban life in the nineteenth century? How might a sketch of a modern, urban American apartment building differ in terms of the types of people who reside in a single building?

To complete this activity online, go to the Online Study Guide at bedfordstmartins.com/mckaywest.

724

variations, but the age-old pattern of great economic inequality remained firmly intact.

The People and Occupations of the Middle Classes

By the beginning of the twentieth century, the diversity and range within the urban middle class were striking. Indeed, it is more meaningful to think not of a single middle class but of a confederation of middle classes whose members engaged in occupations requiring mental, rather than physical, skill.

At the top of the middle class stood the upper middle class, composed mainly of the most successful business families from banking, industry, and large-scale commerce. As people in the upper middle class gained in income and progressively lost all traces of radicalism after the trauma of 1848, they were almost irresistibly drawn toward the aristocratic lifestyle. And although the genuine hereditary aristocracy constituted only a tiny minority in every European country, it retained imposing wealth, unrivaled social prestige, and substantial political influence. This was especially true in central and eastern Europe, where the monarch—the highest-ranking noble of them all—continued to hold great political power.

The topmost reaches of the upper middle class tended to merge with the old aristocracy to form a new upper class of at most 5 percent of the population. Much of the aristocracy welcomed this development. Having experienced a sharp decline in its relative income in the course of industrialization, the landed aristocracy had met big business coming up the staircase and was often delighted to trade titles, country homes, and snobbish elegance for good hard cash. Some of the best bargains were made through marriages to American heiresses. Correspondingly, wealthy aristocrats tended increasingly to exploit their agricultural and mineral resources as if they were business people.

Below the wealthy upper middle class were much larger, much less wealthy, and increasingly diversified middle-class groups. Here were the moderately successful industrialists and merchants as well as professionals in law and medicine. This was the middle middle class, solid and quite comfortable but lacking great wealth. Below it were independent shopkeepers, small traders, and tiny manufacturers—the lower middle class. Both of these traditional elements of the middle class grew modestly with economic development.

As industry and technology expanded in the nineteenth century, a growing demand developed for experts with specialized knowledge, and advanced education soared in importance among the middle classes. Engineering, for example, emerged from the world of skilled labor as a full-fledged profession with considerable prestige and many branches. Architects, chemists, accountants, and surveyors, to name only a few, first achieved professional standing in this period. They established criteria for advanced training and certification and banded together in organizations to promote and defend their interests.

Management of large public and private institutions also emerged as a kind of profession as governments provided more services and as very large corporations such as railroads came into being. Government officials and many private executives were not capitalists in the sense that they owned business enterprises, but public and private managers did have specialized knowledge and the capacity to earn a good living. And they shared most of the values of the business-owning entrepreneurs and the older professionals.

Industrialization also expanded and diversified the lower middle class. The number of independent, property-owning shopkeepers and small business people grew, and so did the number of white-collar employees— a mixed group of traveling salesmen, bookkeepers, store managers, and clerks who staffed the offices and branch stores of large corporations. White-collar employees were propertyless and often earned no more than the better-paid skilled or semiskilled workers did. Yet white-collar workers were fiercely committed to the middle class and to the ideal of upward mobility. In the Balkans, for example, clerks let their fingernails grow very long to distinguish themselves from people who worked with their hands. The tie, the suit, and soft, clean hands were no less subtle marks of class distinction than were wages.

Relatively well educated but without complex technical skills, many white-collar groups aimed at achieving professional standing and the accompanying middle-class status. Elementary school teachers largely succeeded in this effort. From being miserably paid part-time workers in the early nineteenth century, teachers rode the wave of mass education to respectable middle-class status and income. Nurses also rose from the lower ranks of unskilled labor to precarious middle-class standing. Dentistry was taken out of the hands of working-class barbers and placed in the hands of highly trained (and middle-class) professionals.

Middle-Class Culture and Values

In spite of growing occupational diversity and conflicting interests, the middle classes were loosely united by a certain style of life and culture. Food was the largest item in the household budget, for middle-class people liked to eat very well. The European middle classes consumed meat in abundance, and a well-off family might spend 10 percent of its substantial earnings on meat and fully 25 percent of its income on food and drink. Spending on food was also great because the dinner party was this class's favored social occasion. A wealthy family might give a lavish party for eight to twelve almost every

A Corner of the Table With photographic precision, the French artist Paul-Émile Chabas (1869–1937) captures the elegance and intimacy of a sumptuous dinner party. Throughout Europe, members of the upper middle class and aristocracy enjoyed dinners like this with eight or nine separate courses, beginning with appetizers and ending with coffee and liqueurs. (Archives Charmet/The Bridgeman Art Library)

riages, ever-expensive items in the city, were additional signs of rising social status.

Rich businessmen devoted less time to business and more time to "culture" and easy living than was the case in less wealthy or well-established families. The keystones of culture and leisure were books, music, and travel. The long realistic novel, the heroics of composers Wagner and Verdi, the diligent striving of the dutiful daughter at the piano, and the packaged tour to a foreign country were all sources of middle-class pleasure.

In addition to their material tastes, the middle classes generally agreed upon a strict code of behavior and morality. This code laid great stress on hard work, self-discipline, and personal achievement. Men and women who fell into crime or poverty were generally assumed to be responsible for their own circumstances. Christian morality was reaffirmed by this code and was preached tirelessly by middle-class people. Drunkenness and gambling were denounced as vices; sexual purity and fidelity were celebrated as virtues. In short, the middle-class person was supposed to know right from wrong and was expected to act accordingly.

week, whereas more modest households would settle for once a month.

The middle-class wife could cope with this endless procession of meals, courses, and dishes because she had both servants and money at her disposal. Indeed, the employment of at least one full-time maid to cook and clean was the clearest sign that a family had crossed the cultural divide separating the working classes from what some contemporary observers called the "servant-keeping classes." The greater a family's income, the greater the number of servants it employed. Food and servants together absorbed about 50 percent of income at all levels of the middle class.

Well fed and well served, the middle classes were also well housed by 1900. Many prosperous families rented, rather than owned, their homes. Apartment living, complete with tiny rooms for servants under the eaves of the top floor, was commonplace. And, just as the aristocracy had long divided the year between palatial country estates and lavish townhouses during "the season," so the upper middle class purchased country places or built beach houses for weekend and summer use.

By 1900 the middle classes were also quite clothes-conscious. The factory, the sewing machine, and the department store had all helped reduce the cost and expand the variety of clothing. Middle-class women were particularly attentive to the dictates of fashion. (See "Living in the Past: Nineteenth-Century Women's Fashion," page 728.) Private coaches and car-

The People and Occupations of the Working Classes

About four out of five people belonged to the working classes at the beginning of the twentieth century. Many members of the working classes—that is, people whose livelihoods depended primarily on physical labor and who did not employ domestic servants—were still small landowning peasants and hired farm hands. This was especially true in eastern Europe. In western and central Europe, however, the typical worker had left the land. In Great Britain, less than 8 percent of the people worked in agriculture, and in rapidly industrializing Germany only 25 percent were employed in agriculture and forestry. Even in less industrialized France,

less than 50 percent of the people depended on the land in 1900.

The urban working classes were even less unified and homogeneous than the middle classes. In the first place, economic development and increased specialization expanded the traditional range of working-class skills, earnings, and experiences. Meanwhile, the old sharp distinction between highly skilled artisans and unskilled manual workers gradually broke down. To be sure, highly skilled printers and masons as well as unskilled dockworkers and common laborers continued to exist. But between these extremes there appeared ever more semi-skilled groups, many of which were composed of factory workers and machine tenders (Figure 23.2). In the second place, skilled, semiskilled, and unskilled workers developed widely divergent lifestyles and cultural values, and their differences contributed to a keen sense of social status and hierarchy within the working classes. The result was great variety and limited class unity.

Highly skilled workers, who made up about 15 percent of the working classes, became known as the **labor aristocracy**. These workers earned only about two-thirds of the income of the bottom ranks of the servant-keeping classes, but that was fully twice as much as the earnings of unskilled workers. The most "aristocratic" of the highly skilled workers were construction bosses and factory foremen, men who had risen from the ranks and were fiercely proud of their achievement. The labor aristocracy also included members of the traditional highly skilled handicraft trades that had not been mechanized or placed in factories, like cabinetmakers, jewelers, and printers.

The labor aristocracy as a whole was under constant long-term pressure. Gradually, factory methods were being extended to more crafts, and many skilled artisans were replaced by lower-paid semiskilled factory workers. Traditional wood-carvers and watchmakers virtually disappeared, for example, as the making of furniture and timepieces now took place in factories. At the same time, the labor aristocracy was consistently being enlarged by new kinds of skilled workers such as shipbuilders and railway locomotive engineers. Thus the labor elite remained in a state of flux as individuals and whole crafts moved in and out of it.

To maintain this precarious standing, the upper working class adopted distinctive values and strait-laced, almost puritanical behavior. Like the middle classes, the labor aristocracy was strongly committed to the family and to economic improvement. Families in the upper working class saved money regularly, worried about their children's education, and valued good housing. Wives seldom sought employment outside the home. Despite these similarities, skilled workers viewed themselves

Figure 23.2 The Urban Social Hierarchy

Aristocracy

Middle classes
- Upper
- Middle
- Lower

Working classes
- Highly skilled: the "labor aristocracy"
- Semiskilled
- Unskilled

labor aristocracy The highly skilled workers, such as factory foremen and construction bosses, who made up about 15 percent of the working classes from about 1850 to 1914.

The Labor Aristocracy This group of British foremen is attending the International Exhibition in Paris in 1862. Their "Sunday best" includes the silk top hats and long morning coats of the properties classes, but they definitely remain workers, the proud leaders of laboring people. (© The Board of Trustees of the Victoria & Albert Museum)

LIVING IN THE PAST

IN THE LATER NINETEENTH CENTURY fashionable clothing, especially for middle-class women, became the first modern consumer industry as buyers snapped up the constantly changing ready-to-wear goods sold by large department stores. Before the twentieth century, when society fragmented into many different groups expressing themselves in many dress styles, clothing patterns focused mainly on perceived differences in class and gender. Most changes in women's fashion originated in Paris in the nineteenth century. The crinoline dresses shown here were worn exclusively by aristocratic and wealthy middle-class Frenchwomen in the 1850s and 1860s. These expensive dresses, flawlessly tailored by skilled seamstresses, abounded in elaborate embroidery, rich velvety materials, and fancy accessories. The circular spread of the gowns was created by the crinoline, a slip with a metal hoop that held the skirt out on all sides. Underneath women wore the corset, the century's most characteristic women's undergarment, which was laced up tightly in back and which pressed unmercifully from the breasts to the hips.

By 1875, as shown in this painting of a middle-class interior (opposite, top), the corset still binds, but the crinoline hoop was replaced by the bustle, a cotton fan with steel reinforcement that pushed the dress out in back to exaggerate gender differences. Worn initially by the wealthy elite, a cheaper ready-to-wear bustle could be purchased throughout Europe from a department store or mail-order catalogue, and it soon became the standard for middle-class women. Emulating the elite in style, conventional middle-class women shopped carefully, scouting for sales, and drew a boundary separating themselves from working-class women, who wore simple cotton clothes, just as the wealthy had tried to differentiate themselves from the middle class earlier in the century.

By century's end alternative styles of dress began to emerge. The young middle-class Englishwoman in this 1893 photo has chosen a woman's tailored suit, the only major English innovation in nineteenth-century women's fashion. This "alternative dress" combined the tie, suit jacket, vest, and straw hat — all initially items of male attire — with typical feminine elements, such as the skirt and gloves. The practical, socially accepted dress appealed to the growing number of women in paid employment in the 1890s. By the early part of the twentieth century the corset had given way entirely to the more flexible brassiere and the mainstream embrace of loose-fitting garments, as illustrated by this 1910 French advertisement.

Crinoline dresses, Paris, 1859.
(Mary Evans Picture Library/The Image Works)

PARIS FASHIONS FOR SEPTEMBER.

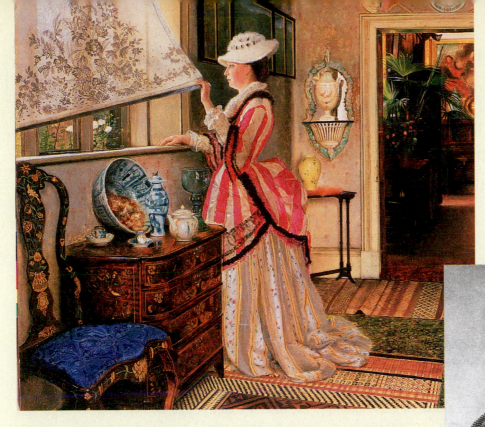

Summer dress with bustle, England, 1875.
(Roy Miles, Esq./The Bridgeman Art Library)

Alternative dress, England, 1893.
(Manchester City Art Galleries)

QUESTIONS FOR ANALYSIS

1. What does the image from 1859 tell you about the life of these women (their work, leisure activities, and so on)? What implications, if any, do you think the later styles shown here had on women's lives? On class distinctions?

2. What does the impractical, restrictive clothing in these images reveal about society's view of women during this period? What is the significance of the emergence of alternative styles of dress?

3. Historian Diana Crane has argued that women's departure from a dominant style can be seen as a symbolic, nonverbal assertion of independence and equality with men. Do you agree? Did the greater freedom of movement in clothing in the twentieth century reflect the emerging emancipation of Western women? Or was the coquettish femininity of loose, flowing dresses only a repackaging of the dominant culture's sharply defined gender boundaries?

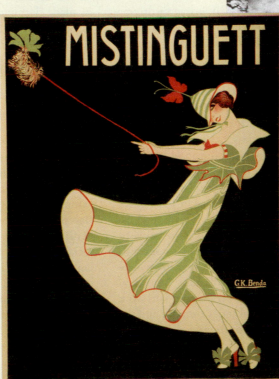

Loose-fitting dress, France, 1910. (© Corbis)

> **❝** Drunkenness was by far the commonest cause of dispute and misery in working class homes. On account of it one saw many a decent family drift down through poverty into total want. **❞**

— **ENGLISH SLUM DWELLER**

not as aspirants to the middle class but as the pacesetters and natural leaders of all the working classes. Well aware of the degradation not so far below them, they practiced self-discipline and stern morality. They generally frowned on heavy drinking and sexual permissiveness. As one German skilled worker somberly warned, "The path to the brothel leads through the tavern" and from there quite possibly to drastic decline or total ruin for person and family.[4]

Below the labor aristocracy stood an enormously complex sector of the labor world, comprising both semiskilled and unskilled urban workers. Workers in the established crafts—carpenters, bricklayers, pipe fitters—stood near the top of the semiskilled hierarchy, often flirting with (or sliding back from) the labor elite. A large number of the semiskilled were factory workers, including substantial numbers of unmarried women, who earned highly variable but relatively good wages and whose relative importance in the labor force was increasing.

sweated industries Poorly paid handicraft production, often by married women paid by the piece and working at home.

Below the semiskilled workers was a larger group of unskilled workers that included day laborers such as longshoremen, wagon-driving teamsters, teenagers, and every kind of "helper." Many of these people had real skills and performed valuable services, but they were unorganized and divided, united only by the common fate of meager earnings. The same lack of unity characterized street vendors and market people—self-employed workers who competed savagely with each other and with the established shopkeepers of the lower middle class.

One of the largest components of the unskilled group was domestic servants, whose numbers grew steadily in the nineteenth century. In Great Britain, for example, one out of every seven employed persons in 1911 was a domestic servant. The great majority were women; indeed, one out of every three girls in Britain between the ages of fifteen and twenty was a domestic servant. Throughout Europe and America, a great many female domestics in the cities were recent migrants from rural areas. As in earlier times, domestic service was hard work at low pay with limited personal independence and the danger of sexual exploitation. For the full-time general maid in a lower-middle-class family, there was an unending routine of babysitting, shopping, cooking, and cleaning. In the great households, the girl was at the bottom of a rigid hierarchy of status-conscious butlers and housekeepers.

Nonetheless, domestic service had real attractions for "rough country girls" with strong hands and few specialized skills. Marriage prospects were better, or at least more varied, in the city. And though wages were low, they were higher and more regular than in hard agricultural work. Finally, as one London observer noted, young girls and other migrants were drawn to the city by "the contagion of numbers, the sense of something going on, the theaters and the music halls, the brightly lighted streets and busy crowds—all, in short, that makes the difference between the Mile End fair on a Saturday night, and a dark and muddy country lane, with no glimmer of gas and with nothing to do."[5]

Many young domestics from the countryside made successful transitions to working-class wife and mother. Yet with an unskilled or unemployed husband, a growing family, and limited household income, many working-class wives had to join the broad ranks of working women in the **sweated industries**. These industries flowered after 1850 and resembled the old putting-out and cottage industries of earlier times (see Chapter 18). The women normally worked at home and were paid by the piece, not by the hour. They and their young children earned pitiful wages and lacked any job security. Some women decorated dishes or embroidered linens, or took in laundry for washing and ironing. The majority made clothing, especially after the advent of the sewing machine. An army of poor women, usually working at home, accounted for much of the inexpensive ready-made clothes displayed on department store racks and in tiny shops.

Working-Class Leisure and Religion

Notwithstanding the hard physical labor and their lack of wealth, the urban working classes sought fun and recreation, and they found both. Across the face of Europe, drinking remained unquestionably the favorite leisure-time activity of working people. For many middle-class moralists as well as moralizing historians since, love of drink has been a curse of the modern age—a sign of social dislocation and popular suffering. Certainly, drinking was deadly serious business. One English slum dweller recalled that "drunkenness was by far the commonest cause of dispute and misery in working class homes. On account of it one saw many a decent family drift down through poverty into total want."[6]

Generally, however, heavy problem drinking declined in the late nineteenth century as it became less socially acceptable. This decline reflected in part the moral leadership of the upper working class. At the same time, drinking became more publicly acceptable. Cafés and pubs became increasingly bright, friendly places. Working-class political activities, both moderate and radical, were also concentrated in taverns and pubs. Moreover, social drinking in public places by married couples and sweethearts became an accepted and widespread practice for the first time. This greater participation by women undoubtedly helped civilize the world of drink and hard liquor.

The two other leisure-time passions of working-class culture were sports and music halls. A great decline in "cruel sports," such as bullbaiting and cockfighting, had occurred throughout Europe by the late nineteenth century. Their place was filled by modern, commercialized spectator sports, of which racing and soccer were the most popular. There was a great deal of gambling on sports events, and for many a working person a desire to decipher racing forms provided a powerful incentive toward literacy. Music halls and vaudeville theaters, the working-class counterparts of middle-class opera and classical theater, were enormously popular throughout Europe. In 1900 there were more than fifty such halls and theaters in London alone. Music hall audiences were thoroughly mixed, which may account for the fact that drunkenness, premarital sex, marital difficulties, and mothers-in-law were all favorite themes of broad jokes and bittersweet songs.

In more serious moments, religion continued to provide working people with solace and meaning. The eighteenth-century vitality of popular religion in Catholic countries and the Protestant rejuvenation exemplified by German Pietism and English Methodism (see Chapter 19) carried over into the nineteenth century. Indeed, many historians see the early nineteenth century as an age of religious revival. Yet historians also recognize that by the last few decades of the nineteenth century, a considerable decline in both church attendance and church donations was occurring in most European countries. And it seems clear that this decline was greater for the urban working classes than for their rural counterparts or for the middle classes.

Why did working-class church attendance decline? Part of the reason was that the construction of churches failed to keep up with the rapid growth of urban population, especially in new working-class neighborhoods. Equally important, however, was the fact that throughout the nineteenth century both Catholic and Protestant churches were normally seen as they saw themselves—as conservative institutions defending social order and custom. Therefore, as the European working classes became more politically conscious, they tended to see the established (or quasi-established) "territorial church" as

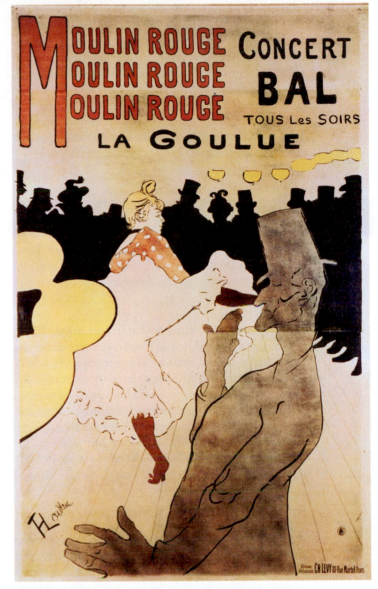

Big City Nightlife The most famous dance hall and cabaret in Paris was the Moulin Rouge. There La Goulue ("the Glutton"), who is featured on this poster, performed her provocative version of the cancan and reigned as the queen of Parisian sensuality. This is one of many colorful posters done by Henri de Toulouse-Lautrec (1864–1901), who combined stupendous creativity and dedicated debauchery in his short life. (Bridgeman-Giraudon/Art Resource, NY)

allied with their political opponents. Especially the men of the urban working classes developed vaguely anti-church attitudes, even though they remained neutral or positive toward religion. They tended to regard regular church attendance as "not our kind of thing"—not part of urban working-class culture.

The pattern was different in the United States. There, most churches also preached social conservatism in the nineteenth century. But because church and state had always been separate and because there was always a host of competing denominations and even different religions, working people identified churches much less with the political and social status quo. Instead, individual churches in the United States were often closely identified with an ethnic group rather than with a social class, and churches thrived, in part, as a means of asserting ethnic identity. This same process did occur in Europe if the church or synagogue had never been linked to the state and served as a focus for ethnic cohesion. Irish Catholic churches in Protestant Britain and Jewish synagogues in Russia were outstanding examples.

The Changing Family

How did working-class and middle-class families change as they coped with the challenges and the opportunities of the developing urban civilization? ■

Urban life wrought many fundamental changes in the family. By the second half of the nineteenth century the family had stabilized considerably after the disruption of the late eighteenth and early nineteenth centuries. The home became more important for both men and women. The role of women and attitudes toward children underwent substantial change, and adolescence emerged as a distinct stage of life. These are but a few of the transformations that affected all social classes in varying degrees.

Premarital Sex and Marriage

By 1850 the preindustrial pattern of lengthy courtship and mercenary marriage for financial gain was pretty well dead among the working classes. In its place, the ideal of romantic love had triumphed. Couples were ever more likely to come from different, even distant, towns and to be more nearly the same age, further indicating that romantic sentiment was replacing tradition and financial considerations.

Economic considerations in marriage began to decline among the middle classes after 1850, but by no means did they disappear entirely. In France dowries and elaborate legal marriage contracts were common practice among the middle classes in the later nineteenth century, and marriage remained for many families one of life's most crucial financial transactions. A popular author advised young Frenchmen that "marriage is in general a means of increasing one's credit and one's fortune and of insuring one's success in the world."[7] This preoccupation with money led many middle-class men in France and elsewhere to marry late, after they had been established economically, and to choose women considerably younger than themselves. Age differences

between husband and wife became a source of tension in many middle-class marriages.

A young woman of the middle class found her romantic life carefully supervised by her well-meaning mother, who schemed for a proper marriage and guarded her daughter's virginity like the family's credit. (See "Listening to the Past: Stephan Zweig on Middle-Class Youth and Sexuality," page 734.) After marriage, middle-class morality sternly demanded fidelity.

Middle-class boys were watched, too, but not as vigilantly. By the time they reached late adolescence, they had usually attained considerable sexual experience with maids or prostitutes.

In the early nineteenth century, sexual experimentation before marriage also triumphed for society as a whole, as did illegitimacy. The illegitimacy explosion that had begun in 1750 continued through the 1840s, at which point one-third of the births in many large European cities was occurring outside of wedlock (see Chapter 19). The rising rate of illegitimacy was reversed in the second half of the nineteenth century: in western, northern, and central Europe, more babies were born to married mothers.

Some observers have argued that this shift reflected the growth of puritanism and a lessening of sexual permissiveness among the unmarried. This explanation, however, is unconvincing because the percentage of working-class brides who were pregnant continued to be high and showed little or no tendency to decline after 1850. In many parts of urban Europe around 1900, as many as one woman in three was going to the altar an expectant mother. Moreover, unmarried people almost certainly used the affordable condoms and diaphragms the industrial age had made available to prevent pregnancy, at least in predominately Protestant countries.

Thus unmarried young people were probably engaging in just as much sexual activity as their parents and grandparents who had created the illegitimacy explosion of 1750 to 1850. But in the later nineteenth century, pregnancy for a young single woman, which a couple might see as the natural consequence of a serious relationship, led increasingly to marriage and the establishment of a two-parent household. This important development reflected the growing respectability of the working classes as well as their gradual economic improvement. Skipping out was less acceptable, and marriage was less of an economic challenge. The urban working-class couple of the late nineteenth century thus became more stable, and that stability strengthened the family as an institution.

Prostitution

Sexual activity certainly existed outside of committed relationships in the nineteenth century, as it undoubtedly always had. In Paris alone, 155,000 women were registered as prostitutes between 1871 and 1903, and 750,000 others were suspected of prostitution in the same years. Men of all classes visited prostitutes, but the middle and upper classes supplied much of the motivating cash. Thus, though many middle-class men abided by the publicly professed code of stern puritanical morality, others indulged their appetites for prostitutes and sexual promiscuity.

My Secret Life, the anonymous eleven-volume autobiography of an English sexual adventurer from the servant-keeping classes, provides a remarkable picture of such a man.[8] Beginning at an early age with a maid, the author becomes progressively obsessed with sex and devotes his life to living his sexual fantasies. In almost every one of his innumerable encounters all across Europe, this man of wealth simply buys his pleasure. Usually meetings are arranged in a businesslike manner: regular and part-time prostitutes quote their prices; working-class girls are corrupted by hot meals and baths.

Obviously atypical in its excesses, *My Secret Life* does reveal the dark side of sex and class in urban society. Frequently thinking of their wives largely in terms of money, family, and social position, the men of the comfortable classes often purchased sex and even affection from poor girls both before and after marriage. Moreover, the great continuing differences between rich and poor made for every kind of debauchery and sexual exploitation. The sternly moral women (and men) of the upper working class detested this sad reality and tried to shield their daughters from it. For many poor young women, however, prostitution, like domestic service, was a stage of life and not a permanent employment. Having done it for a while in their twenties, they went on to marry (or live with) men of their own class and establish homes and families.

Kinship Ties

Within working-class homes, ties to relatives after marriage—kinship ties—were generally very strong. Most newlyweds tried to live near their parents, though not in the same house. Indeed, for many married couples in later-nineteenth-century cities, ties to mothers and fathers, uncles and aunts, were more important than ties to unrelated acquaintances.

People turned to their families for help in coping with sickness, unemployment, death, and old age. Although governments typically provided more welfare services by 1900, the average couple and their children inevitably faced crises. Funerals, for example, brought sudden demands, requiring a large outlay for special clothes, carriages, and burial services. Unexpected death

> **❝ Marriage is in general a means of increasing one's credit and one's fortune and of insuring one's success in the world. ❞**
> —**Popular French author**

or desertion could leave the bereaved or abandoned, especially widows and orphans, in need of financial aid or perhaps a foster home. Relatives responded hastily to such cries, knowing full well that their own time of need and repayment would undoubtedly come.

Relatives were also valuable at less tragic moments. If a couple was quite poor, an aged relation often moved in to cook and mind the children so that the wife could earn badly needed income outside the home. Members of a large family group often lived in the same neighborhood, and they frequently shared Sunday dinners, outgrown clothing, and useful information.

Gender Roles and Early Feminism

Industrialization and the growth of modern cities brought great changes to the lives of European women of all classes. These changes were particularly consequential for married women, and most women did marry in the nineteenth century.

After 1850 the work of most wives became increasingly distinct and separate from that of their husbands. Husbands became wage earners in factories and offices, while wives tended to stay home and manage households and care for children. The preindustrial pattern among both peasants and cottage workers, in which husbands and wives worked together and divided up household duties and child rearing, declined. Instead, as economic conditions improved, most men expected only married women in poor families to work outside the home. Thus many historians have stressed that the societal ideal in nineteenth-century Europe became a strict division of labor by gender and rigidly constructed separate spheres: the wife as mother and homemaker, the husband as wage earner and breadwinner.

This rigid gender division of labor meant that married women faced great obstacles when they needed—or wanted—to move into the man's world of paid employment outside the home. Husbands were unsympathetic or hostile. Well-paying jobs were off-limits to women, and a woman's wage was almost always less than a man's, even for the same work.

Moreover, married women were subordinated to their husbands by law and lacked many basic legal rights. In England a wife had no legal identity and hence no right

LISTENING TO THE PAST

Growing up in Vienna in a prosperous Jewish family, Stephan Zweig (zwighg) (1881–1942) became an influential voice calling for humanitarian values and international culture in early-twentieth-century Europe. Passionately opposed to the First World War, Zweig wrote poetry, plays, and novels. But he was most famous for his biographies: shrewd psychological portraits of historical figures such as Magellan and Marie Antoinette.

After Hitler came to power in 1933, Zweig lived in exile until his death in 1942. Zweig's last work was The World of Yesterday *(1943), one of the truly fascinating autobiographies of the twentieth century. In the following passage, Zweig recalls the romantic experiences and the sexual separation of middle-class youth before the First World War.*

An elegant ball for upper-class youth, with debutantes, junior officers, and vigilant chaperons watching in the background. (State Russian Museum, St. Petersburg, Russia/The Bridgeman Art Library)

❝ During the eight years of our higher schooling [beyond grade school], something had occurred which was of great importance to each one of us: we ten-year-olds had grown into virile young men of sixteen, seventeen, and eighteen, and Nature began to assert its rights. . . . It did not take us long to discover that those authorities in whom we had previously confided — school, family, and public morals — manifested an astonishing insincerity in this matter of sex. But what is more, they also demanded secrecy and reserve from us in this connection. . . .

This "social morality," which on the one hand privately presupposed the existence of sexuality and its natural course, but on the other would not recognize it openly at any price, was doubly deceitful. While it winked one eye at a young man and even encouraged him with the other "to sow his wild oats," as the kindly language of the home put it, in the case of a woman it studiously shut both eyes and acted as if it were blind. That a man could experience desires, and was permitted to experience them, was silently admitted by custom. But to admit frankly that a woman could be subject to similar desires, or that creation for its eternal purposes also required a female polarity, would have transgressed the conception of the "sanctity of womanhood." In the pre-Freudian era, therefore, the axiom was agreed upon that a female person could have no physical desires as long as they had not been awakened by man, and that, obviously, was officially permitted only in marriage. But even in those moral times, in Vienna in particular, the air was full of dangerous erotic infection, and a girl of good family had to live in a completely sterilized atmosphere, from the day of her birth until the day when she left the altar on her husband's arm. In order to protect young girls, they were not left alone for a single moment. . . . Every book which they read was inspected, and above all else, young girls were constantly kept busy to divert their attention from any possible dangerous thoughts. They had to practise the piano, learn singing and drawing, foreign languages, and the history of literature and art. They were educated and overeducated. But while the aim was to make them as educated and as socially correct as possible, at the same time society anxiously took great pains that they should remain innocent of all natural things to a degree unthinkable today. A young girl of good family was not allowed to have any idea of how the male body was formed, or to know how children came into the world, for the angel was to enter into matrimony not only physically untouched, but completely "pure" spiritually as well. "Good breeding," for a young girl of that time, was identical with ignorance of life; and this ignorance ofttimes lasted for the rest of their lives. . . .

What possibilities actually existed for a young man of the middle-class world? In all the others, in the so-called lower classes, the problem was no problem at all. . . . In most of our Alpine villages the number of natural children greatly exceeded the legitimate ones. Among the proletariat, the worker, before he could get married, lived with another worker in free love. . . . It was only in our middle-class society that such a remedy as an early marriage was scorned. . . . And so there was an artificial interval of six, eight, or ten years between actual manhood and manhood as society accepted it; and in this interval the young man had to take care of his own "affairs" or adventures.

Those days did not give him too many opportunities. Only a very few particularly rich young men could afford the luxury of keeping a mistress, that is, taking an apartment and paying her expenses. And only a very few fortunate young men achieved the literary ideal of love of the times — the only one which it was permitted to describe in novels — an affair with a married woman. The others helped themselves for the most part with shopgirls and waitresses, and this offered little inner satisfaction. . . . But, generally speaking, prostitution was still the foundation of the erotic life outside of marriage; in a certain sense it constituted a dark underground vault over which rose the gorgeous structure of middle-class society with its faultless, radiant façade.

The present generation has hardly any idea of the gigantic extent of prostitution in Europe before the [First] World War. Whereas today it is as rare to meet a prostitute on the streets of a big city as it is to meet a wagon in the road, then the sidewalks were so sprinkled with women for sale that it was more difficult to avoid than to find them. To this was added the countless number of "closed houses," the night clubs, the cabarets, the dance parlours with their dancers and singers, and the bars with their "come-on" girls. At that time female wares were offered for sale at every hour and at every price. . . . And this was the same city, the same society, the same morality, that was indignant when young girls rode bicycles, and declared it a disgrace to the dignity of science when Freud in his calm, clear, and penetrating manner established truths that they did not wish to be true. The same world that so pathetically defended the purity of womanhood allowed this cruel sale of women, organized it, and even profited thereby.

We should not permit ourselves to be misled by sentimental novels or stories of that epoch. It was a bad time for youth. The young girls were hermetically locked up under the control of the family, hindered in their free bodily as well as intellectual development. The young men were forced to secrecy and reticence by a morality which fundamentally no one believed or obeyed. Unhampered, honest relationships — in other words, all that could have made youth happy and joyous according to the laws of Nature — were permitted only to the very few. 🙶

Source: Excerpts from pp. 67, 76–78, 81–83, 88 in *The World of Yesterday* by Stephan Zweig, translated by Helmut Ripperger. Copyright © 1943 by the Viking Press, Inc. Used with permission of Viking Penguin, a division of Penguin Group (USA), Inc. Copyright © William Verlag AG, Zurich (Switzerland). Reprinted with permission.

QUESTIONS FOR ANALYSIS

1. According to Zweig, how did the sex lives of young middle-class women and young middle-class men differ? What accounted for these differences?

2. What were the differences between the sex lives of the middle class and those of the "so-called lower classes"? What was Zweig's opinion of these differences?

3. Zweig ends with a value judgment: "It was a bad time for youth." Do you agree or disagree? Why?

to own property in her own name. Even the wages she might earn belonged to her husband. In France the Napoleonic Code (see Chapter 20) also enshrined the principle of female subordination and gave the wife few legal rights regarding property, divorce, and custody of the children.

With all women facing discrimination in education and employment and with middle-class women suffering especially from a lack of legal rights, there is little wonder that some women rebelled and began the long-continuing fight for equality of the sexes and the rights of women. Their struggle proceeded on two main fronts. First, following in the steps of women such as Mary Wollstonecraft (see Chapter 20), organizations founded by middle-class feminists campaigned for equal legal rights for women as well as access to higher education and professional employment. These middle-class feminists argued that unmarried women and middle-class widows with inadequate incomes simply had to have more opportunities to support themselves. Middle-class feminists also recognized that paid (as opposed to unpaid) work could relieve the monotony that some women found in their sheltered middle-class existence and put greater meaning into their lives.

In the later nineteenth century, these organizations scored some significant victories, such as the 1882 law giving English married women full property rights. More women gradually found professional and white-collar employment, especially after about 1880. But progress was slow and hard won. For example, in Germany before 1900, women were not admitted as fully registered students at a single university. Determined pioneers had to fight with tremendous fortitude to break through sexist barriers to advanced education and subsequent professional employment. (See "Individuals in Society: Franziska Tiburtius," page 737.) In the years before 1914, middle-class feminists increasingly focused their attention on political action and fought for the right for women to vote.

Women inspired by utopian and especially Marxian socialism (see Chapter 22) blazed a second path. Often scorning the programs of middle-class feminists, socialist women leaders argued that the liberation of working-class women would come only with the liberation of the entire working class through revolution. In the meantime, they championed the cause of working women and won some practical improvements, especially in Germany, where the socialist movement was most effectively organized. In a general way, these different approaches to women's issues reflected the diversity of classes in urban society.

The Importance of Homemaking

In recent years some scholars have been rethinking gender roles within the long-term development of consumer behavior and household economies. First, they identified an eighteenth-century "industrious revolu-

The Well-Managed Home This painting humanizes the concept of separate spheres and suggests how many homemakers with modest resources made their dwellings happy and appealing with hard work and housekeeping skills. With her clean laundry folded and fresh vegetables carried home beside her market baskets, this woman may soon be thinking of preparing dinner for her returning breadwinner. (V&A Images, London, Art Resource, NY)

tion" that saw many wives turning from work for household consumption — making the family's clothes, for example — to working for cash income to buy finished manufactured goods (see Chapter 19). In the industrial era, these scholars have reinterpreted the gender roles associated with separate spheres as rational consumer behavior. They argue that the "breadwinner-homemaker" household developed from about 1850 onward in order to improve the lives of all family members, especially in the working classes.[9] Thus husbands specialized in earning an adequate cash income — the "family wage" that labor unions demanded — and wives specialized in managing the home.

In doing so, the wife was able to produce desirable goods that simply could not be bought in a market, such as improved health, better eating habits, and better behavior. For example, higher wages from the breadwinner could buy more raw food, but only the homemaker's careful selection, processing, and cooking would allow the family to benefit from increased spending on food.

The homemaker's managerial skills thus enabled the couple to maximize household well-being.

Although the reinterpretation of late-nineteenth-century gender roles in terms of a breadwinner-homemaker partnership is a matter of debate, it fits rather well with some key aspects of family life after 1850. As women's horizons narrowed, and as home and children became the typical wife's main concerns, her control and influence there apparently became increasingly strong throughout Europe. Among the English working classes, it was the wife who generally determined how the family's money was spent. In many families, the husband gave all his earnings to his wife to manage, and he received only a small allowance in return. All the major domestic decisions, from the children's schooling and religious instruction to the selection of new furniture or a new apartment, were hers. In France women had even greater power in their assigned domain. One English feminist noted in 1908 that "though legally women occupy a much inferior status

INDIVIDUALS IN SOCIETY

WHY DID A SMALL NUMBER OF WOMEN in the late nineteenth century brave great odds and embark on professional careers? And how did a few of them manage to reach their objectives? The career and personal reflections of Franziska Tiburtius (tigh-bur-TEE-uhs), a pioneer in German medicine, suggest that talent, determination, and economic necessity were critical ingredients.*

Like many women of her time who would study and pursue professional careers, Franziska Tiburtius (1843–1927) was born into a property-owning family of modest means. The youngest of nine children on a small estate in northeastern Germany, the sensitive child wilted under a harsh governess but flowered with a caring teacher and became an excellent student. Graduating at sixteen and needing to support herself, Tiburtius had few opportunities. A young woman from a "proper" background could work as a governess or a teacher without losing her respectability and spoiling her matrimonial prospects, but that was about it. She tried both avenues. Working for six years as a governess in a noble family and no doubt learning that poverty was often one's fate in this genteel profession, she then turned to teaching. Called home from her studies in Britain in 1871 to care for her brother, who had contracted typhus as a field doctor in the Franco-Prussian War, she found her calling. She decided to become a medical doctor.

Supported by her family, Tiburtius's decision was truly audacious. In all Europe, only the University of Zurich in republican Switzerland accepted female students. Moreover, if it became known that she had studied medicine and failed, she would never get a job as a teacher. No parent would entrust a daughter to an "emancipated" radical who had carved up dead bodies! Although the male students at the university sometimes harassed the women with crude pranks, Tiburtius thrived. The revolution of the microscope and the discovery of microorganisms

was rocking Zurich, and she was fascinated by her studies. She became close friends with a fellow female medical student from Germany, Emilie Lehmus, with whom she would form a lifelong partnership in medicine. She did her internship with families of cottage workers around Zurich and loved her work.

Graduating at age thirty-three in 1876, Tiburtius went to stay with her brother—the doctor in Berlin. Though well qualified to practice, she ran into pervasive discrimination. She was not even permitted to take the state medical exams and could practice only as an unregulated (and unprofessional) "natural healer." But after persistent fighting with the bureaucrats, she was able to display her diploma and practice as "Franziska Tiburtius, M.D. University of Zurich." She and Lehmus were in business.

Soon the two women realized their dream and opened a clinic, subsidized by a wealthy industrialist, for women factory workers. The clinic filled a great need and was soon treating many patients. A room with beds for extremely sick women was later expanded into a second clinic.

Tiburtius and Lehmus became famous. For fifteen years, they were the only women doctors in all Berlin. An inspiration for a new generation of women, they added the wealthy to their thriving practice. But Tiburtius's clinics always concentrated on the poor, providing them with subsidized and up-to-date treatment. Talented, determined, and working with her partner, Tiburtius experienced fully the joys of personal achievement and useful service. Above all, Tiburtius overcame the tremendous barriers raised up against women seeking higher education and professional careers, and this provided an inspiring model for those who dared to follow.

Franziska Tiburtius, pioneering woman physician in Berlin. (Ullstein Bilderdienst/ The Granger Collection, New York)

QUESTIONS FOR ANALYSIS

1. Analyze Franziska Tiburtius's life. What lessons do you draw from it? How do you account for her bold action and success?
2. In what ways was Tiburtius's career related to improvements in health in urban society and to the expansion of the professions?

*This portrait draws on Conradine Lück, *Frauen: Neun Lebensschicksale* (Reutlingen: Ensslin & Laiblin, n.d.), pp. 153–185.

than men [in France], in practice they constitute the superior sex. They are the power behind the throne."[10]

Women ruled at home partly because running the urban household was a complicated, demanding, and valuable task. Twice-a-day food shopping, penny-pinching, economizing, and the growing crusade against dirt—not to mention child rearing—constituted a full-time occupation. Working yet another job for wages outside the home had limited appeal for most married women unless the earnings were essential for family survival. Still, many married women in the working classes did make a monetary contribution to family income by taking in a boarder or doing piecework at home in the sweated industries (see page 730). The wife also guided the home because a good deal of her effort was directed toward pampering her husband as he expected. In countless humble households, she saw that he had meat while she ate bread, that he relaxed by the fire while she did the dishes.

The woman's guidance of the household went hand in hand with the increased pride and emotional importance of home and family. The home she ran was idealized as a warm shelter in a hard and impersonal urban world. According to one historian, "'Home, sweet home,' first heard in the 1870s, had become 'almost a second national anthem.'"[11] By 1900 home and family were what life was all about for millions of people of all classes.

Married couples also developed stronger emotional ties to each other. Even in the comfortable classes, marriages in the late nineteenth century were based more on sentiment and sexual attraction than they had been earlier in the century, as money and financial calculation declined in importance. Affection and eroticism became more central to the couple after marriage. Gustave Droz (droh), whose bestselling *Mr., Mrs., and Baby* went through 121 editions between 1866 and 1884, saw love within marriage as the key to human happiness. He condemned men who made marriage sound dull and practical, men who were exhausted by prostitutes and rheumatism and who wanted their young wives to be little angels. He urged women to follow their hearts and marry men more nearly their own age:

> *A husband who is stately and a little bald is all right, but a young husband who loves you and who drinks out of your glass without ceremony, is better. Let him, if he ruffles your dress a little and places a kiss on your neck as he passes. Let him, if he undresses you after the ball, laughing like a fool. You have fine spiritual qualities, it is true, but your little body is not bad either and when one loves, one loves completely. Behind these follies lies happiness.*[12]

Many French marriage manuals of the late 1800s stressed that women had legitimate sexual needs, such as the "right to orgasm." Perhaps the French were a bit more enlightened in these matters than other nation-

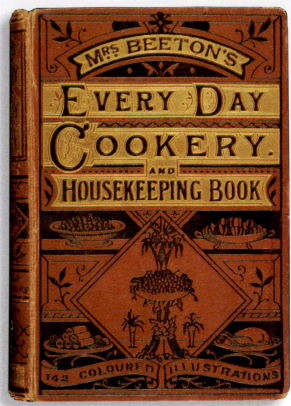

Every Day Cookery and Housekeeping Book The publication of cookbooks and household guides proliferated in the nineteenth century. Mrs. Beeton's bestselling guide offered women housekeeping tips and a wealth of recipes for the homemaker to share with her family. (Graphic Arts Division, Princeton University Library)

alities. But the rise of public socializing by couples in cafés and music halls as well as franker affection within the family suggests a more erotic, pleasurable intimate life for women throughout Western society. This, too, helped make the woman's role as mother and homemaker acceptable and even satisfying.

Child Rearing

Another striking sign of deepening emotional ties within the family was the growing love and concern that mothers gave their tiny infants. Because so many babies in preindustrial Western society died so early in life, mothers of that era often avoided making strong emotional commitments to newborns in order to shield themselves from recurrent heartbreak. Early emotional bonding and a willingness to make real sacrifices for the welfare of the infant were beginning to spread among the comfortable classes by the end of the eighteenth century, but the ordinary mother of modest means adopted new attitudes only as the nineteenth century progressed. The baby became more important, and women became better mothers.

" We want to get ahead, and our daughter should have things better than my wife and sisters did. "

—GERMAN SKILLED WORKER

Mothers increasingly breast-fed their infants, for example, rather than paying wet nurses to do so. Breast-feeding involved sacrifice—a temporary loss of freedom, if nothing else. Yet in an age when there was no good alternative to mother's milk, it saved lives. This surge of maternal feeling also gave rise to a wave of specialized books on child rearing and infant hygiene, such as Droz's phenomenally successful book. Droz urged fathers to get into the act and pitied those "who do not know how to roll around on the carpet, play at being a horse and a great wolf, and undress their baby."[13] Another sign, from France, of increased affection is that fewer illegitimate babies were abandoned as foundlings after about 1850. Moreover, the practice of swaddling disappeared completely. Instead, ordinary mothers allowed their babies freedom of movement and delighted in their spontaneity.

The loving care lavished on infants was matched by greater concern for older children and adolescents. They, too, were wrapped in the strong emotional ties of a more intimate and protective family. For one thing, European women began to limit the number of children they bore in order to care adequately for those they had. It was evident by the end of the nineteenth century that the birthrate was declining across Europe (Figure 23.3), and it continued to do so until after World War II. The Englishwoman who married in the 1860s, for example, had an average of about six children; her daughter marrying in the 1890s had only four; and her granddaughter marrying in the 1920s had only two or possibly three.

The most important reason for this revolutionary reduction in family size, in which the comfortable and well-educated classes took the lead, was parents' desire to improve their economic and social position and that of their children. Children were no longer an economic asset in the later nineteenth century. By having fewer youngsters, parents could give those they had valuable advantages, from music lessons and summer vacations to long, expensive university educations and suitable dowries. A young German skilled worker with only one child spoke for many in his class when he said, "We want to get ahead, and our daughter should have things better than my wife and sisters did."[14]

Thus the growing tendency of couples in the late nineteenth century to use a variety of contraceptive

Life Is Everywhere Emotional ties within ordinary families grew stronger in the nineteenth century, and parents gave their children more love and better care. Painted in 1888 by N. A. Yaroshenko, this outstanding example of Russia's realist tradition of a loving mother and child looking out the window of a railway car while a group of men look on approvingly reflects these new attitudes toward children. The emotional beauty of this painting is darkened, however, by the destination of these passengers: exile in Siberia. (Sovfoto)

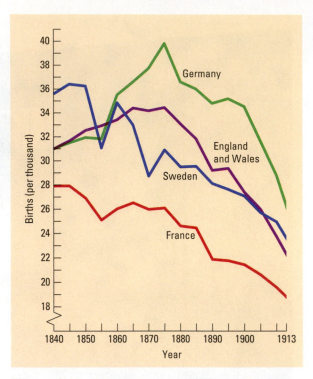

Figure 23.3 **The Decline of Birthrates in England and Wales, France, Germany, and Sweden, 1840–1913** Women had fewer babies for a variety of reasons, including the fact that their children were increasingly less likely to die before reaching adulthood. How does this compare with Figure 23.1 on page 721?

methods—rhythm method, withdrawal method, and mechanical devices—certainly reflected increased concern for children. Indeed, many parents, especially in the middle classes, probably became too concerned about their children, unwittingly subjecting them to an emotional pressure cooker of almost unbearable intensity. The result was that many children, especially adolescents, came to feel trapped and in need of greater independence.

Prevailing biological and medical theories led parents to believe in the possibility that their own emotional characteristics were passed on to their offspring and that they were thus directly responsible for any abnormality in a child. The moment the child was conceived was thought to be of enormous importance for its future health and vitality, and thus women were warned against getting pregnant during a time of illness or unhappiness. The youthful "sexual excess" of the father might also curse future generations. Although this was true in the case of syphilis, which could be transmitted to unborn children, the rigid determinism of such views left little scope for the child's individual development.

Another area of excessive parental concern was the sexual behavior of their children. Masturbation was

viewed with horror, for it represented an act of independence and even defiance. Diet, clothing, games, and sleeping were carefully regulated. Girls were discouraged from riding horses and bicycling because rhythmic friction simulated masturbation. Boys were dressed in trousers with shallow and widely separated pockets.

Attempts to repress the child's sexuality were a source of unhealthy tension, often made worse by the rigid division of gender roles within the family. It was widely believed that mother and child loved each other easily but that relations between father and child were necessarily difficult and often tragic. The father was a stranger; his world of business was far removed from the maternal world of spontaneous affection. Moreover, the father was demanding, often expecting the child to succeed where he himself had failed and making his love conditional on achievement.

Sigmund Freud (1856–1939), the Viennese founder of psychoanalysis, formulated the most striking analysis of the explosive dynamics of the family, particularly the middle-class family in the late nineteenth century. A physician by training, Freud began his career treating mentally ill patients. He noted that the hysteria of his patients appeared to originate in bitter early childhood experiences wherein the child had been obliged to repress strong feelings. When these painful experiences were recalled and reproduced under hypnosis or through the patient's free association of ideas, the patient could be brought to understand the basis of his or her unhappiness and eventually deal with it.

One of Freud's most influential ideas concerned the tensions resulting from the son's instinctive competition with the father for the mother's love and affection. More generally, Freud postulated that much of human behavior is motivated by unconscious emotional needs whose nature and origins are kept from conscious awareness by various mental devices he called defense mechanisms. Freud concluded that much unconscious psychological energy is sexual energy, which is repressed and precariously controlled by rational thinking and moral rules. If Freud exaggerated the sexual and familial roots of adult behavior, that exaggeration was itself a reflection of the tremendous emotional intensity of family life in the late nineteenth century.

The working classes probably had more avenues of escape from such tensions than did the middle classes. Unlike their middle-class counterparts, who remained economically dependent on their families until a long education was finished or a proper marriage secured, working-class boys and girls went to work when they reached adolescence. Earning wages on their own, they could bargain with their parents for greater independence within the household by the time they were sixteen or seventeen. If they were unsuccessful, they could and did leave home to live cheaply as paying lodgers in other working-class homes. Thus the young person from the working classes broke away from the family more easily when emotional ties became oppressive. In the twentieth century, middle-class youths would follow this lead.

Science and Thought

What major changes in science and thought reflected and influenced the new urban society? ■

Major changes in Western science and thought accompanied the emergence of urban society. Several aspects of these complex intellectual developments stand out as especially significant. First, scientific knowledge in many areas expanded rapidly. Breakthroughs in chemistry, physics, and electricity profoundly influenced the Western worldview and spurred the creation of new products and whole industries. The natural and social sciences were also established as highly respected fields of study. In addition, between about the 1840s and the 1890s, European literature underwent a shift from soaring romanticism to tough-minded realism.

The Triumph of Science in Industry

As the pace of scientific advancements quickened and resulted in greater practical benefits, science exercised growing influence on human thought. The intellectual achievements of the scientific revolution (see Chapter 17) had resulted in few such benefits, and theoretical knowledge had also played a relatively small role in the Industrial Revolution in England (see Chapter 21). But breakthroughs in industrial technology in the late eighteenth century enormously stimulated basic scientific inquiry as researchers sought to explain theoretically how such things as steam engines and blast furnaces actually worked. The result was an explosive growth of fundamental scientific discoveries from the 1830s onward. And in contrast to earlier periods, these theoretical discoveries were increasingly transformed into material improvements for the general population.

A perfect example of the translation of better scientific knowledge into practical human benefits was the work of Louis Pasteur and his followers in biology and the medical sciences (see page 721). Another was the development of the branch of physics known as **thermodynamics**. Building on Isaac Newton's laws of mechanics and on studies of steam engines, thermodynamics investigated the relationship between heat and mechanical energy. By midcentury, physicists had formulated the fundamental laws of thermodynamics, which were then applied to mechanical engineering, chemical processes,

and many other fields. The law of conservation of energy held that different forms of energy—such as heat, electricity, and magnetism—could be converted but neither created nor destroyed. Nineteenth-century thermodynamics demonstrated that the physical world was governed by firm, unchanging laws.

Chemistry and electricity were two other fields characterized by extremely rapid scientific progress. And in both fields, "science was put in the service of industry," as the influential economist Alfred Marshall (1842–1924) argued at the time. Chemists devised ways of measuring the atomic weight of different elements, and in 1869 the Russian chemist Dmitri Mendeleev (men-duh-LAY-uhf) (1834–1907) codified the rules of chemistry in the periodic law and the periodic table. Chemistry was subdivided into many specialized branches, such as organic chemistry—the study of the compounds of carbon. Applying theoretical insights gleaned from this new field, researchers in large German chemical companies discovered ways of transforming the dirty, useless coal tar that accumulated in coke ovens into beautiful, expensive synthetic dyes for the world of fashion. German production of synthetic dyes soared, and by 1900 German chemical companies controlled 90 percent of world production.

Electricity, a scientific curiosity in 1800, was totally transformed by a century of tremendous technological advancement. It became a commercial form of energy, first used in communications (the telegraph and underwater cables), then in electro-chemistry (refining aluminum, for example), and finally in central power generation (for lighting, transportation, and industrial motors). By 1890, the internal combustion engine fueled by petroleum was an emerging competitor.

The successful application of scientific research in the fast-growing electrical and organic chemical industries between 1880 and 1913 provided a model for other industries. Systematic "R & D"—research and development—was born in the late nineteenth century. Above all, the burst of industrial creativity and technological innovation, which is often called the **second industrial revolution**, promoted strong economic growth in the later nineteenth century. This ongoing economic development was a leading force driving the urban improvement and the rising standard of living considered in this chapter.

The triumph of science and technology had three other significant consequences. First, though ordinary citizens continued to lack detailed scientific knowledge, everyday experience and innumerable articles in

> **thermodynamics** A branch of physics built on Newton's laws of mechanics that investigated the relationship between heat and mechanical energy.
>
> **second industrial revolution** The burst of industrial creativity and technological innovation that promoted strong economic growth toward the end of the nineteenth century.

Madrid in 1900 This wistful painting of a Spanish square on a rainy day, by Enrique Martinez Cubells y Ruiz (1874–1917), includes a revealing commentary on how scientific discoveries transformed urban life. Coachmen wait atop their expensive hackney cabs for a wealthy clientele, while modern electric streetcars that carry the masses converge on the square from all directions. In this way the development of electricity brought improved urban transportation and enabled the city to expand to the suburbs. (Museo Municipal, Madrid/The Bridgeman Art Library)

newspapers and magazines impressed the importance of science on the popular mind. Second, as science became more prominent in popular thinking, the philosophical implications of science formulated in the Enlightenment spread to broad sections of the population. Natural processes appeared to be determined by rigid laws, leaving little room for either divine intervention or human will. Yet scientific and technical advances had also fed the Enlightenment's optimistic faith in human progress, which now appeared endless and automatic to many middle-class minds. Third, the methods of science acquired unrivaled prestige after 1850. For many, the union of careful experiment and abstract theory was the only reliable route to truth and objective reality. The "unscientific" intuitions of poets and the revelations of saints seemed hopelessly inferior.

Darwin and Natural Selection

Scientific research also progressed rapidly outside of the world of industry and technology, sometimes putting forth direct challenges to traditional beliefs. In geology, for example, Charles Lyell (1797–1875) effectively discredited the long-standing view that the earth's surface had been formed by short-lived cataclysms, such as biblical floods and earthquakes. Instead, according to Lyell's principle of uniformitarianism, the same geological processes that are at work today slowly formed the earth's surface over an immensely long time. Similarly, the evolutionary view of biological development, first proposed by the Greek Anaximander in the sixth century B.C.E., re-emerged in a more modern form in the work of French naturalist Jean Baptiste Lamarck (1744–1829). Lamarck asserted that all forms of life had arisen through a long process of continuous adjustment to the environment.

Lamarck's work was flawed—he believed that the characteristics parents acquired in the course of their lives could be inherited by their children—and was not accepted, but it helped prepare the way for Charles Darwin (1809–1882), the most influential of all nineteenth-century evolutionary thinkers. As the official naturalist on a five-year scientific cruise to Latin America and the South Pacific beginning in 1831, Darwin carefully collected specimens of the different animal species he encountered on the voyage. Back in England, convinced by fossil evidence and by his friend Lyell that the earth and life on it were immensely ancient, Darwin came to doubt the general belief in a special divine creation of each species of animal. Instead, he concluded, all life had gradually evolved from a common ancestral origin in an unending "struggle for survival." After long hesitation, Darwin published his research, which immediately attracted wide attention.

Darwin's great originality lay in suggesting precisely how biological evolution might have occurred. His theory is summarized in the title of his work *On the Origin of Species by the Means of Natural Selection* (1859). Decisively influenced by the gloomy theory of Thomas Malthus (MAL-thuhs) that populations naturally grow faster than their food supplies (see Chapter 21), Darwin argued that chance differences among the members of a given species help some survive while others die. Thus the variations that prove useful in the struggle for survival are selected naturally, and they gradually spread to the entire species through reproduction. Darwin did not explain why such variations occurred in the first place, and not until the early twentieth century did the study of genetics and the concept of mutation provide some answers.

Darwin's theory had a powerful and many-sided influence on European thought and the European middle classes. He was hailed as the great scientist par excellence, the "Newton of biology," who had revealed once again the powers of objective science, and his findings had a significant impact on the young discipline of social science.

Social Science

From the 1830s onward, many thinkers tried to apply the objective methods of science to the study of society. Using the critical thinking methods of the eighteenth-

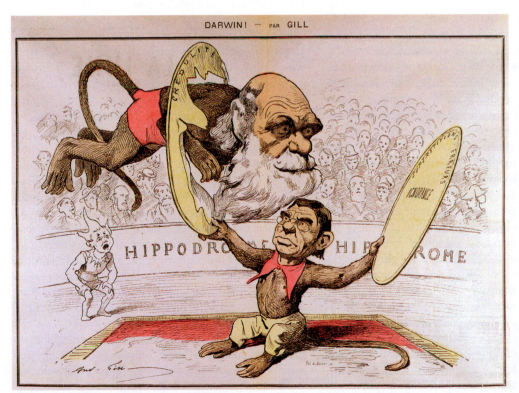

Satirizing Darwin's Ideas
The heated controversies over Darwin's theory of evolution also spawned innumerable jokes and cartoons. This cartoon depicts a bearded Charles Darwin and the French philosopher and atheistic materialist Emile Littré performing as monkeys in a circus as they supposedly break through ignorance and superstition. (Musée de la Ville de Paris, Musée Carnavalet/Archives Charmet/The Bridgeman Art Library)

century philosophes (see Chapter 17), the new "social scientists" studied massive sets of numerical data that governments had begun to collect on everything from children to crime and from population to prostitution. Social scientists developed new statistical methods to analyze these facts "scientifically" and supposedly to test their theories. As a result, the systems of the leading nineteenth-century social scientists were typically more unified, all-encompassing, and dogmatic than those of the philosophes. Karl Marx was a prime example (see Chapter 22).

Another extremely influential system builder was French philosopher Auguste Comte (kont) (1798–1857). Initially a disciple of the utopian socialist Saint-Simon (see Chapter 22), Comte wrote the six-volume *System of Positive Philosophy* (1830–1842), which was largely overlooked during the romantic era. But when the political failures of 1848 completed the swing to realism, Comte's philosophy came into its own. Its influence has remained great to this day.

Comte postulated that all intellectual activity progresses through predictable stages:

> *The great fundamental law . . . is this:—that each of our leading conceptions—each branch of our knowledge—passes successively through three different theoretical conditions: the Theological, or fictitious; the Metaphysical, or abstract; and the Scientific, or positive. . . . The first is the necessary point of departure of human understanding, and the third is the fixed and definitive state. The second is merely a transition.*[15]

By way of example, Comte noted that the prevailing explanation of cosmic patterns had shifted, as knowledge of astronomy developed, from the will of God (the theological) to the will of an orderly nature (the metaphysical) to the rule of unchanging laws (the scientific). Later, this same intellectual progression took place in increasingly complex fields—physics, chemistry, and, finally, the study of society. Comte believed that by applying the scientific method, also called the positivist method, his new discipline of sociology would soon discover the eternal laws of human relations. This colossal achievement would in turn enable expert social scientists to impose a disciplined harmony and well-being on less enlightened citizens. Dismissing the "fictions" of traditional religions, Comte became the chief priest of the religion of science and rule by experts.

Comte's stages of knowledge exemplify the nineteenth-century fascination with the idea of **evolution** and dynamic development so

prominent in Darwin's theory of natural selection. Thinkers in many fields, such as the romantic historians and "scientific" Marxists, shared and applied this basic concept. Reinforced by Darwin's findings, the teachings of secularists such as Comte and Marx scornfully dismissed religious belief in favor of agnostic or atheistic materialism. In the great cities, especially, religion was on the defensive.

Many thinkers went a step further and applied Darwin's theory of biological evolution to human affairs. English philosopher Herbert Spencer (1820–1903) saw the human race as driven forward to ever-greater specialization and progress by a brutal economic struggle that determined the "survival of the fittest." The poor were the ill-fated weak; the prosperous were the chosen strong. Not surprisingly, Spencer and other **Social Darwinists** were especially popular with the upper middle class.

Realism in Literature

In literature, the key themes of **realism** emerged in the 1840s and continued to dominate Western culture and style until the 1890s. Realist writers believed that literature should depict life exactly as it was. Forsaking poetry for prose and the personal, emotional viewpoint of the romantics for strict, scientific objectivity, the realists simply observed and recorded—content to let the facts speak for themselves.

The major realist writers focused their extraordinary powers of observation to create fiction based on contemporary everyday life. Emphatically rejecting the romantic search for the exotic and the sublime, they energetically pursued the typical and the commonplace. Beginning with a dissection of the middle classes, from which most of them sprang, many realists eventually focused on the working classes, especially the urban working classes, which had been neglected in imaginative literature before this time. The realists put a microscope to many unexplored and taboo subjects—sex, strikes, violence, alcoholism—and hastened to report that slums and factories teemed with savage behavior. Many shocked middle-class critics denounced realism as ugly sensationalism wrapped provocatively in pseudo-scientific declarations and crude language.

Unlike the romantics, who had gloried in individual freedom and an unlimited universe, realists were strict determinists. Human beings, like atoms, were components of the physical world, and all human actions were caused by unalterable natural laws. Heredity and environment determined human behavior; good and evil were merely social conventions.

The realist movement began in France, where romanticism had never been completely dominant, and three of its greatest practitioners—Balzac, Flaubert, and Zola—were French. Honoré de Balzac (1799–1850)

evolution The idea, applied by thinkers in many fields, that stresses gradual change and continuous adjustment.

Social Darwinists A group of thinkers who applied the theory of biological evolution to human affairs and saw the human race as driven by an unending economic struggle that would determine the survival of the fittest.

realism A literary movement that stressed the depiction of life as it actually was.

spent thirty years writing a vastly ambitious panorama of postrevolutionary French life. Known collectively as *The Human Comedy*, this series of nearly one hundred books vividly portrays more than two thousand characters from virtually all sectors of French society. Balzac pictures urban society as grasping, amoral, and brutal. In *Le Père Goriot* (1835), the hero, a poor student from the provinces, eventually surrenders his idealistic integrity to feverish ambition and society's pervasive greed.

Madame Bovary (1857), the masterpiece of Gustave Flaubert (floh-BEHR) (1821–1880), is far narrower in scope than Balzac's work, but unparalleled in its depth and accuracy of psychological insight. Unsuccessfully prosecuted as an outrage against public morality and religion, Flaubert's carefully crafted novel tells the ordinary, even banal, story of a frustrated middle-class housewife who has an adulterous love affair and is betrayed by her lover. Without moralizing, Flaubert portrays the provincial middle class as petty, smug, and hypocritical.

Émile Zola (1840–1902) was most famous for his seamy, animalistic view of working-class life. But he also wrote gripping, carefully researched stories featuring the stock exchange, the big department store, and the army, as well as urban slums and bloody coal strikes. Like many later realists, Zola sympathized with socialism, a sympathy evident in his overpowering novel *Germinal* (1885).

Realism quickly spread beyond France. In England, Mary Ann Evans (1819–1880), who wrote under the pen name George Eliot, brilliantly achieved a more deeply felt, less sensational kind of realism. Her great novel *Middlemarch: A Study of Provincial Life* (1871–1872) examines masterfully the ways in which people are shaped by their social medium as well as their own inner strivings, conflicts, and moral choices. Thomas Hardy (1840–1928) was more in the Zola tradition. His novels, such as *Tess of the D'Urbervilles* (1891) and *The Return of the Native* (1878), depict men and women frustrated and crushed by fate and bad luck.

The greatest Russian realist Count Leo Tolstoy (1828–1910) combined realism in description and character development with an atypical moralizing, which came to dominate his later work. Tolstoy's greatest work is *War and Peace* (1864–1869), a monumental novel set against the historical background of Napoleon's invasion of Russia in 1812. Tolstoy probed deeply into the lives of a multitude of unforgettable characters, such as the ill-fated Prince Andrei; the shy, fumbling Pierre; and the enchanting Natasha. Tolstoy went to great pains to develop his fatalistic theory of history, which regards free will as an illusion and the achievements of even the greatest leaders as only the channeling of historical necessity. Yet Tolstoy's central message is one that most of the people discussed in this chapter would have readily

Edouard Manet, *Emile Zola* The young novelist's sensitivity and strength of character permeate this famous portrait by the great French painter Edouard Manet. Focusing on nuances and subtle variations, Manet was at first denounced by the critics, and after Zola lost a newspaper job defending Manet they became close friends. Manet was strongly influenced by Japanese prints, seen in the background. (Erich Lessing/Art Resource, NY)

accepted: human love, trust, and everyday family ties are life's enduring values.

Thoroughgoing realism (or "naturalism," as it was often called) arrived late in the United States, most arrestingly in the work of Theodore Dreiser (1871–1945). His first novel, *Sister Carrie* (1900), a story of an ordinary farm girl who does well by going wrong in Chicago, so outraged conventional morality that the publisher withdrew the book. The United States subsequently became a bastion of literary realism in the twentieth century after the movement had faded away in Europe.

LOOKING BACK LOOKING AHEAD

WHEN EUROPEANS in northwestern Europe looked back at the economic and social landscape in the early twentieth century, they had good reason to feel that the promise of the Industrial Revolution was being realized. The dark days of urban squalor and brutal working hours had given way after 1850 to a gradual rise in the standard of living for all classes. Scientific discoveries were combining with the applied technology of public health and industrial production to save lives and drive continued economic growth.

Moreover, social and economic advance seemed to be matched by progress in the political sphere. The years following the dramatic failure of the revolutions of 1848 saw the creation of unified nation-states in Italy and Germany, and after 1870 nationalism and the nation-state reigned in Europe. Although the rise of nationalism created tensions among the European countries, these tensions would not explode until 1914 and the outbreak of the First World War. Instead, the most aggressive and destructive aspects of European nationalism found their initial outlet in the final and most powerful surge of Western overseas expansion. Thus Europe, transformed by industrialization and nationalism, rushed after 1875 to seize territory and build new or greatly expanded authoritarian empires in Asia and Africa.

CHAPTER REVIEW

■ What was life like in the cities, and how did urban life change in the nineteenth century? (p. 718)

The revolution in industry had a drastic impact on the urban environment. Because it was economically advantageous to locate new industrial factories and offices in urban areas, urban populations grew at unprecedented rates. Living conditions sharply declined, largely because governments were slow to react and the people, ignorant of the connection between cleanliness and good health, were content to live in squalor. When governments finally took the initiative in the mid-nineteenth century to clean up the cities, general public health improved greatly. Society also benefited from scientific advancements. A new understanding of germ control, improved medical techniques, and new vaccines all led to lower mortality rates in urban areas. Finally, better urban planning and new public transportation systems relieved overcrowding.

■ What did the emergence of urban industrial society mean for rich and poor and those in between? (p. 723)

At the top levels of society, the upper middle class expanded its wealth and power as it emulated the aristocracy in material acquisitions and leisure pursuits. The middle and lower middle classes also expanded and gained income, and their occupations became much more diverse with the Industrial Revolution. The working classes saw an overall improvement in their economic condition, but they still struggled, especially the lower working classes. Large numbers of poor women in particular continued to labor as workers in sweated industries and as domestic servants in order to satisfy the demands of their masters in the servant-keeping classes. The nineteenth century also witnessed a decline in church attendance among urban workers, who may have equated organized religion with the old conservative regimes in an era of progress.

■ How did working-class and middle-class families change as they coped with the challenges and the opportunities of the developing urban civilization? (p. 732)

Major changes in family life accompanied the more complex and diversified class system. Especially among the working classes, family life became more stable, more loving, and less mercenary as society generally improved its standard of living. Among the middle classes, marrying continued to serve as a means for economic gain, and emotional benefits were slower to come. At the same time gender roles for men and women of all classes became sharply defined and rigidly separate. The working class increasingly adopted a breadwinner-homemaker division of labor, while middle-class women lacked important legal rights and were frozen out of professional employment. The number of children per family dropped steadily in the second half of the eighteenth century, as parental love and concern for their offspring tended to strengthen.

■ What major changes in science and thought reflected and influenced the new urban society? (p. 741)

The scientific discoveries of the nineteenth century had many practical benefits for the general population. New vaccines, synthetic fabric dyes, and the myriad applications of electricity all contributed to economic growth and a better quality of life for urban society. In turn, ordinary people gained a new awareness and appreciation of science, which began to chip away at their traditional religious understanding of the world. Darwin's widely hailed theory of natural selection, for example, challenged the general belief in divine creation. New social scientists such as Marx and Comte rejected religion and sought to analyze human behavior based on objective statistics. In the realm of literature, novelists such as Balzac and Zola abandoned romantic idealism and wrote about the harsh realities of life's struggles. More generally, literary realism reflected Western society's growing faith in science, material progress, and evolutionary thinking.

Suggested Reading

Anderson, Bonnie S., and Judith P. Zinsser. *A History of Their Own: Women in Europe from Prehistory to the Present*, vol. 2, rev. ed. 2000. An excellent wide-ranging survey.

Barnes, David S. *The Great Stink of Paris and the Nineteenth-Century Struggle Against Filth and Germs*. 2006. An outstanding introduction to sanitary developments and attitudes toward public health.

Coontz, Stephanie. *Marriage, a History: From Obedience to Intimacy, or How Love Conquered Marriage*. 2005. A lively investigation of the historical background to current practice.

De Vries, Jan. *The Industrious Revolution: Consumer Behavior and the Household Economy, 1850 to the Present*. 2008. A major interpretative analysis focusing on married couples and their strategies.

Gottlieb, Beatrice. *The Family in the Western World*. 1993. A wide-ranging synthesis.

Hunt, Tristram. *Building Jerusalem: The Rise and Fall of the Victorian City*. 2006. Considers British urban life and civic pride.

Maynes, Mary Jo. *Taking the Hard Road: Life Course in French and German Workers' Biographies in the Era of Industrialization*. 1995. Includes fascinating stories that provide insight into how workers saw themselves.

Olsen, Donald J. *The City as a Work of Art: London, Paris, and Vienna*. 1988. An architectural feast.

Perrot, Michelle, ed. *A History of Private Life*. 1990. A fascinating multivolume work.

Pilbeam, Pamela. *The Middle Classes in Europe, 1789–1914: France, Germany, Italy, and Russia*. 1990. A stimulating introduction to middle-class life.

Schmiechen, James, and Kenneth Carls. *The British Market Hall: A Social and Architectural History*. 1999. A pathbreaking and beautiful study of Britain's enclosed markets and how they revolutionized the sale of food.

Thompson, F. M. L. *The Rise of Respectable Society: A Social History of Victorian Britain, 1830–1900*. 1986. A laudable survey.

Weiner, Jonathan. *The Beak of the Finch: The Story of Evolution in Our Time*. 1994. A prize-winning, highly readable account of Darwin and evolution.

Notes

1. S. Marcus, "Reading the Illegible," in *The Victorian City: Images and Realities*, ed. H. J. Dyos and Michael Wolff, vol. 1 (London: Routledge & Kegan Paul, 1973), p. 266.

2. Quoted in E. Chadwick, *Report on the Sanitary Condition of the Labouring Population of Great Britain*, ed. M. W. Flinn (Edinburgh: University of Edinburgh Press, 1965; original publication, 1842), pp. 315–316.

3. J. McKay, *Tramways and Trolleys: The Rise of Urban Mass Transport in Europe* (Princeton, N.J.: Princeton University Press, 1976), p. 81.

4. Quoted in R. P. Neuman, "The Sexual Question and Social Democracy in Imperial Germany," *Journal of Social History* 7 (Winter 1974): 276.

5. Quoted in J. A. Banks, "The Contagion of Numbers," in *The Victorian City: Images and Realities*, ed. H. J. Dyos and Michael Wolff, vol. 1 (London: Routledge & Kegan Paul, 1973), p. 112.

6. Quoted in R. Roberts, *The Classic Slum: Salford Life in the First Quarter of the Century* (Manchester, U.K.: University of Manchester Press, 1971), p. 95.

7. Quoted in T. Zeldin, *France, 1848–1945*, vol. 1 (Oxford, U.K.: Clarendon Press, 1973), p. 288.

8. For a thorough discussion see S. Marcus, *The Other Victorians: A Study of Sexuality and Pornography in Mid-Nineteenth-Century England* (New York: Basic Books, 1966).

9. See the pioneering work of J. de Vries, *The Industrious Revolution: Consumer Behavior and the Household Economy* (Cambridge, U.K.: Cambridge University Press, 2008), especially pp. 186–237.

10. Quoted in Zeldin, *France*, p. 346.

11. Roberts, *The Classic Slum*, p. 35.

12. Quoted in Zeldin, *France*, p. 295.

13. Quoted ibid., p. 328.

14. Quoted in Neuman, "The Sexual Question," p. 281.

15. A. Comte, *The Positive Philosophy of Auguste Comte*, trans. H. Martineau, vol. 1 (London: J. Chapman, 1853), pp. 1–2.

Key Terms

utilitarianism (p. 719)

germ theory (p. 721)

labor aristocracy (p. 727)

sweated industries (p. 730)

thermodynamics (p. 741)

second industrial revolution (p. 741)

evolution (p. 744)

Social Darwinists (p. 744)

realism (p. 744)

For practice quizzes and other study tools, visit the Online Study Guide at **bedfordstmartins.com/mckaywest**.

For primary sources from this period, see ***Sources of Western Society*, Second Edition**.

For Web sites, images, and documents related to topics in this chapter, visit Make History at **bedfordstmartins.com/mckaywest**.

24

The Age of Nationalism

1850–1914

The revolutions of 1848 closed one era and opened another. Urban industrial society began to take a strong hold on the continent and in the young United States, as it already had in Great Britain. Internationally, the repressive peace and diplomatic stability of Metternich's time were replaced by a period of war and rapid change. In thought and culture, exuberant romanticism gave way to hardheaded realism. In the Atlantic economy, the hard years of the 1840s were followed by good times and prosperity throughout most of the 1850s and 1860s. Perhaps most important of all, Western society progressively developed, for better or worse, a new and effective organizing principle capable of coping with the many-sided challenge of the dual revolution and the emerging urban civilization. That principle was nationalism — dedication to an identification with the nation-state.

The triumph of nationalism is an enormously significant historical development that was by no means completely predictable. After all, nationalism had been a powerful force since at least 1789, but it had repeatedly failed to realize its goals, most spectacularly in 1848. Yet by 1914 nationalism had become in one way or another an almost universal faith in Europe and in the United States, a faith that had evolved to appeal not only to predominately middle-class liberals but also to the broad masses of society. ■

Cameraphoto Arte, Venice/Art Resource, NY

Life in the Age of Nationalism. Committed to Italian unity, the people of Venice cheer their uplifted nationalist leader, Daniel Manin, during the unsuccessful revolution of 1848. Scenes like this would be validated in the decades to come as nationalism came to predominate in all levels of society across Europe.

CHAPTER PREVIEW

Napoleon III in France
■ How did Napoleon III seek to reconcile popular and conservative forces in an authoritarian nation-state?

Nation Building in Italy and Germany
■ How did the process of unification in Italy and Germany create conservative nation-states?

Nation Building in the United States
■ In what ways did the United States experience nation building?

The Modernization of Russia and the Ottoman Empire
■ What steps did Russia and the Ottoman Turks take toward modernization, and how successful were they?

The Responsive National State, 1871–1914
■ Why after 1871 did ordinary citizens feel a growing loyalty to their governments?

Marxism and the Socialist Movement
■ Why did the socialist movement grow, and how revolutionary was it?

Napoleon III in France

How did Napoleon III seek to reconcile popular and conservative forces in an authoritarian nation-state? ∎

Early nationalism was generally liberal and idealistic and often democratic and radical as well. In the nineteenth century the ideas of nationhood and popular sovereignty posed a fearful revolutionary threat to conservatives like Metternich. Yet from the vantage point of the twenty-first century, it is clear that nationalism wears many masks: it may be narrowly liberal or democratic and radical, as it was for Giuseppe Mazzini and Jules Michelet (see Chapter 22). Yet nationalism can also flourish in dictatorial states, which may be conservative, fascist, or communist, and which may impose social and economic changes from above. Napoleon I's France had already combined national feeling with authoritarian rule. Significantly, it was Napoleon's nephew, Louis Napoleon, who revived and extended this merger.

France's Second Republic

Although Louis Napoleon Bonaparte had played no part in French politics before 1848, universal male suffrage and widespread popular support gave him three times as many votes as the four other presidential candidates combined in the French presidential election of December 1848. This outcome occurred for several reasons. First, Louis Napoleon had the great name of his uncle, whom romantics had transformed from a dictator into a demigod as they created a Napoleonic legend after 1820. Second, as Karl Marx stressed at the time, middle-class and peasant property owners feared the socialist challenge of urban workers, and they wanted a tough ruler to provide protection. Third, in late 1848 Louis Napoleon had a positive "program" for France, which had been elaborated in widely circulated pamphlets before the election and which guided him through his long reign.

Above all, Louis Napoleon believed that the government should represent the people and that it should try hard to help them economically. But how were these tasks to be done? Parliaments and political parties were not the answer, according to Louis Napoleon. French politicians represented special-interest groups, particularly middle-class ones. The answer was a strong, even authoritarian, national leader, like the first Napoleon, a reformer who would serve all the people, rich and poor. This leader would be linked to each citizen by direct democracy, his sovereignty uncorrupted by politicians and legislative bodies. These political ideas meshed well with Louis Napoleon's vision of national unity and social progress. The state and its leader had a sacred duty to

Paris in the Second Empire The flash and glitter of unprecedented prosperity in the Second Empire come alive in this vibrant contemporary painting. Writers and intellectuals chat with elegant women and trade witticisms with financiers and government officials at the Café Tortoni, a favorite rendezvous for fashionable society. Horse-drawn omnibuses with open top decks mingle with cabs and private carriages on the broad new boulevard. (Lauros/ Giraudon/The Bridgeman Art Library)

provide jobs and stimulate the economy, which would benefit all classes. Louis Napoleon's political and social ideas were at least vaguely understood by large numbers of French peasants and workers in December 1848. To the many common people who voted for him, he appeared to be a strong man and a forward-looking champion of their interests.

Elected to a four-year term by an overwhelming majority, President Louis Napoleon had to share power with a conservative National Assembly, according to the constitution. With some misgivings, he signed a bill to increase greatly the role of the Catholic Church in primary and secondary education, and he approved a law depriving many poor people of the right to vote. He took these conservative measures for two main reasons: he wanted the Assembly to vote funds to pay his personal debts, and he wanted to change the constitution so he could run for a second term.

But in 1851, after the Assembly failed to cooperate, Louis Napoleon began to conspire with key army officers. On December 2, 1851, he illegally dismissed the Assembly and seized power in a coup d'état. There was some armed resistance in Paris and widespread insurrection in the countryside in southern France, but these protests were crushed by the army. Restoring universal male suffrage and claiming to stand above the bickering and divisive politicians, Louis Napoleon called on the French people, as the first Napoleon had done, to legalize his actions. They did: 92 percent voted to make him president for ten years. A year later, 97 percent in a plebiscite made him hereditary emperor.

Napoleon III's Second Empire

Louis Napoleon—who was now proclaimed Emperor Napoleon III—experienced both success and failure between 1852 and 1870. His greatest success was with the economy, particularly in the 1850s. His government encouraged the new investment banks and massive railroad construction that were at the heart of the Industrial Revolution on the continent (see Chapter 21). The government also fostered general economic expansion through an ambitious program of public works, which included rebuilding Paris to improve the urban environment (see Chapter 23). The profits of business people soared with prosperity, the wages of workers more than kept up with inflation, and unemployment declined greatly.

Chronology

1839–1876	Western-style reforms in Ottoman Empire
1852–1870	Reign of Napoleon III in France
1859–1870	Unification of Italy
1861	Freeing of Russian serfs
1861–1865	U.S. Civil War
1866	Austro-Prussian War
1870–1871	Franco-Prussian War
1870–1878	Kulturkampf, Bismarck's attack on Catholic Church
1873	Stock market crash spurs renewed anti-Semitism in central and eastern Europe
1880s	Educational reforms in France create more secular public schools
1880s–1890s	Widespread return to protectionism among European states
1883	First social security laws to help workers in Germany
1890–1900	Massive industrialization surge in Russia
1905	Revolution in Russia
1906–1914	Social reform in Great Britain
1908	Young Turks in power in Ottoman Empire

Louis Napoleon always hoped that economic progress would reduce social and political tensions. This hope was at least partially realized. Until the mid-1860s there was considerable support from France's most dissatisfied group, the urban workers. Napoleon III's regulation of pawnshops and his support of credit unions and better housing for the working classes were evidence of helpful reform and positive concern in the 1850s. In the 1860s, he granted workers the right to form unions and the right to strike—important economic rights denied by earlier governments.

At first, political power remained in the hands of the emperor. He alone chose his ministers, and they had great freedom of action. At the same time, Napoleon III restricted but did not abolish the Assembly. Members were elected by universal male suffrage every six years, and Louis Napoleon and his government took the parliamentary elections very seriously. They tried to entice notable people, even those who had opposed the regime, to stand as government candidates in order to expand the base of support. Moreover, the government used its officials and appointed mayors to spread the word that the election of the government's candidates—and the defeat of the opposition—was the key to roads, tax rebates, and a thousand other local concerns.

In 1857 and again in 1863, Louis Napoleon's system worked brilliantly and produced overwhelming electoral victories. Yet in the 1860s, Napoleon III's electoral system gradually disintegrated. A sincere nationalist, Napoleon had wanted to reorganize Europe on the principle of nationality and gain influence and territory for France and himself in the process. Instead, problems in Italy and the rising power of Prussia led to increasing criticism at home from his Catholic and nationalist supporters. With increasing effectiveness, the middle-class liberals who had always wanted a less authoritarian regime continued to denounce his rule.

Napoleon was always sensitive to the public mood. Public opinion, he once said, always wins the last victory. Thus in the 1860s, he responded to critics by progressively liberalizing his empire. He gave the Assembly greater powers and the opposition candidates greater freedom, which they used to good advantage. In 1869 the opposition, consisting of republicans, monarchists, and liberals, polled almost 45 percent of the vote.

The next year, a sick and weary Louis Napoleon again granted France a new constitution, which combined a basically parliamentary regime with a hereditary emperor as chief of state. In a final great plebiscite on the eve of the disastrous war with Prussia, 7.5 million Frenchmen voted in favor of the new constitution, and only 1.5 million opposed it. Napoleon III's attempt to reconcile a strong national state with universal male suffrage was still evolving and was doing so in a democratic direction.

Nation Building in Italy and Germany

How did the process of unification in Italy and Germany create conservative nation-states? ■

Louis Napoleon's triumph in 1848 and his authoritarian rule in the 1850s provided the old ruling classes of Europe with a new model in politics. To what extent might the expanding urban middle classes and even portions of the growing working classes rally to a strong and essentially conservative national state that also promised change? This was one of the great political questions in the 1850s and 1860s. In central Europe, a resounding answer came with the national unification of Italy and Germany.

Italy to 1850

Italy had never been united prior to 1850. Part of Rome's great empire in ancient times, the Italian peninsula was divided in the Middle Ages into competing city-states that led the commercial and cultural revival of the West with amazing creativity. A battleground for the Great Powers after 1494, Italy was reorganized in 1815 at the Congress of Vienna. The rich northern provinces of Lombardy and Venetia were taken by Metternich's Austria. Sardinia and Piedmont were under the rule of an Italian monarch, and Tuscany, with its famous capital Florence, shared north-central Italy with several smaller states. Central Italy and Rome were ruled by the papacy, which had always considered an independent political existence necessary to fulfill its spiritual mission. Naples and Sicily were ruled, as they had been for almost a hundred years, by a branch of the Bourbons. Metternich was not wrong in dismissing Italy as "a geographical expression" (Map 24.1).

Between 1815 and 1848, the goal of a unified Italian nation captured the imaginations of many Italians. There were three basic approaches. The first was the radical program of the idealistic patriot Giuseppe Mazzini, who preached a centralized democratic republic based on universal male suffrage and the will of the people. (See "Listening to the Past: Herder and Mazzini on the Development of Nationalism," page 694.) The second was that of Vincenzo Gioberti, a Catholic priest who called for a federation of existing states under the presidency of a progressive pope. The third was the program of those who looked for leadership to the autocratic kingdom of Sardinia-Piedmont, much as many Germans looked to Prussia.

The third alternative was strengthened by the failures of 1848, when Austria smashed Mazzini's republicanism. Sardinia's new monarch, Victor Emmanuel, retained the liberal constitution granted by his father under duress in March 1848. This constitution combined a strong monarchy with a fair degree of civil liberties and parliamentary government, with deputies elected by a limited franchise based on income. To some of the Italian middle classes, Sardinia appeared to be a liberal, progressive state ideally suited to drive Austria out of northern Italy and lead a free Italy of independent states. By contrast, Mazzini's brand of democratic republicanism seemed quixotic and too radical.

As for the papacy, the initial cautious support for unification by Pius IX (pontificate 1846–1878) had given way to fear and hostility after he was temporarily driven from Rome during the upheavals of 1848. For a long generation, the papacy would stand resolutely opposed not only to national unification but also to most modern trends. In 1864 in the *Syllabus of Errors*, Pius IX strongly denounced rationalism, socialism, separation of church and state, and religious liberty, denying that "the Roman pontiff can and ought to reconcile and align himself with progress, liberalism, and modern civilization."

Cavour and Garibaldi in Italy

Sardinia had the good fortune of being led by a brilliant statesman, Count Camillo Benso di Cavour (kuh-VOOR), the dominant figure in the Sardinian govern-

Map 24.1 The Unification of Italy, 1859–1870 The leadership of Sardinia-Piedmont, nationalist fervor, and Garibaldi's attack on the kingdom of the Two Sicilies were decisive factors in the unification of Italy.

ment from 1850 until his death in 1861. Cavour came from a noble family, and he made a substantial fortune in business before entering politics. Cavour's national goals were limited and realistic. Until 1859 he sought unity only for the states of northern and perhaps central Italy in a greatly expanded kingdom of Sardinia.

In the 1850s, Cavour worked to consolidate Sardinia as a liberal constitutional state capable of leading northern Italy. His program of highways and railroads, of civil liberties and opposition to clerical privilege, increased support for Sardinia throughout northern Italy. Yet Cavour realized that Sardinia could not drive Austria out of northern Italy without the help of a powerful ally. Accordingly, he worked for a secret diplomatic alliance with Napoleon III against Austria.

Finally, in July 1858 Cavour succeeded and goaded Austria into attacking Sardinia in 1859. Napoleon III came to Sardinia's defense. Then after the victory of the combined Franco-Sardinian forces, Napoleon III did a sudden about-face. Worried by criticism from French Catholics for supporting the pope's declared enemy, Napoleon III abandoned Cavour. He made a compromise peace with the Austrians at Villafranca in July 1859.

Sardinia would receive only Lombardy, the area around Milan, from Austria. The rest of the map of Italy would remain essentially unchanged. Cavour resigned in a rage.

Yet Cavour's plans were salvaged by the skillful maneuvers of his allies in the moderate nationalist movement. While the war against Austria had raged in the north, pro-Sardinian nationalists in Tuscany and the other small states of central Italy had fanned popular revolts and easily toppled their ruling princes. Using and controlling the popular enthusiasm, the middle-class nationalist leaders in central Italy called for fusion with Sardinia. This was not at all what France and the other Great Powers wanted, but the nationalists held firm. Cavour returned to power in early 1860 and gained Napoleon III's support by ceding Savoy and Nice to France. The people of central Italy then voted overwhelmingly to join a greatly enlarged kingdom of Sardinia under Victor Emmanuel. Cavour had achieved his original goal of a northern Italian state (see Map 24.1).

For superpatriots such as Giuseppe Garibaldi (1807–1882), the job of unification was still only half done. The son of a poor sailor, Garibaldi personified the romantic, revolutionary nationalism and republicanism

Garibaldi and Victor Emmanuel The historic meeting in Naples between the leader of Italy's revolutionary nationalists and the king of Sardinia sealed the unification of northern and southern Italy. With the sleeve of his red shirt showing, Garibaldi offers his hand — and his conquests — to the uniformed king and his moderate monarchical government. (Scala/Art Resource, NY)

of Mazzini and 1848. Leading a corps of volunteers against Austria in 1859, Garibaldi emerged in 1860 as an independent force in Italian politics.

Partly to use him and partly to get rid of him, Cavour secretly supported Garibaldi's bold plan to "liberate" the kingdom of the Two Sicilies. Landing on the shores of Sicily in May 1860, Garibaldi's guerrilla band of a thousand **Red Shirts** captured the imagination of the Sicilian peasantry, which rose in bloody rebellion against their landlords. Outwitting the twenty-thousand-man royal army, the guerrilla leader won battles, gained volunteers, and took Palermo. Then Garibaldi and his men crossed to the mainland, marched triumphantly toward Naples, and prepared to attack Rome and the pope. But the wily Cavour quickly sent Sardinian forces to occupy most of the Papal States (but not Rome) and to intercept Garibaldi.

Red Shirts The guerrilla army of Giuseppe Garibaldi, who invaded Sicily in 1860 in an attempt to liberate it, winning the hearts of the Sicilian peasantry.

Cavour realized that an attack on Rome would bring about war with France, and he also feared Garibaldi's radicalism and popular appeal. Thus he immediately organized a plebiscite in the conquered territories. Despite the urging of some radical supporters, the patriotic Garibaldi did not oppose Cavour, and the people of the south voted to join the kingdom of Sardinia. When Garibaldi and Victor Emmanuel rode together through Naples to cheering crowds, they symbolically sealed the union of north and south, of monarch and nation-state.

Cavour had succeeded. He had controlled Garibaldi and had turned popular nationalism in a conservative direction. The new kingdom of Italy, which expanded to include Venice in 1866 and Rome in 1870, was a parliamentary monarchy under Victor Emmanuel, neither radical nor democratic. It was politically unified, but only a half million out of 22 million Italians had the right to vote. The properties classes and the common people remained divided. A great and growing social and cultural gap also separated the progressive, industrializing north from the stagnant, agrarian south. The new Italy was united on paper, but profound divisions remained.

The Growing Austro-Prussian Rivalry

In the aftermath of 1848, the German states were locked in a political stalemate. After Austria and Russia blocked Frederick William's attempt in 1850 to unify Germany "from above," tension grew between Austria and Prussia as each power sought to block the other within the German Confederation (see Chapter 22).

At the same time, powerful economic forces were contributing to the Austro-Prussian rivalry. Austria had not been included initially in the German customs union, or Zollverein, which had been founded in 1834 to stimulate trade and increase the revenue of member states. By the end of 1853 Austria was the only state in the German Confederation that had not joined. Middle-class and business groups in the Zollverein were enriching themselves and finding solid economic reasons to bolster their idealistic support of national unification. Prussia's leading role within the Zollverein gave it a valuable advantage in its struggle against Austria's supremacy in German political affairs.

Prussia had emerged from the upheavals of 1848 with a parliament of sorts, which was in the hands of the wealthy liberal middle class by 1859. Patriotic and longing for national unification, these middle-class representatives also wanted to establish once and for all that the parliament, not the king, had the ultimate political power and that the army was responsible to Prussia's elected representatives. The national uprising in Italy in 1859, however, made a profound impression on Prussia's tough-minded William I (r. 1861–1888). Convinced that great political change and war—perhaps with Austria, perhaps with France—were quite possible, William I and his top military advisers pushed to raise taxes and increase the defense budget in order to double the size of the army. The Prussian parliament, reflecting the middle class's desire for a less militaristic society, rejected the military budget in 1862, and the liberals triumphed completely in new elections. King William then called on Count Otto von Bismarck to head a new ministry and defy the parliament. This was a momentous choice.

Bismarck and the Austro-Prussian War

The most important figure in German history between Martin Luther and Adolf Hitler, Otto von Bismarck (1815–1898) has been the object of enormous interest and debate. A great hero to some, a great villain to others,

Bismarck was above all a master of politics. Born into the Prussian landowning aristocracy and always devoted to his Prussian sovereign, Bismarck had a strong personality and an unbounded desire for power. Yet in his drive to secure power for himself and for Prussia, Bismarck was extraordinarily flexible and pragmatic. "One must always have two irons in the fire," he once said. He kept his options open, pursuing one policy and then another as he moved with skill and cunning toward his goal.

Bismarck first honed his political skills as a high-ranking diplomat for the Prussian government. When he took office as chief minister in 1862, he made a strong but unfavorable impression. His speeches were a sensation and a scandal. Declaring that the government would rule without parliamentary consent, Bismarck lashed out at the middle-class opposition: "The great questions of the day will not be decided by speeches and resolutions—that was the blunder of 1848 and 1849—but by blood and iron."

> **❝ The great questions of the day will not be decided by speeches and resolutions . . . but by blood and iron. ❞**
>
> **—OTTO VON BISMARCK**

Denounced for this view that "might makes right," Bismarck had the Prussian bureaucracy go right on collecting taxes, even though the parliament refused to approve the budget. Bismarck reorganized the army. And for four years, from 1862 to 1866, the voters of Prussia continued to express their opposition by sending large liberal majorities to the parliament.

Opposition at home spurred the search for success abroad. The extremely complicated question of Schleswig-Holstein—two provinces that belonged to Denmark but were members of the German Confederation (Map 24.2)—provided a welcome opportunity. In 1864, when the Danish king tried again, as in 1848, to bring these two provinces into a more centralized Danish state against the will of the German Confederation, Prussia joined Austria in a short and successful war against Denmark. However, Bismarck was convinced that Prussia had to control completely the northern, predominately Protestant part of the German Confederation, which meant expelling Austria from German affairs. After the victory over Denmark, Bismarck's skillful maneuvering had Prussia in a position to force Austria out by war, if necessary. Bismarck knew that a war with Austria would have to be a localized one that would not provoke a mighty alliance against Prussia. By skillfully neutralizing Russia and France, he was in a position to engage in a war of his own making.

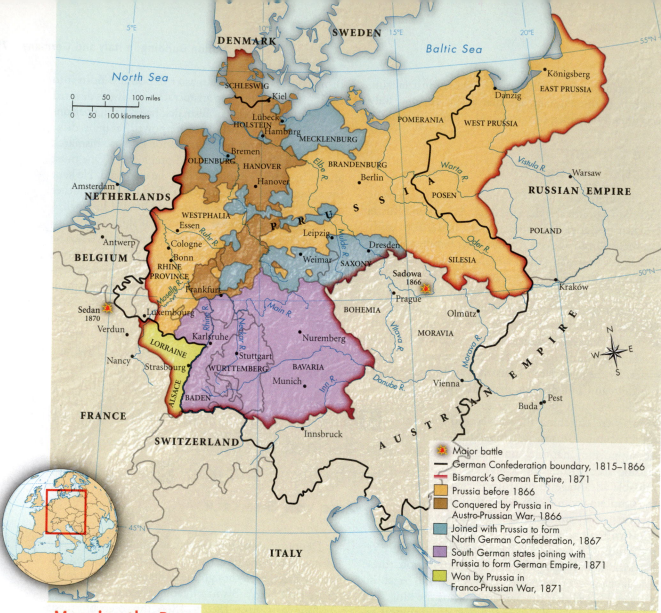

Scale:
0 50 100 miles
0 50 100 kilometers

Legend:
- Major battle
- German Confederation boundary, 1815–1866
- Bismarck's German Empire, 1871
- Prussia before 1866
- Conquered by Prussia in Austro-Prussian War, 1866
- Joined with Prussia to form North German Confederation, 1867
- South German states joining with Prussia to form German Empire, 1871
- Won by Prussia in Franco-Prussian War, 1871

Mapping the Past

Map 24.2 **The Unification of Germany, 1866–1871** This map shows how Prussia expanded and a new German Empire was created through two wars, the Austro-Prussian War of 1866 and the Franco-Prussian War of 1870–1871.

ANALYZING THE MAP What losses did Austria experience in 1866? What territories did France lose as a result of the Franco-Prussian War? Which of the predominately Catholic states of southern Germany joined with Prussia to form the German Empire in 1871?

CONNECTIONS How was central Europe remade and the power of Prussia-Germany greatly increased as a result of the Austro-Prussian War and the Franco-Prussian War?

To complete this activity online, go to the Online Study Guide at bedfordstmartins.com/mckaywest.

The Austro-Prussian War of 1866 lasted only seven weeks. Utilizing railroads to mass troops and the new breech-loading needle gun to achieve maximum firepower, the reorganized Prussian army proved its mettle. It overran northern Germany and defeated Austria decisively at the Battle of Sadowa (SAH-daw-vah) in Bohemia. Anticipating Prussia's future needs, Bismarck offered Austria realistic, even generous, peace terms. Austria paid no reparations and lost no territory to Prussia, although Venetia was ceded to Italy.

But the existing German Confederation was dissolved, and Austria agreed to withdraw from German affairs. Prussia also conquered and annexed several small states north of the Main River and completely dominated the remaining principalities in the newly formed North German Confederation. The mainly Catholic states of the south remained independent while forming alliances with Prussia. Bismarck's fundamental goal of Prussian expansion was being realized (see Map 24.2).

The Taming of the Parliament

Bismarck had long been convinced that the old order he so ardently defended should make peace, on its own terms, with the liberal middle class and the nationalist movement. He realized that nationalism was not necessarily hostile to conservative, authoritarian government. Moreover, Bismarck believed that because of the events of 1848, the German middle class could be led to prefer a national unity under conservative leadership rather than a long, uncertain battle for truly liberal institutions. Thus during the attack on Austria in 1866, he increasingly identified Prussia's fate with the "national development of Germany."

In the aftermath of victory, Bismarck fashioned a federal constitution for the new North German Confederation. Each state retained its own local government, but the king of Prussia became president of the confederation, and the chancellor—Bismarck—was responsible only to the president. The federal government—William I and Bismarck—controlled the army and foreign affairs. There was also a legislature with members of the lower house elected by universal, single-class male suffrage. With this radical innovation, Bismarck opened the door to popular participation and the possibility of going over the head of the middle class directly to the people, much as Napoleon III had done in France. All the while, however, ultimate power rested in the hands of the dominant state of Prussia and its king and army.

In Prussia itself, Bismarck held out an olive branch to the parliamentary opposition. Marshaling all his diplomatic skill, Bismarck asked the parliament to pass a special indemnity bill to approve after the fact all the government's spending between 1862 and 1866. Most of the liberals jumped at the chance to cooperate. With German unity in sight, they repented their "sins." The constitu-tional struggle in Prussia was over, and the German middle class was accepting respectfully the monarchical authority and the aristocratic superiority that Bismarck represented. In the years before 1914, the values of the aristocratic Prussian army officer increasingly replaced those of the middle-class liberal in public esteem and set the social standard.[1]

The Franco-Prussian War

The final act in the drama of German unification followed quickly. Bismarck realized that a patriotic war with France would drive the south German states into his arms. The French obligingly played their part. The apparent issue—whether a distant relative of Prussia's William I might become king of Spain—was only a diplomatic pretext. By 1870 the French leaders of the Second Empire, goaded by Bismarck and alarmed by their powerful new neighbor on the Rhine, had decided on a war to teach Prussia a lesson.

As soon as war against France began in 1870, Bismarck had the wholehearted support of the south German states. With other governments maintaining their neutrality—Bismarck's generosity to Austria in 1866 was paying big dividends—German forces under Prussian leadership decisively defeated the main French army at Sedan on September 1, 1870. Louis Napoleon himself was captured and humiliated. Three days later, French patriots in Paris proclaimed yet another French republic and vowed to continue fighting. But after five months, in January 1871, a starving Paris surrendered,

Proclaiming the German Empire, January 1871 This commemorative painting by Anton von Werner testifies to the nationalistic intoxication in Germany after the victory over France. William I of Prussia stands on a platform surrounded by princes and generals in the famous Hall of Mirrors in the palace of Versailles, while officers from all the units around a besieged Paris cheer and salute him with uplifted swords as emperor of a unified Germany. Bismarck, in white (center), stands between king and army. (akg-images)

and France went on to accept Bismarck's harsh peace terms. By this time, the south German states had agreed to join a new German Empire. The victorious William I was proclaimed emperor of Germany in the Hall of Mirrors in the palace of Versailles. Europe had a nineteenth-century German "sun king" (see Chapter 16). As in the 1866 constitution, the king of Prussia and his ministers had ultimate power in the new German Empire, and the lower house of the legislature was elected by universal male suffrage.

Bismarck and the German Empire imposed a severe penalty on France. France was forced to pay a colossal indemnity of 5 billion francs and to cede the rich eastern province of Alsace and part of Lorraine to Germany. French men and women of all classes viewed the seizure of Alsace and Lorraine as a terrible crime. They could never forget and never forgive, and thus relations between France and Germany after 1871 were tragically poisoned.

The Franco-Prussian War, which Europeans generally saw as a test of nations in a pitiless Darwinian struggle for existence, released an enormous surge of patriotic feeling in Germany. Bismarck's genius, the invincible Prussian army, the solidarity of king and people in a unified nation—these and similar themes were trumpeted endlessly during and after the war. The weakest of the Great Powers in 1862 (after Austria, Britain, France, and Russia), Prussia had become, with fortification by the other German states, the most powerful state in Europe in less than a decade. Most Germans were enormously proud, blissfully imagining themselves the fittest and best of the European species. Semi-authoritarian nationalism and a "new conservatism," which was based on an alliance of the propertied classes and sought the active support of the working classes, had triumphed in Germany.

U.S. Secession, 1860–1861

slaveholding states in very different directions. Northerners extended family farms westward and began building English-model factories in the northeast. By 1850 an industrializing, urbanizing North was also building a system of canals and railroads and attracting most of the European immigrants.

In sharp contrast, industry and cities did not develop in the South, and European immigrants largely avoided the region. Even though three-quarters of all Southern white families were small farmers and owned no slaves in 1850, plantation owners holding twenty or more slaves dominated the economy and society. These profit-minded slave owners used gangs of black slaves to claim a vast new kingdom across the Deep South where cotton was king (Map 24.3). By 1850, this kingdom produced 5 million bales a year and satisfied an apparently insatiable demand from textile mills in Europe and New England.

The rise of the cotton empire greatly expanded slave-based agriculture in the South, spurred exports, and played a key role in igniting rapid U.S. economic growth. The large profits flowing from cotton also led influential Southerners to defend slavery. In doing so, Southern whites developed a strong cultural identity and came to see themselves as a closely knit "we" distinct from the Northern "they." Northern whites viewed their free-labor system as being just and economical and morally superior to slavery. Thus regional antagonisms intensified.

These antagonisms came to a climax after 1848 when a defeated Mexico ceded to the United States a vast area stretching from west Texas to the Pacific Ocean. Debate over the extension of slavery in this new territory caused attitudes to harden on both sides. In Abraham Lincoln's famous words, the United States was a "house divided." Lincoln's election as president in 1860 gave Southern secessionists the chance they had been waiting for. Eventually eleven states left the Union, determined to win their own independence, and formed the Confederate States of America. When Southern troops fired on a Union fort in South Carolina's Charleston harbor, war began.

The long Civil War (1861–1865) was the bloodiest conflict in all of American history, but in the end the South was decisively defeated and the Union preserved. In the aftermath of the war, certain dominant characteristics of American life and national culture took shape. Powerful business corporations emerged, steadfastly supported by the Republican Party during and after the war. The **Homestead Act** of 1862, which gave western land to settlers, and the Thirteenth Amendment

Nation Building in the United States

In what ways did the United States experience nation building? ■

Closely linked to European developments in the nineteenth century, the United States also experienced the full drama of bloody nation building. The "United" States was divided by slavery from its birth, as economic development in the young republic carried free and

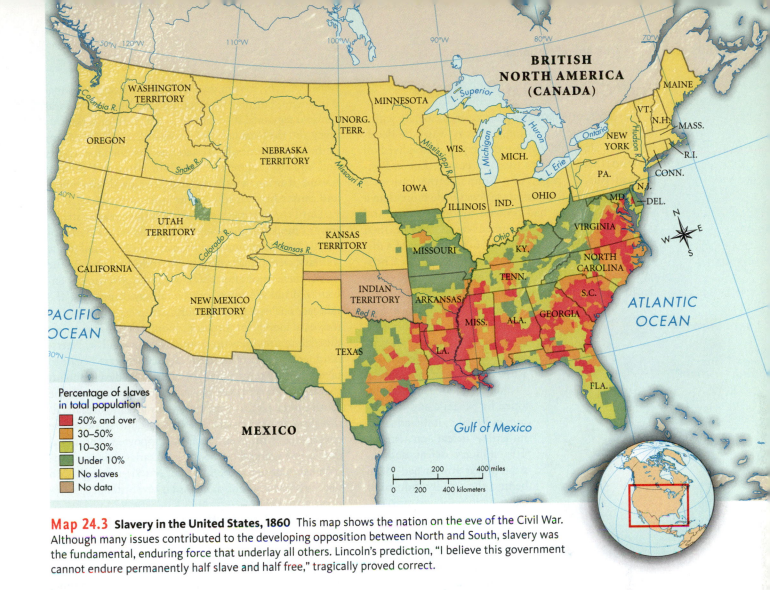

Map 24.3 Slavery in the United States, 1860 This map shows the nation on the eve of the Civil War. Although many issues contributed to the developing opposition between North and South, slavery was the fundamental, enduring force that underlay all others. Lincoln's prediction, "I believe this government cannot endure permanently half slave and half free," tragically proved correct.

Percentage of slaves in total population

- 50% and over
- 30–50%
- 10–30%
- Under 10%
- No slaves
- No data

of 1865, which ended slavery, reinforced the concept of free labor taking its chances in a market economy. Finally, the success of Lincoln and the North in holding the Union together seemed to confirm that the "manifest destiny" of the United States was indeed to straddle a continent as a great world power. Thus a new American nationalism grew out of a civil war.

The Modernization of Russia and the Ottoman Empire

What steps did Russia and the Ottoman Turks take toward modernization, and how successful were they? ∎

The Russian and the Ottoman Empires also experienced profound political crises in the mid-nineteenth century. These crises were unlike those occurring in Italy and Germany, for neither Russia nor the Ottoman Empire aspired to build a single powerful state out of a jumble of principalities. Both empires were already vast multi-national states built on long traditions of military conquest and absolutist rule by elites from the dominant ethnic groups — the Russians and the Ottoman Turks. In the early nineteenth century the governing elites in both states were strongly opposed to representative government and national self-determination, and they continued to concentrate on absolutist rule and competition with other Great Powers.

For both states relentless power politics led to serious trouble. It became clear to the leaders of both empires that they had to embrace the process of **modernization**, defined narrowly as the changes that enable a country to compete effectively with the leading countries at a given time. This limited conception of modernization fits Russia after the Crimean War particularly well, and it helps explain developments in the Ottoman Empire.

Homestead Act A result of the American Civil War that gave western land to settlers, reinforcing the concept of free labor in a market economy.

modernization The changes that enable a country to compete effectively with the leading countries at a given time.

The "Great Reforms" in Russia

In the 1850s, Russia was a poor agrarian society with a rapidly growing population. Industry was little developed, and almost 90 percent of the population lived off the land. (See "Living in the Past: Peasant Life in Post-Reform Russia," page 762.) Bound to the lord on a hereditary basis, the peasant serf was little more than a slave, and serfdom had become the great moral and political issue for the government by the 1840s. Then the Crimean War of 1853 to 1856, arising out of a dispute with France over who should protect certain Christian shrines in the Ottoman Empire, brought crisis. Because the fighting was concentrated in the Crimean peninsula on the Black Sea, Russia's weak transportation network of rivers and wagons failed to supply the distant Russian armies adequately.

France and Great Britain, aided by Sardinia and the Ottoman Empire, inflicted a humiliating defeat on Russia. This military defeat demonstrated that Russia had fallen behind the rapidly industrializing nations of western Europe in many areas. At the very least, Russia needed railroads, better armaments, and reorganization of the army if it was to maintain its international position. Moreover, the disastrous war had caused hardship and raised the specter of massive peasant rebellion. Reform of serfdom was imperative. Military disaster thus forced Tsar Alexander II (r. 1855–1881) and his ministers along the path of rapid social change and general modernization.

The first and greatest of the reforms was the freeing of the serfs in 1861. Human bondage was abolished forever, and the emancipated peasants received, on average, about half of the land. Yet they had to pay fairly high prices for their land, and because the land was owned collectively, each peasant village was jointly responsible for the payments of all the families in the village. Collective ownership and responsibility made it very difficult for individual peasants to improve agricultural methods or leave their villages. Thus old patterns of behavior predominated, and the effects of reform were limited.

Most of the later reforms were also halfway measures. In 1864 the government established a new institution of local government, the zemstvo. Members of this local assembly were elected by a three-class system of towns, peasant villages, and noble landowners. A zemstvo executive council dealt with local problems. Russian liberals hoped that this reform would lead to an elected national parliament, but they were soon disappointed. The local zemstvo remained subordinate to the traditional bureaucracy and the local nobility. More successful was reform of the legal system, which established independent courts and equality before the law. Education and policies toward Russian Jews were also liberalized somewhat, and censorship was relaxed but not removed.

Until the twentieth century, Russia's greatest strides toward modernization were economic rather than political. Transportation and industry, both so vital to the military, were transformed in two industrial surges. The first of these came after 1860, when the government encouraged and subsidized private railway companies. The railroads enabled agricultural Russia to export grain and thus earn money for further economic development. Industrial suburbs grew up around Moscow and St. Petersburg, and a class of modern factory workers began to take shape. Strengthened by industrial development, Russia's military forces began seizing territory to the south and east, greatly exciting many ardent Russian nationalists and superpatriots, who became some of the government's most enthusiastic supporters. Industrial development and the growing proletariat class also contributed mightily to the spread of Marxian thought and the transformation of the Russian revolutionary movement after 1890.

In 1881 Alexander II was assassinated by a small group of anarchist terrorists. The era of reform came to an abrupt end, for the new tsar, Alexander III (r. 1881–1894), was a determined reactionary. Nevertheless, economic modernization sped forward for the second time, as Russia achieved a massive industrialization surge from 1890 to 1900. The key leader was Sergei Witte (suhr-GAY VIH-tuh), the tough, competent minister of finance from 1892 to 1903. Inspired by the writings of Friedrich List (see Chapter 21), Witte believed that the harsh reality of industrial backwardness was threatening Russia's power and greatness. Under Witte's leadership the government built state-owned railroads rapidly, doubling the network to thirty-five thousand miles by the end of the century. Witte established high protective tariffs to build Russian industry, and he put the country on the gold standard of the "civilized world" in order to strengthen Russian finances.

Witte's greatest innovation was to use Westerners to catch up with the West. He encouraged foreigners to build factories in Russia, believing that "the inflow of foreign capital is . . . the only way by which our industry will be able to supply our country quickly with abundant and cheap products."[2] His efforts to entice Westerners to locate their factories in Russia were especially successful in southern Russia. There, in eastern Ukraine, foreign capitalists and their engineers built an enormous and very modern steel and coal industry. In

The Crimean War, 1853–1856

1900 peasants still constituted the great majority of the population, but Russia was industrializing and catching up with the advanced nations of the West.

The Russian Revolution of 1905

Catching up partly meant vigorous territorial expansion, for this was the age of Western imperialism. By 1903 Russia had established a sphere of influence in Chinese Manchuria and was eyeing northern Korea. When the diplomatic protests of equally imperialistic Japan were ignored, the Japanese launched a surprise attack in February 1904. After Japan scored repeated victories, Russia was forced in September 1905 to accept a humiliating defeat.

As is often the case, military disaster abroad brought political upheaval at home. The business and professional classes had long wanted a liberal, representative government. Urban factory workers had all the grievances of early industrialization and were organized in a radical and still illegal labor movement. Peasants had gained little from the era of reforms and were suffering from poverty and overpopulation. At the same time, nationalist sentiment was emerging among the empire's minorities, and subject nationalities, such as the Poles, the Ukrainians, and the Latvians, were calling for self-rule. With the army pinned down in Manchuria, all these currents of discontent converged in the revolution of 1905.

On a Sunday in January 1905, a massive crowd of workers and their families converged peacefully on the Winter Palace in St. Petersburg to present a petition to the tsar. Suddenly troops opened fire, killing and wounding hundreds. The **Bloody Sunday** massacre turned ordinary workers against the tsar and produced a wave of general indignation.

Outlawed political parties came out into the open, and by the summer of 1905 strikes, peasant uprisings, revolts among minority nationalities,

Bloody Sunday A massacre of peaceful protesters at the Winter Palace in St. Petersburg in 1905 that triggered a revolution that overturned absolute tsarist rule and made Russia into a conservative constitutional monarchy.

The October Manifesto of 1905 This painting by the famous realist Ilya Repin captures the riotous joy that seized most moderate, well-educated Russians after Tsar Nicholas II issued the October Manifesto. At long last, they thought, Russia would become a liberal constitutional state, with guaranteed liberties and representative assemblies. (akg-images)

LIVING IN THE PAST

THE CAUTIOUS EMANCIPATION OF 1861, which freed Russian peasants from their noble lords but tied them to their villages, preserved traditional peasant life until the massive industrial surge of the 1890s. Most peasant families continued to live in one- or two-story log cabins strung out along the village's wide dirt road. A cabin typically had a single living room, a storage room (sometimes shared with animals), and a shallow cellar. Simple furniture — a table, benches, storage shelves — was complemented by a large, flat brick oven that was used for both cooking and sleeping. On Saturdays villagers stoked up the communal bathhouse. On Sundays they attended a long Orthodox service in their wooden church, often followed in summer by socializing with family and friends, drinking tea and mild home-made ale, telling stories, and playing the traditional stringed instrument, the balalaika.

In contrast to western Europe, where women had almost never done heavy field work, Russian peasant women always provided much of the hard labor required for plowing, planting, and harvesting. Infertile soil, sparse population, simple hand tools, and short growing seasons demanded intense physical effort from all family members to get the crops planted and harvested before the first hard freeze and the long brutal winter. Since peasant land in Russia followed a common crop rotation and was owned by the entire peasant community, with each family allotted its share of the long strips of crop land according to the family's size, there were no fences to mark off private property rights that did not exist.

Russian peasants always needed additional, nonagricultural, income. Thus both men and women engaged in many crafts and trades, of which weaving, pottery, embroidering, hauling, logging, and carpen-

In this photograph (ca. 1875), members of a Russian family gather outside a typical peasant cabin to enjoy a Sunday break from their labors. (family: The Granger Collection, New York; balalaika: Museum of Fine Arts, Boston/Lebrecht)

Russian agriculture depended on the contribution of women and girls, as this photograph attests. (The Granger Collection, New York)

try were particularly important. Woodworkers, like this peasant barrel maker with his birch-bark shoes and home-made leggings, used an abundant raw material to fashion elaborate dolls and attractive wooden tableware as well as workaday items. Peasants also went to towns and cities for temporary work, and many settled there permanently as industrial workers in the 1890s.

QUESTIONS FOR ANALYSIS

1. How did the abolition of serfdom affect peasant life in Russia?

2. What role did peasant women play in Russian agriculture? Why?

3. How did Russian peasants interact with their environment? In what ways did their environment influence peasants' lives?

This 1895 photo and the wooden nesting dolls highlight the importance of woodworking as a source of secondary income for Russian peasants. (barrel maker: akg-images; nesting dolls: Sergiev Posad Toy Museum, Sergiev Posad, Russia, Photo RK812)

October Manifesto The result of a great general strike in October 1905, it granted full civil rights and promised a popularly elected Duma (parliament) with real legislative power.

Duma The Russian parliament that opened in 1906, elected indirectly by universal male suffrage but controlled after 1907 by the tsar and the conservative classes.

and troop mutinies were sweeping the country. The revolutionary surge culminated in October 1905 in a great paralyzing general strike that forced the government to capitulate. The tsar issued the **October Manifesto**, which granted full civil rights and promised a popularly elected **Duma** (DOO-muh; parliament) with real legislative power. The manifesto split the opposition. Frightened middle-class leaders helped the government repress the uprising and survive as a constitutional monarchy.

On the eve of the opening of the first Duma in May 1906, the government issued the new constitution, the Fundamental Laws. The tsar retained great powers. The Duma, elected indirectly by universal male suffrage, and a largely appointive upper house could debate and pass laws, but the tsar had an absolute veto. As in Bismarck's Germany, the tsar appointed his ministers, who did not need to command a majority in the Duma.

The disappointed, predominately middle-class liberals, the largest group in the newly elected Duma, saw the Fundamental Laws as a step backward. Efforts to cooperate with the tsar's ministers soon broke down, and after months of deadlock, the tsar dismissed the Duma. Thereupon he and his reactionary advisers unilaterally rewrote the electoral law so as to increase greatly the weight of the propertied classes. When elections were held, the tsar could count on a loyal majority in the Duma. His chief minister then pushed through important agrarian reforms designed to break down collective village ownership of land and encourage the more enterprising peasants—his "wager on the strong." In 1914, Russia was partially modernized, a conservative constitutional monarchy with a peasant-based but industrializing economy.

Tanzimat A set of reforms designed to remake the Ottoman Empire on a western European model.

Decline and Reform in the Ottoman Empire

The Ottoman Empire had reached its high point of development under Suleiman the Magnificent in the sixteenth century. By the eighteenth century it was falling rapidly behind western Europe in science, industrial skill,

Area of peasant unrest
Major strikes and mutinies

St. Petersburg
Moscow
RUSSIA
Warsaw
Black Sea

The Russian Revolution of 1905

and military technology. Also during the eighteenth century, Russia's powerful westernized army was able to occupy Ottoman provinces on the Danube River. The danger that the Great Powers of Europe would gradually conquer the Ottoman Empire and divide up its vast territories was real.

Caught up in the Napoleonic wars and losing more territory to Russia, the Ottomans were forced in 1816 to grant Serbia local autonomy. In 1830, the Greeks won their national independence, while French armies began their long and bloody conquest of the Arabic-speaking province of Algeria. The Ottoman Empire was losing territory and power. Another threat to the empire came from within: the rise of Muhammad Ali, the Ottoman governor in Egypt. In 1831, and again in 1839, his French-trained forces occupied the Ottoman provinces of Syria and then Iraq and appeared ready to depose the Ottoman sultan (emperor) Mahmud II (r. 1808–1839). The sultan survived, but only because the European powers forced Muhammad Ali to withdraw. The European powers, minus France, preferred a weak and dependent Ottoman state to a strong and revitalized Muslim entity under a dynamic leader such as Muhammad Ali.

Realizing their precarious position, liberal Ottoman statesmen launched in 1839 an era of radical reforms, which lasted with fits and starts until 1876 and culminated in a constitution and a short-lived parliament. Known as the **Tanzimat** (literally, regulations or orders), these reforms were designed to remake the empire on a western European model. The high point of reform came with Sultan Abdul Mejid's Imperial Rescript of 1857. Articles in the decree called for equality before the law, a modernized administration and military, and religious freedom for Muslims, Christians, and Jews.

Every distinction or designation tending to make any class whatsoever of the subjects of my Empire inferior to another class, on account of their religion, language, or race, shall be forever effaced from the Administrative Protocol. . . .

As all forms of religion are and shall be freely professed in my domains, no subject shall be hindered in the exercise of the religion he professes.[3]

As part of its new policy of tolerance, new commercial laws allowed free importation of foreign goods and permitted foreign merchants to operate freely throughout the empire. Of great importance for later developments, growing numbers among the elite and the upwardly mobile embraced Western education and accepted secular values to some extent.

Pasha Hilim Receiving Archduke Maximilian of Austria As this painting suggests, Ottoman leaders became well versed in European languages and culture. They also mastered the game of power politics, playing one European state off against another and securing the Ottoman Empire's survival. The black servants on the right may be slaves from Sudan. (Miramare Palace Trieste/Dagli Orti/The Art Archive)

Intended to bring revolutionary modernization, the Tanzimat permitted partial recovery but fell short of its goals for several reasons. First, the liberal reforms failed to halt the growth of nationalism among Christian subjects in the Balkans, which resulted in crises and defeats that undermined all reform efforts. Second, the Ottoman initiatives did not curtail the appetite of Western imperialism, which secured a stranglehold on the Ottoman economy.

Finally, equality before the law for all citizens and religious communities actually increased religious disputes, which were in turn exacerbated by the relentless interference of the European powers. This development embittered relations between the religious communities, distracted the government from its reform mission, and split Muslims into secularists and religious conservatives. Many conservative Muslims detested the religious reforms, which they viewed as an impious departure from Islamic tradition and holy law. These Islamic conserva-

tives became the most dependable support of Sultan Abdülhamid (ahb-dool-hah-MEED) (r. 1876–1909), who abandoned the model of European liberalism in his long and repressive reign.

The combination of declining international power and conservative tyranny eventually led to a powerful resurgence of the modernizing impulse among idealistic Turkish exiles in Europe and young army officers in Istanbul. These fervent patriots, the so-called **Young Turks**, seized power in the revolution of 1908, and they forced the sultan to implement reforms. Although they failed to stop the rising tide of anti-Ottoman nationalism in the Balkans, the Young Turks helped prepare the way for the birth of modern secular Turkey after the defeat and collapse of the Ottoman Empire in World War I.

Young Turks Fervent patriots who seized power in the revolution of 1908 in the Ottoman Empire, forcing the conservative sultan to implement reforms.

The Responsive National State, 1871–1914

Why after 1871 did ordinary citizens feel a growing loyalty to their governments? ■

For central and western Europe, the unification of Italy and Germany by "blood and iron" marked the end of a dramatic period of nation building. After 1871 the heartland of Europe was organized into strong national states. Only on the borders of Europe—in Ireland and Russia, in Austria-Hungary and the Ottoman Empire—did subject peoples still strive for national unity and political independence.

General Trends

Despite some major differences between countries, European domestic politics after 1871 had a common framework, the firmly established national state. The common themes within that framework were the emergence of mass politics and growing mass loyalty toward the national state.

For good reason, ordinary people—the masses of an industrializing, urbanizing society—felt increasing loyalty to their governments. More people could vote. By 1914 universal male suffrage had become the rule rather than the exception. This development had as much psychological as political significance. Ordinary men were no longer denied the right to vote because they lacked wealth or education. They felt that they counted; they could influence the government to some extent. They were becoming "part of the system."

The women's suffrage movement also made some gains. By 1913 women could vote in twelve of the western United States. Europe, too, moved slowly in this direction. In 1914 Norway gave the vote to most women. Elsewhere, women such as the English Emmeline Pankhurst were very militant in their demands. They heckled politicians and held public demonstrations. These efforts generally failed before 1914, but they prepared the way for the triumph of the women's suffrage movement immediately after World War I.

As the right to vote spread, politicians and parties in national parliaments represented the people more responsively. The multiparty system prevailing in most countries meant that parliamentary majorities were built

"Votes for Women!" The long-simmering campaign for women's suffrage in England came to a boil after 1903, as militants took to the streets, disrupted political meetings, and tried to storm Parliament. This 1908 illustration shows demonstrators giving a hero's welcome to Mary Leigh, the first suffragette imprisoned for property damage after she threw rocks through the windows of the prime minister's house. Emmeline Pankhurst was also imprisoned after refusing to pay a fine for purportedly kicking and spitting at policemen. Militant suffragettes shared their leader's well-known dedication to "deeds, not words." They proudly wore her portrait badge, a symbol of the lengths they would go for the right to vote. (illustration: The Art Archive; badge: © Museum of London Picture Library)

on shifting coalitions of different parties, and this gave individual parties leverage to obtain benefits for their supporters. Governments also passed laws to alleviate general problems, thereby acquiring greater legitimacy and appearing more worthy of support.

There was a less positive side to building popular support for strong nation-states after 1871. Governments found that they could manipulate national feeling to create a sense of unity and to divert attention away from underlying class conflicts. Conservative and moderate leaders found that workers who voted socialist would rally around the flag in a diplomatic crisis or cheer when distant territory of doubtful value was seized in Africa or Asia. Therefore, after 1871 governing elites frequently used antiliberal and militaristic policies to help manage domestic conflicts, but at the expense of increasing the international tensions that erupted in 1914 in the cataclysm of World War I and the Russian Revolution.

In these same years some fanatics and demagogic political leaders also sought to build extreme nationalist movements by whipping up popular animosity toward imaginary enemies, especially the Jews. The growth of modern anti-Semitism after 1880 epitomized the most negative aspects of European nationalism before the First World War.

The German Empire

Politics in Germany after 1871 reflected many of the general European developments. The new German Empire was a federal union of Prussia and twenty-four smaller states. Much of the everyday business of government was conducted by the separate states, but there was a strong national government with a chancellor—until 1890, Bismarck—and a popularly elected lower house called the **Reichstag** (RIGHKHS-tahg). Although Bismarck refused to be bound by a parliamentary majority, he tried nonetheless to maintain one. This situation gave the political parties opportunities. Until 1878 Bismarck relied mainly on the National Liberals, who had rallied to him after 1866. They supported legislation useful for further economic and legal unification of the country.

Less wisely, they backed Bismarck's attack on the Catholic Church, the so-called **Kulturkampf** (kool-TOOR-kahmpf), or "struggle for civilization." Like Bismarck, the middle-class National Liberals were particularly alarmed by Pius IX and his declaration of papal infallibility in 1870. That dogma seemed to ask German Catholics to put loyalty to their church, a foreign power, above their loyalty to their newly unified nation. Kulturkampf initiatives generally aimed at making the Catholic Church subject to government control. However, only in Protestant Prussia did the Kulturkampf have even limited success, because Catholics throughout the country generally voted for the Center Party, which blocked passage of national laws hostile to the church.

In 1878 Bismarck abandoned his attack on the church and instead courted the Catholic Center Party, whose supporters included many Catholic small farmers in western and southern Germany. By enacting high tariffs on cheap grain from the United States, Canada, and Russia, he won over both the Catholic Center and the Protestant Junkers, who had large landholdings in the east. With the tariffs, then, Bismarck won Catholic and conservative support.

Many other governments followed Bismarck's lead, and the 1880s and 1890s saw a widespread return to protectionism in Europe. France, in particular, established very high tariffs to protect agriculture and industry, peasants and manufacturers, from foreign competition. Thus the European governments were responding effectively to a major economic problem and winning greater loyalty. The general rise of protectionism in this period was also an outstanding example of the dangers of self-centered nationalism: new tariffs led to international name-calling and nasty trade wars.

As for socialism, Bismarck tried to stop its growth in Germany because he genuinely feared its revolutionary language and allegiance to a movement transcending the nation-state. In 1878, after two attempts on the life of William I by radicals (though not socialists), Bismarck used a carefully orchestrated national outcry to ram through the Reichstag a law that strictly controlled socialist meetings and publications and outlawed the Social Democratic Party, which was thereby driven underground. German socialists, however, continued to hold influence, and Bismarck decided to try another tack.

In an attempt to win the support of working-class people, Bismarck urged the Reichstag to take bold action and enact a variety of state-supported social measures. Big business and some conservatives accused Bismarck of creating "state socialism," but Bismarck ably pressed his program in many lively speeches to the nation's representatives and its citizens, as the following excerpt suggests.

Reichstag The popularly elected lower house of government of the new German Empire after 1871.

Kulturkampf Bismarck's attack on the Catholic Church within Germany from 1870 to 1878, resulting from Pius IX's declaration of papal infallibility.

> *Give the working-man the right to work as long as he is healthy; assure him care when he is sick; assure him maintenance when he is old. If you do that, and do not fear the (financial) sacrifice, or cry out at State Socialism as soon as the words "provision for old age" are uttered, . . . then I believe the gentlemen of the Wyden (Social-Democratic) program will sound their bird-call in vain, and that the thronging toward them will cease as soon as working-men see that the Government and legislative bodies are earnestly concerned with their welfare.*[4]

Bismarck and his supporters carried the day and his essentially conservative nation-state pioneered in the provision of social welfare programs. In 1883 he pushed through the Reichstag the first of several modern social security laws to help wage earners. The laws of 1883 and 1884 established national sickness and accident insurance; the law of 1889 established old-age pensions and retirement benefits. Henceforth sick, injured, and retired workers could look forward to some regular benefits from the state. This national social security system, paid for through compulsory contributions by wage earners and employers as well as grants from the state, was the first of its kind anywhere. Bismarck's social security system did not wean workers from voting socialist, but it did give them a small stake in the system and protect them from some of the uncertainties of the complex urban industrial world. This enormously significant development was a product of political competition and government efforts to win popular support.

Increasingly, the great issues in German domestic politics were socialism and the Marxian Social Democratic Party. In 1890 the new emperor, the young, idealistic, and unstable William II (r. 1888–1918), opposed Bismarck's attempt to renew the law outlawing the Social Democratic Party. Eager to rule in his own right and to earn the support of the workers, William II forced Bismarck to resign. After the "dropping of the pilot," German foreign policy changed profoundly and mostly for the worse, but the government did pass new laws to aid workers and to legalize socialist political activity.

Yet William II was no more successful than Bismarck in getting workers to renounce socialism. Indeed, Social Democrats won more and more seats in the Reichstag, becoming Germany's largest single party in 1912. This great electoral victory shocked aristocrats and their wealthy, conservative middle-class allies, heightening the fears of an impending socialist upheaval. Yet the "revolutionary" socialists were actually becoming less radical in Germany. In the years before World War I, the German Social Democratic Party broadened its base by adopting a more patriotic tone, allowing for greater military spending and imperialist expansion. German socialists concentrated instead on gradual social and political reform.

Republican France

Although Napoleon III's reign made some progress in reducing antagonisms between classes, the war with Prussia undid these efforts, and in 1871 France seemed hopelessly divided once again. The patriotic republicans who proclaimed the Third Republic in Paris after the military disaster at Sedan refused to admit defeat. They defended Paris with great heroism for weeks, living off rats and zoo animals until they were starved into submission by German armies in January 1871. When national elections then sent a large majority of conservatives and monarchists to the National Assembly and France's new leaders decided they had no choice but to surrender Alsace (al-SAS) and Lorraine to Germany, the traumatized Parisians exploded in patriotic frustration and proclaimed the Paris Commune in March 1871. Vaguely radical, the leaders of the Commune wanted to govern Paris without interference from the conservative French countryside. The National Assembly, led by aging politician Adolphe Thiers (TEE-ehr), would hear none of it. The Assembly ordered the French army into Paris and brutally crushed the Commune. Twenty thousand people died in the fighting. As in June 1848, it was Paris against the provinces, French against French.

Out of this tragedy, France slowly formed a new national unity, achieving considerable stability before 1914. How is one to account for this? Luck played a part. Until 1875 the monarchists in the "republican" National Assembly had a majority but could not agree who should be king. The compromise Bourbon candidate refused to rule except under the white flag of his absolutist ancestors—a completely unacceptable condition for many supporters of moderate, constitutional monarchy. In the meantime, Thiers's destruction of the radical Commune and his other firm measures showed the fearful provinces and the middle class that the Third Republic might be moderate and socially conservative. France therefore retained the republic, though reluctantly. As President Thiers cautiously said, this was "the government which divides us least."

Another stabilizing factor was the skill and determination of the moderate republican leaders in the early years. The most famous of these was Léon Gambetta (gam-BEH-tuh), the son of an Italian grocer, a warm, easygoing, unsuccessful lawyer who had turned professional politician. By 1879 the great majority of members of both the upper and the lower houses of the National Assembly were republicans, and the Third Republic had firm foundations after almost a decade.

The moderate republicans sought to preserve their creation by winning the hearts and minds of the next generation. Trade unions were fully legalized, and France acquired a colonial empire. More important, a series of laws between 1879 and 1886 established free compulsory elementary education for both girls and boys. At the same time, they greatly expanded the state system of public tax-supported schools. In France and throughout the Western world, the general expansion of public education served as a critical nation-building tool in the late nineteenth century. In France most elementary and much secondary education had traditionally been in the parochial schools of the Catholic Church, which had long been hostile to republics and to much of secular life. Free compulsory elementary education in France became secular republican education.

Although the educational reforms of the 1880s disturbed French Catholics, many of them rallied to the republic in the 1890s. The limited acceptance of the

Captain Alfred Dreyfus   Leaving an 1899 reconsideration of his original court martial, Dreyfus receives an insulting "guard of dishonor" from soldiers whose backs are turned. (Roger-Viollet/Getty Images)

ened. In France only the growing socialist movement, with its very different and thoroughly secular ideology, stood in opposition to patriotic, republican nationalism.

Great Britain and Ireland

Britain in the late nineteenth century has often been seen as a shining example of peaceful and successful political evolution, where an effective two-party parliament skillfully guided the country from classical liberalism to full-fledged democracy with hardly a misstep. This view of Great Britain is not so much wrong as it is incomplete. After the right to vote was granted to males of the solid middle class in 1832, opinion leaders and politicians wrestled with the uncertainties of a further expansion of the franchise. In 1867 the Second Reform Bill of Benjamin Disraeli and the Conservatives extended the vote to all middle-class males and the best-paid workers in order to broaden the Conservative Party's traditional base of aristocratic and landed support. After 1867 English political parties and electoral campaigns became more modern, and the "lower orders" appeared to vote as responsibly as their "betters." Hence the Third Reform Bill of 1884 gave the vote to almost every adult male.

While the House of Commons was drifting toward democracy, the House of Lords was content to slumber nobly. Between 1901 and 1910, however, the House of Lords tried to reassert itself. Acting as supreme court of the land, it ruled against labor unions in two important decisions. And after the Liberal Party came to power in 1906, the Lords vetoed several measures passed by the Commons, including the so-called **People's Budget**, which was designed to increase spending on social welfare services. The Lords finally capitulated, as they had with the Reform Bill of 1832 (see Chapter 22), when the king threatened to create enough new peers to pass the bill, and aristocratic conservatism yielded to popular democracy once and for all.

The result was that extensive social welfare measures, slow to come to Great Britain, were passed in a spectacular rush between 1906 and 1914. During those years, the Liberal Party, inspired by the fiery Welshman David Lloyd George (1863–1945), substantially raised taxes on the rich as part of the People's Budget. This income helped the government pay for national health insurance, unemployment benefits, old-age pensions, and a host of other social measures. The state was integrating the urban masses socially as well as politically.

modern world by the more liberal Pope Leo XIII (pontificate 1878–1903) eased tensions between church and state. Unfortunately, the **Dreyfus affair** changed all that.

In 1894 Alfred Dreyfus, a Jewish captain in the French army, was falsely accused and convicted of treason. His family never doubted his innocence and fought to reopen the case, enlisting the support of prominent republicans and intellectuals such as novelist Émile Zola. In 1898 and 1899, the case split France apart. On one side was the army, which had manufactured evidence against Dreyfus, joined by anti-Semites and most of the Catholic establishment. On the other side stood the civil libertarians and most of the more radical republicans.

This battle, which eventually led to Dreyfus's being declared innocent, revived republican feeling against the church. Between 1901 and 1905, the government severed all ties between the state and the Catholic Church after centuries of close relations. The salaries of priests and bishops were no longer paid by the government, and all churches were given to local committees of lay Catholics. Catholic schools were put on their own financially and soon lost a third of their students. The state school system's power of indoctrination was greatly strength-

Dreyfus affair   A divisive case in which Alfred Dreyfus, a Jewish captain in the French army, was falsely accused and convicted of treason. The Catholic Church sided with the anti-Semites against Dreyfus; after Dreyfus was declared innocent, the French government severed all ties between the state and the church.

People's Budget   A bill proposed after the Liberal Party came to power in England in 1906, it was designed to increase spending on social welfare services, but was initially vetoed in the House of Lords.

This record of accomplishment was only part of the story, however. On the eve of World War I, the unanswered question of Ireland brought Great Britain to the brink of civil war. The terrible Irish famine fueled an Irish revolutionary movement. Thereafter, the English slowly granted concessions, such as the abolition of the privileges of the Anglican Church and rights for Irish peasants. Liberal prime minister William Gladstone (1809–1898), who had proclaimed twenty years earlier that "my mission is to pacify Ireland," introduced bills to give Ireland self-government in 1886 and in 1893. They failed to pass, but in 1913 Irish nationalists in the British Parliament finally gained a home-rule bill for Ireland.

Thus Ireland, the emerald isle, was on the brink of achieving self-government. Yet Ireland was composed of two peoples. As much as the Irish Catholic majority in the southern counties wanted home rule, precisely that much did the Irish Protestants of the northern counties of Ulster come to oppose it. Motivated by the accumulated fears and hostilities of generations, the Protestants of Ulster refused to submerge themselves in a Catholic Ireland, just as Irish Catholics had refused to submit to a Protestant Britain.

The Ulsterites vowed to resist home rule in northern Ireland. By December 1913 they had raised one hundred thousand armed volunteers, and they were supported by much of English public opinion. Thus in 1914 the Liberals in the House of Lords introduced a compromise home-rule bill that did not apply to the northern counties. This bill, which openly betrayed promises made to Irish nationalists, was rejected, and in September the original home-rule bill was passed but simultaneously suspended for the duration of the hostilities — the momentous Irish question had been overtaken by an earth-shattering world war in August 1914.

Irish developments illustrated once again the power of national feeling and national movements in the nineteenth century. Moreover, they were proof that governments could not elicit greater loyalty unless they could capture and control that elemental current of national feeling. Though Great Britain had much going for it — power, Parliament, prosperity — none of these availed in the face of the conflicting nationalisms created by Catholics and Protestants in northern Ireland. Similarly, progressive Sweden was powerless to stop the growth of the Norwegian national movement, which culminated in Norway's breaking away from Sweden and becoming a fully independent nation in 1905. In this light, one can also see how hopeless was the case of the Ottoman Empire in Europe in the later nineteenth century. It was only a matter of time before the Serbs, Bulgarians, and Romanians would break away.

The Austro-Hungarian Empire

The dilemma of conflicting nationalisms in Ireland helps one appreciate how desperate the situation in the Austro-Hungarian Empire had become by the early twentieth century. In 1849 Magyar nationalism had driven Hungarian patriots to declare an independent Hungarian republic, which was savagely crushed by Russian and Austrian armies (see Chapter 22). Throughout the 1850s, Hungary was ruled as a conquered territory, and Emperor Francis Joseph and his bureaucracy tried hard to centralize the state and Germanize the language and culture of the different nationalities.

Then in the wake of defeat by Prussia in 1866, a weakened Austria was forced to strike a compromise and establish the so-called dual monarchy. The empire

NO HOME RULE

LET OUR FLAG RUN OUT STRAIGHT IN THE WIND, THE OLD RED SHALL BE FLOATED AGAIN

WHEN THE RANKS THAT ARE THINNED SHALL BE THINNED, WHEN THE NAMES THAT ARE TWENTY ARE TEN.

ULSTER !

"No Home Rule" Posters like this one helped to incite pro-British, anti-Catholic sentiment in the northern Irish counties of Ulster before the First World War. The rifle raised defiantly and the accompanying rhyme are a thinly veiled threat of armed rebellion and civil war. (Reproduced with the kind permission of the Trustees of the National Museums & Galleries of Northern Ireland. Photograph © Ulster Museum, Belfast)

was divided in two, and the nationalistic Magyars gained virtual independence for Hungary. Henceforth, each half of the empire agreed to deal with its own ethnic minorities. The two states were joined only by a shared monarch and common ministries for finance, defense, and foreign affairs.

In Austria ethnic Germans were only one-third of the population, and in 1895 many Germans saw their traditional dominance threatened by Czechs, Poles, and other Slavs. A particularly emotional issue in the Austrian parliament was the language used in government and elementary education at the local level. From 1900 to 1914 the parliament was so divided that ministries generally could not obtain a majority and ruled instead by decree. Efforts by both conservatives and socialists to defuse national antagonisms by stressing economic issues that cut across ethnic lines were largely unsuccessful.

In Hungary the Magyar nobility in 1867 restored the constitution of 1848 and used it to dominate both the Magyar peasantry and the minority populations until 1914. Only the wealthiest one-fourth of adult males had the right to vote, making the parliament the creature of the Magyar elite. Laws promoting the use of the Magyar (Hungarian) language in schools and government were rammed through and bitterly resented, especially by the Croatians and Romanians. While Magyar extremists campaigned loudly for total separation from Austria, the radical leaders of the subject nationalities dreamed in turn of independence from Hungary. Unlike most major countries, which harnessed nationalism to strengthen the state after 1871, the Austro-Hungarian Empire was progressively weakened and destroyed by it.

Jewish Emancipation and Modern Anti-Semitism

Revolutionary changes in political principles and the triumph of the nation-state brought equally revolutionary changes in Jewish life in western and central Europe. The decisive turning point came in 1848, when Jews formed part of the revolutionary vanguard in Vienna and Berlin and the Frankfurt Assembly endorsed full rights for German Jews. In 1871 the constitution of the new German Empire consolidated the process of Jewish emancipation in central Europe. It abolished all restrictions on Jewish marriage, choice of occupation, place of residence, and property ownership. Exclusion from government employment and discrimination in social relations remained. However, according to one leading historian, by 1871 "it was widely accepted in Central Europe that the gradual disappearance of anti-Jewish prejudice was inevitable."[5] The process of emancipation presented Jews with challenges and opportunities. Traditional Jewish occupations, such as court financial agent, village moneylender, and peddler, were undermined by free-market reforms, but careers in

business, the professions, and the arts were opening to Jewish talent. Many Jews responded energetically and successfully. Active in finance and railroad building, European Jews excelled in wholesale and retail trade, consumer industries, journalism, medicine, and law. By 1871 a majority of Jewish people in western and central Europe had improved their economic situation and entered the middle classes. Most Jewish people also identified strongly with their respective nation-states and with good reason saw themselves as patriotic citizens.

Vicious anti-Semitism reappeared after the stock market crash of 1873, beginning in central Europe. Drawing on long traditions of religious intolerance, ghetto exclusion, and periodic anti-Jewish riots and expulsions, this anti-Semitism was also a modern development, building on the general reaction against liberalism. Modern anti-Semitism whipped up resentment against Jewish achievement and Jewish "financial control," while fanatics claimed that the Jewish race (rather than the Jewish religion) posed a biological threat to the German people. Anti-Semitic beliefs were particularly popular among conservatives, extremist nationalists, and people who felt threatened by Jewish competition, such as small shopkeepers, officeworkers, and professionals.

Anti-Semites also created modern political parties to attack and degrade Jews. In Austrian Vienna in the early 1890s, Karl Lueger (LOO-guhr) and his "Christian socialists" won striking electoral victories, spurring Theodor Herzl to turn from German nationalism and advocate political **Zionism** and the creation of a Jewish state. (See "Individuals in Society: Theodor Herzl," page 772.) Lueger, the popular mayor of Vienna from 1897 to 1910, combined fierce anti-Semitic rhetoric with municipal ownership of basic services, and he appealed especially to the German-speaking lower middle class—and an unsuccessful young artist named Adolf Hitler.

> **Zionism** A movement toward Jewish political nationhood started by Theodor Herzl.

Before 1914 anti-Semitism was most oppressive in eastern Europe, where Jews also suffered from terrible poverty. In the Russian empire, where there was no Jewish emancipation and 4 million of Europe's 7 million Jewish people lived in 1880, officials used anti-Semitism to channel popular discontent away from the government and onto the Jewish minority. Russian Jews were denounced as foreign exploiters who corrupted national traditions, and in 1881–1882 a wave of violent pogroms commenced in southern Russia. The police and the army stood aside for days while peasants looted and destroyed Jewish property. Official harassment continued in the following decades, and some Russian Jews turned toward self-emancipation and the vision of a Zionist settlement in Palestine. Large numbers also emigrated to western Europe and the United States. About 2.75 million Jews left eastern Europe between 1881 and 1914.

Theodor Herzl

INDIVIDUALS IN SOCIETY

IN SEPTEMBER 1897, ONLY DAYS AFTER HIS VISION AND ENERGY had called into being the First Zionist Congress in Basel, Switzerland, Theodor Herzl (1860–1904) assessed the results in his diary: "If I were to sum up the Congress in a word — which I shall take care not to publish — it would be this: At Basel I founded the Jewish state. If I said this out loud today I would be greeted by universal laughter. In five years perhaps, and certainly in fifty years, everyone will perceive it."*

Herzl's buoyant optimism, which so often carried him forward, was prophetic. Leading the Zionist movement until his death at age forty-four in 1904, Herzl guided the first historic steps toward modern Jewish political nationhood and the creation of Israel in 1948. Theodor Herzl was born in Budapest, Hungary, into an upper-middle-class, German-speaking Jewish family. When Herzl was eighteen, his family moved to Vienna, where he studied law. As a university student, he soaked up the liberal beliefs of most well-to-do Viennese Jews, who also championed the assimilation of German culture. Wrestling with his nonreligious Jewishness and his strong pro-German feeling, Herzl embraced German nationalism and joined a German dueling fraternity.

There he discovered that full acceptance required openly anti-Semitic attitudes and a repudiation of all things Jewish. This Herzl could not tolerate, and he resigned. After receiving his law degree, he embarked on a literary career. In 1889 Herzl married into a wealthy Viennese Jewish family, but he and his socialite wife were mismatched and never happy together.

Herzl achieved considerable success as both a journalist and a playwright. His witty comedies focused on the bourgeoisie, including Jewish millionaires trying to live like aristocrats. Accepting many German stereotypes, Herzl sometimes depicted eastern Jews as uneducated and grasping. But as a dedicated, highly educated liberal, he mainly believed that the Jewish shortcomings he perceived were the results of age-old persecution and would disappear through education and assimilation. Herzl also took a growing pride in Jewish steadfastness in the face of victimization and suffering. He savored memories of his early Jewish education and going with his father to the synagogue.

The emergence of modern anti-Semitism (see page 771) shocked Herzl, as it did many acculturated Jewish Germans. Moving to Paris in 1891 as the correspondent for Vienna's leading liberal newspaper, Herzl studied politics and pondered recent historical developments. He then came to a bold conclusion, published in 1896 as *The Jewish State: An Attempt at a Modern Solution to the Jewish Question*. According to Herzl, Jewish assimilation had failed, and attempts to combat anti-Semitism would never succeed. Only by building an independent Jewish state could the Jewish people achieve dignity and renewal.

Theodor Herzl. (Library of Congress)

Herzl developed his political nationalism, or Zionism, before the anti-Jewish agitation accompanying the Dreyfus affair, which only served to strengthen his faith in his analysis. Generally rebuffed by skeptical Jewish elites in western and central Europe, Herzl turned for support to youthful idealists and the poor Jewish masses. He became an inspiring man of action, rallying the delegates to the annual Zionist congresses, directing the growth of the worldwide Zionist organization, and working himself to death. Herzl also understood that national consciousness required powerful emotions and symbols, such as a Jewish flag. Flags build nations, he said, because people "live and die for a flag."

Putting the Zionist vision before non-Jews and world public opinion, Herzl believed in international diplomacy and political agreements. He traveled constantly to negotiate with European rulers and top officials, seeking their support in securing territory for a Jewish state, usually in the Ottoman Empire. Aptly described by an admiring contemporary as "the first Jewish statesman since the destruction of Jerusalem," Herzl proved most successful in Britain. He paved the way for the 1917 Balfour Declaration, which solemnly pledged British support for a "Jewish homeland" in Palestine.

QUESTIONS FOR ANALYSIS

1. Describe Theodor Herzl's background and early beliefs. Do you see a link between Herzl's early German nationalism and his later Zionism?

2. Why did Herzl believe an independent Jewish state with its own national flag was necessary?

3. How did Herzl work as a leader to turn his Zionist vision into a reality?

*Quotes are from Theodor Herzl, *The Diaries of Theodor Herzl*, trans. and ed. with an introduction by Marvin Lowenthal (New York: Grosset & Dunlap, 1962), pp. 224, 22, xxi.

Austreibung der Juden aus Russland.

GRUSS AUS *Leipzig, d. 15. Aug. 99. Mit freundlichem Grüße und Ihr Ow. Kaminski*

Picturing the Past

"The Expulsion of the Jews from Russia" So reads this postcard, correctly suggesting that Russian government officials often encouraged popular anti-Semitism and helped drive many Jews out of Russia in the late nineteenth century. The road signs indicate that these poor Jews are crossing into Germany, where they will find a grudging welcome and a meager meal at the Jolly Onion Inn. Other Jews from eastern Europe settled in France and Britain, thereby creating small but significant Jewish populations in both of these countries for the first time since they had expelled most of their Jews in the Middle Ages. (Alliance Israelite Universelle, Paris/Archives Charmet/The Bridgeman Art Library)

ANALYZING THE IMAGE The inset image in the upper-right corner shows an armed German soldier at the table, carefully watching the Jewish refugees. What similarity do you see between this and the larger image on the postcard to suggest how Jewish refugees were treated in Germany as compared to Russia? The postcard was sent on August 15, 1899, from Leipzig, Germany, and the message is in German. To whom might this card have been sent and what message might the postcard convey to the recipient?

CONNECTIONS What famous event marked the rise of vicious anti-Semitism in the late nineteenth century, and what characterized the modern anti-Semitism of this period? Did the Jews like the ones shown on this postcard find an acceptable haven in Germany in the period before World War I?

To complete this activity online, go to the Online Study Guide at **bedfordstmartins.com/mckaywest**.

Marxism and the Socialist Movement

Why did the socialist movement grow, and how revolutionary was it? ■

Nationalism served, for better or worse, as a new unifying principle. But what about socialism? Socialist parties, which were generally Marxian parties dedicated to an international proletarian revolution, grew rapidly in these years. Did this mean that national states had failed to gain the support of workers? Certainly, many prosperous and conservative citizens were greatly troubled by the socialist movement. And numerous historians have portrayed the years before 1914 as a time of increasing conflict between revolutionary socialism, on the one hand, and a nationalist alliance of the conservative aristocracy and the prosperous middle class, on the other.

The Socialist International

The growth of socialist parties after 1871 was phenomenal. (See "Listening to the Past: Adelheid Popp, the Making of a Socialist," page 776.) Neither Bismarck's antisocialist laws nor his extensive social security system checked the growth of the German Social Democratic Party, which espoused the Marxian ideology. By 1912 it had millions of followers—mostly people from the working classes—and was the largest party in the Reichstag. Socialist parties also grew in other countries, though nowhere else with such success. In 1883 Russian exiles in Switzerland founded the Russian Social Democratic Party, and various socialist parties were unified in 1905 in the French Section of the Workers International. Belgium and Austria-Hungary also had strong socialist parties.

As the name of the French party suggests, Marxian socialist parties were eventually linked together in an international organization. Marx believed that "the working men have no country," and he had urged proletarians of all nations to unite. Marx himself played an important role in founding the First International of socialists—the International Working Men's Association. In the following years, he battled successfully to control the organization and used its annual meetings as a means of spreading his realistic, "scientific" doctrines of inevitable socialist revolution. Then Marx enthusiastically embraced the passionate, radical patriotism of the Paris Commune and its terrible conflict with the French National Assembly as a giant step toward socialist revolution. This impetuous action frightened many of his early sup-porters, especially the more moderate British labor leaders. The First International collapsed.

Yet international proletarian solidarity remained an important objective for Marxists. In 1889, as the individual parties in different countries grew stronger, socialist leaders came together to form the Second International, which lasted until 1914. The International was only a federation of national socialist parties, but it had a great psychological impact. Every three years, delegates from the different parties met to interpret Marxian doctrines and plan coordinated action. May 1 (May Day) was declared an annual international one-day strike, a day of marches and demonstrations. A permanent executive for the International was established. Many feared and many others rejoiced in the growing power of socialism and the Second International.

Unions and Revisionism

Was socialism really radical and revolutionary in these years? On the whole, it was not. As socialist parties grew and attracted large numbers of members, they looked more and more toward gradual change and steady improvement for the working class and less and less toward revolution. The mainstream of European socialism became militantly moderate; that is, socialists increasingly combined radical rhetoric with sober action.

"Greetings from the May Day Festival" Workers participated enthusiastically in the annual one-day strike on May 1 in Stuttgart, Germany, to honor internationalist socialist solidarity, as this postcard suggests. Speeches, picnics, and parades were the order of the day, and workers celebrated their respectability and independent culture. Picture postcards like this one and the one on page 773 developed with railroads, mass travel, and high-speed printing. (akg-images)

Workers themselves were progressively less inclined to follow radical programs. There were several reasons for this. As workers gained the right to vote and to participate politically in the nation-state, they focused their attention more on elections than on revolutions. And as workers won real, tangible benefits, this furthered the process. Workers were also not immune to patriotic education and indoctrination during military service, and many responded positively to drum-beating parades and aggressive foreign policy as they loyally voted for socialists. Nor were workers a unified social group.

Perhaps most important of all, workers' standard of living rose gradually but substantially after 1850 as the promise of the Industrial Revolution was at least partially realized. In Great Britain, for example, workers could buy almost twice as much with their wages in 1906 as in 1850, and most of the increase came after 1870. Workers experienced similar gradual increases in most continental countries after 1850, though much less strikingly in late-developing Russia. The quality of life in urban areas improved dramatically as well. For all these reasons, workers tended more and more to become militantly moderate: they demanded gains, but they were less likely to take to the barricades in pursuit of them.

The growth of labor unions reinforced this trend toward moderation. In the early stages of industrialization, modern unions were generally prohibited by law. A famous law of the French Revolution had declared all guilds and unions illegal in the name of "liberty" in 1791. In Great Britain, attempts by workers to unite were considered criminal conspiracies after 1799. Other countries had similar laws that obviously hampered union development. Unions were considered subversive bodies to be hounded and crushed.

From this sad position workers struggled to escape. Great Britain led the way in 1824 and 1825 when unions won the right to exist but (generally) not the right to strike. After the collapse of Robert Owen's attempt to form one big union in the 1830s (see Chapter 21), new and more practical kinds of unions appeared. Limited primarily to highly skilled workers such as machinists and carpenters, these "new model unions" concentrated on winning better wages and hours through collective bargaining and compromise. This approach helped pave the way to full acceptance in Britain in the 1870s, and after 1890 unions for unskilled workers developed.

Developments in Germany, the most industrialized, socialized, and unionized continental country by 1914, were particularly instructive. German unions were not granted important rights until 1869, and until the antisocialist law was repealed in 1890, they were frequently harassed by the government as socialist fronts. The result was that as late as 1895, there were only about 270,000 union members in a male industrial workforce of nearly 8 million. Then, with German industrialization still

Driven by the movement of the working classes which is daily becoming stronger, a social reaction has set in against the exploiting tendencies of capital.

—EDUARD BERNSTEIN

storming ahead and almost all legal harassment eliminated, union membership skyrocketed, reaching roughly 3 million in 1912.

This great expansion both reflected and influenced the changing character of German unions. Increasingly, unions in Germany focused on bread-and-butter issues— wages, hours, working conditions—rather than on the dissemination of pure socialist doctrine. Genuine collective bargaining, long opposed by socialist intellectuals as a "sellout," was officially recognized as desirable by the German Trade Union Congress in 1899. When employers proved unwilling to bargain, a series of strikes forced them to change their minds. In 1913 alone, over ten thousand collective bargaining agreements benefiting 1.25 million workers were signed.

The German trade unions and their leaders were in fact, if not in name, thoroughgoing revisionists. **Revisionism**—that most awful of sins in the eyes of militant Marxists in the twentieth century—was an effort by various socialists to update Marxian doctrines to reflect the realities of the time. Thus the socialist Eduard Bernstein (1850–1932) argued in 1899 in his *Evolutionary Socialism* that many of Marx's predictions had been proved false.

> **revisionism** An effort by moderate socialists to update Marxian doctrines to reflect the realities of the time.

Social conditions have not developed to such an acute opposition of things and classes as is depicted in the Communist Manifesto. . . . The number of members of the possessing classes to-day is not smaller but larger. . . .

In all advanced countries we see the privileges of the capitalist bourgeoisie yielding step by step to democratic organizations. Under the influence of this, and driven by the movement of the working classes which is daily becoming stronger, a social reaction has set in against the exploiting tendencies of capital.[6]

Therefore, Bernstein argued, socialists should reform their doctrines and tactics. They should combine with other progressive forces to win continued evolutionary gains for workers through legislation, unions, and further economic development. These views were denounced as heresy by the German Social Democratic

Adelheid Popp, the Making of a Socialist

LISTENING TO THE PAST

Nationalism and socialism appeared locked in bitter competition in Europe before 1914, but they actually complemented each other in many ways. Both faiths were secular as opposed to religious, and both fostered political awareness. A working person who became interested in politics and developed nationalist beliefs might well convert to socialism at a later date.

This was the case for Adelheid Popp (1869–1939), a self-taught working woman who became an influential socialist leader. Born into a desperately poor working-class family in Vienna and remembering only a "hard and gloomy childhood," she was forced by her parents to quit school at age ten to begin full-time work. She struggled with low-paying piecework for years before she landed a solid factory job, as she recounts in the following selection from her widely read autobiography. Always an avid reader, Popp became the editor of a major socialist newspaper for German working women. She then told her life story so that all working women might share her truth: "Socialism could change and strengthen others, as it did me."

[Finally] I found work again; I took everything that was offered me in order to show my willingness to work, and I passed through much. But at last things became better. [At age fifteen] I was recommended to a great factory which stood in the best repute. Three hundred girls and about fifty men were employed. I was put in a big room where sixty women and girls were at work.

Against the windows stood twelve tables, and at each sat four girls. We had to sort the goods which had been manufactured, others had to count them, and a third set had to brand on them the mark of the firm. We worked from 7 A.M. to 7 P.M. We had an hour's rest at noon, half-an-hour in the afternoon. . . . I had never yet been paid so much. . . .

I seemed to myself to be almost rich. . . . [Yet] from the women of this factory one can judge how sad and full of deprivation is the lot of a factory worker. In none of the neighbouring factories were the wages so high; we were envied everywhere. Parents considered themselves fortunate if they could get their daughters of fourteen in there on leaving school. . . . And even here, in this paradise, all were badly nourished. Those who stayed at the factory for the dinner hour would buy themselves for a few pennies a sausage or the leavings of a cheese shop. . . . In spite of all the diligence and economy, every one was poor, and trembled at the thought of losing her work. All humbled themselves, and suffered the worst injustice from the foremen, not to risk losing this good work, not to be without food. . . .

I did not only read novels and tales; I had begun . . . to read the classics and other good books. I also began to take an interest in public events. . . . I was not democratically inclined. I was full of enthusiasm then for emperors, and kings and highly placed personages played no small part in my fancies. . . . I bought myself a strict Catholic paper, that criticised very adversely the workers' movement, which was attracting notice. Its aim was to educate in a patriotic and religious direction. . . . I took the warmest interest in the events that occurred in the royal families, and I took the death of the Crown Prince of Austria so much to heart that I wept a whole day. . . . Political events [also] held me in suspense. The possibility of a war with Russia roused my patriotic enthusiasm. I saw my brother already returning from the battlefield covered with glory. . . .

When a particularly strong anti-Semitic feeling was noticeable in political life, I sympathised with it for a time. A broad sheet, "How Israel Attained Power and Sovereignty over all the Nations of the Earth," fascinated me. . . .

About this time an Anarchist group was active. Some mysterious murders which had taken place were ascribed to the Anarchists, and the police made use of them to oppress the rising workmen's movement. . . . I followed the trial of the Anarchists with passionate sympathy. I read all the speeches, and because, as always happens, Social Democrats, whom the authorities really wanted to attack, were among the accused,

Party and later by the entire Second International. Yet the revisionist, gradualist approach continued to gain the tacit acceptance of many German socialists, particularly in the trade unions.

Moderation found followers elsewhere. In France the great socialist leader Jean Jaurès (1859–1914) formally repudiated revisionist doctrines in order to establish a unified socialist party, but he remained at heart a gradualist and optimistic secular humanist. Questions of revolution also split Russian Marxists.

Socialist parties before 1914 had clear-cut national characteristics. Russians and socialists in the Austro-Hungarian Empire tended to be the most radical. The German party talked revolution and practiced reformism, greatly influenced by its enormous trade-union movement. The French party talked revolution and tried

1890 engraving of a meeting of workers in Berlin.
(Bildarchiv Preussischer Kulturbesitz/Art Resource, NY)

I learned their views. I became full of enthusiasm. Every single Social Democrat . . . seemed to me a hero. . . . There was unrest among the workers . . . and demonstrations of protest followed. When these were repeated the military entered the "threatened" streets. . . . In the evenings I rushed in the greatest excitement from the factory to the scene of the disturbance. The military did not frighten me; I only left the place when it was "cleared."

Later on my mother and I lived with one of my brothers who had married. Friends came to him, among them some intelligent workmen. One of these workmen was particularly intelligent, and . . . could talk on many subjects. He was the first Social Democrat I knew. He brought me many books, and explained to me the difference between Anarchism and Socialism. I heard from him, also for the first time, what a republic was, and in spite of my former enthusiasm for royal dynasties, I also declared myself in favour of a republican form of government. I saw everything so near and so clearly, that I actually counted the weeks which must still elapse before the revolution of state and society would take place. From this workman I received the first Social Democratic party organ. . . . I first learned from it to understand and judge of my own lot. I learned to see that all I had suffered was the result not of a divine ordinance, but of an unjust organization of society. . . .

In the factory I became another woman. . . . I told my [female] comrades all that I had read of the workers' movement. Formerly I had often told stories when they had begged me for them. But instead of narrating . . . the fate of some queen, I now held forth on oppression and exploitation. I told of accumulated wealth in the hands of a few, and introduced as a contrast the shoemakers who had no shoes and the tailors who had no clothes. On breaks I read aloud the articles in the Social Democratic paper and explained what Socialism was as far as I understood it. . . . [While I was reading] it often happened that one of the clerks passing by shook his head and said to another clerk: "The girl speaks like a man." ❱❱

Source: Slightly adapted from A. Popp, *The Autobiography of a Working Woman*, trans. E. C. Harvey (Chicago: F. G. Browne, 1913), pp. 29, 34–35, 39, 66–69, 71, 74, 82–90.

QUESTIONS FOR ANALYSIS

1. How did Popp describe and interpret work in the factory?

2. According to her autobiography, what accounts for Popp's nationalist sentiments early on? How and why did she become a Social Democrat?

3. Was Popp likely to lead other working women to socialism by reading them articles from socialist newspapers? Why or why not?

to practice it, unrestrained by a trade-union movement that was both very weak and very radical. In England the socialist but non-Marxian Labour Party, reflecting the well-established union movement, was formally committed to gradual reform. In Spain and Italy, Marxian socialism was very weak. There anarchism, seeking to smash the state rather than the bourgeoisie, dominated radical thought and action.

In short, socialist policies and doctrines varied from country to country. Socialism itself was to a large extent "nationalized" behind the imposing façade of international unity. This helps explain why when war came in 1914, almost all socialist leaders and most workers supported their governments.

LOOKING BACK LOOKING AHEAD

IN 1900, THE TRIUMPH of nationalism in Europe seemed almost complete. Only in eastern Europe, in the three aging multinational empires of Austria-Hungary, Russia, and the Ottomans, did several nationalities still struggle to form their own states. Elsewhere the ethnically unified nation-state, resting solidly upon the continent's ongoing industrialization and its emerging urban society, governed with the consent and even the devotion of its citizens. Responsive and capable of tackling many practical problems, the European nation-state of 1900 was in part the realization of ideologues and patriots like Mazzini and the middle-class liberals active in the unsuccessful revolutions of 1848. Yet whereas early nationalists had envisioned a Europe of free peoples and international peace, the nationalists of 1900 had been nurtured in the traditional competition between European states and the wars of unification in the 1850s and 1860s. This generation of nationalists reveled in the strength of their unity, and the nation-state became a system of power.

Thus after 1870, at the same time the responsive nation-state improved city life and brought social benefits to ordinary people, Europe's leading countries also projected raw power throughout the world. In the expanding colonies of Asia and Africa, the nations of Britain, France, Germany, and Russia seized territory, fought brutal colonial wars, and built authoritarian empires. Moreover, in Europe itself the universal faith in nationalism, which usually reduced social tensions within states, promoted a bitter, almost Darwinian, competition between states. Thus European nationalism threatened the very progress and unity it had helped to build. In 1914, the power of unified nation-states would turn on itself, unleashing the First World War and doling out self-inflicted wounds of enormous proportions to all of Europe's peoples.

CHAPTER REVIEW

■ How did Napoleon III seek to reconcile popular and conservative forces in an authoritarian nation-state? (p. 750)

Elected president of France in 1848 and then named emperor in 1852, Napoleon III combined authoritarian rule with economic growth and positive measures for the poor. Believing that representative government got in the way of reform and progress, Napoleon III aimed to serve the people directly. He also maintained widespread support by allowing his regime to evolve in a democratic direction, staying in power until France was defeated by Prussia in 1870.

■ How did the process of unification in Italy and Germany create conservative nation-states? (p. 752)

In Italy, Cavour joined traditional diplomacy and war against Austria with nationalist uprisings in central Italy to expand the constitutional monarchy of Sardinia-Piedmont. Cavour then called on Garibaldi's revolutionary patriotism to kindle peasant revolt in southern Italy and succeeded in merging the south and the north together in a conservative nation-state under Victor Emmanuel. In Prussia Bismarck also combined traditional statecraft with national feeling. Ruling without the consent of parliament and reorganizing the army, Bismarck succeeded in making Prussia the dominant German state and in driving Austria out of German affairs in 1866. War with France completed the unification process, expanding the power of Prussia and its king in a new German Empire, and instilling in all Germans a strong sense of national pride.

■ In what ways did the United States experience nation building? (p. 758)

The question of slavery divided the early Northern and Southern U.S. states for both economic and political reasons. With westward expansion in the mid-nineteenth century, debates over slavery came to the fore, causing the Southern states to secede and leading to a civil war. The Northern states prevailed, and the Union was preserved. The postwar years saw unique national characteristics arise and seemed to confirm America's destiny as a great world power.

■ What steps did Russia and the Ottoman Turks take toward modernization, and how successful were they? (p. 759)

In autocratic Russia, defeat in the Crimean War posed a regime-threatening crisis, which led to the emancipation of the serfs and economic modernization that featured railroad building, military improvements, and industrialization. Political reform was limited, however, and even after the revolution of 1905 led to a popularly elected Duma, the tsar retained very great power. The Ottoman Empire also sought to modernize to protect the state, but it was considerably less successful. Faced with resistance by Christian nationalists and conservative Muslims, and economically hindered by Western imperialism, the modernization efforts failed to salvage the Ottoman sultan's progressive regime.

■ Why after 1871 did ordinary citizens feel a growing loyalty to their governments? (p. 766)

After 1871 nationalism — the commitment to the nation-state — became the general European creed, nurtured in large part by patriotic education and fueled by foreign wars and increasingly advanced militaries. In addition, most states enacted universal male suffrage and electoral politics, providing citizens with a greater sense of belonging. Representative governments also produced specific social and economic improvements, such as state-sponsored pensions, protective tariffs, and a rising standard of living, that benefited ordinary citizens.

■ Why did the socialist movement grow, and how revolutionary was it? (p. 773)

The socialist movement grew because it became the champion of working-class interests in the emerging urban society and in domestic politics. Socialist leaders in many countries also supported international revolutionary Marxism in theory, but in practice they usually concentrated on bread-and-butter gains for union members. Thus pre-1914 socialism was militantly moderate and not very revolutionary.

Suggested Reading

Berend, Ivan T. *History Derailed: Central and Eastern Europe in the Long Nineteenth Century.* 2003. Focuses on industrialization and its consequences.

Clyman, Toby W., and Judith Vowles, eds. *Russia Through Women's Eyes: Autobiographies from Tsarist Russia.* 1999. An eye-opening collection detailing women's experiences in Russia.

Fink, Carole. *Defending the Rights of Others: The Great Powers, the Jews, and the International Protection, 1878–1938.* 2004. Skilled consideration of the cruelty and tragedy of ethnic conflict and minority oppression.

Finley, C. *The Turks in World History.* 2005. An exciting reconsideration of the Turks in long-term perspective.

Geary, Dick, ed. *Labour and Socialist Movements in Europe Before 1914.* 1989. An excellent collection that examines labor movements in several different countries.

Grenville, J. A. S. *Europe Reshaped, 1850–1978*, 2d ed. 2000. A careful analysis of political developments in the leading states.

Hennock, E. P. *The Origins of the Welfare State in England and Germany, 1850–1914.* 2007. Compares Germany's statist approach with England's response to demands from below.

Hobsbawm, Eric. *The Age of Empire, 1875–1914.* 1987. A classic interpretative work.

Kitchen, Martin. *The Cambridge Illustrated History of Germany.* 1996. Features handsome pictures and a readable text.

Ridley, Jasper. *Phoenix: Garibaldi.* 2001. A thorough study of the world-renowned revolutionary nationalist.

Schulze, Hagen, and William E. Yuill. *States, Nations and Nationalism: From the Middle Ages to the Present.* 1996. An important study that explores the resurgence of European nationalism since the fall of communism.

Slezkine, Yuri. *The Jewish Century.* 2004. A brilliant interpretation of Jewish achievement in the modern era.

Tombs, Robert. *France, 1814–1914.* 1996. An impressive survey with a useful bibliography.

Vital, David. *A People Apart: The Jews in Europe, 1789–1939.* 1999. An engaging and judicious survey.

Key Terms

Red Shirts (p. 754)
Homestead Act (p. 758)
modernization (p. 759)
Bloody Sunday (p. 761)
October Manifesto (p. 764)
Duma (p. 764)
Tanzimat (p. 764)
Young Turks (p.765)
Reichstag (p. 767)
Kulturkampf (p. 767)
Dreyfus affair (p. 769)
People's Budget (p. 769)
Zionism (p. 771)
revisionism (p. 775)

Notes

1. H. Schulze, *States, Nations and Nationalism: From the Middle Ages to the Present* (Oxford, U.K.: Blackwell, 1994), pp. 222–223, 246–247.
2. Quoted by J. McKay, *Pioneers for Profit: Foreign Entrepreneurship and Russian Industrialization, 1885–1913* (Chicago: University of Chicago Press, 1970), p. 11.
3. E. Van Dyck, *Report upon the Capitulations of the Ottoman Empire Since the Year 1150* (Washington, DC: United States Printing Office, 1881, 1882), part 1, pp. 106–107.
4. W. Dawson, *Bismarck and State Socialism* (London: Swan Sonnenschein & Co., 1890), pp. 63–64.
5. R. Seltzer, *Jewish People, Jewish Thought: The Jewish Experience in History* (New York: Macmillan, 1980), p. 533.
6. Eduard Bernstein, *Evolutionary Socialism: A Criticism and Affirmation*, trans. Edith Harvey (New York: B. W. Huebsch, 1909), pp. x–xvi, quoted in J. H. Hexter et al., *The Traditions of the Western World* (Chicago: Rand McNally, 1967), pp. 797–798.

For practice quizzes and other study tools, visit the Online Study Guide at **bedfordstmartins.com/mckaywest**.

For primary sources from this period, see *Sources of Western Society*, **Second Edition**.

For Web sites, images, and documents related to topics in this chapter, visit Make History at **bedfordstmartins.com/mckaywest**.

25

The West and the World

1815–1914

While industrialization and nationalism were transforming urban and agricultural life throughout Europe, Western society itself was reshaping the world. At the peak of its power and pride, the West entered the third and most dynamic phase of the aggressive expansion that had begun with the Crusades and continued with the great discoveries and the rise of seaborne colonial empires. An ever-growing stream of products and ideas flowed out of Europe in the nineteenth century. Hardly any corner of the globe was left untouched. At the same time millions of Europeans picked up stakes and emigrated abroad, primarily to North and South America but also to Australia, North and South Africa, and Asiatic Russia.

The most spectacular manifestations of Western expansion came in the late nineteenth century when the leading European nations established or enlarged their far-flung political empires. This political annexation of territory in the 1880s — the "new imperialism," as it is often called by historians — was the capstone of Europe's underlying economic and technological transformation. More directly, Europe's new imperialism rested on a formidable combination of superior military might and strong authoritarian rule, and it posed a brutal challenge to African and Asian peoples. Different societies met this Western challenge in different ways and with changing tactics, as we shall see. Nevertheless, by 1914 non-Western elites in many lands were rallying their peoples and leading an anti-imperialist struggle for dignity and genuine independence that would eventually triumph after 1945. ∎

Living in the Age of New Imperialism. The late nineteenth century witnessed the spread of European empires abroad and the intertwining of the lives of Europeans and native populations. Here European tourists look on at the well-tended trees and handsome buildings of Cairo's new quarter, a result of European involvement in modernizing the city.

CHAPTER PREVIEW

Industrialization and the World Economy
■ What were some of the global consequences of European industrialization between 1815 and 1914?

The Great Migration
■ How was massive migration an integral part of Western expansion?

Western Imperialism, 1880–1914
■ How and why after 1875 did European nations rush to build political empires in Africa and Asia?

Responding to Western Imperialism
■ What was the general pattern of non-Western responses to Western expansion, and how did India, Japan, and China meet the imperialist challenge?

Industrialization and the World Economy

What were some of the global consequences of European industrialization between 1815 and 1914? ■

The Industrial Revolution created, first in Great Britain and then in continental Europe and North America, a tremendously dynamic economic system. In the course of the nineteenth century, that system was extended across the face of the earth. Some of this extension into non-Western areas was peaceful and beneficial for all concerned, for the West had many products and techniques the rest of the world desired. If peaceful methods failed, however, Europeans used their superior military power to force non-Western nations to open their doors to Western economic interests. In general, Westerners fashioned the global economic system so that the largest share of the ever-increasing gains from trade, technology, and migration flowed to the West and its propertied classes.

The Rise of Global Inequality

The Industrial Revolution in Europe marked a momentous turning point in human history. Those regions of the world that industrialized in the nineteenth century (mainly Europe and North America) increased their wealth and power enormously in comparison to those that did not. A gap between the industrializing regions and the nonindustrializing or **Third World** regions (mainly Africa, Asia, and Latin America) opened up and grew steadily throughout the nineteenth century. Moreover, this pattern of uneven global development became institutionalized, or built into the structure of the world economy. Thus we evolved a "lopsided world," a world of rich lands and poor.

Third World A term that refers to the non-industrialized nations of Africa, Asia, and Latin America as a single unit.

In recent years historical economists have been charting the long-term evolution of this gap, and Figure 25.1 summarizes the findings of one important study. Three main points stand out. First, in 1750 the average standard of living was no higher in Europe as a whole than in the rest of the world. Second, it was industrialization that opened the gaps in average wealth and well-being among countries and regions. Third, income per person stagnated in the Third World before 1913, in striking contrast to the industrializing regions. Only after 1945, in the era of political independence and decolonization, did Third World countries finally make some real economic progress, beginning in their turn the critical process of industrialization.

The rise of these enormous income disparities, which are poignant indicators of equal disparities in food and

British Ships and Shipbuilders The British continued to dominate international trade before the First World War. This handsome membership certificate of the British shipbuilders union features the vessels that tied the world together economically. Britain's thriving shipbuilding industry was concentrated in southern Scotland. (Trade Union Congress, London/ The Bridgeman Art Library)

clothing, health and education, life expectancy and general material well-being, has generated a great deal of debate. One school of interpretation stresses that the West used science, technology, capitalist organization, and even its critical world-view to create its wealth and greater physical well-being. Another school argues that the West used its political and economic power to steal much of its riches, continuing in the nineteenth and twentieth centuries the rapacious colonialism born of the era of expansion. Because these issues are complex and there are few simple answers, it is helpful to consider them in the context of world trade in the nineteenth century.

The World Market

Commerce between nations has always stimulated economic development. In the nineteenth century, Europe directed an enormous increase in international commerce. Great Britain took the lead in cultivating export markets for its booming industrial output, as British manufacturers looked first to Europe and then around the world.

Take the case of cotton textiles. By 1820 Britain was exporting 50 percent of its production. Europe bought 50 percent of these cotton textile exports, while India bought only 6 percent. Then as European nations and the United States erected protective tariff barriers and promoted domestic industry, British cotton textile manufacturers aggressively sought and found other foreign markets in non-Western areas. By 1850 India was buying 25 percent and Europe only 16 percent of a much larger total. As a British colony, India could not raise tariffs to protect its ancient cotton textile industry, and thousands of Indian weavers lost their livelihoods.

In addition to its dominance in the export market, Britain was also the world's largest importer of goods. From the repeal of the Corn Laws in 1846 (see Chapter 22) to the outbreak of World War I in 1914, Britain remained the world's emporium, where not only agricultural products and raw materials but also manufactured goods entered freely. Free access to Britain's market stimulated the development of mines and plantations in many non-Western areas.

International trade also grew as transportation systems improved. Wherever railroads were built, they drastically reduced transportation costs, opened new economic opportunities, and called forth new skills and attitudes. Much of the railroad construction undertaken in Latin America, Asia, and Africa connected seaports with inland cities and regions, as opposed to linking and developing cities and regions within a given country. Thus railroads dovetailed admirably with Western economic interests, facilitating the inflow and sale of Western manufactured goods and the export and the development of local raw materials.

The power of steam revolutionized transportation by sea as well as by land. Steam power began to supplant sails on the oceans of the world in the late 1860s. Passenger and freight rates tumbled as ship design

Figure 25.1 **The Growth of Average Income per Person in the Third World, Developed Countries, and Great Britain, 1750–1970** Growth is given in 1960 U.S. dollars and prices.

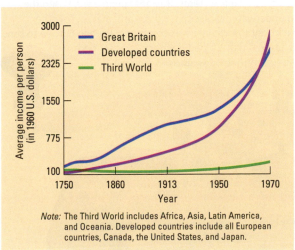

Note: The Third World includes Africa, Asia, Latin America, and Oceania. Developed countries include all European countries, Canada, the United States, and Japan.

became more sophisticated, and the intercontinental shipment of low-priced raw materials became feasible. The opening of the Suez and Panama Canals shortened global transport time considerably. In addition, port facilities were modernized to make loading and unloading cheaper, faster, and more dependable.

The revolution in land and sea transportation encouraged European entrepreneurs to open up vast new territories around the world and develop agricultural products and raw materials there for sale in Europe. Improved transportation enabled Asia, Africa, and Latin America to ship not only the traditional tropical products—spices, tea, sugar, coffee—but also new raw materials for industry, such as jute, rubber, cotton, and coconut oil.

New communications systems directed the flow of goods across global networks. Transoceanic telegraph cables inaugurated rapid communications among the financial centers of the world. While a British tramp freighter steamed from Calcutta to New York, a broker in London was arranging by telegram for it to carry an American cargo to Australia. The same communications network conveyed world commodity prices instantaneously.

As their economies grew, Europeans began to make massive foreign investments beginning about 1840. By the outbreak of World War I in 1914, Europeans had invested more than $40 billion abroad. Great Britain, France, and Germany were the principal investing countries (Map 25.1). The great gap between rich and poor within Europe meant that the wealthy and moderately well-to-do could and did send great sums abroad in search of interest and dividends.

Most of the capital exported did not go to European colonies or protectorates in Asia and Africa. About three-quarters of total European investment went to other European countries, the United States and Canada, Australia and New Zealand, and Latin America. Europe found its most profitable opportunities for investment in construction of the railroads, ports, and utilities that were necessary to settle and develop the lands in such places as Australia and the Americas. By lending money for a foreign railroad, Europeans also enabled white settlers to buy European rails and locomotives and to develop sources of cheap food and raw materials. Much of this investment was peaceful and mutually beneficial for lenders and borrowers. The victims were Native American Indians and Australian aborigines, who were decimated by the diseases, liquor, and weapons of an aggressively expanding Western society.

The Opening of China

Europe's relatively peaceful development of robust offshoots in sparsely populated North America, Australia, and much of Latin America absorbed huge quantities of goods, investments, and migrants. Yet Europe's economic and cultural penetration of old, densely populated civilizations was also profoundly significant. With such civilizations Europeans also increased their trade and profit, and they were prepared to use force, if necessary, to attain their desires. This was what happened in China, a striking example of the pattern of intrusion into non-Western lands.

Traditional Chinese civilization was self-sufficient. For centuries China had sent more goods and inventions to Europe than it had received, and this was still the case in the early nineteenth century. Trade with Europe was carefully regulated by the Chinese imperial government—the Qing (ching), or Manchu, Dynasty—which required all foreign merchants to live in the southern port of Guangzhou (Canton) and to buy and sell only to licensed Chinese merchants. Practices considered harmful to Chinese interests were strictly forbidden.

For years the little community of foreign merchants in Canton had to accept the Chinese system. By the 1820s, however, the dominant group, the British, were flexing their muscles. Moreover, in the smoking of opium—that "destructive and ensnaring vice" denounced by Chinese decrees—British merchants had found something that the Chinese really wanted. Grown legally in British-occupied India, opium was smuggled into China, where its use and sale were illegal. Huge profits and growing addiction led to a rapid increase in sales. By 1836 the aggressive goal of the British merchants in Canton was an independent British colony in China and "safe and unrestricted liberty" in their Chinese trade. Spurred on by economic motives, they pres-

A Revolution in Communications The development of the electromagnetic telegraph in the 1840s permitted rapid long-distance communications for the first time in history. Governments quickly saw the telegraph's revolutionary implications for waging war and invested in the building of telegraph systems. Business people then used the telegraph and underwater cables to tie the world market together. The "Camelback" key shown here was commonly used in Europe to send the "dots and dashes" that trained operators transcribed into messages. (John D. Jenkins, www.sparksmuseum.com)

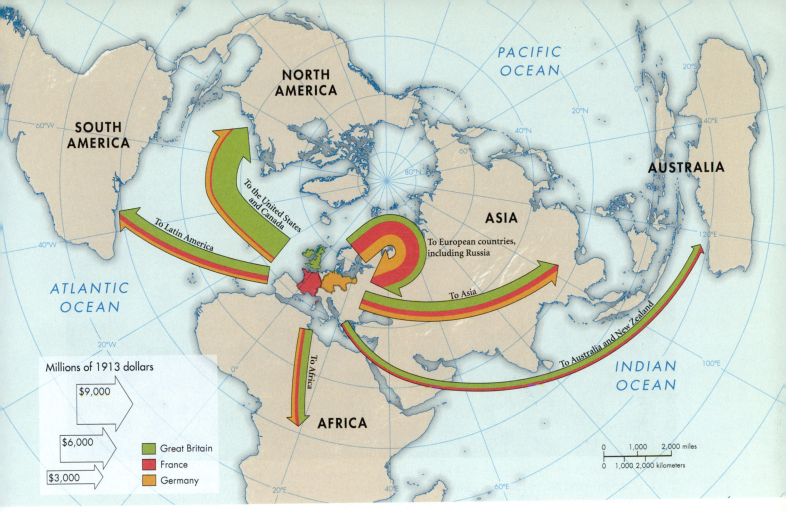

NORTH AMERICA

SOUTH AMERICA

AUSTRALIA

ASIA

To European countries, including Russia

To the United States and Canada

To Latin America

ATLANTIC OCEAN

PACIFIC OCEAN

To Asia

To Africa

To Australia and New Zealand

INDIAN OCEAN

AFRICA

Millions of 1913 dollars

$9,000

$6,000

$3,000

Great Britain
France
Germany

0   1,000   2,000 miles
0   1,000 2,000 kilometers

Map 25.1 European Investment to 1914 Foreign investment grew rapidly after 1850, and Britain, France, and Germany were the major investing nations. As this map suggests, most European investment was not directed to the African and Asian areas seized by the new imperialism after 1880.

sured the British government to take decisive action and enlisted the support of other British manufacturers with visions of vast Chinese markets to be opened.

At the same time, the Qing government decided that the **opium trade** had to be stamped out. It was ruining the people and stripping the empire of its silver, which was going to British merchants to pay for the opium. The government began to prosecute Chinese drug dealers vigorously, and in 1839 it sent special envoy Lin Zexu to Canton to deal with the crisis. Lin Zexu dealt harshly with Chinese who purchased opium, and he seized the opium stores of the British merchants, who then withdrew to the barren island of Hong Kong. He sent a famous letter justifying his policy to Queen Victoria in London. (See "Listening to the Past: Lin Zexu and Yamagata Aritomo, Confronting Western Imperialism," page 808.) Explaining the government's determination to stop the opium trade, Lin Zexu also wrote: "Our great unified Qing Empire regards itself as responsible for the habits and morals of its subjects and cannot rest content to see any of them become victims of a deadly poison."[1]

The wealthy, well-connected British merchants appealed to their allies in London for support, and the

British government responded. It also wanted free, unregulated trade with China, as well as the establishment of diplomatic relations on the European model, complete with ambassadors, embassies, and published treaties. Using troops from India and being in control of the seas, Britain occupied several coastal cities and forced China to give in to British demands. In the Treaty of Nanking in 1842, the imperial government was required to cede the island of Hong Kong to Britain forever, pay an indemnity of $100 million, and open up four large cities to unlimited foreign trade with low tariffs.

opium trade The sale of opium—grown legally in British-occupied India—by British merchants in China, where the drug was illegal; it became a destructive and ensnaring vice of the Chinese.

With Britain's new power over Chinese commerce, the opium trade flourished, and Hong Kong developed rapidly as an Anglo-Chinese enclave. China continued to accept foreign diplomats in Beijing (Peking), the imperial capital, but disputes over trade between China and the Western powers continued. Finally, there was a second round of foreign attack between 1856 and 1860, culminating in the occupation of Beijing by seventeen thousand British and French troops and the intentional

Britain and China at War Britain capitalized on its overwhelming naval superiority in its war against China, as shown in this British painting celebrating a dramatic moment in a crucial 1841 battle near Guangzhou. Having received a direct hit from a steam-powered British ironclad, a Chinese sailing ship explodes into a wall of flame. The Chinese lost eleven ships and five hundred men in the two-hour engagement; the British suffered only minor damage. (National Maritime Museum, London)

burning of the emperor's summer palace. Another round of harsh treaties gave European merchants and missionaries greater privileges and protection and forced the Chinese to accept trade and investment on unfavorable terms for several more cities. Thus did Europeans use military aggression to blow a hole in the wall of Chinese seclusion and open the country to foreign trade and foreign ideas.

Japan and the United States

China's neighbor Japan had its own highly distinctive civilization and even less use for Westerners. European traders and missionaries first arrived in Japan in the sixteenth century. By 1640 Japan had reacted quite negatively to their presence. The government decided to seal off the country from all European influences in order to preserve traditional Japanese culture and society. When American and British whaling ships began to appear off Japanese coasts almost two hundred years later, the policy of exclusion was still in effect. An order of 1825 commanded Japanese officials to "drive away foreign vessels without second thought."[2]

Japan's unbending isolation seemed hostile and barbaric to the West, particularly to the United States. It complicated the practical problems of shipwrecked American sailors and the provisioning of whaling ships and China traders sailing in the eastern Pacific. It also thwarted the hope of trade and profit. Moreover, Americans shared the self-confidence and dynamism of expanding Western society, and they felt destined to play a great role in the Pacific. To Americans it seemed the duty of the United States to force the Japanese to share their ports and behave as a "civilized" nation.

After several unsuccessful American attempts to establish commercial relations with Japan, Commodore Matthew Perry steamed into Edo (now Tokyo) Bay in 1853. Relying on **gunboat diplomacy** and threatening to attack, Perry demanded diplomatic negotiations with the emperor. Japan entered a grave crisis. Some Japanese warriors urged resistance, but senior officials realized how defenseless their cities were against naval bombardment. Shocked and humiliated, they reluctantly signed a treaty with the United States that opened two ports and permitted trade. Over the next five years, more treaties spelled

gunboat diplomacy The use or threat of military force to coerce a government into economic or political agreements.

out the rights and privileges of the Western nations and their merchants in Japan. Japan was "opened." What the British had done in China with war, the Americans had done in Japan with the threat of war.

Western Penetration of Egypt

Egypt's experience illustrates not only the explosive power of the expanding European economy and society but also their seductive appeal. European involvement in Egypt also led to a new model of formal political control, which European powers applied widely in Africa and Asia after 1882.

Of great importance in African and Middle Eastern history, the ancient land of the pharaohs had since 525 B.C.E. been ruled by a succession of foreigners, most recently by the Ottoman Turks. In 1798 French armies under young General Napoleon Bonaparte invaded the Egyptian part of the Ottoman Empire and occupied the territory for three years. Into the power vacuum left by the French withdrawal stepped an extraordinary Albanian-born Turkish general, Muhammad Ali (1769–1849).

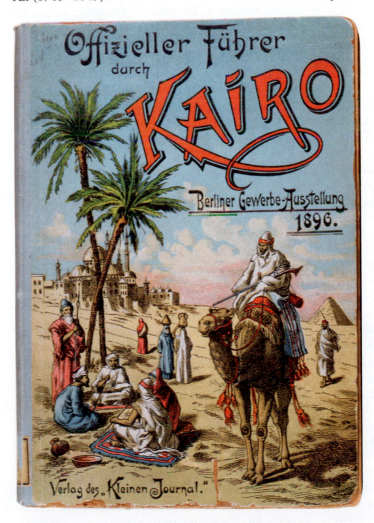

First appointed governor of Egypt in 1805 by the Turkish sultan, Muhammad Ali set out to build his own state on the strength of a large, powerful army organized along European lines. He drafted for the first time the illiterate, despised peasant masses of Egypt, and he hired French and Italian army officers to train these raw recruits and their Turkish officers. The government was also reformed, new lands were cultivated, and communications were improved. By the end of his reign in 1848, Muhammad Ali had established a strong and virtually independent Egyptian state, to be ruled by his family on a hereditary basis within the Turkish empire.

Muhammad Ali's policies of modernization attracted large numbers of Europeans to the banks of the Nile. The port city of Alexandria had more than fifty thousand Europeans by 1864. Europeans served not only as army officers but also as engineers, doctors, government officials, and police officers. Others turned to trade, finance, and shipping.

To pay for his ambitious plans, Muhammad Ali encouraged the development of commercial agriculture. This development had profound implications. Egyptian peasants were poor but largely self-sufficient, growing food for their own consumption on state-owned lands allotted to them by tradition. Faced with the possibility of export agriculture, high-ranking officials and members of Muhammad Ali's family began carving large private landholdings out of the state domain. The new landlords made the peasants their tenants and forced them to grow cash crops such as cotton and rice geared to European markets. Thus Egyptian landowners "modernized" agriculture, but to the detriment of peasant well-being.

These trends continued under Muhammad Ali's grandson Ismail (ihs-MAH-eel), who in 1863 began his sixteen-year rule as Egypt's khedive (kuh-DEEV), or prince. Educated at France's leading military academy, Ismail was a westernizing autocrat. The large irrigation networks he promoted caused cotton production and exports to Europe to boom, and with his support the

Egyptian Travel Guide Ismail's efforts to transform Cairo were fairly successful. As a result European tourists could more easily visit the country that their governments dominated. Ordinary Europeans were lured to exotic lands by travel books like this colorful "Official Guide" to an exhibition on Cairo held in Berlin. (Private Collection/Archives Charmet/The Bridgeman Art Library)

My country is no longer in Africa, we now form part of Europe.

—ISMAIL

Suez Canal was completed by a French company in 1869. The Arabic of the Egyptian masses replaced the Turkish of the foreign conquerors as the official language; young Egyptians educated in Europe spread new skills; and Cairo acquired modern boulevards and Western hotels. As Ismail proudly declared, "My country is no longer in Africa, we now form part of Europe."[3]

The Suez Canal, 1869

Yet Ismail was too impatient and reckless. His projects were enormously expensive, and by 1876 Egypt owed foreign bondholders a colossal debt that it could not pay. France and Great Britain intervened and forced Ismail to appoint French and British commissioners to oversee Egyptian finances so that the Egyptian debt would be paid in full. This momentous decision marked a sharp break with the past. Throughout most of the nineteenth century, Europeans had used military might and political force primarily to make sure that non-Western lands would accept European trade and investment. Now Europeans were going to determine the state budget and effectively rule Egypt.

Foreign financial control evoked a violent nationalistic reaction among Egyptian religious leaders, young intellectuals, and army officers. In 1879, under the leadership of Colonel Ahmed Arabi, they formed the Egyptian Nationalist Party. Continuing diplomatic pressure, which forced Ismail to abdicate in favor of his weak son, Tewfiq (r. 1879–1892), resulted in bloody anti-European riots in Alexandria in 1882. A number of Europeans were killed, and Tewfiq and his court had to flee to British ships for safety. When the British fleet bombarded Alexandria, more riots swept the country, and Colonel Arabi led a revolt. But a British expeditionary force put down the rebellion and occupied all of Egypt.

The British said their occupation was temporary, but British armies remained in Egypt until 1956. They maintained the façade of the khedive's government as

great migration The mass movement of people from Europe in the nineteenth century; one reason that the West's impact on the world was so powerful and many-sided.

an autonomous province of the Ottoman Empire, but the khedive was a mere puppet. British rule did result in tax reforms and somewhat better conditions for peasants, while foreign bondholders received their interest and Egyptian nationalists nursed their injured pride.

British rule in Egypt also provided a new model for European expansion in densely populated lands. Such expansion was based on military force, political domination, and a self-justifying ideology of beneficial reform. This model was to predominate until 1914. Thus did Europe's Industrial Revolution lead to tremendous political as well as economic expansion throughout the world after 1880.

The Great Migration

How was massive migration an integral part of Western expansion? ■

A poignant human drama was interwoven with economic expansion: millions of people pulled up stakes and left their ancestral lands in the course of history's greatest migration. To millions of ordinary people for whom the opening of China and the interest on the Egyptian debt had not the slightest significance, this great movement was the central experience in the saga of Western expansion. It was, in part, because of this **great migration** that the West's impact on the world in the nineteenth century was so powerful and many-sided.

The Pressure of Population

In the early eighteenth century, the growth of European population entered its third and decisive stage, which continued unabated until the early twentieth century (Figure 25.2). Birthrates eventually declined in the nineteenth century, but so did death rates, mainly because of the rising standard of living and secondarily because of the revolution in medicine (see Chapter 23). Thus the population of Europe (including Asiatic Russia) more than doubled, from approximately 188 million in 1800 to roughly 432 million in 1900.

These figures actually understate Europe's population explosion, for between 1815 and 1932 more than 60 million people left Europe. The migrants went primarily to the "areas of European settlement"—North and South America, Australia, New Zealand, and Siberia—where they contributed to a rapid growth in numbers. Since population grew more slowly in Africa and Asia than in Europe and the Americas, as Figure 25.2 shows, Europeans and people of predominately European origin jumped from about 24 percent of the world's total in 1800 to about 38 percent on the eve of World War I.

The growing number of Europeans provided further impetus for Western expansion, and it was a driving

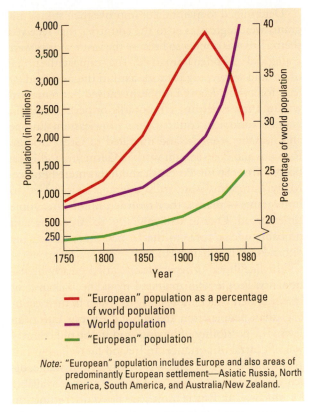

Figure 25.2 **The Increase of European and World Populations, 1750–1980** Europeans and peoples of predominantly European origin became a growing percentage of total world population between roughly 1750 and 1914.

Legend for Figure 25.2:
- "European" population as a percentage of world population
- World population
- "European" population

Note: "European" population includes Europe and also areas of predominantly European settlement—Asiatic Russia, North America, South America, and Australia/New Zealand.

force behind emigration. As in the eighteenth century, the rapid increase in numbers put pressure on the land and led to land hunger and relative overpopulation in area after area. In most countries, migration increased twenty years after a rapid growth in population, as many children of the baby boom grew up, saw little available land and few opportunities, and migrated. This pattern was especially prevalent when rapid population increase predated extensive industrial development, which offered the best long-term hope of creating jobs within the country and reducing poverty. Thus millions of country folk went abroad as well as to nearby cities in search of work and economic opportunity.

Before looking at the people who migrated, let us consider three facts. First, the number of men and women who left Europe increased rapidly at the end of the nineteenth century and leading up to World War I. As Figure 25.3 shows, more than 11 million left in the first decade of the twentieth century, over five times the number departing in the 1850s. The outflow of migrants was clearly a defining characteristic of European society for the entire period.

Second, different countries had very different patterns of movement. As Figure 25.3 also shows, people left Britain and Ireland (which are not distinguished in the British figures) in large numbers from the 1840s on. This emigration reflected not only rural poverty but also the movement of skilled industrial technicians and the preferences shown to British migrants in the British Empire. Ultimately, about one-third of all European

Figure 25.3 **Emigration from Europe by Decades, 1851–1940** Emigration from Europe grew greatly until the outbreak of World War I in 1914, and it declined rapidly thereafter.

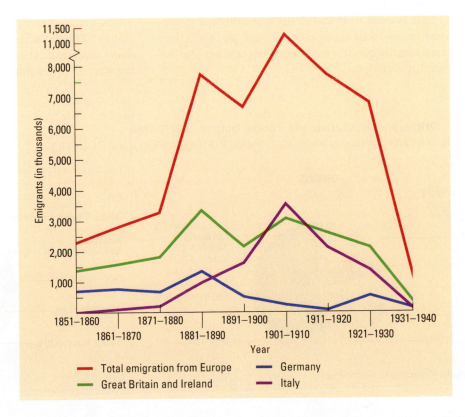

Legend for Figure 25.3:
- Total emigration from Europe
- Great Britain and Ireland
- Germany
- Italy

migrants between 1840 and 1920 came from the British Isles. German migration was quite different. It grew irregularly after about 1830, reaching a first peak in the early 1850s and another in the early 1880s. Thereafter it declined rapidly, for Germany's rapid industrialization was providing adequate jobs at home. This pattern contrasted sharply with that of Italy. More and more Italians left the country right up to 1914, reflecting severe problems in Italian villages and relatively slow industrial growth. Thus migration patterns mirrored social and economic conditions in the various European countries and provinces.

Third, although the United States did absorb the largest overall number of European migrants, fewer than half of all migrants went to the United States. Asiatic Russia, Canada, Argentina, Brazil, Australia, and New Zealand also attracted large numbers, as Figure 25.4 shows. Moreover, migrants accounted for a larger proportion of the total population in Argentina, Brazil, and Canada than it did in the United States. The common American assumption that European migration meant migration to the United States is quite inaccurate.

European Migrants

What kind of people left Europe, and what were their reasons for doing so? The European migrant was generally an energetic small farmer or skilled artisan trying hard to stay ahead of poverty, not a desperately impoverished landless peasant or urban proletarian. These small peasant landowners and village craftsmen typically left Europe because their traditional way of life was threatened by too little land, estate agriculture, and cheap factory-made goods. (See "Living in the Past: The Immigrant Experience," page 792.)

Determined to maintain or improve their status, migrants were a great asset to the countries that received them. This was doubly so because the vast majority were young and very often unmarried. They came in the prime of life and were ready to work hard in the new land, at least for a time. Many Europeans moved but remained within Europe, settling temporarily or permanently in another European country. Jews from eastern Europe and peasants from Ireland migrated to Great Britain, Russians and Poles sought work in Germany, and Latin peoples from Spain, Portugal, and Italy entered France. Many Europeans were truly migrants as opposed to immigrants—that is, they returned home after some time abroad. One in two migrants to Argentina and probably one in three to the United States eventually returned to their native land.

The likelihood of repatriation varied greatly by nationality. People who migrated from the Balkans, for instance, were much more likely to return to their countries than people from Ireland and eastern European Jews. The possibility of buying land in the old country was of central importance. In Ireland (as well as in England and Scotland) land was tightly held by large, often absentee landowners, and little land was available for purchase. In Russia most Jews faced discrimination and were forced to live in the Pale of Settlement (see Chapter 17), and most Russian land was held by non-Jews. Therefore, when Irish farmers and Russian Jewish artisans migrated in search of opportunity, it was basically a once-and-for-all departure.

The mass movement of Italians illustrates many of the characteristics of European migration. As late as the 1880s, three of every four Italians depended on agriculture. With the influx of cheap North American wheat, many small landowning peasants whose standard of living was falling began to leave their country. Many Ital-

Figure 25.4 Origins and Destinations of European Emigrants, 1851–1960
European emigrants came from many countries; almost half of them went to the United States.

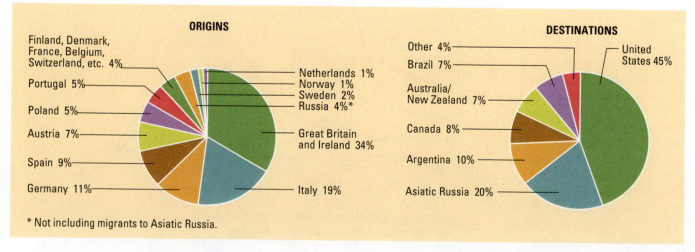

An Italian Custom in Argentina Italian immigrants introduced the game of bocce to Argentina, where it took hold and became a popular recreation for men. Dressed up in their Sunday best, these Argentinean laborers are totally focused on the game, which is somewhat like horseshoes or shuffleboard. (Hulton Archive/Getty Images)

> **Either we get decent human rights or else let us go wherever our eyes may lead us.**
>
> —SPOKESMAN FOR KIEV JEWISH COMMUNITY

ians went to the United States, but before 1900 more went to Argentina and Brazil.

Many Italians had no intention of settling abroad permanently. Some called themselves "swallows." After harvesting their own wheat and flax in Italy, they "flew" to Argentina to harvest wheat between December and April. Returning to Italy for the spring planting, they repeated this exhausting process. This was a very hard life, but a frugal worker could save $250 to $300 in the course of a season, at a time when an Italian agricultural worker earned less than $1 a day in Italy.

Ties of family and friendship played a crucial role in the movement of peoples. Many people from a given province or village settled together in rural enclaves or tightly knit urban neighborhoods thousands of miles away. Very often a strong individual—a businessman, a religious leader—would blaze the way, and others would follow, forming a "migration chain."

Many landless young European men and women were spurred to leave by a spirit of revolt and independence. In Sweden and in Norway, in Jewish Russia and in Italy, these young people felt frustrated by the small privileged classes, which often controlled both church and government and resisted demands for change and greater opportunity. Many a young Norwegian seconded the passionate cry of Norway's national poet, Martinius

Bjørnson (BYURN-sawn): "Forth will I! Forth! I will be crushed and consumed if I stay."[4] Many young Jews wholeheartedly agreed with a spokesman of Kiev's Jewish community in 1882, who summed up his congregation's growing defiance in the face of brutal discrimination: "Our human dignity is being trampled upon, our wives and daughters are being dishonored, we are looted and pillaged; either we get decent human rights or else let us go wherever our eyes may lead us."[5]

Thus for many, migration was a radical way to "get out from under." Migration slowed down when the people won basic political and social reforms, such as the right to vote, equality before the law, and social security.

Asian Migrants

Not all migration was from Europe. A substantial number of Chinese, Japanese, Indians, and Filipinos—to name only four key groups—responded to rural hardship with temporary or permanent migration. At least 3 million Asians (as opposed to more than 60 million Europeans) moved abroad before 1920. Most went as indentured laborers to work under incredibly difficult conditions on the plantations or in the gold mines of Latin America, southern Asia, Africa, California, Hawaii,

LIVING IN THE PAST

BETWEEN 1800 AND 1930, 60 MILLION EUROPEANS left their homelands in search of better lives. About half moved to the United States; between 1890 and 1925 over 20 million men, women, and children passed through the Ellis Island Immigration Station in New York City harbor. During these years, southern and eastern Europeans, such as Italians, Poles, and Russian Jews, far outnumbered the northern Euro-

peans who had predominated in the mid-nineteenth-century wave of migration to the United States. Today over 40 percent of Americans are descendants of people who went through immigration control on Ellis Island. These figures give some idea of the immense number of people involved in this great migration, but statistics hardly capture what it was like to pull up stakes and move to America.

Transporting migrants across the North Atlantic was big business. Well-established steamship companies such as Cunard, White Star, and Hamburg-America advertised inexpensive fares and good accommodations. The reality was usually different. For the vast majority who could afford only third-class passage in the steerage compartment (so called because it was located near the ship's rudder), the eight- to fourteen-day journey overseas from Naples, Hamburg, or Liverpool was cramped, cold, and unsanitary. Yet poor job prospects and religious or political persecution at home — and the lure of America's booming economy — led many to take the journey.

Once they arrived at Ellis Island, steerage passengers were subjected to a four- to five-hour examination in the Great Hall. Physicians checked their health. Customs officers inspected legal documents. Bureaucrats administered intelligence tests and evaluated the migrants' financial and moral status. The exams worried and sometimes insulted the new arrivals. As one Polish-Jewish immigrant remembered, "They asked us questions. 'How much is two and one? How much is two and two?' But the next young girl, also from our city, went and they asked her, 'How do you wash stairs, from the top or from the bottom?' She says, 'I don't come to America to wash stairs.'"*

Migrants with obvious illnesses were required to stay in the island's hospital for several weeks to see if they improved. Sick passengers whom officials judged either a threat to public health or a likely drain on public finances were sent home. Suspected anarchists and, later, Bolsheviks were also deported.

*"Immigration: Ellis Island," http://library.thinkquest.org/20619/Eivirt.html (16 February 2010).

Italian poster advertising sailings to the United States, Brazil, Uruguay, Argentina, and Central America, 1906. (National Archives, RG85: 51411/53)

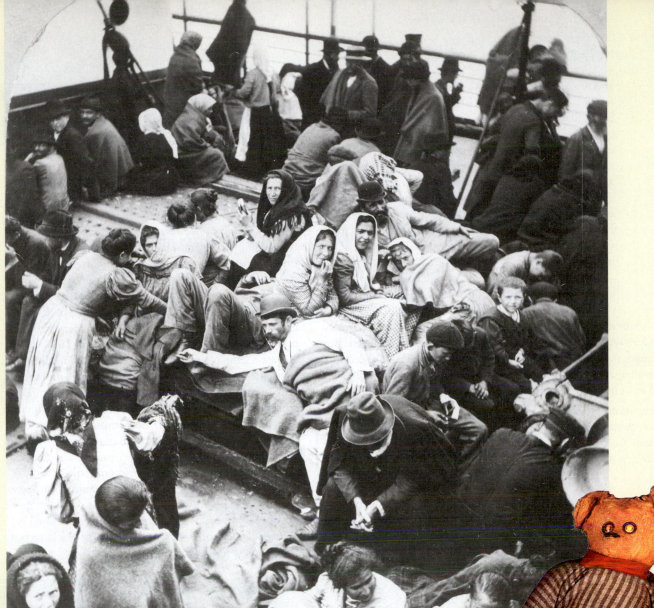

By today's standards, it was remarkably easy for those seeking to establish permanent residency to enter the United States: only about 2 percent of all migrants were denied entry. After they cleared processing, the new arrivals were ferried to New York City, where they either stayed or moved to other industrialized cities of the northeast and Midwest. The migrants typically took unskilled jobs for low wages, but by keeping labor costs down, they fueled the rapid industrialization of late-nineteenth-century America. They furthermore transformed the United States from a land of predominately British and northern European settlers into the multicultural melting pot of myth and fame.

QUESTIONS FOR ANALYSIS

1. Why did so many Europeans make the difficult and sometimes dangerous transatlantic trip to the United States?

2. What were the main concerns of U.S. immigration officials as they evaluated the new arrivals? Did U.S. officials treat immigrants fairly?

Conditions for steerage passengers were cramped, as evidenced by this photo from 1902. Passengers were limited to bringing only their most cherished possessions, such as the teddy bear from Switzerland and the Hebrew prayer book from Poland, both of which made the crossing with their owners in 1921. (steerage: The Granger Collection, New York; prayer book: Karen Yamauchi, photographer/NPS, lent by Florence Ercolano; teddy bear: Karen Yamauchi, photographer/NPS, gift of Gertrude Schneider)

and Australia. White estate owners very often used Asians to replace or supplement blacks after the suppression of the slave trade.

In the 1840s, for example, there was a strong demand for field hands in Cuba, and the Spanish government actively recruited Chinese laborers. Between 1853 and 1873, when such migration was stopped, more than 130,000 Chinese laborers went to Cuba. The majority spent their lives as virtual slaves. The great landlords of Peru also brought in more than 100,000 workers from China in the nineteenth century, and there were similar movements of Asians elsewhere.

Such migration from Asia would undoubtedly have grown to much greater proportions if planters and mine owners in search of cheap labor had been able to hire as many Asian workers as they wished. But they could not. Asians fled the plantations and gold mines as soon as possible, seeking greater opportunities in trade and towns. There they came into conflict with local populations, whether in Malaya, East Africa, or areas settled by Europeans. These European settlers demanded a halt to Asian migration. By the 1880s, Americans and Australians were building **great white walls**—discriminatory laws designed to keep Asians out.

A crucial factor in the migrations before 1914 was, therefore, the general policy of "whites only" in the open lands of possible permanent settlement. This, too, was part of Western dominance in the increasingly lopsided world. Largely successful in monopolizing the best overseas opportunities, Europeans and people of European ancestry reaped the main benefits from the great migration. By 1913 people in Australia, Canada, and the United States all had higher average incomes than people in Great Britain, still Europe's wealthiest nation.

great white walls Laws designed by Americans and Australians to keep Asians from settling in their countries in the 1880s.

new imperialism The late-nineteenth-century drive by European countries to create vast political empires abroad.

Western Imperialism, 1880–1914

How and why after 1875 did European nations rush to build political empires in Africa and Asia? ▪

The expansion of Western society reached its apex between about 1880 and 1914. In those years, the leading European nations not only continued to send massive streams of migrants, money, and manufactured goods around the world, but also rushed to create or enlarge vast political empires abroad. This political empire building contrasted sharply with the economic penetration of non-Western territories between 1816 and 1880, which had left a China or a Japan "opened" but politically independent. By contrast, the empires of the late nineteenth century recalled the old European colonial empires of the seventeenth and eighteenth centuries and led contemporaries to speak of the **new imperialism**.

Characterized by a frantic rush to plant the flag over as many people and as much territory as possible, the new imperialism had momentous consequences. It resulted in new tensions among competing European states, and it led to wars and threats of war with non-European powers. The new imperialism was aimed primarily at Africa and Asia. It put millions of black, brown, and yellow peoples directly under the rule of whites.

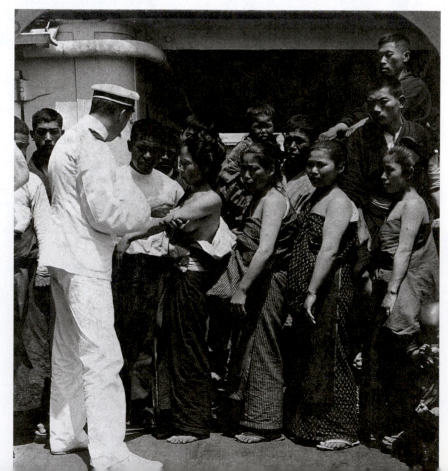

Vaccinating Migrants Bound for Hawaii, 1904
First Chinese, then Japanese, and finally Koreans and Filipinos went across the Pacific in large numbers to labor in Hawaii on American-owned sugar plantations in the late nineteenth century. The native Hawaiians had been decimated by disease, creating a severe labor shortage for Hawaii's plantation economy. (Corbis)

The European Presence in Africa Before 1880

Prior to 1880, European nations controlled only 10 percent of the African continent, and their possessions were hardly increasing. The French had begun conquering Algeria in 1830, and by 1880 substantial numbers of French, Italian, and Spanish colonists had settled among the overwhelming Arab majority there. Yet the overall effect on Africa was minor.

At the southern tip of the continent, Britain had taken possession of the Dutch settlements at Cape Town during the wars with Napoleon I. This British takeover of the Cape Colony had led disgruntled Dutch cattle ranchers and farmers in 1835 to make their so-called Great Trek into the interior, where they fought the Zulu and Xhosa peoples for land. After 1853, while British colonies such as Canada and Australia were beginning to evolve toward self-government, the Boers or **Afrikaners** (a-frih-KAH-nuhrz), as the descendants of the Dutch in the Cape Colony were beginning to call themselves, proclaimed their political independence and defended it against British armies. By 1880 Afrikaner and British settlers, who detested each other, had wrested control of much of South Africa from the Zulu, Xhosa, and other African peoples.

Other than the French presence in the north and the British and Afrikaners in the south, Africa was largely free of Westerners. European trading posts and forts dating back to the Age of Discovery and the slave trade sparsely dotted the coast of West Africa. The Portuguese maintained a loose hold on their old possessions in Angola and Mozambique. Elsewhere over the great mass of the continent, Europeans did not rule.

After 1880, the situation changed drastically. In a spectacular manifestation of the new imperialism, European countries jockeyed for territory in Africa, breaking sharply with previous patterns of colonization and diplomacy.

The Scramble for Africa After 1880

Between 1880 and 1900, Britain, France, Germany, and Italy scrambled for African possessions as if their national livelihoods depended on it (Map 25.2). By 1900 nearly the whole continent had been carved up and placed under European rule: only Ethiopia in northeast Africa, which was able to fight off Italian invaders, and Liberia on the West African coast, which had been settled by freed slaves from the United States, remained independent. In all other African territories, the Euro-

pean powers tightened their control and established colonial governments in the years before 1914.

The Dutch settler republics also succumbed to imperialism, but the final outcome was different. The British, led by Cecil Rhodes (1853–1902) in the Cape Colony, leapfrogged over the two Afrikaner states—Orange Free State and the Transvaal—in the early 1890s and established protectorates over Bechuanaland (bech-WAH-nuh-land) (now Botswana) and Rhodesia (now Zimbabwe and Zambia), named in honor of its founder. Although unable to undermine the stubborn Afrikaners in the Transvaal, English-speaking capitalists like Rhodes developed fabulously rich gold mines there, and the British eventually conquered their white rivals in the bloody South African War (1899–1902). In 1910 the old Afrikaner territories were united with the old Cape Colony and the eastern province of Natal in a new Union of South Africa, established—unlike any other territory in Africa—as a largely "self-governing" colony. This enabled the defeated Afrikaners to use their numerical superiority over the British settlers to gradually take political power, as even the most educated nonwhites lost the right to vote outside the Cape Colony. (See "Individuals in Society: Cecil Rhodes," page 798.)

Afrikaners Descendants of the Dutch settlers in the Cape Colony in southern Africa.

In the complexity of the European seizure of Africa, certain events and individuals stand out. Of enormous importance was the British occupation of Egypt in 1882, which established the new model of formal political control (see pages 787–788). There was also the role of Leopold II of Belgium (r. 1865–1909), an energetic, strong-willed monarch of a tiny country with a lust for distant territory. As early as 1861, he had laid out his vision of expansion: "The sea bathes our coast, the world lies before us. Steam and electricity have annihilated distance, and all the nonappropriated lands on the surface of the globe can become the field of our operations and of our success."[6]

By 1876 Leopold was focusing on central Africa. Subsequently, he formed a financial syndicate under his personal control to send Henry M. Stanley, a sensation-seeking journalist and part-time explorer, to the Congo basin. Stanley was able to establish trading stations, sign "treaties" with African chiefs, and plant Leopold's flag. Leopold's actions alarmed the French, who quickly sent out an expedition under Pierre de Brazza. In 1880 de Brazza signed a treaty of protection with the chief of the large Teke tribe and began to establish a French protectorate on the north bank of the Congo River.

The Struggle for South Africa, 1878

Map legend:
- British territory
- Boer republics
- Battle

KALAHARI DESERT · ATLANTIC OCEAN · TRANSVAAL · ZULULAND · ORANGE FREE STATE · CAPE COLONY · Cape Town · INDIAN OCEAN

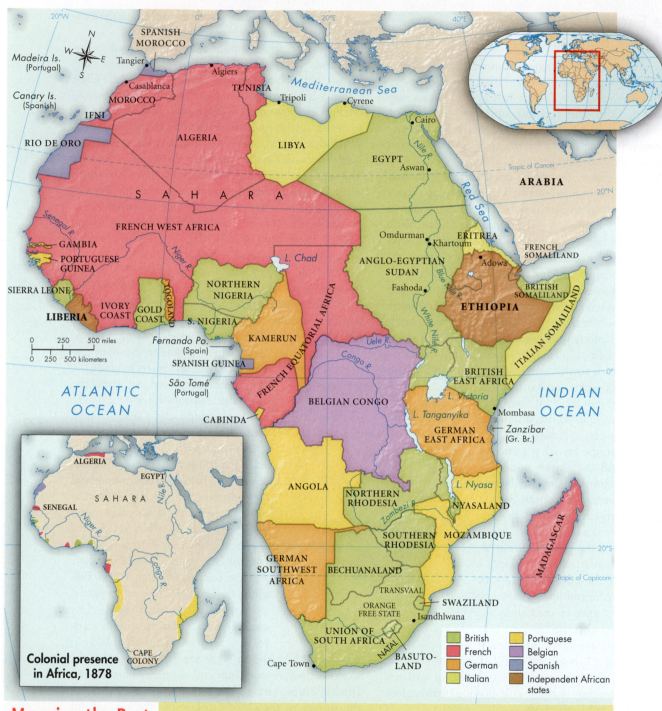

Colonial presence in Africa, 1878

Legend:
- British
- French
- German
- Italian
- Portuguese
- Belgian
- Spanish
- Independent African states

Mapping the Past

Map 25.2 The Partition of Africa The European powers carved up Africa after 1880 and built vast political empires. European states also seized territory in Asia in the nineteenth century, although some Asian states and peoples managed to maintain their political independence (see Map 25.3, page 800). Compare the patterns of European imperialism in Africa and Asia, using this map and Map 25.3.

ANALYZING THE MAP What European countries were leading imperialist states in both Africa and Asia, and what lands did they hold? What countries in Africa and Asia maintained their political independence? What did the United States and Japan have in common in Africa and Asia?

CONNECTIONS The late nineteenth century was the high point of European imperialism. What were the motives behind the rush for land and empire in Africa and Asia?

To complete this activity online, go to the Online Study Guide at bedfordstmartins.com/mckaywest.

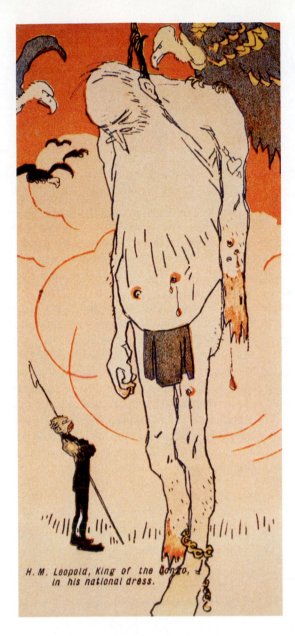

H. M. Leopold, King of the Congo, in his national dress.

European Imperialism at Its Worst This 1908 English cartoon, "Leopold, King of the Congo, in his national dress," focuses on the barbaric practice of cutting off the hands and feet of Africans who refused to gather as much rubber as Leopold's company demanded. In 1908 an international human rights campaign forced the Belgian king to cede his personal fief to the Belgian state. (The Granger Collection, New York)

1880, Bismarck, like many other European leaders at the time, had seen little value in colonies. Then in 1884 and 1885, as political agitation for expansion increased, Bismarck did an abrupt about-face, and Germany established protectorates over a number of small African kingdoms and tribes in Togo, the Cameroons region, southwest Africa, and, later, East Africa. In acquiring colonies, Bismarck cooperated against the British with France's Jules Ferry, an ardent republican who also embraced imperialism. With Bismarck's tacit approval, the French pressed southward from Algeria, eastward from their old forts on the Senegal coast, and northward from their protectorate on the Congo River.

Meanwhile, the British began enlarging their West African enclaves and impatiently pushed northward from the Cape Colony and westward from Zanzibar. Their thrust southward from Egypt was blocked in Sudan by fiercely independent Muslims who massacred a British force at Khartoum in 1885.

A decade later, another British force, under General Horatio H. Kitchener, moved cautiously and more successfully up the Nile River, building a railroad to supply arms and reinforcements as it went. Finally, in 1898 these British troops met their foe at Omdurman (ahm-duhr-MAHN) (see Map 25.2), where Muslim tribesmen armed with spears charged time and time again, only to be cut down by the recently invented Maxim machine gun. In the somber words of one English observer, "It was not a battle but an execution. The bodies were not in heaps . . . but they spread evenly over acres and acres."[7] In the end, eleven thousand brave Muslim tribesmen lay dead, while only twenty-eight Britons had been killed.

Continuing up the Nile after the Battle of Omdurman, Kitchener's armies found that a small French force had already occupied the village of Fashoda (fuh-SHOH-duh). Locked in imperial competition with Britain ever since the British occupation of Egypt, France had tried to beat the British to one of Africa's last unclaimed areas—the upper reaches of the Nile. The result was a serious diplomatic crisis and the threat of war. Eventually, wracked by the Dreyfus affair (see Chapter 24) and unwilling to fight, France backed down and withdrew its forces, allowing the British to take over.

> **Berlin conference**
> A meeting of European leaders held in 1884 and 1885 in order to lay down some basic rules for imperialist competition in sub-Saharan Africa.

Leopold's buccaneering intrusion into the Congo area raised the question of the political fate of Africa. By 1882 Europe had caught "African fever." There was a gold rush mentality, and the race for territory was on. To lay down some basic rules for this new and dangerous game of imperialist competition in sub-Saharan Africa, Jules Ferry of France and Otto von Bismarck (see Chapter 24) of Germany arranged an international conference on Africa in Berlin in 1884 and 1885. The **Berlin conference** established the principle that European claims to African territory had to rest on "effective occupation" in order to be recognized by other states. This meant that Europeans would push relentlessly into interior regions from all sides and that no single European power would be able to claim the entire continent. The conference recognized Leopold's personal rule over a neutral Congo free state and agreed to work to stop slavery and the slave trade in Africa.

The Berlin conference coincided with Germany's sudden emergence as an imperial power. Prior to about

Cecil Rhodes

INDIVIDUALS IN SOCIETY

CECIL RHODES (1853–1902) EPITOMIZED THE DYNAMISM and the ruthlessness of the new imperialism. He built a corporate monopoly, claimed vast tracts in Africa, and established the famous Rhodes scholarships to develop colonial (and American) leaders who would love and strengthen the British Empire. But to Africans, he left a bitter legacy.

Rhodes came from a large middle-class family and at seventeen went to southern Africa to seek his fortune. He soon turned to diamonds, newly discovered at Kimberley, picked good partners, and was wealthy by 1876. But Rhodes, often called a dreamer, wanted more. He entered Oxford University, while returning periodically to Africa, and his musings crystallized in a belief in progress through racial competition and territorial expansion. "I contend," he wrote, "that we [English] are the finest race in the world and the more of the world we inhabit the better it is for the human race."*

Rhodes's belief in British expansion never wavered. In 1880 he formed the De Beers Mining Company, and by 1888 his firm monopolized southern Africa's diamond production and earned fabulous profits. Rhodes also entered the Cape Colony's legislature and became the all-powerful prime minister from 1890 to 1896.

His main objective was to dominate the Afrikaner republics and to impose British rule on as much land as possible beyond their northern borders. Working through a state-approved private company financed in part by De Beers, Rhodes's agents forced and cajoled African kings to accept British "protection," then put down rebellions with Maxim machine guns. Britain thus obtained a great swath of empire on the cheap.

But Rhodes, like many high achievers obsessed with power and personal aggrandizement, went too far. He backed, and then in 1896 declined to call back, a failed invasion of the Transvaal, which was designed to topple the Dutch-speaking republic. Repudiated by top British leaders who had encouraged his plan, Rhodes had to resign as prime minister. In declining health, he continued to agitate against the Afrikaner republics. He died at age forty-nine as the South African War (1899–1902) ended.

In accounting for Rhodes's remarkable but flawed achievements, both sympathetic and critical biographers stress his imposing size, enormous energy, and powerful personality. His ideas were commonplace, but he believed in them passionately, and he could persuade and inspire others to follow his lead. Rhodes the idealist was nonetheless a born negotiator, a crafty deal maker who believed that everyone could be had for a price. According to his most insightful biographer, Rhodes's homosexuality — discreet, partially repressed, and undeniable — was also "a major component of his magnetism and his success."†

*Robert Rotberg, *The Founder: Cecil Rhodes and the Pursuit of Power* (New York: Oxford University Press, 1988), p. 150.

†Ibid., p. 408.

Never comfortable with women, he loved male companionship. He drew together a "band of brothers," both gay and straight, to share in the pursuit of power.

Rhodes cared nothing for the rights of blacks. Ever a combination of visionary and opportunist, he looked forward to an eventual reconciliation of Afrikaners and British in a united white front. Therefore, as prime minister of the Cape Colony, he broke with the colony's liberal tradition and supported Afrikaner demands to reduce drastically the number of black voters and limit black freedoms. This helped lay the foundation for the Union of South Africa's brutal policy of racial segregation known as *apartheid* after 1948.

QUESTIONS FOR ANALYSIS

1. In what ways does Rhodes's career epitomize the new imperialism in Africa?
2. How did Rhodes relate to Afrikaners and to black Africans? How do you account for the differences and the similarities?

Cecil Rhodes, after crushing the last African revolt in Rhodesia in 1896. (Brown Brothers)

The British conquest of Sudan exemplifies the general process of empire building in Africa. The fate of the Muslim force at Omdurman was eventually inflicted on all native peoples who resisted European rule: they were blown away by vastly superior military force. But however much the European powers squabbled for territory and privilege around the world, they always had the sense to stop short of actually fighting each other. Imperial ambitions were not worth a great European war.

Imperialism in Asia

Although the sudden division of Africa was more spectacular, Europeans also extended their political control in Asia. In 1815 the Dutch ruled little more than the island of Java in the East Indies. Thereafter they gradually brought almost all of the three-thousand-mile archipelago under their political authority, though — in good imperialist fashion — they had to share some of the spoils with Britain and Germany. In the critical decade of the 1880s, the French under the leadership of Ferry took Indochina. India, Japan, and China also experienced a profound imperialist impact (Map 25.3).

Two other great imperialist powers, Russia and the United States, also acquired rich territories in Asia. Russia moved steadily forward on two fronts throughout the nineteenth century. Russians conquered Muslim areas to the south in the Caucasus and in Central Asia, reaching the border of Afghanistan in 1885. Russia also proceeded to nibble greedily on China's outlying provinces in the Far East, especially in the 1890s.

The great conquest by the United States was the Philippines, taken from Spain in 1898 after the Spanish-American War. When it quickly became clear that the United States had no intention of granting independence, Philippine patriots rose in revolt and were suppressed only after long, bitter fighting. Some Americans protested the taking of the Philippines, but to no avail. Thus another great Western power joined the imperialist ranks in Asia.

Causes of the New Imperialism

Many factors contributed to the late-nineteenth-century rush for territory and empire, which was in turn one aspect of Western society's generalized expansion in the age of industry and nationalism. It is little wonder that controversies have raged over interpretation of the new imperialism, especially since authors of every persuasion have often exaggerated particular aspects in an attempt to prove their own theories. Yet despite complexity and controversy, basic causes are clearly identifiable.

Economic motives played an important role in the extension of political empires, especially in the British Empire. By the late 1870s, France, Germany, and the United States were industrializing rapidly behind ris-

French Seizure of Madagascar Africans in Madagascar transport a French diplomat in 1894, shortly before France annexed the island. (Snark/Art Resource, NY)

ing tariff barriers. Great Britain was losing its early lead and facing increasingly tough competition in foreign markets. In this new economic climate, Britain came to value old possessions, especially its vast colony of India, which it had exploited most profitably for more than a century. When continental powers began to grab Asian and African territory in the 1880s, the British followed suit immediately. They feared that France and Germany would seal off their empires with high tariffs and that future economic opportunities would be lost forever.

Actually, the overall economic gains of the new imperialism proved quite limited before 1914. The new colonies were simply too poor to buy much, and they offered few immediately profitable investments. Nonetheless, even the poorest, most barren desert was jealously prized, and no territory was ever abandoned. This was because colonies became important for political and diplomatic reasons. Each leading country saw colonies as crucial to national security and military power. For instance, safeguarding the Suez Canal played a key

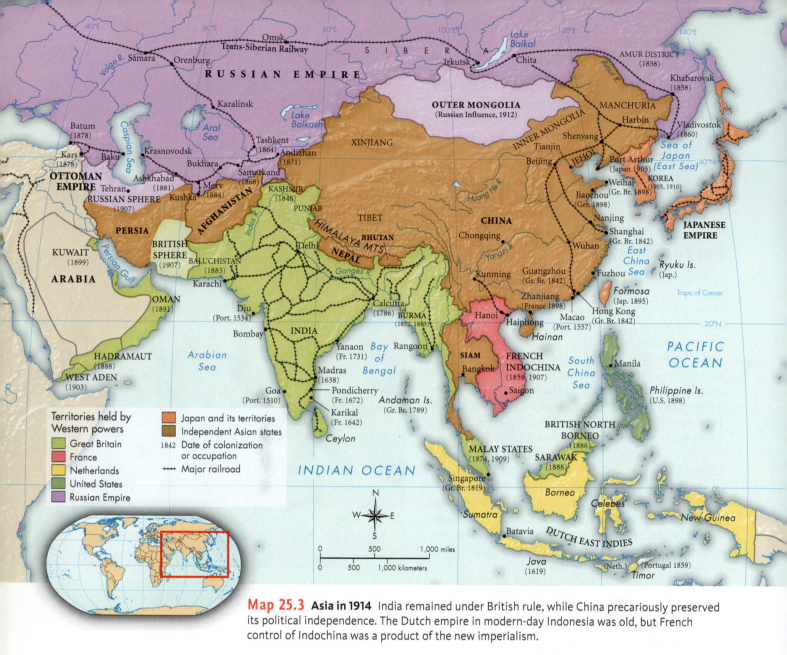

Map 25.3 Asia in 1914 India remained under British rule, while China precariously preserved its political independence. The Dutch empire in modern-day Indonesia was old, but French control of Indochina was a product of the new imperialism.

role in the British occupation of Egypt, and protecting Egypt in turn led to the bloody conquest of Sudan. Far-flung possessions guaranteed ever-growing navies the safe havens and the dependable coaling stations they needed in time of crisis or war.

Many people were convinced that colonies were essential to great nations. "There has never been a great power without great colonies," wrote one French publicist. The famous and influential nationalist historian of Germany, Heinrich von Treitschke (HAHYN-rihkh fuhn TRIGHCH-kuh), spoke for many when he wrote: "Every virile people has established colonial power. . . . All great nations in the fullness of their strength have desired to set their mark upon barbarian lands and those who fail to participate in this great rivalry will play a pitiable role in time to come."[8]

Treitschke's harsh statement reflects not only the increasing aggressiveness of European nationalism after Bismarck's wars of German unification, but also Social

Darwinian theories of brutal competition among races. As one prominent English economist argued, the "strongest nation has always been conquering the weaker . . . and the strongest tend to be best." Thus European nations, which were seen as racially distinct parts of the dominant white race, had to seize colonies to show they were strong and virile. Moreover, since racial struggle was nature's inescapable law, the conquest of "inferior" peoples was just. "The path of progress is strewn with the wreck . . . of inferior races," wrote one professor in 1900. "Yet these dead peoples are, in very truth, the stepping stones on which mankind has risen to the higher intellectual and deeper emotional life of today."[9] Social Darwinism and harsh racial doctrines fostered imperialist expansion.

So did the industrial world's unprecedented technological and military superiority. Three aspects were particularly important. First, the rapidly firing Maxim machine gun, so lethal at Omdurman in Sudan, was an

Tools for Empire Building Western technological advances aided Western political ambitions in Africa and Asia. The Maxim machine gun shown at far right was highly mobile and could lay down a continuous barrage that would decimate charging enemies, as in the slaughter of Muslim tribesmen at the Battle of Omdurman in the Sudan. Quinine was also very important to empire building. First taken around 1850 in order to prevent the contraction of the deadly malaria disease, quinine enabled European soldiers and officials to move safely into the African interior and overwhelm native peoples. (gun: Lordprice Collection/Alamy; quinine: Wellcome Library, London)

ultimate weapon in many another unequal battle. Second, newly discovered quinine proved no less effective in controlling attacks of malaria, which had previously decimated whites in the tropics whenever they left breezy coastal enclaves and dared to venture into mosquito-infested interiors. Third, the combination of the steamship and the international telegraph permitted Western powers to quickly concentrate their firepower in a given area when it was needed. Never before—and never again after 1914—would the technological gap between the West and non-Western regions of the world be so great.

Social tensions and domestic political conflicts also contributed mightily to overseas expansion. In Germany, in Russia, and in other countries to a lesser extent, contemporary critics of imperialism charged conservative political leaders with manipulating colonial issues in order to divert popular attention from the class struggle at home and to create a false sense of national unity. Thus imperial propagandists relentlessly stressed that colonies benefited workers as well as capitalists, providing jobs and cheap raw materials that raised workers' standard of living. Government leaders and their allies in the tabloid press successfully encouraged the masses to savor foreign triumphs and glory in the supposed increase in national prestige. In short, conservative leaders defined imperialist development as a national necessity, which they used to justify the status quo and their hold on power.

Finally, certain special-interest groups in each country were powerful agents of expansion. Shipping companies wanted lucrative subsidies. White settlers demanded more land and greater protection. Missionaries and humanitarians wanted to spread religion and stop the slave trade within Africa. Military men and colonial officials, whose role has often been overlooked, foresaw rapid advancement and highly paid positions in growing empires. The actions of such groups pushed the course of empire forward.

A "Civilizing Mission"

Western society did not rest the case for empire solely on naked conquest and a Darwinian racial struggle or on power politics and the need for naval bases on every ocean. Imperialists developed additional arguments in order to satisfy their consciences and answer their critics.

A favorite idea was that Europeans could and should "civilize" more primitive nonwhite peoples. According to this view, nonwhites would eventually receive the benefits of modern economies, cities, advanced medicine, and higher standards of living. In time, they might be ready for self-government and Western democracy. Thus the French spoke of their sacred "civilizing mission." In 1899 Rudyard Kipling (1865–1936), who wrote masterfully of Anglo-Indian life and was perhaps the most influential British writer of the 1890s, exhorted Europeans (and Americans in the United States) to unselfish service in distant lands in his poem "The White Man's Burden":

> *Take up the White Man's Burden—*
> *Send forth the best ye breed—*
> *Go bind your sons to exile*
> *To serve your captives' need,*
> *To wait in heavy harness,*
> *On fluttered folk and wild—*
> *Your new-caught, sullen peoples*
> *Half-devil and half-child.*[10]

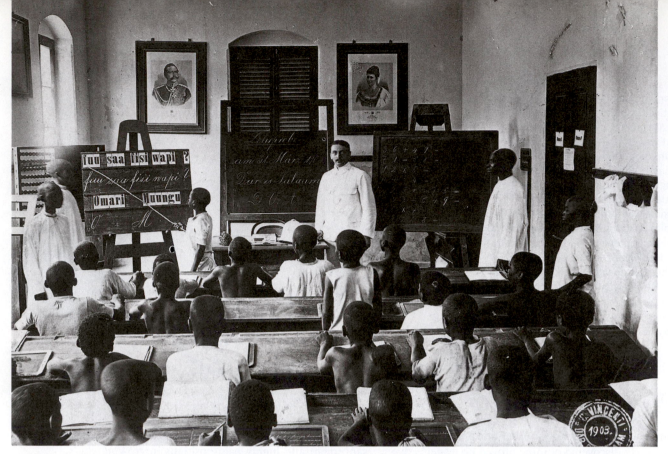

A Missionary School A Swahili schoolboy leads his classmates in a reading lesson in Dar es Salaam in German East Africa before 1914, as portraits of Emperor William II and his wife look down on the classroom. Europeans argued that they were spreading the benefits of a superior civilization with schools like this one, which is unusually well-built and furnished because of its strategic location in the capital city. (Ullstein Bilderdienst/The Granger Collection, New York)

Many Americans accepted the ideology of the **white man's burden**. It was an important factor in the decision to rule, rather than liberate, the Philippines after the Spanish-American War. Like their European counterparts, these Americans believed that their civilization had reached unprecedented heights and that they had unique benefits to bestow on all "less advanced" peoples. Another argument was that imperial government protected natives from tribal warfare as well as from cruder forms of exploitation by white settlers and business people.

white man's burden The idea that Europeans could and should civilize more primitive nonwhite peoples and that imperialism would eventually provide nonwhites with modern achievements and higher standards of living.

Peace and stability under European control also facilitated the spread of Christianity. In Africa Catholic and Protestant missionaries competed with Islam south of the Sahara, seeking converts and building schools to spread the Gospel. Many Africans' first real contact with whites was in mission schools. Some peoples, such as the Ibo in Nigeria, became highly Christianized.

Such occasional successes in black Africa contrasted with the general failure of missionary efforts in India, China, and the Islamic world. There Christians often preached in vain to peoples with ancient, complex religious beliefs. Yet the number of Christian believers around the world did increase substantially in the nineteenth century, and missionary groups kept trying.

Critics of Imperialism

The expansion of empire aroused sharp, even bitter, critics. A forceful attack was delivered in 1902, after the unpopular South African War, by radical English economist J. A. Hobson (1858–1940) in his *Imperialism*, a work that influenced Lenin and others. Hobson contended that the rush to acquire colonies was due to the economic needs of unregulated capitalism, particularly the need of the rich to find outlets for their surplus capital. Yet, Hobson argued, imperial possessions did not pay off economically for the country as a whole. Only unscrupulous special-interest groups profited from them, at the expense of both the European taxpayer and the natives. Moreover, Hobson argued that the quest for empire diverted popular attention away from domestic reform and the need to reduce the great gap between rich and poor. These and similar arguments were not very persuasive, however. Most people then (and now) were sold on the idea that imperialism was economically profitable for the homeland, and a broad and genuine enthusiasm for empire developed among the masses.

Hobson and many other critics struck home, however, with their moral condemnation of whites imperiously ruling nonwhites. They rebelled against crude Social Darwinian thought. "O Evolution, what crimes are committed in thy name!" cried one foe. Another sardonically coined a new beatitude: "Blessed are the strong, for they shall prey on the weak."[11] Kipling and his kind were lampooned as racist bullies whose rule rested on brutality, racial contempt, and the Maxim machine gun. Henry Labouchère, a member of Parliament and prominent spokesman for this position, mocked Kipling's famous poem:

> Pile on the Brown Man's burden!
> And if ye rouse his hate,
> Meet his old-fashioned reasons
> With Maxims up to date,
> With shells and Dum-Dum bullets
> A hundred times plain
> The Brown Man's loss must never
> Imply the White Man's gain.[12]

Similarly, in 1902 in *Heart of Darkness* Polish-born novelist Joseph Conrad (1857–1924) castigated the "pure selfishness" of Europeans in "civilizing" Africa; the main character, once a liberal scholar, turns into a savage brute.

Critics charged Europeans with applying a degrading double standard and failing to live up to their own noble ideals. At home Europeans had won or were winning representative government, individual liberties, and a certain equality of opportunity. In their empires, Europeans imposed military dictatorships on Africans and Asians; forced them to work involuntarily, almost like slaves; and discriminated against them shamelessly. Only by renouncing imperialism, its critics insisted, and giving captive peoples the freedoms Western society had struggled for since the French Revolution would Europeans be worthy of their traditions. Europeans who denounced the imperialist tide provided colonial peoples with a Western ideology of liberation.

Responding to Western Imperialism

What was the general pattern of non-Western responses to Western expansion, and how did India, Japan, and China meet the imperialist challenge? ■

To peoples in Africa and Asia, Western expansion represented a profoundly disruptive assault. Everywhere it threatened traditional ruling classes, local economies, and existing ways of life. Christian missionaries and European secular ideologies challenged established beliefs and values. Non-Western peoples experienced a crisis of identity, one made all the more painful by the power and arrogance of the white intruders.

The Pattern of Response

Generally, the initial response of African and Asian rulers to aggressive Western expansion was to try to drive the unwelcome foreigners away. This was the case in China, Japan, and upper Sudan, as we have seen. Violent antiforeign reactions exploded elsewhere again and again, but the superior military technology of the industrialized West almost invariably prevailed. Beaten in battle, many Africans and Asians concentrated on preserving their cultural traditions at all costs. Others found themselves forced to reconsider their initial hostility. Some (such as Ismail of Egypt) concluded that the West was indeed superior in some ways and that it was therefore necessary to reform their societies and copy some European achievements, especially if they wished to escape full-blown Western political rule. Thus it is possible to think of responses to the Western impact as a spectrum, with "traditionalists" at one end, "westernizers" or "modernizers" at the other, and many shades of opinion in between. Both before and after European domination, the struggle among these groups was often intense. With time, however, the modernizers tended to gain the upper hand.

When the power of both the traditionalists and the modernizers was thoroughly shattered by superior force, the great majority of Asians and Africans accepted imperial rule. Political participation in non-Western lands was historically limited to small elites, and the masses were used to doing what their rulers told them to do. In these circumstances Europeans, clothed in power and convinced of their righteousness, governed smoothly and effectively. They received considerable support from both traditionalists (local chiefs, landowners, religious leaders) and modernizers (Western-educated professional classes and civil servants).

Nevertheless, imperial rule was in many ways an imposing edifice built on sand. Support for European rule among the conquered masses was shallow and weak. Thus the native people followed with greater or lesser enthusiasm a few determined personalities who came to oppose the Europeans. Such leaders always arose, both when Europeans ruled directly and when they manipulated native governments, for at least two basic reasons.

First, the nonconformists—the eventual anti-imperialist leaders—developed a burning desire for human dignity. They came to feel that such dignity was incompatible with foreign rule. Second, and somewhat ironically, potential leaders found in the Western world the ideologies and justification for their protest. They discovered liberalism, with its credo of civil liberty and political self-determination. They echoed the demands of anti-imperialists in Europe and America that the West live up to its own ideals. Above all, they found themselves attracted to modern nationalism, which asserted that every people had the right to control its own destiny. After 1917 anti-imperialist revolt would find another weapon in Lenin's version of Marxian socialism. Thus the anti-imperialist search for dignity drew strength from Western thought and culture, as is particularly apparent in the development of three major Asian countries—India, Japan, and China.

Empire in India

India was the jewel of the British Empire, and no colonial area experienced a more profound British impact. Unlike Japan and China, which maintained a real or precarious independence, and unlike African territories, which were annexed by Europeans only at the end of the nineteenth century, India was ruled more or less absolutely by Britain for a very long time.

Arriving in India on the heels of the Portuguese in the seventeenth century, the British East India Company had conquered the last independent native state by 1848. The last "traditional" response to European rule—the attempt by the established ruling classes to drive the white man out by military force—was broken in India in 1857 and 1858. Those were the years of the **Great Rebellion** (which the British called a "mutiny"), when an insurrection by Muslim and Hindu mercenaries in the British army spread throughout northern and central India before it was finally crushed, primarily by loyal native troops from southern India. Britain then ruled India directly until Indian independence was gained in 1947.

After 1858 India was ruled by the British Parliament in London and administered by a tiny, all-white civil service in India. In 1900 this elite consisted of fewer than 3,500 top officials, for a population of 300 million. The British white elite, backed by white officers and native troops, was competent and generally well-disposed toward the welfare of the Indian peasant masses. Yet it practiced strict job discrimination and social segregation, and most of its members quite frankly considered the jumble of Indian peoples and castes to

The Great Rebellion, 1857–1858

CHINA
TIBET
NEPAL
Delhi
INDIA
GOA (Port.)
Arabian Sea
Bay of Bengal
Ceylon

■ Under British control
□ Area of rebellion

Great Rebellion The 1857 and 1858 insurrection by Muslim and Hindu mercenaries in the British army that spread throughout northern and central India before finally being crushed.

be racially inferior. As Lord Kitchener, one of the most distinguished top military commanders in India, stated:

> It is this consciousness of the inherent superiority of the European which has won for us India. However well educated and clever a native may be, and however brave he may prove himself, I believe that no rank we can bestow on him would cause him to be considered an equal of the British officer.[13]

British women played an important part in the imperial enterprise, especially after the opening of the Suez Canal in 1869 made it much easier for civil servants and businessmen to bring their wives and children with them to India. These British families tended to live in their own separate communities, where they occupied large houses with well-shaded porches, handsome lawns, and a multitude of servants. It was the wife's responsibility to manage this complex household. Many officials' wives learned to relish their duties, and they directed their households and servants with the same self-confident authoritarianism that characterized British political rule in India.

A small minority of British women—many of them feminists, social reformers, or missionaries, both married and single—sought to go further and shoulder the "white women's burden" in India, as one historian has described it.[14] These women tried especially to improve the lives of Indian women, both Hindu and Muslim, and to move them closer through education and legislation to the better conditions that they believed Western women had attained. Their greatest success was educating some elite Hindu women who took up the cause of reform.

With British men and women sharing a sense of mission as well as strong feelings of racial and cultural superiority, the British acted energetically and introduced many desirable changes to India. Realizing that they needed well-educated Indians to serve as skilled subordinates in the government and army, the British established a modern system of progressive secondary education in which all instruction was in English. Thus through education and government service, the British offered some Indians excellent opportunities for both economic and social advancement. High-caste Hindus, particularly quick to respond, emerged as skillful intermediaries between the British rulers and the Indian people, and soon they formed a new elite profoundly influenced by Western thought and culture.

This new bureaucratic elite played a crucial role in modern economic development, which was a second result of British rule. Irrigation projects for agriculture, the world's third-largest railroad network for good communications, and large tea and jute plantations geared to the world economy were all developed. Unfortunately, the lot of the Indian masses improved little, for

❝ However well educated and clever a native may be, . . . I believe that no rank we can bestow on him would cause him to be considered an equal of the British officer. ❞

—LORD KITCHENER

the increase in production was eaten up by population increase.

Finally, with a well-educated, English-speaking Indian bureaucracy and modern communications, the British created a unified, powerful state. They placed under the same general system of law and administration the different Hindu and Muslim peoples and the vanquished kingdoms of the entire subcontinent—groups that had fought each other for centuries and had been repeatedly conquered by Muslim and Mongol invaders. It was as if Europe, with its many states and varieties of Christianity, had been conquered and united in a single great empire.

In spite of these achievements, the decisive reaction to European rule was the rise of nationalism among the Indian elite. No matter how anglicized and necessary a member of the educated classes became, he or she could never become the white ruler's equal. The top jobs, the best clubs, the modern hotels, and even certain railroad compartments were sealed off to brown-skinned Indians. The peasant masses might accept such inequality as the latest version of age-old oppression, but the well-educated, English-speaking elite eventually could not. For the elite, racial discrimination meant injured pride and bitter injustice. It flagrantly contradicted those cherished Western concepts of human rights and equality. Moreover, it was based on dictatorship, no matter how benign.

By 1885, when educated Indians came together to found the predominately Hindu Indian National Congress, demands were increasing for the equality and self-government that Britain had already granted white-settler colonies, such as Canada and Australia. By 1907, emboldened in part by Japan's success (see the next section), the radicals in the Indian National Congress were calling for complete independence. Although there were sharp divisions between Hindus and Muslims, Indians were finding an answer to the foreign challenge. The common heritage of British rule and Western ideals, along with the reform and revitalization of the Hindu religion, had created a genuine movement for national independence.

Imperial Complexities in India
Britain permitted many native princes to continue their rule, if they accepted British domination. This photo shows a road-building project designed to facilitate famine relief in a southern native state. Officials of the local Muslim prince and their British "advisers" watch over workers drawn from the Hindu majority. (Nizam's Good Works Project—Famine Relief: Road Building, Aurangabad 1895–1902, from Judith Mara Gutman, *Through Indian Eyes*. Courtesy, Private Collection)

The Example of Japan

When Commodore Matthew Perry arrived in Japan in 1853 with his crude but effective gunboat diplomacy, Japan was a complex feudal society. At the top stood a figurehead emperor, but real power was in the hands of a hereditary military governor, the shogun. With the help of a warrior nobility known as samurai, the shogun governed a country of hard-working, productive peasants and city dwellers. Often poor and restless, the intensely proud samurai were humiliated by the sudden American intrusion and the unequal treaties with Western countries.

Meiji Restoration The restoration of the Japanese emperor to power in 1867, leading to the subsequent modernization of Japan.

When foreign diplomats and merchants began to settle in Yokohama, radical samurai reacted with a wave of antiforeign terrorism and antigovernment assassinations between 1858 and 1863. The imperialist response was swift and unambiguous. An allied fleet of American, British, Dutch, and French warships demolished key forts, further weakening the power and prestige of the shogun's government. Then in 1867, a coalition led by patriotic samurai seized control of the government with hardly any bloodshed and restored the political power of the emperor. This was the **Meiji Restoration**, a great turning point in Japanese development.

The immediate, all-important goal of the new government was to meet the foreign threat. The battle cry of the Meiji (MAY-jee) reformers was "Enrich the state and strengthen the armed forces." Yet how were these tasks to be done? In an about-face that was one of history's most remarkable chapters, the young but well-trained, idealistic but flexible leaders of Meiji Japan dropped their antiforeign attacks. Convinced that Western civilization was indeed superior in its military and industrial aspects, they initiated from above a series of measures to reform Japan along modern lines. In the broadest sense, the Meiji leaders tried to harness the power inherent in Europe's dual revolution in order to protect their country and catch up with the West.

In 1871 the new leaders abolished the old feudal structure of aristocratic, decentralized government and formed a strong unified state. Following the example of the French Revolution, they dismantled the four-class legal system and declared social equality. They decreed

A Busy Store in Meiji Japan Commercial life was extremely vigorous in Japan before it was opened to Western influence, and Tokyo was already one of the world's largest cities. This colorful print from the Meiji era shows how sophisticated Japanese consumers have adopted various aspects of Western dress. This reflects Japan's willingness to borrow from the West to maintain its independence and meet the Western challenge. (Arthur Sackler Gallery, Smithsonian Institution, Washington, D.C.: Gift of Ambassador and Mrs. William Leonhart, S1998.44a–c)

freedom of movement in a country where traveling abroad had been a most serious crime. They created a free, competitive, government-stimulated economy. Japan began to build railroads and modern factories. Thus the new generation adopted many principles of a free, liberal society, and, as in Europe, such freedom resulted in a tremendously creative release of human energy.

Yet the overriding concern of Japan's political leadership was always a powerful state and a strong military. (See "Listening to the Past: Lin Zexu and Yamagata Aritomo, Confronting Western Imperialism," page 808.) A powerful modern navy was created, and the army was completely reorganized along European lines, with three-year military service required for all males and a professional officer corps. This army of draftees effectively put down disturbances in the countryside, and in 1877 it was used to crush a major rebellion by feudal elements protesting the loss of their privileges. Japan also borrowed rapidly and adapted skillfully the West's science and modern technology, particularly in industry, medicine, and education. Many Japanese were encouraged to study abroad, and the government paid large salaries to attract foreign experts. These experts were replaced by trained Japanese as soon as possible.

By 1890, when the new state was firmly established, the wholesale borrowing of the early restoration had given way to more selective emphasis on those things foreign that were in keeping with Japanese tradition. Following the model of the German Empire, Japan established an authoritarian constitution and rejected democracy. The power of the emperor and his ministers was vast, that of the legislature limited.

Japan successfully copied the imperialism of Western society. Expansion not only proved that Japan was strong; it also cemented the nation together in a great mission. Having "opened" Korea with the gunboat diplomacy of imperialism in 1876, Japan decisively defeated China in a war over Korea in 1894 and 1895 and took Formosa (modern-day Taiwan). In the next years, Japan competed aggressively with the leading European powers for influence and territory in China, particularly in Manchuria. There Japanese and Russian imperialism met and collided. In 1904 Japan attacked Russia without warning, and after a bloody war, Japan emerged with a valuable foothold in China, Russia's former protectorate over Port Arthur (see Map 25.3). By 1910, with the annexation of Korea, Japan had become a major imperialist power.

Japan became the first non-Western country to use an ancient love of country to transform itself and thereby meet the many-sided challenge of Western expansion. Moreover, Japan demonstrated convincingly that a modern Asian nation could defeat and humble a great Western power. Many Chinese and Vietnamese nationalists were fascinated by Japan's achievement. Japan provided patriots throughout Asia and Africa with an inspiring example of national recovery and liberation.

Toward Revolution in China

In 1860 the two-hundred-year-old Qing Dynasty in China appeared on the verge of collapse. Efforts to repel foreigners had failed, and rebellion and chaos wracked the country. Yet the government drew on its traditional strengths and made a surprising comeback that lasted more than thirty years.

Two factors were crucial in this reversal. First, the traditional ruling groups temporarily produced new and effective leadership. Loyal scholar-statesmen and generals quelled disturbances such as the great Tai Ping (tigh-PIHNG) rebellion. The remarkable empress dowager Tzu Hsi (tsoo shee) governed in the name of her young son, combining shrewd insight with vigorous action to revitalize the bureaucracy.

Second, destructive foreign aggression lessened, for the Europeans had obtained their primary goal of commercial and diplomatic relations. Indeed, some Europeans contributed to the dynasty's recovery. A talented Irishman effectively reorganized China's customs office, increasing government tax receipts, and a sympathetic American diplomat represented China in foreign lands, helping to strengthen the central government. Such efforts dovetailed with the dynasty's efforts to adopt some aspects of Western government and technology while maintaining traditional Chinese values and beliefs.

The parallel movement toward domestic reform and limited cooperation with the West collapsed under the blows of Japanese imperialism. The Sino-Japanese War of 1894 to 1895 and the subsequent harsh peace treaty revealed China's helplessness in the face of aggression, triggering a rush for foreign concessions and protectorates in China. At the high point of this rush in 1898, it appeared that the European powers might actually divide China among themselves, as they had recently divided Africa. Probably only the jealousy each nation felt toward its imperialist competitors saved China from partition. In any event, the tempo of foreign encroachment greatly accelerated after 1894.

China's precarious position after the war with Japan led to a renewed drive for fundamental reforms. Like the leaders of the Meiji Restoration, some modernizers saw salvation in Western institutions. In 1898 they convinced the young emperor to launch a desperate **hundred days of reform** in an attempt to meet the foreign challenge. More radical reformers, such as the revolutionary Sun Yatsen (soun yaht-SEN) (1866–1925), who came from the peasantry and was educated

hundred days of reform
A series of Western-style reforms launched in 1898 by the Chinese government in an attempt to meet the foreign challenge.

LISTENING TO THE PAST

For centuries China was the world's largest and most self-sufficient state, and in 1800 the Qing (Manchu) Dynasty was still upholding China's traditional sovereignty and majesty. Foreign merchants could only trade with licensed Chinese merchants through the port of Guangzhou (Canton) on the south China coast. By 1830, however, British merchants were also smuggling highly addictive opium into China and earning colossal illegal profits.

In 1838 the Chinese government moved aggressively to deal with the crisis. It dispatched Lin Zexu, an energetic top official, to Guangzhou to stamp out the opium trade. Lin dealt harshly with Chinese buyers and then confiscated the opium stores of the British merchants. He also wrote a famous letter to Queen Victoria, calling on her to help end the drug trade and explaining why the Chinese government had acted. Neither Lin's action nor his eloquent letter, a portion of which follows, was successful. British armies attacked, China was "opened," and the opium trade continued.

Lin Zexu, Letter to Queen Victoria

His Majesty the Emperor comforts and cherishes foreigners as well as Chinese: he loves all the people of the world without discrimination. Whenever profit is found, he wishes to share it with all men; whenever harm appears, he likewise will eliminate it on behalf of all mankind. His heart is in fact the heart of the universe.

Generally speaking, the succeeding rulers of your honorable country have been respectful and obedient. Time and again they have sent petitions to China, saying: "We are grateful to His Majesty the Emperor for the impartial and favorable treatment he has granted to the citizens of my country who have come to China to trade. . . ."

As this trade has lasted for a long time, there are bound to be unscrupulous as well as honest traders. Among the unscrupulous are those who bring opium to China to harm the Chinese; they succeed so well that this poison has spread far and wide in all the provinces. You, I hope, will certainly agree that people who pursue material gains to the great detriment of the welfare of others can be neither tolerated by Heaven nor endured by men. . . .

I have heard that the areas under your direct jurisdiction such as London, Scotland, and Ireland do not produce opium; it is produced instead in your Indian possessions. . . . In these possessions the English people . . . also open factories to manufacture this terrible drug. As months accumulate and years pass by, the poison they have produced increases in its wicked intensity, and its repugnant odor reaches as high as the sky. Heaven is furious with anger, and all the gods are moaning with pain. It is hereby suggested that you destroy and plow under all of these opium plants and grow food crops instead, while issuing an order to punish severely anyone who dares to plant opium poppies again. . . .

Since a foreigner who goes to England to trade has to obey the English law, how can an Englishman not obey the Chinese law when he is physically within China? The present law calls for the imposition of the death sentence on any Chinese who has peddled or smoked opium. Since a Chinese could not peddle or smoke opium if foreigners had not brought it to China, it is clear that the true culprits are the opium traders from foreign countries. Being the cause of other people's death, why should they be spared from capital punishment? A murderer of one person is subject to the death sentence; just imagine how many people opium has killed! This is the rationale behind the new law which says that any foreigner who brings opium to China will be sentenced to death by hanging or beheading. Our purpose is to eliminate this poison once and for all and to the benefit of all mankind.

European traders and missionaries arrived in Japan in the sixteenth century, but in 1640 the government expelled the Europeans in order to preserve the existing Japanese culture and society. Three centuries later, Japan met the challenge of the West by adopting many of the methods and technologies of the West. Yamagata Aritomo (1838–1922) contributed significantly to this effort and its success.

Born into the military nobility known as the samurai, Yamagata Aritomo joined in the Meiji Restoration (see page 806), and to him fell the task of strengthening the armed forces, which the Meiji reformers had separated from the civilian officials. Traveling to Europe and carefully studying European armies and navies, he returned home in 1872 and wrote the memorandum reprinted here, "Opinion on Military Affairs and Conscription." The next year, he helped reorganize Japanese society by writing a new law calling for a Japanese army drafted from the whole male population, on the Western pattern. No longer would fighting be the province of samurai alone.

Yamagata Aritomo, "Opinion on Military Affairs and Conscription"

A military force is required to defend the country and protect its people. Previous laws of this country inculcated in the minds of the samurai those basic functions, and there was no separation between the civilian and military affairs. Nowadays civilian officials and military officials have separate functions, and the

The new Japanese army in about 1870, wearing Western uniforms and marching in formation. (Laurie Platt Winfrey, Inc./The Granger Collection, New York)

practice of having the samurai serve both functions has been abandoned. It is now necessary to select and train those who can serve the military functions, and herein lies the change in our military system. . . .

The creation of a standing army for our country is a task which cannot be delayed. . . .

The so-called reservists do not normally remain within military barracks. During peacetime they remain in their homes, and in an emergency they are called to service. All of the countries in Europe have reservists, and amongst them Prussia has most of them. There is not a single able-bodied man in Prussia who is not trained in military affairs. Recently Prussia and France fought each other and the former won handily. . . .

It is recommended that our country adopt a system under which any able-bodied man twenty years of age be drafted into military service, . . . and after completion of a period of service, they shall be returned to their homes. In this way every man will become a soldier, and not a single region in the country will be without defense. Thus our defense will become complete.

The second concern of the Ministry is coastal defense. This includes building of warships and constructing coastal batteries. Actually, battleships are moveable batteries. Our country has thousands of miles of coastline, and any remote corner of our country can become the advance post of our enemy. . . .

At a time like this it is very clear where the priority of this country must lie. We must now have a well-trained standing army supplemented by a large number of reservists. We must build warships and construct batteries. We must train officers and soldiers. We must manufacture and store weapons and ammunitions. The nation may consider that it cannot bear the expenses . . . [but] we cannot do without our defense for a single day. 〞

Sources: Excerpt from "A Letter to Queen Victoria" by Lin Tse-hsu (Zexu) in *China in Transition: 1517–1911*, edited and translated by Dun Jen Li, pp 64–66. Copyright © 1967 by D. Van Nostrand Company, Inc. "Opinion on Military Affairs and Conscription" from *Japan: A Documentary History*, ed. David J. Lu. (Armonk, N.Y.: M. E. Sharpe, 1997), pp. 315–318. Translation © 1997 by David J. Lu. Reprinted by permission of M. E. Sharpe, Inc. All rights reserved. Not for reproduction.

QUESTIONS FOR ANALYSIS

1. According to Lin, why did China move against the drug trade, and why should Queen Victoria help?

2. What measures does Yamagata advocate? Why? What lessons does he draw from Europe?

3. What similarities and differences do you see in the situations and the thinking of Lin and Yamagata?

Le Petit Parisien

SUPPLÉMENT LITTÉRAIRE ILLUSTRÉ

DIRECTION: 18, rue d'Enghien, PARIS

TOUS LES JOURS
Le Petit Parisien
5 CENTIMES.

TOUS LES JEUDIS
SUPPLÉMENT LITTÉRAIRE
5 CENTIMES.

Picturing the Past

Demonizing the Boxer Rebellion For months this Sunday supplement to a very popular French newspaper ran gruesome front page pictures of ferocious Boxers burning buildings, murdering priests, and slaughtering Chinese Christians. Whipping up European outrage about native atrocities was a prelude to harsh reprisals by the Western Powers. (Mary Evans Picture Library/The Image Works)

ANALYZING THE IMAGE What is happening in this picture? How would you characterize the mood of the crowd?

CONNECTIONS The images of Africans in Madagascar (page 799), Egyptians (painting and exhibition guide, pages 781 and 787), and the Chinese shown here were all drawn by European artists for Europeans. What, if any, similarities do these images share? What do they suggest to Europeans at home about colonial empires abroad and the native peoples who lived there? How does the perspective in the prints by Japanese artists for a Japanese audience (pages 806 and 809) differ?

To complete this activity online, go to the Online Study Guide at bedfordstmartins.com/mckaywest.

in Hawaii by Christian missionaries, sought to overthrow the dynasty altogether and establish a republic.

The efforts at radical reform by the young emperor and his allies threatened the Qing establishment and the empress dowager Tzu Hsi, who had dominated the court for the past quarter of a century. Pulling a palace coup, she and her supporters imprisoned the emperor, rejected the reform movement, and put reactionary officials in charge. Hope for reform from above was crushed.

A violent reaction swept the country, encouraged by the Qing court and led by a secret society that foreigners called the Boxers. These Boxers blamed China's ills on foreigners, especially the foreign missionaries whom they accused of traveling through China and telling the Chinese that their customs were primitive and their beliefs were wrong. Above all, the conservative, patriotic, antiforeign Boxers charged the foreign missionaries with undermining the Chinese reverence for their ancestors and thereby threatening the Chinese family and the entire society. In the agony of defeat and unwanted reforms, the Boxers and other secret societies struck out at their enemies. In northeastern China, more than two hundred foreign missionaries and several thousand Chinese Christians were killed, prompting threats and demands from Western governments. The empress dowager answered by declaring war, hoping that the Boxers might relieve the foreign pressure on the Qing Dynasty.

The imperialist response was swift and harsh. After the Boxers besieged the embassy quarter in Beijing, foreign governments organized an international force of twenty thousand soldiers to rescue their diplomats and punish China. Beijing was occupied and plundered by Western armies. In 1901 China was forced to accept a long list of penalties, including a heavy financial indemnity payable over forty years.

The years after this heavy defeat were ever more troubled. Anarchy and foreign influence spread as the power and prestige of the Qing Dynasty declined still further. Antiforeign, antigovernment revolutionary groups agitated and plotted. Finally in 1912, a spontaneous uprising toppled the Qing Dynasty. After thousands of years of emperors and empires, a loose coalition of revolutionaries proclaimed a Western-style republic and called for an elected parliament. The transformation of China under the impact of expanding Western society entered a new phase, and the end was not in sight.

LOOKING BACK LOOKING AHEAD

IN THE EARLY TWENTIETH century, educated Europeans had good reason to believe that they were living in an age of progress. The ongoing triumphs of industry and science and the steady improvements in the standard of living from about 1850 were undeniable, and it was generally assumed that these favorable trends would continue. There had also been progress in the political realm. The bitter class conflicts that culminated in the bloody civil strife of 1848 had given way in most European countries to stable nation-states with elected legislative bodies that reflected the general population, responded to real problems, and enjoyed popular support. Moreover, there had been no general European war since Napoleon I had been defeated in 1815. Only the brief, limited wars connected with German and Italian unification at mid-century had broken the peace in the European heartland.

In the global arena, peace was much more elusive. In the name of imperialism, Europeans (and North Americans) used war and the threat of war to open markets and punish foreign governments around the world. Although criticized by some intellectuals and leftists such as J. A. Hobson, these foreign campaigns in the late nineteenth century resonated with European citizens and stimulated popular nationalism. Like fans in a sports bar, the peoples of Europe followed their teams and cheered them on to victories that were almost certain. Thus imperialism and nationalism reinforced and strengthened each other in Europe, especially after 1875.

This was a dangerous development. Easy imperialist victories over weak states and poorly armed non-Western peoples encouraged excessive pride and led Europeans to underestimate the fragility of their accomplishments. Imperialism also made nationalism more aggressive and militaristic. And as European imperialism was dividing the world after 1875, the leading European states were also dividing themselves into two opposing military alliances. Thus when the two armed camps stumbled into war in 1914, there would be a superabundance of nationalistic fervor, patriotic sacrifice, and military destruction.

CHAPTER REVIEW

■ What were some of the global consequences of European industrialization between 1815 and 1914? (p. 782)

In the nineteenth century, global inequality in income and well-being increased markedly as a growing gap opened up between the industrializing West and the regions of Africa, Asia, and Latin America. Drawing on the advantages of this growing gap in industry and technology, the West entered the third and most dynamic phase of its centuries-old expansion into non-Western lands. In so doing, Western nations promoted a prodigious growth of world trade and investment, forced reluctant countries such as China and Japan into the globalizing economy, and profitably subordinated many lands to their own economic interests.

■ How was massive migration an integral part of Western expansion? (p. 788)

In response to population pressures at home and economic opportunities abroad, Western nations also sent forth millions of emigrants to the sparsely populated areas of European settlement in North and South America, Australia, and Asiatic Russia. As industrialization took hold and provided more decent jobs at home, migration from countries like Germany slowed. But Europeans continued to migrate in large numbers until war came in 1914. Migration from Asia was much more limited, mainly because European settlers raised high barriers to prevent the settlement of Asian immigrants.

■ How and why after 1875 did European nations rush to build political empires in Africa and Asia? (p. 794)

After 1875, Western countries used a combination of brute force and the self-justifying ideology of a "civilizing mission" to carve out vast political empires in Africa and rushed to establish political influence in Asia. There were many reasons for this empire building, but economic motives, political competition, and superior military technology were particularly important. In addition, many Europeans justified imperialist expansion on the basis of civilizing and Christianizing primitive peoples, whom they believed they were racially superior to.

■ What was the general pattern of non-Western responses to Western expansion, and how did India, Japan, and China meet the imperialist challenge? (p. 803)

African and Asian peoples attempted to defend themselves against the armies and navies of Western imperialism, but they were generally defeated in battle. They then had to develop different strategies. Traditionalists concentrated on preserving their culture, while modernists sought to introduce reforms capable of revitalizing their societies, often turning to Western concepts such as liberalism and, above all, nationalism. In India, an English-speaking elite developed after the failure of the Great Rebellion of 1857, and by 1885 a new Indian National Congress was calling for complete independence. In Japan, the remarkable leaders of the Meiji Restoration turned to Western models to escape Western domination, proclaiming legal equality, modernizing the military, and embracing modern industry and science. The reform movement in China was weaker and less successful, contributing to the fall of the Qing Dynasty in 1912 and the proclamation of a Western-style republic. By 1914 non-Western elites in all three countries were engaged in a national anti-imperialist struggle for dignity, genuine independence, and modernization.

Suggested Reading

Bagchi, Amiya Kumar. *Perilous Passage: Mankind and the Ascendancy of Capital*. 2005. A spirited radical critique of the "rise of the West."

Conklin, Alice. *A Mission to Civilize: The French Republican Ideal and West Africa, 1895–1930*. 1997. An outstanding examination of French imperialism.

Conrad, Joseph. *Heart of Darkness*. 1902. A novel that unforgettably probes European imperial motives.

Cook, Scott B. *Colonial Encounters in the Age of High Imperialism*. 1996. A stimulating overview with a very readable account of the explorer Stanley and central Africa.

Crews, Robert. *For Prophet and Tsar: Islam and Empire in Russia and Central Asia*. 2006. Considers neglected aspects of Russian imperialism.

Curtin, P., et al. *African History: From Earliest Times to Independence*, 2d ed. 1995. An excellent brief introduction to Africa in the age of imperialism.

Ebrey, Patricia Buckley. *The Cambridge Illustrated History of China*. 1999. A lively and beautiful work by a leading specialist.

Fage, J. D. *A History of Africa*, 3d ed. 1995. A highly recommended account.

Goodlad, Graham. *British Foreign and Imperial Policy, 1865–1919*. 2000. A lively examination of Britain's leading position in European imperialism.

Hochschild, Adam. *King Leopold's Ghost: A Story of Greed, Terror, and Heroism in Colonial Africa, 1895–1930*. 1997. A chilling account of Belgian imperialism in the Congo.

Mahfouz, H. *Palace of Desire*. 1991. A great novelist's compelling portrait of an Egyptian family and its social setting before 1914.

Maier, Charles S. *Among Empires: American Ascendancy and Its Predecessors*. 2006. Examines imperial power in history and how well America measures up.

Marshall, P. J., ed. *Cambridge Illustrated History of the British Empire*. 1996. A stunning pictorial history.

Midgley, Clare, ed. *Gender and Imperialism*. 1998. Examines the complex questions related to European women and imperialism.

Rotberg, Robert I. *The Founder: Cecil Rhodes and the Pursuit of Power*. 1988. Examines the imperialist's mind and times with great acuity.

Walthall, Anne. *Japan: A Cultural, Social, and Political History*. 2006. A concise, up-to-date overview covering a broad range of developments.

Notes

1. Quoted in A. Waley, *The Opium War Through Chinese Eyes* (New York: Macmillan, 1958), p. 29.
2. Quoted In J. W. Hall, *Japan, from Prehistory to Modern Times* (New York: Delacorte Press, 1970), p. 250.
3. Quoted in Earl of Cromer, *Modern Egypt* (London, 1911), p. 48.
4. Quoted in T. Blegen, *Norwegian Migration to America*, vol. 2 (Northfield, MN: Norwegian-American Historical Association, 1940), p. 468.
5. Quoted in I. Howe, *World of Our Fathers* (New York: Harcourt Brace Jovanovich, 1975), p. 290.
6. Quoted in W. L. Langer, *European Alliances and Alignments, 1871–1890* (New York: Vintage Books, 1931), p. 290.
7. Quoted in J. Ellis, *The Social History of the Machine Gun* (New York: Pantheon Books, 1975), pp. 86, 101.
8. Quoted in G. H. Nadel and P. Curtis, eds., *Imperialism and Colonialism* (New York: Macmillan, 1964), p. 94.
9. Quoted in W. L. Langer, *The Diplomacy of Imperialism*, 2d ed. (New York: Alfred A. Knopf, 1951), pp. 86, 88.
10. Rudyard Kipling, *The Five Nations* (London, 1903).
11. Quoted in Langer, *The Diplomacy of Imperialism*, p. 88.
12. Quoted in Ellis, *The Social History of the Machine Gun*, pp. 99–100.
13. Quoted in K. M. Panikkar, *Asia and Western Dominance: A Survey of the Vasco da Gama Epoch of Asian History* (London: George Allen & Unwin, 1959), p. 116.
14. A. Burton, "The White Women's Burden: British Feminists and 'The Indian Women,' 1865–1915," in *Western Women and Imperialism: Complicity and Resistance*, ed. N. Chauduri and M. Strobel (Bloomington: Indiana University Press, 1992), pp. 137–157.

Key Terms

Third World (p. 782)
opium trade (p. 785)
gunboat diplomacy (p. 786)
great migration (p. 788)
great white walls (p. 794)
new imperialism (p. 794)
Afrikaners (p. 795)
Berlin conference (p. 797)
white man's burden (p. 802)
Great Rebellion (p. 804)
Meiji Restoration (p. 806)
hundred days of reform (p. 807)

For practice quizzes and other study tools, visit the Online Study Guide at **bedfordstmartins.com/mckaywest**.

For primary sources from this period, see *Sources of Western Society*, **Second Edition**.

For Web sites, images, and documents related to topics in this chapter, visit Make History at **bedfordstmartins.com/mckaywest**.

26
War and Revolution

1914–1919

In the summer of 1914, the nations of Europe went willingly to war. They believed they had no other choice. Both peoples and governments confidently expected a short war leading to a decisive victory and thought that European society would be able to go on as before. These expectations were almost totally mistaken. The First World War was long, indecisive, and tremendously destructive. To the shell-shocked generation of survivors, it was known simply as the Great War because of its unprecedented scope and intensity.

From today's perspective, it is clear that the First World War was closely connected to the ideals and developments of the previous century. Industrialization, which promised a rising standard of living for the people, now produced horrendous weapons that killed and maimed millions. Imperialism, which promised to "civilize" those the Europeans considered savages, now led to intractable international conflicts. Nationalism, which promised to bring compatriots together in a harmonious nation-state, now encouraged hateful prejudice and chauvinism. The extraordinary violence of world war shook confidence in such nineteenth-century certainties to its core.

The war would also have an enormous impact on the century that followed. The need to provide extensive supplies and countless soldiers for the war effort created mass suffering, encouraged the rise of the bureaucratic state, and brought women in increasing numbers into the workplace. Millions were killed or wounded at the front and millions more grieved these losses. Grand states collapsed: the Russian, Austro-Hungarian, and Ottoman Empires passed into history. The trauma of war contributed to the rise of extremist politics—in the Russian Revolution of 1917 the Bolsheviks established a radical communist regime, and totalitarian fascist movements gained popularity across Europe in the postwar decades. Explaining the war's causes and consequences remains one of the great challenges for historians of modern Europe. ■

Life in World War I. This painting by British artist Paul Nash portrays a supply road on the western front. Nash's somber palate, tiny figures, and Cubist-influenced landscape capture the devastation and anonymous violence of total war.

CHAPTER PREVIEW

The Road to War
■ What caused the First World War, and why did it have significant popular support?

Waging Total War
■ How did the First World War change the nature of modern warfare?

The Home Front
■ What was the impact of total war on civilian populations?

The Russian Revolution
■ What led to the Russian Revolution, and what was its outcome?

The Peace Settlement
■ How did the Allies fashion a peace settlement, and why was it unsuccessful?

The Road to War

What caused the First World War, and why did it have significant popular support? ■

Historians have long debated why Europeans so readily pursued a war that was long and costly and failed to resolve the problems faced by the combatant nations. There was no single most important cause. Growing competition over colonies and world markets, a belligerent arms race, and a series of diplomatic crises sharpened international tensions. On the home front, new forms of populist nationalism strengthened people's unquestioning belief in "my country right or wrong." At the same time, ongoing domestic conflicts encouraged governments to pursue aggressive foreign policies in attempts to bolster national unity. All helped pave the road to war.

Growing International Conflict

The First World War began, in part, because European statesmen failed to resolve the diplomatic problems created by Germany's rise to Great Power status. The Franco-Prussian War and the unification of Germany opened a new era in international relations. By war's end in 1871, France was defeated, and Bismarck had made Prussia-Germany the most powerful nation in Europe (see Chapter 24). Yet, as Bismarck never tired of repeating after 1871, Germany was a "satisfied" power. Within Europe, he claimed, Germany had no territorial ambitions and wanted only peace.

But how was peace to be preserved? Bismarck's first concern was to keep an embittered France diplomatically isolated and without military allies. His second concern was the threat to peace posed by the enormous multinational empires of Austria-Hungary and Russia. Those two had many conflicting interests, particularly in southeastern Europe, where the waning strength of the Ottoman Empire had created a threatening power vacuum in the disputed border territories of the Balkans.

Bismarck's accomplishments in foreign policy were great, but only temporary. From 1871 to the late 1880s, he maintained German leadership in international affairs, and he signed a series of defensive alliances with Austria-Hungary and Russia designed to isolate a hostile France, which was still smarting over the loss of Alsace-Lorraine. Yet in 1890 the new emperor William II incautiously dismissed Bismarck, in part because he disagreed with the chancellor's friendly policy toward Russia. Under William II, Bismarck's carefully planned alliance system began to unravel. Germany refused to renew a nonaggression pact with Russia, the centerpiece of Bismarck's system, in spite of Russian willingness to do so. This fateful departure in foreign affairs prompted long-isolated republican France to court absolutist Russia, offering loans, arms, and support. In early 1894 France and Russia became military allies. As a result, continental Europe was divided into

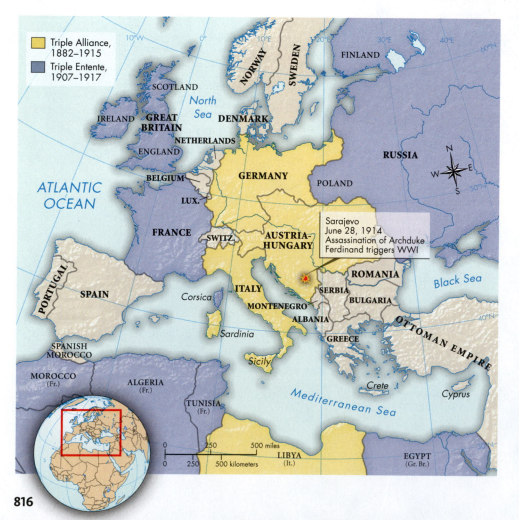

Map 26.1 **European Alliances at the Outbreak of World War I, 1914** At the start of World War I, Europe was divided into two hostile alliances: the Triple Entente of Britain, France, and Russia, and the Triple Alliance of Germany, Austria-Hungary, and Italy. Italy joined the Entente in 1915.

two rival blocs. The **Triple Alliance** of Austria, Germany, and Italy faced an increasingly hostile Dual Alliance of Russia and France, and the German general staff began secret preparations for a war on two fronts (Map 26.1).

As rivalries deepened on the continent, Great Britain's foreign policy became increasingly crucial. Long content with its "splendid [geographical] isolation" and without permanent alliances, Britain after 1891 was the only uncommitted Great Power. Many Germans and some Britons felt that the advanced, racially related Germanic and Anglo-Saxon peoples were natural allies. However, the good relations that had prevailed between Prussia and Great Britain since the mid-eighteenth century gave way to a bitter Anglo-German rivalry.

There were several reasons for this ill-fated development. Commercial rivalry in world markets between Germany and Great Britain increased sharply in the 1890s, as Germany became a great industrial power. Germany's ambitious pursuit of colonies further threatened British interests. Above all, Germany's decision in 1900 to expand greatly its battle fleet posed a challenge to Britain's long-standing naval supremacy.

Increased Anglo-German tensions coincided with the South African War between the British and the Dutch in South Africa, which encouraged worldwide opposition to British imperialism (see Chapter 25). In response, British leaders prudently set about shoring up their exposed position with alliances and agreements. Britain improved its often-strained relations with the United States, concluded an alliance with Japan in 1902, and allied with France in the Anglo-French Entente of 1904, which settled all outstanding colonial disputes between Britain and France.

Alarmed by Britain's ever-closer ties to France, Germany's leaders decided to test the strength of their alliance. In 1905 William II declared that Morocco was an independent, sovereign state and demanded that Germany receive the same trading rights as France. This aggressive saber rattling, termed the First Moroccan Crisis, clearly violated long-standing French colonial interests in the region. William II insisted on an international conference in hopes of settling the Moroccan question to Germany's benefit. But William II's crude bullying only brought France and Britain closer together, and Germany left the conference empty-handed.

The result of the First Moroccan Crisis in 1905 was something of a diplomatic revolution. Britain, France, Russia, and even the United States began to see Germany as a potential threat that might seek to dominate all Europe. At the same time, German leaders began to see sinister plots to encircle Germany and block its development as a world power. In 1907 Russia, battered by its disastrous war with Japan and the revolution of 1905, agreed to settle its quarrels with Great Britain in Persia and Central Asia and signed the Anglo-Russian Agreement. This agreement laid the foundation of the **Triple Entente** (ahn-TAHNT), an alliance between Britain, Russia, and France.

Germany's decision to add a large, enormously expensive fleet of big-gun battleships to its already expanding navy also heightened tensions. German patriots saw a large navy as the legitimate right of a great world

Triple Alliance The alliance of Austria, Germany, and Italy. Italy left the alliance when war broke out in 1914 on the grounds that Austria had launched a war of aggression.

Triple Entente The alliance of Great Britain, France, and Russia in the First World War.

Chronology

1914–1918	World War I
June 28, 1914	Serbian nationalist assassinates Archduke Francis Ferdinand
August 1914	War begins; Ottoman Empire joins the Central Powers
September 1914	Battle of the Marne; German victories on the eastern front
1915	Italy joins the Triple Entente; German submarine sinks the *Lusitania*; Germany halts unrestricted submarine warfare
1915–1918	Armenian genocide; German armies occupy large parts of east-central Europe
1916	Battles of Verdun and the Somme
1916–1918	Antiwar movement spreads throughout Europe; Arab rebellion against Ottoman Empire
1917	Germany resumes unrestricted submarine warfare
March 1917	February Revolution in Russia
April 1917	United States enters the war
October–November 1917	Battle of Caporetto
November 1917	Bolshevik Revolution in Russia; Balfour Declaration on Jewish Homeland in Palestine
1918	Treaty of Brest-Litovsk; revolution in Germany
1918–1920	Civil war in Russia
1919	Treaty of Versailles; Allies invade Turkey
1923	Treaty of Lausanne recognizes Turkish independence

power and as a source of national pride. But British leaders saw the German buildup as a military challenge that forced them to spend the "People's Budget" (see Chapter 24) on battleships rather than on social welfare. In 1909 the London *Daily Mail* hysterically informed its readers that "Germany is deliberately preparing to destroy the British Empire."[1] By then Britain had sided psychologically, if not officially, with France and Russia.

The leading nations of Europe were divided into two hostile camps, both ill-prepared to deal with the worsening situation in the Balkans. Britain, France, and Russia — the members of the Triple Entente — were allied in direct opposition to the German-led Triple Alliance. This unfortunate treaty system only confirmed the failure of all European leaders to incorporate Bismarck's mighty empire permanently and peacefully into the international system. By 1914, many believed that war was inevitable (see Map 26.1).

The Mood of 1914

Diplomatic rivalries and international crises played key roles in the rush to war, but a complete understanding of the war's origins requires an account of the "mood of 1914" — the attitudes and convictions of Europeans around 1914.[2] Widespread militarism (the popular approval of military institutions and their values) and nationalism encouraged leaders and citizens alike to see international relations as an arena for the testing of national power, with war if necessary.

Germany was especially famous for its powerful and aggressive army, but military institutions played a prominent role in affairs of state and in the lives of ordinary people across Europe. In a period marked by diplomatic tensions, politicians relied on generals and military experts to help shape public policy. All the Great Powers built up their armed forces and designed mobilization plans to rush men and weapons to the field of battle. Universal conscription in Germany, France, Italy, Austria-Hungary, and Russia — only Britain still relied on a volunteer army — exposed hundreds of thousands of young men each year to military culture and discipline.

The continent had not experienced a major conflict since the Franco-Prussian War (1870–1871), and Europeans vastly underestimated the destructive potential of modern weapons. Encouraged by the patriotic national press, many believed that war was glorious, manly, and heroic. If they expected another conflict, they thought it would be over quickly. Leading politicians and intellectuals likewise portrayed war as a test of strength that would lead to national unity and renewal. Such ideas

German Militarism   The German emperor William II reviews his troops with the Italian king Victor Emmanuel in front of the royal palace in Potsdam in 1902. Aggressive militarism and popular nationalism helped pave the road to war. (© Scherl/SV-Bilderdienst/The Image Works)

permeated European society. As one German volunteer wrote in his diary as he left for the front in 1914, "I believe that this war is a challenge for our time and for each individual, a test by fire, that we may ripen into manhood, become men able to cope with the coming stupendous years and events."[3]

Support for military values was closely linked to a growing sense of popular nationalism. Since the 1850s, the spread of the idea that members of an ethnic group should live together in a homogeneous, united national state had provoked all kinds of international conflicts over borders and citizenship rights. Nationalism also drove the spiraling arms race and the struggle over colonies. Broad popular commitment to national interests above all else weakened groups that thought in terms of international communities and consequences. Expressions of antiwar sentiment by socialists or women's groups were seen as a betrayal of country in time of need. Inspired by nationalist beliefs, much of the population was ready for war.

Leading statesmen had practical reasons for promoting militarism and nationalism. Political leaders had long used foreign adventurism and diplomatic posturing to distract the people from domestic conflicts. In Great Britain, leaders faced civil war in Northern Ireland and a vocal and increasingly radical women's movement. In Russia, the revolution of 1905 and defeat in the Russo-Japanese War (1904–1905) had greatly weakened support for the tsarist regime. In Germany, the victory of the Marxist Social Democratic Party in the parliamentary elections of 1912 led government authorities to believe the country was falling apart. The French likewise faced difficult labor and budget problems.

Determined to hold onto power and frightened by rising popular movements, ruling classes across Europe were willing to gamble on diplomatic brinksmanship and even war to postpone dealing with intractable social problems. Victory promised to preserve the privileged positions of elites and rally the masses behind the national cause. Patriotic nationalism did bring unity in the

> ❝ I am a Yugoslav nationalist, aiming for the unification of all Yugoslavs, and I do not care what form of state, but it must be free from Austria. ❞
>
> **—GAVRILO PRINCIP**

short run, but the wealthy governing classes underestimated the risk of war to themselves. They had forgotten that great wars and great social revolutions very often go hand in hand.

The Outbreak of War

On June 28, 1914, Archduke Francis Ferdinand, heir to the Austro-Hungarian throne, was assassinated by Serbian revolutionaries during a state visit to the Bosnian capital of Sarajevo (sar-uh-YAY-voh). After a series of failed attempts to bomb the archduke's motorcade, Gavrilo Princip, a fanatical member of the radical group Young Bosnia, shot the archduke and his wife Sophie as they passed by in their automobile. Princip was captured and put on trial, but he remained unrepentant. In court, he proudly asserted, "I am a Yugoslav nationalist, aiming for the unification of all Yugoslavs, and I do not care what form of state, but it must be free from Austria."[4]

Princip's deed, in the crisis-ridden territories of the Balkans on the border between the weakened Ottoman

Nationalist Opposition in the Balkans
This band of well-armed and determined guerrillas from northern Albania was typical of groups fighting against Ottoman rule in the Balkans. Balkan nationalists succeeded in driving the Ottoman Turks out of most of Europe and established an independent Albania in 1912, but their victory increased tensions with Austria-Hungary and among the Great Powers. (Roger-Viollet/Getty Images)

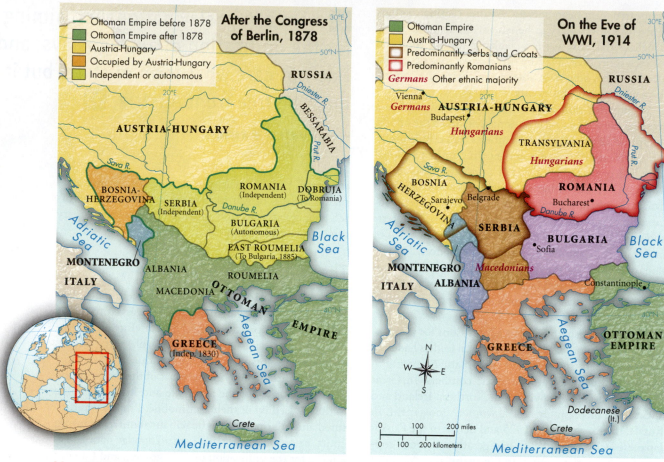

Map 26.2 **The Balkans, 1878–1914** After the Congress of Berlin in 1878, the Ottoman Empire suffered large territorial losses but remained a power in the Balkans. By 1914 Ottoman control had given way to ethnic boundaries that did not follow political boundaries, and Serbian national aspirations threatened Austria-Hungary.

and Austro-Hungarian Empires, led Europe into world war. In the early years of the twentieth century, war in the Balkans—"the tinderbox of Europe"—seemed inevitable. The reason was simple: between 1900 and 1914, the Western powers had successfully forced the Ottoman rulers to give up their European territories (Map 26.2). The ethnic nationalism inspired by these changing state boundaries was destroying the Ottoman Empire and threatening Austria-Hungary. The only questions were what kinds of wars would result and where they would lead.

By the early twentieth century, nationalism in southeastern Europe was on the rise. Independent Serbia in particular was eager to build a state that would include all ethnic Serbs. Serbia was thus openly hostile to Austria-Hungary and the Ottoman Empire, since both states included substantial Serbian minorities within their borders. To block Serbian expansion, Austria in 1908 formally annexed the territories of Bosnia and Herzegovina (hert-suh-goh-VEE-nuh). The southern part of the Austro-Hungarian Empire now included an even larger Serbian population, as well as Croats and Muslims.

Serbians expressed rage but could do nothing without support from Russia, their traditional ally.

The tensions in the Balkans soon erupted into a regional war. In the First Balkan War (1912), Serbia joined Greece and Bulgaria to attack the Ottoman Empire and then quarreled with Bulgaria over the spoils of victory. In the Second Balkan War (1913), Bulgaria attacked its former allies. Austria intervened and forced Serbia to give up Albania. After centuries, nationalism had finally destroyed the Ottoman Empire in Europe. Encouraged by their success against the Ottoman Empire, Balkan nationalists increased their demands for freedom from Austrian control, dismaying the leaders of the multinational Austro-Hungarian Empire. The former hoped and the latter feared that Austria might next be broken apart.

Within this complex context, the assassination of Archduke Francis Ferdinand instigated a five-week period of intense diplomatic activity that culminated in world war. The leaders of Austria-Hungary concluded that Serbia was implicated in the assassination and deserved severe punishment. On July 23 Austria-Hungary presented Serbia with an unconditional ultimatum, including demands that would violate Serbian sovereignty. When Serbia replied moderately but evasively, Austria mobilized its armies and declared war on Serbia on July 28. Thus a desperate multinational Austria-Hungary deliberately chose war to stem the rising tide of hostile nationalism within its borders in a last-ditch attempt to save its existing empire.

From the beginning of the crisis, Germany pushed Austria-Hungary to confront Serbia and thus bore much responsibility for turning a little war into a world war. Emperor William II and his chancellor Theobald von Bethmann-Hollweg realized that war between Austria and Russia was likely, for a resurgent Russia would not stand by, as it had in the Balkan wars, and watch the Austrians crush the Serbs. Yet Bethmann-Hollweg hoped that, although Russia (and its ally France) would go to war, Great Britain would remain neutral, unwilling to fight a war for Russia in the distant Balkans. To take advantage of these conditions, the German chancellor sent a telegram to Austria-Hungary that promised Germany's unconditional support in case of war. Germany's actions encouraged the prowar faction in Vienna to take a hard line against the Serbs at a time when moderation might still have limited the crisis.

In fact, the diplomatic situation quickly spiraled out of control as military plans and timetables began to dictate policy. Russia, a vast country, required much more time to mobilize its armies than did Germany and Austria-Hungary. And since the complicated mobilization plans of the Russian general staff assumed a two-front war with both Austria and Germany, Russia could not mobilize against one without mobilizing against the other. Therefore, on July 29 Tsar Nicholas II ordered full mobilization and in effect declared war. The German general staff also thought in terms of a two-front war. Their misguided **Schlieffen Plan** called for a quick victory over France after a lightning attack through neutral Belgium—the quickest way to reach Paris—before turning on Russia. On August 3 German armies invaded Belgium. Great Britain declared war on Germany the following day.

The speed of the so-called July Crisis created shock, panic, and excitement. In the final days of July and the first few days of August, massive crowds thronged the streets of Paris, London, St. Petersburg, Berlin, and Vienna. Shouting enthusiastic prowar slogans, the excited crowds pushed politicians and military leaders toward the increasingly inevitable confrontation. Events proceeded rapidly, and those who might have opposed the war could do little to prevent its arrival. In a little over a month, a limited Austrian-Serbian war had become a European-wide conflict, and the First World War had begun.

Waging Total War

How did the First World War change the nature of modern warfare? ■

When the Germans invaded Belgium in August 1914, they and everyone else thought that the war would be short and relatively painless. Many sincerely believed that "the boys will be home by Christmas." They were wrong. On the western front in France and the eastern front in Russia, the belligerent armies bogged down in a new and extremely costly kind of war, termed **total war** by German general Erich Ludendorff. Total war meant new roles for soldiers and civilians alike. At the front, total war meant lengthy, violent, and deadly battles fought with all the weapons a highly industrialized society could produce. At home, national economies were geared toward the war effort. Governments revoked civil liberties, and many civilians lost lives or livelihoods as occupying armies moved through their towns and cities. The struggle expanded to include nations and peoples outside Europe. The Middle East, Africa, East Asia, and the United States were all brought into the maelstrom of total war.

Schlieffen Plan Failed German plan calling for a lightning attack through neutral Belgium and a quick defeat of France before turning on Russia.

total war A war in which distinctions between the soldiers on the battlefield and civilians at home are blurred, and where the government plans and controls economic social life in order to supply the armies at the front with supplies and weapons.

Stalemate and Slaughter on the Western Front

In the face of the German invasion, the Belgian army heroically defended its homeland and fell back in good order to join a rapidly landed British army corps near the Franco-Belgian border. With the outbreak of the war, Russian armies immediately attacked eastern Germany, forcing the Germans to transfer much-needed troops to the east. Instead of quickly capturing Paris per the Schlieffen Plan, by the end of August dead-tired German soldiers were advancing slowly along an enormous front in the scorching summer heat.

The Schlieffen Plan

Planned German offensive

Neutral nations

NETHERLANDS
GERMANY
Brussels
Rhine R.
BELGIUM
LUX.
Paris
Reims
Metz
Seine R.
Marne R.
FRANCE
SWITZ.

0   100   200 mi.
0   100   200 km.

Map 26.3 World War I in Europe and the Middle East, 1914–1918 Trench warfare on the western front was concentrated in Belgium and northern France (inset), while the war in the east encompassed an enormous territory.

Legend (main map):
- Triple Entente and allies
- Central Powers and allies
- Greatest extent of territory gained by Germany-Austria
- German submarine war zone
- Neutral nations
- Farthest advance by Central Powers on date marked
- Farthest advance by Entente Powers on date marked
- British naval blockade
- Major battle

The Western Front (inset legend):
- Germany, 1914
- Greatest extent of territory gained by Germany, Sept. 1914
- Front at beginning of 1915
- German offensive, Summer 1918
- Major battle

On September 6 the French attacked a gap in the German line at the Battle of the Marne. For three days, France threw everything into the attack. At one point, the French government desperately requisitioned all the taxis of Paris to rush reserves to the troops at the front. Finally, the Germans fell back. France had been miraculously saved (Map 26.3).

With the armies stalled, both sides began to dig trenches to protect themselves from machine-gun fire. By November 1914, an unbroken line of four hundred miles of defensive trenches extended from the Belgian coast through northern France and on to the Swiss frontier. Armies on both sides dug in behind rows of trenches, mines, and barbed wire defenses, and slaughter on the western front began in earnest. The cost in lives of **trench warfare** was staggering, the gains in territory minuscule. For ordinary soldiers, conditions in the trenches were atrocious. (See "Living in the Past: Life and Death on the Western Front," page 824.) Recently invented weapons, the products of an industrial age, made battle impersonal, traumatic, and extremely deadly. The machine gun, hand grenades, poison gas, flame-throwers, long-range artillery, the airplane, and the tank were all used to maximum effect, some for the first time. All favored the defense, increased casualty rates, and revolutionized the practice of war.

The high commands of the combatant nations, who had learned military tactics and strategy in the nineteenth century, hardly understood trench warfare. For four years the generals repeated the same mistakes, mounting massive offensives designed to achieve decisive breakthroughs. Brutal frontal assaults against highly fortified trenches might overrun the enemy's front line, but attacking soldiers rarely captured any substantial territory. A French soldier described the bloody reality of high-tech warfare and the anonymous, almost unreal qualities of hand-to-hand combat between the trenches:

I went over the top, I ran, I shouted, I hit, I can't remember where or who. I crossed the wire, jumped over holes, crawled through shell craters still stinking of explosives, men were falling, shot in two as they ran; shouts and gasps were half muffled by the sweeping surge of gunfire. But it was like a nightmare mist all around me. . . . Now my part in it is over for a few minutes. . . . Something is red over there; something is burning. Something is red at my feet: blood.[5]

The French and British offensives of 1915 never gained more than three miles of territory from the enemy. In 1916 the unsuccessful German campaign against Verdun cost some 700,000 lives on both sides and ended in a draw, the opposing trenches still in place. The results in 1917 were little better. In hard-fought battles on all fronts, millions of young men were wounded or lost their lives for no real gain.

The Battle of the Somme, a great British offensive undertaken in the summer of 1916 in northern France, exemplified the horrors of trench warfare. The battle began with a weeklong heavy artillery bombardment on the German line, intended to cut the barbed wire fortifications, decimate the enemy trenches, and prevent the Germans from making an effective defense. For seven days and nights the British artillery fired nonstop on the German lines, expending 3 million shells. On July 1 the British went "over the top." Fortified by a double shot of harsh navy rum, the troops gathered in their trenches that morning. At precisely 7:30 A.M., line officers ordered the attack. The troops climbed out of the trenches and moved into no-man's land in the direction of the German lines, dug into a series of ridges about half a mile away.

At the beginning of the bombardment, the Germans fled into their dugouts — underground shelters dug deep into the trenches — where they suffered with little water, food, or sleep. But they survived. As the British soldiers neared the German lines and the shelling stopped, the Germans emerged from their bunkers, set up their machine guns, and mowed down the approaching troops. In many places, the wire had not been cut by the bombardment, so the struggling attackers, slowed down by heavy packs weighing over fifty-five pounds, made especially easy targets. About 20,000 British men were killed and 40,000 wounded on the first day of the attack, a crushing defeat that shook troop morale and public opinion. The battle dragged on until November, and in the end the British did push the Germans back — a whole seven miles. Some 420,000 British, 200,000 French, and 600,000 Germans were killed or wounded defending an insignificant piece of land. The war ground on.

trench warfare A type of fighting used in World War I behind rows of trenches, mines, and barbed wire; the cost in lives was staggering and the gains in territory minimal.

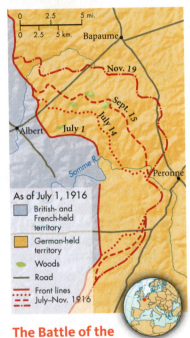

The Battle of the Somme, 1916

0   2.5   5 mi.
0   2.5   5 km.

Bapaume
Nov. 19
Sept. 15
July 15
Albert
July 1
July 14
Somme R.
Peronne

As of July 1, 1916
■ British- and French-held territory
■ German-held territory
● Woods
— Road
--- Front lines July–Nov. 1916

The Widening War

On the eastern front, the slaughter did not immediately degenerate into trench warfare, and the fighting was dominated by Germany. Repulsing the initial Russian attacks, the Germans won major victories at the Battles of Tannenberg and the Masurian Lakes in August

LIVING IN THE PAST

HARDSHIP AND TEDIUM ALTERNATED with spasms of indescribable violence on the western front. Enlisted men rotated in and out of position, at best spending two weeks at base, two weeks in reserve positions, and two weeks in the trenches on the front lines. They had little leave time to visit loved ones at home, though they exchanged literally billions of letters and postcards with friends and family. At the front,

mud and vermin, bad food, damp and cold, and wretched living quarters were the norm. Soldiers spent most of their time repairing rough trenches and dugouts and standing watch for an enemy they rarely saw.

During periods of combat, modern weapons like mustard gas, the machine gun, and long-range artillery resulted in horrific violence. Units were often decimated in poorly planned frontal assaults, and comrades could rarely retrieve the wounded and dead from no-man's land between the lines. Bodies, mangled by high explosives, were ground into the mud and disappeared, or became part of the earthworks themselves. A British soldier described the appalling effects: "the last I saw of him was two arms straining madly at the ground, blood pouring from his mouth while legs and body sank into a shellhole filled with water."*

The statistics tell a no less staggering story. Between 10 and 13 million combatants on all sides died during the war, and some 21 million were wounded. One historian estimates that fully half of all dead soldiers went either missing or unidentified; the tidy rows of crosses in military cemeteries mask a horrible reality. The maimed veteran—traumatized by shell shock or missing limbs or facial features—became an inescapable element of postwar life and culture.

For the dead and wounded, American president Woodrow Wilson's words rang true: World War I was indeed "the war to end all wars." Things were less clear for the survivors. The Peace Treaty of Versailles offered relief from the fighting, but hardly resolved the underlying issues. After 1918 anxious Europeans had to come to terms with numbing losses and the harsh realities of the postwar world.

*Quoted in Denis Winter, *Death's Men: Soldiers of the Great War* (London: Penguin, 1979), p. 180.

This French postcard celebrates victory over the Germans in the 1914 campaign and idealizes the harsh reality of trench warfare. (akg-images)

and September 1914. Russia had also put real pressure on the relatively weak Austro-Hungarian army, but by 1915 the eastern front had stabilized in Germany's favor. A staggering 2.5 million Russian soldiers had been killed, wounded, or captured. German armies occupied huge swaths of the Russian empire in central Europe, including ethnic Polish, Belorussian, and Baltic territories. Yet Russia was not knocked out of the war, marking another failure of the Schlieffen Plan.

To govern the occupied territories in central Europe, the Germans installed a vast military bureaucracy, with some 15,000 army administrators and professional specialists. Anti-Slavic prejudice dominated the mindset of the occupiers. The local Slavs were seen as savages and ethnic "mongrels" who were unable to work like "other, more joyously productive races," as one administrator reported. The military administration used prisoners of war and refugees as forced labor and stole animals and crops from local farmers: 90,000 horses, 140,000 heads of cattle, and 767,000 pigs were used to supply the occupying army or sent home to Germany. About one-third of the civilian population was killed or became

Soldiers "going over the top." (Pictoral Press Ltd/Alamy)

QUESTIONS FOR ANALYSIS

1. How did highly industrialized warfare affect the everyday experience of enlisted men in the First World War?

2. What were the effects of modern weaponry, and how did it change the way soldiers were buried?

3. How do these images differ in their depiction of war? What might the postcard artist and the photographer have intended in showing these views of World War I?

Soldiers wore gas masks like this American-made one as protection from enemy artillery that fired shells containing poisonous gas. (Collection Memorial de la Bataille de Verdun)

refugees under this brutal occupation. In the long run, the German state hoped to turn these territories into German possessions, a chilling forerunner of Nazi policies in World War II.[6]

The changing tides of victory and hopes for territorial gains brought neutral countries into the war (see Map 26.3). Italy, a member of the Triple Alliance since 1882, had declared its neutrality in 1914 on the grounds that Austria had launched a war of aggression. Then in May 1915 Italy joined the Triple Entente of Great Britain, France, and Russia in return for prom-

ises of Austrian territory. The war along the Italian-Austrian front was bitter and deadly and cost some 600,000 Italian lives.

In October 1914 the Ottoman Empire joined Austria and Germany, by then known as the Central Powers. The following September Bulgaria decided to follow the Ottoman Empire's lead in order to settle old scores with Serbia. The Balkans, with the exception of Greece, were occupied by the Central Powers.

The entry of the Ottoman Turks carried the war into the Middle East. Heavy fighting between the

Writing Home from the Front Cramped within the tight network of trenches on the western front, a British soldier writes a letter home while his compatriots rest before the next engagement. The post was typically the only connection between soldiers and their relatives, and over 28 billion pieces of mail passed between home and front on all sides during the war. Mass-produced postcards such as this one often displayed fantasies about loved ones at home. (photo: Courtesy of the Trustees of the Imperial War Museum; postcard: Imperial War Museum/The Art Archive)

Ottomans and the Russians enveloped the Armenians, who lived on both sides of the border and had experienced brutal repression by the Turks in 1909. When in 1915 some Armenians welcomed Russian armies as liberators, the Ottoman government, with German support, ordered a mass deportation of its Armenian citizens from their homeland. In this murderous example of modern ethnic cleansing, now termed the Armenian genocide, a million innocent civilians died from murder, starvation, and disease.

In 1915, at the Battle of Gallipoli, British forces tried and failed to take the Dardanelles and Constantinople from the Ottoman Turks. The invasion force was pinned down on the beaches, and the ten-month-long battle cost the Turks 300,000 and the British 265,000 men killed, wounded, or missing.

The British were more successful at inciting the Arabs to revolt against their Turkish rulers. They bargained with the foremost Arab leader, Hussein ibn-Ali (1856–1931), who was a direct descendant of the prophet Muhammad and the chief magistrate (*sharif*) of Mecca, the holiest city in the Muslim world. Controlling much of the Ottoman Empire's territory along the Red Sea, an area known as the Hejaz (see Map 26.5, on page 844), Hussein managed in 1915 to win vague British commitments for an independent Arab kingdom. Thus in

The Armenian Genocide, 1915–1918

Black Sea

Constantinople

GREECE

RUSSIAN EMPIRE

Caspian Sea

OTTOMAN EMPIRE

PERSIA (IRAN)

☐ Armenian ethnic area

● Massacre and deportation site (size indicates relative death toll)

■ Modern Armenia

1916 Hussein revolted against the Turks, proclaiming himself king of the Arabs. He joined forces with the British under T. E. Lawrence, who in 1917 helped lead Arab soldiers in a successful guerrilla war against the Turks on the Arabian peninsula.

Similar victories were eventually scored in the Ottoman province of Iraq. Britain occupied the southern Iraqi city of Basra in 1914 and captured Baghdad in 1917. In September 1918 British armies and their Arab allies rolled into Syria. This offensive culminated in the triumphal entry of Hussein's son Faisal (FIGH-suhl) into Damascus. Arab patriots in Syria and Iraq now expected a large, unified Arab nation-state to rise from the dust of the Ottoman collapse — though in the event they were disappointed by the Western Powers (see page 843).

The war spread to colonial Africa and East Asia as well. Instead of revolting as the Germans hoped, the colonial subjects of the British and French generally supported the Allied powers. Colonized peoples helped local British and French commanders seize Germany's colonies around the globe. More than a million Africans and Asians served in the various armies of the warring powers; more than double that number served as porters to carry equipment. The French, facing a shortage of young men, made especially heavy use of colonial troops.

In April 1917 the United States declared war on Germany, another crucial development in the expanding conflict. American intervention grew out of the war at sea and general sympathy for the Triple Entente. At the beginning of the war, Britain and France established a naval blockade to strangle the Central Powers. No neutral cargo ship was permitted to sail to Germany. In early 1915 Germany retaliated with the murderously effective submarine, a new weapon that violated traditional niceties of fair warning under international law.

In May 1915 a German submarine sank the British passenger liner *Lusitania*, claiming more than 1,000 lives, among them 139 U.S. citizens. President Woodrow Wilson protested vigorously, using the tragedy to incite American public opinion against the Germans. As a result, Germany halted its submarine warfare for almost two years; the alternative was almost certain war with the United States.

Early in 1917 the German military command — confident that improved submarines could starve Britain into submission before the United States could come to its rescue — resumed unrestricted submarine warfare. This was a reckless gamble, and the United States declared war on Germany. Eventually the United States tipped the balance in favor of the Triple Entente and its allies.

Armenian Deportation   In 1915 when some Armenians welcomed Russian armies as liberators after years of persecution, the Ottoman government ordered a genocidal mass deportation of its Armenian citizens from their homeland in the empire's eastern provinces. This photo, taken from a hotel window in Kharpert by a German businessman in 1915, shows Turkish guards marching Armenian men off to prison, where they were tortured to death. A million Armenians died from murder, starvation, and disease during World War I. (Courtesy of the Armenian Library, Watertown, Mass.)

The Home Front

What was the impact of total war on civilian populations? ■

The war's impact on civilians was no less massive than it was on the men crouched in the trenches. Total war encouraged the growth of state bureaucracies, changed the lives of ordinary women and men, and by the end inspired mass antiwar protest movements.

Mobilizing for Total War

In August 1914 many people greeted the outbreak of hostilities enthusiastically. In every country, ordinary folk believed that their nation was right to defend itself from foreign aggression. With the exception of a few extreme left-wingers, even socialists supported the war. Yet by mid-October generals and politicians had begun to realize that victory would require more than patriotism. Each combatant country experienced a desperate need for men and weapons. To keep the war machine from sputtering to a stop, national leaders aggressively intervened in society and the economy.

By the late nineteenth century the responsive national state had already shown an eagerness to manage the welfare of its citizens (see Chapter 24). Now the state intruded even further into people's daily lives. Each combatant state established new government ministries to mobilize soldiers and armaments and to provide care for war widows and wounded veterans. Censorship offices controlled news about the course of the war. Free-market capitalism was abandoned, at least for the duration. Instead, government planning boards set mandatory production goals, established rationing programs, and set limits on wages and prices. Based on tremendously productive industrial economies controlled from above, government management yielded an effective—and therefore immensely destructive—war effort on all sides.

Germany went furthest in developing a planned economy to wage total war. As soon as war began, Walter Rathenau, the talented Jewish industrialist in charge of Germany's largest electric company, convinced the government to set up the War Raw Materials Board to ration and distribute raw materials. Under Rathenau's direction, every useful material from foreign oil to barnyard manure was inventoried and rationed. Moreover, the board launched successful attempts to produce substitutes, such as synthetic rubber and synthetic nitrates, needed to make explosives and essential to the blockaded German war machine. Food was also rationed in accordance with physical need. At the same time, Germany failed to tax the war profits of private firms heavily enough. This failure contributed to massive deficit

German Ration Card The burdens of total war forced governments to control the distribution of the most basic goods, including food. This German ration card from 1915 has tear-away coupons for weekly allotments of potatoes. (Private Collection Newbury/The Art Archive)

financing, inflation, the growth of a black market, and the eventual re-emergence of class conflict.

Following the terrible Battles of Verdun and the Somme in 1916, German military leaders forced the Reichstag to accept the Auxiliary Service Law, which required all males between seventeen and sixty to work only at jobs considered critical to the war effort. Women also worked in war factories, mines, and steel mills, where they labored, like men, at heavy and dangerous jobs. With the passage of the law, many more women followed. People lived on little more than one thousand calories a day. War production increased while some Germans starved to death.

After 1917 Germany's leaders ruled by dictatorial decree. Generals Hindenburg and Ludendorff drove Chancellor Bethmann-Hollweg from office. With the support of the newly formed ultra-conservative and prowar Fatherland Party, the generals established a military dictatorship. Hindenburg called for the ultimate mobilization for total war. Germany could win, he said, only "if all the treasures of our soil that agriculture and industry can produce are used exclusively for the conduct of War. . . . All other considerations must come second."[7] Thus in Germany total war led to the establishment of history's first "totalitarian" society, a model for future national socialists.

Only Germany was directly ruled by a military government, yet leaders in all the belligerent nations took power from parliaments, suspended civil liberties, and ignored democratic procedures. After 1915 the British Ministry of Munitions organized private industry to produce for the war, allocated labor, set wage and price rates, and settled labor disputes. In France a weakened parliament met in secret, and the courts jailed pacifists who dared criticize the state. Once the United States entered the war, new federal agencies such as the War Labor Board and the War Industries Board regulated industry, labor relations, and agricultural production. The war may have been deadly for citizen armies, but it was certainly good for the growth of the bureaucratic nation-state.

The Social Impact

The social impact of total war was no less profound than the economic impact, though again there were important national variations. National conscription sent millions of men to the front, exposing many to foreign lands for the first time in their lives. The insatiable needs of the military created a tremendous demand for workers, and jobs were readily available. This situation—seldom, if ever, seen before 1914, when unemployment

> **❝** . . . if all the treasures of our soil that agriculture and industry can produce are used exclusively for the conduct of War. . . . All other considerations must come second. **❞**
>
> **—GENERAL HINDENBURG**

and poverty had been facts of urban life—brought momentous changes.

The need for workers meant greater power and prestige for labor unions. Unions now cooperated with war governments on workplace rules, wages, and production schedules in return for real participation in important decisions. The entry of labor leaders and unions into policymaking councils paralleled the entry of socialist leaders into the war governments. Both reflected a new government openness to the needs of those at the bottom of society.

The role of women also changed dramatically. In every country, large numbers of women left home and domestic service to work in industry, transportation, and offices. The production of vast amounts of arms and ammunition required huge numbers of laborers, and women moved into skilled industrial jobs long

Women Factory Workers Building a Truck, London, 1917 Millions of men on all sides were drafted to fight in the war, creating a serious labor shortage. When women left home to fill jobs formerly reserved for men, they challenged traditional gender roles. (© Hulton-Deutsch Collection/Corbis)

considered men's work only. Some women believed that the war promised to permanently break down the barriers between men's and women's work. One French woman argued that

> Like you [men] — we [women] are ambitious. Give us the chance to learn the inner workings of the engineering trade, so that one day we may become overseers and forewomen. The prospect that one might rise through the ranks and so gain a better future is a powerful stimulant.[8]

Moreover, women became highly visible in public — not only as munitions workers but also as bank tellers and mail carriers, and even as police officers, firefighters, and farm laborers. Women also served as auxiliaries and nurses at the front. (See "Individuals in Society: Vera Brittain," at right.)

The war expanded the range of women's activities and helped change attitudes about gender, but the long-term results were mixed. Women across Europe gained experience in jobs previously reserved for men, and as a result of women's many-sided war effort, the United States, Britain, Germany, Poland, and other countries granted women the right to vote immediately after the war. At the war's end, however, millions of demobilized soldiers demanded their jobs back, and governments forced women out of the workplace. Their employment gains were mostly temporary, except in nursing and social work, already considered "women's work." The great dislocations of war loosened sexual morality, and some women bobbed their hair, shortened their skirts, and smoked in public. Yet supposedly "loose" women were often criticized for betraying their soldier-husbands away at the front. And women's rights movements faded in the 1920s and 1930s, in large part because feminist leaders found it difficult to regain momentum after the crisis of war.

To some extent, the war promoted greater social equality, blurring class distinctions and lessening the gap between rich and poor. This blurring was most apparent in Great Britain, where the bottom third of the population generally lived better than they ever had, for the poorest gained most from the severe shortage of labor. Elsewhere, greater equality was reflected in full employment, rationing according to physical needs, and a sharing of hardships. In general, European society became more uniform and egalitarian, in spite of some war profiteering.

Death itself had no respect for traditional social distinctions. It savagely decimated the young aristocratic officers who led the charge, and it fell heavily on the mass of drafted peasants and unskilled workers who followed, leading commentators to speak of a "lost generation." Yet death often spared highly skilled workers and foremen. Their lives were too valuable to squander at the front, for they were needed to train the newly recruited women and older unskilled men laboring valiantly in war plants at home.

Growing Political Tensions

During the first two years of war, many soldiers and civilians supported their governments. Belief in a just cause and patriotic nationalism united peoples behind their national leaders. Each government used rigorous censorship and crude propaganda to bolster popular support. German propaganda pictured black soldiers from France's African empire raping German women, while the French and British ceaselessly recounted and exaggerated German atrocities in Belgium and elsewhere. Patriotic posters and slogans, slanted news, and biased editorials inflamed national hatreds and helped control public opinion, encouraging soldiers to continue fighting.

Despite such efforts, by the spring of 1916 people were beginning to crack under the strain of total war. On May 1 that year, several thousand demonstrators in Berlin heard the radical socialist leader Karl Liebknecht (1871–1919) attack the costs of the war effort. Liebknecht was immediately arrested and imprisoned, but his daring action electrified Europe's far left. Strikes and protest marches over inadequate food flared up on every home front. In April 1916 Irish nationalists in Dublin took advantage of this situation and revolted against British rule in the great Easter Rebellion. A week of bitter fighting passed before the rebels were crushed and their leaders executed. In France, Georges Clemenceau (zhorzh kleh-muhn-SOH) (1841–1929) established a virtual dictatorship, pouncing on strikers and jailing without trial journalists and politicians who dared to suggest a compromise peace with Germany.

On all sides, soldiers' morale began to decline. Numerous French units refused to fight after the disastrous French offensive of May 1917. Only tough military justice for mutiny leaders and a tacit agreement with the troops that there would be no more grand offensives enabled the new general in chief, Henri-Philippe Pétain (pay-TAN), to restore order. Facing defeat, wretched conditions at the front, and growing hopelessness, Russian soldiers deserted in droves, providing fuel for the Russian Revolution of 1917. After the murderous Battle of Caporetto in northern Italy in 1917, the Italian army collapsed in despair. In the massive battles of 1916 and 1917, the British armies had been "bled dry." Only the promised arrival of fresh troops from the United States stiffened the resolve of the allies.

The strains were even worse for the Central Powers. In October 1916, a young socialist assassinated the chief minister of Austria. The following month, when the aging Emperor Francis Joseph died, a symbol of unity disappeared. In spite of absolute censorship, political dissatisfaction and conflicts among nationalities grew. Both Czech and Yugoslav leaders demanded independent states for their peoples. In April 1917 Austria's chief minister summed up the situation in the gloomiest possible terms. The country and army were

INDIVIDUALS IN SOCIETY

ALTHOUGH THE GREAT WAR UPENDED MILLIONS OF LIVES, it struck Europe's young people with the greatest force. For Vera Brittain (1893–1970), as for so many in her generation, the war became life's defining experience, which she captured forever in her famous autobiography, *Testament of Youth* (1933).

Brittain grew up in a wealthy business family in northern England, bristling at small-town conventions and discrimination against women. Very close to her brother Edward, two years her junior, Brittain read voraciously and dreamed of being a successful writer. Finishing boarding school and beating down her father's objections, she prepared for Oxford's rigorous entry exams and won a scholarship to its women's college. Brittain also fell in love with Roland Leighton, an equally brilliant student from a literary family and her brother's best friend. All three, along with two more close friends, Victor Richardson and Geoffrey Thurlow, confidently prepared to enter Oxford in late 1914.

When war suddenly loomed in July 1914, Brittain shared with millions of Europeans a thrilling surge of patriotic support for her government, a prowar enthusiasm she later played down in her published writings. She wrote in her diary that her "great fear" was that England would declare its neutrality and commit the "grossest treachery" toward France.* She supported Roland's decision to enlist, agreeing with his glamorous view of war as "very ennobling and very beautiful." Later, exchanging anxious letters with Roland in France in 1915, Brittain began to see the conflict in personal, human terms. She wondered if any victory or defeat could be worth Roland's life.

Struggling to quell her doubts, Brittain redoubled her commitment to England's cause and volunteered as an army nurse. For the next three years she served with distinction in military hospitals in London, Malta, and northern France, repeatedly torn between the vision of noble sacrifice and the reality of human tragedy. She lost her sexual inhibitions caring for mangled male bodies, and she longed to consummate her love with Roland. Awaiting his return on leave on Christmas Day in 1915, she was greeted instead with a telegram: Roland had been killed two days before.

Vera Brittain was marked forever by her wartime experiences. (Vera Brittain Archive, William Ready Division of Archives and Research Collections, McMaster University Library)

Roland's death was the first of the devastating blows that eventually overwhelmed Brittain's idealistic patriotism. In 1917 first Geoffrey and then Victor died from gruesome wounds. In early 1918, as the last great German offensive covered the floors of her war-zone hospital with maimed and dying German prisoners, the bone-weary Vera felt a common humanity and saw only more victims. A few weeks later Edward—her last hope—died in action. When the war ended, she was, she said, a "complete automaton," with "my deepest emotions paralyzed if not dead."

Returning to Oxford and finishing her studies, Brittain gradually recovered. She formed a deep, restorative friendship with another talented woman writer, Winifred Holtby, published novels and articles, and became a leader in the feminist campaign for gender equality. She also married and had children. But her wartime memories were always with her. Finally, Brittain succeeded in coming to grips with them in *Testament of Youth*, her powerful anti-war autobiography. The unflinching narrative spoke to the experiences of an entire generation and became a runaway bestseller. Above all, Brittain captured the ambivalent, contradictory character of the war, when millions of young people found excitement, courage, and common purpose but succeeded only in destroying their lives with their superhuman efforts and futile sacrifices. Becoming ever more committed to pacifism, Brittain opposed England's entry into World War II.

QUESTIONS FOR ANALYSIS

1. What were Brittain's initial feelings toward the war? How and why did they change as the conflict continued?

2. Why did Brittain volunteer as a nurse, as many women did? How might wartime nursing have influenced women of her generation?

3. In portraying the ambivalent, contradictory character of World War I for Europe's youth, was Brittain describing the character of all modern warfare?

*Quoted in the excellent study by P. Berry and M. Bostridge, *Vera Brittain: A Life* (London: Virago Press, 2001), p. 59; additional quotations are from pp. 80 and 136.

Picturing the Past

Wartime Propaganda Posters This famous French propaganda poster from 1918 (left) proclaims "They shall not pass" and expresses the French determination to hold back the German invaders at any cost. The American recruitment poster from 1917 (right) encourages "fighting men" to "join the Navy." (French poster: Archives Municipales Versailles/Gianni Dagli Orti/The Art Archive; American poster: Museum of the City of New York/The Art Archive)

ANALYZING THE IMAGE How would you describe the soldier and sailor pictured on these posters? What messages about the war do the posters convey?

CONNECTIONS The "They shall not pass" poster was created after France had been at war for four years, while the naval recruitment poster came out before American troops were actively engaged overseas. How might the country of origin and the date of publication have affected the messages conveyed?

To complete this activity online, go to the Online Study Guide at bedfordstmartins.com/mckaywest.

exhausted. Another winter of war would bring revolution and disintegration.

Germans on the home front likewise suffered immensely from the burdens of total war. The British naval blockade greatly limited food imports, and scarcity and poorly implemented rationing plans had horrific results: some 750,000 German civilians starved to death. For the rest, heavy rationing of basic goods such as matches, bread, cooking oil, and meat undermined morale. The national political unity of the first year of the war collapsed as the social conflicts of prewar Germany re-emerged. A growing minority of moderate so-

cialists in the Reichstag called for a compromise "peace without annexations or reparations."

Such a peace was unthinkable for the conservatives and military leaders in the Fatherland Party. So also was the surge in revolutionary agitation and strikes by war-weary workers that occurred in early 1917. When the bread ration was further reduced in April, more than 200,000 workers and women struck and demonstrated for a week in Berlin, returning to work only under the threat of prison and military discipline. That same month, radicals left the Social Democratic Party to form the Independent Social Democratic Party; in 1918 they would found the German Communist Party. Thus militaristic Germany, like its ally Austria-Hungary (and its enemy France), was beginning to crack in 1917. Yet it was Russia that collapsed first and saved the Central Powers—for a time.

The Russian Revolution

What led to the Russian Revolution, and what was its outcome? ■

The Russian Revolution of 1917 was one of modern history's most momentous events. Directly related to the growing tensions of World War I, it had significance far beyond the wartime agonies of a single European nation. For some, the revolution was Marx's socialist vision come true; for others, it was the triumph of dictatorship. To all, it presented a radically new prototype of state and society.

The Fall of Imperial Russia

Like its allies and its enemies, Russia had embraced war with patriotic enthusiasm in 1914. At the Winter Palace, while throngs of people knelt and sang "God save the tsar," Tsar Nicholas II (r. 1894–1917) repeated the oath Alexander I had sworn in 1812 during Napoleon's invasion of Russia (see Chapter 20), vowing never to make peace as long as the enemy stood on Russian soil. Russia's lower house of parliament, the Duma, voted to support the war. Conservatives anticipated expansion in the Balkans, while liberals and most socialists believed that alliance with Britain and France would bring democratic reforms. For a moment, Russia was united.

Enthusiasm for the war soon waned as better-equipped German armies inflicted terrible losses. By 1915 substantial numbers of Russian soldiers were sent to the front without rifles; they were told to find their arms among the dead. Russia's battered peasant army nonetheless continued to fight, and Russia moved toward full mobilization on the home front. The Duma and organs of local government set up special committees to coordinate defense, industry, transportation, and agriculture. These efforts improved the military situation, but overall Russia mobilized less effectively than the other combatants.

One problem was weak leadership. Under the constitution resulting from the revolution of 1905 (see Chapter 24), the tsar had retained complete control over the bureaucracy and the army. A kindly but narrow-minded aristocrat, Nicholas II failed to form a close partnership with his citizens. He distrusted the publicly elected Duma and resisted popular involvement in government, relying instead on the old bureaucratic apparatus. As a result, the Duma, the educated middle classes, and the masses became increasingly critical of the tsar's leadership. In September 1915 parties ranging from conservative to moderate socialist formed the Progressive bloc, which called for a completely new government responsible to the Duma instead of the tsar. In answer, Nicholas temporarily adjourned the Duma. The tsar then announced that he was traveling to the front in order to lead and rally Russia's armies, leaving the government in the hands of his wife, the strong-willed and autocratic Tsarina Alexandra.

His departure was a fatal turning point. In his absence, Tsarina Alexandra arbitrarily dismissed loyal political advisers and turned to her court favorite, the disreputable and unpopular Rasputin. Rasputin was an uneducated Siberian preacher whose influence with the tsarina rested on his purported healing powers. Alexis, who was Alexandra's only son and heir to the throne, suffered from the rare blood disease hemophilia. Rasputin claimed that only he could stop the bleeding, using his miraculous powers. In a desperate attempt to right the situation and end unfounded rumors that Rasputin was the empress's lover, three members of the high aristocracy murdered Rasputin in December 1916. The ensuing scandal further undermined support for the tsarist government.

Imperial Russia had entered a terminal crisis. Despite limited success against the Austrians in the summer of 1916, heavy casualties, bad food and equipment, and concern for those at home led to opposition in the ranks. Tens of thousands of soldiers deserted, swelling the number of the disaffected at home. By early winter 1917, the cities were wracked by food shortages, heating fuel was in short supply, and the economy was breaking down. In mid-March violent street demonstrations broke out in Petrograd (formerly St. Petersburg), spread to the factories, and then engulfed the city. From the front, the tsar ordered the army to open fire on the protesters, but the soldiers refused to shoot and joined the revolutionary crowd. The Duma declared a provisional government on March 12, 1917. Three days later, Nicholas abdicated.

The Provisional Government

This **February Revolution** that led to the establishment of the provisional government and the abdication of the tsar was the result of an unplanned uprising of hungry, angry people in the capital, but it was eagerly accepted throughout the country. (The name of the revolution matches the Russian calendar, which used to use a different dating system.)

February Revolution
Unplanned uprisings accompanied by violent street demonstrations begun in March 1917 (old calendar February) in Petrograd, Russia, that led to the abdication of the tsar and the establishment of a provisional government.

The patriotic upper and middle classes embraced the prospect of a more determined war effort, while workers anticipated better wages and more food. After generations of autocracy, the provisional government established equality before the law; freedom of religion, speech, and assembly; and the right of unions to organize and strike.

Petrograd Soviet A huge, fluctuating mass meeting of two to three thousand workers, soldiers, and socialist intellectuals modeled on the revolutionary soviets of 1905.

Yet both liberal and moderate socialist leaders of the provisional government rejected these broad political reforms. Though the Russian people were sick of fighting, the new leaders also refused to take Russia out of the war. A new government formed in May 1917 included the fiery agrarian socialist Alexander Kerensky, who became prime minister in July. He refused to confiscate large landholdings and give them to peasants, fearing that such drastic action would only complete the disintegration of Russia's peasant army. For the patriotic Kerensky, as for other moderate socialists, the continuation of war was still a national duty. Human suffering and war-weariness grew, testing the limited strength of the provisional government.

From its first day, the provisional government had to share power with a formidable rival—the **Petrograd Soviet** (or council) of Workers' and Soldiers' Deputies. Modeled on the revolutionary soviets of 1905, the Petrograd Soviet comprised two to three thousand workers, soldiers, and socialist intellectuals. Seeing itself as a true grassroots product of revolutionary democracy, the Soviet acted as a parallel government. It issued its own radical orders, weakening the authority of the provisional government.

The most famous edict of the Petrograd Soviet was Army Order No. 1, issued in May 1917, which stripped officers of their authority and placed power in the hands of elected committees of common soldiers. Designed primarily to protect the revolution from resistance by the aristocratic officer corps, the order led to a collapse of army discipline.

In July 1917 the provisional government ordered a poorly considered summer offensive against the Germans. The campaign was a miserable failure, and peas-

The Radicalization of the Russian Army Russian soldiers inspired by the Bolshevik cause carry banners with Marxist slogans calling for revolution and democracy, around July 1917. One reads "All Power to the Proletariat," a telling response to the provisional government's failure to pull Russia out of the war. Sick of defeat and wretched conditions at the front, the tsar's troops welcomed Lenin's promises of "Bread, Land, and Peace" and were enthusiastic participants in the Russian Revolution. (Hulton/Getty Images)

ant soldiers began "voting with their feet." They deserted in droves, returning to their villages to help their families get a share of the land, which peasants were seizing as they settled old scores in a great agrarian upheaval. Russia was descending into anarchy in the summer of 1917. It was an unparalleled opportunity for the most radical and talented of Russia's many revolutionary leaders, Vladimir Ilyich Lenin (1870–1924).

Lenin and the Bolshevik Revolution

Lenin's life had been dedicated to the cause of revolution. Born into the middle class, he became an enemy of imperial Russia when his older brother was executed for plotting to kill the tsar in 1887. As a law student, Lenin eagerly studied Marxist socialism, which began to win converts among radical intellectuals as industrialization surged forward in Russia in the 1890s. A pragmatic and flexible thinker, Lenin updated Marx's revolutionary philosophy to address existing conditions in Russia.

Three interrelated concepts were central for Lenin. First, he stressed that only violent revolution could destroy capitalism. He tirelessly denounced all theories of a peaceful evolution to socialism as a betrayal of Marx's message of violent class conflict. Second, Lenin argued that under certain conditions a socialist revolution was possible even in a nonindustrialized agrarian country like Russia. The Russian industrial working class was admittedly tiny, but peasants, like workers, were numerous, poor, and exploited, and they could thus take the place of Marx's traditional working class in the coming conflict.

Third, Lenin believed that the possibility of revolution was determined more by human leadership than by vast historical laws. He called for a highly disciplined workers' party strictly controlled by a small, dedicated elite of intellectuals and professional revolutionaries like himself. Unlike ordinary workers and trade-union officials, this elite would never be seduced by short-term gains. It would not stop until revolution brought it to power. Lenin's version of Marxism had a major impact on events in Russia and ultimately changed the way future revolutionaries undertook radical revolt around the world.

Lenin's ideas did not go unchallenged by other Russian Marxists. At meetings of the Russian Social Democratic Labor Party in London in 1903, matters came to a head. Lenin demanded a small, disciplined, elitist party, while his opponents wanted a more democratic party with mass membership. The Russian Marxists

Key Events of the Russian Revolution

August 1914	Russia enters the war
1916–1917	Tsarist government in crisis
March 1917	February Revolution; establishment of provisional government; tsar abdicates
April 1917	Lenin returns from exile
July 1917	Bolshevik attempt to seize power fails
October 1917	Bolsheviks gain a majority in the Petrograd Soviet
November 7, 1917	Bolsheviks seize power; Lenin named head of new communist government
March 1918	Treaty of Brest-Litovsk; Trotsky becomes head of the Red Army
1918–1920	Civil war
1920	Civil war ends; Lenin and Bolshevik-Communists take control of Russia

promptly split into two rival factions. Lenin called his camp the **Bolsheviks**, or "majority group"; his opponents were Mensheviks, or "minority group." The Bolsheviks had only a tenuous majority of a single vote, but Lenin kept the name for propaganda reasons and developed the revolutionary party he wanted: tough, disciplined, and led from above.

Unlike most other socialists, Lenin had not rallied around the national flag in 1914. Observing events from neutral Switzerland, where he lived in exile to avoid persecution by the tsar's police, Lenin viewed the war as a product of imperialist rivalries and a marvelous opportunity for socialist revolution. After the February Revolution of 1917, the German government provided the impatient Lenin, his wife, and about twenty trusted colleagues with safe passage across Germany and back into Russia. The Germans hoped that Lenin would undermine the sagging war effort of the provisional government. They were not disappointed. Arriving triumphantly at Petrograd's Finland Station on April 3, Lenin attacked at once. To the astonishment of the local Bolsheviks, he rejected all cooperation with what he called the "bourgeois" provisional government. His slogans were radical in the extreme: "All power to the soviets"; "All land to the peasants"; "Stop the war now." Lenin was a superb tactician. His promises of "Bread, Land, and Peace" spoke to the expectations of suffering workers, peasants, and soldiers alike, and earned the Bolsheviks substantial popular support. The moment for revolution was at hand.

Yet Lenin and the Bolsheviks almost lost the struggle for Russia. An attempt to seize power in July collapsed, and Lenin went into hiding. This temporary setback

Bolsheviks Lenin's radical, revolutionary arm of the Russian party of Marxian socialism, which successfully installed a dictatorial socialist regime in Russia.

Lenin Rallies Soldiers
Lenin, known for his fiery speeches, addresses Red Army soldiers in Moscow in the midst of the Russian civil war, May 1920. Leon Trotsky, the leader of the Red Army, stands on the podium stairs to the right. (Mansell/Time Life Images/Getty Images)

made little difference in the long run. Intrigue between Kerensky, who became prime minister in July, and his commander in chief, General Lavr Kornilov, resulted in Kornilov's leading a feeble coup against the provisional government in September. In the face of this rightist counter-revolutionary threat, the Bolsheviks were re-armed and redeemed. Kornilov's forces disintegrated, but Kerensky lost all credit with the army, the only force that might have saved democratic government in Russia.

Trotsky and the Seizure of Power

Throughout the summer, the Bolsheviks greatly increased their popular support. Party membership soared from 50,000 to 240,000, and in October the Bolsheviks gained a fragile majority in the Petrograd Soviet. Now Lenin's supporter Leon Trotsky (1879–1940), a spell-binding revolutionary orator and radical Marxist, bril-liantly executed the Bolshevik seizure of power.

Painting a vivid but untruthful picture of German and counter-revolutionary plots, Trotsky convinced the Petrograd Soviet to form a special military-revolutionary committee in October and make him its leader. Thus military power in the capital passed into Bolshevik hands. On the night of November 6, militants from Trotsky's committee joined with trusted Bolshevik soldiers to seize government buildings and pounce on members of the provisional government. Then they went on to the Con-gress of Soviets where a Bolshevik majority—roughly 390 of 650 excited delegates—declared that all power had passed to the soviets and named Lenin head of the new government. John Reed, a sympathetic American

journalist, described the enthusiasm that greeted one of Lenin's speeches at the congress:

Now Lenin, gripping the edge of the reading stand . . . stood there waiting, apparently oblivious to the long-rolling ovation, which lasted several minutes. When it finished, he said simply, "We shall now proceed to construct the Socialist order!" Again that overwhelming human roar.[9]

The Bolsheviks came to power for three key reasons. First, by late 1917 democracy had given way to anarchy: power was there for those who would take it. Second, in Lenin and Trotsky the Bolsheviks had an utterly de-termined and superior leadership, which both the tsar-ist and the provisional governments lacked. Third, as Reed's comments suggest, the Bolsheviks appealed to soldiers and urban workers who were exhausted by war, weary of tsarist autocracy, and ready for radical changes. With time, many Russians would become bitterly disap-pointed with the Bolshevik regime, but for the moment they had good reason to hope for peace, better living conditions, and a more equitable society.

Dictatorship and Civil War

The truly monumental accomplishment of Lenin, Trotsky, and the rest of the Bolsheviks was not taking power, but keeping it. Over the next four years, the Bolsheviks conquered the chaos they had helped create and began to build a communist society. The conspira-tors became conquerors. How was this done?

Lenin had the genius to profit from developments over which he and the Bolsheviks had little control.

Since summer, a peasant revolution had swept across Russia, as impoverished peasants invaded and divided among themselves the estates of the landlords and the church. Thus when Lenin mandated land reform from above, he merely approved what peasants were already doing. Popular unrest had also spread to the cities. Urban workers established their own local soviets or committees and demanded direct control of individual factories. This, too, Lenin ratified with a decree in November 1917.

The Bolsheviks cleverly proclaimed their regime a "provisional workers' and peasants' government," promising that a freely elected Constituent Assembly would draw up a new constitution. But free elections in November produced a stunning setback: the Bolsheviks won only 23 percent of the elected delegates. The Socialist Revolutionary Party—the peasants' party—had a clear majority with about 40 percent of the vote. The Constituent Assembly met for only one day, on January 18, 1918. It was then permanently disbanded by Bolshevik soldiers acting under Lenin's orders. Thus just two months after the Bolshevik victory, Lenin began to form a one-party state.

Unlike many of his colleagues, Lenin acknowledged that Russia had effectively lost the war with Germany and that the only realistic goal was peace at any price. That price was very high. Germany demanded that the Soviet government give up all its western territories.

These areas were inhabited by Poles, Finns, Lithuanians, and other non-Russians—people who had been conquered by the tsars over three centuries and put into the "prisonhouse of nationalities," as Lenin had earlier called the Russian empire.

At first, Lenin's fellow Bolsheviks refused to accept such great territorial losses. But when German armies resumed their unopposed march into Russia in February 1918, Lenin had his way in a very close vote. A third of old Russia's population was sliced away by the **Treaty of Brest-Litovsk** (BREHST lih-TAWFSK), signed with Germany in March 1918. With peace, Lenin escaped the disaster of continued war and could pursue his goal of absolute political power for the Bolsheviks—now also called Communists—within Russia.

The war's end and the destruction of the democratically elected Constituent Assembly inspired armed opposition to the Bolshevik regime. People who had supported self-rule in November saw that once again they were getting dictatorship from the capital. The officers of the old army rejected the peace treaty and organized the so-called White opposition to the Bolsheviks in southern Russia, Ukraine, and Siberia and west of Petrograd. The Whites came from many social groups

Treaty of Brest-Litovsk
Peace treaty signed in March 1918 between the Central Powers and Russia that ceded Russian territories containing a third of the Russian empire's population to the Central Powers.

Spreading Communism Bolshevik supporters and propagandists worked diligently to enlist the backing of ordinary people across Russia. Standing in front of a portrait of Lenin, this bearded agitator explains the benefits of the Bolshevik program to a group of Russian peasants. (Bettmann/Corbis)

and were united only by their hatred of communism and the Bolsheviks—the Reds.

By the summer of 1918, Russia was in a full-fledged civil war. Fully eighteen self-proclaimed regional governments—several of which represented minority nationalities—were challenging Lenin's government in Moscow. By the end of the year, White armies were on the attack. In October 1919 they closed in on central Russia from three sides, and it appeared they might triumph. They did not.

Lenin and the Red Army beat back the counter-revolutionary White armies for several reasons. Most important, the Bolsheviks had quickly developed a better army. Once again, Trotsky's leadership was decisive. At first the Bolsheviks had preached democracy in the military and even elected officers in 1917. But beginning in March 1918, Trotsky became war commissar of the newly formed Red Army. He re-established strict discipline and the draft. Soldiers deserting or disobeying an order were summarily shot. Moreover, Trotsky made effective use of former tsarist army officers, who were actively recruited and given unprecedented powers over their troops. In short, Trotsky formed a disciplined and effective fighting force, which repeatedly defeated the Whites in the field.

war communism The application of centralized state control during the Russian civil war, in which the Bolsheviks seized grain from peasants, introduced rationing, nationalized all banks and industry, and required everyone to work.

Other conditions favored the Bolsheviks. Strategically, the Reds controlled central Russia and the crucial cities of Moscow and Petrograd. The Whites attacked from the fringes and lacked coordination. Moreover, the poorly defined political program of the Whites was a mishmash of liberal republicanism and monarchism, and it never united the Bolshevik's enemies under a progressive democratic banner. And while the Bolsheviks promised the ethnic minorities in Russian-controlled territories substantial autonomy, the nationalist Whites wished to preserve the tsarist empire.

The Bolsheviks mobilized the home front for the war effort by establishing a system of centralized controls called **war communism**. All banks and industries were nationalized, and private enterprise was outlawed. Bolshevik commissars introduced rationing, seized grain from peasants to feed the cities, and maintained strict workplace discipline. Although these measures contributed to a breakdown of normal economic activity, they maintained labor discipline and kept the Red Army supplied with men and material.

Revolutionary terror also contributed to the Communist victory. Lenin and the Bolsheviks set up a fearsome secret police known as the Cheka, dedicated to suppressing counter-revolutionaries of all types. During the civil war, the Cheka imprisoned and executed without trial tens of thousands of supposed class enemies. Victims included clergymen, aristocrats and wealthy Russian bourgeoisie, deserters from the Red Army, and political opponents of all kinds, including the tsar and his family, who were executed in July 1918. The so-called Red Terror of 1918–1920 helped establish the secret police as a central tool of the new communist government.

Foreign military intervention to support the White armies in the civil war also ironically helped the Bolsheviks. For a variety of reasons, but primarily to stop the spread of communism, the Western Allies (including the United States, Britain, France, and Japan) sent troops to support the Whites. Yet their efforts were limited and halfhearted. In 1919 Westerners were sick of war, and few politicians wanted to get involved in a new military crusade. Thus Allied intervention did not aid the Whites effectively, though it did permit the Bolsheviks to appeal to the patriotic nationalism of ethnic Russians, in particular former tsarist army officers who objected to foreign involvement in Russian affairs.

By the spring of 1920, the White armies were almost completely defeated, and the Bolsheviks had retaken much of the territory ceded to Germany under the Treaty of Brest-Litovsk. The Red Army reconquered Belarus and Ukraine, both of which had gained a brief moment of independence at the end of World War I. Building on this success, the Bolsheviks moved westward into Polish territory, but they were halted on the outskirts of Warsaw in August 1920 by troops under the leadership of the Polish field marshal and chief of state Jozef Pilsudski. The defeat halted Bolshevik attempts to spread communism into western Europe, though in 1921 the Red Army overran the independent nationalist governments of the Caucasus. The Russian civil war was over. Despite losses to Poland, the Bolsheviks had won an impressive victory.

Ceded after Treaty of Brest-Litovsk, 1918
Bolshevik territory, 1919
Occupied by Allies, 1919
White Army forces
Boundary of U.S.S.R., 1921

NORWAY
SWEDEN
FINLAND
Barents Sea
Archangel
Petrograd
Moscow
Warsaw
BELARUS
RUSSIA
POLAND
UKRAINE
ROMANIA
BULGARIA
Black Sea
Caspian Sea
TURKEY

The Russian Civil War, 1917–1922

The Peace Settlement

How did the Allies fashion a peace settlement, and why was it unsuccessful? ◼

Even as civil war spread in Russia and chaos engulfed much of eastern Europe, the war in the west was coming to an end. In the spring of 1918, the German high command launched a desperate attack against France. This offensive failed, and the United States, Britain,

"The Deceiving Brothers Have Fallen Upon Us!" This pro-Bolshevik propaganda poster from the Russian civil war is loaded with symbolism. It draws on the Greek myth of Hercules battling the hydra to depict the enemies of the revolution as a many-headed snake. Ugly caricatures of Germany, France, Tsar Nicholas, Britain, and the church bleed from the blows of a powerful Russian worker, who embodies the revolutionary working class. At the bottom of the page, a lengthy poem calls on the Russian people to stand together to defeat the "deceiving brothers," and in the background a booming industrial landscape represents the development that will follow Bolshevik victory. (The New York Public Library/Art Resource, NY)

and France defeated Germany. The guns of world war finally fell silent, and the victorious Western Allies came together in Paris to establish a lasting peace. Expectations were high; optimism was almost unlimited.

The Allies soon worked out terms for peace with Germany and for the creation of the peacekeeping League of Nations. Nevertheless, the hopes of peoples and politicians were disappointed, for the peace settlement of 1919 turned out to be a failure. Rather than lasting peace, the immediate postwar years brought economic crisis and violent political conflict.

The End of the War

In early 1918 the German leadership decided that the time was ripe for a last-ditch, all-out attack on France. The defeat of Russia had released men and materials for the western front. The looming arrival of fresh U.S. troops and the growth of dissent at home quickened German leaders' resolve, and General Ludendorff and company fell on France once more in the great spring offensive of 1918. German armies came within thirty-five miles of Paris, but Ludendorff's exhausted, overextended forces never broke through. They were stopped in July at the second Battle of the Marne, where 140,000 American soldiers saw action. The late but massive American intervention tipped the scales in favor of Allied victory.

By September British, French, and American armies were advancing steadily on all fronts, and a panicky General Ludendorff realized that Germany had lost the war. Not wanting to shoulder the blame, he insisted that moderate politicians should take responsibility for the defeat. On October 4 the German emperor formed a new, more liberal civilian government to sue for peace.

As negotiations over an armistice dragged on, the frustrated German people rose up in revolt. On November 3 sailors in Kiel mutinied, and throughout northern Germany soldiers and workers began to establish revolutionary councils on the Russian soviet model. The same day, Austria-Hungary surrendered to the Allies and began breaking apart. Revolution broke out in Germany, and masses of workers demonstrated for peace in Berlin. With army discipline collapsing, Emperor William II abdicated and fled to Holland. Socialist leaders in Berlin proclaimed a German republic on November 9 and agreed to tough Allied terms of surrender. The armistice went into effect on November 11, 1918. The war was over.

Revolution in Austria-Hungary and Germany

Military defeat brought turmoil and revolution to Austria-Hungary and Germany, as it had to Russia. Having started the war to preserve an imperial state, the Austro-Hungarian Empire perished in the attempt.

The independent states of Austria, Hungary, and Czechoslovakia, and a larger Romania, were carved out of its territory (Map 26.4). A greatly expanded Serbian monarchy gained control of the western Balkans and took the name Yugoslavia. For four months in 1919, until conservative nationalists seized power, Hungary became an independent Soviet republic. Austria-Hungary no longer existed.

In late 1918 Germany likewise experienced a dramatic revolution that resembled the Russian Revolution of March 1917. In both cases, a genuine popular uprising welled up from below, toppled an authoritarian monarchy, and created a liberal provisional republic. In both countries, liberals and moderate socialist politicians struggled with more radical workers' and soldiers' councils (or soviets) for political dominance. In Germany, however, moderates from the Social Democratic Party and their liberal allies held on to power and established the Weimar Republic—a democratic government that would lead Germany for the next fifteen years. Their success was a deep disappointment for the Russian Bolsheviks, who had hoped that a more radical revolution in Germany would help spread communism across the European continent.

There were several reasons for the German outcome. The great majority of the Marxist politicians in the Social Democratic Party were not revolutionaries and were really moderates, as they had been before the war. They wanted political democracy and civil liberties and favored the gradual elimination of capitalism. They were also German nationalists, appalled by the prospect of civil war and revolutionary terror. Of crucial importance was the fact that the moderate Social Democrats quickly came to terms with the army and big business, which helped prevent Germany from reaching total collapse.

Yet the triumph of the German Social Democrats brought violent chaos to Germany in 1918–1919. The new republic was attacked from both sides of the political spectrum. Radical communists led by Karl Liebknecht and Rosa Luxemburg and their supporters in the councils tried to seize control of the government in the Spartacist Uprising in Berlin in January 1919. The moderate Social Democrats called in nationalist Free Corps militias, bands of demobilized soldiers who had kept their weapons, to crush the uprising. Liebknecht and Luxemburg were arrested and then brutally murdered by Free Corps soldiers. In Bavaria, a short-lived Soviet-style republic was violently overthrown on government orders by the Free Corps. Nationwide strikes by leftist workers and a short-lived military takeover—the Kapp Putsch—were also repressed by the central government.

By the summer of 1920, the situation had calmed down, but the new republican government faced deep discontent. Communists and radical socialists blamed

Map showing territorial changes in Europe after World War I with the following labels:

FINLAND • Helsinki
NORWAY • Oslo
SWEDEN • Stockholm
ESTONIA • Tallinn
Petrograd (St. Petersburg)
LATVIA • Riga
Moscow •
LITHUANIA • Vilnius
DENMARK • Copenhagen
IRELAND
GREAT BRITAIN • London
NETHERLANDS • Amsterdam
Danzig
POLISH CORRIDOR
EAST PRUSSIA
SOVIET UNION
North Sea
Baltic Sea
GERMANY • Berlin
• Weimar
POLAND • Warsaw
Vstula R.
Kiev •
RHINELAND • Cologne
BELGIUM • Brussels
Rhine R.
Versailles • Paris • LUX.
SAAR
LORRAINE
ALSACE • Strasbourg
• Frankfurt
Prague •
CZECHOSLOVAKIA
GALICIA
Dniester R.
Dnieper R.
ATLANTIC OCEAN
FRANCE
Loire R.
Geneva • Bern
SWITZ.
Locarno •
Milan •
• Venice
Po R.
Genoa •
Rapallo •
S. TYROL
Vienna •
AUSTRIA
HUNGARY • Budapest
• Trieste
Zagreb •
CROATIA
Belgrade •
BESSARABIA
ROMANIA • Bucharest
Garonne R.
Rhône R.
PORTUGAL
SPAIN
Elba
Corsica
ITALY
Sardinia
Rome •
Naples •
MONTENEGRO (To Yugoslavia 1921)
Sarajevo •
YUGOSLAVIA
SERBIA
Danube R.
BULGARIA • Sofia
Black Sea
ALBANIA
GREECE • Athens
Mediterranean Sea
Sicily
Crete
TURKEY • Izmir
Constantinople •

Legend:
— Boundaries of German, Russian, and Austro-Hungarian Empires in 1914
■ New and reconstituted nations
■ Demilitarized or Allied occupation zone

0   100   200 miles
0   100   200 kilometers

Mapping the Past

Map 26.4 Territorial Changes After World War I World War I brought tremendous changes to eastern Europe. New nations and new boundaries were established, and a dangerous power vacuum was created by the relatively weak states established between Germany and Soviet Russia.

ANALYZING THE MAP What territory did Germany lose, and to whom? Why was Austria referred to as a head without a body in the 1920s? What new independent states were formed from the old Russian empire?

CONNECTIONS How were the principles of national self-determination applied to the redrawing of Europe after the war, and why didn't this theory work in practice?

To complete this activity online, go to the Online Study Guide at bedfordstmartins.com/mckaywest.

the Social Democrats for the murders of Liebknecht and Luxemburg and the repression of the Bavarian Soviet. Right-wing nationalists, including the new Nazi Party, despised the government from the start. They spread the myth that the German army had never actually lost the war—instead, the nation was "stabbed in the back" by socialists and pacifists at home. In Germany, the end of the war brought only a fragile sense of political stability.

The Treaty of Versailles

In January 1919 over seventy delegates from twenty-seven nations met in Paris to hammer out a peace accord. The conference produced the **Treaty of Versailles**, which laid out the terms of the postwar settlement and was signed by the victorious Allies and the defeated Germany. The peace negotiations inspired great expectations.

Treaty of Versailles The 1919 peace settlement that ended war between Germany and the Allied powers.

❝ [The victors] were journeying to Paris . . . to found a new order in Europe. We were preparing not Peace only, but Eternal Peace. ❞

—BRITISH DIPLOMAT

A young British diplomat later wrote that the victors "were journeying to Paris . . . to found a new order in Europe. We were preparing not Peace only, but Eternal Peace."[10]

This idealism was greatly strengthened by U.S. President Wilson's January 1918 peace proposal, the **Fourteen Points**. The proposal called for open diplomacy, a reduction in armaments, freedom of commerce and trade, and the establishment of a **League of Nations**, an international body designed to provide a place for peaceful resolution of world problems. Perhaps most important, Wilson demanded that the peace be based on the notion of **national self-determination**, meaning that peoples should be able to choose their own national governments through democratic majority-rule elections, and live free from outside interference in territories with clearly defined permanent borders. Despite the general optimism inspired by these ideas, the conference and the treaty itself quickly generated disagreement.

The controlling powers at the conference were termed the "Big Three": the United States, Great Britain, and France. Germany, Austria-Hungary, and Russia were excluded from the conference, though their lands were placed on the negotiating table. Italy was included, but its role was quite limited. The conference included smaller nations as well, from the Middle East, Africa, and East Asia, but their concerns, for the most part, were simply ignored.

Almost immediately upon their arrival in Paris, the Big Three began to quarrel. President Wilson, who was wildly cheered by European crowds as the champion of democratic international cooperation, was almost obsessed with creating the League of Nations. Wilson insisted that this question come first, for he passionately believed that only a permanent international organization could avert future wars. Wilson had his way, although prime ministers Lloyd George of Great Britain and especially Georges Clemenceau of France were unenthusiastic. They were primarily concerned with punishing Germany.

The question of what to do with Germany in fact dominated discussions among the Big Three. Clemenceau wanted Germany to pay for its aggression. The war in the west had been fought on French soil, and like most French people, Clemenceau wanted revenge, economic retribution, and lasting security for France. This, he believed, required the creation of a buffer state between France and Germany, the permanent demilitarization of Germany, and vast German reparations. Lloyd George supported Clemenceau, but was less harsh. Wilson disagreed. Clemenceau's demands seemed vindictive, and they violated Wilson's sense of Christian morality and the principle of national self-determination. By April the countries attending the conference were deadlocked on the German question, and Wilson packed his bags to go home.

In the end, Clemenceau was convinced that France could not afford to face Germany alone in the future and agreed to a compromise. He gave up the French demand for a Rhineland buffer state in return for a formal defensive alliance with the United States and Great Britain. Under the terms of this alliance, both Wilson and Lloyd George promised that their countries would come to France's aid in the event of a German attack. The Allies moved quickly to finish the settlement, believing that further adjustments would be possible within the dual framework of a strong Western alliance and the League of Nations.

The Treaty of Versailles was the key to the settlement. Its terms redrew the map of Europe, and the war's losers paid the price. The new independent nations carved out of the Austro-Hungarian and Russian Empires included Poland, Czechoslovakia, Finland, the Baltic states, and Yugoslavia. The Ottoman Empire (which had fought on the German side) was split apart, its territories placed under the control of the victors. Germany's African and Asian colonies were given to France, Britain, and Japan as League of Nations mandates or administered territories, though Germany's losses within Europe were relatively minor, thanks to Wilson. Alsace-Lorraine was returned to France. Ethnic Polish territories seized by Prussia during the eighteenth-century partition of Poland (see Chapter 17) were returned to the new Polish state. Predominately German Danzig was also placed within the Polish border, but as a self-governing city under League of Nations protection. Germany had to limit its army to one

Fourteen Points Wilson's 1918 peace proposal calling for open diplomacy, a reduction in armaments, freedom of commerce and trade, the establishment of the League of Nations, and national self-determination.

League of Nations A permanent international organization, established during the 1919 Paris peace conference, designed to protect member states from aggression and avert future wars.

national self-determination The notion that people should be able to live free from outside interference in nations with clearly defined borders, and should be able to choose their own national governments through democratic majority-rule elections.

hundred thousand men and agree to build no military fortifications in the Rhineland.

More harshly, in Article 231, the famous **war guilt clause**, the Allies declared that Germany (with Austria) was solely responsible for the war. Germany therefore had to pay reparations equal to all civilian damages caused by the fighting. This unfortunate and much-criticized clause expressed French and to some extent British demands for revenge. For the Germans, reparations were a crippling financial burden. Moreover, the war guilt clause was a cutting insult to German national pride. Many Germans believed wartime propaganda that had repeatedly claimed that Germany was an innocent victim, forced into war by a circle of barbaric enemies.

When presented with the treaty, the new German government protested vigorously. But there was no alternative, especially since the people of Germany were still starving because the Allies had not yet lifted their naval blockade. On June 28, 1919, German representatives of the ruling moderate Social Democrats and the Catholic Party signed the treaty in Louis XIV's hall of mirrors at Versailles, where Bismarck's empire had been joyously proclaimed almost fifty years before (see Chapter 24).

The rapidly concluded Versailles treaty was far from perfect, but within the context of war-shattered Europe it was a beginning. Germany had been punished, but not dismembered. A new world organization complemented a traditional defensive alliance of satisfied powers: Britain, France, and the United States. The remaining serious problems, the Allies hoped, could be worked out in the future. Moreover, Allied leaders had seen speed as essential for another reason. They detested Lenin and feared that his Bolshevik Revolution might spread. They realized that their best answer to Lenin's unending calls for worldwide upheaval was peace and tranquillity for war-weary peoples.

Yet the great hopes of early 1919 had turned to ashes by the end of the year. The Western alliance had collapsed, and a grandiose plan for permanent peace had given way to a fragile European truce. There were several reasons for this turn of events. First, the U.S. Senate and, to a lesser extent, the American people rejected Wilson's handiwork. Republican senators led by Henry Cabot Lodge believed that the treaty gave away Congress's constitutional right to declare war and demanded changes in the articles. In failing health, Wilson, with narrow-minded self-righteousness, rejected all attempts at compromise. In doing so, he ensured that the treaty would never be ratified by the United States in any form and that the United States would never join the League of Nations. Moreover, the Senate refused to ratify Wilson's treaties forming a defensive alliance with France and Great Britain. America in effect had turned its back on

Europe. The Wilson-Lodge fiasco and the newly found gospel of isolationism represented a tragic renunciation of America's responsibility. Using U.S. actions as an excuse, Great Britain too refused to ratify its defensive alliance with France. Bitterly betrayed by its allies, France stood alone.

The principle of national self-determination, which had engendered such enthusiasm after the war, was good in theory but flawed in practice. Even in Europe, the borders of new states such as Poland, Czechoslovakia, and Yugoslavia cut through a jumble of ethnic and religious groups who often despised each other. The new central European nations would prove to be economically weak and politically unstable, the focus of conflict in the interwar years. In the colonies, desires for self-determination were simply ignored. The Great Powers happily received Germany's colonies but were hardly ready to give up their own. The problems with self-determination were particularly evident in the fate of the territories of the former Ottoman Empire, where the victorious Allies paid little attention to the desires of the native peoples of the Middle East.

war guilt clause An article in the Treaty of Versailles that declared that Germany (with Austria) was solely responsible for the war and had to pay reparations equal to all civilian damages caused by the fighting.

The Peace Settlement in the Middle East

Although Allied leaders at Versailles focused mainly on European questions, they also imposed a political settlement on what had been the Ottoman Empire. This settlement brought radical and controversial changes to the Middle East. In short, the Ottoman Empire was broken up, Britain and France expanded their power and influence in the Middle East, and Arab nationalists felt cheated and betrayed.

The British government had encouraged the wartime Arab revolt against the Ottoman Turks (see page 826) and had even made vague promises of an independent Arab kingdom. However, when the fighting stopped, the British and the French chose instead to honor secret wartime agreements to divide and rule the Ottoman lands. Most important was the Sykes-Picot Agreement of 1916, named after British and French diplomats. In the secret accord, Britain and France basically agreed that France would receive modern-day Lebanon and Syria and much of southern Turkey, and that Britain would receive Palestine, Transjordan, and Iraq. Thus the Allies never truly intended to grant Arab self-determination after the war. When Britain and France set about implementing their secret plans after the armistice, Arab nationalists reacted with surprise and resentment.

British plans for the Ottoman province of Palestine also angered Arab nationalists. The **Balfour Declaration** of November 1917, written by British foreign secretary Arthur Balfour, had declared that Britain favored a "National Home for the Jewish People" in Palestine, but without prejudicing the civil and religious rights of the non-Jewish communities already living in Palestine. Some members of the British cabinet believed that the declaration would appeal to German, Austrian, and American Jews and thus help the British war effort. Others sincerely supported the Zionist vision of a Jewish homeland (see Chapter 24), which they hoped would also help Britain maintain control of the Suez Canal. In any event, Palestinian Arabs were dismayed.

In 1914 Jews accounted for about 11 percent of the population in the three Ottoman districts that would

Balfour Declaration A 1917 British statement that declared British support of a National Home for the Jewish People in Palestine.

subsequently be lumped together by the British to form Palestine; the rest of the population was predominantly Arab. Yet both groups understood that the National Home for the Jewish People mentioned in the Balfour Declaration implied the establishment of some kind of Jewish state that would violate majority rule. Moreover, a state founded on religious and ethnic exclusivity was out of keeping with both Islamic and Ottoman tradition, which had historically been more tolerant of religious diversity and minorities than the Christian monarchs or nation-states in Europe.

Though Arab leaders attended the Versailles Peace Conference, efforts to secure autonomy in the Middle East came to nothing. Only the kingdom of Hejaz—today part of Saudi Arabia—was granted independence (Map 26.5). In response, Arab nationalists came together in Damascus as the General Syrian Congress in 1919 and unsuccessfully called again for political independence. (See "Listening to the Past: Resolution of the

Map 26.5 The Partition of the Ottoman Empire, 1914–1923 By 1914 the Ottoman Turks had been pushed out of the Balkans, and their Arab provinces were on the edge of revolt. That revolt, in alliance with the British, erupted during the First World War and contributed greatly to the Ottoman defeat. Refusing to grant independence to the Arabs, the Allies established League of Nations mandates and replaced Ottoman rulers in Syria, Iraq, Transjordan, and Palestine.

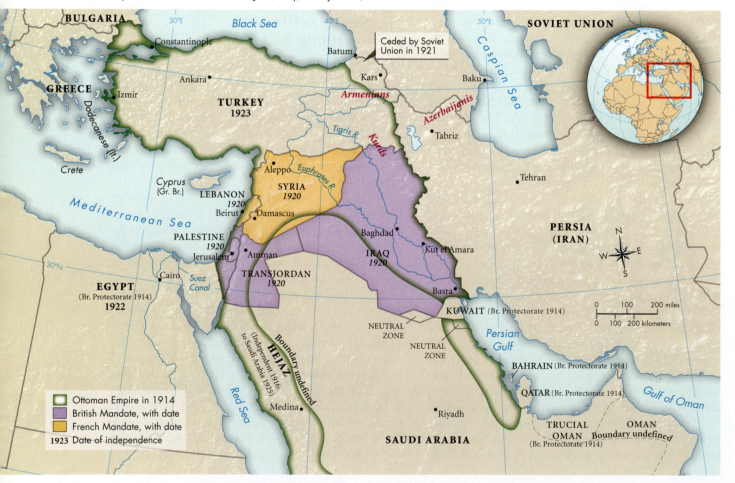

General Syrian Congress at Damascus," page 846.) The Congress proclaimed Syria an independent kingdom, and a similar congress declared Iraqi independence.

The Western reaction was swift and decisive. A French army stationed in Lebanon attacked Syria, taking Damascus in July 1920. The Arab government fled, and the French took over. Meanwhile, the British put down an uprising in Iraq with bloody fighting and established effective control there. Brushing aside Arab opposition, the British mandate in Palestine furthermore formally incorporated the Balfour Declaration and its commitment to a Jewish national home. Western imperialism, in the form of League of Nations mandates, appeared to have replaced Ottoman rule in the Arab Middle East.

The Allies sought to impose even harsher terms on the defeated Turks than on the "liberated" Arabs. A treaty forced on the helpless Ottoman sultan dismembered the Turkish heartland. Great Britain and France occupied parts of modern-day Turkey, and Italy and Greece also claimed shares. There was a sizable Greek minority in western Turkey, and Greek nationalists wanted to build a modern Greek empire modeled on long-dead Christian Byzantium. In 1919 Greek armies carried by British ships landed on the Turkish coast at Smyrna (SMUHR-nuh) and advanced unopposed into the interior, while French troops moved in from the south. Turkey seemed finished.

Yet Turkey survived the postwar invasions. Led by Mustafa Kemal (1881–1938), the Turks refused to acknowledge the Allied dismemberment of their country and gradually mounted a forceful resistance. Kemal had directed the successful Turkish defense at the Battle of Gallipoli with Britain, and despite staggering losses, the newly established Turkish army repulsed the invaders. The Greeks and their British allies sued for peace. In 1923, after long negotiations, the resulting Treaty of Lausanne (loh-ZAN) recognized the territorial integrity of a truly independent Turkey and solemnly abolished the hated Capitulations that the European powers had imposed over the centuries to give their citizens special privileges in the Ottoman Empire.

Kemal, a nationalist without religious faith, believed that Turkey should modernize and secularize along Western lines. He established a republic, had himself elected

Prince Faisal at the Versailles Peace Conference, 1919 Standing in front, Faisal is supported by his allies and black slave. Nur-as-Said, an officer in the Ottoman army who joined the Arab revolt, is second from the left, and the British officer T. E. Lawrence — popularly known as Lawrence of Arabia — is fourth from the left in back. Faisal failed to win political independence for the Arabs, as the British backed away from the vague promises they had made during the war. (Courtesy of the Trustees of the Imperial War Museum)

LISTENING TO THE PAST

President Wilson insisted at Versailles that the right of self-determination should be applied to the conquered Ottoman territories, and he sent an American commission of inquiry to Syria, even though the British and French refused to participate. The commission canvassed political views throughout greater Syria, and its long report with many documents reflected public opinion in the region in 1919.

To present their view to the Americans, Arab nationalists from present-day Syria, Lebanon, Israel, and Jordan came together in Damascus as the General Syrian Congress and passed the following resolution on July 2, 1919.

❝ We the undersigned members of the General Syrian Congress, meeting in Damascus on Wednesday, July 2nd, 1919, . . . provided with credentials and authorizations by the inhabitants of our various districts, Moslems, Christians, and Jews, have agreed upon the following statement of the desires of the people of the country who have elected us to present them to the American Section of the International Commission; the fifth article was passed by a very large majority; all the other articles were accepted unanimously.

1. We ask absolutely complete political independence for Syria within these boundaries. [Describes the area including the present-day states of Syria, Lebanon, Israel, and Jordan.]

2. We ask that the Government of this Syrian country should be a democratic civil constitutional Monarchy on broad decentralization principles, safeguarding the rights of minorities, and that the King be the Emir Faisal, who carried on a glorious struggle in the cause of our liberation and merited our full confidence and entire reliance.

3. Considering the fact that the Arabs inhabiting the Syrian area are not naturally less gifted than other more advanced races and that they are by no means less developed than the Bulgarians, Serbians, Greeks, and Roumanians at the beginning of their independence, we protest against Article 22 of the Covenant of the League of Nations, placing us among the nations in their middle stage of development which stand in need of a mandatory power.

4. In the event of the rejection by the Peace Conference of this just protest for certain considerations that we may not understand, we, relying on the declarations of President Wilson that his object in waging war was to put an end to the ambition of conquest and colonization, can only regard the mandate mentioned in the Covenant of the League of Nations as equivalent to the rendering of economical and technical assistance that does not prejudice our complete independence. And desiring that our country should not fall prey to colonization and believing that the American Nation is farthest from any thought of colonization and has no political ambition in our country, we will seek the technical and economical assistance from the United States of America, provided that such assistance does not exceed 20 years.

5. In the event of America not finding herself in a position to accept our desire for assistance, we will seek this assistance from Great Britain, also provided that such assistance does not infringe the complete independence and unity of our country and that the duration of such assistance does not exceed that mentioned in the previous article.

6. We do not acknowledge any right claimed by the French Government in any part whatever of our Syrian country and refuse that she should assist us or

Palestinian Arabs protest against large-scale Jewish migration into Palestine.
(Roger-Viollet/Getty Images)

have a hand in our country under any circumstances and in any place.

7. We oppose the pretensions of the Zionists to create a Jewish commonwealth in the southern part of Syria, known as Palestine, and oppose Zionist migration to any part of our country; for we do not acknowledge their title but consider them a grave peril to our people from the national, economical, and political points of view. Our Jewish compatriots shall enjoy our common rights and assume the common responsibilities.

8. We ask that there should be no separation of the southern part of Syria, known as Palestine, nor of the littoral western zone, which includes Lebanon, from the Syrian country. We desire that the unity of the country should be guaranteed against partition under whatever circumstances.

9. We ask complete independence for emancipated Mesopotamia [today's Iraq] and that there should be no economical barriers between the two countries. . . .

The noble principles enunciated by President Wilson strengthen our confidence that our desires emanating from the depths of our hearts, shall be the decisive factor in determining our future; and that President Wilson and the free American people will be our supporters for the realization of our hopes, thereby proving their sincerity and noble sympathy with the aspiration of the weaker nations in general and our Arab people in particular.

We also have the fullest confidence that the Peace Conference will realize that we would not have risen against the Turks, with whom we had participated in all civil, political, and representative privileges, but for their violation of our national rights, and so will grant us our desires in full in order that our political rights may not be less after the war than they were before, since we have shed so much blood in the cause of our liberty and independence.

We request to be allowed to send a delegation to represent us at the Peace Conference to defend our rights and secure the realization of our aspirations. **"**

Source: "Resolution of the General Syrian Congress at Damascus, 2 July 1919," from the King-Crane Commission Report, in *Foreign Relations of the United States: Paris Peace Conference*, 1919, 12:780–781.

QUESTIONS FOR ANALYSIS

1. What kind of state did the delegates want?

2. Did the delegates view their "Jewish compatriots" and the Zionists in different ways? Why?

3. How did the delegates appeal to American sympathies?

president, and created a one-party system—partly inspired by the Bolshevik example—to transform his country. The most radical reforms pertained to religion and culture. For centuries, most of the intellectual and social activities of believers had been regulated by Islamic religious authorities. Profoundly influenced by the example of western Europe, Kemal set out to limit the place of religion and religious leaders in daily affairs. He decreed a revolutionary separation of church and state, promulgated law codes inspired by European models, and established a secular public school system. Women received rights that they never had before. By the time of his death in 1938, Kemal had implemented much of his revolutionary program. He had moved Turkey much closer to Europe, foretelling current efforts by Turkey to join the European Union as a full-fledged member.

The Human Costs

World War I broke empires, inspired revolutions, and changed national borders on a world scale. It also had immense human costs, and ordinary people in the combatant nations struggled to deal with its legacy in the years that followed. The raw numbers are astonishing: estimates vary, but total deaths on the battlefield numbered between 10 and 13 million soldiers. Germany had the highest number of military casualties, with about 2 million dead and 4 million wounded. France had the highest proportionate number of losses; about 1.2 million were killed, or one out of every ten adult males. The other belligerents paid a high price as well (Figure 26.1). Between 7 and 10 million civilians died because of the war and war-related hardships, and another 20 million people died in the worldwide influenza epidemic that followed the war in 1918.

The vast number of violent deaths and the scope of trench warfare made proper burials difficult, if not impossible. Soldiers were typically interred where they fell, and by 1918 there were thousands of ad hoc military cemeteries scattered across northern France and Flanders. When remains were gathered, the chaos and danger of the battlefield limited accurate identification. After the war, the bodies were moved to more formal cemeteries, but hundreds of thousands remained unidentified. British and German soldiers ultimately remained in foreign soil, in graveyards managed by national commissions. After some delay, the bodies of most of the French combatants were brought home to local cemeteries.

Millions of ordinary people grieved, turning to family, friends, neighbors, and the church for comfort. Towns and villages across Europe raised public memorials to honor the dead and held memorial ceremonies on important anniversaries: on November 11, the day the war ended; in Britain on July 1 to commemorate the Battle of the Somme. These were poignant and often tearful moments for participants. For the first time, each nation built a tomb of the unknown soldier as a national memorial site. Memorials were also built on the main battlefields of the war. All expressed the general need to recognize the great sorrow and suffering caused by so much death.

The victims of the First World War included millions of widows and orphans and huge numbers of disabled and emotionally scarred veterans. Some 10 million soldiers came home disfigured or mutilated. Governments tried to take care of the disabled and the survivor families, but there was never enough money to adequately fund pensions and job training programs. Artificial limbs were expensive, uncomfortable, and awkward, and employers rarely wanted disabled workers on the payroll. Crippled veterans were often forced to beg on the streets, a common sight for the next decade.

The German case is instructive. Nearly 10 percent of German civilians were direct victims of the war, and taking care of them was one of the most difficult problems faced by the new German government. Veterans groups organized to lobby for state support, and fully one-third of the federal budget of the Weimar Republic was tied up in war-related pensions and benefits. With the onset of the Great Depression in 1929, benefits were cut, leaving bitter veterans vulnerable to Nazi propagandists who paid homage to the sacrifices of the war even as they called for the overthrow of the republican government. The human cost of the war thus had another steep price: across Europe, newly formed radical right-wing parties, including the German National Socialists and the Italian Fascists, successfully manipulated popular feelings of loss and resentment to undermine fragile parliamentary governments.

Figure 26.1 Casualties of World War I The losses of World War I were the highest ever for a war in Europe. These numbers are approximate because of problems with record keeping caused by the destructive nature of total war.

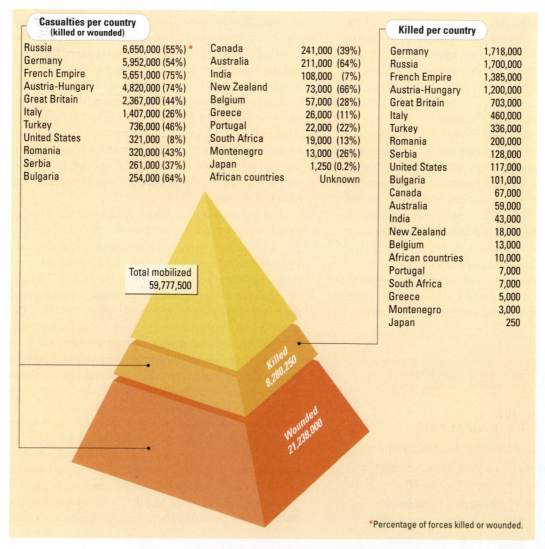

Casualties per country (killed or wounded)			
Russia	6,650,000 (55%) *	Canada	241,000 (39%)
Germany	5,952,000 (54%)	Australia	211,000 (64%)
French Empire	5,651,000 (75%)	India	108,000 (7%)
Austria-Hungary	4,820,000 (74%)	New Zealand	73,000 (66%)
Great Britain	2,367,000 (44%)	Belgium	57,000 (28%)
Italy	1,407,000 (26%)	Greece	26,000 (11%)
Turkey	736,000 (46%)	Portugal	22,000 (22%)
United States	321,000 (8%)	South Africa	19,000 (13%)
Romania	320,000 (43%)	Montenegro	13,000 (26%)
Serbia	261,000 (37%)	Japan	1,250 (0.2%)
Bulgaria	254,000 (64%)	African countries	Unknown

Killed per country	
Germany	1,718,000
Russia	1,700,000
French Empire	1,385,000
Austria-Hungary	1,200,000
Great Britain	703,000
Italy	460,000
Turkey	336,000
Romania	200,000
Serbia	128,000
United States	117,000
Bulgaria	101,000
Canada	67,000
Australia	59,000
India	43,000
New Zealand	18,000
Belgium	13,000
African countries	10,000
Portugal	7,000
South Africa	7,000
Greece	5,000
Montenegro	3,000
Japan	250

Total mobilized
59,777,500

Killed
8,280,250

Wounded
21,238,000

*Percentage of forces killed or wounded.

Disabled French Veterans The war killed millions of soldiers and left many more permanently disabled, making the sight of men missing limbs or disfigured in other ways a common one in the 1920s. (Bettmann/Corbis)

LOOKING BACK LOOKING AHEAD

WHEN CHIEF OF THE GERMAN General Staff Count Helmuth von Moltke imagined the war of the future in a letter to his wife in 1905, his comments were surprisingly accurate. "It will become a war between peoples which will not be concluded with a single battle," the general wrote, "but which will be a long, weary struggle with a country that will not acknowledge defeat until the whole strength of its people is broken."[11] As von Moltke foresaw, World War I broke peoples and nations. The trials of total war increased the power of the centralized state and in the end brought down the Austro-Hungarian, Ottoman, and Russian Empires. The brutal violence shocked and horrified observers across the world; ordinary citizens were left to mourn their losses.

Despite high hopes for Wilson's Fourteen Points, the Treaty of Versailles hardly brought a lasting peace. The war's disruptions encouraged the radical political struggles of the 1920s and 1930s and the rise of totalitarian regimes across Europe, which led to the even more extreme violence of the Second World War. Indeed, some historians believe that the interwar years of 1914 to 1945 might mostly accurately be labeled a modern European Thirty Years' War, since the problems unleashed in August 1914 were only really resolved in the 1950s. This strong assertion contains a great amount of truth. For all of Europe, World War I was a revolutionary conflict of gigantic proportions with lasting traumatic effects.

CHAPTER REVIEW

■ What caused the First World War, and why did it have significant popular support? (page 816)

The immediate cause of the war was the assassination of the heir to the Austro-Hungarian throne by a Serbian nationalist who sought to unify all Serbs in one national state. Backed by Germany, Austria-Hungary reacted harshly, setting off a chain of diplomatic and political events that turned a potentially little war into a world war. The assassination set into play a number of other long-term conflicts, including the diplomatic problems created by Germany's rise to Great Power status after the Franco-Prussian War. By 1912 Europe was divided into two hostile alliances: the Triple Alliance (Germany, Austria, and Italy) on one side and the Dual Alliance (France and Russia) on the other. Diplomatic crises in the colonies and the Balkans, and an arms race between Germany and Britain, increased international tensions. The mood of 1914 was another important factor. Political leaders and ordinary people shared strong feelings of nationalism and believed that military action would be a honorable test of national strength. Europeans underestimated the effects of modern weapons, and leading statesmen willingly engaged in aggressive foreign policy to distract from social tensions at home. Thus the start of the war cannot be blamed on a single factor.

■ How did the First World War change the nature of modern warfare? (page 821)

The violence of a new type of "total war" helps explain why so many died and so many were crippled physically and psychologically. Total war required service by soldiers and civilians alike. New weapons such as the machine gun and poison gas made the war especially deadly. Generals adapted slowly to these new weapons, and men died by the millions. Trench warfare favored the defender, and both sides saw only minimal territorial gains despite enormous losses. On the eastern front, Russians made initial gains in Germany, only to be pushed back into Russia where millions were killed or starved to death. On both the eastern and western fronts, the war degenerated into a persistent stalemate. As it ground on, neutral countries were brought into the conflict, which eventually spread to the Middle East and into some parts of colonial East Asia and Africa.

■ What was the impact of total war on civilian populations? (page 828)

To meet the growing demand for men and weapons, governments began to control many aspects of economic and social life. The result of the need to mobilize entire societies and economies for total war was an administrative revolution that greatly increased the power of the central state.

The need for workers led to growing power and prestige of labor unions and to the entry of women into the workplace. Women received new rights and experimented with new roles, though the long-term results were mixed. As the war ground on, protests against it grew. In addition, countries such as Germany experienced strikes and protest marches over inadequate food supplies. Soldiers deserted in growing numbers, contributing to increasing political tensions at home. Overall, though, civilian populations achieved greater social equality through full employment and the sharing of hardships.

■ What led to the Russian Revolution, and what was its outcome? (page 833)

Severe losses in the war, an ineffective war effort, and poor leadership by Nicholas II created conditions that led to the February Revolution of 1917. After the tsar abdicated, a new provisional government was created. Returning from exile, Lenin and his Bolshevik Party built popular support for his brand of Marxist socialism among war-weary soldiers and the urban poor. Led by the brilliant tactician Trotsky, Lenin and the Bolsheviks took advantage of anarchy in the capital to seize power. The Bolsheviks established a radical regime, smashed existing capitalist institutions, and stayed in power with a new kind of authoritarian rule that posed a powerful ongoing revolutionary challenge to Europe and its colonial empires.

■ How did the Allies fashion a peace settlement, and why was it unsuccessful? (page 838)

The "war to end war" did not bring peace—only a fragile truce. The Big Three powers of the United States, Great Britain, and France had to compromise to reach a settlement. The resulting Treaty of Versailles redrew the map of Europe, dissolving the Austro-Hungarian and Ottoman Empires. But in the west, the Allies failed to maintain their wartime solidarity. Germany, angered by the war guilt clause, remained unrepentant, and the financial burden of war reparations sowed the seeds for World War II. Moreover, the victory of national self-determination in eastern Europe created small, weak states and thus a power vacuum between a still-powerful Germany and a potentially mighty communist Russia. Europeans refused to extend the rights of self-determination to colonized peoples in Africa, Asia, and the Arab Middle East. As in Europe, the borders of the new nation-states often ignored the diversity of peoples on the ground, and so left unresolved problems for the postwar world.

Suggested Reading

Audoin-Rouzeau, Stéphane. *Men at War, 1914–1918: National Sentiment and Trench Journalism in France During the First World War*. 1992. Reconstructs the everyday life of the ordinary French soldier on the western front.

Davis, Belinda J. *Home Fires Burning: Food, Politics, and Everyday Life in Berlin in World War I*. 2000. A moving account of women struggling to feed their families and their protests against the imperial German state.

Fitzpatrick, Sheila. *The Russian Revolution 1917–1932*. 1982. An important interpretation that considers the long-term effects of the revolution.

Fromkin, David. *A Peace to End All Peace*. 2001. A brilliant reconsideration of the collapse of the Ottoman Empire and its division by the Allies.

Gatrell, Peter. *Russia's First World War: A Social and Economic History*. 2005. An excellent resource for students and specialists.

Grayzel, Susan R. *Women and the First World War*. 2002. This useful introduction offers an overview of women's experience of war across Europe.

Horne, John N., and Larry Kramer. *German Atrocities 1914: A History of Denial*. 2001. An evenhanded and revealing account of the atrocities committed by the German army in occupied Belgium.

Hull, Isabel V. *Absolute Destruction: Military Culture and the Practices of War in Imperial Germany*. 2005. A controversial book about the military culture that dominated German society from the Franco-Prussian to the First World War.

Joll, James. *The Origins of the First World War*. 1992. A thorough review of the causes of the war that brings together military, diplomatic, economic, political, and cultural history.

Keegan, John. *The Face of Battle: A Study of Agincourt, Waterloo, and the Somme*. 1983. A famous study by a famous historian that compares the Battle of the Somme to other famous battles.

Liulevicius, Vejas Gabriel. *War Land on the Eastern Front: Culture, National Identity, and German Occupation in World War I*. 2000. An important and pathbreaking work on the eastern front.

Macmillan, Margaret. *Paris, 1919: Six Months That Changed the World*. 2001. A comprehensive, exciting account of all aspects of the peace conference.

Mosse, George. *Fallen Soldiers: Reshaping the Memory of the World Wars*. 1990. A pathbreaking yet accessible account of how Europeans remembered the world wars.

Neiberg, Michael S. *Fighting the Great War: A Global History*. 2006. A lively and up-to-date account.

Read, Christopher. *From Tsar to Soviets: The Russian People and Their Revolution, 1917–1921*. 1996. A fine narrative of the events of the Russian Revolution.

Remarque, Erich Maria. *All Quiet on the Western Front*. 1928. This novel remains one of the most moving fictional treatments of World War I.

Whalen, Richard. *Bitter Wounds: German Victims of the Great War*. 1984. An excellent treatment of the human costs of the war in Germany.

Winter, Jay. *Rites of Memory, Sites of Mourning: The Great War in European Cultural History*. 1998. A new interpretation of the way Europeans came to terms with the war, by a well-respected historian in the field.

Notes

1. Quoted in J. Remak, *The Origins of World War I* (New York: Holt, Rinehart & Winston, 1967), p. 84.
2. On the mood of 1914, see J. Joll, *The Origins of the First World War* (New York: Longman, 1992), pp. 199–233.
3. Quoted in George L. Mosse, *Fallen Soldiers: Reshaping the Memory of the World Wars* (New York: Oxford University Press, 1990), p. 64.
4. Quoted in Noel Malcolm, *Bosnia: A Short History* (New York: New York University Press, 1996), p. 153.
5. Quoted in S. Audoin-Rouzeau, *Men at War, 1914–1918: National Sentiment and Trench Journalism in France During the First World War* (Oxford, U.K.: Berg, 1992), p. 69.
6. V. G. Liulevicius, *War Land on the Eastern Front: Culture, National Identity, and German Occupation in World War I* (New York: Cambridge University Press, 2000), pp. 54–89; quotation on p. 71.
7. Quoted in F. P. Chambers, *The War Behind the War, 1914–1918* (London: Faber & Faber, 1939), p. 168.
8. Quoted in L. L. Downs, *Manufacturing Inequality: Gender Divisions in the French and British Metalworking Industries, 1914–1939* (Ithaca, N.Y.: Cornell University Press, 1995), p. 95.
9. John Reed, *Ten Days That Shook the World* (New York: International Publishers, 1967), p. 126.
10. Quoted in H. Nicolson, *Peacemaking 1919* (New York: Grosset & Dunlap Universal Library, 1965), pp. 8, 31–32.
11. Quoted in C. Barnett, *The Swordbearers: Supreme Command in the First World War* (New York: Morrow, 1964), p. 40.

Key Terms

Triple Alliance (p. 817)
Triple Entente (p. 817)
Schlieffen Plan (p. 821)
total war (p. 821)
trench warfare (p. 823)
February Revolution (p. 833)
Petrograd Soviet (p. 834)
Bolsheviks (p. 835)
Treaty of Brest-Litovsk (p. 837)
war communism (p. 838)
Treaty of Versailles (p. 841)
Fourteen Points (p. 842)
League of Nations (p. 842)
national self-determination (p. 842)
war guilt clause (p. 843)
Balfour Declaration (p. 844)

For practice quizzes and other study tools, visit the Online Study Guide at **bedfordstmartins.com/mckaywest**.

For primary sources from this period, see *Sources of Western Society*, **Second Edition**.

For Web sites, images, and documents related to topics in this chapter, visit Make History at **bedfordstmartins.com/mckaywest**.

27
The Age of Anxiety

(akg-images. © Estate of George Grosz/Licensed by VAGA, New York, NY)

1900–1940

When Allied diplomats met in Paris in early 1919 with their optimistic plans for building a lasting peace, most people looked forward to happier times. After the terrible trauma of total war, they hoped that life would return to normal and would make sense in the familiar prewar terms of peace, prosperity, and progress. Their hopes were in vain. The First World War and the Russian Revolution had mangled too many things beyond repair. Life would no longer fit neatly into the old molds.

Instead, great numbers of men and women felt themselves increasingly adrift in a strange, uncertain, and uncontrollable world. They saw themselves living in an age of anxiety and continual crisis. Radical developments in the arts and sciences challenged received wisdom of all kinds. Political stability remained elusive, and the Great Depression in 1929 shocked the status quo. Democratic liberalism was besieged by the rise of authoritarian and fascist governments, and another world conflict seemed imminent. In the early 1920s the French poet and critic Paul Valéry (va-lay-REE) (1871–1945) described the widespread "impression of darkness" in this age of anxiety, where "almost all the affairs of men remain in a terrible uncertainty. We think of what has disappeared, and we are almost destroyed by what has been destroyed; we do not know what will be born, and we fear the future, not without reason."[1] Valéry's words captured the sense of gloom and foreboding that dominated the decades between the world wars. ∎

Life in the Age of Anxiety. Dadaist George Grosz's *Inside and Outside* is a disturbing image of the class conflict wrought by the economic crises of the 1920s. Wealthy and bestial elites celebrate a luxurious New Year's Eve "inside," while "outside" a disabled veteran begs in vain for money from uncaring passersby.

CHAPTER PREVIEW

Uncertainty in Modern Thought
■ In what ways did new and sometimes radically experimental ideas in philosophy, religion, physics, psychology, and literature reflect the general crisis in Western thought?

Modernism in Architecture, Art, and Music
■ How did modernism revolutionize architecture, painting, and music?

An Emerging Consumer Society
■ How did the emerging consumer society and mass culture of the interwar years change the everyday lives of ordinary men and women?

The Search for Peace and Political Stability
■ How did the democratic leaders of the 1920s deal with deep-seated instability and try to establish real peace and prosperity?

The Great Depression, 1929–1939
■ What caused the Great Depression, and how did the Western democracies respond to this challenge?

Uncertainty in Modern Thought

In what ways did new and sometimes radically experimental ideas in philosophy, religion, physics, psychology, and literature reflect the general crisis in Western thought? ■

The decades surrounding the First World War—from the 1880s to the 1930s—brought intense cultural and intellectual experimentation. Dramatic changes shook the fields of philosophy, science, and literature. After the war, these new ideas spread rapidly. Western society began to question and even abandon many of the cherished values and beliefs that had guided it since the eighteenth-century Enlightenment and the nineteenth-century triumph of industrial development and scientific advance. Ordinary people found many of these revolutionary ideas unsettling. In response, many turned to Christianity, which experienced a remarkable revival in this period.

Modern Philosophy

Before 1914 most people still believed in Enlightenment philosophies of progress, reason, and individual rights. At the turn of the century, supporters of these philosophies had some cause for optimism. Political rights were gradually spreading to women and workers, and the rising standard of living, the taming of the city, and the growth of state-supported social programs suggested that things were indeed improving. Such developments en-

couraged faith in the ability of a rational human mind to understand the universe through intellectual investigation. Just as there were laws of science, many thinkers felt that there were laws of society that rational human beings could discover and then wisely act on.

Nevertheless, as the nineteenth century drew to a close, a small group of serious thinkers and creative writers mounted a determined attack on these well-worn optimistic ideas. These critics rejected the general faith in progress and the rational human mind. The German philosopher Friedrich Nietzsche (NEE-chuh) (1844–1900) was particularly influential. Nietzsche worked as a professor of classical languages at the University of Basel until ill health forced him to retire at an early age. Never a systematic philosopher, he wrote as a prophet in a provocative and poetic style. In the first of his *Untimely Meditations* (1873), he argued that ever since classical Athens, the West had overemphasized rationality and stifled the authentic passions and animal instincts that drive human activity and true creativity.

Nietzsche went on to question the conventional values of Western society. He believed that reason, democracy, progress, and respectability were outworn social and psychological constructs whose influence was suffocating self-realization and excellence. Though he was the son of a Lutheran minister, Nietzsche famously rejected religion. In his 1877 book *On the Genealogy of Morals*, he claimed that Christianity embodied a "slave morality" that glorified weakness, envy, and mediocrity. In one of his most famous lines, a wise fool proclaims that "God is dead," metaphorically murdered by lackadaisical modern Christians who no longer really believed in him.

"Existence Precedes Essence"
Slogans such as this one captured the basic meaning of the philosophy of existentialism by underscoring the meaninglessness of human life and helped turn French intellectual Jean-Paul Sartre into a public celebrity. Here Sartre gives a radio interview in 1948 as his intellectual partner Simone de Beauvoir looks on. (Bettmann/Corbis)

Nietzsche painted a dark world, perhaps foreshadowing his loss of sanity in 1889. The West was in decline; false values had triumphed. The death of God left people disoriented and depressed. According to Nietzsche, the only hope for the individual was to accept the meaninglessness of human existence and then make that very meaninglessness a source of self-defined personal integrity and hence liberation. In this way, at least a few superior individuals could free themselves from the humdrum thinking of the masses and become true heroes.

Little read during his active years, Nietzsche's works attracted growing attention in the early twentieth century. Artists and writers experimented with his ideas, which were fundamental to the rise of the philosophy of existentialism in the 1920s. Subsequent generations have remade Nietzsche to suit their own needs, and his influence remains enormous to this day.

The growing dissatisfaction with established ideas before 1914 was apparent in other important thinkers. In the 1890s French philosophy professor Henri Bergson (1859–1941) argued that immediate experience and intuition were as important as rational and scientific thinking for understanding reality. According to Bergson, a religious experience or a mystical poem was often more accessible to human comprehension than was a scientific law or a mathematical equation.

Another thinker who challenged the certainties of rational thinking was French socialist Georges Sorel (1847–1922). Sorel concluded that Marxian socialism was an inspiring but unprovable religion, rather than a scientific truth as Marx himself had argued. Socialism would shatter capitalist society, Sorel believed, through a great general strike of all working people inspired by a myth of revolution. Sorel rejected democracy and believed that the masses of the new socialist society would have to be tightly controlled by a small revolutionary elite.

The First World War accelerated the revolt against established certainties in philosophy, but that revolt went in two very different directions. In English-speaking countries, the main development was the acceptance of logical positivism in university circles. In the continental countries, the primary development in philosophy was existentialism.

Logical positivism was truly revolutionary. Adherents of this worldview argued that what we know about human life must be based on rational facts and direct

1919	Treaty of Versailles; Freudian psychology gains popularity; Keynes, *Economic Consequences of the Peace*; Rutherford splits the atom; Bauhaus school founded
1920s	Existentialism, Dadaism, and surrealism gain prominence
1922	Eliot, *The Waste Land*; Joyce, *Ulysses*; Woolf, *Jacob's Room*; Wittgenstein writes on logical empiricism
1923	French and Belgian armies occupy the Ruhr
1924	Dawes Plan
1925	Berg's opera *Wozzeck* first performed; Kafka, *The Trial*
1926	Germany joins the League of Nations
1927	Heisenberg's principle of uncertainty
1928	Kellogg-Briand Pact
1929	Faulkner, *The Sound and the Fury*
1929–1939	Great Depression
1933	The National Socialist Party takes power in Germany
1935	Riefenstahl's documentary film *The Triumph of the Will*
1936	Formation of Popular Front in France

observation. They concluded that theology and most of traditional philosophy was meaningless because even the most cherished ideas about God, eternal truth, and ethics were impossible to prove using logic. This outlook is often associated with the Austrian philosopher Ludwig Wittgenstein (VIT-guhn-shtighn) (1889–1951), who later immigrated to England, where he trained numerous disciples. Wittgenstein argued in his pugnacious *Tractatus Logico-Philosophicus* (Essay on Logical Philosophy) in 1922 that philosophy is only the logical clarification of thoughts, and that therefore it should concentrate on the study of language, which expresses thoughts. In his view, the great philosophical issues of the ages—God, freedom, morality, and so on—are quite literally senseless, a great waste of time, for neither scientific experiments nor the logic of mathematics could demonstrate their validity. Statements about such matters reflected only the personal preferences of a given individual. As Wittgenstein put it in the famous last sentence of his work, "Of what one cannot speak, of that one must keep silent." Logical positivism, which has remained dominant in England and the United States to this day, drastically reduced the scope of philosophical inquiry and offered little solace to ordinary people.

logical positivism A philosophy that sees meaning in only those beliefs that can be empirically proven, and that therefore rejects most of the concerns of traditional philosophy, from the existence of God to the meaning of happiness, as nonsense.

On the continent, others looked for answers in **existentialism**. This new philosophy loosely united highly diverse and even contradictory thinkers in a search for usable moral values in a world of anxiety and uncertainty. Modern existentialism had many forerunners, including Nietzsche and the Danish religious philosopher Søren Kierkegaard (1813–1855). The philosophy gained recognition in Germany in the 1920s when philosophers Martin Heidegger and Karl Jaspers found a sympathetic audience among disillusioned postwar university students. These existentialist writers placed great emphasis on the loneliness and meaninglessness of human existence in a godless world and the individual's need to come to terms with the fear caused by this situation.

existentialism A philosophy that stresses the meaninglessness of existence and the importance of the individual in searching for moral values in an uncertain world.

Most existential thinkers in the twentieth century were atheists. Often inspired by Nietzsche, who had proclaimed the death of God, they did not believe that a supreme being had established humanity's fundamental nature and given life its meaning. In the words of the famous French existentialist Jean-Paul Sartre (ZHAWN-pawl SAHR-truh) (1905–1980), "existence precedes essence." By that, Sartre meant that there are no God-given, timeless truths outside or independent of individual existence. Only after they are born do people struggle to define their essence, entirely on their own. According to thinkers like Sartre, existence itself is absurd. Human beings are terribly alone, for there is no God to help them. They are left to confront the inevitable arrival of death and so are hounded by despair. The crisis of the existential thinker epitomized the modern intellectual crisis—the shattering of beliefs in God, reason, and progress.

Existentialists did recognize that human beings must act in the world. Indeed, in the words of Sartre, "man is condemned to be free." Because life is meaningless, existentialists believe that individuals are forced to create their own meaning and define themselves through their actions. Such radical freedom is frightening, and Sartre concluded that most people try to escape their unwanted freedom by structuring their lives around conventional social norms. According to Sartre, to escape is to live in "bad faith," to hide from the hard truths of existence. To live authentically, individuals must become "engaged" and choose their own actions in full awareness of their inescapable responsibility for their own behavior. Existentialism thus had a powerful ethical component. It placed great stress on individual responsibility and choice, on "being in the world" in the right way.

Existentialism came of age in France during and immediately after World War II. The terrible conditions of that war, discussed in the next chapter, reinforced the existential view of and approach to life. On the one hand, the armies of the German dictator Hitler had conquered most of Europe and unleashed a hideous reign of barbarism. On the other hand, men and women had more than ever to define themselves by their actions. Specifically, individuals had to choose whether to resist Hitler or accept and even abet tyranny. Joining the French resistance, as Sartre did, represented a clear choice between good and evil, and perhaps even life and death. After World War II, leading French existentialists such as Sartre and Albert Camus (1913–1960) became enormously influential. They offered powerful but unsettling answers to the profound moral issues and the crises of the first half of the twentieth century.

The Revival of Christianity

Though philosophers such as Nietzsche, Wittgenstein, and Sartre all argued that religion had little to teach people in a modern age, the decades after the First World War witnessed a tenacious revival of Christian thought. Christianity and religion in general had been on the defensive in intellectual circles since the Enlightenment. In the years before 1914, some theologians, especially Protestant ones, had felt the need to interpret Christian doctrine and the Bible so that they did not seem to contradict science, evolution, and common sense. In these circles, Christ was seen primarily as a great moral teacher, and the mysterious, spiritual aspects of his divinity were played down. Indeed, some modern theologians were embarrassed by the miraculous, unscientific aspects of Christianity and turned away from them.

Especially after World War I, a number of thinkers and theologians began to revitalize the fundamentals of Christianity. Sometimes described as Christian existentialists because they shared the loneliness and despair of atheistic existentialists, they stressed human beings' sinful nature, the need for faith, and the mystery of God's forgiveness. The revival of fundamental Christian belief after World War I was fed by the rediscovery of the work of the nineteenth-century Danish theologian Søren Kierkegaard (1813–1855), whose ideas became extremely influential. Kierkegaard (KIHR-kuh-gahrd) believed it was impossible for ordinary individuals to prove the existence of God, but he rejected the notion that Christianity was an empty practice. In his classic work *Sickness unto Death* (1849), Kierkegaard mastered his religious doubts by suggesting that people must take a "leap of faith" and accept the existence of an objectively unknowable but nonetheless awesome and majestic God.

In the 1920s the Swiss Protestant theologian Karl Barth (1886–1968) propounded similar ideas. In a series of brilliant and influential writings, Barth argued that human beings were imperfect, sinful creatures whose reason and will are hopelessly flawed. Religious truth is therefore made known to human beings only through God's grace, not through reason. People have to accept

God's word and the supernatural revelation of Jesus Christ with awe, trust, and obedience, not reason or logic.

Among Catholics, the leading existential Christian was Gabriel Marcel (1887–1973). Born into a cultivated French family, Marcel found in the Catholic Church an answer to what he called the postwar "broken world." Catholicism and religious belief provided the hope, humanity, honesty, and piety for which he hungered. Flexible and gentle, Marcel and his countryman Jacques Maritain (1882–1973) denounced anti-Semitism and supported closer ties with non-Catholics.

After 1914 religion became much more relevant and meaningful to thinking people than it had been before the war. In addition to Marcel and Maritain, many other illustrious intellectuals turned to religion between about 1920 and 1950. Poets T. S. Eliot and W. H. Auden, novelists Evelyn Waugh and Aldous Huxley, historian Arnold Toynbee, writer C. S. Lewis, psychoanalyst Karl Stern, physicist Max Planck, and philosopher Cyril Joad were all either converted to religion or attracted to it for the first time. Religion, often of a despairing, existential variety, was one meaningful answer to uncertainty and anxiety. In the words of a famous Roman Catholic convert, English novelist Graham Greene, "One began to believe in heaven because one believed in hell."[2]

The New Physics

Progressive minds believed that science, unlike religion and philosophical speculation, was based on hard facts and controlled experiments. Ever since the scientific revolution of the seventeenth century, scientific advances and their implications had greatly influenced the beliefs of thinking people. By the late nineteenth century, science was one of the main pillars supporting Western society's optimistic and rationalistic worldview. Unchanging natural laws seemed to determine physical processes and permit useful solutions to more and more problems. All this was comforting, especially to people who were no longer committed to traditional religious beliefs. And all this was challenged by the new physics.

An important first step toward the new physics was the discovery at the end of the nineteenth century that atoms were not like hard, permanent little billiard balls. They were actually composed of many far-smaller, fast-moving particles, such as electrons and protons. Polish-born physicist Marie Curie (1867–1934) and her French husband, Pierre, discovered that radium constantly emits subatomic particles and thus does not have a constant atomic weight. Building on this and other work in radiation, German physicist Max Planck (1858–1947) showed in 1900 that subatomic energy is emitted in uneven little spurts, which Planck called "quanta," and not in a steady stream, as previously believed. Planck's

The Christian Revival Swiss theologian Karl Barth helped rejuvenate Protestant thought in the 1920s by arguing for the awesome and unknowable nature of God. The liberal Barth, shown delivering a sermon in 1946, remained a powerful advocate of religious tolerance in the decades after World War II. (Ullstein Bild/akg-images)

discovery called into question the old sharp distinction between matter and energy: the implication was that matter and energy might be different forms of the same thing. The old view of atoms as the stable basic building blocks of nature, with a different kind of unbreakable atom for each of the ninety-two chemical elements, was badly shaken.

In 1905 the German-Jewish genius Albert Einstein (1879–1955) went further than the Curies and Planck in undermining Newtonian physics. His famous **theory of special relativity** postulated that time and space are relative to the viewpoint of the observer and that only the speed of light is constant for all frames of reference in the universe. In order to make his revolutionary and

theory of special relativity Albert Einstein's theory that time and space are relative to the observer and that only the speed of light remains constant.

En amerikansk tecknares bekymmer för framtiden.

Dä professorn äntligen efter årslånga experiment lyckades sönderdela en atom.

Unlocking the Power of the Atom
Many of the fanciful visions of science fiction came true in the twentieth century, although not exactly as first imagined. This 1927 Swedish cartoon satirizes a professor who has split the atom and unwittingly destroyed his building and neighborhood in the process. In the Second World War professors harnessed the atom in bombs and decimated faraway cities and foreign civilians. (Mary Evans Picture Library/The Image Works)

paradoxical idea somewhat comprehensible to the non-mathematical layperson, Einstein used analogies involving moving trains. For example, if a woman in the middle of a moving car got up and walked forward to the door, she had gone, relative to the train, a half car length. But relative to an observer on the embankment, she had gone farther. In addition, Einstein's theory stated clearly that matter and energy are interchangeable and that even a particle of matter contains enormous levels of potential energy. Einstein's ideas unified an apparently infinite universe with the incredibly small, fast-moving subatomic world. In comparison, the closed framework of the Newtonian physics developed during the scientific revolution, exemplified by Newton's supposedly immutable laws of motion and mechanics, was quite limited (Chapter 17).

The 1920s opened the "heroic age of physics," in the apt words of Ernest Rutherford (1871–1937), one of its leading pioneers. Breakthrough followed breakthrough. In 1919 Rutherford showed that the atom could be split. By 1944 seven subatomic particles had been identified, the most important of which was the neutron. The neutron's capacity to pass through other atoms allowed for an even more intense bombardment of matter, leading to chain reactions of unbelievable force. This discovery was fundamental to the subsequent construction of the atomic bomb.

Although few nonscientists understood this revolution in physics, the implications of the new theories and discoveries, as presented by newspapers and popular writers, were disturbing to millions of men and women in the 1920s and 1930s. In 1927, for example,

German physicist Werner Heisenberg (VER-nuhr HIGH-zuhn-buhrg) (1901–1976) formulated the "uncertainty principle," which postulates that nature itself is ultimately unknowable and unpredictable. Heisenberg suggested that the universe lacked any absolute objective reality. Everything was "relative," that is, dependent on the observer's frame of reference. Such ideas caught on among ordinary people, who found the unstable, relativistic world described by the new physicists strange and troubling. Instead of Newton's dependable, rational laws, there seemed to be only tendencies and probabilities in an extraordinarily complex and uncertain universe. Like modern philosophy, physics no longer provided comforting truths about natural laws or optimistic answers about humanity's place in an understandable world.

Freudian Psychology

With physics presenting an uncertain universe so unrelated to ordinary human experience, questions regarding the power and potential of the human mind assumed special significance. The findings and speculations of Sigmund Freud (Chapter 23) were particularly influential, yet also deeply disturbing.

Before Freud, poets and mystics had probed the unconscious and irrational aspects of human behavior. But most professional scientific psychologists assumed that the conscious mind processed sense experiences in a rational and logical way. Human behavior in turn was the result of rational calculation—of "thinking." Freud developed a very different view of the human psyche beginning in the late 1880s. Basing his insights on the analysis of dreams and of hysteria, Freud concluded that human behavior was basically irrational, governed by the unconscious, a sort of mental reservoir that contained vital instinctual drives and powerful memories. The unconscious was unknowable to the conscious mind but it deeply influenced people's behavior, so that they were often unaware of the source or meaning of their actions.

Elaborating on these ideas, Freud described three structures of the self—the **id**, the **ego**, and the **superego**—that were basically at war with one another. The primitive, irrational id was entirely unconscious. The source of sexual, aggressive, and pleasure-seeking instincts, the id sought immediate fulfillment of all desires and was totally amoral. The id was kept in check by the superego, the conscience or internalized voice of parental or social control. For Freud, the superego was also irrational. It was overly strict and puritan, and it was constantly in conflict with the pleasure-seeking id. The third component of human psychology was the ego, the rational self that was mostly conscious and worked to negotiate between the demands of the id and the superego.

For Freud, the healthy individual possessed a strong ego that effectively balanced the id and superego. Neurosis, or mental illness, resulted when the three structures were somehow out of balance. Since the id's instinctual drives were extremely powerful, the ever-present danger for individuals and whole societies was that unacknowledged drives might overwhelm the control mechanisms of the ego in a violent, distorted way. Freud's famous "talking cure"—in which neurotic patients lay back on a couch and shared their innermost thoughts with the psychoanalyst—was an attempt to resolve such unconscious tensions and restore the rational ego to its predominant role.

Yet Freud, like Nietzsche, believed that the mechanisms of rational thinking and traditional moral values could be too strong. In his famous book *Civilization and Its Discontents* (1930), Freud argued that civilization was possible only when individuals renounced their irrational instincts in order to live peaceably in groups. Such renunciation made communal life possible, but it left basic instincts unfulfilled and so led to widespread unhappiness. Freud gloomily concluded that Western civilization was itself inescapably neurotic.

Freudian psychology and clinical psychiatry had become an international movement by 1910, but only after 1919 did they receive popular attention, especially in northern Europe and the United States. Many opponents and even some enthusiasts interpreted Freud as saying that the first requirement for mental health was an uninhibited sex life. Thus after the First World War, the popular interpretation of Freud reflected and encouraged growing sexual experimentation, particularly among middle-class women. For more serious students, the psychology of Freud and his followers drastically undermined the old easy optimism about the rational and progressive nature of the human mind.

Twentieth-Century Literature

Western literature was deeply influenced by the general intellectual climate of pessimism, relativism, and alienation. The great nineteenth-century novelists had typically written as all-knowing narrators, describing realistic characters and their relationships to an understandable, if sometimes harsh, society. Writers now developed new techniques to express new realities. In the twentieth century, many authors adopted the limited, often confused viewpoint of a single individual. Like Freud, these novelists focused their attention on the complexity and irrationality of the human mind, where feelings, memories, and desires are forever scrambled. The great French novelist Marcel Proust (1871–1922), in his semi-autobiographical

id, ego, and superego
Freudian terms to describe the three parts of the self and the basis of human behavior, which Freud saw as basically irrational.

Freud's Couch As part of his "talking cure," Austrian neurologist Sigmund Freud invited neurotic patients to lie back on a couch and speak about their dreams and innermost thoughts. This famous photo shows Freud's couch in his office in Vienna. His theories about the unconscious and instinctual motivation of human behavior cast doubt on Enlightenment ideals of rationalism and progress. (© Edmund Engelman)

Remembrance of Things Past (1913–1927), recalled bittersweet memories of childhood and youthful love and tried to discover their innermost meaning. To do so, Proust lived like a hermit in a soundproof Paris apartment for ten years, withdrawing from the present to dwell on the past.

Serious novelists also used the **stream-of-consciousness technique** with its reliance on internal monologues to explore the psyche. In *Jacob's Room* (1922), Virginia Woolf (1882–1941) created a novel made up of a series of internal monologues in which she tried to capture the inner voice in prose. In this and other stories, Woolf portrayed characters whose ideas and emotions from different periods of time bubble up as randomly as from a patient on a psychoanalyst's couch. William Faulkner (1897–1962), one of America's greatest twentieth-century novelists, used the same technique in *The Sound and the Fury* (1929), much of

stream-of-consciousness technique A literary technique, found in works by Virginia Woolf, James Joyce, and others, that uses interior monologue—a character's thoughts and feelings as they occur—to explore the human psyche.

whose intense drama is confusedly seen through the eyes of a man who is mentally disabled.

The most famous stream-of-consciousness novel is *Ulysses*, published by Irish novelist James Joyce (1882–1941) in 1922. Into an account of a single day in the life of an ordinary man, Joyce weaves an extended ironic parallel between his hero's aimless wanderings through the streets and pubs of Dublin and the adventures of Homer's hero Ulysses on his way home from Troy. *Ulysses* was surely one of the most disturbing novels of its generation. Abandoning any sense of a conventional plot, breaking formal rules of grammar, and blending foreign words, puns, bits of knowledge, and scraps of memory together in bewildering confusion, the language of *Ulysses* is intended to mirror modern life itself: a gigantic riddle waiting to be unraveled. Joyce furthermore included frank descriptions of the main character's sexual thoughts and encounters. In Great Britain and the United States, the novel was considered obscene and was banned until the early 1930s.

As creative writers turned their attention from society to the individual and from realism to psychological relativity, they rejected the idea of progress. Some described "anti-utopias," nightmare visions of things to come. In 1918 an obscure German high school teacher named Oswald Spengler (1880–1936) published *The Decline of the West*, which quickly became an international sensation. According to Spengler, every culture experiences a life cycle of growth and decline. Western civilization, in Spengler's opinion, was in its old age and would soon be overtaken by the rise of East Asia. T. S. Eliot (1888–1965), in his famous poem *The Waste Land* (1922), likewise depicted a world of growing desolation:

> *April is the cruelest month, breeding*
> *Lilacs out of the dead land, mixing*
> *Memory and desire, stirring*
> *Dull roots with spring rain. . . .*
> *What are the roots that clutch, what branches grow*
> *Out of this stony rubbish? Son of man,*
> *You cannot say, or guess, for you know only*
> *A heap of broken images, where the sun beats,*
> *And the dead tree gives no shelter, the cricket no relief,*
> *And the dry stone no sound of water.*[3]

With its biblical references and its images of a ruined and wasted nature and general human incomprehension, Eliot's poem expressed the widespread despair that followed the First World War. Writer Franz Kafka (1883–1924) also portrayed an incomprehensible, alienated world. Kafka's novels *The Trial* (1925) and *The Castle* (1926), as well as his famous novella *The Metamorphosis* (1915)—in which the main character turns into a giant insect—portray helpless individuals crushed by inexplicably hostile forces. The German-Jewish Kafka died young, at forty-one, and so did not see the world of his nightmares materialize in the Nazi state. In these and many other works, authors between the wars used new literary techniques and dark imagery to portray the widespread unease of the age of anxiety.

Modernism in Architecture, Art, and Music

How did modernism revolutionize architecture, painting, and music? ■

Like the scientists and intellectuals who were part of the same modern culture, creative artists rejected old forms and old values. **Modernism** in architecture, art, and music meant constant experimentation and a search for new kinds of expression. Even today the modernism of the immediate prewar years and the 1920s still seems strikingly fresh and original. And though many people find the varied modern visions of the arts strange and disturbing, the first half of the twentieth century, so dismal in many respects, stands as one of Western civilization's great artistic eras.

Architecture and Design

Already in the late nineteenth century, architects inspired by modernism had begun to transform the physical framework of urban society. The United States, with its rapid urban growth and lack of rigid building traditions, pioneered in the new architecture. In the 1890s the Chicago school of architects, led by Louis H. Sullivan (1856–1924), used cheap steel, reinforced concrete, and electric elevators to build skyscrapers and office buildings lacking almost any exterior ornamentation. In the first decade of the twentieth century, Sullivan's student Frank Lloyd Wright (1869–1959) built a series of radically modern houses featuring low lines, open interiors, and mass-produced building materials. Europeans were inspired by these and other American examples of functional construction, like the massive, unadorned grain elevators of the Midwest.

Promoters of modern architecture argued that buildings and living spaces in general should be ordered according to a new principle: **functionalism**. Buildings, like industrial products, should be useful and "functional"—that is, they should serve, as well as possible, the purpose for which they were made. According to the Franco-Swiss architect Le Corbusier (luh cowr-booz-YAY) (1887–1965), one of the great champions of modernism, "a house is a machine for living in."[4]

Corbusier's polemical work *Towards a New Architecture*, published in 1923, laid out a series of guidelines meant to revolutionize building design. Corbusier argued that architects should adopt the latest technologies in their construction practices. They should no longer decorate their buildings with fancy ornamentation, but should rather find beauty in the clean straight lines of practical construction and efficient machinery. The resulting buildings, fashioned according to what was soon called the "international style," were typically symmetrical rectangles made of concrete, glass, and steel.

In Europe architectural leadership centered in German-speaking countries until Hitler took power in 1933. In 1911 twenty-eight-year-old Walter Gropius (1883–1969) broke sharply with the past in his design of the Fagus shoe factory at Alfeld, Germany—a clean, light, elegant building of glass and iron. In 1919 Gropius merged the schools of fine and applied arts at Weimar into a single interdisciplinary school, the **Bauhaus**. The Bauhaus brought together many leading modern architects, designers, and theatrical innovators. Working as an effective, inspired team, they combined the study of fine art, including painting and sculpture, with the study of applied art in the crafts of printing, weaving, and furniture making. Throughout the 1920s the Bauhaus,

modernism A label given to the artistic and cultural movements of the late nineteenth and early twentieth centuries, which were typified by radical experimentation that challenged traditional forms of artistic expression.

functionalism The principle that buildings, like industrial products, should serve as well as possible the purpose for which they were made.

Bauhaus A German interdisciplinary school of fine and applied arts that brought together many leading modern architects, designers, and theatrical innovators.

LIVING IN THE PAST

EUROPEAN DESIGN MOVEMENTS OF THE EARLY TWENTIETH CENTURY had a lasting impact on everyday lifestyles. Many ordinary elements of living, from apartment buildings to interior furnishings, were transformed by modernist experimentation. The Bauhaus (or House of Building), an institute founded in Germany by architect Walter Gropius in 1919, exemplified modern design at its most original and influential. It attracted an international array of highly talented artists, designers, architects, and students, including the Russian painter Wassily Kandinsky, the Swiss artist Paul Klee, and the Hungarian-Jewish photographer and painter László Moholy-Nagy.

The instructors and students at the Bauhaus sought to revolutionize product design by unifying art, craft, and technology. They argued that everyday objects should openly reflect the highly rationalized, industrialized, and modern society in which — and for which — they were made.

Bauhaus adherents believed that form should follow function and that, as director Mies van der Rohe put it in a famous aphorism, "less is more." The result was streamlined, functional designs stripped of all ornamentation that were nonetheless works of great style and lasting beauty.

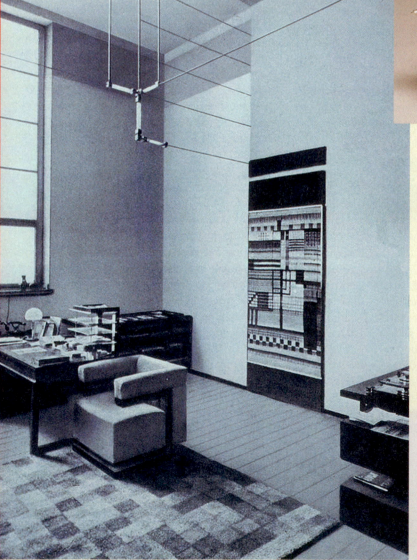

The angular, streamlined furnishings shown in the Bauhaus director's office (ca. 1923) exemplify the school's attempt to use modern materials and design to combine beautiful form and practical function in everyday goods, as do the chair designed by Marcel Breuer and the teapot by Marianne Brandt, the head of the Bauhaus metal workshop. (office: Courtesy, University of California, San Diego/ARTstor Slide Gallery. © 2010 Artists Rights Society [ARS], New York/VGBK, Bonn; chair: Digital Image © The Museum of Modern Art/Licensed by SCALA/Art Resource; teapot: Image © The Metropolitan Museum of Art/Art Resource, NY. © 2010 Artists Rights Society [ARS], New York/VG Bild-Kunst, Bonn)

The Bauhaus School in Dessau, Germany, designed by Walter Gropius in 1925–1926. (imagebroker/alamy)

Bauhaus designers created extensive public buildings as well as common household goods. Working-class housing projects, industrial factories, and private residences all were designed and built by Bauhaus architects. At home, no everyday item was too insignificant to be treated as an object of high design. The industrial ethos of the Bauhaus was brought to bear on textiles, typography, furniture, and even teapots and dishware. The famous steel tube and leather "Wassily chair," created by German designer Marcel Breuer, exemplified Bauhaus concepts and remains a classic icon of modernism. Such goods were mass-produced and marketed at affordable prices, bringing high-concept design into the lives of ordinary Europeans.

In 1933 Adolf Hitler and the Nazi Party, zealous opponents of modern art of all kinds, shut down the Bauhaus Institute. Many of the institute's prominent teachers and students fled Nazi persecution. Gropius, Breuer, Mies van der Rohe, and numerous others moved to the United States, where they helped spread Bauhaus ideas around the world after the end of the Second World War.

QUESTIONS FOR ANALYSIS

1. How do the Bauhaus designs shown here reflect the modern industrial society in which they were created?

2. Why did Bauhaus designers work in so many different fields? Why is their work still influential today?

with its stress on functionalism and good design for everyday life, attracted enthusiastic students from all over the world. It had a great and continuing impact. (See "Living in the Past: Modern Design for Everyday Use," at left.)

Another leading modern architect, Ludwig Mies van der Rohe (1886–1969), followed Gropius as director of the Bauhaus in 1930. Like many modernist intellectuals, he immigrated to the United States to escape the repressive Nazi regime. His classic steel-frame and glass-wall Lake Shore Apartments in Chicago, built between 1948 and 1951, epitomized the triumph of the modernist international style in the great building boom that followed the Second World War.

New Artistic Movements

In the decades surrounding the First World War, the visual arts, like other realms of culture, experienced radical change and experimentation. For the last several centuries, artists had tried to portray accurate representations of reality. Now a new artistic avant-garde emerged to challenge the assumptions of their elders. From Impressionism and Expressionism to Dadaism and surrealism, a sometimes bewildering array of artistic movements followed one after another. Modern painting and sculpture became increasingly abstract. Artists turned their backs on figurative representation and began to break down form into its constituent parts: lines, shapes, and colors.

Berlin, Munich, Moscow, Vienna, New York, and especially Paris became famous for their radical artistic undergrounds. Commercial art galleries and exhibition halls exhibited the new work, and schools and institutions, such as the Bauhaus, emerged to train a generation in modern techniques. Young artists flocked to these urban cultural centers to participate in the new movements, earn a living making art, and perhaps change the world with their revolutionary ideas.

One of the earliest and best-known modernist movements was Impressionism, which blossomed in Paris in the 1870s. French artists such as Claude Monet (1840–1926) and Edgar Degas (1834–1917) and the American Mary Cassatt (1844–1926), who settled in Paris in 1875, tried to portray their sensory "impressions" in their work. Impressionists looked to the world around them for subject matter, and they turned their backs on traditional themes such as battles, religious scenes, and wealthy elites. Monet's colorful and atmospheric paintings of farmland haystacks and Degas's many pastel drawings of ballerinas exemplify the way Impressionists moved toward abstraction. Capturing a fleeting moment of color and light, in often blurry and quickly painted images, was far more important than portraying a heavily detailed and precise rendering of an actual object.

By the 1890s new artistic movements had emerged alongside of Impressionism. Postimpressionists and Expressionists, such as Vincent van Gogh (1853–1890), built on Impressionist motifs of color and light but added a deep psychological element to their pictures, reflecting the attempt to search within the self and reveal (or express) deep inner feelings on the canvas. Some groups directly challenged the art world status quo. In Vienna, the Secessionists—so named because they broke with or seceded from traditional Viennese art institutions in 1897—created rich, colorful images that were highly decorative but also deeply expressive of inner feelings. *The Kiss*, a well-known painting by the Viennese painter Gustav Klimt (1862–1918), exemplifies the way Secessionists created abstract works rooted in the depths of emotion, in this case love and sensuality.

In Paris in 1907 the famous painter Pablo Picasso, along with other artists, established Cubism—a highly analytical approach to art concentrated on a complex

Dadaism An artistic movement of the 1920s and 1930s that attacked all accepted standards of art and behavior and delighted in outrageous conduct.

geometry of zigzagging lines and sharply angled overlapping planes. About three years later came the ultimate stage in the development of abstract, nonrepresentational art. Artists such as the Russian-born Wassily Kandinsky (VAS-uh-lee kan-DIHN-skee) (1866–1944) turned away from nature completely. "The observer," said Kandinsky, "must learn to look at [my] pictures . . . as form and color combinations . . . as a representation of mood and not as a representation of *objects*."[5]

The shock of World War I encouraged further radicalization. In 1916 a group of artists and intellectuals in exile in Zurich, Switzerland, championed a new movement they called **Dadaism**, which attacked all the familiar standards of art and delighted in outrageous behavior. The war had shown once and for all that life was meaningless, the Dadaists argued, so art should be meaningless as well. Dadaists tried to shock their audiences with what they called "anti-art," works and public performances that were entirely nonsensical. A famous example is a reproduction of Leonardo da Vinci's *Mona Lisa* in which the famous painting is ridiculed with a hand-drawn mustache and an obscene inscription. After the war, Dadaism became an international movement, spreading to Paris, New York, and particularly Berlin in the early 1920s.

After 1924 many Dadaists were attracted to surrealism. Surrealists such as Salvador Dali (1904–1989) were deeply influenced by Freudian psychology and portrayed images of the unconscious in their art. They painted fantastic worlds of wild dreams and uncomfortable symbols, where watches melted and giant metronomes beat time in precisely drawn but impossible alien landscapes.

Many modern artists sincerely believed that art had a radical mission. By calling attention to the supposed bankruptcy of mainstream society, art had the power to produce radical social change. Beyond producing art, groups such as the Dadaists and the surrealists wrote radical and sometimes nonsensical manifestos meant to spread their ideas and challenge conventional assumptions of all kinds. Dadaist Richard Huelsenbeck's *Collective Dada Manifesto* of 1920 captured the playfulness of Dada but also the movement's serious critical edge:

> *Art in its execution and direction is dependent on the time in which it lives, and artists are creatures of their epoch. The highest art will be that which in its conscious content presents the thousandfold problems of the day, the art which has been visibly shattered by the explosions of last week, which is forever trying to collect its limbs after yesterday's crash. . . . Dada is the international expression of our times, the great rebellion of artistic movements, the artistic reflex of all these offensives, peace congresses, riots in the vegetable market. . . . Blast the bloodless abstraction of expressionism! Blast the literary hollowheads and their theories for improving the world! . . . To be against this manifesto is to be a Dadaist!*[6]

The Shock of the Avant-Garde Dadaist Hugo Ball recites his nonsense poem "Karawane" at the notorious Cabaret Voltaire in Zurich, Switzerland, in 1916. Avant-garde artists such as Ball consciously used their work to overturn familiar artistic conventions and challenge the assumptions of the European middle classes. (Apic/Getty Images)

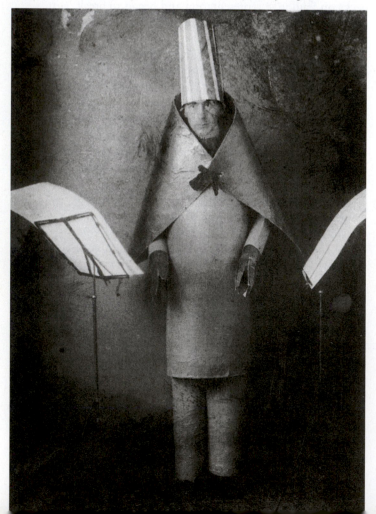

As such words suggest, by the 1920s art had become increasingly politicized. Many avant-garde artists sided with the far left; some became committed communists. Such artists and art movements had a difficult time surviving the political crises of the 1930s. Between 1933 and 1945, when the National Socialist (Nazi) Party came to power in Germany and brought a second world war to the European continent, hundreds of artists and intellectuals migrated to the United States to escape the war and the repressive Nazi state. After World War II, New York greatly benefited from this transfusion of talent and replaced Paris and Berlin as the capital of modern art.

Modern Music

Developments in modern music were strikingly parallel to those in painting. Composers, too, attempted to express emotional intensity in radically experimental forms. The ballet *The Rite of Spring* by composer Igor Stravinsky (1882–1971) practically caused a riot when it was first

> **❝ Dada is the international expression of our times, the great rebellion of artistic movements. . . . Blast the bloodless abstraction of expressionism! ❞**
>
> **—RICHARD HUELSENBECK**

performed in Paris in 1913 by a famous Russian dance company. The combination of pulsating, dissonant rhythms from the orchestra pit and the earthy representation of lovemaking by the strangely dressed dancers on the stage was a shocking, almost pornographic enactment of a primitive fertility rite.

After the First World War, when irrationality and violence had seemed to pervade human experience, modernism flourished in opera and ballet. One of the most famous and powerful examples was the opera *Wozzeck*, by Alban Berg (1885–1935), first performed

Salvador Dali, *Metamorphosis of Narcissus* Dali was a leader of the surrealist art movement, which emerged in the late 1920s. Surrealists were deeply influenced by the theories of Sigmund Freud and used strange and evocative symbols to capture the inner workings of dreams and the unconscious in their work. In this 1937 painting, Dali plays with the Greek myth of Narcissus, who fell in love with his own reflection and drowned in a pool. What mysterious significance, if any, lies behind this surreal reordering of everyday reality? (Tate, London/Art Resource, NY. © 2010 Salvador Dali, Gala-Salvador Dali Foundation/Artists Rights Society [ARS], New York)

Musical Modernism Dancers in Russian composer Igor Stravinsky's avant-garde opera *The Rite of Spring* perform at the Paris premiere. The dissonant music, wild sets and costumes, and unpredictable dance movements shocked and insulted the audience, which rioted on the opening night in May 1913. (Lebrecht/The Image Works)

in Berlin in 1925. Blending a half-sung, half-spoken kind of dialogue with harsh, atonal music, *Wozzeck* is a gruesome tale of a soldier driven by Kafka-like inner terrors and vague suspicions of unfaithfulness to murder his mistress.

Some composers turned their backs on long-established musical conventions. Just as abstract painters arranged lines and color but did not draw identifiable objects, so modern composers arranged sounds without creating recognizable harmonies. Led by Viennese composer Arnold Schönberg (SHUHN-buhrg) (1874–1951), they abandoned traditional harmony and tonality. The musical notes in a given piece were no longer united and organized by a key; instead they were independent and unrelated. Schönberg's twelve-tone music of the 1920s arranged all twelve notes of the scale in an abstract mathematical pattern, or "tone row." This pattern sounded like no pattern at all to the ordinary listener and could be detected only by a highly trained eye studying the musical score. Accustomed to the harmonies of classical and romantic music, audiences generally resisted modern atonal music. Only after the Second World War did it begin to win acceptance.

An Emerging Consumer Society

How did the emerging consumer society and mass culture of the interwar years change the everyday lives of ordinary men and women? ▪

After the First World War, European society experienced fundamental changes in the basic consumption of goods and services. Modern business forms of credit, retail, and advertising helped sell increasing numbers of mass-produced goods—the products of a highly industrialized factory system—to ever-larger numbers of people. With the arrival of cinema and radio, the leisure time of ordinary people was increasingly dominated by commercial entertainment. These changes had roots in the prosperous decades before World War I and would not be fully consolidated until the consumer revolution of the 1950s and 1960s. Yet in the years between the end of World War I in 1918 and the start of World War II in 1939 the outlines of a modern consumer society emerged with startling clarity.

Mass Culture

The emerging consumer society of the 1920s is a good example of the way technological developments can lead to widespread social change. The arrival of a highly industrialized manufacturing system dedicated to mass-producing inexpensive goods, the establishment of efficient transportation systems that could bring these goods to national markets, and the rise of professional advertising experts and agencies to sell them were all part of a revolution in the way consumer goods were made, marketed, and used by ordinary people. Contemporaries viewed the new mass culture as a distinctly modern aspect of everyday life. It seemed that consumer goods themselves were modernizing society by changing so many ingrained habits. Some people embraced the new ways, while others worried that the changes wrought by an increasingly unavoidable consumer culture threatened familiar values and precious traditions.

Critics had good reason to worry. Mass-produced goods indeed had a profound impact on the lives of ordinary people. Housework and private life were increasingly organized around an array of modern appliances, from telephones and radios to electric ovens, washing machines, and refrigerators. The aggressive marketing of fashionable clothing and personal care products, such as shampoos, perfume, and makeup, encouraged a cult of youthful "sex appeal"; individual attractiveness was increasingly determined by the use of brand-name products. The mass production and marketing of automobiles and the rise of established tourist agencies opened roads to increased mobility and travel.

Commercialized mass entertainment likewise prospered and began to dominate the way people spent their leisure time. Movies and radio thrilled millions (see page 869). Professional sporting events drew throngs of fans. Thriving print media brought readers an astounding variety of newspapers, inexpensive books, and glossy illustrated magazines. Flashy restaurants, theatrical revues, and nightclubs competed for evening customers.

Department stores epitomized the emergence of consumer society. Already well established across Europe and the United States by the 1890s, by the 1920s they had become veritable cornucopias of commerce. The typical store had over forty departments that sold an enticing variety of goods, including clothing, magazines, housewares, food, and spirits. The larger stores included travel bureaus, movie theaters, and refreshment stands. Aggressive advertising campaigns, youthful and attractive salespeople, and easy credit and return policies attracted customers in droves.

> **❝** [The] woman of today refuses to be regarded as a physically weak being . . . and seeks to support herself through gainful employment. . . . Her task is to clear the way for equal rights for women in all areas of life. **❞**
>
> —**German feminist**

The emergence of modern consumer culture both undermined and reinforced existing social differences. On one hand, consumerism helped democratize Western society. Since everyone could purchase any good, if he or she had the means, mass culture helped break down old social barriers between class, region, and religion. Yet it also reinforced social differences. Manufacturers soon realized they could profit by marketing goods to specific groups. Catholics, for example, could purchase their own popular literature and inexpensive devotional items, and young people eagerly bought the latest fashions marketed directly to them. The expense of many items meant that only the wealthy could purchase them. Automobiles and, in the 1920s, even vacuum cleaners cost so much that ownership became a sign of status.

The changes in women's lives were particularly striking. The new household items transformed the way women performed housework. Advice literature of all kinds encouraged housewives to rush out and buy the latest appliances so they could "modernize" their domestic labor. In public, consumer culture brought growing visibility to women, especially the young. Girls and young women worked behind the counters and shopped in the aisles of department stores, and they went out on the street alone in ways unthinkable in the nineteenth century. Contemporaries spoke repeatedly about the arrival of the **"new woman,"** a surprisingly independent female who could vote and held a job, spent her salary on the latest fashions, applied makeup and smoked cigarettes, and used her sex appeal to charm any number of young men. "The woman of yesterday," wrote one German feminist in 1929, yearned for marriage and children and "honor[ed] the achievements of the 'good old days.'" The new "woman of today," she continued, "refuses to be regarded as a physically weak being . . . and seeks to support herself through gainful employment. . . . She is organically bound up with the economic and cultural developments of the last few decades. Her task is to clear the way for equal rights for women in all areas of life."[7] Despite such enthusiasm,

"new woman" Somewhat stereotypical image of the modern and independent working woman popular in the 1920s.

the new woman was in some ways a stereotype, a product of marketing campaigns dedicated to selling consumer goods to the masses. Few young women could afford to live up to the image promoted in the mass press, even if they had jobs. Yet the changes associated with the First World War (see Chapter 26) and the emergence of consumer society did loosen traditional limits on women's behavior.

The emerging consumer culture generated a chorus of complaint from cultural critics of all stripes. On the left, socialist writers worried that the appeal of mass culture was undermining working-class radicalism, creating passive consumers rather than active class-conscious revolutionaries. On the right, conservatives complained that money spent on poor-quality mass-produced goods sapped the livelihood of industrious artisans and undermined proud national traditions. Religious leaders believed that modern consumerism encouraged rampant individualism and that greedy materialism was replacing spirituality. Many others bemoaned the loose morals of

Picturing the Past

The New Woman: Image or Reality?   A young woman enjoys a drink at the Romanesque Café in Berlin in 1924. The independence of this "new woman," wearing fashionable clothes with a revealing hemline and lacking an escort, transgressed familiar gender roles and shocked and fascinated contemporaries. Images of the new woman appeared in movies, illustrated magazines, and advertisements, such as this German poster selling "this winter's perfume." (café: Bildarchiv Preussischer Kulturbesitz/Art Resource, NY; advertisement: Lordprice Collection/Alamy)

ANALYZING THE IMAGE   How do these portrayals of the new woman challenge conventional gender roles? Do you think the woman in the Berlin café was influenced by advertisements for consumer products such as perfume and clothing?

CONNECTIONS   What role did the emergence of a modern consumer culture play in the way contemporaries understood the new woman? Did consumer goods marketed to women open doors for liberating behavior, or did they set new standards that limited women's options?

To complete this activity online, go to the Online Study Guide at bedfordstmartins.com/mckaywest.

the new woman and fretted over the decline of traditional family values.

Despite such criticism—which would continue after World War II—consumer society was here to stay. Ordinary people enjoyed the pleasures of mass consumption, and individual identities were tied ever more closely to modern mass-produced goods. Yet the Great Depression of 1929 (see page 874) would make actual participation in the new world of goods fleeting and elusive. The promise of prosperity would only truly be realized during the great economic boom that followed the Second World War.

The Appeal of Cinema

Nowhere was the influence of mass culture more evident than in the rapid growth of standardized commercial entertainment, especially cinema and radio. Both became major industries in the interwar years, and an eager public enthusiastically embraced the new media. Across Europe and the United States, many millions spent their hard-earned money and their leisure hours watching movies or listening to radio broadcasts. The arrival of the modern mass media overshadowed and began to replace the traditional arts and amusements of people in villages and small towns, changing familiar ways of life.

Cinema first emerged in the United States around 1880, driven in part by the inventions of Thomas Edison. By 1910 American directors and business people had set up "movie factories," at first in the New York area and then in Los Angeles. Europeans were quick to follow. By 1914 Great Britain, France, Germany, and Italy, among others, had established their own small production companies. World War I quickened the pace. National leaders realized that movies offered distraction to troops and citizens and were furthermore an effective means of spreading propaganda. Audiences lined up to see *The Battle of the Somme*, a British film released in August 1916 that was frankly intended to encourage popular support for the war. The effect of this early example of national propaganda was immediate and heart wrenching. "The tears in many people's eyes and the silence that prevailed when I saw the film showed that every heart was full of love and sympathy for our soldiers," wrote one viewer to the *London Times* that September.[8]

Cinema became a true mass medium in the 1920s, the golden age of silent film. The United States was again a world leader, but European nations also established important national studios. Germany's Universal Film Company (or UFA) was particularly renowned. In the massive Babelsberg Studios just outside Berlin, talented directors produced classic Expressionist films such as *Nosferatu* (1922), a creepy vampire story, and *Metropolis* (1927), about a future society in the midst of a working-class revolt. Such films used the latest production techniques, thrilling audiences with fast and slow motion, montage sequences, unsettling close-ups, and strange dissolves.

Film making was big business on an international scale. Studios competed to place their movies on foreign screens, and by 1926 U.S. money was drawing German directors and stars to Hollywood and consolidating America's international domination. European theater owners were sometimes forced to book whole blocks of American films to get the few pictures they really wanted; in response, European governments set quotas on the number of U.S. films they imported. This system put European producers at a disadvantage until "talkies" permitted a revival of national film industries in the 1930s, particularly in France.

Motion pictures would remain the central entertainment of the masses until after the Second World War. Growing numbers of ordinary people flocked to the gigantic movie palaces built across Europe in the mid-1920s, splendid theaters that could seat thousands. There they viewed the latest features, which were reviewed by critics in newspapers and flashy illustrated magazines. Cinema audiences grew rapidly in the 1930s. In Great Britain in the late 1930s, one in every four adults went to the movies twice a week, and two in five went at least once a week. Other countries had similar figures.

As these numbers suggest, motion pictures could be powerful tools of indoctrination, especially in countries with dictatorial regimes. Lenin encouraged the development of Soviet film making, believing that the new medium was essential to the social and ideological transformation of the country. Beginning in the mid-1920s, a series of epic films, the most famous of which were directed by Sergei Eisenstein (1898–1948), brilliantly dramatized the communist view of Russian history. In Nazi Germany a young and immensely talented woman film maker, Leni Riefenstahl (REE-fuhn-shtahl) (1902–2003) directed a masterpiece of documentary propaganda, *The Triumph of the Will*, based on the 1934 Nazi Party rally at Nuremberg. Riefenstahl combined stunning aerial photography with images of joyful crowds welcoming Hitler, the Nazi leader, and mass processions of young Nazi fanatics. Her film, released in 1935, was a brilliant and all-too-powerful documentary of Germany's Nazi rebirth.

The Arrival of Radio

Like film, radio became a full-blown mass medium in the 1920s. Experimental sets were available in the 1880s; the work of Italian inventor Guglielmo Marconi (1874–1937) around 1900 and the development of the vacuum tube in 1904 made possible primitive transmissions of speech and music. But the first major public broadcasts of special events in Great Britain and the United

States occurred only in 1920. Lord Northcliffe, who had pioneered in journalism with the inexpensive, mass-circulation *Daily Mail*, sponsored a broadcast of "only one artist . . . the world's very best, the soprano Nellie Melba."[9] Singing from London in English, Italian, and French, Melba was heard simultaneously all over Europe on June 16, 1920. This historic event captured the public's imagination and launched the meteoric career of radio.

Every major country quickly established national broadcasting networks. In the United States such networks were privately owned and were financed by advertising, but in Europe the typical pattern was direct control by the government. In Great Britain, for example, Parliament set up an independent public corporation, the British Broadcasting Corporation (BBC), supported by licensing fees. Whatever the institutional framework, radio became popular and influential. By the late 1930s

more than three out of every four households in both democratic Great Britain and dictatorial Germany had at least one cheap mass-produced radio.

Like the movies, radio was well suited for political propaganda. Dictators such as Mussolini and Hitler controlled the airwaves and could reach enormous national audiences with their frequent dramatic speeches. In democratic countries, politicians such as American president Franklin Roosevelt and British prime minister Stanley Baldwin effectively used informal "fireside

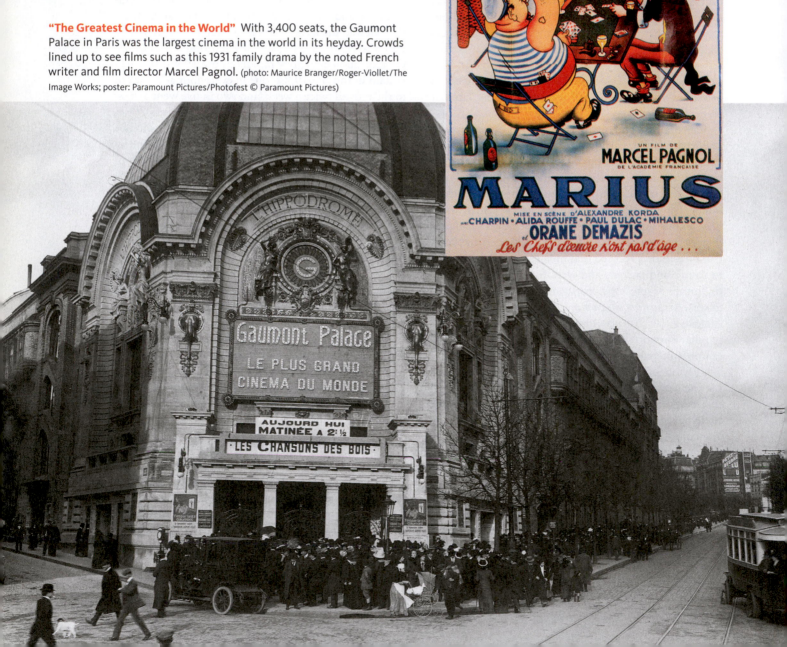

"The Greatest Cinema in the World" With 3,400 seats, the Gaumont Palace in Paris was the largest cinema in the world in its heyday. Crowds lined up to see films such as this 1931 family drama by the noted French writer and film director Marcel Pagnol. (photo: Maurice Branger/Roger-Viollet/The Image Works; poster: Paramount Pictures/Photofest © Paramount Pictures)

chats" to bolster their popularity. The new media of mass culture offered audiences pleasant distractions but were at the same time potentially dangerous instruments of political manipulation.

The Search for Peace and Political Stability

How did the democratic leaders of the 1920s deal with deep-seated instability and try to establish real peace and prosperity? ■

As established patterns of thought and culture were challenged and mangled by the ferocious impact of World War I, so too was the political fabric stretched and torn. The Versailles settlement had established a shaky truce, not a solid peace. Thus national leaders faced a gigantic task as they sought to create a stable international order within the general context of intellectual crisis and revolutionary cultural change.

The pursuit of real and lasting peace proved difficult for many reasons. Germany hated the Treaty of Versailles. France was fearful and isolated. Britain was undependable, and the United States had turned its back on European problems. Eastern Europe was in ferment, and no one could predict the future of communist Russia. Moreover, the international economic situation was poor and greatly complicated by war debts and disrupted patterns of trade. Yet from 1925 to late 1929, it appeared that peace and stability were within reach. When the economic collapse of the 1930s mocked these hopes and brought the rise of brutal dictators, the disillusionment of liberals in the democracies intensified.

Germany and the Western Powers

Germany was the key to lasting peace. Yet to Germans of all political parties, the Treaty of Versailles represented a harsh dictated peace, to be revised or repudiated as soon as possible. Germany still had the potential to become the strongest country in Europe and remained a source of instability. Moreover, with ominous implications for the future, France and Great Britain did not see eye to eye on Germany. By the end of 1919, France wanted to stress the harsh elements in the Treaty of Versailles. Most of the war in the west had been fought on French soil, and the expected costs of reconstruction, as well as of repaying war debts to the United States, were staggering. Thus French politicians believed that massive reparations from Germany were a vital economic necessity. And after having compromised with President Wilson only to be betrayed by America's failure to ratify the treaty, many French leaders saw strict implementation of all provisions of the Treaty of Versailles as France's

last best hope. Large reparation payments could hold Germany down indefinitely, and France would realize its goal of security.

The British soon felt differently. Prewar Germany had been Great Britain's second-best market in the entire world, and after the war a healthy, prosperous Germany appeared to be essential to the British economy. Many English people agreed with the analysis of the young English economist John Maynard Keynes (caynz) (1883–1946), who eloquently denounced the Treaty of Versailles in his famous *Economic Consequences of the Peace* (1919). According to Keynes's interpretation, astronomical reparations and harsh economic measures would impoverish Germany, encourage Bolshevism, and increase economic hardship in all countries. "There are no precedents of the indemnity imposed on Germany under the present treaty," he wrote. "The policy of reducing Germany to servitude for a generation, of degrading the lives of millions of human beings, and of depriving a whole nation of happiness should be abhorrent and detestable."[10] Only a complete revision of the foolish treaty could save Germany—and Europe. Keynes's attack engendered much public discussion and became very influential. It created sympathy for Germany in the English-speaking world, which often paralyzed English and American leaders in their relations with Germany between the First and Second World Wars.

❝ **The policy of reducing Germany to servitude for a generation, of degrading the lives of millions of human beings, and of depriving a whole nation of happiness should be abhorrent and detestable.** ❞

— **JOHN MAYNARD KEYNES**

The British were also suspicious of France's army—the largest in Europe, and authorized at Versailles to occupy the German Rhineland until 1935—and of France's foreign policy. Ever since 1890 France had looked to Russia as a powerful ally against Germany. But with Russia hostile and communist, and with Britain and the United States unwilling to make any firm commitments, France turned to the newly formed states of eastern Europe for diplomatic support. In 1921 France signed a mutual defense pact with Poland and associated itself closely with the so-called Little Entente, an alliance that joined Czechoslovakia, Romania, and Yugoslavia against defeated and bitter Hungary.

While French and British leaders drifted in different directions, the Allied reparations commission completed its work. In April 1921 it announced that Germany had to pay the enormous sum of 132 billion gold marks ($33 billion) in annual installments of 2.5 billion gold marks. Facing possible occupation of more of its territory, the young German republic—generally known as the Weimar Republic—made its first payment in 1921.

Then in 1922, wracked by rapid inflation and political assassinations and motivated by hostility and arrogance as well, the Weimar Republic announced its inability to pay more. It proposed a moratorium on reparations for three years, with the clear implication that thereafter reparations would be either drastically reduced or eliminated entirely.

The British were willing to accept a moratorium on reparations, but the French were not. Led by their tough-minded prime minister, Raymond Poincaré (1860–1934), they decided they had to either call Germany's bluff or see the entire peace settlement dissolve to France's great disadvantage. So, despite strong British protests, in early January 1923 armies of France and its ally Belgium moved out of the Rhineland and began to occupy the Ruhr district, the heartland of industrial Germany, creating the most serious international crisis of the 1920s. If forcible collection proved impossible, France would use occupation to paralyze Germany and force it to accept the Treaty of Versailles.

Strengthened by a wave of patriotism, the German government ordered the people of the Ruhr to stop working and passively resist the French occupation. The coal mines and steel mills of the Ruhr fell silent, leaving 10 percent of Germany's total population out of work. The French answer to passive resistance was to seal off the Ruhr and the entire Rhineland from the rest of Germany, letting in only enough food to prevent starvation. German opinion was in-

censed when the French sent over forty thousand colonial troops from North and West Africa to control the territory. German propagandists labeled the colonial occupying troops the "black shame," warning that the African soldiers were savages, eager to brutalize civilians and assault German women. Such accounts were entirely unfounded; they expressed the all-too-common racial prejudice of the time. This racial panic nonetheless intensified German-French tensions.

By the summer of 1923, France and Germany were engaged in a great test of wills. French armies could not collect reparations from striking workers at gunpoint. But French occupation was paralyzing Germany and its economy. Faced with the need to support the striking Ruhr workers and their employers, the German government began to print money to pay its bills, causing runaway inflation. Prices soared as German money rapidly lost all value. People went to the store with big bags of banknotes; they returned home with handfuls of groceries. The accumulated savings of many retired and middle-class people were wiped out. Catastrophic inflation cruelly mocked the old middle-class virtues of thrift, caution, and self-reliance. Many Germans felt betrayed. They hated and blamed the Western governments, their own government, big business, the Jews, the workers, and the communists for their misfortune. Right-wing nationalists including Adolf Hitler and the newly established Nazi Party eagerly capitalized on the widespread feelings of discontent.

French Occupation of the Ruhr, 1923–1925

"German Women Protest the Colored Occupation on the Rhine"
In 1923 the French army occupied the industrial district of the Ruhr in Germany in an effort to force reparations payments. The occupying forces included colonial troops from West Africa, and Germans responded with a racist propaganda campaign that cast the West African troops as uncivilized savages. (Stiftung Deutsches Historiches Museum, Berlin, P62/1483.2)

Protest der deutschen Frauen gegen die farbige Besatzung am Rhein

In August 1923, as the mark lost value and political unrest grew throughout Germany, Gustav Stresemann (GOOS-tahf SHTRAY-zuh-mahn) (1878–1929) assumed leadership of the government. Stresemann adopted an attitude of compromise. He called off passive resistance in the Ruhr and in October agreed in principle to pay reparations, but asked for a re-examination of Germany's ability to pay. Poincaré accepted. His hard line was becoming increasingly unpopular with French citizens, and it was hated in Britain and the United States. (See "Individuals in Society: Gustav Stresemann," page 875.)

More generally, in both Germany and France, power was finally passing to more moderate leaders who realized that continued confrontation was a destructive, no-win situation. Thus, after five long years of hostility and tension, culminating in a kind of undeclared war in the Ruhr in 1923, Germany and France decided to give compromise and cooperation a try. The British, and even the Americans, were willing to help. The first step was a reasonable agreement on the reparations question.

Hope in Foreign Affairs

In 1924 an international committee of financial experts headed by American banker Charles G. Dawes met to re-examine reparations from a broad perspective. The resulting **Dawes Plan** (1924) was accepted by France, Germany, and Britain. Germany's yearly reparations were reduced and linked to the level of German economic prosperity. Germany would also receive large loans from the United States to promote economic recovery. In short, Germany would get private loans from the United States in order to pay reparations to France and Britain, thus enabling those countries to repay the large war debts they owed the United States.

This circular flow of international payments was complicated and risky, but for a while it worked. The German republic experienced a shaky economic recovery. With continual inflows of American capital, Germany paid about $1.3 billion in reparations in 1927 and 1928, enabling France and Britain to repay the United States. In this way the Americans belatedly played a part in the general economic settlement that, though far from ideal, facilitated the worldwide recovery of the late 1920s.

This economic settlement was matched by a political settlement. In 1925 the leaders of Europe signed a number of agreements at Locarno, Switzerland. Germany and France solemnly pledged to accept their common border, and both Britain and Italy agreed to fight either France or Germany if one invaded the other. Stresemann reluctantly agreed to settle boundary disputes with Poland and Czechoslovakia by peaceful means, but did not agree to permanent borders to Ger-

many's east. In response, France promised those countries military aid if Germany attacked them. The refusal to settle Germany's eastern borders angered the Poles, and though the "spirit of Locarno" lent some hope to those seeking security and stability in international affairs, political tensions deepened in eastern Europe.

Other developments strengthened hopes for international peace. In 1926 Germany joined the League of Nations, and in 1928 fifteen countries signed the Kellogg-Briand Pact, initiated by French prime minister Aristide Briand and U.S. secretary of state Frank B. Kellogg. The signing states agreed to "renounce [war] as an instrument of international policy" and settle international disputes peacefully. The pact made no provisions for action in case war actually occurred and in fact did little to halt the arrival of the Second World War in 1939. It nonetheless fostered a cautious optimism in the late 1920s and encouraged the hope that the United States would accept its responsibilities as a great world power by contributing to European stability.

Hope in Democratic Government

Domestic politics also offered reason to hope. During the occupation of the Ruhr and the great inflation, republican government in Germany had appeared on the verge of collapse. In 1923 communists momentarily entered provincial governments, and in November an obscure politician named Adolf Hitler leaped onto a table in a beer hall in Munich and proclaimed a "national socialist revolution." But Hitler's plot to seize control of the government was easily crushed, and Hitler was sentenced to prison, where he outlined his theories and program in his book *Mein Kampf* (My Struggle). Throughout the 1920s, Hitler's National Socialist Party attracted support primarily from fanatical anti-Semites, ultra-nationalists, and disgruntled ex-servicemen. In 1928 his party had just twelve insignificant seats in the Reichstag. Indeed, after 1923 liberal democracy seemed to take root in Weimar Germany. A new currency was established, and the economy stabilized.

The moderate businessmen who tended to dominate the various German coalition governments were convinced that economic prosperity demanded good relations with the Western Powers, and they supported parliamentary government at home. Stresemann himself was a man of this class, and he was the key figure in every government until his death in 1929. Elections were held regularly, and republican democracy appeared to have growing support among a majority of Germans.

> **Dawes Plan** War reparations agreement that reduced Germany's yearly payments, made payment dependent on economic prosperity, and granted large U.S. loans to promote recovery.

There were, however, sharp political divisions in the country. Many unrepentant nationalists and monarchists populated the right and the army. Members of Germany's recently formed Communist Party were noisy and active on the left. The Communists, directed from Moscow, reserved their greatest hatred and sharpest barbs for their cousins the Social Democrats, whom they endlessly accused of betraying the revolution. The working classes were divided politically, but a majority supported the nonrevolutionary but socialist Social Democrats.

The situation in France was similar to that in Germany. Communists and Socialists battled for the support of the workers. After 1924 the democratically elected government rested mainly in the hands of coalitions of moderates, and business interests were well represented. France's great accomplishment was the rapid rebuilding of its war-torn northern region. The expense of this undertaking led, however, to a large deficit and substantial inflation. By early 1926, the franc had fallen to 10 percent of its prewar value, causing a severe crisis. Poincaré was recalled to office, while Briand remained minister for foreign affairs. The Poincaré government proceeded to slash spending and raise taxes, restoring confidence in the economy. The franc was stabilized at about one-fifth of its prewar value, and the economy remained fairly stable until 1930.

Britain, too, faced challenges after 1920. The wartime trend toward greater social equality continued, however, helping maintain social harmony. The great problem was unemployment. In June 1921 almost 2.2 million people—23 percent of the labor force—were out of work, and throughout the 1920s unemployment hovered around 12 percent. Yet the state provided unemployment benefits to those without jobs and supplemented the payments with subsidized housing, medical aid, and increased old-age pensions. These and other measures kept living standards from seriously declining, defused class tensions, and pointed the way toward the welfare state Britain would establish after World War II.

Relative social harmony was accompanied by the rise of the Labour Party as a determined champion of the working classes and of greater social equality. Committed to the kind of moderate revisionist socialism that had emerged before World War I (see Chapter 24), the Labour Party replaced the Liberal Party as the main opposition to the Conservatives. The new prominence of the Labour Party reflected the decline of old liberal ideals of competitive capitalism, limited government control, and individual responsibility. In 1924 and 1929, the Labour Party under Ramsay MacDonald (1866–1937) governed the country with the support of the smaller Liberal Party. Yet Labour moved toward socialism gradually and democratically, so that the middle

Great Depression

A worldwide economic depression from 1929 through 1939, unique in its severity and duration and with slow and uneven recovery.

classes were not overly frightened as the working classes won new benefits.

The British Conservatives showed the same compromising spirit on social issues. In 1922 Britain granted southern, Catholic, Ireland full autonomy after a bitter guerrilla war, thereby removing a key source of prewar friction. Despite conflicts such as the 1926 strike by hard-pressed coal miners, which led to an unsuccessful general strike, social unrest in Britain was limited in the 1920s and 1930s. Thus developments in both international relations and the domestic politics of the leading democracies gave cause for optimism in the late 1920s.

The Great Depression, 1929–1939

What caused the Great Depression, and how did the Western democracies respond to this challenge? ■

This fragile optimism was short-lived. Beginning in 1929, a massive economic downturn struck the entire world with ever-greater intensity, and recovery was slow and uneven. Contemporaries labeled the economic crisis the **Great Depression**, to emphasize its severity and duration. Only with the Second World War did the depression disappear in much of the world.

The social and political consequences of the Great Depression were enormous. Mass unemployment and failing farms made insecurity and unemployment a reality for millions of ordinary people (Map 27.1). In Europe and the United States, governments instituted a variety of social welfare programs intended to manage the crisis. Yet the prolonged economic collapse shattered the fragile political stability of the mid-1920s and encouraged the growth of extremists on both ends of the political spectrum. Democratic government faltered, and authoritarian fascist parties gained power across Europe.

The Economic Crisis

Though economic activity was already declining moderately in many countries by early 1929, the crash of the stock market in the United States in October of that year initiated a worldwide crisis. The American economy had prospered in the late 1920s, but there were large inequalities in income and a serious imbalance between actual investment and stock market speculation. Thus net investment—in factories, farms, equipment, and the like—actually fell from $3.5 billion in 1925 to $3.2 billion in 1929. In the same years, as money flooded into stocks, the value of shares traded on the

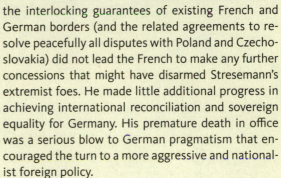

INDIVIDUALS IN SOCIETY

THE GERMAN FOREIGN MINISTER GUSTAV STRESEMANN (1878–1929) is a controversial historical figure. Hailed by many as a hero of peace, he was denounced as a traitor by radical German nationalists and then by Hitler's Nazis. After World War II, revisionist historians stressed Stresemann's persistent nationalism and cast doubt on his peaceful intentions. Weimar Germany's most renowned leader is a fascinating example of the restless quest for convincing historical interpretation.

Stresemann's origins were modest. His parents were Berlin innkeepers and retailers of bottled beer, and of their five children only Gustav was able to attend high school. Attracted first to literature and history, Stresemann later turned to economics, earned a doctoral degree, and quickly reached the top as a manager and director of German trade associations. A highly intelligent extrovert with a knack for negotiation, Stresemann became a deputy in the German Reichstag (parliament) in 1907 as a business-oriented liberal and nationalist. When World War I erupted, he believed, like most Germans, that Germany had acted defensively and was not at fault. He emerged as a strident nationalist and urged German annexation of conquered foreign territories. Germany's collapse in defeat and revolution devastated Stresemann. He seemed a prime candidate for the hateful extremism of the far right.

Yet although Stresemann opposed the Treaty of Versailles as an unjust and unrealistic imposition, he turned back toward the center. He accepted the new Weimar Republic and played a growing role in the Reichstag as the leader of his own small pro-business party. His hour came in the Ruhr crisis, when French and Belgian troops occupied the district. Named chancellor in August 1923, he called off passive resistance and began talks with the French. His government also quelled communist uprisings; put down rebellions in Bavaria, including an attempted coup by Hitler; and ended runaway inflation with the introduction of a new currency. Stresemann fought to preserve German unity, and he succeeded.

Voted out as chancellor in November 1923, Stresemann remained as foreign minister in every German government until his death in 1929. Proclaiming a policy of peace and agreeing to pay reparations, he achieved his greatest triumph in the Locarno agreements of 1925 (see page 873). But the interlocking guarantees of existing French and German borders (and the related agreements to resolve peacefully all disputes with Poland and Czechoslovakia) did not lead the French to make any further concessions that might have disarmed Stresemann's extremist foes. He made little additional progress in achieving international reconciliation and sovereign equality for Germany. His premature death in office was a serious blow to German pragmatism that encouraged the turn to a more aggressive and nationalist foreign policy.

Stresemann was no fuzzy pacifist. Historians debunking his legend are right in seeing an enduring patriotism in his defense of German interests. But Stresemann, like his French counterpart Aristide Briand, was a statesman of goodwill who wanted peace through mutually advantageous compromise. A realist trained by business and politics in the art of the possible, Stresemann also reasoned that Germany had to be a satisfied and equal partner if peace was to be secure. His unwillingness to guarantee Germany's eastern borders (see Map 26.4 on page 841), which is often criticized as contributing to the coming of the Second World War, reflected his conviction that keeping some Germans under Polish and Czechoslovakian rule created a ticking time bomb in Europe.

Stresemann was no less convinced that war on Poland would almost certainly re-create the Allied coalition that had crushed Germany in 1918.[*] His insistence on the necessity of peace in the east as well as the west was prophetic. Hitler's 1939 invasion of Poland resulted in an even mightier coalition that almost annihilated Germany in 1945.

QUESTIONS FOR ANALYSIS

1. What did Gustav Stresemann do to promote reconciliation in Europe? How did his policy toward France differ from that toward Poland and Czechoslovakia?
2. What is your interpretation of Stresemann? Does he arouse your sympathy or your suspicion and hostility? Why?

[*]Robert Grathwol, "Stresemann: Reflections on His Foreign Policy," *Journal of Modern History* 45 (March 1973): 52–70.

Foreign Minister Gustav Stresemann of Germany (right) leaves a meeting with Aristide Briand, his French counterpart. (Corbis)

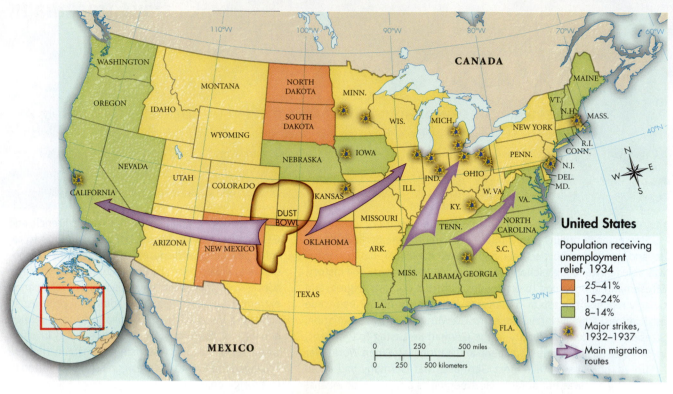

United States

Population receiving unemployment relief, 1934

- 25–41%
- 15–24%
- 8–14%
- Major strikes, 1932–1937
- Main migration routes

Europe

Unemployed workers, 1932

- 25–32%
- 15–24%
- No comparable data available
- Major strikes and riots, 1930s

Mapping the Past

Map 27.1 The Great Depression in the United States and Europe, 1929–1939 These maps show that unemployment was high almost everywhere, but that national and regional differences were also substantial.

ANALYZING THE MAP Which European countries had the highest rate of unemployment? How do the rates of people on unemployment relief in the United States compare to the percentage of unemployed workers in Europe? In the United States, what were the main channels of migration for workers?

CONNECTIONS What tactics of reform and recovery did European nations use to combat the deprivations of the Great Depression?

To complete this activity online, go to the Online Study Guide at bedfordstmartins.com/mckaywest.

exchanges soared from $27 billion to $87 billion. Such inflated prices should have raised serious concerns about economic solvency, but even experts failed to predict the looming collapse.

The American stock market boom was built on borrowed money. Many wealthy investors, speculators, and people of modest means had bought stocks by paying only a small fraction of the total purchase price and borrowing the remainder from their stockbrokers. Such buying "on margin" was extremely dangerous. When prices started falling, the hard-pressed margin buyers either had to put up more money, which was often impossible, or sell their shares to pay off their brokers. Thousands of people started selling all at once. The result was a financial panic. Countless investors and speculators were wiped out in a matter of days or weeks.

The consequences were swift and severe. Stripped of wealth and confidence, battered investors and their fellow citizens started buying fewer goods. Prices fell, production began to slow down, and unemployment began to rise. Soon the entire American economy was caught in a spiraling decline.

The financial panic in the United States triggered an international financial crisis. Throughout the 1920s, American bankers and investors had lent large amounts of capital to many countries. Once the panic broke, New York bankers began recalling these short-term loans. Gold reserves began to flow rapidly out of European countries, particularly Germany and Austria, toward the United States. It became very hard for European business people to borrow money, and the panicky public began to withdraw its savings from the banks. These banking problems eventually led to the crash of the largest bank in Austria in 1931 and then to general financial chaos. The recall of private loans by American bankers also accelerated the collapse in world prices when businesses around the world dumped industrial goods and agricultural commodities in a frantic attempt to get cash to pay what they owed.

The financial crisis led to a general crisis of production: between 1929 and 1933, world output of goods fell by an estimated 38 percent. As this happened, each country turned inward and tried to manage the crisis alone. In 1931, for example, Britain went off the gold standard, refusing to convert banknotes into gold, and reduced the value of its money. Britain's goal was to make its goods cheaper and therefore more salable in the world market. But because more than twenty nations, including the United

States in 1934, also went off the gold standard, few countries gained a real advantage. Similarly, country after country followed the example of the United States when in 1930 it raised protective tariffs to their highest levels ever and tried to seal off shrinking national markets for American producers only. Such actions further limited international trade. Within this context of fragmented and destructive economic nationalism, a halting recovery only began in 1933.

Although opinions differ, two factors probably best explain the relentless slide to the bottom from 1929 to early 1933. First, the international economy lacked leadership able to maintain stability when the crisis came. Neither Britain nor the United States—the world's economic leaders at the time—successfully stabilized the international economic system in 1929. The United States, which had momentarily played a positive role after the occupation of the Ruhr, cut back its international lending and erected high tariffs.

The second factor was poor national economic policy in almost every country. Governments generally cut their budgets when they should have raised spending and run large deficits in order to stimulate their economies. After World War II, such a "counter-cyclical policy," advocated by John Maynard Keynes, became a well-established weapon against downturn and depression. But in the 1930s, Keynes's prescription was generally regarded with horror by orthodox economists.

Mass Unemployment

The lack of large-scale government spending contributed to the rise of mass unemployment. As the financial crisis led to cuts in production, workers lost their jobs and had little money to buy goods. In Britain, where unemployment had averaged 12 percent in the 1920s, it averaged more than 18 percent between 1930 and 1935. Far worse was the case of Germany, where in 1932 one in every three workers was jobless. In the United States, unemployment had averaged only 5 percent in the 1920s. In 1932 it soared to about 33 percent: 14 million people were out of work (see Map 27.1). Only by pumping new money into the economy could the government increase demand and break the vicious cycle of decline.

Mass unemployment created great social problems. Poverty increased dramatically, although in most countries unemployed workers generally received some kind of

British Unemployment, 1932

Insured workers unemployed
- More than 35%
- 25–35%
- 15–24%
- Less than 15%

LISTENING TO THE PAST

Periodic surges in unemployment were an old story in capitalist economies, but the long-term joblessness of millions in the Great Depression was something new and unexpected. In Britain especially, where the depression followed a weak postwar recovery, large numbers suffered involuntary idleness for years at a time. Whole families lived "on the dole," the weekly welfare benefits paid by the government.

One of the most insightful accounts of unemployed workers was written by the British journalist and novelist George Orwell (1903–1950), who studied the conditions in northern England and wrote The Road to Wigan Pier *(1937), an excerpt of which follows. An independent socialist who distrusted rigid Marxism, Orwell believed that socialism could triumph in Britain if it came to mean commonsense "justice and liberty" for a broad sector of the working classes. Orwell's disillusionment with authoritarian socialism and Soviet-style communism pervades his other famous works,* Animal Farm *(1945) and* 1984 *(1949).*

❝ When you see the unemployment figures quoted at two millions, it is fatally easy to take this as meaning that two million people are out of work and the rest of the population is comparatively comfortable. . . . [Adding in the destitute,] you might take the number of underfed people in England (for *everyone* on the dole or thereabouts is underfed) as being, at the very most, five millions.

This is an enormous under-estimate, because, in the first place, the only people shown on unemployment figures are those actually drawing the dole — that is, in general, heads of families. An unemployed man's dependants do not figure on the list unless they too are drawing a separate allowance. . . . In addition there are great numbers of people who are in work but who, from a financial point of view, might equally be unemployed, because they are not drawing anything that can be described as a living wage.

Allow for these and their dependants, throw in as before the old-age pensioners, the destitute and other nondescripts, and you get an *underfed* population of well over ten millions. . . . Take the figures for Wigan, which is typical enough of the industrial and mining districts. . . . The total population of Wigan is a little under 87,000; so that at any moment more than one person in three out of the whole population — not merely the registered workers — is either drawing or living on the dole. . . .

Nevertheless, in spite of the frightful extent of unemployment, it is a fact that poverty — extreme poverty — is less in evidence in the industrial North than it is in London. Everything is poorer and shabbier, there are fewer motor-cars and fewer well-dressed people; but also there are fewer people who are obviously destitute. . . . In the industrial towns the old communal way of life has not yet broken up, tradition is still strong and almost everyone has a family — potentially, therefore, a home. In a town of 50,000 or 100,000 inhabitants there is no casual and as it were unaccounted-for population; nobody sleeping in the streets, for instance. Moreover, there is just this to be said for the unemployment regulations, that they do not discourage people from marrying. A man and wife on twenty-three shillings a week are not far from the starvation line, but they can make a home of sorts; they are vastly better off than a single man on fifteen shillings. . . .

But there is no doubt about the deadening, debilitating effect of unemployment upon everybody, married or single, and upon men more than upon women. . . . Everyone who saw Greenwood's play *Love on the Dole* must remember that dreadful moment when the poor, good, stupid working man beats on the table and cries out, "O God, send me some work!" This was not dramatic exaggeration, it was a touch from life. That cry must have been uttered, in almost those words, in tens of thousands, perhaps hundreds of thousands of English homes, during the past fifteen years.

But, I think not again — or at least, not so often. . . . When people live on the dole for years at a time they grow used to it, and drawing the dole, though it remains unpleasant, ceases to be shameful. Thus the old, independent, workhouse-fearing tradition is undermined. . . .

So you have whole populations settling down, as it were, to a lifetime of the P.A.C. . . . Take, for instance,

meager unemployment benefits or public aid that prevented starvation. (See "Listening to the Past: George Orwell on Life on the Dole," above.) Millions of people lost their spirit, condemned to an apparently hopeless search for work. Homes and ways of life were disrupted in millions of personal tragedies. Young people postponed marriages, and birthrates fell sharply. There was an increase in suicide and mental illness. Poverty or the threat of poverty became a grinding reality. In 1932 the workers of Manchester, England, appealed to their city officials — a typical plea echoed throughout the Western world:

Poster used in the British election campaign of 1931, when unemployment rose to a new record high. (Conservative Research Department/The Bridgeman Art Library)

of cheap smart clothes since the war. The youth who leaves school at fourteen and gets a blind-alley job is out of work at twenty, probably for life; but for two pounds ten on the hire-purchase system he can buy himself a suit which, for a little while and at a little distance, looks as though it had been tailored in Savile Row. The girl can look like a fashion plate at an even lower price. . . . You can stand on the street corner, indulging in a private daydream of yourself as Clark Gable or Greta Garbo, which compensates you for a great deal. . . .

Trade since the war has had to adjust itself to meet the demands of underpaid, underfed people, with the result that a luxury is nowadays almost always cheaper than a necessity. One pair of plain solid shoes costs as much as two ultra-smart pairs. . . . And above all there is gambling, the cheapest of all luxuries. Even people on the verge of starvation can buy a few days' hope ("Something to live for," as they call it) by having a penny on a sweepstake. . . . Twenty million people are underfed but literally everyone in England has access to a radio. What we have lost in food we have gained in electricity. Whole sections of the working class who have been plundered of all they really need are being compensated, in part, by cheap luxuries which mitigate the surface of life.

Do you consider all this desirable? No, I don't. But it may be that the psychological adjustment which the working class are visibly making is the best they could make in the circumstances. They have neither turned revolutionary nor lost their self-respect; merely they have kept their tempers and settled down to make the best of things on a fish-and-chip standard. The alternative would be God knows what continued agonies of despair; or it might be attempted insurrections which, in a strongly governed country like England, could only lead to futile massacres and a régime of savage repression. 》

Source: Excerpts from Chapter V in *The Road to Wigan Pier* by George Orwell. Copyright © 1958 and renewed 1986 by the Estate of Sonia B. Orwell. Reprinted by permission of Houghton Mifflin Harcourt Publishing Company, from *The Complete Works of George Orwell* by George Orwell. Copyright © George Orwell, 1986. Reproduced by permission of Bill Hamilton as the Literary Executor of the Estate of the Late Sonia Brownell Orwell and Seeker & Warburg Ltd.

the fact that the working class think nothing of getting married on the dole. . . . Life is still fairly normal, more normal than one really has the right to expect. Families are impoverished, but the family-system has not broken up. The people are in effect living a reduced version of their former lives.

Instead of raging against their destiny they have made things tolerable by lowering their standards. But they don't necessarily lower their standards by cutting out luxuries and concentrating on necessities; more often it is the other way about — the more natural way, if you come to think of it. Hence the fact that in a decade of unparalleled depression, the consumption of all cheap luxuries has increased. The two things that have probably made the greatest difference of all are the movies and the mass-production

QUESTIONS FOR ANALYSIS

1. According to Orwell, "extreme poverty" was less visible in the northern industrial towns than in London. How did family relations contribute to social stability in the face of growing poverty?

2. What were the consequences of long-term unemployment for English workers? How did joblessness change attitudes and behaviors?

3. Judging from Orwell's description, did radical revolution seem likely in England in the Great Depression? Why?

We tell you that thousands of people . . . are in desperate straits. We tell you that men, women, and children are going hungry. . . . We tell you that great numbers are being rendered distraught through the stress and worry of trying to exist without work. . . . If you do not do this — if you do not provide useful work for the unemployed — what, we ask, is your alternative? Do not imagine that this colossal tragedy of unemployment is going on endlessly without some fateful catastrophe. Hungry men are angry men.[11]

Only strong government action could deal with mass unemployment, a social powder keg preparing to explode.

Homelessness in London The Great Depression of the 1930s disrupted the lives of millions across the United States and Europe. The frustration and agony of unemployment are evident in this common scene of unemployed and homeless Londoners wrapping themselves in newspaper against the cold. (Mary Evans Picture Library/The Image Works)

The New Deal in the United States

The Great Depression and the response to it marked a major turning point in American history. President Herbert Hoover (r. 1929–1933) and his administration initially reacted to the stock market crash and economic decline with dogged optimism but limited action. When the full force of the financial crisis struck Europe in the summer of 1931 and boomeranged back to the United States, people's worst fears became reality. Banks failed; unemployment soared. Between 1929 and 1932 industrial production fell by about 50 percent.

In these tragic circumstances, Franklin Delano Roosevelt (r. 1933–1945) won a landslide presidential victory in 1932 with grand but vague promises of a "New Deal for the forgotten man." Roosevelt's basic goal was to reform capitalism in order to preserve it. Though Roosevelt rejected socialism and government ownership of industry in 1933, he nonetheless advocated forceful government intervention in the economy

and instituted a broad range of government-supported social programs designed to stimulate the economy and provide jobs for ordinary people. Across Europe, governments engaged in similar actions in desperate attempts to relieve the economic crisis.

In the United States, innovative federal programs promoted agricultural recovery, a top priority. Almost half of the American population still lived in rural areas, and American farmers were hard hit by the depression. Roosevelt took the United States off the gold standard and devalued the dollar in an effort to raise American prices and rescue farmers. The Agricultural Adjustment Act of 1933 also aimed at raising prices and farm income by limiting agricultural production. These planning measures worked for a while, and in 1936 farmers repaid Roosevelt with overwhelming support.

The most ambitious attempt to control and plan the economy was the National Recovery Administration (NRA). Intended to reduce competition and fix prices and wages for everyone's benefit, the NRA broke with

> ❝ Do not imagine that this colossal tragedy of unemployment is going on endlessly without some fateful catastrophe. Hungry men are angry men. ❞

—WORKERS IN MANCHESTER, ENGLAND

the cherished American tradition of free competition and aroused conflicts among business people, consumers, and bureaucrats. It did not work well and was declared unconstitutional in 1935.

Roosevelt and his advisers then attacked the key problem of mass unemployment directly. The federal government accepted the responsibility of employing directly as many people as financially possible. New agencies were created to undertake a vast range of projects. The most famous of these was the Works Progress Administration (WPA), set up in 1935. One-fifth of the entire U.S. labor force worked for the WPA at some point in the 1930s, constructing public buildings, bridges, and highways. The WPA was enormously popular, and the hope of a government job helped check the threat of social revolution in the United States.

In 1935 the U.S. government also established a national social security system with old-age pensions and unemployment benefits. The National Labor Relations Act of 1935 gave union organizers the green light by declaring collective bargaining to be the policy of the United States. Union membership more than doubled from 4 million in 1935 to 9 million in 1940. In general, between 1935 and 1938 government rulings and social reforms chipped away at the privileges of the wealthy and tried to help ordinary people.

Relief programs like the WPA were part of the New Deal's fundamental commitment to use the federal government to provide for the welfare of all Americans. This commitment marked a profound shift from the traditional stress on family support and community responsibility. Embraced by a large majority in the 1930s, this shift in attitudes proved to be one of the New Deal's most enduring legacies.

Yet despite undeniable accomplishments in social reform, the New Deal was only partly successful as a response to the Great Depression. At the height of the recovery in May 1937, 7 million workers were still unemployed, in contrast to a high of 15 million in 1933. The economic situation then worsened seriously in the recession of 1937 and 1938, and unemployment had risen to a staggering 10 million when war broke out in Europe in September 1939. The New Deal never did pull the United States out of the depression; it took the Second World War to do that.

The Scandinavian Response to the Depression

Of all the Western democracies, the Scandinavian countries under Social Democratic leadership responded most successfully to the challenge of the Great Depression. Having grown steadily in the late nineteenth century, the Social Democrats became the largest political party in Sweden and then in Norway after the First World War. In the 1920s they passed important social reform legislation for both peasants and workers and developed a unique kind of socialism. Flexible and nonrevolutionary, Scandinavian socialism grew out of a strong tradition of cooperative community action. Even before 1900 Scandinavian agricultural cooperatives had shown how individual peasant families could join together for everyone's benefit. Labor leaders and capitalists were also inclined to work together.

When the economic crisis struck in 1929, socialist governments in Scandinavia built on this pattern of cooperative social action. Sweden in particular pioneered in the use of large-scale deficits to finance public works and thereby maintain production and employment. In ways that paralleled some aspects of Roosevelt's New Deal, Scandinavian governments also increased such social welfare benefits as old-age pensions, unemployment insurance, subsidized housing, and maternity allowances. All this spending required a large bureaucracy and high taxes, first on the rich and then on practically everyone. Yet both private and cooperative enterprise thrived, as did democracy. Some observers saw Scandinavia's welfare socialism as an appealing middle way between sick capitalism and cruel communism or fascism.

Recovery and Reform in Britain and France

In Britain MacDonald's Labour government and then, after 1931, the Conservative-dominated coalition government followed orthodox economic theory. The budget was balanced, but spending was tightly controlled and unemployed workers received barely enough welfare to live. Despite government lethargy, the economy recovered considerably after 1932. By 1937 total production was about 20 percent higher than in 1929. In fact, for Britain the years after 1932 were actually somewhat

Oslo Breakfast Scandinavian socialism championed cooperation and practical welfare measures, playing down strident rhetoric and theories of class conflict. The Oslo breakfast exemplified the Scandinavian approach. It provided every schoolchild in the Norwegian capital with a good breakfast free of charge. (Courtesy, Directorate for Health and Social Affairs, Oslo)

better than the 1920s had been, the opposite of the situation in the United States and France.

This good but by no means brilliant performance reflected the gradual reorientation of the British economy. After going off the gold standard in 1931 and establishing protective tariffs in 1932, Britain concentrated increasingly on the national, rather than the international, market. The old export industries of the Industrial Revolution, such as textiles and coal, continued to decline, but new industries, such as automobiles and electrical appliances, grew in response to British home demand. Moreover, low interest rates encouraged a housing boom. By the end of the decade, there were highly visible differences between the old, depressed industrial areas of the north and the new, growing areas of the south. These developments encouraged Britain to look inward and avoid unpleasant foreign entanglements.

Because France was relatively less industrialized and more isolated from the world economy, the Great Depression came late. But once the depression hit France, it stayed and stayed. Decline was steady until 1935, and a short-

Popular Front A short-lived New Deal–inspired alliance in France led by Léon Blum that encouraged the union movement and launched a far-reaching program of social reform.

lived recovery never brought production or employment back up to predepression levels. Economic stagnation both reflected and heightened an ongoing political crisis. There was no stability in government. As before 1914, the French parliament was made up of many political parties that could never cooperate for long. In 1933, for example, five coalition cabinets formed and fell in rapid succession.

The French lost the underlying unity that had made government instability bearable before 1914. Fascist-type organizations agitated against parliamentary democracy and looked to Mussolini's Italy and Hitler's Germany for inspiration. In February 1934 French fascists rioted and threatened to take over the republic. At the same time, the Communist Party and many workers opposed to the existing system were looking to Stalin's Russia for guidance. The vital center of moderate republicanism was weakened by attacks from both sides.

Frightened by the growing strength of the fascists at home and abroad, the Communists, the Socialists, and the Radicals formed an alliance — the **Popular Front** — for the national elections of May 1936. Their clear victory reflected the trend toward polarization. The number of Communists in the parliament jumped dramatically from 10 to 72, while the Socialists, led by Léon Blum, became the strongest party in France, with 146 seats. The really quite moderate Radicals slipped badly, and the conservatives lost ground to the far right.

In the next few months, Blum's Popular Front government made the first and only real attempt to deal with the social and economic problems of the 1930s in France. Inspired by Roosevelt's New Deal, the Popular Front encouraged the union movement and launched a far-reaching program of social reform, complete with paid vacations and a forty-hour workweek. Popular with workers and the lower middle class, these measures were quickly sabotaged by rapid inflation and cries of revolution from fascists and frightened conservatives. Wealthy people sneaked their money out of the country, labor unrest grew, and France entered a severe financial crisis. Blum was forced to announce a "breathing spell" in social reform.

Political dissension in France was encouraged by the Spanish Civil War (1936–1939), during which authoritarian fascist rebels overthrew the democratically elected republican government. Communists demanded that France support the Spanish republicans, while many French conservatives would gladly have joined Hitler and Mussolini in aiding the Spanish fascists. Extremism grew, and France itself was within sight of civil war. Blum was forced to resign in June 1937, and the Popular Front quickly collapsed. An anxious and divided France drifted aimlessly once again, preoccupied by Hitler and German rearmament.

LOOKING BACK LOOKING AHEAD

THE DECADES BEFORE and especially after World War I brought intense intellectual and cultural innovation. The results were both richly productive and deeply troubling. From T. S. Eliot's poem "The Waste Land" to Einstein's theory of special relativity and the sleek glass and steel buildings of the Bauhaus, the intellectual products of the time stand among the highest achievement of Western arts and sciences. At the same time, mass culture, embodied in cinema, radio, and an emerging consumer culture, had transformative effects on everyday life. Yet the modern vision was often bleak and cold. The arrival of consumer society undermined traditional values, contributing to feelings of disorientation and pessimism. The situation was worsened by ongoing political and economic turmoil. The Treaty of Versailles had failed to create a lasting peace or resolve the question of Germany's role in postwar Europe. The Great Depression revealed the fragility of the world economic system and cast millions out of work. In the end, perhaps, the era's intellectual achievements and the overall sense of crisis and anxiety were closely related.

Writing in 1930, Sigmund Freud captured the general mood of gloom and foreboding. "Men have gained control over the forces of nature to such an extent that . . . they would have no difficulty in exterminating one another to the last man," wrote the famous psychologist. "They know this, and hence comes a large part of their current unrest, their unhappiness and their mood of anxiety."[12] Freud's dark words reflected the extraordinary human costs of World War I and the horrific power of modern weaponry. They also expressed his despair over the growing popularity of repressive dictatorial regimes. During the interwar years, many grand European nations—including Italy, Germany, Spain, Poland, Portugal, Austria, and Hungary—would fall one by one to authoritarian or fascist dictatorships, and so succumb to the temptations of totalitarianism. Liberal democracy was severely weakened. European stability was threatened by the radical programs of Soviet Communists on the left and fascists on the right, and Freud uncannily predicted the great conflict to come.

CHAPTER REVIEW

■ **In what ways did new and sometimes radically experimental ideas in philosophy, religion, physics, psychology, and literature reflect the general crisis in Western thought? (p. 854)**

After the First World War, Western intellectual life underwent a general crisis marked by pessimism, uncertainty, and fascination with irrational forces. Philosophers, building on the prewar writings of Nietzsche, rejected the traditional philosophical questions, focusing instead on the rules of language or an existential morality. Christianity experienced a fundamentalist revival, albeit of an existentialist nature that stressed the sins of humanity and the unknowable mystery of God. Einstein's theories reordered the universe and overturned Newtonian physics, and Freudian psychology privileged the power of the irrational in human thought. Ceaseless experimentation and rejection of old forms characterized literature and reflected the unease of this period. In short, almost every field of Western thought experienced revolutionary change.

■ **How did modernism revolutionize architecture, painting, and music? (p. 861)**

Modernism had a powerful impact on many cultural endeavors in the decades around World War I. Architects such as Walter Gropius, director of the Bauhaus, promoted stripped-down glass and steel buildings that emphasized function over form and that formed the basis of the international style after World War II. Modern schools of painting, from the Impressionists to the Dadaists and surrealists, broke with past traditions, producing images that were increasingly radical and abstract. Arnold Schönberg and other musicians wrote dissonant, atonal music that discarded familiar melodies and harmonies. Such disturbing works reflected the crises of the age of anxiety but also became classic examples of modern Western art and culture.

■ **How did the emerging consumer society and mass culture of the interwar years change the everyday lives of ordinary men and women? (p. 866)**

Modern consumer society brought inexpensive mass-produced goods of all kinds to ordinary men and women, including household appliances, clothing, shampoos and makeup, and automobiles. The use of leisure time was likewise transformed by mass culture. Motion pictures and radio provided entertainment and relaxation for the masses, even as dictatorial governments used the new media for political propaganda. Consumer culture was enormously popular because it offered escape from the hard realities of everyday life. But new forms of consumerism also generated

debate and controversy, particularly among those worried about the decline of traditional values and lifestyles, and the arrival of the Great Depression made the purchase of even basic consumer goods increasingly difficult.

■ **How did the democratic leaders of the 1920s deal with deep-seated instability and try to establish real peace and prosperity? (p. 871)**

The Treaty of Versailles left defeated Germany and the victorious Allies bitterly divided. The question of German reparations soon led to political stalemate, French occupation of Germany's Ruhr district, runaway German inflation, and the prospect of a general European collapse. In 1923 courageous new leaders turned to compromise. Led by Stresemann in Germany and Briand in France and backed by Great Britain and the United States, the new leaders worked out a complicated financial and political settlement that led to economic recovery and fragile political stability. Germany recovered, France rebuilt its war-ravaged areas, and Britain's Labour Party expanded social services, but the stability such measures achieved was short-lived.

■ **What caused the Great Depression, and how did the Western democracies respond to this challenge? (p. 874)**

The Great Depression grew out of the fragile international financial system and a speculative boom in the U.S. stock market in the 1920s. The stock market crash in 1929 shattered international banking and triggered a disastrous downward spiral in prices and production, bringing massive unemployment to millions of workers. Turning inward to cope with the economic crisis and the related social problems, the Western democracies responded with relief measures, extended unemployment benefits, labor reforms, and social concern. These measures eased distress and prevented revolutions in the leading nations, but with the significant exception of the Scandinavian countries, the Western democracies failed to restore prosperity, eliminate high unemployment, or prevent widespread disillusionment. The old liberal ideals of individual rights and responsibilities, elected government, and economic freedom declined and appeared outmoded to many citizens.

Suggested Reading

Berend, Ivan T. *Decades of Crisis: Central and Eastern Europe Before World War II.* 2001. An up-to-date study of this complex region.

Berghahn, Volker R. *Europe in the Era of Two World Wars: From Militarism and Genocide to Civil Society.* 2006. A short and stimulating account.

Bullock, Alan, ed. *The Twentieth Century: A Promethean Age.* 1971. Particularly noteworthy because it is a lavish visual feast combined with penetrating essays on major developments.

Burrow, J. W. *The Crisis of Reason: European Thought, 1848–1914.* 2002. A rewarding intellectual history.

Cawood, Ian. *Britain in the Twentieth Century.* 2003. A useful national survey.

Eksteins, Modris. *Rites of Spring: The Great War and the Birth of the Modern Age.* 1989. A penetrating analysis of the links between World War I and modern culture and politics.

Exra, Elizabeth. *European Cinema.* 2004. A concise history of European film and movie industries from their origins to the present.

Kertzer, David I., and Marzio Barbagli, eds. *The History of the European Family,* vol. 3: *Family Life in the Twentieth Century.* 2003. A distinguished collection of essays by experts.

Kracauer, Siegfried. *From Caligari to Hitler: A Psychological History of the German Film.* 1947. An early and critical look at the Weimar-era German film industry by a contemporary critic that remains a cultural studies classic.

McMillan, James F. *Twentieth-Century France: Politics and Society, 1898–1991.* 1992. A recommended national survey.

Paxton, Robert O. *Europe in the Twentieth Century.* 2004. An excellent account of contemporary history with a liberal viewpoint.

Roberts, Mary Louise. *Civilization Without Sexes: Reconstructing Gender in Postwar France, 1917–1927.* 1994. A fascinating interpretation of gender roles in France after the First World War.

Schwartz, Vanessa R. *Spectacular Realities: Early Mass Culture in Fin-de-Siècle Paris.* 1999. Explores the foundation of modern mass culture in late-nineteenth-century Paris.

Slater, Don. *Consumer Culture and Modernity.* 1997. An informative review of scholarly interpretations of consumer society.

Weitz, Eric. *Weimar Germany: Promise and Tragedy.* 2007. A thorough exploration of modern art, culture, and politics in interwar Germany.

Winders, James A. *European Culture Since 1848: From Modernism to Postmodern and Beyond.* 1998. A lively and accessible account.

Notes

1. P. Valéry, *Variety,* trans. M. Cowley (New York: Harcourt Brace, 1927), pp. 27–28.
2. G. Greene, *Another Mexico* (New York: Viking Press, 1939), p. 3.
3. T. S. Eliot, "The Waste Land," in *The Norton Anthology of Poetry Revised,* ed. A. W. Allison et al. (New York: Norton, 1975), p. 1034.
4. C. E. Jeanneret-Gris (Le Corbusier), *Towards a New Architecture* (London: J. Rodker, 1931), p. 15.
5. Quoted in A. H. Barr, Jr., *What Is Modern Painting?* 9th ed. (New York: Museum of Modern Art, 1966), p. 25.
6. R. Huelsenbeck, "Collective Dada Manifesto (1920)," in *The Dada Painters and Poets,* ed. Robert Motherwell and Jack D. Flam (Boston: G. K. Hall, 1981), pp. 242–246.
7. Elsa Herrmann, *This Is the New Woman* (1929), quoted in *The Weimar Republic Sourcebook,* ed. A. Kaes, M. Jay, and E. Dimendberg (Berkeley: University of California Press, 1994), pp. 206–208.
8. Quoted in R. Smither, ed., *The Battles of the Somme and Ancre* (London: Imperial War Museum, 1993), p. 67.
9. Quoted in A. Briggs, *The Birth of Broadcasting,* vol. 1 (London: Oxford University Press, 1961), p. 47.
10. J. M. Keynes, *The Economic Consequences of the Peace* (1919), quoted in M. A. Kishlansky, *Sources of the West: Readings in Western Civilization* (New York: Pearson Longman, 2008), p. 252.
11. Quoted in S. B. Clough et al., eds., *Economic History of Europe: Twentieth Century* (New York: Harper & Row, 1968), pp. 243–245.
12. S. Freud, *Civilization and Its Discontents* (New York: W. W. Norton, 1961), p. 112.

Key Terms

logical positivism (p. 855)
existentialism (p. 856)
theory of special relativity (p. 857)
id, ego, and superego (p. 859)
stream-of-consciousness technique (p. 860)
modernism (p. 861)
functionalism (p. 861)
Bauhaus (p. 861)
Dadaism (p. 864)
"new woman" (p. 867)
Dawes Plan (p. 873)
Great Depression (p. 874)
Popular Front (p. 882)

For practice quizzes and other study tools, visit the Online Study Guide at **bedfordstmartins.com/mckaywest**.

For primary sources from this period, see *Sources of Western Society*, **Second Edition**.

For Web sites, images, and documents related to topics in this chapter, visit Make History at **bedfordstmartins.com/mckaywest**.

28

Dictatorships and the Second World War

1919–1945

The intense wave of artistic and cultural innovation in the 1920s and 1930s, which shook the foundations of Western thought, was paralleled by radical developments in the realm of politics. In the age of anxiety, communist and fascist states undertook determined assaults on democratic government and individual rights across Europe. On the eve of the Second World War, popularly elected governments survived only in Great Britain, France, Czechoslovakia, the Low Countries, Scandinavia, and Switzerland.

Across the 1920s and 1930s, totalitarian regimes in the communist Soviet Union and fascist Italy and Germany practiced a ruthless and dynamic tyranny. Their attempts to revolutionize state and society went far beyond familiar forms of conservative authoritarianism. Communist and fascist states ruled with unprecedented severity. They promised to greatly improve the lives of ordinary citizens and intervened radically in those lives in pursuit of utopian schemes of social engineering. Their drive for territorial expansion threatened neighboring nations and put the democracies on the defensive. The human costs were appalling. Millions died as Stalin forced communism on the Soviet Union in the 1930s. Attempts to build a "racially pure" New Order in Europe by Hitler's Nazi Germany led to the deaths of millions more in World War II and the Holocaust.

Such brutalities may seem a thing of the distant past that "can't happen again." Yet horrible atrocities in Cambodia, Bosnia, and Rwanda show that they continue to plague the world in our time. It remains vital that we understand Europe's era of overwhelming violence in order to guard against the possibility of its recurrence in the future. ■

Life at Auschwitz. This rough painting by an anonymous inmate of the Auschwitz-Birkenau Nazi concentration camp is preserved on the ceiling of a camp barracks. Guarded by SS officers, prisoners labor on a drainage canal under the worst conditions, while two carry a dead worker off the field.

CHAPTER PREVIEW

Authoritarian States
■ How did radical totalitarian dictatorship differ from conservative authoritarianism, and in what ways were communism and fascism totalitarian systems?

Stalin's Soviet Union
■ How did Stalin and the Communist Party build a modern totalitarian state in the Soviet Union?

Mussolini and Fascism in Italy
■ How did Mussolini's dictatorship come to power and govern in Italy?

Hitler and Nazism in Germany
■ How did Hitler gain power, what policies did totalitarian Nazi Germany pursue, and why did they lead to World War II?

The Second World War
■ How did Germany and Japan create enormous empires, and how were they defeated by the Allies?

Authoritarian States

How did radical totalitarian dictatorship differ from conservative authoritarianism, and in what ways were communism and fascism totalitarian systems? ■

Both conservative and radical dictatorships swept through Europe in the 1920s and 1930s. Although these two types of dictatorship shared some characteristics and sometimes overlapped in practice, in essence they were quite different. Conservative authoritarian regimes were long established in Europe. Radical totalitarian dictatorships, based on the ideologies of Stalinist communism and fascism, were a new and frightening development aimed at the radical reconstruction of existing society.

Conservative Authoritarianism and Radical Totalitarian Dictatorships

The traditional form of antidemocratic government in European history was conservative authoritarianism. Like Catherine the Great in Russia and Metternich in Austria, the leaders of such governments relied on obedient bureaucracies in their efforts to control society. Liberals, democrats, and socialists were often jailed or exiled, but old-fashioned authoritarian governments were limited in their power and objectives. They had neither the ability nor the desire to control many aspects of their subjects' lives. These governments largely limited their demands to taxes, army recruits, and passive acceptance. As long as the people did not try to change the system, they often had considerable personal independence.

After the First World War, authoritarianism revived, especially in the less-developed eastern part of Europe. But new kinds of radical dictatorship that went much further than conservative authoritarianism emerged in the Soviet Union, Germany, and to some extent Italy and other countries. Communist dictatorship had ruled the Soviet Union since the Russian Revolution (see Chapter 26). Fascist dictators took over in Italy in 1922 and in Germany in 1933. By the start of World War II, fascist governments controlled Spain, Portugal, Austria, Hungary, and Romania. And both Communist and fascist political parties were well established in all major European nations, where they ran for parliamentary office even as they challenged the very basis of liberal democracy.

Some scholars use the term **totalitarianism** to describe these radical dictatorships, which made unprec-

totalitarianism A radical dictatorship that exercises "total claims" over the beliefs and behavior of its citizens by taking control of the economic, social, intellectual, and cultural aspects of society.

edented "total claims" on the beliefs and behavior of their citizens. The totalitarian model emphasizes the characteristics that fascist and communist dictatorships had in common, and the term gained prominence after World War II. Scholars showed that the one-party totalitarian state used violent political repression and intense propaganda to gain complete power. But it did not stop there. Increasingly, the state tried to dominate the economic, social, intellectual, and cultural aspects of people's lives. Deviation from the norm, even in art or family behavior, could become a crime.

Most historians agree that totalitarianism owed much to the experience of total war in 1914–1918 (see Chapter 26). World War I required state governments to limit individual liberties and intervene in the economy in order to achieve one supreme objective: victory. The brutality of the war eroded the ideal of individual rights; after so many casualties, the value of one life seemed far less important than the good of the entire nation. Totalitarian politicians were inspired by the example of the modern state at war. They showed a callous disregard for human life and greatly expanded the power of the state in pursuit of social control.

Communist and fascist dictatorships shared other characteristics. Both violently rejected parliamentary government and liberal values. Classical liberalism (see Chapter 22) sought to limit the power of the state and protect the rights of the individual. Totalitarians, on the other hand, believed that liberal individualism undermined equality and unity. They rejected democracy in favor of one-party political systems ruled from the top.

A charismatic leader typically dominated the totalitarian state — Stalin in the Soviet Union, Mussolini in Italy, Hitler in Germany. All three created political parties of a new kind, dedicated to promoting idealized visions of collective harmony. They used force and terror to intimidate and destroy political opponents and pursued policies of imperial expansion to exploit other lands. They censored the mass media and instituted propaganda campaigns meant to advance their goals. Finally, and perhaps most important, totalitarian governments engaged in massive projects of state-controlled social engineering dedicated to replacing individualism with a unified "people" capable of exercising the collective will.

Communism and Fascism

Communism and fascism clearly shared a desire to revolutionize state and society. Yet some scholars argue that the differences between the two systems are more important than the similarities, and so move beyond the totalitarian model. What were the main differences between these two systems? To answer this question, it is important to consider the way ideology, or a guiding political philosophy, was linked to the use of state-sponsored repression and violence.

Following Marx, Soviet Communists strove to create an international brotherhood of workers. In this idealized communist utopia, class differences would supposedly disappear, resulting in a society free of capitalist inequality (see Chapter 22). In pursuit of this social leveling, the Soviet government under Stalin aggressively intervened in all walks of life. Under Stalinism—the name given to the Communist system under Stalin—the state used force to destroy the upper and middle classes. The Stalinist state nationalized private property, pushed rapid industrialization, and collectivized agriculture (see pages 891–896). As the Stalinization of Soviet society proceeded in the late 1920s and the 1930s, millions lost their livelihoods and their lives.

The fascist vision of a new society was quite different. Leaders who embraced **fascism**, such as Mussolini and Hitler, claimed that they were striving to build a new community on a national—not an international—level. Extreme nationalists and often racists, fascists glorified war and the military and sought to destroy independent working-class movements. For them, the nation was the highest embodiment of the people, and the powerful leader was supposedly the materialization of the people's collective will.

Like communists, fascists promised to improve the lives of ordinary workers. Fascist governments intervened in the economy, but unlike communist regimes they did not try to level class differences and nationalize private property. Instead, they countered the vision of communist equality with the ideal of a community rooted in the bonds of nationalism. In the ideal fascist state, society would no longer be a battlefield of class versus class or individual self-interest. Instead, all strata and classes would work together to build a harmonious national community.

Communists and fascists differed in another crucial respect: the question of race. Where communists sought to build a new world around the destruction of class differences, fascists typically sought to build a new national community grounded in racial homogeneity. Fascists embraced the doctrine of **eugenics**, a pseudoscience that maintained that the selective breeding of human beings could improve the general characteristics of a national population. Eugenics was popular throughout the United States and Europe in the 1920s and 1930s, and many scientists, doctors, and government bureaucrats viewed it as a legitimate means of social planning and improvement. But fascists, especially the German National Socialists or Nazis, pushed these ideas to their limit.

Adopting ideologies of eugenics, the Nazis believed that the German nation had to be "purified" of outsider groups. Jews, Gypsies, homosexuals, the mentally and physically disabled, and others were deemed unable to contribute to the nation's "racial stock" and needed to be segregated or eliminated. Such ideas ultimately led to the Holocaust, the attempt to purge Germany and Europe of all Jews and other groups who were deemed

Chronology

1921	New Economic Policy (NEP) in U.S.S.R.
1922	Mussolini seizes power in Italy
1924–1929	Buildup of Nazi Party in Germany
1927	Stalin comes to power in U.S.S.R.
1928	Stalin's first five-year plan
1929	Lateran Agreement; start of collectivization in Soviet Union
1929–1939	Great Depression
1931	Japan invades Manchuria
1932–1933	Famine in Ukraine
1933	Hitler appointed chancellor in Germany; Nazis begin control of state and society
1935	Mussolini invades Ethiopia
1936	Start of great purges under Stalin; Spanish civil war begins
1937	Japanese army attacks China
1939	Germany occupies Czech lands and invades western Poland; Britain and France declare war on Germany, starting World War II; Soviet Union occupies eastern Poland
1940	Germany defeats and occupies France
1940	Battle of Britain
1941	Germany invades U.S.S.R.; Japan attacks Pearl Harbor; United States enters war
1941–1945	The Holocaust
1942–1943	Battle of Stalingrad
1944	Allied invasion at Normandy
1945	Soviet and U.S. forces enter Germany; United States drops atomic bombs on Japan; World War II ends

fascism A movement characterized by extreme, often expansionist nationalism, antisocialism, a dynamic and violent leader, and glorification of war and the military.

eugenics A pseudoscientific doctrine that maintains that the selective breeding of human beings can improve the general characteristics of a national population, which helped inspire Nazi ideas about "race and space" and ultimately contributed to the Holocaust.

Picturing the Past

The Appeal of Propaganda Totalitarian leaders used extensive propaganda campaigns to enlist the support of the masses. Italian dictator Benito Mussolini repeatedly linked his regime to the glory of ancient Rome. Here he has donned the costume of a legionnaire to lead a parade in front of the Roman Coliseum (top). The Soviet dictator Stalin presented himself as the friend of all humankind. In this propaganda poster (bottom), titled "The Great Stalin, the Banner of Friendship of the Peoples of the U.S.S.R.," he receives flowers from a diverse group of Soviet citizens, including ethnic Russians and East and Central Asians. This idealized testament to peaceful coexistence within the Soviet empire masked the tensions aroused by Russian domination. (Mussolini: Stefano Bianchetti/Corbis; Stalin: Bedford/St. Martin's)

ANALYZING THE IMAGE How do these images present the role of the dictatorial leader? How do they represent the relationship between the leader and the led?

CONNECTIONS How might these idealized portrayals have helped build support for their respective regimes? Was there any truth behind the propaganda?

To complete this activity online, go to the Online Study Guide at bedfordstmartins.com/mckaywest.

"undesirable" by mass killing during World War II (see page 912). Though the Soviets sometimes persecuted specific ethnic groups, they never attempted to destroy a group entirely. Communists, in fact, denounced eugenics and never sought to build a society based on race or biological engineering.

Perhaps because both championed the revolutionary overthrow of existing society, communists and fascists were sworn and deadly enemies. The result was a great clash of ideologies, which was in large part responsible for the horrific destruction and loss of life in the middle of the twentieth century. Explaining the nature of totalitarian dictatorships thus remains a crucial project for historians, even as they look more closely at the ideological differences between communism and fascism.

One important set of questions explores the way dictatorial regimes generate popular consensus. Neither Hitler nor Stalin ever achieved the total control each sought. Nor did they rule alone; modern dictators need the help of large state bureaucracies and large numbers of ordinary people. Which was more important for generating popular support: terror and coercion, or practical material rewards? Why did so many people seem to approve of dictatorial rule, even as it cost the lives of millions? When, why, and how did people resist the demands of tyranny? Seeking answers to such questions leads us toward what Holocaust survivor Primo Levi called the "gray zone" of moral compromise, which defined everyday life in totalitarian societies. (See "Individuals in Society: Primo Levi," page 915.)

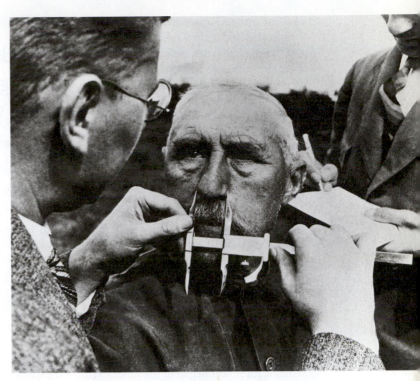

Eugenics in Nazi Germany Nazi "race scientists" believed they could use the eugenic methods of social engineering to build a powerful Aryan race. In this photograph, published in a popular magazine in 1933, a clinician measures a man's nose. Such pseudoscientific methods were used to determine an individual's supposed "racial value." (Hulton-Deutsch Collection/Corbis)

Stalin's Soviet Union

How did Stalin and the Communist Party build a modern totalitarian state in the Soviet Union? ▪

Lenin's harshest critics claim that he established the basic outlines of a modern totalitarian dictatorship after the Bolshevik Revolution and during the Russian civil war. If this is so, then Joseph Stalin (1879–1953) certainly finished the job. A master of political infighting, Stalin cautiously consolidated his power and eliminated his enemies in the mid-1920s. Then in 1928, as undisputed leader of the ruling Communist Party, Stalin launched the first **five-year plan**—the "revolution from above," as he so aptly termed it.

The 1928 five-year plan and those that followed were extremely ambitious. They marked the beginning of a radical attempt to transform Soviet society into a communist state. The ultimate goal was to generate new attitudes, new loyalties, and a new socialist humanity. The means chosen by Stalin and the small Communist Party elite in order to do so were constant propaganda, enormous sacrifice by the people, harsh repression that included purges and executions, and rewards for those

who followed the party line. Thus the Soviet Union in the 1930s became a dynamic modern totalitarian state.

From Lenin to Stalin

By spring 1921 Lenin and the Bolsheviks had won the civil war, but they ruled a shattered and devastated land. Many farms were in ruins, and food supplies were exhausted. In southern Russia drought combined with the ravages of war to produce the worst famine in generations. Industrial production had broken down completely. In the face of economic disintegration, riots by peasants and workers, and an open rebellion by previously pro-Bolshevik sailors at Kronstadt, the tough but ever-flexible Lenin changed course. He repressed the Kronstadt rebels, and in March 1921 he replaced war communism (see Chapter 26) with the **New Economic Policy (NEP)**, which re-established limited economic freedom in an attempt to rebuild agriculture

five-year plan A plan launched by Stalin in 1928, and termed the "revolution from above," aimed at modernizing the Soviet Union and creating a new communist society with new attitudes, new loyalties, and a new socialist humanity.

New Economic Policy (NEP) Lenin's 1921 policy to re-establish limited economic freedom in an attempt to rebuild agriculture and industry in the face of economic disintegration.

and industry. During the civil war, the Bolsheviks had simply seized grain without payment. Now peasant producers were permitted to sell their surpluses in free markets, and private traders and small handicraft manufacturers were allowed to reappear. Heavy industry, railroads, and banks, however, remained wholly nationalized.

The NEP was a political and economic success. Politically, it was a necessary but temporary compromise with the Soviet Union's overwhelming peasant majority. Realizing that his government was not strong enough to take land from the peasants and turn them into state workers, Lenin made a deal with the only force capable of overturning his government. The NEP brought rapid economic recovery, and by 1926 industrial output surpassed, and agricultural production was almost equal to, prewar levels.

As the economy recovered and the government partially relaxed its censorship and repression, an intense struggle for power began in the inner circles of the Communist Party, for Lenin had left no chosen successor when he died in 1924. The principal contenders were Stalin and Trotsky. The son of a shoemaker, Joseph Dzhugashvili (joo-guhsh-VEEL-yih)—later known as Stalin—had studied for the priesthood but was expelled from his seminary. By 1903 he was a Bolshevik revolutionary in southern Russia.

Stalin was a good organizer but a poor speaker and writer, and he had no experience outside of Russia. Trotsky, a great and inspiring leader who had planned the 1917 takeover and then created the victorious Red Army, appeared to have all the advantages in the struggle to take power. Yet Stalin won because he was more effective at gaining the all-important support of the party, the only genuine source of power in the one-party state. Rising to general secretary of the party's Central Committee in 1922, he used his office to win friends and allies with jobs and promises.

Stalin also won because he was better able to relate Marxian teaching to Soviet realities in the 1920s. Stalin developed a theory of "socialism in one country" that was more appealing to the majority of communists than was Trotsky's doctrine of "permanent revolution." Stalin argued that the Russian-dominated Soviet Union had the ability to build socialism on its own. Trotsky maintained that socialism in the Soviet Union could succeed only if a socialist revolution swept throughout Europe. To many Russian communists, Trotsky's views sold their country short and promised risky conflicts with capitalist countries. Stalin's willingness to break with the NEP and "build socialism" at home appealed to young militants in the party, who detested the capitalist-appearing NEP.

> ❝ We are fifty or a hundred years behind the advanced countries. We must make good this distance in ten years. Either we do it, or we shall go under. ❞
>
> —JOSEPH STALIN

With cunning skill, Stalin gradually achieved supreme power between 1922 and 1927. First he allied with Trotsky's personal enemies to crush Trotsky, and then he moved against all who might challenge his ascendancy, including his former allies. Stalin's final triumph came at the party congress of December 1927, which condemned all "deviation from the general party line" formulated by Stalin. The dictator and his followers were then ready to launch the revolution from above, radically changing the lives of millions of ordinary Russians.

The Five-Year Plans

The party congress of 1927, which ratified Stalin's consolidation of power, marked the end of the NEP and the beginning of the era of socialist five-year plans. The first five-year plan had staggering economic objectives. In just five years, total industrial output was to increase by 250 percent. Heavy industry, the preferred sector, was to grow even faster. Agricultural production was slated to increase by 150 percent, and one-fifth of the peasants in the Soviet Union were scheduled to give up their private plots and join socialist collective farms. By 1930 economic and social change was sweeping the country.

Stalin unleashed his "second revolution" for a variety of interrelated reasons. There were, first of all, ideological considerations. Like Lenin, Stalin and his militant supporters were deeply committed to socialism as they understood it. They feared a gradual restoration of capitalism, wished to promote the working classes, and were eager to abolish the NEP's private traders, independent artisans, and property-owning peasants.

Economic motivations were also important. A fragile economic recovery stalled in 1927 and 1928, and a new socialist offensive seemed necessary to ensure industrial and agricultural growth. Economic development would allow the U.S.S.R. to catch up with the West and so overcome traditional Russian "backwardness." As Stalin said in 1931, pressing for ever-greater speed and sacrifice, "We are fifty or a hundred years behind the advanced countries. We must make good this distance in ten years. Either we do it, or we shall go under." (See "Listening to the Past: Stalin Justifies the Five-Year Plan," page 894.)

The independent peasantry remained a major problem. For centuries the peasants had wanted to own the land, and finally they had it. Sooner or later, the communists reasoned, the peasants would embrace conservative capitalism and pose a threat to the regime. At the same time, the mainly urban communists believed that the feared and despised "class enemy" in the villages could be squeezed to provide the enormous sums needed for all-out industrialization.

To resolve these issues, in 1929 Stalin ordered the **collectivization of agriculture**—the forced consolidation of individual peasant farms into large, state-controlled enterprises. Peasants all over the Soviet Union were compelled to move off their small plots onto large state-run farms, where their tools, livestock, and produce would be held in common and central planners could control their work.

The increasingly repressive measures instituted by the state focused on the **kulaks**, the class of well-off peasants who had benefited the most from the market policies of the NEP. The kulaks were actually a very small group, but they were held up as a great enemy of progress, and Stalin called for their "liquidation" and seizure of their land. Stripped of land and livestock, many starved or were deported to forced-labor camps for "re-education."

The forced collectivization of agriculture led to disaster. Peasant resistance caused chaos in the countryside, and large numbers of farmers slaughtered their animals and burned their crops rather than turn them over to state commissars. Between 1929 and 1933, the number of horses, cattle, sheep, and goats in the Soviet Union fell by at least half. Nor were the state-controlled collective farms more productive. The output of grain barely increased, and collectivized agriculture was unable to make any substantial financial contribution to Soviet industrial development in the first five-year plan.

In Ukraine the drive against peasants snowballed into an assault on Ukrainians in general, who had sought independence from Soviet rule after the First World War. In 1932, as collectivization and deportations continued, Stalin and his associates set levels of grain deliveries for the Ukrainian collective at excessively high levels, and they refused to relax those quotas or even allow

food relief when Ukrainian communist leaders reported that starvation was occurring. The result was a terrible man-made famine in Ukraine in 1932 and 1933, which probably claimed 6 million lives.

Collectivization was a cruel but real victory for Stalinist ideologues. Its human cost was staggering. Millions of people died as a direct result—more than the total number of deaths in World War I. Yet by the end of 1938, fully 93 percent of peasant families had been herded onto collective farms, effectively neutralizing them as a political threat. Yet the opposition of the peasantry had forced the supposedly all-powerful state to make modest concessions. Peasants secured the right to limit a family's labor on the state-run farms and to cultivate tiny family plots, which provided them with much of their food. In 1938 these family plots produced 22 percent of all Soviet agricultural produce on only 4 percent of all cultivated land.

The industrial side of the five-year plans was more successful—indeed, quite spectacular. A huge State Planning Commission, the "Gosplan," oversaw the program by setting production goals and controlling deliveries of raw and finished materials. This was a complex and difficult task, and production bottlenecks and slowdowns often resulted. In addition, Stalinist planning

> **collectivization of agriculture**
> The forcible consolidation of individual peasant farms into large state-controlled enterprises in the Soviet Union under Stalin.
>
> **kulaks** The better-off peasants who were stripped of land and livestock under Stalin and were generally not permitted to join collective farms; many of them starved or were deported to forced-labor camps for "re-education."

Day Shift at Magnitogorsk Beginning in 1928, Stalin's government issued a series of ambitious five-year plans designed to rapidly industrialize the Soviet Union. The plans focused primarily on boosting heavy industry and included the building of a gigantic steel complex at Magnitogorsk in the Ural Mountains. Here steelworkers review production goals at the Magnitogorsk foundry. (Sovfoto)

Stalin Justifies the Five-Year Plan

LISTENING TO THE PAST

On February 4, 1931, Joseph Stalin delivered the following address, entitled "No Slowdown in Tempo!" to the First Conference of Soviet Industrial Managers. Published the following day in Pravda, the newspaper of the Communist Party, and widely publicized at home and abroad, Stalin's speech reaffirmed the leader's commitment to the breakneck pace of industrialization and collectivization set forth in the first five-year plan.

Arguing that more sacrifices were necessary, Stalin sought to rally the people and generate support for the party's program. His address captures the spirit of Soviet public discourse in the early 1930s.

Stalin's concluding idea, that Bolsheviks needed to master technology and industrial management, reflected another major development. The Soviet Union was training a new class of communist engineers and technicians, who were beginning to replace foreign engineers and "bourgeois specialists," Russian engineers trained in tsarist times who were grudgingly tolerated after the revolution.

It is sometimes asked whether it is not possible to slow down the tempo somewhat, to put a check on the movement. No, comrades, it is not possible! The tempo must not be reduced! On the contrary, we must increase it as much as is within our powers and possibilities. This is dictated to us by our obligations to the workers and peasants of the U.S.S.R. This is dictated to us by our obligations to the working class of the whole world.

To slacken the tempo would mean falling behind. And those who fall behind get beaten. But we do not want to be beaten. No, we refuse to be beaten! One feature of the history of old Russia was the continual beatings she suffered because of her backwardness. She was beaten by the Mongol khans, . . . the Turkish beys, . . . and the Japanese barons. All beat her—because of her backwardness, cultural backwardness, political backwardness, industrial backwardness, agricultural backwardness. They beat her because to do so was profitable and could be done with impunity. . . . Such is the law of the exploiters—to beat the backward and the weak. It is the jungle law of capitalism. You are backward, you are weak—therefore you are wrong; hence you can be beaten and enslaved. You are mighty—therefore you are right; hence we must be wary of you. That is why we must no longer lag behind.

In the past we had no fatherland, nor could we have had one. But now that we have overthrown capitalism and power is in our hands, in the hands of the people, we have a fatherland, and we will uphold its independence. Do you want our socialist fatherland to be beaten and to lose its independence?

"Our program is realistic," Stalin proclaims on this poster, "because it is you and me working together." (David King Collection)

generally favored heavy industry over the production of consumer goods, often leading to shortages of basic necessities. Despite such problems, Soviet industry produced about four times as much in 1937 as it had in 1928. No other major country had ever achieved such rapid industrial growth. Forced industrial growth went hand in hand with urban development: more than 25 million people migrated to cities during the 1930s, mostly peasants who left their villages to become laborers in Russia's growing industrial centers.

Steel was the idol of the Stalinist age. The Soviet state needed heavy machinery for rapid development, and an industrial labor force was created almost overnight as peasant men and women began working in the huge steel mills and plants built across the country. Between 1930 and 1932, independent trade unions lost most of their power. The government could assign workers to any job anywhere in the country, and an internal passport system ensured that individuals could not move without the permission of the police. When factory manag-

If you do not want this, you must put an end to its backwardness in the shortest possible time and develop a genuine Bolshevik tempo in building up its socialist economy. There is no other way. That is why Lenin said on the eve of the October Revolution: "Either perish, or overtake and outstrip the advanced capitalist countries."

We are fifty or a hundred years behind the advanced countries. We must make good this distance in ten years. Either we do it, or we shall go under. That is what our obligations to the workers and peasants of the U.S.S.R. dictate to us.

But we have yet other, more serious and more important, obligations. They are our obligations to the world proletariat. . . . We achieved victory not solely through the efforts of the working class of the U.S.S.R., but also thanks to the support of the working class of the world. Without this support we would have been torn to pieces long ago. . . .

Why does the international proletariat support us? How did we merit this support? By the fact that we were the first to hurl ourselves into the battle against capitalism, we were the first to establish working-class state power, we were the first to begin building socialism. By the fact that we are engaged on a cause which, if successful, will transform the whole world and free the entire working class. But what is needed for success? The elimination of our backwardness, the development of a high Bolshevik tempo of construction. We must march forward in such a way that the working class of the whole world, looking at us, may say:

There you have my advanced detachment, my shock brigade, my working-class state power, my fatherland; they are engaged on their cause, *our* cause, and they are working well; let us support them against the capitalists and promote the cause of the world revolution. Must we not justify the hopes of the world's working class, must we not fulfill our obligations to them? Yes, we must if we do not want to utterly disgrace ourselves.

Such are our obligations, internal and international.

As you see, they dictate to us a Bolshevik tempo of development.

I will not say that we have accomplished nothing in regard to management of production during these years. In fact, we have accomplished a good deal. . . . But we could have accomplished still more if we had tried during this period really to master production, the technique of production, the financial and economic side of it. In ten years at most we must make good the distance that separates us from the advanced capitalist countries. We have all the "objective" possibilities for this. The only thing lacking is the ability to make proper use of these possibilities.

And that depends on us. *Only* on us! . . . If you are a factory manager—interfere in all the affairs of the factory, look into everything, let nothing escape you, learn and learn again. Bolsheviks must master technique. It is time Bolsheviks themselves became experts. . . .

It is said that it is hard to master technique. That is not true! There are no fortresses that Bolsheviks cannot capture. We have solved a number of most difficult problems. We have overthrown capitalism. We have assumed power.

We have built up a huge socialist industry. We have transferred the middle peasants on the path of socialism. We have already accomplished what is most important from the point of view of construction. What remains to be done is not so much: to study technique, to master science. And when we have done that we shall develop a tempo of which we dare not even dream at present. And we shall do it if we really want to. **"**

Source: Joseph Stalin, "No Slowdown in Tempo!" *Pravda*, February 5, 1931, excerpted from "Reading No. 14" in *Soviet Economic Development: Operation Outstrip, 1921–1965*, by Anatole G. Mazour.

QUESTIONS FOR ANALYSIS

1. What reasons does Stalin give to justify an unrelenting "Bolshevik" tempo of industrial and social change? In the light of history, which reason seems most convincing? Why?

2. Imagine that the year is 1931 and you are a Soviet student reading Stalin's speech. Would Stalin's determination inspire you, frighten you, or leave you cold? Why?

3. Some historians argue that Soviet socialism was a kind of utopianism, where the economy, the society, and even human beings could be completely remade and perfected. What utopian elements do you see in Stalin's declaration?

ers needed more hands, they called on their counterparts on the collective farms, who sent them millions of "unneeded" peasants over the years.

Workers typically lived in deplorable conditions in hastily built industrial cities such as Magnitogorsk (Magnetic Mountain City) in the Ural mountains. Yet they also experienced some benefits of upward mobility. In a letter published in the Magnitogorsk newspaper, an ordinary electrician described the opportunities created by rapid industrialization:

In old tsarist Russia, we weren't even considered people. We couldn't dream about education, or getting a job in a state enterprise. And now I'm a citizen of the USSR. Like all citizens I have the right to a job, to education, to leisure. . . . In 1931, I came to Magnitogorsk. From a common laborer I have turned into a skilled worker. . . . I live in a country where one feels like living and learning. And if the enemy should attack this country, I will sacrifice my life in order to destroy the enemy and save my country.[1]

We should read such words with care, since they appeared in a state-censored publication. Yet the enthusiasm was at least partly authentic. The great industrialization drive, concentrated between 1928 and 1937, was an awe-inspiring achievement purchased at enormous sacrifice on the part of ordinary Soviet citizens.

Life and Culture in Soviet Society

The aim of Stalin's five-year plans was to create a new kind of society with a strong industrial economy and a powerful army. Stalin and his helpers were good Marxian economic determinists. Once everything was owned by the state, they believed, a socialist society composed of committed socialists would inevitably emerge. Their utopian vision of a new humanity floundered, but they did build a new society whose broad outlines existed into the mid-1980s. Life in this society had both good and bad aspects.

Because consumption was reduced to pay for investment, there was little improvement in the average standard of living in the years before World War II. Studies show that the average nonfarm wage purchased only about half as many goods in 1932 as it had in 1928. After 1932 real wages rose slowly, but by 1937 workers could still buy only about 60 percent of what they had bought in 1928 and less than in 1913. Collectivized peasants experienced greater hardships.

Daily life was difficult in Stalin's Soviet Union. Many people lived primarily on black bread and wore old, shabby clothing. There were constant shortages, although very heavily taxed vodka was always readily available. Housing was a particularly serious problem. Millions were moving into the cities, but the government built few new apartments. A relatively lucky family received one room for all its members and shared both a kitchen and a toilet with others on the floor.

Life was hard but by no means hopeless. Idealism and ideology had real appeal for many communists and ordinary citizens, who saw themselves heroically building the world's first socialist society while capitalism crumbled in a worldwide depression and degenerated into fascism in the West. This optimistic belief in the future of the Soviet Union also attracted many disillusioned Westerners to communism in the 1930s.

On a more practical level, Soviet workers did receive important social benefits, such as old-age pensions, free medical services, free education, and day-care centers for children. Unemployment was almost unknown. Finally, there was the possibility of personal advancement.

The keys to improving one's position were specialized skills and technical education. Rapid industrialization required massive numbers of trained experts, such as skilled workers, engineers, and plant managers. Thus the Stalinist state broke with the egalitarian policies of the 1920s and provided tremendous incentives to those

who could serve its needs. It paid the mass of unskilled workers and collective farmers very low wages, but it dangled high salaries and special privileges before its growing technical and managerial elite. This elite joined with the political and artistic elites in a new upper class, whose members were rich and powerful.

The radical transformation of Soviet society had a profound impact on women's lives. Marxists had traditionally believed that both capitalism and middle-class husbands exploited women. The Russian Revolution of 1917 immediately proclaimed complete equality of rights for women. In the 1920s divorce and abortion were made easily available, and women were urged to work outside the home. After Stalin came to power, he reversed this trend. The government now revoked many laws supporting women's emancipation in order to strengthen the traditional family and build up the state's population.

The most lasting changes for women involved work and education. Peasant women continued to work on farms, and millions of women toiled in factories and in heavy construction, building dams, roads, and steel mills in summer heat and winter frost. The Soviets also opened higher education to women, who could now enter the ranks of the better-paid specialists in industry and science. Medicine practically became a woman's profession. By 1950, 75 percent of all doctors in the Soviet Union were women.

Alongside such advances, Soviet society demanded great sacrifices from women. The vast majority of women had to work outside the home. Wages were so low that it was almost impossible for a family or couple to live only on the husband's earnings. Men continued to dominate the very best jobs. Finally, rapid change and economic hardship led to many broken families, creating further physical and emotional strains for women. In any event, the massive mobilization of women was a striking characteristic of the Soviet state.

Culture was thoroughly politicized for propaganda and indoctrination purposes. Party activists lectured workers in factories and peasants on collective farms while newspapers, films, and radio broadcasts endlessly recounted socialist achievements and capitalist plots. Whereas the 1920s had seen considerable experimentation in modern art and theater, in the 1930s intellectuals were ordered by Stalin to become "engineers of human minds." They were instructed to exalt the lives of ordinary workers and glorify Russian nationalism. Russian history was rewritten so that early tsars such as Ivan the Terrible and Peter the Great became worthy forerunners of the greatest Russian leader of all — Stalin. Writers and artists who could effectively combine genuine creativity and political propaganda became the darlings of the regime.

Stalin seldom appeared in public, but his presence was everywhere — in portraits, statues, books, and quotations from his "sacred" writings. Although the government persecuted religion and turned churches into "museums of atheism," the state had both an earthly religion and a high priest—Marxism-Leninism and Joseph Stalin.

Stalinist Terror and the Great Purges

In the mid-1930s, the great offensive to build socialism and a new society culminated in ruthless police terror and a massive purging of the Communist Party. First used by the Bolsheviks in the civil war to maintain their power, terror as state policy was revived in the collectivization drive against the peasants. The top members of the party and government publicly supported Stalin's initiatives, but there was some grumbling. At a small gathering in November 1932, even Stalin's wife complained bitterly about the misery of the people and the horrible famine in Ukraine. Stalin showered her with insults, and she died that same night, apparently by her own hand. In late 1934 Stalin's number-two man, Sergei Kirov, was mysteriously murdered. Although Stalin himself probably ordered Kirov's murder, he blamed the assassination on what he called "fascist agents" within the Communist Party. Stalin used the incident to launch a reign of terror that purged the party of supposed traitors and solidified his own control.

Murderous state-sponsored repression picked up steam over the next two years. It culminated in the "great purge" of 1936–1938, a series of spectacular public show trials in which false evidence, often gathered using torture, was used to incriminate party administrators and

Red Army leaders. In August 1936 sixteen "Old Bolsheviks"—prominent leaders who had been in the party since the Russian Revolution (see Chapter 26)—confessed to all manner of contrived plots against Stalin in Moscow; all were executed. Then in 1937 the secret police arrested a mass of lesser party officials and newer members, torturing them and extracting confessions for more show trials. In addition to the party faithful, union officials, managers, intellectuals, army officers, and countless ordinary citizens were accused of counterrevolutionary activities and struck down. At least 8 million people were arrested, and millions of these were executed or never returned from prisons and forced-labor camps.

Stalin and the remaining party leadership recruited 1.5 million new members to take the place of those purged. Thus more than half of all Communist Party members in 1941 had joined since the purges, and they experienced rapid social advance. Often the children of workers, they had usually studied in the new technical schools, and they soon proved capable of managing the government and large-scale production. Despite its human costs, the great purges brought substantial practical rewards to this new generation of committed communists. They would serve Stalin effectively until his death in 1953, and they would govern the Soviet Union until the early 1980s.

Stalin's mass purges remain baffling, for most historians believe that those purged posed no threat and were innocent of their supposed crimes. Certainly the highly publicized purges sent a warning to the people: no one was secure; everyone had to serve the party and its leader

Life in a Forced-Labor Camp
Deported peasants and other political prisoners work under the most dehumanizing conditions to build the Stalin–White Sea Canal in far northern Russia, around 1933. In books and plays, Stalin's followers praised the project as a model for the regeneration of "reactionaries" and "kulak exploiters" through the joys of socialist work. (David King Collection)

with redoubled devotion. Some scholars have argued that the terror was part of a fully developed totalitarian state, which must always fight real or imaginary enemies.

The long-standing interpretation that puts the blame for the great purges on Stalin has nevertheless been challenged. Some historians argue that Stalin's fears about resistance to his rule were exaggerated but real. Moreover, many in the party and in the general population shared his fears. Bombarded with ideology and political slogans, the population responded energetically to Stalin's directives. Investigations and trials snowballed into mass hysteria, resulting in a modern witch-hunt that claimed millions of victims. In this view of the 1930s, a deluded Stalin found large numbers of willing collaborators for crime as well as for achievement.[2]

Mussolini and Fascism in Italy

How did Mussolini's dictatorship come to power and govern in Italy? ■

Mussolini's fascist movement and his seizure of power in 1922 were important steps in the rise of dictatorships in Europe between the two world wars. Mussolini began his political career as a revolutionary socialist, but after World War I he turned against the working class and successfully sought the support of conservatives. Mussolini and his supporters were the first to call themselves "fascists"—revolutionaries determined to create a new totalitarian state based on extreme nationalism and militarism. Few scholars today would argue that Mussolini succeeded. His dictatorship was brutal and theatrical, but it included elements of conservative authoritarianism as well as dynamic totalitarianism.

The Seizure of Power

In the early twentieth century, Italy was a liberal state with civil rights and a constitutional monarchy. On the eve of World War I, the parliamentary regime finally granted universal male suffrage, and Italy appeared to be moving toward democracy. But there were serious problems. Much of the Italian population was still poor, and many peasants were more attached to their villages and local interests than to the national state. Moreover, the papacy, many devout Catholics, conservatives, and landowners remained strongly opposed to liberal institutions and to the

Black Shirts Mussolini's private militia that destroyed socialist newspapers, union halls, and Socialist Party headquarters, eventually pushing Socialists out of the city governments of northern Italy.

middle-class lawyers and politicians who ran the country largely for their own benefit. Relations between church and state were often tense. Class differences were also extreme, leading to the development of a powerful revolutionary socialist movement. Only in Italy among the main European countries did the radical left wing of the Socialist Party gain leadership as early as 1912, and only in Italy did the Socialist Party unanimously oppose World War I from the very beginning.

The war worsened the political situation. Having fought on the side of the Allies almost exclusively for purposes of territorial expansion, the parliamentary government bitterly disappointed Italian nationalists with Italy's modest gains at Versailles. Workers and peasants also felt cheated: to win their support during the war, the government had promised social and land reform, which it did not deliver after the war.

Instead, unemployment and inflation soared after the war ended, creating mass hardship. The Russian Revolution, which promised ordinary workers a way out, energized Italy's revolutionary socialist movement. The Italian Socialist Party followed the Bolshevik example, and radical workers and peasants began occupying factories and seizing land in 1920. These actions scared and mobilized the property-owning classes. Moreover, after the war the pope lifted his ban on participation by Catholics in Italian politics, and a strong Catholic party quickly emerged. Thus by 1921 revolutionary socialists, antiliberal conservatives, and anxious property owners were all opposed—though for different reasons—to the liberal parliamentary government.

Into these crosscurrents of unrest and fear stepped the blustering, bullying Benito Mussolini (1883–1945). Son of a village schoolteacher and a poor blacksmith, Mussolini began his political career as a Socialist Party leader and radical newspaper editor before World War I. In 1914, powerfully influenced by antidemocratic cults of violent action, the young Mussolini urged that Italy join the Allies, a stand for which he was expelled from the Italian Socialist Party. Later Mussolini fought at the front and was wounded in 1917. Returning home, he began organizing bitter war veterans like himself into a band of fascists—from the Italian word for "a union of forces."

At first Mussolini's program was a radical combination of nationalist and socialist demands, including territorial expansion, benefits for workers, and land reform for peasants. As such, it competed directly with the well-organized Socialist Party and failed to get off the ground. When Mussolini saw that his violent verbal assaults on rival Socialists won him growing support from conservatives and the frightened middle classes, he shifted gears in 1920 and became a sworn enemy of socialism.

Mussolini and his private militia of **Black Shirts** grew increasingly violent. Typically, a band of fascist toughs would roar off in trucks at night and swoop down on a few isolated Socialist organizers, beating them up and force-feeding them almost deadly doses of castor oil. Few people were killed, but socialist newspapers, union halls, and local Socialist Party headquarters were destroyed, and the Black Shirts managed to push Socialists out of city governments in northern Italy.

Fascism soon became a mass movement. A skillful politician, Mussolini convinced his followers that they were not just opposing the "Reds" but also making a revolution of their own, forging a strong, dynamic movement that would help the little people against the established interests. As the government collapsed in 1922, largely because of the chaos created by his Black Shirt militias, Mussolini stepped forward as the savior of order and property. Striking a conservative note in his speeches and gaining the support of army leaders, Mussolini demanded the resignation of the existing government. In October 1922 a band of armed fascists marched on Rome to threaten the king and force him to appoint Mussolini prime minister of Italy. The threat worked. Victor Emmanuel III (r. 1900–1946), who had no love for the old liberal politicians, asked Mussolini to take over the government and form a new cabinet. Thus, af-

ter widespread violence and a threat of armed uprising, Mussolini seized power using the legal framework of the Italian constitution.

The Regime in Action

Mussolini became prime minister in 1922, yet his long-term political intentions were by no means clear until 1924. Some of his radical Black Shirt supporters wished to immediately construct a revolutionary fascist state. Mussolini's ministers, however, included old conservatives, moderates, and even Socialists, and he at first moved cautiously to establish control. He promised a "return to order" and consolidated his support among Italian elites. Fooled by Mussolini's apparent moderation, the Italian parliament passed a new electoral law that gave two-thirds of the representatives in the parliament to the party that won the most votes. This change allowed the Fascist Party and its allies to win an overwhelming majority in April 1924. Shortly thereafter, a group of fascist extremists kidnapped and murdered the Socialist politician Giacomo Matteotti (JAHK-oh-moh mat-tee-OH-tee). This outrage alarmed Mussolini's opponents, and a group of prominent

Fascist Youth on Parade Totalitarian governments in Italy and Nazi Germany established mass youth organizations to instill the values of national unity and train young soldiers for the state. These members of the Balila, Italy's fascist youth organization, raise their rifles in salute at a mass rally in 1939. (Hulton-Deutsch Collection/Corbis)

parliamentary leaders demanded that Mussolini's armed squads be dissolved and all violence be banned.

Mussolini may not have ordered Matteotti's murder, but he took advantage of the resulting political crisis. After first hesitating, he charged forward. Declaring his desire to "make the nation Fascist," he imposed a series of repressive measures. The government ruled by decree, abolished freedom of the press, and organized fixed elections. Mussolini arrested his political opponents, disbanded all independent labor unions, and put dedicated Fascists in control of Italy's schools. Mussolini trumpeted his goal in a famous slogan of 1926: "Everything in the state, nothing outside the state, nothing against the state." By the end of that year, Italy was a one-party dictatorship under Mussolini's unquestioned leadership.

Mussolini's Fascist Party drew support from broad sectors of the population, in large part because he was willing to compromise with the traditional elites that controlled the army, the economy, and the state. He never tried to purge these groups or even move very vigorously against them. He left big business to regulate itself, and there was no land reform. Mussolini also drew increasing support from the Catholic Church. In the **Lateran Agreement** of 1929, he recognized the Vatican as a tiny independent state, and he agreed to give the church significant financial support. The pope expressed his satisfaction and urged Italians to support Mussolini's government. Because he was forced to compromise with these conservative elites, Mussolini never established complete totalitarian control.

Mussolini's government nonetheless proceeded with attempts to bring fascism to Italy. The state engineered popular consent by staging massive rallies and sporting events, creating fascist youth and women's movements, and providing new welfare benefits. Newspapers, radio, and film promoted a "cult of the Duce" (leader), portraying Mussolini as a powerful strongman who embodied the highest qualities of the Italian people.

Like other fascist regimes, Mussolini's government was vehemently opposed to liberal feminism and promoted instead traditional gender roles. The "new fascist man" was supposed to be a virile, patriotic warrior; at the same time his wife was the guardian of the home who raised children to support the values of the fascist state. Some women found great satisfaction in their devotion to family, national service, and the Italian "race":

> *Be it in the family, be it in the state, we Italian women are always ready to sacrifice petty personal vanity and outward appearances to collaborate effectively with work and advice toward spiritual unity, toward real uplift, with absolute dedication of our persons to the Chief [Mussolini] to whom we have vowed our faith and our love.*[3]

Mussolini also gained popularity by manipulating popular pride in the grand history of the ancient Roman Empire. "Fascism, in its entirety, is the resurrection of Roman-ness," wrote one enthusiast. Propagandists criticized liberalism and parliamentary government as foreign imports that violated "Roman" traditions.[4]

Mussolini matched his aggressive rhetoric with military action: Italian armies invaded the African nation of Ethiopia in October 1935. After surprising setbacks at the hands of the poorly armed Ethiopian army, the Italians won in 1936, and Mussolini could proudly declare that Rome again had its empire. The brutal colonial war shocked international opinion and cemented ties between Italy and Nazi Germany. After a visit to Berlin in the fall of 1937, the Italian dictator pledged support for Hitler and promised that Italy and Germany would "march together right to the end."[5]

Deeply influenced by Hitler's example (see below), Mussolini's government passed a series of anti-Jewish racial laws in 1938. The laws were unpopular, and the fascist government did not aggressively persecute Jews until late in World War II, when Italy was under Nazi control. Nor did Mussolini establish a truly ruthless police state. Only twenty-three political prisoners were condemned to death between 1926 and 1944. Mussolini's fascist Italy, though repressive and undemocratic, was never really totalitarian.

Italy's Ethiopian Campaign, 1935–1936

SUDAN (Gr. Br.)
ERITREA (It.)
FRENCH SOMALILAND
Addis Ababa
BRITISH SOMALILAND
ETHIOPIA
ITALIAN SOMALILAND
KENYA (Gr. Br.)
INDIAN OCEAN

→ Italian campaigns, 1935–1936

Lateran Agreement A 1929 agreement that recognized the Vatican as an independent state, with Mussolini agreeing to give the church heavy financial support in return for public support from the pope.

Hitler and Nazism in Germany

How did Hitler gain power, what policies did totalitarian Nazi Germany pursue, and why did they lead to World War II? ■

The most frightening dictatorship developed in Nazi Germany. A product of Hitler's tactical genius as well as of Germany's social and political situation, National Socialism (or Nazism) shared some of the characteristics of Italian fascism. But Nazism was far more interventionist than its Italian counterpart. Under Hitler, the Nazi dictatorship smashed or took over most independent organizations, established firm control over the German state and society, and violently persecuted the Jewish population. Truly totalitarian in its aspirations, the dynamism of Nazi Germany, based on racial aggression and territorial expansion, led to history's most destructive war.

The Roots of National Socialism

National Socialism grew out of many complex developments, of which the most influential were extreme nationalism and racism. These two ideas captured the mind of the young Adolf Hitler (1889–1945), and he dominated Nazism until the end of World War II.

The son of a successful Austrian customs official, Hitler spent his childhood in small towns in Austria. He was a mediocre student who dropped out of high school at age fourteen. Hitler then moved to Vienna, where he was exposed to extreme Austro-German nationalists who believed Germans to be a superior people and the natural rulers of central Europe. They advocated union with Germany and violent expulsion of "inferior" peoples as the means of maintaining German domination of the Austro-Hungarian Empire.

In Vienna Hitler eagerly absorbed this virulent anti-Semitism and a deep hatred of Slavs. He developed an unshakable belief in the crudest distortions of Social Darwinism (see Chapter 25), the superiority of Germanic races, and the inevitability of racial conflict. The Jews, he claimed, directed an international conspiracy of finance capitalism and Marxian socialism against German culture, German unity, and the German people.

Hitler was not alone. Racist anti-Semitism became wildly popular on the far right wing of European politics in the decades surrounding the First World War. Such irrational beliefs, rooted in centuries of Christian anti-Semitism, were given pseudoscientific legitimacy by nineteenth-century developments in biology and eugenics. These ideas came to define Hitler's worldview and would play an immense role in the ideology and actions of National Socialism.

Hitler greeted the outbreak of the First World War as a salvation. The struggle and discipline of war gave life meaning, and Hitler served bravely as a dispatch carrier on the western front. When Germany was defeated

Events Leading to World War II

1919	Treaty of Versailles is signed
1920	Founding of National Socialist German Workers' Party (Nazis)
1922	Mussolini seizes power in Italy
1927	Stalin takes full control in the Soviet Union
1929–1939	Great Depression
1931	Japan invades Manchuria
January 1933	Hitler is appointed chancellor of Germany
March 1933	Reichstag passes the Enabling Act, granting Hitler absolute dictatorial power
October 1933	Germany withdraws from the League of Nations
1935	Nuremberg Laws deprive Jews of all rights of citizenship
March 1935	Hitler announces German rearmament
October 1935	Mussolini invades Ethiopia and receives Hitler's support
March 1936	German armies move unopposed into the demilitarized Rhineland
1936–1939	Civil war in Spain, culminating in taking of power by fascist regime under Franco
October 1936	Rome-Berlin Axis created
1937	Japan invades China
March 1938	Germany annexes Austria
September 1938	Munich Conference: Britain and France agree to German seizure of the Sudetenland from Czechoslovakia
March 1939	Germany occupies the rest of Czechoslovakia; appeasement ends in Britain
August 1939	Nazi-Soviet pact is signed
September 1, 1939	Germany invades Poland
September 3, 1939	Britain and France declare war on Germany

in 1918, Hitler's world was shattered. Convinced that Jews and Marxists had "stabbed Germany in the back," he vowed to fight on.

In late 1919 Hitler joined a tiny extremist group in Munich called the German Workers' Party. In addition to denouncing Jews, Marxists, and democrats, the German Workers' Party promised a uniquely German National Socialism that would abolish the injustices of capitalism and create a mighty "people's community." By 1921 Hitler had gained absolute control of this small but growing party, which had been renamed the National Socialist German Workers' Party, or Nazis, in 1920. Hitler became a master of mass propaganda and political showmanship. In wild, histrionic speeches, he worked his

National Socialism A movement born of extreme nationalism and racism, led by Adolf Hitler, that ruled Germany from 1933 to 1945 and forced Europe into the Second World War.

audience into a frenzy with demagogic attacks on the Versailles treaty, Jews, war profiteers, and Germany's Weimar Republic.

Party membership multiplied tenfold after early 1922. In late 1923 the Weimar Republic seemed on the verge of collapse, and Hitler, inspired by Mussolini's recent victory, organized an armed uprising in Munich—the so-called Beer Hall Putsch. Despite the failure of the poorly planned coup and Hitler's arrest, National Socialism had been born.

Hitler's Road to Power

At his trial, Hitler violently denounced the Weimar Republic, and he gained enormous publicity. From the failed revolt, Hitler concluded that he had to come to power through electoral competition rather than armed rebellion. He used his brief prison term to dictate his book *Mein Kampf* (My Struggle). Here Hitler laid out his basic ideas on "racial purification" and territorial expansion that would increasingly define National Socialism.

In *Mein Kampf* Hitler claimed that Germans were a "master race" that needed to defend its "pure blood" from groups he labeled "racial degenerates," including Jews, Slavs, and others. The German race was destined to triumph and grow, and, according to Hitler, it needed *Lebensraum* (living space). This space could be found to Germany's east, in central Europe, which Hitler claimed was inhabited by the "subhuman" Slavs and Jews. The future dictator portrayed a sweeping vision of war and conquest in which the German master race would colonize and ultimately replace these "subhumans" across east-central Europe. He championed the idea of the leader-dictator or *Führer* (FYOUR-uhr), whose unlimited power would embody the people's will and lead the German nation to victory. These ideas—a deadly combination of race and space—would ultimately propel Hitler's Germany into the Second World War.

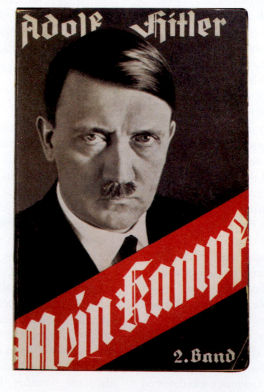

Cover of Hitler's *Mein Kampf* Nazi dictator Adolf Hitler wrote *Mein Kampf* (My Struggle) in 1923 while serving a prison sentence for armed rebellion against the democratic German government. The book, which sold millions of copies during Hitler's rule, presents his detailed plans for the "racial purification" of Germany and the expansion of the German state. How does the cover photo convey the idea of powerful leadership? (Bildarchiv Preussischer Kulturbesitz/Art Resource, NY)

In the years of relative prosperity and stability between 1924 and 1929, Hitler built up the Nazi Party. By 1928 it had a hundred thousand members. To appeal to middle-class voters, Hitler de-emphasized the anti-capitalist elements of National Socialism and vowed to fight communism. The Nazis still remained a small splinter group in 1928, when they received only 2.6 percent of the vote in the general elections and twelve seats in the Reichstag, the German parliament. There the Nazi deputies pursued the legal strategy of using democracy to destroy democracy.

The Great Depression of 1929 brought the ascent of National Socialism. Now Hitler promised German voters economic as well as political salvation. His appeals for "national rebirth" appealed to a broad spectrum of voters, including middle- and lower-middle-class groups—small business owners, officeworkers, artisans, and peasants—as well as skilled workers striving for middle-class status. Seized by panic as bankruptcies increased, unemployment soared, and the communists made dramatic election gains, voters deserted the conservative and moderate parties for the Nazis. In the election of 1930 the Nazis won 6.5 million votes and 107 seats, and in July 1932 they gained 14.5 million votes—38 percent of the total. They were now the largest party in the Reichstag.

The breakdown of democratic government helped the Nazis seize power. Unable to gain the support of a majority in the Reichstag, in summer 1930 Chancellor Heinrich Brüning (BROU-nihng) dissolved the parliament. He convinced the president, the aging war hero General Hindenburg, to authorize rule by decree under Article 48 of the constitution, which allowed the central government to govern without the consent of the parliament. Brüning tried to overcome the economic crisis by cutting back government spending and ruthlessly forcing down prices and wages. His conservative policies intensified Germany's economic collapse and convinced many voters that the country's republican leaders were stupid and corrupt, adding to Hitler's appeal.

Division on the left also contributed to Nazi success. Even though the two left-wing parties together outnumbered the Nazis in the Reichstag, the Communists refused to cooperate with the Social Democrats. German communists had long competed with the socialists for the allegiance of the working classes. Now in the crisis of the early 1930s, they failed to resolve their differences and mount an effective opposition to the Nazi takeover.

Finally, Hitler excelled in the dirty backroom politics of the decaying Weimar Republic. In 1932 Hitler cleverly gained the support of conservative politicians and key leaders in the army and big business. These people thought they could use Hitler for their own advantage, to resolve the political crisis, but also to get increased military spending, fat contracts, and tough measures against workers. They accepted Hitler's demand to be appointed chancellor in a coalition government, reasoning that he could be used and controlled. On January 30, 1933, Adolf Hitler, leader of the largest party in Germany, was legally appointed chancellor by President Hindenburg.

State and Society in Nazi Germany

Hitler moved rapidly and skillfully to establish an unshakable dictatorship that would pursue the Nazi program of race and space. First, Hitler and the Nazi Party worked to consolidate their power. To maintain legal appearances, Hitler called for new elections. In February 1933, in the midst of a violent electoral campaign, the Reichstag building was partly destroyed by fire. Hitler blamed the Communist Party, and he convinced President Hindenburg to sign dictatorial emergency acts that abolished freedom of speech and assembly as well as most personal liberties.

The façade of democratic government was soon torn asunder. When the Nazis won only 44 percent of the vote in the elections, Hitler outlawed the Communist Party and arrested its parliamentary representatives. Then on March 23, 1933, the Nazis pushed through the Reichstag the so-called **Enabling Act**, which gave Hitler absolute dictatorial power for four years. Armed with the Enabling Act, the Nazis moved to smash or control all independent organizations. Their deceitful stress on legality, coupled with divide-and-conquer techniques, disarmed the opposition until it was too late for effective resistance.

Germany became a one-party Nazi state. Elections were farces. The new regime took over the government bureaucracy intact, installing Nazis in top positions. At the same time, they created a series of overlapping Nazi Party organizations responsible solely to Hitler. As research in recent years has shown, the resulting system of dual government was riddled with rivalries, contradictions, and inefficiencies. The Nazi state was often disorganized and lacked the all-encompassing unity that its propagandists claimed. Yet this fractured system suited Hitler and his purposes. The lack of unity encouraged competition among state personnel, who worked to outdo each other to fulfill Hitler's vaguely expressed goals. The Führer thus played the established bureaucracy against his personal party government and maintained dictatorial control.

Once the Nazis were firmly in command of the government, Hitler and the party turned their attention to constructing a National Socialist society defined by national unity and racial exclusion. First the Nazis attacked their political enemies. Communists, Social Democrats, and trade-union leaders were forced out of their jobs or arrested and taken to hastily built concentration camps. The Nazis outlawed strikes and abolished independent labor unions, which were replaced by the Nazi-controlled German Labor Front.

Hitler then purged the Nazi Party of its more extremist elements. The Nazi storm troopers (the SA), the quasi-military band of 3 million toughs in brown shirts who had fought communists and beaten up Jews before the Nazis took power, now expected top positions in the army. Some SA radicals even talked of a "second revolution" that would create equality among all Germans by sweeping away the capitalist system. Now that the Nazis were in power, however, Hitler was eager to win support of the traditional military and maintain social order. He decided that the leadership of the SA had to be eliminated. On the night of June 30, 1934, Hitler's elite personal guard — the SS — arrested and shot without trial roughly a thousand SA leaders and other political enemies. Afterward the SS grew rapidly. Under its methodical, ruthless leader Heinrich Himmler (1900–1945), the SS took over the political police and the concentration camp system.

The Nazi Party instituted a policy it called "coordination" that was meant to force society to conform to National Socialist ideology. Professional people — doctors and lawyers, teachers and engineers — saw their previously independent organizations swallowed up by Nazi associations. Publishing houses were put under Nazi control, and universities and writers were quickly brought into line. Democratic, socialist, and Jewish literature was put on ever-growing blacklists. Passionate students and pitiful professors burned forbidden books in public squares. Modern art and architecture — which the Nazis considered "degenerate" — were ruthlessly prohibited. Life became violently anti-intellectual. By 1934 a brutal dictatorship characterized by frightening dynamism and obedience to Hitler was largely in place.

Acting on its vision of racial purity, the party began a many-faceted campaign against those they deemed incapable of making a positive contribution to the "master race." The Nazis persecuted a number of

Enabling Act An act pushed through the Reichstag by the Nazis that gave Hitler absolute dictatorial power for four years.

supposedly undesirable groups based on their reputed racial characteristics. Jews headed the list, but Slavic peoples, Gypsies (Sinti and Roma), homosexuals, Jehovah's Witnesses, people considered handicapped, and a loosely defined group of so-called asocials were also targets of ostracism and brutal state-sponsored repression.

In what some historians term the Nazi "racial state," barbarism and race hatred were institutionalized with the force of science and law.[6] New university academies, such as the German Society for Racial Research, wrote studies that measured and defined racial differences; prejudice was thus presented in the guise of enlightened science, a means for creating a strong national race. The ethical breakdown was exemplified in a series of sterilization laws, which led to the forced sterilization of some four hundred thousand "undesirable" citizens.

From the beginning, German Jews were a special object of Nazi persecution. By the end of 1934, most Jewish lawyers, doctors, professors, civil servants, and musicians had been banned from their professions. In 1935 the infamous Nuremberg Laws classified as Jewish anyone having three or more Jewish grandparents. The Nuremberg Laws also outlawed marriage and sexual relations between Jews and those defined as German and deprived Jews of all rights of citizenship. Conversion to Christianity and abandonment of the Jewish faith made no difference. In their commentary on the Nuremberg Laws, two leading German lawyers made the close connections between "blood" and the legal definition of citizenship quite clear:

> *What is German, and what either benefits or harms the German people and the Reich, can only be known by those of German blood. . . . Only he who is a racial comrade can be a citizen. Only one who is of German blood, no matter what his religious faith, can be a racial comrade. Therefore no Jew can be a racial comrade.*[7]

For the vast majority of German citizens not targeted by such laws, the creation of a demonized outsider group may well have contributed to feelings of national unity and support for the Hitler regime.

In late 1938 the assault on the Jews accelerated. During a well-organized wave of violence known as Kristallnacht (the night of broken glass), Nazi gangs smashed windows, looted Jewish-owned shops, and destroyed homes and synagogues. German Jews were then rounded up and made to pay for the damage. Confronted with ever-increasing prejudice, by 1939 some 300,000 of Germany's 500,000 Jews had emigrated, sacrificing almost all their property in order to leave Germany. Some Germans privately opposed these outrages, but most went along or looked the other way. This lack of opposition reflected anti-Semitism to a degree still being debated by historians, but it certainly revealed the strong popular support enjoyed by Hitler's government.

Popular Support for National Socialism

Why did millions of ordinary Germans back a brutally repressive regime? A combination of coercion and reward enlisted popular support for the racial state. Using the secret police and the growing concentration camp system in a reign of ruthless terror, the regime persecuted its political and "racial" enemies. Yet for the large majority of ordinary German citizens who were not Jews, communists, or members of other outsider groups, Hitler's government brought new opportunities. The German "master race" clearly benefited from Nazi ideologies of race and space.

Hitler had promised the masses economic recovery—"work and bread"—and he delivered. The Nazi state launched a large public works program to help pull Germany out of the depression. Work began on superhighways, offices, gigantic sports stadiums, and public housing, which created jobs and instilled pride in national recovery. By 1938 unemployment had fallen to 2 percent, and there was a shortage of workers. Thus between 1932 and 1938, the standard of living for the average employed worker increased moderately. Business profits rose sharply.

The persecution of Jews brought substantial benefits to ordinary Germans. As Jews were forced out of their jobs and then their homes, Germans stepped in to take their place. In a process known as Aryanization (named after the "Aryan master race" prized by the Nazis for their supposedly pure German blood), many Jews were forced to sell their businesses to "racially pure" Germans at rock-bottom prices. For millions of so-called Aryans, a rising standard of living—at whatever ethical price—was tangible evidence that Nazi promises were more than show and propaganda.

Economic recovery was accompanied by a great wave of social and cultural innovation intended to construct what Nazi propagandists called the *Volksgemeinschaft*—a people's community for all racially pure Germans. The party organized mass organizations to spread Nazi ideology and enlist volunteers for the Nazi cause. Millions of Germans joined the Hitler Youth, the League of German Women, and the German Labor Front. The Nazi Winter Relief charity drives, with captains on almost every block, handed out donations to the needy. Mass rallies, such as annual May Day celebrations and Nazi Party conventions in Nuremberg, brought together thousands of participants. Reports on such events in the Nazi-controlled press brought the message home to millions more.

The Nazis made great attempts to control the private lives and leisure time of ordinary Germans. State-sponsored "Strength Through Joy" programs set up exercise classes, beautified workplaces, and took working-class Germans on free vacations. A series of newly invented holidays, from Hitler's birthday to "people's Christmas" encouraged Germans to celebrate the values of the racial state at home. The government promised prosperity and proudly touted a glittering array of inexpensive and enticing people's products. Items such as the Volkswagen (the people's car) were intended to link individual desires for consumer goods to the collective ideology of the people's community. (See "Living in the Past: Nazi Propaganda and Consumer Goods," page 906.) Though such programs faltered as the state turned its resources toward rearmament for the approaching war (see page 909), they suggested to all that the regime sincerely wished to improve German living standards.

Women played a special role in the Nazi state. Promising to "liberate women from women's liberation," Nazi ideologues championed a return to traditional family values. They outlawed abortion, discouraged women from holding jobs or obtaining higher education, and glorified domesticity and motherhood.

Women were cast as protectors of the hearth and home and were instructed to raise young boys and girls in accordance with Nazi ideals. In the later 1930s, facing labor shortages, the Nazis reluctantly reversed course and encouraged women to enter the labor force. At the same time, the millions of women enrolled in Nazi mass organizations, which organized charity drives and other social programs, experienced a new sense of community in public activities.

Few historians today believe that Hitler and the Nazis brought about a real social revolution, as an earlier generation of scholars often argued. Yet Hitler's rule corresponded to a time of economic growth, and Nazi propagandists continually triumphed the supposed accomplishments of the regime. The vision of the people's community, the national pride of German recovery, and the feelings of belonging created by acts of racial exclusion led many Germans to support the regime. Hitler himself remained popular with broad sections of the population well into the war.

Mothers in the Fatherland Nazi ideologues promoted strictly defined gender roles for men and women, the Nazi state implemented a variety of social programs to encourage "racially correct" women to stay home and raise "Aryan" children. This colorful poster portrays the joy of motherhood and calls for donations to the Mother and Child division of the National Socialist People's Welfare office. A woman who had four children was awarded the bronze Cross of Honor for the German Mother (above). The medal came with a letter of appreciation signed by Hitler. (poster: akg-images; medal: Private Collection/Peter Newark Military Pictures/The Bridgeman Art Library)

LIVING IN THE PAST

IT IS EASY TO FORGET THAT THE VOLKSWAGENS that zip around America's streets today got their start in Hitler's Germany, introduced as part of a Nazi campaign to provide inexpensive but attractive consumer goods to the *Volk* (the People). Marketed to Aryans, but not to Jews and other "racial enemies," the Volkswagen (or People's Car) and other People's Products, including the People's Radio, the People's Refrigerator, and even the People's Single Family Home, symbolized a return to German prosperity. As these advertisements suggest, the appeal of material abundance was a central plank in Nazi propaganda.

Despite Hitler's promise of a "new, happier age" that would "make the German people rich,"* many of these consumer goods remained out of reach of ordinary Germans. The Volkswagen was a case in point. The car was sold by subscription, and a customer made weekly deposits into a savings account. When the balance was paid off, the customer would receive a car. By the end of the Nazi regime, some 340,000 Germans had opened such savings accounts. Yet because of problems with production, the car's relatively high price, and the concentration on armaments production in the late 1930s, not even one People's Car was delivered to a private customer.

In contrast, the People's Radio was a unique success. The modest VE-301 radio was much cheaper than standard models, and between 1934 and 1942, the number of Germans who owned radios doubled. Many people could now sit at home and listen to broadcasts ranging from popular and classical music to speeches from regime leaders like Minister of Propaganda Joseph Goebbels, whose tirades were so inescapable that Germans nicknamed the VE-301 the "Goebbels snout."

QUESTIONS FOR ANALYSIS

1. What do these images suggest about everyday life in Nazi Germany? What do they reveal about the aspirations of the German people for a good life in the 1930s?

2. Consider why both the government and the commercial manufacturers attached the prefix "Volk," or People, to products like the Volkswagen. What larger message did these two groups seek to convey through the use of this prefix?

3. How are these images similar to advertisements today? How are they different?

*Peter Fritzsche, *Life and Death in the Third Reich* (Cambridge, Mass.: Harvard University Press, 2008), p. 59.

This 1938 advertisement for the Volkswagen, produced by the Nazi Strength Through Joy organization, highlights the pleasures of a family vacation. (Deutsches Historisches Museum, Berlin/DHM Sebastian Ahlers/The Bridgeman Art Library)

"All Germany listens to the Führer on the People's Radio." (poster: Bundesarchiv Koblenz Plak 003-022-025; radio: Victoria & Albert Museum/V&A Picture Library)

Not all Germans supported Hitler, however, and a number of German groups actively resisted him after 1933. But opponents of the Nazis were never unified, which helps account for their lack of success. In addition, the regime clamped down: tens of thousands of political enemies were imprisoned, and thousands were executed. In the first years of Hitler's rule, the principal resisters were communists and socialists in the trade unions, groups smashed by the expansion of the SS system. A second group of opponents arose in the Catholic and Protestant churches. However, their efforts were directed primarily at preserving religious life, not at overthrowing Hitler. In 1938 and again during the war, a few high-ranking army officers, who feared the consequences of Hitler's reckless aggression, plotted against him, but all were unsuccessful.

Aggression and Appeasement

The nazification of German society fulfilled only part of the larger Nazi agenda. Even as it built up the people's community, the regime aggressively pursued policies meant to achieve territorial expansion for the supposedly superior German race. At first, Hitler carefully camouflaged his expansionist foreign policy. Germany was still militarily weak, and the Nazi leader loudly proclaimed his peaceful intentions. Germany's withdrawal from the League of Nations in October 1933, however, indicated that Gustav Stresemann's policy of peaceful cooperation was dead (see Chapter 27). Then in March 1935 Hitler openly proclaimed that Germany would no longer abide by the disarmament clauses of the Treaty of Versailles. He established a military draft and began to build up the German army. France, Italy, and Great Britain protested strongly and warned against future aggressive actions.

Yet the emerging united front against Hitler quickly collapsed. Britain adopted a policy of **appeasement**, granting Hitler everything he could reasonably want (and more) in order to avoid war. British appeasement, which practically dictated French policy, was motivated in large part by the pacifism of a population still horrified by the memory of the First World War. As in Germany, many powerful conservatives in Britain underestimated Hitler. They believed that Soviet communism was the real danger and that Hitler could be used to stop it. Such strong anticommunist feelings made an alliance between the Western Powers and Stalin unlikely.

appeasement The British policy toward Germany prior to World War II that aimed at granting Hitler whatever he wanted, including western Czechoslovakia, in order to avoid war.

When Hitler suddenly marched his armies into the demilitarized Rhineland in March 1936, brazenly violating the Treaties of Versailles and Locarno (Map 28.1), Britain refused to act. France could do little without British support. Emboldened, Hitler moved ever more aggressively in international affairs. He enlisted powerful allies in the Nazi cause. Italy and Germany established the so-called Rome-Berlin Axis in 1936. Japan, also under the rule of a fascist dictatorship, joined the Axis alliance.

At the same time, Germany and Italy intervened in the Spanish civil war (1936–1939), where their military aid helped General Francisco Franco's revolutionary fascist movement defeat the democratically elected republican government. Republican Spain's only official aid in the fight against Franco came from the Soviet Union, for public opinion in Britain and especially in France was hopelessly divided on whether to intervene.

In late 1937 Hitler moved forward with plans to crush Austria and Czechoslovakia as the first step in his long-contemplated drive for living space in the east. By threatening Austria with invasion, Hitler forced the Austrian chancellor to put local Nazis in control of the government in March 1938. The next day, in the Austrian Anschluss (annexation), German armies moved in unopposed, and Austria became two more provinces of Greater Germany (see Map 28.1).

Simultaneously, Hitler demanded that territories inhabited mostly by ethnic Germans in western Czechoslovakia—the Sudetenland—be ceded to Nazi Germany. Though democratic Czechoslovakia was allied with France and the Soviet Union and prepared to defend itself, appeasement triumphed again. In September 1938 British prime minister Arthur Neville Chamberlain flew to Germany three times in fourteen days. In these negotiations, Chamberlain and the French agreed with Hitler that Germany should immediately take over the Sudetenland. Returning to London from the Munich Conference, Chamberlain told cheering crowds that he had secured "peace with honor . . . peace for our time." Sold out by the Western Powers, Czechoslovakia gave in.

Chamberlain's peace was short-lived. In March 1939 Hitler's armies invaded and occupied the rest of Czechoslovakia. The effect on Western public opinion was electrifying. This time, there was no possible rationale of self-determination for Nazi aggression, since Hitler was seizing ethnic Czechs and Slovaks as captive peoples.

Map 28.1 **The Growth of Nazi Germany, 1933–1939** Until March 1939 Hitler's conquests brought ethnic Germans into the Nazi state; then he turned on the Slavic and Jewish peoples he had always hated. He stripped Czechoslovakia of its independence and prepared to attack Poland in September 1939.

"Peace in Our Time" British prime minister Neville Chamberlain speaks at the London airport on his return from a meeting with Adolf Hitler in Munich in September 1938. In return for acceptance of the German annexation of the Czech Sudetenland, Hitler promised to halt foreign aggression, and Chamberlain famously announced that he had negotiated "peace in our time" with the Nazi leader. Less than a year later, Germany invaded Poland and Europe was at war. (Hulton Archive/Getty Images)

When Hitler next used the question of German minorities in Danzig as a pretext to confront Poland, a suddenly militant Chamberlain declared that Britain and France would fight if Hitler attacked his eastern neighbor. Hitler did not take these warnings seriously and pressed on.

In August 1939, in an about-face that stunned the world, sworn enemies Hitler and Stalin signed a so-called nonaggression pact that in fact paved the road to war. Each dictator promised to remain neutral if the other became involved in open hostilities. An attached secret protocol ruthlessly divided Poland and east-central Europe into German and Soviet zones. Stalin agreed to the pact because he remained distrustful of Western intentions and Hitler offered immediate territorial gain.

For Hitler, everything was now set. On September 1, 1939, German armies and warplanes smashed into Poland from three sides. Two days later, Britain and France, finally true to their word, declared war on Germany. The Second World War had begun.

The Second World War

How did Germany and Japan create enormous empires, and how were they defeated by the Allies? ■

Nazi Germany's unlimited ambition unleashed an apocalyptic cataclysm of world war. Hitler's armies quickly conquered much of western and eastern Europe, establishing a vast empire of death and destruction based on Nazi ideas of race and space. At the same time, Japa-

nese armies overran much of Southeast Asia and created their own racial empire. This reckless aggression brought together a coalition of unlikely but powerful allies determined to halt the advance of fascism: Britain, the United States, and the Soviet Union. After years of slaughter that decimated much of Europe and East Asia, this "Grand Alliance" decisively defeated the Axis powers.

German Victories in Europe

Using planes, tanks, and trucks in the first example of a blitzkrieg, or "lightning war," Hitler's armies crushed Poland in four weeks. While the Soviet Union quickly took its part of the booty—the eastern half of Poland and the independent Baltic states of Lithuania, Estonia, and Latvia—French and British armies prepared their defenses in the west.

In spring 1940 the Nazi lightning war struck again. After occupying Denmark, Norway, and Holland, German motorized columns broke into France through southern Belgium, split the Franco-British forces, and trapped the entire British army on the French beaches of Dunkirk. By heroic efforts, the British withdrew their troops but not their equipment, and France was taken by the Nazis. By July 1940 Hitler ruled practically all of western continental Europe. Italy was an ally; Romania, Hungary, and Bulgaria joined the Axis powers; and the Soviet Union, Spain, and Sweden were friendly neutrals. Only Britain, led by the uncompromising Winston Churchill (1874–1965), remained unconquered.

To prepare for an amphibious invasion of Britain, Germany sought to gain control of the air. In the Battle of Britain, which began in July 1940, up to a thousand

German Bombers over Warsaw Germany opened its September 1939 attack on Poland by subjecting the Polish capital to repeated bombardment. By the end of the war, both sides had engaged in massive air campaigns against civilian targets, taking the lives of millions of civilians and leading finally to the use of the atomic bomb against Japan in 1945. (INTERFOTO/Alamy)

German planes a day attacked British airfields and key factories, dueling with British defenders high in the skies. Losses were heavy on both sides. In September 1940 Hitler angrily turned from military objectives to indiscriminate bombing of British cities in an attempt to break British morale. British aircraft factories increased production, and the heavily bombed people of London defiantly dug in. By October Britain was beating Germany three to one in the air war, and the Battle of Britain was over. Unsuccessful in Britain, the Nazi war machine turned south and invaded and occupied Greece and the Balkans.

New Order Hitler's program based on racial imperialism, which gave preferential treatment to the Nordic peoples; the French, an "inferior" Latin people, occupied a middle position, and Slavs and Jews were treated harshly as "subhumans."

Hitler now allowed his lifetime obsession of creating a vast eastern European empire ruled by the master race to dictate policy. In June 1941 German armies attacked the Soviet Union along a vast front, breaking the Nazi-Soviet pact (Map 28.2). By October Leningrad was practically surrounded, most of Ukraine had been conquered, and Moscow was besieged. But the Soviets did not collapse, and when a severe winter struck German armies outfitted in summer uniforms, the invaders were stopped. Stalled in Russia, Hitler and his allies still ruled over a vast European empire stretching from the outskirts of Moscow to the English Channel. Hitler, the Nazi leadership, and the loyal German army were positioned to greatly accelerate construction of their New Order in Europe.

Europe Under Nazi Occupation

Hitler's **New Order** was based firmly on the guiding principle of National Socialism: racial imperialism. Occupied peoples were treated according to their place on the Nazi racial hierarchy. All were subject to harsh policies dedicated to ethnic cleansing and the plunder of resources for the Nazi war effort.

Within the New Order, the so-called Nordic peoples—the Dutch, Norwegians, and Danes—received preferential treatment, for the Germans believed they were racially related to the Aryan master race. Here the Nazis established puppet governments of various kinds; though most people hated the conquerors, the Nazis found collaborators willing to rule these states in accord with German needs. France was divided into two parts. The German army occupied the north, including Paris. The southeast remained nominally independent. There the aging Marshal Henri-Philippe Pétain formed a new French government—the so-called Vichy (VIH-shee) regime—that adopted many aspects of National Socialist ideology and willingly placed French Jews in the hands of the Nazis.

In all conquered territories, the Nazis used a variety of techniques to enrich Germans and support the war

Map 28.2 World War II in Europe and Africa, 1939–1945 This map shows the extent of Hitler's empire before the Battle of Stalingrad in late 1942 and the subsequent advances of the Allies until Germany surrendered on May 7, 1945. Compare this map with Map 28.1 on page 908 to trace the rise and fall of the Nazi empire over time.

Legend:
- Axis powers and their allies
- Occupied by Germany and its allies
- Allied powers and their allies
- Neutral nations
- Boundary of Greater Germany
- Major battle

Map labels and annotations:
- NORWAY, Oslo
- SWEDEN, Stockholm
- FINLAND, Helsinki
- Siege of Leningrad, Sept. 1941–Jan. 1944
- Leningrad
- Germans repulsed, Dec. 1941
- Moscow, Oct. 1941–Jan. 1942
- SOVIET UNION
- Smolensk, Tula
- Russian front, spring 1944
- ESTONIA, Riga, LATVIA, LITHUANIA
- BELARUS, Pinsk
- Kursk, July–Aug. 1943
- Siege of Stalingrad, Aug. 21, 1942–Jan. 31, 1943
- Russian front, Nov. 1942
- Dnieper, Aug.–Dec. 1943
- Russian front, Dec. 1941
- Stalingrad
- NORTHERN IRELAND
- North Sea
- DENMARK, Copenhagen
- Baltic Sea
- Germany surrenders, May 8, 1945
- Siege, Sept. 1939; Uprising, Aug.–Sept. 1944
- Posen, Warsaw
- POLAND, Kraków
- Kiev
- UKRAINE
- IRELAND
- GREAT BRITAIN
- Battle of Britain, fall 1940
- NETHERLANDS, London
- Berlin
- Russian front, Feb. 1945
- Dunkirk
- BELGIUM
- Rhine R., Vistula R.
- Invasion of Normandy, June 6, 1944
- ATLANTIC OCEAN
- Paris
- Battle of the Bulge, Dec. 1944
- Western front, Feb. 1945
- GERMANY
- SLOVAKIA
- Danube R.
- Vienna
- HUNGARY, Budapest
- Yalta
- FRANCE
- Axis troops occupy Vichy France, Nov. 10 and 11, 1942
- Vichy
- SWITZERLAND
- VICHY FRANCE
- Po R.
- Bologna
- CROATIA
- ROMANIA, Bucharest
- Danube R.
- Black Sea
- SERBIA, Sofia
- Italian front Feb. 1945
- Corsica
- ITALY
- Rome (Liberated June 1944)
- Monte Cassino, May 1944
- Salerno, Sept. 1943
- ALBANIA
- BULGARIA
- PORT. (Portugal)
- Lisbon
- Madrid
- SPAIN
- Ebro R.
- Sardinia
- Allies Invade Sicily and Italy, July–Sept. 1943
- GREECE
- Ankara
- TURKEY
- SPANISH MOROCCO, GIBRALTAR (Gr. Br.)
- Casablanca, Nov. 1942
- MOROCCO (Fr.)
- Axis troops evacuated, May 1943
- Sicily
- Sicily, July 1943
- Malta (Gr. Br.)
- Battle for Crete May 20–June 1, 1941
- Athens
- Crete (Gr.)
- Cyprus (Gr. Br.)
- SYRIA (Fr. Mandate)
- IRAQ (Br. Mandate)
- LEBANON (Fr. Mandate)
- PALESTINE (Br. Mandate)
- TRANS-JORDAN (Br. Mandate)
- ALGERIA (Vichy France)
- TUNISIA (Fr.)
- Joined Allies, Nov. 1942
- Mediterranean Sea
- El Alamein, summer 1942
- Suez Canal
- Nile R.
- Cairo
- SAUDI ARABIA
- LIBYA (It.)
- EGYPT
- Adriatic Sea
- 0   200   400 miles
- 0   200   400 kilometers

Compare this map with Map 28.1 on page 908

Mapping the Past

Map 28.2 **World War II in Europe and Africa, 1939–1945** This map shows the extent of Hitler's empire before the Battle of Stalingrad in late 1942 and the subsequent advances of the Allies until Germany surrendered on May 7, 1945. Compare this map with Map 28.1 on page 908 to trace the rise and fall of the Nazi empire over time.

ANALYZING THE MAP   What was the first country conquered by Hitler (see Map 28.1)? Locate Germany's advance and retreat on the Russian front in December 1941, November 1942, spring 1944, and February 1945. How does this compare to the position of British and American forces on the battlefield at similar points in time?

CONNECTIONS   What implications might the battle lines on February 1945 have had for the postwar settlement in Europe?

To complete this activity online, go to the Online Study Guide at bedfordstmartins.com/mckaywest.

Vichy France, 1940

effort. Occupied nations were forced to pay for the costs of the war and for the occupation itself, and the price was high. Nazi administrators stole goods and money from local Jews, set currency exchanges at favorable rates, and forced occupied peoples to accept worthless wartime scrip. Soldiers were encouraged to steal but also to purchase goods at cheap exchange rates and send them home. A flood of plunder reached Germany, which helped maintain high living standards and preserved popular morale well into the war. Nazi victory furthermore placed national Jewish populations across Europe under German control, and so eased the planning and implementation of the mass murder of Europe's Jews.

In the occupied territories on the eastern front, German rule was ruthless and deadly. From the start, the Nazi leadership had cast the war in the east as a war of annihilation. They now set out to build a vast eastern colonial empire where Jews would be exterminated and Poles, Ukrainians, and Russians would be enslaved and forced to die out. According to the plans, ethnic German peasants would resettle the resulting abandoned lands. In pursuit of such goals, large parts of western Poland were incorporated into Germany. Another part of Poland was set up as the General Government and placed under the rule of a merciless civilian administration.

With the support of military commanders, German policemen, and bureaucrats in the occupied territories, Nazi administrators and Himmler's elite SS corps now implemented a program of destruction and annihilation to create a "mass settlement space" for racially pure Germans. Across the east, the Nazi armies destroyed cities and factories, stole crops and farm animals, and subjected conquered peoples to forced starvation and mass murder. The murderous sweep of Nazi occupation destroyed the lives of millions, as the example of

Nazi Occupation of Poland and East-Central Europe, 1939–1942

Belarus makes clear. There fewer than 7 million of the 9 million original inhabitants were still in the country when the Red Army liberated the territory in 1944. Of these, 3 million were homeless. In Belarus the Nazis killed some 700,000 Soviet prisoners of war, 550,000 Jews, 340,000 peasants and refugees, and 100,000 members of other groups. In addition more than 380,000 people were transported to Germany to work as forced laborers.[8]

In response to such atrocities, small but determined underground resistance groups fought back. They were hardly unified. Communists and socialists often disagreed with more centrist or nationalist groups on long-term goals and short-term tactics. In Yugoslavia, for example, communist and royalist military resistance groups attacked the Germans, but also each other. The resistance nonetheless presented a real challenge to the Nazi New Order. Poland, under German occupation longer than any other nation, had the most determined and well-organized resistance. The Nazis had closed all Polish universities and outlawed national newspapers, but the Poles organized secret classes and maintained a thriving underground press. Underground members of the Polish Home Army, led by the government in exile in London, passed intelligence about German operations to the Allies and committed sabotage; communist groups in Poland likewise attacked the Nazis. The famous French resistance undertook similar actions, as did groups in Italy, Greece, Russia, and the Netherlands.

The German response was swift and deadly. The Nazi army and the SS tortured captured resistance members and executed hostages in reprisal for attacks. Responding to actions undertaken by resistance groups, the German army murdered the male populations of Lidice (Czechoslovakia) and Oradour (France) and leveled the entire towns—brutal examples of Nazi barbarism in pursuit of a racial New Order in occupied Europe.

The Holocaust

The ultimate abomination of Nazi racism was the condemnation of all European Jews and other peoples considered racially inferior to extreme racial persecution and then annihilation in the **Holocaust**, a great spasm of racially inspired mass murder that took place during the Second World War.

Immediately after taking power, the Nazis began to use social, legal, and economic means to persecute Jews and other "undesirable" groups. Between 1938 and 1940, persecution turned deadly in the Nazi euthanasia (mercy killing) campaign, an important step toward genocide. Just as Germany began the war, some 70,000 people with physical and mental disabilities were forced into special hospitals, barracks, and camps. Deemed by Nazi administrators as "unworthy lives" who might "pollute" the German race, they were murdered in cold blood. The victims were mostly ethnic Germans, and the euthanasia campaign was stopped after church leaders and ordinary families spoke out. The staff involved took what they learned in this program with them to the extermination camps the Nazis would soon build in the east (Map 28.3).

The German victory over Poland in 1939 brought some 3 million Jews under Nazi control. Jews living in German-occupied territories were soon forced to move into centralized urban areas known as ghettos. In walled-off districts in cities large and small — two of the most important were in Warsaw and Lodz — hundreds of thousands of Polish Jews were forced to live in highly crowded and unsanitary conditions, without real work or adequate sustenance. Over 500,000 people died in the Nazi ghettos.

The racial violence reached new extremes when the German war of annihilation against the Soviet Union opened in 1941. Three military death squads known as Special Action Units (*Einsatzgruppen*) and other military groups followed the advancing German armies into central Europe. With systematic intent, they moved from town to town shooting Jews and other target populations. The victims of these mobile killing units were often forced to dig their own graves in local woods or country fields before they were shot down. In this way the German armed forces murdered some 2 million innocent civilians.

In late 1941 Hitler and the Nazi leadership, in some still-debated combination, ordered the SS to implement the mass murder of all Jews in Europe. What the Nazi leadership called the "final solution of the Jewish question" had begun. The Germans set up an industrialized killing machine that remains unparalleled. The SS established an extensive network of concentration camps, industrial complexes, and railroad transport lines to imprison and murder Jews and other so-called undesirables, and to exploit their labor before they died. In the occupied eastern territories, the surviving residents of the ghettos were loaded onto trains and taken to camps such as Auschwitz-Birkenau, the best known of the Nazi killing centers, where over 1 million people — the vast majority of them Jews — were murdered in gas chambers. Some few were put to work as expendable laborers. The Jews of Germany and then of occupied western and central Europe were likewise rounded up, put on trains, and sent to the camps. Even after it was quite clear that Germany would lose the war, the killing continued.

The murderous attack on European Jews was the ultimate monstrosity of Nazi racism and racial imperialism. By 1945 the Nazis had killed about 6 million Jews. (See "Individuals in Society: Primo Levi," page 915.) Who was responsible for this terrible crime? Historians continue to debate this critical question. Some lay the

The Holocaust The Nazi drive to establish a racial empire in east-central Europe led to the Holocaust, the mass murder of approximately 6 million Jews during World War II. The Nazis also persecuted and killed millions of Slavic peoples, Gypsies (Sinta and Roma), Soviet prisoners of war, communists, and other groups deemed undesirable by the Nazi state. In this horrifying photograph, German soldiers and members of the Reich Labor Service look on as a member of a Special Action Unit (*Einsatzgruppe*) executes a Ukrainian Jew who kneels at the edge of a mass grave. (Library of Congress, LC-USZ61-671)

guilt on Hitler and the Nazi leadership, arguing that ordinary Germans had little knowledge of the extermination camps or were forced to participate by Nazi terror and totalitarian control. Other scholars conclude that far more Germans knew about and were at best indifferent to the fate of "racial inferiors."

Yet the question remains: what inspired those who actually worked

Holocaust The systematic effort of the Nazi state to exterminate all European Jews and other groups deemed racially inferior during the Second World War.

Map 28.3 **The Holocaust, 1941–1945** The leadership of Nazi Germany established an extensive network of ghettos and concentration and extermination camps to persecute their political opponents and those people deemed "racially undesirable" by the regime. The death camps, where the Nazi SS systematically murdered millions of European Jews, Soviet prisoners of war, and others, were located primarily in Nazi-occupied territories in eastern Europe, but the conditions in the concentration camps within Germany's borders were almost as brutal.

in the killing machine—the "desk murderers" in Berlin who sent trains to the east, the soldiers in the military units who shot Jews in the Polish forests, the guards at Auschwitz? Some historians believe that extremist and widely shared anti-Semitism led "ordinary Germans" to become Hitler's "willing executioners." Others argue that heightened peer pressure, the desire to advance in the ranks, and the need to prove one's strength under the most brutalizing wartime violence turned average Germans into reluctant killers. The conditioning of racist Nazi propaganda clearly played a role. Whatever the motivation, numerous Germans were somehow prepared to join the SS ideologues and perpetrate ever-greater crimes, from mistreatment to arrest to mass murder.[9]

Japanese Empire and the War in the Pacific

The racist war of annihilation in Europe was matched by racially inspired warfare in East Asia. In response to political divisions and economic crisis, a fascist government had taken control of Japan in the 1930s. As in Nazi Germany and fascist Italy, the Japanese system was highly nationalistic and militaristic and was deeply committed to imperial expansion. The Japanese shared extremist European ideas about racial hierarchy, but with a twist. According to Japanese theorists, the Asian races were far superior to western Aryans. In speeches, schools, and newspapers, ultranationalists eagerly voiced the extreme anti-Western views that had risen in the 1920s and 1930s. They glorified the warrior virtues of honor

INDIVIDUALS IN SOCIETY

MOST JEWS DEPORTED TO AUSCHWITZ WERE MURDERED as soon as they arrived, but the Nazis made some prisoners into slave laborers, and a few of them survived. Primo Levi (1919–1987), an Italian Jew who was one of these laborers, lived to become one of the most influential witnesses to the Holocaust and its death camps.

Like much of Italy's small Jewish community, Levi's family belonged to the urban professional classes. Primo graduated from the University of Turin with highest honors in chemistry in 1941. But starting in 1938, when Italy introduced racial laws, he had faced growing discrimination, and in 1943 he joined the antifascist resistance movement. Quickly captured, he was deported to Auschwitz with 650 Italian Jews in February 1944. Stone-faced SS men picked only 96 men, Levi among them, and 29 women from this transport to work in their respective labor camps; the rest were gassed upon arrival.

Levi and his fellow Jewish prisoners were kicked, punched, stripped, branded with tattoos, crammed into huts, and worked unmercifully. Hoping for some sign of prisoner solidarity in this terrible environment, Levi found only a desperate struggle of each against all and enormous status differences among prisoners. Many stunned and bewildered newcomers, beaten and demoralized by their bosses — the most privileged prisoners — simply collapsed and died. Others struggled to secure their own privileges, however small, because food rations and working conditions were so abominable that ordinary Jewish prisoners perished in two to three months.

Sensitive and noncombative, Levi found himself sinking into oblivion. But instead of joining the mass of the "drowned," he became one of the "saved" — a complicated surprise with moral implications that he would ponder all his life. As Levi explained in *Survival in Auschwitz* (1947), the usual road to salvation in the camps was some kind of collaboration with German power. Savage German criminals were released from prison to become brutal camp guards; non-Jewish political prisoners competed for jobs entitling them to better conditions; and, especially troubling for Levi, a small number of Jewish men plotted and struggled for the power of life and death over other Jewish prisoners.

Though not one of these Jewish bosses, Levi believed that he himself, like almost all survivors, had entered the "gray zone" of moral compromise. "Nobody can know for how long and under what trials his soul can resist before yielding or breaking," Levi wrote. "The harsher the oppression, the more widespread among the oppressed is the willingness, with all its infinite nuances and motivations, to collaborate."* According to Levi, there were no saints in the concentration camps: the Nazi system degraded its victims, forcing them to commit sometimes bestial acts against their fellow prisoners in order to survive.

For Levi, compromise and salvation came from his profession. Interviewed by a German technocrat for work in the camp's synthetic rubber program, Levi spoke fluent German, including scientific terminology, and so was chosen for this relatively easy labor. Work in the warm camp laboratory offered Levi opportunities to pilfer equipment that could then be traded to other prisoners for food and necessities. Levi also gained critical support from three prisoners who refused to do wicked and hateful acts. And he counted "luck" as essential for his survival: in the camp infirmary with scarlet fever in February 1945 as advancing Russian armies prepared to liberate the camp, Levi was not evacuated by the Nazis and shot to death like most Jewish prisoners.

After the war Primo Levi was haunted by the nightmare that the Holocaust would be ignored or forgotten. Ashamed that so many people whom he considered better than himself had perished, and wanting the world to understand the genocide in all its complexity so that never again would people tolerate such atrocities, he turned to writing about his experiences. He grappled tirelessly with his vision of individual choice and moral ambiguity in a hell designed to make the victims collaborate and persecute each other. Bearing witness to the Holocaust, Levi wrote and lectured tirelessly to preserve the memory of Jewish victims and guilty Nazis.

Primo Levi, who never stopped thinking, writing, and speaking about the Holocaust. (Giansanti/Corbis Sygma)

QUESTIONS FOR ANALYSIS

1. Describe Levi's experience at Auschwitz. How did camp prisoners treat each other? Why?
2. What does Levi mean by the "gray zone"?
3. Will a vivid historical memory of the Holocaust help to prevent future genocide?

*Primo Levi, *The Drowned and the Saved* (New York: Vintage, 1989), pp. 43, 60. See also Levi, *Survival in Auschwitz: The Nazi Assault on Humanity*, rev. ed. 1958 (London: Collier Books, 1961). These powerful testimonies are highly recommended.

and sacrifice and proclaimed that Japan would liberate East Asia from Western colonialists.

Japan soon acted on its racial-imperial ambitions. In 1931 Japanese armies invaded and occupied Manchuria, a vast territory bordering northeastern China. In 1937 Japan brutally invaded China itself. Seeking to cement ties with the fascist regimes of Europe, in 1940 the Japanese entered into a formal alliance with Italy and Germany, and in summer 1941 Japanese armies occupied southern portions of the French colony of Indochina (now Vietnam and Cambodia).

The goal was to establish what the Japanese called the Greater East Asia Co-Prosperity Sphere. Under the slogan "Asia for Asians," propagandists maintained that Japanese expansion was intended to liberate East Asian people from the hated Western colonialists. By promising to create a mutually advantageous union for long-term development, the Japanese tapped currents of nationalist sentiment, and most local populations were glad to see the Western Powers go.

But the Co-Prosperity Sphere was a sham. Real power remained in the hands of Japanese military commanders and their superiors in Tokyo, and the occupiers exploited local peoples for Japan's wartime needs. In addition, the Japanese often exhibited great cruelty toward civilian populations and prisoners of war, which aroused local populations against the invaders. Nonetheless, the ability of the Japanese to defeat the Western colonial powers set a powerful example for national liberation groups in East Asia in the years of decolonization that followed World War II.

Japanese expansion in the Pacific evoked a sharp response from the U.S. administration under President Roosevelt, and Japan's leaders came to believe that war with the United States was inevitable. After much debate they decided to launch a surprise attack on the U.S. fleet in Pearl Harbor in the Hawaiian Islands. On December 7, 1941, the Japanese sank or crippled every American battleship, but by chance all the American aircraft carriers were at sea and escaped unharmed. Pearl Harbor brought the Americans into the war in Europe and Asia in a spirit of anger and revenge.

As the Americans mobilized for war, Japanese armies overran more European and American colonies in Southeast Asia. By May 1942 Japan controlled a vast empire (Map 28.4) and was threatening Australia. The Americans pushed back and engaged the Japanese in a series of hard-fought naval battles. In July 1943 the Americans and their Australian allies opened a successful island-hopping campaign that slowly forced Japan out of its conquered territories. The war in the Pacific was extremely brutal—a "war without mercy," in the words of a leading American scholar—and atrocities were committed on both sides. A product of spiraling violence, mutual hatred, and dehumanizing racial stereotypes, the fighting intensified as the United States moved toward Japan.[10]

The "Hinge of Fate"

While the Nazis and the Japanese built their savage empires, Great Britain, the United States, and the Soviet Union joined together in a military pact Churchill termed the Grand Alliance. This was a matter of chance more than choice. Only the Japanese surprise attack had brought the isolationist United States into the war. Moreover, the British and Americans were determined opponents of Soviet communism, and disagreements between the Soviets and the capitalist powers sowed mutual distrust. Stalin repeatedly urged Britain and the United States to open a second front to relieve pressure on Soviet forces by attacking the Germans in western Europe, but Churchill and Roosevelt refused until the summer of 1944. Despite such tensions, the overriding goal of defeating the Axis powers brought together these reluctant allies.

To ease tensions, the Grand Alliance agreed on a policy of "Europe first." Only after Hitler was defeated would the Allies mount an all-out attack on Japan, the lesser threat. The Allies also agreed to concentrate on immediate military needs, postponing tough political questions about the eventual peace settlement that might have divided them. To further encourage mutual trust, the Allies adopted the principle of the unconditional surrender of Germany and Japan. This policy cemented the Grand Alliance because it denied Hitler any hope of dividing his foes. It also meant that Soviet and Anglo-American armies would almost certainly be forced to invade and occupy all of Germany, and that Japan would fight to the bitter end.

The military resources of the Grand Alliance were awesome. The United States harnessed its vast industrial base to wage global war and in 1943 outproduced not only Germany, Italy, and Japan, but all of the rest of the world combined. Great Britain became an impregnable floating fortress, a gigantic frontline staging area for the decisive blow to the heart of Germany. After a determined push, the Soviet Union's military strength was so great that it might well have defeated Germany without Western help. Stalin drew heavily on the heroic resolve of the Soviet people, especially those in the central Russian heartland. Broad-based Russian nationalism, as opposed to narrow communist ideology, became a powerful unifying force in what the Soviet people appropriately called the Great Patriotic War of the Fatherland.

The combined might of the Allies forced back the Nazi New Order on all fronts (see Map 28.2). In North Africa, heavy fighting between British and Axis forces had resulted in significant German advances. At the Battle of El Alamein (el al-uh-MAYN) in May 1942, British forces decisively defeated combined German and Italian armies and halted the Axis penetration of North Africa. Winston Churchill called the battle the "hinge of fate" that cemented Allied victory. Shortly

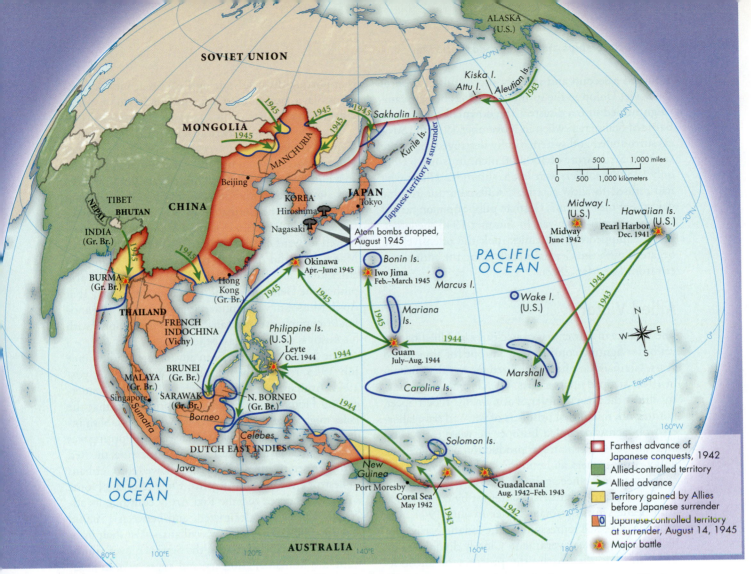

Map 28.4 World War II in the Pacific In 1942 Japanese forces overran an enormous amount of territory, which the Allies slowly recaptured in a long, bitter struggle. As this map shows, Japan still held a large Asian empire in August 1945 when the unprecedented devastation of atomic warfare suddenly forced it to surrender.

thereafter, an Anglo-American force landed in Morocco and Algeria. These French possessions, which were under the control of Pétain's Vichy government, went over to the Allies. Fearful of an Allied invasion across the Mediterranean, in November 1942 German forces occupied Vichy France, and the collaborationist French government effectively ceased to exist.

After driving the Axis powers out of North Africa, in spring 1943 U.S. and British forces invaded Sicily and then mainland Italy. Mussolini was overthrown by a coup d'état, and the new Italian government publicly accepted unconditional surrender. The Germans had anticipated such a move. Nazi armies invaded and seized control of northern and central Italy, and German paratroopers rescued Mussolini in a daring raid and put him at the head of a puppet government. Facing stiff German resistance, the Allies battled their way up the Italian peninsula. The Germans still held northern Italy, but they were clearly on the defensive.

The spring of 1943 brought crucial Allied victories at sea and in the air. In the first years of the war, Ger-

man submarines had successfully attacked North Atlantic shipping, severely hampering the British war effort. New antisubmarine technologies favored the Allies. Soon massive convoys of hundreds of ships were streaming across the Atlantic, bringing much-needed troops and supplies from the United States to Britain.

The German air force had never really recovered from its defeat in the Battle of Britain. With almost unchallenged air superiority, the United States and Britain now mounted massive bombing raids on German cities to maim industrial production and break civilian morale. By the war's end, hardly a German city of any size remained untouched, and many—including Dresden, Hamburg, Berlin, and Cologne—lay in ruins.

Great Britain and the United States had made critical advances in the western theater of operations, but the German forces suffered worse defeats at the hands of the Red Army on the eastern front. Although the Germans had almost captured the major cities of Moscow and Leningrad in early winter 1941, they were forced back by determined Soviet counterattacks. The Germans mounted a second and initially successful invasion of the Soviet Union in the summer of 1942, but the campaign turned into a disaster. The downfall came at the Battle of Stalingrad, when in November 1942 the Soviets surrounded and systematically destroyed the entire German Sixth Army of 300,000 men. In January 1943 only 123,000 soldiers were left to surrender. Hitler, who had refused to allow a retreat, suffered a catastrophic defeat. For the first time, German public opinion turned decisively against the war. In summer 1943 the larger, better-equipped Soviet armies took the offensive and began to push the Germans back along the entire eastern front (see Map 28.2).

Allied Victory

The balance of power was now clearly in Allied hands, yet bitter fighting continued in Europe for almost two years. Germany, less fully mobilized for war than Britain in 1941, stepped up its efforts. The German war industry, under the Nazi minister of armaments Albert Speer, put to work millions of prisoners of war and slave laborers from across occupied Europe. Between early 1942 and July 1944, German war production tripled despite heavy Anglo-American bombing.

German resistance against Hitler also failed to halt the fighting. An unsuccessful attempt by conservative army leaders to assassinate Hitler in July 1944 only brought increased repression by the fanatic Nazis who had taken over the government. Closely disciplined by the regime, frightened by the prospect of unconditional surrender, and terrorized by Nazi propaganda

that portrayed the advancing Russian armies as rapacious Slavic beasts, the Germans fought on with suicidal resolve.

On June 6, 1944, American and British forces under General Dwight Eisenhower landed on the beaches of Normandy, France, in history's greatest naval invasion. In a hundred dramatic days, more than 2 million men and almost half a million vehicles pushed inland and broke through the German lines. Rejecting proposals to strike straight at Berlin in a massive attack, Eisenhower moved forward cautiously on a broad front. Not until March 1945 did American troops cross the Rhine and enter Germany. By spring of 1945 the Allies had also pushed the Germans out of the Italian peninsula. That April, Mussolini was captured in northern Italy by anti-fascist communist partisans and executed, along with his mistress and other fascist leaders.

The Soviets, who had been advancing steadily since July 1943, reached the outskirts of Warsaw by August 1944. Anticipating German defeat, the Polish underground Home Army ordered an uprising, so that the Poles might take the city on their own and establish independence from the Soviets. The Warsaw Uprising was a tragic miscalculation. Citing military pressure, the Red Army refused to enter the city and allowed the Germans to destroy the Polish insurgents. Only after the Home Army surrendered did the Red Army continue its advance. Warsaw was decimated, and between 150,000 and 200,000 Poles—mostly civilians—lost their lives.

Over the next six months, the Soviets moved southward into Romania, Hungary, and Yugoslavia. In January 1945 the Red Army crossed Poland into Germany,

German Prisoners of War After the Battle of Stalingrad
Wrapped in coats and blankets to protect against the bitter Russian winter, these German prisoners of war were marched through the destroyed streets of Stalingrad after their defeat in February 1943. The battle was a major turning point that marked the start of the destruction of Nazi Germany. Hundreds of thousands of soldiers on both sides lost their lives, and of the approximately 100,000 German prisoners taken by the Red Army only about 5,000 returned home after the war. (Corbis)

Nuclear Wasteland at Hiroshima Only a handful of buildings remain standing in the ruins of Hiroshima in September 1945. Fearing the costs of a prolonged ground and naval campaign against the Japanese mainland, the United States dropped atomic bombs on Hiroshima and Nagasaki in August 1945. The bombings ended the war and opened the nuclear age. (AP Images)

and on April 26 met American forces on the Elbe River. The Allies had closed their vise on Nazi Germany and had overrun Europe. As Soviet forces fought their way into Berlin, Hitler committed suicide in his bunker, and on May 8 the remaining German commanders capitulated.

The war in the Pacific also drew to a close. In spite of repeated U.S. victories, Japanese troops had continued to fight with enormous courage and determination. American commanders believed the conquest of Japan might cost a million American casualties and claim 10 to 20 million Japanese lives. In fact, Japan was almost helpless, its industry and dense, fragile wooden cities largely destroyed by intense American bombing. Yet the Japanese seemed determined to fight on, ready to die for a hopeless cause.

On August 6 and 9, 1945, after much discussion at the upper levels of the U.S. government, American planes dropped atomic bombs on Hiroshima and Nagasaki in Japan. The mass bombing of cities and civilians, one of the terrible new practices of World War II, now ended in the final nightmare—unprecedented human destruction in a single blinding flash. On August 14, 1945, the Japanese announced their surrender. The Second World War, which had claimed the lives of more than 50 million soldiers and civilians, was over.

LOOKING BACK
LOOKING AHEAD

THE FIRST HALF of the twentieth century brought almost unimaginable violence and destruction, leading historian Eric Hobsbawm to label the era the "age of catastrophe."[11] Shaken by the rapid cultural change and economic collapse that followed the tragedy of World War I, many Europeans embraced the radical politics of communism and fascism. For some, visions of a classless society or a racially pure national community offered a way out of the age of anxiety. Totalitarian dictators like Stalin and Hitler capitalized on the desire for social order, building dictatorial regimes that demanded total allegiance to an ideological vision. Even as these regimes rewarded supporters and promised ordinary people a new age, they ruthlessly repressed their enemies, real and imagined. The vision proved fatal: the great clash of ideologies that emerged in the 1920s and 1930s led to history's most deadly war, killing millions and devastating large swathes of Europe and East Asia.

Only the reluctant Grand Alliance of the liberal United States and Great Britain with the communist Soviet Union was able to defeat the Axis powers. After 1945, fascism was finished, discredited by total defeat and the postwar revelation of the Holocaust. To make sure, the Allies would occupy the lands of their former enemies. Rebuilding a devastated Europe proved a challenging but in the end manageable task: once recovery took off, the postwar decades brought an economic boom that led to levels of prosperity unimaginable in the interwar years. Maintaining an alliance between the capitalist West and the communist East was something else. Trust quickly broke down. Europe was divided into two hostile camps, and Cold War tensions between East and West would dominate European and world politics for the next fifty years.

CHAPTER REVIEW

■ How did radical totalitarian dictatorship differ from conservative authoritarianism, and in what ways were communism and fascism totalitarian systems? (p. 888)

Conservative authoritarianism was a familiar form of government in Europe. Such states were concerned with preserving the status quo. They limited political participation but for the most part did not interfere in the lives of their citizens. Totalitarian dictatorships, such as Stalin's Soviet Union, Hitler's Germany, and to some extent Mussolini's Italy, were very different. Using censorship, propaganda, and harsh repression, communists and fascists tried to gain total control over their populations in order to construct radically new societies. Both types of totalitarian societies sought to remake state and society, but communists tried to build a classless international brotherhood of workers while fascists placed the nation above all. The Nazis, the most extreme fascists, tried to construct a state based on racial exclusion.

■ How did Stalin and the Communist Party build a modern totalitarian state in the Soviet Union? (p. 891)

Stalin consolidated his power in the 1920s, and in 1928 he launched the five-year plans. In doing so, Stalin's Soviet Union asserted a total claim on the lives of its citizens. It posed ambitious goals in the form of rapid state-directed industrialization and savage collectivization of agriculture. And it found enthusiastic supporters who believed that Stalin and the Communist Party were building their kind of socialism and a new socialist personality at home. Relentless propaganda and the great purges reinforced the party's unlimited control of its citizens.

■ How did Mussolini's dictatorship come to power and govern in Italy? (p. 898)

Mussolini began as a socialist, but he turned to the right when he received growing support from conservatives. His private militia of Black Shirts used intimidation and violence to take over the government. Coming to power "legally" with the king's help, Mussolini proclaimed the revolutionary totalitarian character of his one-party rule, implementing state control of the press and education, rigging elections, and disbanding all labor unions. Nevertheless, his fascist party received broad support, in part because he was willing to compromise with the army and business leaders. In this way, Mussolini's government retained many elements of conservative authoritarianism, such as compromising with the Catholic Church and keeping women in traditional roles.

■ How did Hitler gain power, what policies did totalitarian Nazi Germany pursue, and why did they lead to World War II? (p. 900)

Failing to overthrow the government in an attempted coup in 1923, Hitler came to power legally in 1933 by promising voters national renewal and economic recovery from the Great Depression. His policies appeared to help the economy, and he quickly established a one-party totalitarian regime with ambitious goals and widespread popular support. Through legal manipulation, repression, and violence, the Nazis controlled all aspects of the German state and society. But whereas Stalin concentrated on building socialism at home, Hitler and the Nazi elite aimed at unlimited territorial and racial aggression on behalf of a master race against Jews and other peoples they deemed undesirable. He proceeded gradually at first, and Britain and France sought to appease him with various diplomatic concessions. Hitler's unprovoked attack on Poland in 1939 brought a military response from Britain and France and the beginning of World War II.

■ **How did Germany and Japan create enormous empires, and how were they defeated by the Allies? (page 909)**

Germany used force to implement a policy of territorial expansion based on race and space, first with the Western European democracies, then with its eastern neighbors in a quest to create living space for a German master race. Hitler's forces overran much of western and eastern Europe, plundered the occupied territories to enrich Germans and support the war effort, and annihilated millions of Jews and other "subhumans." Allied with Germany after Pearl Harbor, Japan too had racial-imperial ambitions and used its army to invade Manchuria, China, and other parts of Southeast Asia in order to create a Japanese empire under the pretense of "Asia for Asians." But unlimited aggression unwittingly forged a mighty coalition led by Britain, the Soviet Union, and the United States. This Grand Alliance held together to smash the racist Nazi empire in Europe and destroy Japan's vast, overextended empire in the Pacific.

Suggested Reading

Aly, Götz. *Hitler's Beneficiaries: Plunder, Racial War, and the Nazi Welfare State*. 2005. A controversial interpretation of popular support for the Hitler regime focused on the material benefits of wartime plunder.

Applebaum, Anne. *Gulag: A History*. 2004. An excellent study of Soviet police terror.

Bergen, Doris. *War and Genocide: A Concise History of the Holocaust*, 2d ed. 2009. A concise and accessible discussion of National Socialism and the murderous Nazi assault on European Jews and other groups.

Bosworth, R. J. B. *Mussolini's Italy: Life Under the Fascist Dictatorship, 1915–1945*. 2007. An outstanding study of Italy under Mussolini.

Browning, Christopher R. *Ordinary Men: Reserve Police Battalion 101 and the Final Solution in Poland*, 2d ed. 2001. A carefully researched, unnerving account of German atrocities in Poland during World War II.

Burleigh, Michael. *The Third Reich: A New History*. 2001. A splendid accomplishment that refurbishes the concept of totalitarianism.

Conquest, Robert. *The Great Terror: A Reassessment*. 1991. An excellent account of Stalin's purges of the 1930s.

Fitzpatrick, Sheila, and Michael Geyer, eds. *Beyond Totalitarianism: Stalinism and Nazism Compared*. 2009. A collection of essays that challenges the usefulness of the totalitarian model by comparing the two dictatorships.

Kaplan, Marion A. *Between Dignity and Despair: Jewish Life in Nazi Germany*. 1998. A deeply moving book about the Jewish response to the Holocaust, with a compelling focus on women's history.

Kotkin, Stephen. *Magnetic Mountain: Stalinism as Civilization*. 1995. An extraordinary account of Stalinism and forced industrialization in the 1930s.

Merridale, Catherine. *Ivan's War: Life and Death in the Red Army, 1939–1945*. 2007. A fascinating account of ordinary Soviet soldiers.

Ransel, David L. *Village Mothers: Three Generations of Change in Russia and Tataria*. 2005. A pathbreaking study based on oral histories made in the 1990s.

Roberts, David D. *The Totalitarian Experiment in Twentieth-Century Europe: Understanding the Poverty of Great Politics*. 2006. Makes a case for the totalitarian model by comparing Stalinism, Nazism, and Italian fascism.

Weinberg, Gerhard L. *World at Arms: A Global History of World War II*, new ed. 2005. A masterful military history of World War II that places Europe in global context.

Williamson, D. G. *The Age of the Dictators: A Study of the European Dictatorships, 1918–53*. 2007. An accessible overview.

Notes

1. Quoted in S. Kotkin, *Magnetic Mountain: Stalinism as a Civilization* (Berkeley: University of California Press, 1997), pp. 221–222.
2. R. Thurston, *Life and Terror in Stalin's Russia, 1934–1941* (New Haven, Conn.: Yale University Press, 1996), esp. pp. 16–106; also M. Malia, *The Soviet Tragedy: A History of Socialism in Russia, 1917–1991* (New York: Free Press, 1995), pp. 227–270.
3. Quoted in V. de Grazia, *How Fascism Ruled Women: Italy, 1922–1945* (Berkeley: University of California Press, 1992), p. 236.
4. Quoted in C. Duggan, *A Concise History of Italy* (New York: Cambridge University Press, 1994), p. 227.
5. Quoted in ibid, p. 234.
6. M. Burleigh and W. Wippermann, *The Racial State: Germany 1933–1945* (New York: Cambridge University Press, 1991).
7. W. Stuckart and H. Globke, "Commentary on the German Racial Law" (1936), quoted in G. Mosse, *Nazi Culture: A Documentary History* (New York: Schocken, 1981), p. 332.
8. On the German occupation of Belarus, see C. Gerlach, "German Economic Interests, Occupation Policy, and the Murder of the Jews in Belorussia, 1941–43," in U. Herbert, ed., *National Socialist Extermination Policies: Contemporary German Perspectives and Controversies* (New York: Berghan Books, 2000), pp. 210–239. See also M. Allen, *The Business of Genocide: The SS, Slave Labor, and the Concentration Camps* (Chapel Hill: University of North Carolina Press, 2002), pp. 270–285.
9. D. Goldhagen, *Hitler's Willing Executioners: Ordinary Germans and the Holocaust* (New York: Vintage Books, 1997); for an alternate explanation see C. Browning, *Ordinary Men: Reserve Police Battalion 101 and the Final Solution in Poland* (New York: Harper, 1992).
10. J. Dower, *War Without Mercy: Race and Power in the Pacific War* (New York: Pantheon, 1986).
11. E. Hobsbawm, *The Age of Extremes: A History of the World, 1914–1991* (New York: Vintage, 1996), p. 21.

Key Terms

totalitarianism (p. 888)
fascism (p. 889)
eugenics (p. 889)
five-year plan (p. 891)
New Economic Policy (NEP) (p. 891)
collectivization of agriculture (p. 893)
kulaks (p. 893)
Black Shirts (p. 898)
Lateran Agreement (p. 900)
National Socialism (p. 901)
Enabling Act (p. 903)
appeasement (p. 907)
New Order (p. 910)
Holocaust (p. 912)

For practice quizzes and other study tools, visit the Online Study Guide at **bedfordstmartins.com/mckaywest**.

For primary sources from this period, see ***Sources of Western Society*, Second Edition**.

For Web sites, images, and documents related to topics in this chapter, visit Make History at **bedfordstmartins.com/mckaywest**.

29
Cold War Conflict and Consensus

1945–1965

The defeat of the Nazis and their allies in 1945 left Europe in ruins, but also laid the basis for one of Western civilization's most remarkable recoveries. In the immediate postwar years, Europeans struggled to overcome the effects of rampant death and destruction, and the victorious Allies worked to shape an effective peace treaty. Disagreements between the Soviet Union and the Western allies emerged during the peace process and quickly led to an apparently endless Cold War between the two new superpowers — the United States and the Soviet Union.

Europe was divided into a Soviet-aligned Eastern bloc and a U.S.-aligned Western bloc, and Cold War rivalry spurred military, economic, and technological competition. Amid these overarching tensions, battered western Europe fashioned a great renaissance, building strong democratic institutions and vibrant economies. After a period of political repression, the Soviet Union and the East Bloc also saw some reforms, leading to stability there as well.

But the postwar period was by no means peaceful. Anti-Soviet uprisings across eastern Europe led to military intervention and tragedy for thousands. Colonial independence movements in the developing world sometimes erupted in violence, even after liberation was achieved. Cold War hostilities had an immense impact on the decolonization process, often to the detriment of formerly colonized peoples.

Global Cold War conflicts notwithstanding, the postwar decades witnessed the construction of a surprisingly durable consensus in both communist eastern Europe and liberal western Europe. At the same time, changing class structures, new roles for women and youths, and new migration patterns had a profound impact on European society, laying the groundwork for major transformations in the decades to come. ∎

Georgios Makkas/Alamy

Life in Eastern Europe. This relief sculpture, a revealing example of socialist realism from 1952 that portrays a mail carrier, industrial workers, and peasants, adorns the wall of the central post office in Banská Bystrica, a regional capital in present-day Slovakia (the former Czechoslovakia). Citizens in the Soviet satellite nations of the East Bloc frequently saw similar works of public art, which idealized the dignity of ordinary laborers and the advantages of communism.

CHAPTER PREVIEW

Postwar Europe and the Origins of the Cold War
■ How did the events at the close of World War II contribute to the emergence of the Cold War, and how did the U.S.-Soviet rivalry affect life in Europe?

The Western Renaissance
■ Why did western Europe recover so successfully, and what were the sources of postwar stability?

Soviet Eastern Europe
■ What was the pattern of postwar rebuilding and development in the Soviet Union and communist eastern Europe?

The End of Empires
■ What circumstances led to the postwar colonial independence movements, and how did the Cold War influence the process?

Postwar Social Transformations
■ How did large-scale changes in social structures and relations contribute to European stability on both sides of the iron curtain?

Postwar Europe and the Origins of the Cold War

How did the events at the close of World War II contribute to the emergence of the Cold War, and how did the U.S.-Soviet rivalry affect life in Europe? ■

In 1945 triumphant American and Soviet soldiers came together and embraced on the banks of the Elbe River in the heart of vanquished Germany. At home, in the United States and in the Soviet Union, the soldiers' loved ones erupted in joyous celebration. Yet millions had perished in the war, Europe was devastated, and countless refugees wandered through the rubble.

The victors now faced the momentous challenges of rebuilding the shattered European nations, dealing with Nazi criminals, and creating a lasting peace. Reconstruction began, and war crimes were punished, but the Allies failed to truly cooperate in peacemaking. Motivated by different goals and hounded by misunderstandings, the United States and the Soviet Union soon found themselves at loggerheads. By the end of 1947 Europe was rigidly divided into East and West Blocs allied with the Soviet Union and the United States, respectively. The resulting Cold War was waged around the world for the next forty years as the competing superpowers engaged in an all-out competition for political, military, and technological superiority.

The Legacies of the Second World War

In the summer of 1945 Europe lay in ruins. Across the continent, the fighting had destroyed cities and landscapes and had obliterated buildings, factories, farms, rail tracks, roads, and bridges. Many cities — including Leningrad, Warsaw, Vienna, Budapest, Rotterdam, and Coventry — were completely devastated. Surviving cities such as Prague and Paris were left relatively unscathed, mostly by chance. The Germans had engaged in bombing attacks against London and other cities, destroying vast swathes of property and killing tens of thousands of innocent civilians. Allied air assaults on civilian targets were even more destructive. British and American bombers had flattened Hamburg, Dresden, and other German cities large and small, with great loss of life. As opposing armies seesawed between Warsaw and Moscow, the scorched earth policy had left few buildings stand-

Displaced Persons in the Ruins of Berlin The end of the war in 1945 stopped the fighting, but not the suffering. For the next two years, millions of displaced persons wandered the streets of Europe searching for sustenance, lost family members, and a place to call home. (Fred Rampage/Getty Images)

ing. Postwar observers compared the remaining rubble piles to moonscapes.

The human costs of the Second World War are almost incalculable (Map 29.1). The death toll far exceeded the mortality figures for World War I. The war killed at least 20 million Soviets, including soldiers and civilians. Between 9 and 11 million noncombatants lost their lives in Nazi concentration camps, including 6 million Jews and over 220,000 Sinti and Roma Gypsies. One out of every five Poles died in the war, including 3 million of Poland's 3.25 million Jews. German deaths numbered 5 million, only 3 million of them soldiers. France and Britain both lost fewer soldiers than in World War I, but the British civilian population suffered 60,000 dead and 300,000 wounded. Over 400,000 U.S. soldiers died in the European and Pacific campaigns, and other nations across Europe and the globe also lost staggering numbers. The best estimates are that about 50 million human beings perished in the conflict.

The destruction of war furthermore left tens of millions homeless—25 million in the Soviet Union and 20 million in Germany alone, joined by countless French, Czechs, Poles, Italians, and others. The wartime policies of Hitler and Stalin had forced some 30 million people from their homes in the hardest hit nations of east-central Europe. The end of the war and the start of the peace increased their numbers. Some 13 million ethnic Germans fled west before the advancing Soviet troops or were forced to leave the states of eastern Europe under the terms of the peace accords. Forced laborers from Poland, France, the Balkans, and other nations, brought to Germany by the Nazis, now sought to go home. A woman in Berlin described the flow of refugees passing through the city in spring 1945:

> The streets were filled with small, tired caravans of people. . . . Most were headed east. All the vehicles looked the same: pitiful handcarts piled high with sacks, crates, and trunks. Often I saw a woman or an older child in front, harnessed to a rope, pulling the cart forward, with the smaller children or a grandpa pushing from behind. There were people perched on top, too, usually very little children or elderly relatives. The old people look terrible amid all the junk, the men as well as the women—pale, dilapidated, apathetic. Half-dead sacks of bones.[1]

These **displaced persons** or DPs—their numbers increased by concentration camp survivors, released prisoners of war, and hundreds of thousands of orphaned children—searched for food and shelter. From 1945 to 1947 the newly established United Nations Relief and Rehabilitation Administration (UNRRA) opened over 760 DP camps and spent $10 billion to house, feed, clothe, and repatriate the refugees.

For DPs, going home was not always the best option. Soviet and Eastern European nationals who had spent time in the West were seen as politically unreliable by the new Stalinist regimes of the Soviet bloc. Many faced prison terms, exile to labor camps in the Siberian gulag, and even execution upon their return. Jewish DPs faced unique problems. Their communities had been destroyed, there was persistent anti-Semitism, and for the most part they were not welcome in their former homelands. Many stayed in special Jewish DP camps in Germany for years. After the creation of Israel in 1948 (see page 947), over 330,000 European Jews left the continent where they had experienced so much suffering and destruction for the new Jewish state. By 1957, when the last DP camp closed, the UNRRA had cared for and resettled many millions of refugees under the most difficult conditions.

Postwar authorities were also left to deal with the crimes committed by the Nazis. Across Europe and

displaced persons Postwar refugees, including 13 million Germans, former Nazi prisoners and forced laborers, and orphaned children.

Chronology

1945	Yalta Conference; end of World War II; Potsdam Conference; Nuremberg trials
1945–1960s	Decolonization of Asia and Africa
1945–1965	United States takes lead in Big Science
1947	Truman Doctrine; Marshall Plan
1948	Founding of Israel
1948–1949	Berlin airlift
1949	Creation of East and West Germany; formation of NATO; establishment of COMECON
1950–1953	Korean War
1953	Death of Stalin
1955–1964	Khrushchev rises to power; de-Stalinization of Soviet Union
1955	Warsaw Pact founded
1956	Pasternak, *Doctor Zhivago*; Suez crisis
1957	Formation of Common Market
1961	Building of Berlin Wall
1962	Cuban missile crisis; Solzhenitsyn, *One Day in the Life of Ivan Denisovich*
1964	Brezhnev replaces Khrushchev as Soviet leader

Refugee movements
Baltic →
Czech →
Finns →
Germans →
Poles →
Russians →

City substantially destroyed
Allied occupation of Germany and Austria, 1945–1955
Territory lost by Germany
Territory gained by Soviet Union

Peoples settled by International Refugee Organization →

0   100   200 miles
0 100 200 kilometers

Mapping the Past

Map 29.1 **The Aftermath of World War II in Europe, ca. 1945–1950** By 1945 millions of people displaced by war and territorial changes were on the move. The Soviet Union and Poland took land from Germany, which the Allies partitioned into occupation zones. Those zones subsequently formed the basis of the East and West German states. Austria was detached from Germany, but the Soviets subsequently permitted Austria to reunify as a neutral state.

ANALYZING THE MAP Which groups fled west? Who went east? How would you characterize the general direction of most of these movements?

CONNECTIONS What does the widespread movement of people at the end of the war suggest about the war? What does it suggest about the ensuing political climate?

To complete this activity online, go to the Online Study Guide at bedfordstmartins.com/mckaywest.

particularly in the east, almost 100,000 Germans and Austrians were convicted of wartime crimes. Many more were investigated or indicted. Collaborators, those non-Germans who had assisted the occupying forces, were also punished. In the days and months immediately after the war, spontaneous acts of retribution brought some collaborators to account. In both France and Italy, unofficial groups seeking revenge summarily executed some 25,000 persons. French women accused of "horizontal collaboration" — having sexual relations with men in the occupying German forces — were publicly humiliated by angry mobs. Newly established postwar governments quickly established authority over questions of guilt and punishment, and in trials across

Europe collaborators were sanctioned or sentenced to prison. A minority received the death sentence.

In Germany, Allied occupation governments set up denazification procedures meant to identify former Nazi Party members and punish those responsible for the worst crimes of the National Socialist state. At the Nuremberg trials (1945–1946), an international military tribunal organized by the four Allied powers — the Soviet Union, the United States, Britain, and France — tried and sentenced the highest-ranking Nazi military and civilian leaders who had survived the war. The twenty-two defendants were charged with war crimes and crimes against humanity. After chilling testimony from victims of the regime, which revealed the full systematic horror of Nazi atrocities, twelve were sentenced to death.

The Nuremberg trials marked the last time the four Allies worked together to punish former Nazis. As the Cold War developed and the Soviets and the Western allies drew increasingly apart, each carried out separate denazification programs in its own zone of occupation. In the West, U.S. military courts at first actively prosecuted leading Nazis. But the huge numbers implicated in Nazi crimes, West German opposition to the proceedings, and the need for stability in the looming Cold War made thorough denazification impractical. Except for the worst offenders, the West had quietly shelved denazification by 1948. The process was similar in the Soviet zone. At first, punishment was swift and harsh. About 45,000 former party officials, upper-class industrialists, and large landowners were identified as Nazis and sentenced to prison or death. As in the West, however, former Nazis who cooperated with the new regime could avoid prosecution, and many soon found leading positions in government and industry in both the Soviet and U.S. zones.

In the years immediately after the war, ordinary people across Europe came to terms with the war and slowly regained normal lives, working at steady civilian jobs, living in good housing, and raising families. Still, the revelation of Nazi barbarism, the destruction of so many lives, and the great disruptions of the postwar years had deeply shaken European confidence. As German philosopher Theodor Adorno wrote in 1951, "There can be no poetry after Auschwitz." Against this background of postwar ruin, despair, and slow recovery, the victorious Allies struggled to shape a reasonable and lasting peace.

The Peace Accords and Cold War Origins

The most powerful allies in the wartime coalition — the Soviet Union and the United States — began to quarrel almost as soon as the unifying threat of Nazi Germany disappeared. The hostility between the Eastern and Western superpowers was the sad but logical outgrowth of military developments, wartime agreements, and long-standing political and ideological differences that stretched back to the Russian Revolution (see Chapter 26).

In the early phases of the Second World War, the Americans and the British made military victory their highest priority. They avoided discussion of Stalin's war aims and the shape of the eventual peace settlement. Stalin received a military alliance only and no postwar commitments. Yet the United States and Britain did not try to take advantage of the Soviet Union's precarious position in 1942 because they feared that hard bargaining would encourage Stalin to consider making a separate peace with Hitler. They focused instead on the policy of unconditional surrender to solidify the alliance. By late 1943 discussion about the shape of the postwar world could no longer be postponed. The conference that the "Big Three" — Stalin, Roosevelt, and Churchill — held in the Iranian capital of Teheran in November 1943 thus proved of crucial importance in determining subsequent events.

At the Teheran Conference, the Big Three jovially reaffirmed their determination to crush Germany, discussed Poland's postwar borders, and crafted a strategy to win the war. Stalin, concerned that the Soviet Union was bearing the brunt of the fighting, asked his allies to relieve his armies by opening a second front in France. Churchill, fearful of the military dangers of a direct attack, argued that American and British forces should follow up their Italian campaign with an indirect attack on Germany through the Balkans. Roosevelt, however, agreed with Stalin that an American-British frontal assault through France would be better. This agreement was part of Roosevelt's general effort to meet Stalin's wartime demands whenever possible, and it had momentous political implications. It meant that the Soviet and the American-British armies would come together in defeated Germany along a north-south line and that only Soviet troops would liberate eastern Europe. Thus the basic shape of postwar Europe was emerging even as the fighting continued.

When the Big Three met again in February 1945 at Yalta on the Black Sea in southern Russia, advancing Soviet armies were within a hundred miles of Berlin. The Red Army had occupied Poland as well as Bulgaria, Romania, Hungary, part of Yugoslavia, and much of Czechoslovakia. The temporarily stalled American-British forces had yet to cross the Rhine into Germany. Moreover, the United States was far from defeating Japan. In short, the Soviet Union's position was strong and America's weak.

There was little the increasingly sick and apprehensive Roosevelt could do but double his bet on Stalin's peaceful intentions. The Allies agreed at the Yalta Conference that each of the victorious powers would occupy

The Big Three In 1945 a triumphant Winston Churchill, an ailing Franklin Roosevelt, and a determined Stalin met at Yalta in southern Russia to plan for peace. Cooperation soon gave way to bitter hostility, and the decisions made by these leaders transformed the map of Europe. (Franklin D. Roosevelt Presidential Library)

a separate zone of Germany, and that the Germans would pay heavy reparations to the Soviet Union. At American insistence, Stalin agreed to declare war on Japan after Germany was defeated. As for Poland, the Big Three agreed that the Soviet Union would permanently incorporate the eastern Polish territories its army had occupied at the start of the war, and that Poland would be compensated with German lands to the west. They also agreed in an ambiguous compromise that eastern European governments were to be freely elected but pro-Russian.

The Yalta compromise over elections in eastern Europe broke down almost immediately. Even before the conference, Bulgaria and Poland were under the control of communists who had arrived home from the eastern front with the Red Army. Elsewhere in eastern Europe, the advancing Soviets formed coalition governments that included Social Democrats and other leftist parties, but reserved key government posts for Moscow-trained communists. At the postwar Potsdam Conference of July 1945, the long-avoided differences over eastern Europe finally surged to the fore. The compromising Roosevelt had died and had been succeeded by the more determined President Harry Truman (r. 1945–1953), who demanded immediate free elections throughout eastern Europe. Stalin refused point-blank. "A freely elected government in any of these East European countries would be anti-Soviet," he admitted simply, "and that we cannot allow."[2]

Here, then, were the keys to the much-debated origins of the Cold War. When the Allies were fighting Germany, they could maintain an alliance of necessity. As the war drew to a close, however, long-standing hostility between East and West reemerged. Mutual distrust, anxious security concerns, and antagonistic desires for economic and territorial control now destroyed the former partnership.

Stalin, who had lived through two enormously destructive German invasions, was determined to establish a defensive buffer zone of sympathetic states around the Soviet Union and at the same time expand the reach of communism and the Soviet state. Stalin believed that only communists could be truly dependable allies, and that free elections would result in independent and possibly hostile governments on his western border. With Soviet armies in central Europe, there was no way short of war for the United States to control the region's political future. War was out of the question, and Communist regimes would govern in east-central Europe for the next forty-five years. The United States, for its part, wished to maintain liberal democracy and free-market capitalism in western Europe. The Americans quickly showed that they were willing to use their vast political, economic, and military power to maintain predominance in their own sphere of influence.

West Versus East

The Cold War escalated over the next five years as both sides hardened their positions. In May 1945, as the fighting ended, Truman abruptly cut off all aid to the ailing Soviet Union. In October he declared that the United States would never recognize any government established by force against the free will of its people. In March

1946 former British prime minister Churchill ominously informed an American audience that an "iron curtain" had fallen across the continent, dividing Germany and all of Europe into two antagonistic camps (Map 29.2).

Stalin had indeed consolidated his hold on eastern Europe. Recognizing that communists could not take power in free elections, he purged the last remaining noncommunist elements from the coalition governments set up after the war and established Soviet-style one-party communist dictatorships. Stalin's seizure of power in Czechoslovakia in February 1948, after the Czech Communist Party had won significant electoral support, was particularly antidemocratic. It greatly strengthened Western fears of limitless communist expansion.

In the West, the large, well-organized Communist Parties of France and Italy returned to what they called the "struggle against capitalist imperialism." They criticized the growing role of the United States in western Europe and challenged their own governments with violent rhetoric and large strikes. At the same time, communist revolutionaries were waging bitter civil wars in Greece and China (see below and page 947). By the spring of 1947 it appeared to many Americans that Stalin and the Soviet Union were determined to export communism by subversion throughout Europe and around the world.

The United States responded with the **Truman Doctrine**, aimed at "containing" communism to areas already occupied by the Red Army. The United States, President Truman promised, would use diplomatic, economic, and even military means to resist the expansion of communism anywhere on the globe. At first, Truman asked Congress for military aid to Greece and Turkey, countries that Britain, weakened by war and financially overextended, could no longer protect. With American support, both remained in the Western bloc. The U.S. government restructured its military to meet the Soviet threat, pouring money into defense spending and testing nuclear weapons. The

Truman Doctrine America's policy geared to containing communism to those countries already under Soviet control.

Map 29.2 **Cold War Europe in the 1950s** The Cold War divided Europe into two hostile military alliances that formed to the east and west of an "iron curtain."

> ❝ Our policy [of aid] is not directed against any country or doctrine but against hunger, poverty, desperation, and chaos. ❞
>
> **—U.S. SECRETARY OF STATE GEORGE C. MARSHALL**

American determination to enforce containment hardened when the Soviets exploded their own atomic bomb in 1949. Emotional, moralistic denunciations of Stalin and communist Russia emerged as part of American public life. At home and abroad, the United States engaged in an anticommunist crusade.

The expansion of the U.S. military was only one aspect of Truman's policy of containment. In 1947 western Europe was still on the verge of economic collapse. Food was scarce across the continent, inflation was high, and black markets flourished. Recognizing that an economically and politically stable western Europe could be an effective block against the popular appeal of communism, U.S. Secretary of State George C. Marshall offered Europe economic aid—the **Marshall Plan**—to help it rebuild. As Marshall wrote in a State Department bulletin:

> *The truth of the matter is that Europe's requirements for the next three or four years of foreign food and other essential products—principally from America—are so much greater than her present ability to pay that she must have substantial additional help or face economic, social, and political deterioration of a very grave character. . . . Our policy [of aid] is not directed against any country or doctrine but against hunger, poverty, desperation, and chaos. Its purpose should be the revival of a working economy in the world so as to permit the emergence of political and social conditions in which free institutions can exist.*[3]

The Marshall Plan was one of the most successful foreign aid programs in history. When it ended in 1951, the United States had given about $13 billion in aid (equivalent to over $200 billion in today's dollars) to fifteen western European nations, and Europe's economy was on the way to recovery. Marshall Plan funding was initially offered to East Bloc countries as well, but fearing Western interference in the Soviet sphere, Stalin rejected the offer. In 1949 the Soviets established the **Council for Mutual Economic Assistance (COME-** CON), an economic organization of communist states intended to rebuild the East Bloc independently of the West. The generous aid of the Marshall Plan was limited to countries in the Western bloc, increasing Cold War tensions.

In the late 1940s Berlin, the capital city of Germany, was on the front line of the Cold War. Like the rest of Germany, Berlin had been divided among the victorious Allies into east and west zones. In June 1948 the Western allies replaced the currency in West Germany and West Berlin, a first move in plans to establish a separate West German state. This action violated the peace accords, and in response Stalin blocked all traffic through the Soviet zone of Germany to Berlin in an attempt to reunify the city under Soviet control. Acting firmly, the Western allies coordinated around-the-clock flights of hundreds of planes over the Soviet roadblocks, supplying provisions to West Berliners and thwarting Soviet efforts to swallow up the western half of the city. After 324 days, the Berlin airlift had proven successful, and the Soviets backed down.

The U.S. success in breaking the Berlin blockade had several lasting results. First, it paved the way for the creation of two separate German states in 1949: the Federal Republic of West Germany, aligned with the United States, and the German Democratic Republic (or East Germany), aligned with the Soviet Union. Germany would remain divided into two separate states for the next fifty years, a radical solution to the "German problem" that satisfied people fearful of the nation's possible military resurgence.

The Berlin crisis also seemed to show that containment worked, and thus strengthened U.S. resolve to maintain a military presence in western Europe. In 1949 the United States formed **NATO** (the North Atlantic Treaty Organization), an anti-Soviet military alliance of Western governments. As one British diplomat put it, NATO was designed "to keep the Russians out, the Americans in, and the Germans down."[4] With U.S. backing, West Germany joined NATO in 1955 and was allowed to rebuild its military so as to defend western Europe against possible Soviet attack. West Germany was now firmly allied with the West. The Soviets countered in 1955 by organizing the **Warsaw Pact**, a military alliance among the satellite nations of eastern Europe. In both political and military terms, Europe was divided into two hostile blocs.

Marshall Plan American plan for providing economic aid to western Europe to help it rebuild.

Council for Mutual Economic Assistance (COMECON) An economic organization of communist states meant to help rebuild eastern Europe under Soviet auspices.

NATO The North Atlantic Treaty Organization, an anti-Soviet military alliance of Western governments.

Warsaw Pact Soviet-backed military alliance of eastern European nations.

The Berlin Airlift Standing in the rubble of their bombed-out city in 1948, a German crowd in the American section awaits the arrival of a U.S. transport plane flying in over the Soviet blockade. The crisis over Berlin was a dramatic indication of growing tensions among the former Allies, which resulted in the division of Europe into two hostile camps. (Time Life Pictures/Getty Images)

The superpower confrontation that emerged from the ruins of World War II took shape in central Europe and Germany, but it quickly spread around the globe. The Cold War turned hot in East Asia. When the Soviet-backed communist army of North Korea invaded South Korea in 1950, President Truman swiftly sent U.S. troops. In 1953 a fragile truce was negotiated, and the fighting stopped. The United States thus extended its policy of containment to Asia but drew back from an attack on communist China and possible nuclear war. In the end the Korean War was indecisive: Korea remained divided between the communist north and the liberal south. The war nonetheless showed that while the superpowers might maintain a fragile peace in Europe, they were perfectly willing to engage in open conflict in non-Western territories (see also page 944).

In the decade after World War II, the Soviet-American confrontation became institutionalized and formed the bedrock of the long Cold War era, which lasted until 1989, with intermittent periods of relaxation. For the next forty-five years, the superpowers would struggle to win political influence and territorial control, and also to achieve technological superiority. Cold War hostilities directly fostered a nuclear arms race, the U.S. and Soviet space programs, and the computer revolution,

all made possible by stunning achievements in science and technology.

Big Science and New Technologies

With the advent of the Second World War, pure theoretical science had already lost its impractical innocence when it was joined with practical technology (applied science) on a massive scale. Most leading university scientists went to work on top-secret projects to help their governments fight the war. The development by British scientists of radar to detect enemy aircraft was a particularly important outcome of this new kind of sharply focused research. The air war also greatly stimulated the development of rocketry and jet aircraft and spurred further work on electronic computers that calculated the complex mathematical relationships between fast-moving planes and anti-aircraft shells to increase the likelihood of a hit. The most spectacular and deadly result of directed scientific research during the war was the atomic bomb, which showed the world both the awesome power and the heavy moral responsibilities of modern science and its high priests.

The impressive results of directed research during World War II inspired a new model for science — Big

Science. By combining theoretical work with sophisticated engineering in a large organization, Big Science could tackle extremely difficult problems, from new and improved weapons for the military to better products for consumers. Big Science was extremely expensive, requiring large-scale financing from governments and large corporations. Highly specialized modern scientists and technologists typically worked as members of a team in a large bureaucratic organization, where the individual was very often a small cog in a great machine.

Throughout the Cold War, in both the capitalist United States and the socialist Soviet Union, the government stepped in to provide generous funding for scientific activity. Populous, victorious, and wealthy, the United States took the lead in Big Science after World War II. Between 1945 and 1965 government spending on scientific research and development in the United

States grew five times as fast as the national income, and by 1965 such spending took 3 percent of all U.S. income. As the Soviet Union recovered, it too devoted heavy subsidies to scientific research.

One reason for the parallel between the two countries was that science was not demobilized in either country after the war. Scientists remained a critical part of every major military establishment, and a large portion of all postwar scientific research supported the growing Cold War arms race. New weapons such as missiles, nuclear submarines, and spy satellites demanded breakthroughs no less remarkable than those responsible for radar and the first atomic bomb. After 1945 roughly one-quarter of all men and women trained in science and engineering in the West — and perhaps more in the Soviet Union — were employed full-time in the production of weapons to kill other humans. By the 1960s both sides had enough

МЫ—МИРНЫЕ ЛЮДИ,

НО НАШ БРОНЕПОЕЗД СТОИТ НА ЗАПАСНОМ ПУТИ!

Picturing the Past

A Soviet View of the Arms Race This propaganda poster from the 1950s reads, "We are a peaceful people, but our armored train stands in ready reserve." The reference to the armored train recalls the Bolshevik use of trains in combat against the White armies during the Russian civil war of the early 1920s. (Sovfoto)

ANALYZING THE IMAGE What does the "armored train" of the 1950s look like? How does the artist portray the Soviet people, and how does this supposedly peaceful image express Cold War hostility?

CONNECTIONS Why might the Soviet citizens again need protection, and why would the artist reference the Russian civil war? How did the emergence of Big Science contribute to the global confrontation between the superpowers?

To complete this activity online, go to the Online Study Guide at **bedfordstmartins.com/mckaywest.**

nuclear firepower to destroy each other and the rest of the world many times over.

Sophisticated science, lavish government spending, and military needs all came together in the space race of the 1960s. In 1957 the Soviets used long-range rockets developed in their nuclear weapons program to put a satellite in orbit. In 1961 they sent the world's first cosmonaut circling the globe. Embarrassed by Soviet triumphs, the United States made an all-out commitment to catch up with the Soviets and landed a crewed spacecraft on the moon in 1969. Four more moon landings followed by 1972.

Advanced nuclear weapons and the space race would have been impossible without the concurrent revolution in computer technology. The search for better weaponry in World War II had boosted the development of sophisticated data-processing machines, including the electronic Colossus computer used by the British to break German military codes. The massive mainframe ENIAC (Electronic Numerical Integrator and Computer), built for the U.S. Army at the University of Pennsylvania, went into operation in 1945. The invention of the transistor in 1947 further hastened the spread of computers. From the mid-1950s on, bulky vacuum tubes were increasingly replaced by this small, efficient electronic switching device. By the 1960s sophisticated computers were indispensable tools for a variety of military, commercial, and scientific uses, foreshadowing the rise of personal computers in the decades to come.

Big Science also had more humane and tangible results for ordinary people. During the postwar green revolution, directed research into agriculture greatly increased the world's food supplies. Farming was industrialized and became more and more productive per acre, and far fewer people worked in rural areas. The application of scientific techniques to industrial processes also made consumer goods less expensive and more readily available to larger numbers of people. The transistor, for example, was applied to computers but was also used in portable radios and kitchen appliances, and in any number of other electronic consumer products. In sum, in both the East and the West Blocs, epoch-making inventions and new technologies created new sources of material well-being and entertainment as well as destruction.

The Western Renaissance

Why did western Europe recover so successfully, and what were the sources of postwar stability? ■

As the Cold War divided Europe into two blocs, the future appeared bleak. Economic conditions were the worst in generations, and Europe was weak and divided, a battleground for Cold War ambitions. Yet Europe recovered, with the nations of western Europe in the vanguard.

In less than a generation, western Europeans constructed democratic political institutions that paved the way for unprecedented economic growth. A true consumer revolution brought improved living standards and a sense of prosperity to ever-larger numbers of people. Western European countries also entered collective economic agreements and established the European Economic Community, the first steps toward broad European unity. It was an amazing rebirth—a true renaissance.

The Search for Political and Social Consensus

After the war, economic conditions in western Europe were terrible. Infrastructure of all kinds barely functioned, and runaway inflation and a thriving black market testified to severe shortages and hardships. In 1948, as Marshall Plan dollars poured in, however, the battered economies of western Europe began to improve. The outbreak of the Korean War in 1950 further stimulated economic activity, and Europe entered a period of rapid economic progress that lasted into the late 1960s. Never before had the European economy grown so fast.

There were many reasons for this stunning economic performance. American aid got the process off to a fast start. Moreover, economic growth became a basic objective of all western European governments, for leaders and voters alike were determined to avoid a return to the dangerous and demoralizing stagnation of the 1930s.

The postwar governments in western Europe thus embraced new political and economic policies that led to a remarkably lasting social consensus. They turned to liberal democracy and generally adopted Keynesian economics (see Chapter 28) in successful attempts to stimulate their economies. In addition, whether they leaned to the left or to the right, national leaders applied an imaginative mixture of government planning and free-market capitalism to promote economic growth. They relied on limited regulation of the economy and established generous welfare provisions for both workers and the middle classes. This consensual framework for good government lasted until the middle of the 1970s, when Western governments responded to a stubborn economic crisis by cutting state spending and turning to the right.

In politics, the Nazi occupation and the war had discredited old ideas and old leaders, and a new team of European politicians emerged to guide national recovery. Across the West, newly formed Christian Democratic parties became important power brokers. Rooted in the Catholic parties of the prewar decades (see Chapters 24 and 28), the **Christian Democrats** offered voters tired of radical politics a center-right vision

Christian Democrats
Center-right political parties that rose to power in western Europe after the Second World War.

of reconciliation and recovery. The socialists and the communists, active in the resistance against Hitler, also increased their power and prestige, especially in France and Italy. They, too, provided fresh leadership and pushed for social change and economic reform.

Across much of continental Europe, the Christian Democrats defeated their left-wing competition. In Italy the Christian Democrats were the leading party in the first postwar elections in 1946, and in early 1948 they won an absolute majority in the parliament in a landslide victory. In France the Popular Republican Movement, a Christian Democratic party, provided some of the best postwar leaders after General Charles de Gaulle (duh-GOHL) resigned from the office of prime minister in January 1946. West Germans, too, chose a Christian Democratic government that governed West Germany from 1949 until 1966.

As they provided effective leadership for their respective countries, the Christian Democrats drew inspiration from a common Christian and European heritage. They steadfastly rejected authoritarianism and narrow nationalism and placed their faith in democracy and liberalism. They were steadfast cold warriors, and their anticommunist rhetoric was harsh and unrelenting. Rejecting the class politics of the left, they championed a return to traditional family values, a vision with great appeal after a war that left many broken families and destitute households; the Christian Democrats often received a majority of women's votes.

Following their U.S. allies, the Christian Democrats advocated free-market economics and promised voters prosperity and ample consumer goods. At the same time, they instituted welfare measures such as education subsidies, family and housing allowances, public transportation, and public health insurance throughout continental Europe. When necessary, Christian Democratic leaders accepted the need for limited government planning. In France the government established modernization commissions for key industries, and state-controlled banks funneled money into industrial development. In postwar West Germany, the Christian Democrats broke decisively with the straitjacketed Nazi economy and promoted a "social-market economy" based on a combination of free-market liberalism, some state intervention, and an extensive social welfare network.

By contrast, in Great Britain the social-democratic Labour Party took power after the war and ambitiously tried to establish a "cradle-to-grave" welfare state. Although the Labour Party suffered defeats throughout much of the 1950s and early 1960s, its Conservative opponents maintained much of the welfare state when they came to power. Many British industries were nationalized, or placed under state control, including banks, iron and steel industries, utilities and public transportation networks, and even the famous travel agency Thomas Cook and Sons. The British government gave its citizens free medical services and hospital care, generous retirement pensions, and unemployment benefits, all subsidized by progressive taxation. Even though wartime austerity and rationing programs were in place until the mid-1950s, Britain offered the most comprehensive coverage outside the extensive welfare systems set up in the Scandinavian countries. In eastern and western Europe alike, state-sponsored welfare measures meant that, by the early 1960s, Europeans had more food, better homes, and longer lives than ever before.

Western Europe's recovery was spectacular in the generation after 1945. By the late 1950s, contemporaries were talking about a widespread "economic miracle" that had brought robust growth to most western European countries. The booming economy complemented political transformation and social reform, creating solid foundations for a new European stability.

Toward European Unity

The political and social consensus that emerged in the postwar decade was accompanied by the first tentative steps on the long road toward a more unified Europe. Christian Democrats were particularly committed to cultural and economic cooperation, and other groups shared their dedication. Many Europeans believed that only a new "European nation" could effectively rebuild the war-torn continent and reassert the continent's influence in world affairs.

A number of new financial arrangements and institutions encouraged slow but steady moves toward European unity, as did cooperation with the United States. The Bretton Woods agreement of 1944 had already linked Western currencies to the U.S. dollar and established the International Monetary Fund and the World Bank to facilitate free markets and world trade. To receive Marshall Plan aid, the European states were required by the Americans to cooperate with one another, leading to the creation of the Organization for European Economic Cooperation (OEEC) and the Council of Europe in 1948, both of which promoted commerce and international cooperation among European nations.

European federalists hoped that the Council of Europe would quickly evolve into a European parliament with sovereign rights, but this did not happen. Britain, with its vast empire and its close relationship with the United States, consistently opposed conceding real political power—sovereignty—to the council. Many continental nationalists and communists agreed with the British. Frustrated in the direct political approach, European federalists turned to economics as a way of working toward genuine unity. In 1950 two far-seeing French statesmen, the planner Jean Monnet and Foreign Minister Robert Schuman, called for a special international organization to control and integrate all European steel and coal production. Christian Democratic governments in West Germany, Italy, Belgium, the Netherlands, and Luxembourg accepted the French idea and founded the European Coal and Steel Community in 1951 (the British steadfastly refused to join). The immediate economic goal—a single continental steel and coal market without national tariffs or quotas—was rapidly realized. The more far-reaching political goal was to bind the six member nations so closely together economically that war among them would eventually become unthinkable and virtually impossible.

In 1957 the six nations of the Coal and Steel Community signed the Treaty of Rome, which created the European Economic Community, generally known as the **Common Market**. The first goal of the treaty was a gradual reduction of all tariffs among the six in order to create a single market almost as large as that of the United States. Other goals included the free movement of capital and labor and common economic policies and institutions. The Common Market created a solid foundation for economic growth; it encouraged trade among European states, promoted global exports, and helped build shared resources for the modernization of national industries. The movement toward European unity thus brought increased transnational cooperation, and at the same time bolstered national self-interest.

The development of the Common Market fired imaginations and encouraged hopes of rapid progress toward political as well as economic union. In the 1960s, however, these hopes were frustrated by a resurgence of more traditional nationalism. France again took the lead. French president Charles de Gaulle, elected to office in 1959, was at heart a romantic nationalist. De Gaulle viewed the United States as the main threat to genuine French (and European) independence. He withdrew all French military forces from what he called an "American-controlled" NATO, developed France's own nuclear weapons, and vetoed the scheduled advent of majority rule within the Common Market. Thus the 1950s and 1960s established a lasting pattern: Europeans would establish ever-closer economic ties, but the Common Market remained a union of independent sovereign states.

Common Market The European Economic Community, created by six western European nations in 1957 as part of a larger search for European unity.

The Consumer Revolution

In the late 1950s western Europe's rapidly expanding economy led to a rising standard of living and remark-

Life and Leisure in the Consumer Revolution By the late 1950s a rapidly expanding economy was making more consumer goods available to more people on both sides of the iron curtain, transforming the way they spent their leisure time. British teens listened to the latest rock 'n' roll hits on long-playing record albums. The *Six-Five Special* album pictured here featured recordings from the successful BBC television series of the same name. Consumer goods were not as readily available in the East, and the state controlled what goods were produced. Citizens of communist Czechoslovakia could tune into state-censored television broadcasts on this Czech-made ten-inch tabletop receiver. (television: Martin Hajek/Visual Connection Archive; album: Science Museum/Science & Society Picture Library)

able growth in the number and availability of standardized consumer goods. Modern consumer society had precedents in the decades before the Second World War (see Chapter 28), but these years saw the arrival of a veritable consumer revolution: as the percentage of income spent on necessities such as housing and food declined dramatically, near full employment and high wages meant that more Europeans could buy more things than ever before. Shaken by war and eager to rebuild their homes and families, western Europeans eagerly embraced the new products of consumer society. Like Americans, they filled their houses and apartments with modern appliances such as washing machines, and they eagerly purchased the latest entertainment devices of the day: radio sets, record players, and televisions.

The purchase of consumer goods was greatly facilitated by the increased use of installment purchasing, which allowed people to buy on credit. With the expansion of social security safeguards reducing the need to accumulate savings for hard times and old age, ordinary people were increasingly willing to take on debt, and new banks and credit unions offered loans for consumer purchases on easy terms. Free-market economics and government promotion of the consumer sector were thus quite successful. For example, the European automobile industry expanded phenomenally after lagging far behind that of the United States since the 1920s. In 1948 there were only 5 million cars in western Europe; by 1965 there were 44 million. Car ownership was democratized and became possible for better-paid workers.

The consumer revolution included a vast array of small, everyday goods that changed both lifestyles and attitudes, as a young woman growing up in 1950s Wales remembered:

> We began to acquire material possessions. A car (but no television), a hoover (but no fridge). Presents became more lavish. By the end of the decade I was the proud owner of a transistor radio, an alarm clock . . . a hula hoop, and even a few new clothes (my first pair of jeans was purchased, against fierce opposition, out of saved-up pocket money). It is difficult to be sure to what extent this was the result of our own rise in the world and how much a product of the general surge in consumerism. However, it certainly left me with the feeling I was lucky. I was constantly being reminded by my eldest sister that "when I was your age, we never had. . . ."[5]

The consumer revolution had powerful ramifications in an era of Cold War competition. Politicians in both the East and the West claimed that their respective systems could best provide citizens with ample consumer goods. (See "Listening to the Past: The Nixon-Khrushchev 'Kitchen Debate,'" page 942.) In the competition over consumption, Western free markets clearly surpassed Eastern planned economies in the production and distribution of inexpensive products. Western leaders championed the arrival of prosperity and promised new forms of social equality based on equal access to consumer goods rather than forced class leveling—as in the hated East Bloc. As the West German minister

Rebellion in East Germany In June 1953 disgruntled construction workers in East Berlin walked off the job to protest low pay and high work quotas, setting off a nationwide rebellion against the Communist regime. The protesters could do little against the Soviet tanks and troops who entered the country to put down the revolt. (Bildarchiv Preussischer Kulturbesitz/Art Resource, NY)

of economics claimed in a 1957 speech, only liberal capitalism—not communist planning—would "lead the German people out of misery and despair to a happier future, prosperity, and social security."[6] The race to provide ordinary people with higher living standards would be a central if often overlooked aspect of the Cold War, as Soviet eastern Europe struggled to catch up to Western standards of prosperity.

Soviet Eastern Europe

What was the pattern of postwar rebuilding and development in the Soviet Union and communist eastern Europe? ▪

While western Europe surged ahead economically after the Second World War and increased its independent political power as American influence gradually waned, eastern Europe followed a different path. The Soviet Union first tightened its grip on the "liberated" nations of eastern Europe under Stalin and then refused to let go. Though limited reforms after Stalin's death led to some economic improvement and limited gains in freedoms, postwar recovery in eastern Europe proceeded along Soviet lines, and political and social developments there were strongly influenced by changes in the Soviet Union.

Postwar Life Under Stalin

The "Great Patriotic War of the Fatherland" had fostered Russian nationalism and a relaxation of dictatorial terror. It also had produced a rare but real unity between Soviet rulers and most Russian people. Having made a heroic war effort, the vast majority of the Soviet people hoped in 1945 that a grateful party and government would grant greater freedom and democracy. Such hopes were soon disappointed.

Even before the war ended, Stalin was moving the Soviet Union back toward rigid dictatorship. As early as 1944 the leading members of the Communist Party were given a new motivating slogan: "The war on Fascism ends, the war on capitalism begins."[7] By early 1946 Stalin was arguing that war was inevitable as long as capitalism existed. Working to extend communist influence across the globe, the Soviets established the Cominform, or Communist Information Bureau, an international organization dedicated to maintaining Russian control over Communist parties abroad, in western as well as eastern Europe. Stalin's new foreign foe in the West served as an excuse for re-establishing a harsh dictatorship in the Soviet Union itself. Stalin reasserted the Communist Party's complete control of the government and his absolute mastery of the party. Rigid ideological indoctrination, attacks on religion, and the absence of civil liberties were soon facts of life for citizens of the Soviet empire. Millions of supposed political enemies were sent to prison, exile, or forced-labor camps.

The new satellite states in Soviet-controlled east-central Europe, including Poland, Hungary, Czechoslovakia, Romania, Albania, Bulgaria, and East Germany, were remade on the Soviet model. Though there were significant differences in what was soon known as the East Bloc, developments followed a similar pattern. Popular Communist leaders who had led the resistance against Germany were ousted as Stalin sought to create obedient instruments of domination in eastern Europe. With Soviet backing, national Communist Parties established one-party dictatorships subservient to the Communist Party in Moscow. Dissenters were arrested, imprisoned, and sometimes executed. Show trials of supposedly disloyal Communist Party leaders in Romania and Czechoslovakia in the early 1950s testified to the unrestrained influence of the Soviet Communists and Stalin's urge to establish complete control—as well as his increasing paranoia.

Only Josip Broz Tito (TEE-toh) (1892–1980), the resistance leader and Communist chief of Yugoslavia, was able to proclaim independence and successfully resist Soviet domination. Tito stood up to Stalin in 1948, and because there was no Russian army in Yugoslavia, he got away with it. Yugoslavia became communist but remained outside of the Soviet-dominated East Bloc. The country prospered as a multiethnic state until it began to break apart in the 1980s.

Within the East Bloc, the newly installed communist governments moved quickly to restructure national economies along Soviet lines. East Germany, Hungary, and Romania—countries that had fought against Russia in World War II—were forced to pay substantial war reparations to the Soviet Union. In East Germany, the Russians seized factories and equipment, even tearing up railroad tracks and sending the rails to the Soviet Union. At the same time, Communist authorities introduced Soviet-style five-year plans (see Chapter 28) to cope with the enormous task of economic reconstruction. Most industries and businesses across the East Bloc were nationalized (turned over to state ownership). Such efforts recast economic life in the Stalinist mold and created great disruptions in everyday life, even as they laid the groundwork for industrial development later in the decade. (See "Living in the Past: A Model Socialist Steel Town," page 938.)

Communist planners gave top priority to heavy industry and the military, and neglected consumer goods and housing. In addition, East Bloc leaders were suspicious of Western-style consumer culture. An overabundance of consumer goods, they believed, created waste and encouraged rampant individualism and social inequality. Thus, for practical and ideological reasons, the provision of consumer goods clearly lagged in the East

A Model Socialist Steel Town

LIVING IN THE PAST

STEEL WAS KING IN THE POSTWAR SOVIET BLOC. On both sides of the iron curtain, economic recovery required the development of heavy industry, but socialist planners were especially eager to promote large-scale industrial production centered on coal, iron, and steel. Following Soviet examples, East Bloc countries built model socialist cities, including Nowa Huta (NOH-vuh HOO-tuh; New Foundry), a steel town erected in the early 1950s on the outskirts of Kraków, Poland.

Nowa Huta was one of the grandest construction projects of the Stalinist era. An entire city surrounded the massive Lenin steelworks, both built with Soviet assistance. By the mid-1960s Polish leaders bragged that Nowa Huta produced more steel per day than any foundry in Europe.

The monumental Central Square, complete with an imposing statue of Lenin, was the center of the planned city. Streets radiated out into blocks of workers' apartment buildings designed by socialist architects. In theory, Nowa Huta brought together working and living space and included everything a working family might need: green space, department and grocery stores, recreation facilities, kindergartens and schools, cultural centers, and an extensive streetcar system. And indeed, Nowa Huta created real opportunities for Polish workers. Many moved from the farm to the city, where they enjoyed relatively good housing and good wages. Yet workers labored under party oversight and strict workplace discipline, including demanding production quotas, and the pollution from the foundry fouled the air and damaged Kraków's historic architecture.

By 1957 over one hundred thousand people lived in Nowa Huta, most of them employed at the steelworks. At mass rallies and workplace meetings—attendance was mandatory—workers and their families

The main square of Nowa Huta with the Lenin Works foundry in the background. (Sovfoto)

met colleagues and friends and listened to lengthy speeches about the honor of simple labor and the superiority of socialism. Despite protests from workers, who were mostly Catholic, the Communist authorities sought to repress religious belief and refused to build a church until 1966.

According to propagandists, cities like Nowa Huta proved that the East could surpass the West in terms of industrial output while creating humane and equitable living spaces. But the grand experiment reveals one of the weaknesses of the East Bloc economy. By the mid-1970s the steel produced by the "tiger nations" of East Asia was better and less expensive than that made at Nowa Huta, and the foundry could no longer compete in global markets. The Communist Party clung to its vision of the workers' state, and continued government subsidies helped bankrupt the Polish state. Today, much of the plant is closed, but visitors can still explore an important example of socialist planning and ponder everyday life in a model industrial suburb.

QUESTIONS FOR ANALYSIS

1. How did planned cities like Nowa Huta reflect and promote socialist values?

2. Why would Polish leaders continue to support Nowa Huta when its products were no longer competitive?

3. Imagine yourself a worker in Nowa Huta. What would you find appealing about the living conditions? What would you find objectionable?

According to socialist planners, the newly built workers' apartments at Nowa Huta had everything a growing family could want, but the happiness depicted in this staged photo stands in contrast to the difficult working conditions and the state repression of Catholicism that led to popular unrest. (Sovfoto)

This photo from a 1951 May Day parade in Nowa Huta depicts marchers carrying posters of (from left to right) Marx, a Polish Communist leader, Lenin, and Engels. (Wiktor Pental/visavis.pl)

Bloc, leading to popular complaints and disillusionment with the constantly deferred promise of socialism.

Communist regimes also moved aggressively to collectivize agriculture, as they had in the Soviet Union in the 1930s (see Chapter 28). By the early 1950s independent farmers had virtually disappeared in most of the East Bloc. Poland was the exception: there the Stalinist regime tolerated the existence of private agriculture, hoping to maintain stability in the large and potentially rebellious country.

For ordinary eastern Europeans, everyday life was hard throughout the 1950s. Socialist planned economies often led to production problems and persistent shortages of basic household items. Party leaders encouraged workers to perform almost superhuman labor to "build socialism," often for low pay and under poor conditions. In East Germany, popular discontent with this situation led to open revolt in June 1953. A strike by Berlin construction workers protesting poor wages and increased work quotas led to nationwide demonstrations that were put down with Soviet troops and tanks. Over 350 protesters were killed and thousands jailed, though when the revolt was over the East German government instituted reforms designed to meet the most pressing demands of the demonstrators.

Communist censors purged culture and art in aggressive campaigns that reimposed rigid anti-Western ideological conformity. The regime required artists and writers to conform to the dictates of socialist realism, which idealized the working classes and the Soviet Union. Artists who strayed from the party line were denounced, and many talented writers, composers, and film directors were forced to produce works that conformed to the state's political goals. In short, the postwar East Bloc resembled the U.S.S.R. in the 1930s, although police terror was less intense (see Chapter 28).

Reform and De-Stalinization

In 1953 the aging Stalin finally died, and the dictatorship that he had built began to change. Even as Stalin's heirs struggled for power, they realized that reforms were necessary because of the widespread fear and hatred of Stalin's political terrorism. The power of the secret police was curbed, and many forced-labor camps were gradually closed. Change was also necessary to spur economic growth, which had sputtered under Stalin's five-year plans. Moreover, Stalin's belligerent foreign policy had led directly to a strong Western alliance, which isolated the Soviet Union.

The Soviet Communist leadership was badly split on the question of just how much change should be permitted in order to preserve the system. Conservatives

de-Stalinization The liberalization of the post-Stalin Soviet Union led by reformer Nikita Khrushchev.

wanted to make as few changes as possible. Reformers, who were led by Nikita Khrushchev (1894–1971), argued for major innovations. Khrushchev (kroush-CHAWF), who had joined the party as an uneducated coal miner in 1918 and had risen to a high-level position in the 1930s, emerged as the new Soviet premier in 1955.

To strengthen his position and that of his fellow reformers within the party, Khrushchev launched a surprising attack on Stalin and his crimes at a closed session of the Twentieth Party Congress in 1956. In his famous "secret speech," Khrushchev described to the startled Communist delegates how Stalin had "supported the glorification of his own person with all conceivable methods" to build a propagandistic "cult of personality." The delegates applauded when Khrushchev went on to report that Stalin had tortured and murdered thousands of loyal Communists and bungled the country's defense in World War II:

> [Stalin] discarded the Leninist method of convincing and educating . . . for that of administrative violence, mass repressions, and terror. . . . Mass arrests and deportations of many thousands of people, execution without trial and without normal investigation created conditions of insecurity, fear, and even desperation. . . . And what was the result of [Stalin's failed leadership at the Battle for Kharkov]? The Germans surrounded our army concentrations and consequently we lost hundreds of thousands of our soldiers. . . . Not Stalin, but the party as a whole, the Soviet Government, our heroic army . . . the whole Soviet nation — these are the ones who assured victory in the Great Patriotic War. (Tempestuous and prolonged applause.)[8]

The liberalization — or **de-Stalinization**, as it was called in the West — of the Soviet Union was genuine. Khrushchev's secret speech was read at Communist Party meetings held throughout the country, and it strengthened the reform movement. The Communist Party jealously maintained its monopoly on political power, but Khrushchev shook up the party and brought in new members. Some resources were shifted from heavy industry and the military toward consumer goods and agriculture, and Stalinist controls over workers were relaxed. The Soviet Union's low standard of living finally began to improve and continued to rise substantially throughout the booming 1960s.

De-Stalinization also created great ferment among writers and intellectuals who sought cultural freedom, such as the poet Boris Pasternak (1890–1960), who finished his great novel *Doctor Zhivago* in 1956. Published in the West but not in Russia, *Doctor Zhivago* is both a literary masterpiece and a powerful challenge to communism. It tells the story of a prerevolutionary intellectual who rejects the violence and brutality of the revolution of 1917 and the Stalinist years. Pasternak was denounced —

but under Khrushchev he was not shot. Other talented writers followed Pasternak's lead, and courageous editors let the sparks fly. The writer Aleksandr Solzhenitsyn (sohl-zhuh-NEET-suhn) (1918–2008) created a sensation when his *One Day in the Life of Ivan Denisovich* was published in the Soviet Union in 1962. Solzhenitsyn's novel portrays in grim detail life in a Stalinist concentration camp—a life to which Solzhenitsyn himself had been unjustly condemned—and is a damning indictment of the Stalinist past.

Khrushchev was proud of Soviet achievements and liked to boast that East Bloc living standards and access to consumer goods would soon surpass the West. (See "Listening to the Past: The Nixon-Khrushchev 'Kitchen Debate,'" page 942.) Socialist citizens in fact experienced a limited consumer revolution. Their options were more modest than those in the West, but eastern Europeans purchased automobiles, televisions, and other consumer goods in ever-increasing numbers in the 1960s.

Foreign Policy and Domestic Rebellion

Khrushchev also de-Stalinized Soviet foreign policy. "Peaceful coexistence" with capitalism was possible, he argued, and great wars were not inevitable. Khrushchev even made concessions, agreeing in 1955 to real independence for a neutral Austria after ten long years of Allied occupation. Thus there was considerable relaxation of Cold War tensions between 1955 and 1957. At the same time, Khrushchev began wooing the new nations of Asia and Africa—even those that were not communist—with promises and aid.

In the eastern European satellites, de-Stalinization stimulated rebelliousness. Having suffered in silence under Stalin, communist reformers and the masses were quickly emboldened to seek much greater liberty and national independence. Poland took the lead in 1956, when extensive rioting brought a new government to power. The new first secretary of the Polish Communist Party argued that there were "many roads to socialism" and managed to win greater autonomy from Soviet control. The new leadership maintained Communist control even as it tolerated a free peasantry and an independent Catholic Church.

Hungary experienced a real and tragic revolution the same year. Led by students and workers—the classic urban revolutionaries— the people of Budapest installed Imre Nagy, a liberal communist reformer, as their new prime minister in October 1956. Nagy forced Soviet troops to leave the country, but the victory was short-lived. After the new government promised free elections and renounced Hungary's military alliance with Moscow, the Russian leaders ordered an invasion and crushed the national and democratic revolution. Around 2,700 Hungarians died in the revolt. Fighting was bitter until the end, for the Hungarians hoped that the United States would come to their aid. When this did not occur, most people in eastern Europe concluded that their only hope was to strive for small domestic gains while following Russia obediently in foreign affairs. The re-established Communist regime executed the revolt's leaders and sent another 22,000 to prison.

The outcome of the Hungarian uprising weakened support for Soviet-style communism in western Europe; for those who still believed in socialist equality, the brutal repression was deeply discouraging. Across western Europe, tens of thousands of Communist Party members resigned in disgust. At the same time, Western leaders saw that the Soviets would use military force to defend their control over the Communist bloc, and that only open war between East and West had the potential to overturn authoritarian Communist rule. This price was too high, and it seemed that Communist domination of east-central Europe was here to stay.

The Limits of Reform

By late 1962 opposition to Khrushchev's reformist policies had gained momentum in party circles. Khrushchev's Communist colleagues began to see de-Stalinization as a dangerous threat to the dictatorial authority of the party. Moreover, Khrushchev's policy toward the West was erratic and ultimately unsuccessful. In 1958, in a failed attempt to close the open border between East and West Berlin, he ordered the Western allies to evacuate the city within six months. In response, the allies reaffirmed their unity in West Berlin, and Khrushchev backed down. Then in 1961 Khrushchev ordered the East Germans to build a wall between East and West Berlin, thereby sealing off West Berlin in clear violation of existing access agreements between the Great Powers. The recently elected U.S. president, John F. Kennedy (r. 1961–1963), insisted publicly that the United States would never abandon Berlin. Hoping that the Berlin

> **❝** Mass arrests and deportations of many thousands of people, execution without trial and without normal investigation created conditions of insecurity, fear, and even desperation. **❞**
>
> **— NIKITA KHRUSHCHEV**

LISTENING TO THE PAST

During the Cold War, the United States and the Soviet Union waged political battles in Europe and wars of influence in the former colonies. But the two superpowers also sparred over which system — communism or capitalism — provided the best lifestyle for its citizens.

In a late-1950s effort to relieve Cold War tensions, the Americans and Soviets allowed one another to set up public displays in each other's territory. The American National Exhibition in Moscow in 1959 included a model U.S. suburban home, complete with modern kitchen appliances, a television and stereo console, and a Cadillac sedan, all meant to demonstrate the superiority of capitalism to local visitors.

Against this backdrop, U.S. vice president Richard Nixon and Soviet premier Nikita Khrushchev engaged in an impromptu and sometimes ham-fisted argument over the merits of their respective political systems. As this exchange from the famous "kitchen debate" suggests, dishwashers were also on the front line of the Cold War.

KHRUSHCHEV: We want to live in peace and friendship with Americans because we are the two most powerful countries and if we live in friendship then other countries will also live in friendship. But if there is a country that is too war-minded we could pull its ears a little and say: Don't you dare; fighting is not allowed now; this is a period of atomic armament; some foolish one could start a war and then even a wise one couldn't finish the war. Therefore, we are governed by this idea in our policy — internal and foreign. How long has America existed? Three hundred years?

NIXON: One hundred and fifty years.

KHRUSHCHEV: One hundred and fifty years? Well then we will say America has been in existence for 150 years and this is the level she has reached. We have existed not quite 42 years and in another seven years we will be on the same level as America. When we catch you up, in passing you by, we will wave to you. Then if you wish we can stop and say: Please follow up. Plainly speaking, if you want capitalism you can live that way. That is your own affair and doesn't concern us. We can still feel sorry for you but since you don't understand us — live as you do understand. . . . [Wrapping his arms about a Soviet workman.] Does this man look like a slave laborer? [Waving at others.] With men with such spirit how can we lose?

NIXON: [Pointing to American workmen.] With men like that we are strong. But these men, Soviet and American, work together well for peace, even as they have worked together in building this exhibition. This is the way it should be. Your remarks are in the tradition of what we have come to expect — sweeping and extemporaneous. Later on we will both have an opportunity to speak and consequently I will not comment on the various points that you raised, except to say this — this color television is one of the most advanced developments in communication that we have. I can only say that if this competition in which you plan to outstrip us is to do the best for both of our peoples and for peoples everywhere, there must be a free exchange of ideas. After all, you don't know everything.

KHRUSHCHEV: If I don't know everything you don't know anything about communism except fear of it.

NIXON: There are some instances where you may be ahead of us, for example in the development of the thrust of your rockets for the investigation of outer space; there may be some instances in which we are ahead of you — in color television, for instance.

KHRUSHCHEV: No, we are up with you on this, too. We have bested you in one technique and also in the other.

NIXON: You see, you never concede anything.

KHRUSHCHEV: I do not give up.

NIXON: Wait till you see the picture. Let's have far more communication and exchange in this very area that we speak of. We should hear you more on our televisions. You should hear us more on yours.

KHRUSHCHEV: That's a good idea. Let's do it like this. You appear before our people. We will appear before your people. People will see and appreciate this. . . .

NIXON: [Halting Khrushchev at the model kitchen in the model house.] You had a very nice house in your exhibition in New York. My wife and I saw and enjoyed it very much. I want to show you this kitchen. It is like those of our houses in California.

KHRUSHCHEV: [After Nixon calls attention to a built-in panel-controlled washing machine.] We have such things.

NIXON: This is the newest model. This is the kind which is built in thousands of units for direct installation in the houses. [He adds that Americans are interested in making life easier for their women.]

Mr. Khrushchev remarked that in the Soviet Union, they did not have "the capitalist attitude toward women."

NIXON: I think that this attitude toward women is universal. What we want to do is make easier the life of our housewives.

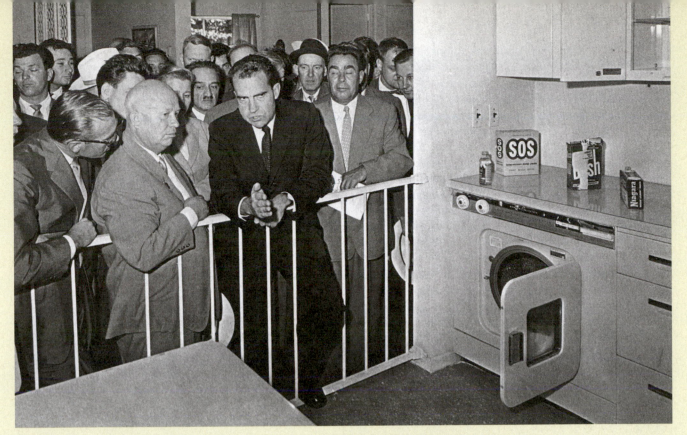

Khrushchev and Nixon discuss the merits of the American way during the famous kitchen debate. (AP Images)

Nixon explained that the house could be built for $14,000 and that most veterans had bought houses for between $10,000 and $15,000.

NIXON: Let me give you an example you can appreciate. Our steelworkers, as you know, are on strike. But any steelworker could buy this house. They earn $3 an hour. This house costs about $100 a month to buy on a contract running 25 to 30 years.

KHRUSHCHEV: We have steelworkers and we have peasants who also can afford to spend $14,000 for a house. . . .

KHRUSHCHEV: Don't you have a machine that puts food into the mouth and pushes it down? Many things you've shown us are interesting but they are not needed in life. They have no useful purpose. They are merely gadgets. We have a saying, if you have bedbugs you have to catch one and pour boiling water into the ear.

NIXON: We have another saying. This is that the way to kill a fly is to make it drink whisky. But we have a better use for whisky. [Aside] I like to have this battle of wits with the Chairman. He knows his business. . . .

KHRUSHCHEV: The Americans have created their own image of the Soviet man and think he is as you want him to be. But he is not as you think. You think the Russian people will be dumbfounded to see these things, but the fact is that newly built Russian houses have all this equipment right now. Moreover, all you have to do to get a house is to be born in the Soviet Union.

You are entitled to housing. I was born in the Soviet Union. So I have a right to a house. In America, if you don't have a dollar — you have the right to choose between sleeping in a house or on the pavement. Yet you say that we are slaves of communism. . . .

NIXON: We do not claim to astonish the Russian people. We hope to show our diversity and our right to choose. We do not wish to have decisions made at the top by government officials who say that all homes should be built in the same way. Would it not be better to compete in the relative merits of washing machines than in the strength of rockets. Is this the kind of competition you want?

KHRUSHCHEV: Yes that's the kind of competition we want. But your generals say: "Let's compete in rockets. We are strong and we can beat you." But in this respect we can also show you something.

NIXON: To me you are strong and we are strong. In some ways, you are stronger. In others, we are stronger. We are both strong not only from the standpoint of weapons but from the standpoint of will and spirit. **"**

Source: Transcript of the "Kitchen Debate" at the opening of the American National Exhibition at Sokolniki Park in Moscow, July 24, 1959.

QUESTIONS FOR ANALYSIS

1. Why do Nixon and Khrushchev spend so much time talking about the lives of workers in the United States and the Soviet Union?

2. Why were consumer goods, such as washing machines and television sets, such important symbols of modernity and progress for both Nixon and Khrushchev?

3. What does the kitchen debate reveal about the different ways in which communist and capitalist leaders viewed women's role in society?

Wall would lessen Cold War tensions, Kennedy nonetheless allowed its construction.

Emboldened and seeing a chance to change the balance of military power decisively, Premier Khrushchev next ordered missiles with nuclear warheads installed in Fidel Castro's communist Cuba in 1962. President Kennedy countered with a naval blockade of Cuba. After a tense diplomatic crisis, Khrushchev agreed to remove the Soviet missiles in return for American pledges not to disturb Castro's regime. In a secret agreement, Kennedy also promised to remove U.S. nuclear missiles from Turkey.

Khrushchev's influence, already slipping, declined rapidly after the Cuban missile crisis. In 1964 the reformist premier was displaced in a bloodless coup, and he spent the rest of his life under house arrest. Under his successor, Leonid Brezhnev (1906–1982), the Soviet Union began a period of stagnation and limited re-Stalinization. Almost immediately, Brezhnev (BREHZH-nehf) and his supporters started talking quietly of Stalin's "good points" and ignoring his crimes. This change informed Soviet citizens that further liberalization could not be expected at home. Soviet leaders, determined never to suffer Khrushchev's humiliation in the face of American nuclear superiority, also launched a massive arms buildup. Yet Brezhnev and company proceeded cautiously in the mid-1960s and avoided direct confrontation with the U.S.

decolonization The postwar reversal of Europe's overseas expansion caused by the rising demand of the colonized peoples themselves, the declining power of European nations, and the freedoms promised by U.S. and Soviet ideals.

Despite popular protests and changes in leadership, the Soviet Union and its satellite countries had achieved some stability by the late 1950s. Communist regimes addressed dissent and uprisings with an effective combination of military force, political repression, and limited economic reform. East and West traded propaganda threats, but both sides basically accepted the division of Europe into spheres of influence. More violent conflicts now took place in the developing world, where decolonization was opening new paths for Cold War confrontation.

The End of Empires

What circumstances led to the postwar colonial independence movements, and how did the Cold War influence the process? ■

In the postwar era, in one of world history's great turning points, Europe's long-standing overseas expansion was dramatically reversed. The retreat from imperial control—what Europeans called **decolonization**—

remade the world map. Some one hundred new nations in Africa, Asia, and the Middle East joined the global community (Map 29.3).

In some cases, decolonization proceeded relatively smoothly, with an orderly transition and little violence. In others, the European powers were determined to preserve colonial rule—long a source of profit and national pride—and colonized peoples won independence only after long and bloody struggles.

The Cold War had a profound impact on decolonization. Anticolonial independence movements often had to choose sides in the struggle between the superpowers, and after independence was won, both the United States and the Soviet Union struggled to exert influence in the former colonies. Liberation from colonial domination was a proud achievement that brought fundamental gains in political freedom, but also left lasting problems for the former colonized and colonizers alike.

Decolonization and the Cold War

The most basic cause of imperial collapse was the rising demand of non-Western peoples for national self-determination, racial equality, and personal dignity. This demand spread from intellectuals to the masses in nearly every colonial territory after the First World War. By 1939 colonial empires had already been shaken, and the Second World War prepared the way for the eventual triumph of independence movements.

European empires had been based on an enormous power differential between the rulers and the ruled, a difference that had greatly declined by 1945. Western Europe was economically devastated and militarily weak immediately after the war. Moreover, the Japanese had driven imperial rulers from large parts of East Asia during the war in the Pacific, shattering the myth of European superiority and invincibility. In East Asia, European imperialists confronted strong anticolonial nationalist movements that had developed under the Japanese occupation.

To some degree, the Great Powers also regarded their empires very differently after 1945 than before 1914, or even before 1939. Empire had rested on self-confidence and self-righteousness; Europeans had believed their superiority to be not only technical and military but also spiritual and moral. The horrors of the Second World War destroyed such complacent arrogance and gave opponents of imperialism much greater influence in Europe. Increasing pressure from the United States, which had long presented itself as an enemy of empire, further encouraged Europeans to let go of their former colonies. Economically weakened, and with their political power and moral authority in tatters, the imperial powers could hardly afford to engage in bloody colonial wars and wanted instead to concentrate on rebuilding at home.

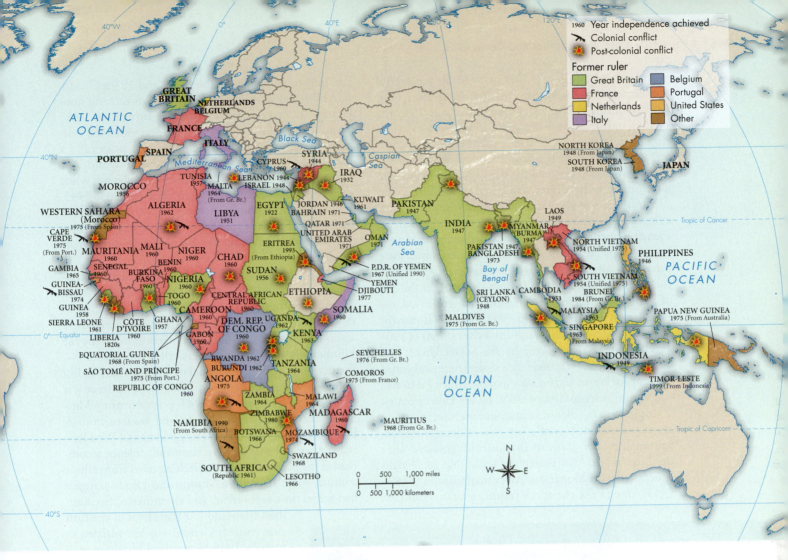

Map 29.3 **Decolonization in Africa and Asia, 1947 to the Present** Divided primarily along religious lines into two states, British India led the way to political independence in 1947. Most African territories achieved statehood by the mid-1960s as European empires passed away, unlamented.

Around the globe, the Cold War had an inescapable impact on decolonization. Liberation from colonial rule had long been a communist goal, a key component of world revolution. The Soviets and Red Chinese advocated rebellion in the developing world and promised native peoples an end to colonial exploitation followed by freedom and equality in a socialist state. They supported communist independence movements with economic and military aid, and the insurgent guerrilla, armed with a Soviet-produced AK-47 machine gun, became the new symbol of Marxist revolution.

Western Europe and particularly the United States offered a competing vision of independence based on free-market economics and liberal democracy. Like the Soviet Union, the United States extended aid and arms to decolonizing nations. The Americans promoted cautious moves toward self-determination in the context of containment, attempting to limit the influence of communism in newly liberated states.

After they had won independence, the leaders of the new nations often found themselves trapped between the superpowers, compelled to voice support for one bloc or the other. Many new leaders followed a policy of **nonalignment**, remaining neutral in the Cold War and playing both sides for what they could get.

nonalignment Policy of postcolonial governments to remain neutral in the Cold War and play both the United States and the Soviet Union for what they could get.

The Struggle for Power in Asia

The first major fight for independence that followed World War II, between the Dutch and anticolonial insurgents in the Dutch East Indies (today's Indonesia), in many ways exemplified decolonization in the Cold War world. The Dutch had been involved in Indonesia since the early seventeenth century (see Chapter 15), and in the crisis that followed the Second World War they hoped to use Indonesia's raw materials, particularly rubber, to support economic recovery. During the war, however, the Japanese had overrun the archipelago and encouraged hopes for independence from Western control. When the Dutch returned in 1945, they faced a determined group of rebels inspired by a powerful combination of nationalism, Marxism, and Islam. Four years of deadly guerrilla war followed, and in 1949 the Netherlands reluctantly accepted Indonesian independence. The new Indonesian president became an effective advocate of nonalignment. He relied on the support of the Indonesian Communist Party but received foreign aid from both the United States and the Soviet Union.

A similar combination of communism and anti-colonialism inspired the independence movement in French Indochina (now Vietnam, Cambodia, and Laos). France desperately wished to maintain control over these prized colonies and tried its best to re-establish colonial rule after the Japanese occupation collapsed at the end of World War II. Despite substantial American aid, the French army was defeated in 1954 by forces under the guerrilla leader Ho Chi Minh (hoh chee mihn) (1890–1969), who was supported by the Soviet Union and China. Indochina was divided: a shaky truce established the states of North and South Vietnam, which led to civil war and subsequent intervention by the United States.

India, Britain's oldest, largest, and most lucrative imperial possession, played a key role in decolonization. Nationalist opposition to British rule coalesced after the First World War under the leadership of British-educated lawyer Mohandas (Mahatma) Gandhi (1869–1948), one of the twentieth century's most significant

and influential figures. In the 1920s and 1930s Gandhi (GAHN-dee) built a mass movement preaching non-violent "noncooperation" with the British. In 1935 Gandhi wrested from the frustrated and unnerved British a new, liberal constitution that was practically a blueprint for independence. The Second World War interrupted progress toward Indian self-rule, but when the Labour Party came to power in Great Britain in 1945, it was ready to relinquish sovereignty. British socialists had always been critical of imperialism, and the heavy cost of governing India had become a large financial burden.

Britain withdrew peacefully, but conflict between India's Hindu and Muslim populations posed a lasting dilemma for the South Asian subcontinent. As independence neared, the Muslim minority grew increasingly anxious about their status in an India dominated by the Hindu majority. Muslim leaders called for partition — the division of India into separate Hindu and Muslim states — and the British agreed. When independence was made official on August 15, 1947, predominantly Muslim territories on India's eastern and western borders became East Pakistan (today Bangladesh) and West Pakistan. A wave of massive migration and violence accompanied the partition of India. Seeking relief from ethnic conflict, some 10 million Muslim and Hindu refugees fled across the new borders, and an estimated five hundred thousand lost their lives in the riots that ensued. Gandhi was assassinated in January 1948 by a radical Hindu nationalist who opposed partition, and Jawaharlal Nehru became Indian prime minister.

As the Cold War heated up in the following decade, Pakistan, an Islamic republic, developed close ties with the United States. Under the leadership of Nehru, India successfully established a liberal, if socialist-friendly, democratic state and maintained a policy of nonalignment, dealing with both the United States and the Soviet Union. Pakistan and India both joined the British Common-

Gandhi Arrives in Delhi, October 1939
From the 1920s until his death in 1948, the Indian anticolonial leader Mahatma Gandhi led a determined and ultimately successful campaign against British imperialism. His advocacy of nonviolent resistance inspired the Indian masses, nurtured Indian national identity, and left a lasting model for later protest movements. Here Gandhi arrives for negotiations with the British viceroy after the outbreak of World War II. (Corbis)

wealth, a voluntary and cooperative association of former British colonies that already included Canada, Australia, and New Zealand.

If Indian nationalism drew on Western parliamentary liberalism, Chinese nationalism developed and triumphed in the framework of Marxist-Leninist ideology. After the withdrawal of the occupying Japanese army in 1945, China erupted in open civil war between Jiang Jieshi (traditionally called Chiang Kai-shek; 1887–1975), the leader of the conservative Guomindang (Kuomintang, National People's Party), and the Chinese communists, headed by Mao Zedong (MAOU dzuh-DOUNG). Stalin gave Mao aid, and the Americans gave Jiang much more. Winning the support of the peasantry by promising to expropriate the holdings of the big landowners, the tougher, better-organized communists forced the Guomindang to withdraw to the island of Taiwan in 1949. Mao and the communists united China's 550 million inhabitants in a strong centralized state. The Chinese communists expelled foreigners and began building a new society that adapted Marxism to Chinese conditions and brought Stalinist-style repression—mass arrests, forced-labor camps, and ceaseless propaganda campaigns—to the Chinese people. The new government also promoted land reform and extended education and health-care programs to the peasantry, and it introduced five-year plans that successfully boosted industrial production.

Independence and Conflict in the Middle East

In some areas of the Middle East, the movement toward political independence went relatively smoothly. The French League of Nations mandates in Syria and Lebanon had collapsed during the Second World War, and Saudi Arabia and Transjordan had already achieved independence from Britain. But events in the British mandate of Palestine and in Egypt showed that decolonization in the Middle East could be a dangerous and difficult process.

As part of the peace accords that followed the First World War, the British government had advocated a Jewish homeland alongside the Arab population (see Chapter 26). This tenuous compromise unraveled after World War II. Neither Jews nor Arabs were happy with British rule, and violence and terrorism mounted on both sides. In 1947 the frustrated British decided to leave

Israel, 1948

Palestine, and the United Nations voted in a nonbinding resolution to divide the territory into two states—one Arab and one Jewish. The Jews accepted the plan and founded the state of Israel in 1948. The Palestinians and the surrounding Arab nations viewed Jewish independence as a betrayal of their own interests, and they attacked the Jewish state as soon as it was proclaimed. The Israelis drove off the invaders and conquered more territory. Roughly nine hundred thousand Arab Palestinians fled or were expelled from their homes, creating a persistent refugee problem. Holocaust survivors from Europe streamed into Israel, as Theodor Herzl's Zionist dream came true (see Chapter 24). The next fifty years saw four more wars between the Israelis and the Arab states and innumerable clashes between Israelis and Palestinians.

The Arab defeat in 1948 triggered a powerful nationalist revolution in Egypt in 1952, led by the young army officer Gamal Abdel Nasser (1918–1970). The revolutionaries drove out the pro-Western king, and in 1954 Nasser became president of an independent Egyptian republic. A crafty politician, Nasser advocated nonalignment and expertly played the superpowers against each other, securing loans from the United States and purchasing Soviet arms.

In July 1956 Nasser abruptly nationalized the foreign-owned Suez Canal Company, the last symbol and substance of Western power in the Middle East. Infuriated, the British and the French, along with the Israelis, secretly planned a military invasion. The resulting Suez crisis marked a watershed in the history of European imperialism. The Israeli army invaded the Sinai Peninsula bordering the canal, and British and French bombers attacked Egyptian airfields. This was, however, the dying gasp of traditional imperial power. World opinion was outraged, and the United States feared that such a blatant show of imperialism would propel the Arab states

The Suez Crisis, 1956

Nationalizing the Suez Canal
Egyptian president Nasser greets cheering crowds in Cairo after the surprise takeover of the Suez Canal. Jubilation throughout Egypt and the Arab world quickly turned to humiliation as invading forces from Israel, Britain, and France crushed the Egyptian army, and a shell-shocked Nasser offered to resign. But the Egyptian masses demanded that he stay, and the charismatic Nasser emerged triumphant after the Americans and Soviets forced Israel, Britain, and France to back down. (Hulton-Deutsch Collection/Corbis)

into the Soviet bloc. The Americans joined with the Soviets to force the British, French, and Israelis to back down. Egyptian nationalism triumphed: Nasser got his canal, and Israel left the Sinai in 1957. The Suez crisis showed that the European powers could no longer maintain their global empires, and it demonstrated the power and appeal of nonalignment.

The African Awakening

In less than a decade, most African states won independence from European imperialism, a remarkable event of world historical importance. In much of the continent south of the Sahara, decolonization proceeded relatively smoothly. Yet the new African states were quickly caught up in the struggles between the Cold War superpowers, and decolonization all too often left a lasting legacy of economic decline and political instability (see Map 29.3).

Starting in 1957 most of Britain's African colonies achieved independence with little or no bloodshed and then entered a very loose association with Britain as members of the British Commonwealth. Ghana, Nigeria, Tanzania, and other nations gained independence in this way, but there were exceptions to this smooth transfer of power. In Kenya in the early 1950s, British forces brutally crushed the Mau Mau rebellion, but nonetheless had to grant Kenyan independence in 1963. In the former British colony of South Africa, white settlers left the Commonwealth in 1961 and declared an independent republic in order to preserve the unequal advantages

of apartheid—an exploitative system of racial segregation enforced by law.

The decolonization of the Belgian Congo was one of the great tragedies of the Cold War. Belgian leaders, profiting from the colony's wealth of natural resources and proud of their small nation's imperial status, maintained a system of apartheid and dragged their feet in granting independence. These conditions sparked an anticolonial movement that grew increasingly aggressive in the late 1950s under the able leadership of the charismatic Patrice Lumumba. In January 1960 the Belgians gave in, hastily announcing that the Congo would be independent six months later, a schedule that was irresponsibly fast. Lumumba was chosen prime minister in democratic elections, but when the Belgians pulled out on schedule, the new government was entirely unprepared. Chaos broke out when the Congolese army rioted against the Belgian military officers who remained in the country.

With substantial financial investments in the Congo, the United States and western Europe worried that the new nation might fall into Soviet hands. U.S. leaders cast Lumumba as a Soviet proxy, an oversimplification of his nonalignment policies, and American anxiety increased when Lumumba turned to the Soviet Union for aid and protection. A cable from the CIA chief in the Congo revealed the way Cold War anxieties framed the situation:

Embassy and station believe Congo experiencing classic Communist takeover government. . . . Whether or not Lumumba actually Commie or just playing Commie game to assist solidifying his power, anti-West forces rapidly increasing power [in] Congo and there may be little time left in which to take action to avoid another Cuba.[9]

In a troubling example of containment in action, the CIA helped implement a military coup against Lumumba, who was assassinated in captivity in January 1961. The Congolese military set up a U.S.-backed dictatorship under the corrupt general Joseph Mobutu. Mobutu ruled until 1997 and became one of the world's wealthiest men, while the Congo remains one of the poorest and most politically troubled nations in the world.

French colonies in Africa followed several roads to independence. Like the British, the French offered most of their African colonies the choice of a total break with France or independence within a kind of French commonwealth. All but one of the new states chose association with France, largely because they identified with French culture and wanted aid from their former colonizer. The French were eager to help — provided their former colonies would accept close ties with France on French terms. As in the past, the French and their Common Market partners, who helped foot the bill, saw themselves as continuing their civilizing mission in sub-Saharan Africa (see Chapter 25). More important, they saw in Africa untapped markets for their industrial goods, raw materials for their factories, outlets for profitable investment, and good temporary jobs for their engineers and teachers.

Things were more difficult in the French colony of Algeria, a large Muslim state on the Mediterranean Sea, where some 500,000 French and Europeans had taken up permanent residency by the 1950s. Nicknamed *pied noirs* (people with black feet), many of these Europeans had raised families in Algeria for three or four generations, and they enforced a two-tiered system of citizenship, maintaining complete control of politics and the economy. When Muslim rebels, inspired by Islamic fundamentalism and communist ideals, established the National Liberation Front (FLN) and revolted against French colonialism in the early 1950s, the presence of the pied noirs complicated matters. Worried about their position in the colony, the pied noirs pressured the French government to help them. In response, the French army sent some 400,000 troops to crush the FLN and put down the revolt.

The resulting Algerian war — long, bloody, and dirty, with numerous atrocities on both sides — lasted from 1954 to 1962. The excesses of the French army included systematic torture, the so-called resettlement or forced relocation of the Muslim population, and attacks on civilians who supported the insurgents. News reports turned French public opinion and indeed the government against the war, but efforts to open peace talks instigated a revolt by the Algerian French and threats of a

French Checkpoint in Algeria, 1962 French soldiers search a civilian in Algiers, the capital of Algeria. Inspired by a potent mix of communism and Islamic radicalism, the Algerian National Liberation Front fought a lengthy and bloody struggle against the French colonial government that finally led to Algerian independence in 1962. (Agence France Presse/Hulton Archive/Getty Images)

coup d'état by the French army. In 1958 the immensely popular General Charles de Gaulle was reinstated as French prime minister as part of the movement to keep Algeria French, and his appointment calmed the army, the pied noirs, and the French public. Yet de Gaulle pragmatically accepted the principle of Algerian self-determination, and in 1962 he ended the conflict. After more than a century of French rule, Algeria became independent, and its European population quickly fled to France.

By the mid-1960s most African states had won independence, some through bloody insurrections. There were exceptions: South African blacks still longed for liberation from apartheid, and the tiny nation of Portugal waged war against independence movements in its colonies of Angola and Mozambique until the 1970s. Even in liberated nations, the colonial legacy had long-term negative effects. African leaders may have expressed support for socialist or democratic principles in order to win aid from the superpowers. In practice, however, corrupt and authoritarian African leaders like Mobutu in the Congo often established lasting authoritarian dictatorships and enriched themselves at the expense of their populations.

Even after decolonization, western European countries managed to increase their economic and cultural ties with their former African colonies in the 1960s and 1970s. Above all, they used the lure of special trading privileges, and provided heavy investment in French- and English-language education to enhance a powerful Western presence in the new African states. This situation led a variety of leaders and scholars to charge that western Europe (and the United States) had imposed a system of neocolonialism on the former colonies. According to this view, neocolonialism was a system designed to perpetuate Western economic domination and undermine the promise of political independence, thereby extending to Africa (and much of Asia) the economic subordination that the United States had established in Latin America in the nineteenth century. Such economic ties were clearly better than open political domination, but, according to critics, they still worked to the former colony's disadvantage.

Postwar Social Transformations

How did large-scale changes in social structures and relations contribute to European stability on both sides of the iron curtain? ■

While Europe staged its astonishing political and economic recovery from the Nazi nightmare, the basic structures of Western society were changing no less rapidly and remarkably. New forms of European migration, a changing class structure, and new roles for women and youths had dramatic impacts on everyday life in postwar Europe. These large-scale changes were experienced differently in communist eastern and democratic western Europe. Nonetheless, such large-scale changes had transformative effects on both sides of the iron curtain. Thus social and cultural trends joined political and economic recovery to build stability in the postwar decades.

Changing Class Structures

Rapid economic growth went a long way toward creating a new society in Europe after the Second World War. European society became more mobile. Old class barriers relaxed, and class distinctions became fuzzier.

Changes in the structure of the middle class were particularly influential in the general drift toward a less rigid class structure. In the nineteenth and early twentieth centuries, the model for the middle class had been the independent, self-employed individual who owned a business or practiced a liberal profession such as law or medicine. Ownership of property—very often inherited property—and strong family ties had often been the keys to wealth and standing within the middle class. After 1945 this pattern declined drastically in western Europe. A new breed of managers and experts—so-called white-collar workers—replaced traditional property owners as the leaders of the middle class. Ability to serve the needs of a big organization largely replaced inherited property and family connections in determining an individual's social position in the middle and upper-middle classes. At the same time, the middle class grew massively and became harder to define.

There were several reasons for these developments. Rapid industrial and technological expansion created a powerful demand for technologists and managers in large corporations and government agencies. Moreover, the old propertied middle class lost control of many family-owned businesses, and many small businesses (including family farms) simply passed out of existence as their former owners joined the ranks of salaried employees.

Similar processes were at work in the communist states of the East Bloc, where class leveling was an avowed goal of the authoritarian socialist state. The forced nationalization of industry, the expropriation of property, and aggressive attempts to open employment opportunities to workers and equalize wage structures effectively reduced class differences. Party members typically received better jobs and more pay, but the income differentials between the top and bottom strata of East Bloc societies were far smaller than those in the West.

In both East and West, managers and civil servants represented the model for a new middle class of salaried specialists. Well-paid and highly trained, often with backgrounds in engineering or accounting, these pragmatic experts were primarily concerned with efficiency and with practical solutions to concrete problems.

The structure of the lower classes also became more flexible and open. There was a mass exodus from farms and the countryside; the population of one of the most traditional and least mobile groups in European society—farmers—drastically declined. Meanwhile, the number of industrial workers in western Europe also began to decline, as new jobs for white-collar and service employees grew rapidly. This change marked a significant transition in the world of labor. In general, European workers were better educated and more specialized than before, and the new workforce bore a greater resemblance to the growing middle class of salaried specialists than to traditional industrial workers. The welfare benefits extended by postwar governments also worked to promote greater social equality by raising lower-class living standards and by being paid for in part by higher taxes on the wealthy.

Patterns of Postwar Migration

Changing patterns of migration also had a significant impact on European society. From the 1850s to the 1930s, countless European immigrants had left the continent for colonies or foreign states, seeking economic opportunity or freedom from political or religious persecution (see Chapter 26). In the 1950s and 1960s the trend reversed. Europeans now saw an influx of migrants into their lands, particularly in the prosperous northwest, where the demand for labor encouraged mass immigration.

Some migration took place within national borders. Declining job prospects in Europe's rural areas encouraged many peasants and small farmers to seek better prospects in the cities. In the poorer nations in southern Europe such as Spain, Portugal, and Italy, millions moved to more developed regions of their own countries. The process was similar in the Soviet bloc, where the forced collectivization of agriculture and state subsidies for heavy industry opened opportunities in urban areas. Before the erection of the Berlin Wall in 1961,

some 3.5 million East Germans also crossed the open border into the Federal Republic of Germany, seeking higher pay and a better life.

Many other Europeans moved across national borders seeking work. The general pattern was from south to north. Workers from less-developed countries like Italy, Spain, and socialist Yugoslavia moved to the industrialized nations of the north, and particularly to war-ravaged Germany, which had lost 5 million people during the Second World War and was in desperate need of able-bodied workers. In the 1950s and 1960s West Germany and other prosperous countries implemented a series of **guest worker programs** that were designed to recruit much-needed labor for the booming economy. West Germany signed labor agreements with Italy, Greece, Spain, Portugal, Yugoslavia, Turkey, and the North African countries of Tunisia and Morocco. By the early 1970s there were 2.8 million foreign workers in Germany and 2.3 million in France, where they made up 11 percent of the French workforce.

Most guest workers were young, unskilled single men who labored for low wages in entry-level jobs and sent much of their pay to their families at home. (See "Individuals in Society: Armando Rodrigues, West Germany's

guest worker programs Government-run programs in western Europe designed to recruit labor for the booming postwar economy.

The *Empire Windrush* Docks in London On June 22, 1948, almost five hundred Jamaicans seeking to emigrate to Great Britain arrived in London on the former troopship *Empire Windrush*. The event symbolized the changing patterns of postwar migration that would bring cultural and ethnic diversity to western Europe. (Keystone/Getty Images)

Armando Rodrigues, West Germany's "One-Millionth Guest Worker"

INDIVIDUALS IN SOCIETY

POPPING FLASHBULBS GREETED PORTUGUESE WORKER ARMANDO RODRIGUES when he stepped off a train in Cologne in September 1964. Celebrated in the national media as West Germany's one-millionth guest worker, Rodrigues was met by government and business leaders — including the minister of labor — who presented him with a motorcycle and a bouquet of carnations. A famous photograph of the event shows a modestly dressed Rodrigues mounted on his bike and surrounded by clapping dignitaries.

In most respects, Rodrigues was hardly different from the many foreign workers recruited to work in West Germany and other northern European countries. Yet given his moment of fame, he is an apt symbol of a troubled labor program that helped turn Germany into a multiethnic society.

By the late 1950s the new Federal Republic desperately needed able-bodied men to fill the low-paying jobs created by rapid economic expansion. West Germany had signed its first bilateral labor agreement with Italy in 1955, and treaties with other Mediterranean countries soon followed.

Rodrigues and hundreds of thousands of other young men signed up for the employment program and then submitted to an arduous application process. Rodrigues traveled from his village to the regional Federal Labor Office, where he filled out forms and took written and medical exams. Months later, after he had received an initial one-year contract from a German employer, Rodrigues and twelve hundred other Portuguese and Spanish men boarded a special train reserved for foreign workers and embarked for the Federal Republic.

For labor migrants, life was hard in West Germany. In the first years of the guest worker program, most recruits were young men between the ages of twenty and forty who were either single or willing to leave their families at home. They typically filled low-level jobs in construction, mines, and factories, and they lived in segregated barracks close to their workplaces, with six to eight workers in a room.

According to official plans, the so-called guest workers were supposed to return home after a specified period of time. Rodrigues went back to Portugal in the late 1970s, but despite government pressure, millions of temporary "guests" raised families and became permanent West German residents, building substantial ethnic minorities in the Federal Republic. Because of strict naturalization laws, however, they could not become West German citizens.

West Germans gave Rodrigues and his fellow migrants a mixed reception. Though they were a welcome source of inexpensive labor, the men who

Armando Rodrigues received a standing ovation and a motorcycle when he got off the train in Cologne in 1964. (DPA/Landov)

emigrated from what West Germans called "the southern lands" faced discrimination and prejudice. "Order, cleanliness, and punctuality seem like the natural qualities of a respectable person to us," wrote one official in 1966. "In the south, one does not learn or know this, so it is difficult [for a person from the south] to adjust here."*

Despite such hostility, foreign workers established a lasting and powerful presence in West Germany, and they were a significant factor in the country's swift economic recovery. Over time, West Germans came to terms with the tensions surrounding cultural integration and ethnic pluralism. Some forty-five years after Rodrigues arrived in Cologne, his motorcycle is on permanent display in the House of History Museum in Bonn. The exhibit is a remarkable testament both to the contribution of migrant labor to West German economic growth and to the benefits of multiculturalism in a democratic German society.

QUESTIONS FOR ANALYSIS

1. How did Rodrigues's welcome at his 1964 reception differ from the general attitude toward guest workers in Germany at the time?

2. What were the long-term costs and benefits of West Germany's labor recruitment policies?

*Quoted in Rita Chin, *The Guest Worker Question in Postwar Germany* (New York: Cambridge University Press, 2007), p. 43.

'One-Millionth Guest Worker,'" at left.) According to government plans, guest workers were supposed to return to their home countries after a specified period. In time, however, they built new lives, and to the dismay of the authorities many chose to live permanently in their adoptive countries. The number of Turkish foreign residents in West Germany soon surpassed the number of members of other ethnic groups, creating a large Turkish Muslim minority in the Federal Republic.

Europe was also changed by **postcolonial migration**, the movement of people from the former colonies (see pages 944–950) and the developing world into the prosperous states of Europe. In contrast to guest workers, who migrated as a result of formal recruitment programs, postcolonial migrants, who could often claim citizenship rights from their former colonizers, moved spontaneously to the former imperial powers. Immigrants from the Caribbean, India, Africa, and Asia moved to Britain; North Africans and especially Algerians moved to France; and Indonesians from the former Dutch East Indies migrated to the Netherlands. Postcolonial migrants also moved to eastern Europe, though in fewer numbers.

postcolonial migration
The postwar movement of people from former colonies and the developing world into Europe.

These new migration patterns had dramatic results. Immigrant labor fueled economic recovery. Growing ethnic diversity changed the face of Europe and enriched the cultural life of the continent. The new residents were not always welcome, however. Adaptation to European lifestyles could be difficult, and migrants often held on to their own languages and lived in separate communities. They faced employment and housing discrimination, and they were targeted by the anti-immigration policies of xenophobic politicians. Some Europeans worried that Muslim migrants from North Africa and Turkey would fail to properly adapt to European values and customs. In the twenty-first century Europeans continue to deal with the challenges of a multiethnic society.

New Roles for Women

The postwar culmination of a one-hundred-year-long trend toward early marriage, early childbearing, and small family size in wealthy urban societies (see Chapter 23) had revolutionary implications for women. Above all, pregnancy and child care occupied a much smaller portion of a woman's life than in earlier times. The postwar baby boom did make for larger families and fairly rapid population growth of 1 to 1.5 percent per year in many European countries, but the long-term decline in birthrates resumed by the 1960s. By the early 1970s about half of Western women were having their last baby by the age of twenty-six or twenty-seven. When the youngest child trooped off to kindergarten, the average mother had more than forty years of life in front of her.

This was a momentous transition. Throughout history male-dominated society insisted on defining most women as mothers or potential mothers, and motherhood was very demanding. In the postwar years, however, motherhood no longer absorbed the energies of a lifetime, and more and more married women looked for new roles in the world of work outside the family.

Women's roles in the workforce also changed after World War II. The ever-greater complexity of the modern economy meant that many women had to go outside the home to find cash income. Three major forces helped women searching for jobs. First, the economy boomed from about 1950 to 1973 and created strong demand for labor. Second, the economy continued its gradual shift away from the old male-dominated heavy industries, such as coal, steel, and shipbuilding, to the more dynamic white-collar service industries in which some women had always worked, such as government, education, trade, and health care. Third, young Western women shared fully in the postwar education revolution (see page 955) and could take advantage of the growing need for officeworkers and well-trained professionals. Thus more and more married women became full-time and part-time wage earners.

In the East Bloc, communist leaders asserted that they had opened up numerous jobs to women, and in large part they were correct. In eastern Europe, women accounted for almost half of all employed persons, and many women made their way into previously male professions, such as medicine and engineering. In western Europe and North America, there was a good deal of variation, with the percentage of married women in the workforce rising from a range of roughly 20 to 25 percent in 1950 to a range of 30 to 60 percent in the 1970s.

All was not easy for women entering paid employment. Married women entering (or re-entering) the labor force faced widespread and long-established discrimination in pay, advancement, and occupational choice in comparison to men. Moreover, many women could find only part-time work. As the divorce rate rose in the 1960s, part-time work, with its low pay and scanty benefits, often meant poverty for many women with teenage children. Finally, in the best of circumstances, married working women still carried most of the child-rearing and housekeeping responsibilities. Trying to live up to society's seemingly contradictory ideals was one reason for

many women to accept part-time employment; women working full-time typically faced an exhausting "double day" — on the job and at home.

The injustices that married women encountered as wage earners contributed greatly to the subsequent movement for women's equality and emancipation. Sexism and discrimination in the workplace — and in the home — grew loathsome and evoked the sense of injustice that drives revolutions and reforms. When in the 1960s a powerful feminist movement arose in the United States and western Europe to challenge the system, it found widespread support among working women.

Youth Culture and the Generation Gap

Postwar Europe also witnessed remarkable changes in youth roles and lifestyles, as the bulging cohort of so-called baby boomers born after World War II created a distinctive and very international youth culture. In the 1950s young people across western Europe and the United States created unique subcultures rooted in fashion and musical taste that set them off from their elders

British Teddy Boys, 1953 These young men are dressed in the "Teddy boy" style with velvet collars, narrow ties, and peg trousers that combine British Edwardian and American fashion. Like other subcultures in the 1950s, the Teds used their appearance to express their youthful rebelliousness. Teddy Boys quickly earned a reputation for street fighting, low-level criminal activity, and attacks on Britain's growing West Indian community. (© Henry Grant Collection/Museum of London)

and fueled anxious comments about a growing "generation gap."

Youth styles in the United States often provided inspiration for movements in Europe. Groups like the British Teddy Boys, the West German *Halbstarken* (half-strongs), and the French *blouson noirs* (black jackets) modeled their rebellious clothing and cynical attitudes on the bad-boy characters played by U.S. film stars such as James Dean and Marlon Brando. American jazz and rock 'n' roll spread rapidly in western Europe, aided by the invention of the long-playing record album (or LP) and the 45 rpm "single" in the late 1940s, and the growth of the corporate music industry. American musicians such as Elvis Presley, Bill Haley and the Comets, and Gene Vincent thrilled youths and worried parents, teachers, and politicians.

Youths played a key role in the consumer revolution. Postwar prosperity gave young people more purchasing power than ever before, and marketing experts and manufacturers quickly recognized that the young people they now called "teenagers" had money to spend. An array of advertisements and products now consciously targeted the youth market. In France, for example, magazine advertising aimed at adolescents grew by 400 percent between 1959 and 1962. As the baby boomers entered their late teens, they eagerly purchased trendy clothing and the latest pop music hits, as well as record players, transistor radios, magazines, hairstyles, and makeup, all marketed for the "young generation."

The new youth culture became an inescapable part of European society. One clear sign of this new presence was the rapid growth in the number of universities—and college students. In contrast to the United States, university education in Europe had been limited for centuries to a small elite. In 1950 only 3 to 4 percent of western European youths went on to higher education. Then, as government subsidies made education more affordable to the masses, enrollments skyrocketed. By 1960 at least three times more students attended some kind of university than they had before World War II, and the number continued to rise sharply until the 1970s.

The rapid expansion of higher education opened new opportunities for the middle and lower classes, but it also meant that classrooms were badly overcrowded. Many students felt that they were not getting the kind of education they needed for jobs in the modern world. At the same time, some reflective students feared that universities would soon do nothing but turn out docile technocrats both to stock and to serve "the establishment." Thus it was no coincidence that students became leaders in a counterculture that attacked the ideals of the affluent society and shocked the West in the late 1960s.

LOOKING BACK LOOKING AHEAD

THE UNPRECEDENTED human and physical destruction of the Second World War left Europeans shaken, searching in the ruins for new livelihoods and a workable political order. A tension-filled peace settlement left the continent divided into two hostile political-military blocs, and the resulting Cold War, complete with the possibility of atomic annihilation, threatened to explode into open confrontation. Albert Einstein voiced a common anxiety when he said, "I do not know with what weapons World War III will be fought, but World War IV will be fought with sticks and stones."

Despite such fears, the division of Europe led to the emergence of a remarkably enduring world system. In the West, liberal democracy and the Western alliance brought social and political consensus. In the East, a combination of political repression and partial reform likewise limited dissent and encouraged stability. During the height of the Cold War, Europe's former colonies won liberation in a process that was often flawed, but that nonetheless resulted in political independence for millions of people. And large-scale transformations, including the rise of Big Science and rapid economic growth, opened new opportunities for women and immigrants and contributed to stability on both sides of the iron curtain.

By the early 1960s Europeans had entered a remarkable age of affluence that almost eliminated real poverty on most of the continent. Superpower confrontations had led not to European war but to peaceful coexistence. The following decades, however, would see substantial challenges to this postwar consensus. Youth revolts and a determined feminist movement, an oil crisis and a deep economic recession, and political dissent and revolution in the socialist bloc would shake and remake the foundations of Western society.

CHAPTER REVIEW

■ **How did the events at the close of World War II contribute to the emergence of the Cold War, and how did the U.S.-Soviet rivalry affect life in Europe? (p. 924)**

The Cold War grew out of the way World War II was fought in Europe and out of deep tensions between the victorious superpowers. Near the end of World War II, American and British forces met Stalin's armies in the middle of Germany and central Europe, so that the war-torn continent was already divided militarily in 1945. In the postwar political settlement, the division became official, and a divided Germany became the epicenter of an East-West Cold War. Stalin gradually established dependent communist dictatorships in eastern Europe to ensure the security of the Soviet Union, and the United States instituted a policy of containment aimed at stopping the spread of communism into western Europe and around the world. Western European nations joined U.S.-backed NATO to protect against Soviet attack, and the Soviet-aligned states formed their own Warsaw Pact in retaliation. As the Cold War matchup in Europe was institutionalized, competition between the two superpowers for military, economic, and technological superiority led to a surge in scientific innovation.

■ **Why did western Europe recover so successfully, and what were the sources of postwar stability? (p. 933)**

Western Europe's success was due to a combination of political recovery and unprecedented economic expansion. Political recovery included the emergence of the Christian Democrats and the movement toward European unity. The center-right Christian Democrats won sweeping victories across continental Europe, ushering in a new era of politics that catered to family values and the rejection of communism. They also promoted a free-market economy but advocated government assistance in such areas as finance and health care. In the mid-1950s economic growth took off for a generation, fueled by Marshall Plan aid and the liberal trade policies of the new Common Market. The resulting consumer revolution brought increasing prosperity to increasing numbers of people.

■ **What was the pattern of postwar rebuilding and development in the Soviet Union and communist eastern Europe? (p. 937)**

Immediately following World War II, Stalin imposed harsh one-party rule in the lands occupied by the Soviet armies, and he reimposed rigid central planning in both the Soviet Union and its eastern European satellite countries. Nationalized industry led to a scarcity of consumer goods, and

ordinary citizens faced difficult lives. In the mid-1950s Khrushchev instituted a policy of de-Stalinization that eased government controls, led to more cultural freedoms, and relaxed Cold War tensions. A modest consumer revolution and a rising standard of living improved everyday life in the Soviet Union in the late 1950s and the 1960s.

■ **What circumstances led to the postwar colonial independence movements, and how did the Cold War influence the process? (p. 944)**

Several causes led to the struggle for postwar independence in the European colonies. First, intellectuals had been calling for colonized peoples to move toward self-determination and racial equality since the early decades of the twentieth century, and their ideas were finally gaining momentum. In addition, World War II had drained Europe of much of the military and economic strength necessary to maintain a hold on its colonies, and Europeans began questioning their own moral authority to undertake a "civilizing mission," given the destruction they had caused in their own nations. In some cases, colonized peoples gained independence through peaceful negotiation with the imperial powers. In others, independence was won only after fierce revolts or all-out wars. Meanwhile, the two postwar superpowers jockeyed for position among the former colonies, their competing ideologies each offering its own version of freedom. As former colonial nations such as France, Belgium, and Great Britain relaxed their hold on their imperial territories, the United States and the Soviet Union struggled for influence. Both provided economic aid and military arms to anticolonial independence movements, leading to proxy wars and the establishment of client states among the new nations in Asia, Africa, and the Middle East.

■ **How did large-scale changes in social structures and relations contribute to European stability on both sides of the iron curtain? (p. 950)**

In the years after 1945 economic expansion led to a more fluid, less antagonistic class structure in western Europe. In eastern Europe, communist policies attacked class distinctions and promised equality for all. Economic growth and social welfare programs drew new workers to European countries, and internal migration, guest worker programs, and postcolonial migration opened Europe to new peoples and cultures. Married women also entered the labor force in growing numbers. The growing prosperity of the postwar era gave young people more money and educational opportunities, spurring the development of a distinct youth culture in the 1960s.

Suggested Reading

Bernstein, Serge. *The Republic of de Gaulle, 1958–1969.* 2006. An outstanding work on France.

Bessel, Richard. *Germany 1945: From War to Peace.* 2009. Examines the extensive destruction of Germany after the war and its transition into the postwar period.

Chamberlain, M. E. *Decolonization: The Fall of European Empires,* 2d ed. 1999. A clear, up-to-date account.

Chin, Rita. *The Guest Worker Question in Postwar Germany.* 2007. An engaging interpretation of postwar migration patterns in the Federal Republic.

Deak, Istav, Jan Tomasz Gross, and Tony Judt, eds. *The Politics of Retribution in Europe: World War II and Its Aftermath.* 2000. A collection of essays on postwar attempts to punish those responsible for Nazi crimes.

de Grazia, Victoria. *Irresistible Empire: America's Advance Through Twentieth-Century Europe.* 2005. Lively, provocative account of the Americanization of Europe from 1900 to the 1950s.

de Senarclens, Pierre. *From Yalta to the Iron Curtain: The Great Powers and the Origins of the Cold War.* 1995. A valuable work on the Cold War.

Eksteins, Modris. *Walking Since Daybreak: A Story of Eastern Europe, World War II, and the Heart of Our Century.* 2000. A powerful, partly autobiographical account that is highly recommended.

Hitchcock, William I. *The Struggle for Europe: The Turbulent History of a Divided Continent, 1945 to the Present.* 2004. A valuable general study with extensive bibliographies.

Jaraush, Konrad. *After Hitler: Recivilizing Germans, 1945–1995.* 2006. A stimulating survey by a distinguished historian.

Judt, Tony. *Postwar: A History of Europe Since 1945.* 2005. A masterful reconsideration, especially strong on smaller countries.

Tipton, Frank B., and Robert Aldrich. *An Economic and Social History of Europe from 1939 to the Present.* 1987. An interesting wide-ranging account.

Westad, Odd Arne. *The Global Cold War: Third World Interventions and the Making of Our Times.* 2007. Up-to-date study of the Cold War's global impact.

Notes

1. Anonymous, *A Woman in Berlin: Eight Weeks in the Conquered City: A Diary* (New York: Metropolitan Books, 2005), pp. 239–240.
2. Quoted in N. Graebner, *Cold War Diplomacy, 1945–1960* (Princeton, N.J.: Van Nostrand, 1962), p. 17.
3. From a speech delivered by George Marshall at Harvard University on June 5, 1947, reprinted in *Department of State Bulletin* (June 15, 1947), pp. 1159–1160.
4. Quoted in T. Judt, *Postwar: A History of Europe Since 1945* (New York: Penguin, 2005), p. 150.
5. Liz Heron, ed., *Truth, Dare or Promise,* quoted in M. H. Hunt, *The World Transformed, 1945 to the Present: A Documentary Reader* (Boston: Bedford/St. Martin's, 2004), pp. 192–193.
6. L. Erhard, *The Economics of Success* (Princeton, N.J.: D. Van Nostrand, 1963), p. 207.
7. Quoted in D. Treadgold, *Twentieth Century Russia,* 5th ed. (Boston: Houghton Mifflin, 1981), p. 442.
8. Nikita Khrushchev, "On the Cult of Personality and Its Consequences" (1956), quoted in J. M. Brophy et al., *Perspectives from the Past* (New York: Norton, 2009), pp. 804–805.
9. Quoted in M. Huband, *The Skull Beneath the Skin: Africa After the Cold War* (Boulder: Westview Press, 2001), p. 9.

Key Terms

displaced persons (p. 925)
Truman Doctrine (p. 929)
Marshall Plan (p. 930)
Council for Mutual Economic Assistance (COMECON) (p. 930)
NATO (p. 930)
Warsaw Pact (p. 930)
Christian Democrats (p. 933)
Common Market (p. 935)
de-Stalinization (p. 940)
decolonization (p. 944)
nonalignment (p. 945)
guest worker programs (p. 951)
postcolonial migration (p. 953)

For practice quizzes and other study tools, visit the Online Study Guide at **bedfordstmartins.com/mckaywest**.

For primary sources from this period, see ***Sources of Western Society*, Second Edition**.

For Web sites, images, and documents related to topics in this chapter, visit Make History at **bedfordstmartins.com/mckaywest**.

30
Challenging the Postwar Order

1960–1991

As Europe entered the 1960s, the consensus established in the postwar era appeared stable and secure. Centrist politicians in western Europe agreed that abundant jobs and extensive state spending on welfare benefits would continue to improve living standards at all levels of society. In the Soviet Union and the East Bloc, although conditions varied country by country, modest economic growth and limited reforms amid continued political repression likewise contributed to a sense of stability. Cold War tensions relaxed, and it seemed that a remarkable age of affluence would ease political differences and lead to social harmony.

In the late 1960s, however, this hard-won consensus began to unravel. In 1968 counterculture protesters across the globe challenged dominant certainties. In the early 1970s the astonishing postwar economic advance ground to a halt, with serious social consequences. In western Europe, a new generation of more conservative political leaders drastically cut welfare benefits to deal with economic decline and growing global competition. New political groups — including feminists and environmentalists, national separatists and new-right populists — criticized centrist politics from across the political spectrum.

In the East Bloc, postwar leaders continued to vacillate between reform and repression, leading to frustrating stagnation. In the 1980s a broad movement to transform the communist system took root in Poland, and efforts to reform and revitalize the communist system in the Soviet Union snowballed out of control. In 1989 revolutions swept away communist rule throughout the entire Soviet bloc as the Cold War reached a dramatic conclusion. ∎

Life in a Divided Europe. Watchtowers, armed guards, and minefields controlled the communist eastern side of the Berlin Wall, the primary symbol of Cold War division in Europe. In the liberal West, to the contrary, ordinary folk turned the easily accessible wall into an ad hoc art gallery — this whimsical graffiti art appeared in the late 1980s.

CHAPTER PREVIEW

Reform and Protest in the 1960s
■ How did social and political changes in the 1960s contribute to growing criticism of the postwar consensus that had emerged in the 1950s?

Changing Consensus in Western Europe
■ How did economic decline in the 1970s contribute to fundamental social and political change in the 1980s in western Europe and North America?

The Decline of "Really Existing Socialism"
■ What internal and external factors weakened communist power in the East Bloc, and how did Soviet leader Mikhail Gorbachev try to reform the system from above?

The Revolutions of 1989
■ Why did anticommunist revolutions sweep through eastern Europe in 1989, and what were the immediate consequences?

Reform and Protest in the 1960s

How did social and political changes in the 1960s contribute to growing criticism of the postwar consensus that had emerged in the 1950s? ■

Looking at the wealth and prosperity of the early 1960s, commentators asserted that western Europe had entered an age of affluence. Compared to the previous fifty years, things looked good. After fifteen years of steady economic expansion, western Europeans began to enjoy the benefits of a well-established modern consumer society, and politics decidedly shifted to the left. Newly elected Social Democratic governments moved to normalize relations with the East Bloc and increased their countries' spending on welfare provisions. In the East, tensions lessened, eased by modest economic growth and forced underground by political repression. On both sides of the iron curtain, it seemed that the stability hammered out in the postwar decades was here to stay.

Challenges to the postwar consensus emerged in the mid-1960s, first in the form of a student counterculture that confronted the values of mainstream society with radical politics and lifestyle rebellions. Discontent spread to the East Bloc as well, particularly in Czechoslovakia, where in

détente The progressive relaxation of Cold War tensions.

1968 a rapid push toward liberalization was crushed by Soviet military force.

Cold War Tensions Thaw

The first decades of postwar reconstruction had been overseen by the center-right Christian Democrats, who successfully shaped the postwar consensus around Cold War politics, free-market economics with limited state intervention, and welfare provisions (see Chapter 29). Now, buoyed by the rapidly expanding economy, the politics shifted to the left. In Britain, the Labour Party returned to power in 1964, after thirteen years in opposition. In the Scandinavian countries of Denmark, Norway, and Sweden, Social Democratic parties maintained a leading role throughout the period. In West Germany, the aging postwar chancellor Konrad Adenauer (1876–1967) retired in 1963, and in 1969 Willy Brandt (1913–1992) became the first Social Democratic West German chancellor; his party would govern Germany until 1982. Even the tough-minded, independent French president Charles de Gaulle resigned in 1969.

One result of the victory of Social Democrats was the policy of **détente** (day-TAHNT), the progressive relaxation of Cold War tensions. While the Cold War continued to rage outside Europe and generally defined relations between the Soviet Union and the United States, western Europe took major steps toward genuine peace along the iron curtain. West German chancel-

A West German Leader Apologizes for the Holocaust In 1970 West German chancellor Willy Brandt knelt before the Jewish Heroes' Monument in Warsaw, Poland, to ask forgiveness for the German mass murder of European Jews and other groups during the Second World War. Brandt's action, captured in photo and film by the onlooking press, symbolized the chancellor's policy of Ostpolitik, the normalization of relations between the East and West Blocs. (AP Images)

lor Willy Brandt took the lead. In December 1970 he flew to Poland for the signing of a historic treaty of reconciliation. In a dramatic moment rich in symbolism, Brandt laid a wreath at the tomb of the Polish unknown soldier and another at the monument commemorating the armed uprising of Warsaw's Jewish ghetto against occupying Nazi armies. Standing before the ghetto memorial, a somber Brandt fell to his knees as if in prayer. "I wanted," Brandt said later, "to ask pardon in the name of our people for a million-fold crime which was committed in the misused name of the Germans."[1]

Brandt's gesture at the Warsaw Ghetto memorial and the treaty with Poland were part of his policy of reconciliation with eastern Europe, termed *Ostpolitik* (German for eastern policy). Brandt aimed at nothing less than a comprehensive peace settlement for central Europe and the two German states established after 1945. The Federal Republic of Germany (West Germany) had from its founding refused to recognize the communist German Democratic Republic (East Germany). West Germany also refused to accept the loss of German territory ceded to Poland and the Soviet Union after 1945.

According to Brandt, the building of the Berlin Wall in 1961 revealed the limitations of West Germany's official hard line toward communist eastern Europe. A new foreign policy was needed. Brandt negotiated treaties with the Soviet Union, Poland, and Czechoslovakia that formally accepted existing state boundaries in return for a mutual renunciation of force or the threat of force. Using the imaginative formula of "two German states within one German nation," Brandt's government also broke decisively with the past and entered into direct relations with East Germany. Brandt aimed for modest practical improvements rather than reunification, which at that point was completely impractical.

The policy of détente reached its high point when the United States, Canada, the Soviet Union, and all European nations (except isolationist Albania and tiny Andorra) signed the Final Act of the Helsinki Conference in 1975. The thirty-five participating nations agreed that Europe's existing political frontiers could not be changed by force. They also solemnly accepted numerous provisions guaranteeing the human rights and political freedoms of their citizens. Although the East did continue to curtail certain domestic freedoms and violate human rights guarantees (see pages 980–982), the

Chronology

1961	Building of Berlin Wall suggests permanence of the East Bloc
1962–1965	Second Vatican Council
1963	Wolf, *Divided Heaven*; Friedan, *The Feminine Mystique*
1964	Civil Rights Act in the United States
1964–1973	U.S. involvement in Vietnam War
1966	Formation of National Organization for Women (NOW)
1968	Soviet invasion of Czechoslovakia; "May events" protests in France
1971	Founding of Greenpeace
1973	OPEC oil embargo
1975	Final Act of the Helsinki Conference
1979	Margaret Thatcher becomes British prime minister; founding of West German Green Party; Soviet invasion of Afghanistan
1985	Mikhail Gorbachev named Soviet premier
1987	United States and Soviet Union sign arms reduction treaty
1989	Soviet withdrawal from Afghanistan
1989–1991	Fall of communism in eastern Europe
December 1991	Dissolution of the Soviet Union

agreement was generally effective in maintaining international peace.

Newly empowered Social Democrats also engaged in reform at home. Building on the welfare systems established in the 1950s, politicians increased state spending on public services even further. Society under western European social democracy was not "socialist," as it was in the Soviet bloc, where economic planning, government ownership, and one-party dictatorships ensured overwhelming state control. To the contrary, Social Democrats maintained a firm commitment to capitalist free markets and democratic electoral politics. At the same time, they viewed welfare provisions as a way to ameliorate the inevitable inequalities of a competitive market economy. As a result, western European democracies spent more and more state funds on health care, education, old-age insurance, and public housing.

By the early 1970s state spending on such programs hovered around 40 percent of the gross domestic product in France, West Germany, and Great Britain. Scandinavia and the Netherlands spent even more, all paid for with very high tax rates. Despite doctrinal differences, the center-right Christian Democrats also supported spending on public benefits and entitlements—as long as the economy prospered. With the economic slowdown of the mid-1970s, growing inflation and un-employment strained state budgets and undermined support for the welfare state consensus (see pages 972–974).

The Affluent Society

The political shift to the left in the 1960s was accompanied by rapid social change across western Europe. High wages meant that more and more people could afford the goods and gadgets provided by the consumer revolution that began in the 1950s (see Chapter 29), and the arrival of a full-blown consumer society had a profound impact on daily life. Labor-saving devices in family homes—vacuum cleaners, refrigerators, washing machines, and many others—transformed women's housework. Later studies showed that these new goods caused women to spend even more time cleaning and cooking to new exacting standards, but at the time electric appliances were considered indispensable to what contemporaries called a "modern lifestyle." The establishment of U.S.-style self-service supermarkets across Europe changed the way food was produced, purchased, and prepared, and threatened to force independent bakers, butchers, and neighborhood grocers out of business. (See "Living in the Past: The Supermarket Revolution," page 964.)

Europeans at all levels of society had more money to spend on leisure time and recreational pursuits. One of the most astonishing leisure-time developments was the blossoming of mass travel and tourism. With month-long paid vacations required by law in most western European countries and with widespread automobile ownership, travel to beaches and ski resorts came within the reach of the middle class and much of the working class. By the late 1960s packaged tours with cheap group airfares and bargain hotel accommodations had made even distant lands easily accessible. At home, more and more Europeans oriented their leisure time around television, watching news and entertainment and the latest American imports in the evenings.

Intellectuals and cultural critics greeted the age of affluence with a chorus of criticism. Some worried that rampant consumerism created a bland conformity that wiped out regional and national traditions and undermined intellectual activity. The great majority of ordinary people, they concluded, now ate the same foods, wore the same clothes, and watched the same programs on television, sapping creativity and individualism. Other critics complained bitterly that these changes threatened to Americanize European culture, but they could do little to stop the spread of consumer culture.

Worries about the Americanization of Europe were overstated—European nations preserved distinctive national cultures even during the consumer revolution—but social change was nonetheless unavoidable. The

moral authority of religious doctrine lost ground before the growing individualism of consumer society. Church membership declined, and fewer Europeans attended regular Sunday services. Even in traditionally Catholic countries, such as Italy, Ireland, and France, outward signs of popular belief seemed to falter. At the Second Vatican Council, convened from 1962 to 1965, Catholic leaders agreed on a number of reforms meant to democratize and renew the church and broaden its appeal. They called for new openness in Catholic theology, and masses would henceforth be said in local languages rather than in Latin, which few could understand. Their resolutions did little to halt the slide toward secularization. In Protestant lands—Great Britain, Scandinavia, the Netherlands, and most of West Germany—the decline in church membership was even greater.

Family ties also weakened in the age of affluence, and the number of adults living alone grew remarkably. Men

Braniff Airways Hostesses, ca. 1968 Sporting the latest "mod" styles, hostesses for Braniff International Airways wear uniforms made by world-renowned Italian fashion designer Emilio Pucci. The 1960s counterculture helped popularize the use of kaleidoscopic fluorescent colors and wild shapes in fashion, the fine arts, and advertising. (Braniff Archives)

and women married later, the nuclear family became smaller and more mobile, and divorce rates rose rapidly. By the 1970s the baby boom of the postwar decades was over, and population growth leveled out and even began to decline in the prosperous nations of northwest Europe.

The Growing Counterculture Movement

One of the dramatic results of economic prosperity and a more tolerant society was the emergence of a youthful counterculture that came of age in the mid-1960s to challenge the assumptions of the affluent society. What accounts for the emergence of the counterculture in the mid-1960s? Simple demographics played an important role. Young soldiers returning home after World War II in 1945 eagerly established families, and the next two decades brought a dramatic increase in the number of births per year in Europe and the United States. The children born during this baby boom grew up in an era of political liberalism and unprecedented material affluence. They learned about the horrors of totalitarian government during World War II, watched as colonial peoples forged new paths to freedom during the decades of decolonization, and worried about the growing conformity that seemed to be an inherent part of consumer society. Impressed by the U.S. civil rights movement and dismayed by ongoing Western imperialism and war, the baby boomers had the education—and perhaps most important the freedom from material want—to act on their concerns about inequality and social justice.

Counterculture movements in both Europe and the United States drew much inspiration from the American civil rights movement. In the late 1950s and early 1960s African Americans effectively challenged institutionalized inequality using legal means, as well as through public demonstrations, sit-ins, and bus boycotts, and threw off a deeply entrenched system of segregation and repression. The landmark Civil Rights Act of 1964, which prohibited discrimination in public services and on the job, and the Voting Rights Act of 1965, which guaranteed all African Americans the right to vote, were the crowning achievements of the long struggle against racism.

If dedicated African Americans and their white supporters could successfully reform entrenched power structures, student leaders reasoned, so could they. At the University of California–Berkeley in 1964 and 1965, students consciously adapted the tactics of the civil rights movement, including demonstrations and sit-ins, to challenge limits on free speech and academic freedom at the university. Their efforts were contagious. Soon students across the United States and in western Europe, where rigid rules controlled student activities at overcrowded

new universities, were engaged in active protests. The youth movement had come of age, and it mounted a determined challenge to the Western consensus.

Dreaming of complete freedom and simpler, purer societies, many student activists in western Europe and the United States embraced an updated, romanticized version of Marxism, creating a movement that came to be known as the **New Left**. Adherents of the New Left argued that Marxism in the Soviet Union had been perverted to serve the needs of a repressive totalitarian state. Western capitalism, with its cold disregard for social equality, was little better. What was needed was a more humanitarian style of socialism, a rather vaguely defined Marxist program that could avoid the worst excesses of both capitalism and Soviet-style communism. New Left critics also attacked what they saw as the conformity of consumer society. The so-called culture industry, they argued, fulfilled only false needs and so contributed to the alienation of Western society.

New Left A movement of students in the West who advocated simpler, purer societies based on an updated, romanticized version of Marxism.

Such rarefied ideas fascinated student intellectuals, but much counterculture activity revolved around a lifestyle rebellion that apparently had broader appeal. Politics and lifestyles merged, a process captured in the popular 1960s slogan "the personal is the political." Nowhere was this more obvious than in the so-called sexual revolution. The 1960s brought frank discussion about sexuality in general, a new willingness to engage in premarital sex, and a growing acceptance of homosexuality. Sexual experimentation was facilitated by the development of the birth-control pill, which could eliminate the risk of unwanted pregnancy and went on the market in most western European countries in the 1960s. By 1970 "the pill" was being taken daily by millions of women across the Western world. Much of the new openness about sex crossed generational lines, but for the young the idea of sexual emancipation was closely linked to radical politics. Sexual openness and "free love," the sixties generation argued, not only moved people beyond traditional norms, but might also form the foundation of a more humane society.

The revolutionary aspects of the sexual revolution are easily exaggerated. According to a poll of German college students taken in 1968, the overwhelming majority wished to establish permanent families on traditional middle-class models. Yet the sexual behavior of young people did change in the 1960s and 1970s. More young people engaged in premarital sexual intercourse, and they did so at an earlier age than ever before. A 1973 study reported that only 4.5 percent of West German youths born in 1945 and 1946 had experienced sexual relations before their seventeenth birthday, but that 32 percent of those born in 1953 and 1954 had done so.[2] Such trends continued in the following decades.

LIVING IN THE PAST

IN FEBRUARY 1961 SUPERMARKET ITALIANI OPENED its first supermarket-style grocery store in Florence, Italy, an ancient city famous for its Renaissance art and culture. The opening was an apparent triumph: some fifteen thousand customers mobbed the store, and police were called in to control the crowd. Owned by a multinational U.S.-based corporation, Supermarket Italiani proudly advertised "self service" — in English — the slogan expressing a new cachet for all things American. Yet all was not well in Florence. Small grocers greeted the supermarket with strikes. Demonstrators called for boycotts. Angry letters to local newspapers complained that Italian traditions were in decay.

No wonder. The supermarket brought dramatic changes. For centuries residents of Florence — like most Europeans — had bought their food from local butchers, bakers, and fruit and vegetable dealers. In these tiny neighborhood stores, a shopkeeper and family greeted customers, discussed quality and price, and gossiped about neighborhood events. Customers could not handle the merchandise, which was sold fresh and in bulk. In a typical exchange, the shopkeeper took an order, calculated the price, weighed and wrapped the goods, and often provided home delivery.

Shopping in a well-lit American-style supermarket changed all that. Consumers entered a much larger store, picked up a cart, and strolled through long aisles stocked with pre-packaged and pre-priced goods. Frozen meat and canned vegetables meant that seasonal items were now available all year round. Competing brands introduced many versions of the same product, and advertising campaigns and cut-rate pricing enticed customers, who paid for all of their food selections in one place: at the checkout counter, where anonymous clerks tallied bills and made change using modern cash registers.

The bright lights and colorful packaging masked changes in both production and consumption. New farming methods, distribution networks, and packaging and advertising industries emerged to meet the demands of supermarket retailing. Supermarketing encouraged the rise of huge international chains such as Aldi, which started as a small chain in postwar

For decades before the supermarket revolution of the 1950s, Europeans shopped in small stores featuring specialty selections, such as this Italian shop selling meats, cheese, and preserved goods. Shoppers asked for items that were displayed behind the counter and were typically served by the store owner or members of the family. (From "50 anni di supermercati," Gallerie fotographiche, larepubblica.it)

In the new supermarkets, customers enjoyed self-service from a vastly expanded array of mass-produced goods, colorfully packaged and displayed on open shelves in long, impersonal aisles. Shoppers in this British supermarket in the 1960s carried their selections in baskets or carts to checkout counters at the front of the store. (Mary Evans Picture Library/ The Image Works)

Germany and now owns over eight thousand stores around the world. At home, the supermarket changed recipes and meal plans as well as household budgets and shopping styles. Supermarkets also transformed city space. Large stores on busy roads meant more traffic, and automobiles and parking lots threatened the very existence of neighborhood corner stores.

This was all new when Supermarket Italiani opened in Florence in 1961. By 1971, however, there were 538 supermarkets in Italy, 1,833 in France, and over 2,000 in West Germany. Though they never entirely displaced small grocers—and never totally dominated the food retail sector, as in the United States—by the 1980s supermarkets were a normal part of everyday life, vivid evidence of how the consumer revolution transformed the way Europeans shopped for, ate, and thought about food.

QUESTIONS FOR ANALYSIS

1. Why did Italians greet the arrival of supermarket shopping with both protest and enthusiasm?
2. In what ways does the supermarket exemplify the consumer revolution that swept through Europe in the late 1950s and the 1960s? What were its implications for family life?

Advertisement for the opening of a new supermarket in France. (From "50 anni di supermercati," Gallerie fotographiche, larepubblica.it)

Swinging London Pop-art decorations on Carnaby Street, the center of swinging London, herald the coming Christmas season in December 1967. (Bettmann/Corbis)

Along with sexual openness, drug use and rock music were at the center of the lifestyle revolt. For "the 68ers"—as the sixties generation in Europe came to be called—using drugs was a way to break free from conventional morals, to "turn on, tune in, and drop out," in the words of the American cult figure Timothy Leary. The popular music of the 1960s championed countercultural lifestyles. Rock bands like the Beatles, the Rolling Stones, and many others sang songs about drugs and casual sex. Counterculture "scenes" developed in cities such as San Francisco, Paris, and West Berlin. Carnaby Street, the center of "swinging London" in the 1960s, was world famous for its clothing boutiques and record stores, underscoring the close connections between generational revolt and consumer culture.

The United States and Vietnam

The growth of the counterculture movement was closely linked to the course of the Vietnam War. Although many student radicals at the time believed that imperialism was the main cause, American involvement in Vietnam was more clearly a product of the Cold War and the policy of containment (see Chapter 29). From the late 1940s on, most Americans and their leaders viewed the world in terms of a constant struggle to stop the spread of communism. As western Europe began to revive and China established a communist government in 1949, efforts to contain communism shifted to Asia. The bloody Korean War (1950–1953) ended in stalemate, but the United States did succeed in preventing a communist victory in South Korea.

After Vietnam won independence from France in 1954, U.S. president Dwight D. Eisenhower (r. 1953–1961) refused to sign the Geneva Accords that temporarily divided the country into two zones—a socialist north and an anticommunist south. When the South Vietnamese government declined to hold free elections that would unify the north and south zones, Eisenhower provided the south with military aid. President John F. Kennedy (r. 1961–1963) later increased the number of American "military advisers" to sixteen thousand, and in 1964 President Lyndon B. Johnson (r. 1963–1969) greatly expanded America's role in the Vietnam conflict, providing South Vietnam with massive military aid and a half million American troops. Though the United States bombed North Vietnam with ever-greater intensity, it did not invade the north or set up a naval blockade. In the end, the American strategy of limited warfare backfired. It was the American people who grew weary and the American leadership that cracked.

The undeclared war in Vietnam, fought nightly on American television, eventually divided the nation. Initial support was strong. The politicians, the media, and the population as a whole saw the war as part of a legitimate defense against communist totalitarianism in all poor countries. But an antiwar movement quickly emerged on college campuses, where the prospect of being drafted to fight savage battles in Asian jungles made male stomachs churn. In October 1965 student protesters joined forces with old-line socialists, New Left intellectuals, and pacifists in antiwar demonstrations in fifty American cities. The protests spread to western Europe. By 1967 a growing number of critics in the United States and Europe denounced the American presence in Vietnam as a criminal intrusion into a complex and distant civil war.

Criticism reached a crescendo after the Vietcong Tet Offensive in January 1968. The communists' first comprehensive attack on major South Vietnamese cities failed militarily, with the Vietcong suffering heavy losses, but the Tet Offensive signaled that the war was not close to ending, as Washington had claimed. America's leaders lost heart, and within months President Johnson announced that he would not stand for re-election and called for negotiations with North Vietnam.

President Richard M. Nixon (r. 1969–1974) sought to gradually disengage America from Vietnam beginning in 1968. Intensifying the continuous bombardment of the enemy while simultaneously pursuing peace talks with the North Vietnamese, Nixon suspended the draft, so hated on college campuses, and cut American forces in Vietnam from 550,000 to 24,000 in four years. In 1973 Nixon finally reached a peace agreement with North Vietnam that allowed remaining American forces to complete their withdrawal, and gave the United States the right to resume bombing if the accords were broken. Fighting declined markedly in South Vietnam, where the South Vietnamese army appeared to hold its own against the Vietcong.

Although the storm of criticism in the United States seemed to have passed, America's disillusionment with the war had far-reaching repercussions. In early 1974, when North Vietnam launched a general invasion against South Vietnamese armies, the U.S. Congress refused to permit any American military response. After more than thirty-five years of battle, the South Vietnamese were forced in 1975 to accept a unified country under a communist dictatorship.

Student Revolts and 1968

The intensification of the Vietnam War in the late 1960s was accompanied by worldwide opposition. Many politically active students believed that the United States was fighting an immoral and imperialistic war against a small and heroic people, and the counterculture became increasingly radical. In European and American cities, students and sympathetic followers organized massive demonstrations against the war, and then extended their protests to support colonial independence movements, to demand an end to the nuclear arms race, and to call for world peace and liberation from social conventions of all kinds.

Youth activism erupted in 1968 in a series of protests and riots that circled the globe. African Americans rioted across the United States after the assassination of civil rights leader Martin Luther King, Jr. Antiwar demonstrators battled police at the Democratic National Convention in Chicago. Police in Mexico City shot and killed several hundred protesters calling for political reform (the exact number of deaths is still unknown), and students in Tokyo demonstrated against the war in Vietnam. Clashes between protesters and police occurred across western Europe and in the East Bloc as well. Students in Warsaw marched to protest government censorship, and youths in Prague were in the forefront of

Student Rebellion in Paris These rock-throwing students in the Latin Quarter of Paris are trying to force education reforms and even topple de Gaulle's government. In May 1968, in a famous example of the protest movements that swept the world in the late 1960s, Parisian rioters clashed repeatedly with France's tough riot police in bloody street fighting. De Gaulle remained in power, but a major reform of French education did follow. (Bruno Barbey/Magnum Photos)

the attempt to radically reform communism from within (see pages 982–983).

One of the most famous and perhaps far-reaching of these revolts occurred in France in May 1968, when angry students and striking workers brought the French economy to a standstill. A group of students inspired by New Left ideals initially occupied buildings and took over the University of Paris. Violent clashes with police followed. When police tried to clear the area around the university on the night of May 10, a pitched street battle took place. At the end of the night, 460 arrests had been made, 367 people were wounded, and protesters had burned about 200 cars. The slogans that appeared on posters put up overnight on the walls in Paris expressed the spirit of the New Left: "Power to the imagination"; "Be realistic, demand the impossible"; "Beneath the paving stones, the beach." The critique of the dehumanization of modern society captured in these slogans reflects both the imagination and also the vagueness of the demands of the counterculture.

The so-called May events might have been a typically short-lived student protest against American involvement in Vietnam and the abuses of capitalism, but the demonstrations triggered a national revolt. By May 18 some 10 million workers were out on strike, and protesters occupied factories across France. For a brief moment, it seemed as if counterculture dreams of a revolution from below would come to pass. The French Fifth Republic was on the verge of collapse, and a shaken President de Gaulle surrounded Paris with troops.

In the end, however, the idealistic goals of the radical students did not really correspond to the bread-and-butter demands of the striking workers. When the government promised workplace reforms, including immediate pay raises, the strikers returned to work. President de Gaulle dissolved the French parliament and called for new elections. His conservative party won almost 75 percent of the seats, showing that the majority of the French people supported neither general strikes nor student-led revolutions. The universities shut down for the summer, and the movement had dissipated by the time fall semester began. The May events marked the high point of counterculture protest in Europe; in the early 1970s the movement declined.

As the political enthusiasm of the counterculture waned, committed activists were divided among themselves about the best way to continue to fight for social change. Some followed what German student leader Rudi Dutschke called "the long march through the institutions" and began to work for change from within the system. They entered national politics and joined emerging feminist, antinuclear, and environmental groups that would play an important role in the coming decades (see pages 974–979).

Other groups, however, followed a more radical path. Across Europe, but particularly in Italy and West Germany, fringe New Left groups tried to bring radical change by turning to violence and terrorism. The Italian Red Brigades and the West German Red Army Faction robbed banks, bombed public buildings, and kidnapped and killed politicians and business leaders. After spasms of violence in the late 1970s—in Italy, for example, the Red Brigades murdered former prime minister Aldo Moro—security forces succeeded in incarcerating most of the terrorist leaders, and the movement fizzled out.

Counterculture protests generated a great deal of excitement and trained a generation of activists, but New Left ideologies focused on alienation and dehumanization captured in slogans like "Power to the imagination" resulted in little practical political change. Lifestyle rebellions involving sex, drugs, and rock music transformed individual behavior, but they hardly led to revolution.

The 1960s in the East Bloc

The building of the Berlin Wall in 1961 suggested that communism was here to stay, and the failure of NATO to intervene showed that the United States and western Europe basically accepted the premise. It also encouraged socialist regimes to experiment with some economic and cultural liberalization. East Bloc economies clearly lagged behind those of the West, exposing the weaknesses of heavy-handed central planning. To address these problems, socialist leaders now implemented cautious forms of decentralization and limited market policies. The results were mixed. Hungary's so-called New Economic Mechanism, which broke up state monopolies, allowed some private retail stores, and encouraged private agriculture, was perhaps most successful. East Germany's New Economic System, inaugurated in 1963, brought limited privatization and also showed moderate success, though it was reversed when the government returned to centralization in the late 1960s. In other East Bloc countries, however, economic growth flagged.

Recognizing that the emphasis on heavy industry could lead to popular discontent, Communist planning commissions redirected resources to the consumer sector. Again, the results varied across the East Bloc. By 1970, for example, ownership of televisions in the more developed nations of East Germany, Czechoslovakia, and Hungary approached that of the West, and other consumer goods were also more available. In Poland, however, the economy stagnated in the 1960s. In the more conservative Albania and Romania, where leaders held fast to Stalinist practices, provision of consumer goods faltered. In general, ordinary people in the East Bloc grew increasingly tired of the shortage of consumer goods that seemed an endemic part of socialist society.

In the 1960s Communist regimes also granted cautious cultural freedoms. In the Soviet Union, the cul-

The East German Trabi This small East German passenger car, produced between 1963 and 1990, was one of the best-known symbols of everyday life in East Germany. Though the cars were notorious for their poor engineering, the growing number of Trabis on East German streets nonetheless testified to the increased availability of consumer goods in the East Bloc in the 1960s and 1970s. (Visual Connection Archive)

tural thaw allowed dissidents like Aleksandr Solzhenitsyn and Boris Pasternak to publish critical works of fiction (see Chapter 29), and this relative tolerance spread to eastern European countries as well. In East Germany, for example, during the Bitterfeld Movement—named after a conference of writers, officials, and workers in Bitterfeld, an industrial city south of Berlin—the regime encouraged intellectuals to take a more critical view of life in the East Bloc, so long as they did not directly oppose communism itself. Author Christa Wolf's novel *Divided Heaven* (1963) is a classic example of the genre. Though her boyfriend immigrates to West Germany in search of better work conditions, the leading character remains committed to building socialism, despite the very real problems she sees in a small-town factory.

Despite some cultural openness, the most outspoken dissidents were harassed and often forced to emigrate to the West, and an underground *samizdat* (SAH-meez-daht) literature critical of communism emerged in the Soviet Union and the East Bloc. The label *samizdat*, a Russian term meaning "self-published," referred to books, periodicals, newspapers, and pamphlets that directly criticized communism and thus went far beyond the limits of criticism accepted by the state. Written and published secretly to avoid regime censors, and then passed hand to hand by dissident readers, samizdat literature emerged in Russia, Poland, and other countries in the mid-1950s and blossomed in the 1960s. These unofficial networks of communication kept critical thought alive and built contacts among dissidents, building the foundation for the protest movements of the 1970s and 1980s.

Modest prosperity and limited cultural tolerance only went so far. The citizens of East Bloc countries sought political liberty as well, and the limits on reform were sharply revealed in Czechoslovakia during the 1968

"Prague spring" (named for the country's capital city). In January 1968 reform elements in the Czechoslovak Communist Party gained a majority and voted out the long-time Stalinist leader in favor of Alexander Dubček (1921–1992), whose new government launched dramatic reforms. Educated in Moscow, Dubček (DOOB-chehk) was a dedicated communist, but he and his allies believed that they could reconcile genuine socialism with personal freedom and internal party democracy. They called for "socialism with a human face" and relaxed state censorship and replaced rigid bureaucratic planning with local decision making by trade unions, managers, and consumers. The reform program proved enormously popular.

Although Dubček remembered the lesson of the Hungarian revolution (see Chapter 29) and constantly proclaimed his loyalty to the Soviet Union and the Warsaw Pact, the determination of the Czechoslovak reformers to build a more liberal and democratic socialism frightened hard-line Communists. These fears were particularly strong in Poland and East Germany, where leaders knew full well that they lacked popular support. Moreover, the Soviet Union feared that a liberalized Czechoslovakia would eventually be drawn to neutrality or even to the democratic West. Thus the East Bloc leadership launched a concerted campaign of intimidation against the Czechoslovak reformers, and five hundred thousand Russian and allied eastern European troops suddenly occupied Czechoslovakia in August 1968. The Czechoslovaks made no attempt to resist militarily, and the arrested leaders surrendered to Soviet demands. The reform program was abandoned, and the Czechoslovak experiment in humanizing communism came to an end.

Shortly after the invasion of Czechoslovakia, Soviet premier Leonid Brezhnev (1906–1982) declared the

The Invasion of Czechoslovakia Armed with Czechoslovakian flags, courageous Czechs in downtown Prague try to stop a Soviet tank and repel the invasion and occupation of their country by the Soviet Union and its eastern European allies. This dramatic confrontation was ultimately unsuccessful. Realizing that military resistance would be suicidal, the Czechs capitulated to Soviet control. (AP Images)

so-called **Brezhnev Doctrine**, according to which the Soviet Union and its allies had the right to intervene in any socialist country whenever they saw the need. The 1968 invasion of Czechoslovakia was the crucial event of the Brezhnev era: it showed that only the threat of the Soviet military was holding the East Bloc together. At the same time, it demonstrated the determination of the ruling elite to maintain the status quo throughout the Soviet bloc, which would last for the next twenty years.

Brezhnev Doctrine
Doctrine created by Leonid Brezhnev that held that the Soviet Union had the right to intervene in any socialist country whenever it saw the need.

Changing Consensus in Western Europe

How did economic decline in the 1970s contribute to fundamental social and political change in the 1980s in western Europe and North America? ■

The great postwar economic boom came to a close in the early 1970s, opening a long period of economic stagnation, widespread unemployment, and social dislocation. Western European leaders drifted to the right, cutting taxes and state spending and selling off state-owned companies. A number of new political groups entered national politics, including feminists and environmentalists on the left and neo-nationalist political parties on the right. By the end of the 1980s the postwar stability based on economic prosperity, generous welfare provisions, and consensus politics had been deeply shaken, and the West had restructured its economy and entered the information age.

Economic Crisis and Hardship

Starting in the early 1970s the West entered into a long period of economic decline. One of the early causes of the downturn was the collapse of the international monetary system, which since 1945 had been based on the American dollar, valued in gold at $35 an ounce. In the postwar decades, the United States spent billions of dollars on foreign aid and foreign wars, weakening the value of American currency. In 1971 President Nixon attempted to reverse this trend by abruptly stopping the exchange of U.S. currency for gold. The value of the dollar fell sharply, and inflation accelerated worldwide. Fixed rates of exchange were abandoned, and great uncertainty replaced postwar predictability in international trade and finance.

Even more damaging to the global economy was the dramatic reversal in the price and availability of energy. The great postwar boom had been fueled in part by cheap oil from the Middle East, which permitted Big Science and other energy-intensive industries—automobiles, chemicals, and electric power—to expand rapidly and lead other sectors of the economy forward (see Chapter 29). The fate of the developed world was thus increasingly linked to this turbulent region, and strains began to show in the late 1960s. In 1967, in the Six-Day War between Israel and its Arab neighbors, Israel quickly defeated Egypt, Jordan, and Syria and expanded its territory in the former territories of Palestine, angering Arab leaders. The conflict exacerbated anti-Western feeling in the Arab states. By 1971 **OPEC**, the Arab-led Organization of Petroleum Exporting Countries, had watched the price of crude oil decline consistently compared with the rising price of Western manufactured goods. OPEC decided to reverse that trend by presenting a united front against Western oil companies.

The stage was set for a revolution in energy prices when Egypt and Syria launched a surprise attack on Israel in October 1973, setting off the fourth Arab-Israeli war. With the help of U.S. military arms, Israel again achieved a quick victory. OPEC then declared an embargo on oil shipments to the United States, Israel's ally, and within a year crude oil prices quadrupled. Western nations realized that the rapid price increase was economically destructive, but together they did nothing. Thus governments, industry, and individuals had no choice other than to deal piecemeal with the so-called oil shock—a "shock" that turned out to be an earthquake.

Coming on the heels of upheaval in the international monetary system, the revolution in energy prices plunged the world into its worst economic decline since the 1930s. The energy-intensive industries that had driven the economy up in the 1950s and 1960s now dragged it down. Unemployment rose, productivity and living standards declined, and inflation soared. By 1976 a modest recovery was in progress, but when a fundamentalist Islamic revolution struck Iran and oil production collapsed in that country in 1979, the price of crude oil doubled, and the world economy succumbed to its second oil shock. Unemployment and inflation rose dramatically before another uneven recovery began in 1982. Economists coined a new term—**stagflation**—to describe the combination of low growth and high inflation that led to a worldwide recession.

Anxious observers, recalling the disastrous consequences of the Great Depression, worried that the Common Market would disintegrate in the face of severe economic dislocation and that economic nationalism would halt steps toward European unity. Yet the Common Market—now officially known as the European Economic Community—continued to attract new members. In 1973 Denmark and Iceland, in addition to Britain, finally joined. Greece joined in 1981, and Portugal and Spain entered in 1986. The nations of the European Economic Community cooperated more closely in international undertakings, and the movement toward unity for western Europe stayed alive.

The developing world was hit hard by slowed growth, and the global economic downturn widened the gap between rich and poor countries. Governments across South America, sub-Saharan Africa, and South Asia borrowed heavily from the United States and western Europe in attempts to restructure their economies, setting the stage for a serious international debt crisis. At the same time, the East Asian countries of Japan and then Singapore, South Korea, and Taiwan started exporting high-tech consumer goods to the West. Competition from these East Asian "tiger economies," whose labor costs were comparatively low, shifted manufacturing jobs away from the highly industrialized countries of northern Europe.

Even as the world economy slowly began recovering in the 1980s, it could no longer create enough jobs to replace those that were lost. By the end of the 1970s, the foundations of economic growth had begun shifting to high-tech information industries, such as computing and biotechnology, and to services, including medicine, banking, and finance. Scholars spoke of the shift as the arrival of "the information age" or **postindustrial society**. Technological advances streamlined the production of many goods, making many industrial jobs superfluous. In western Europe, heavy industry, such as steel, mining, automobile manufacture, and shipbuilding, lost ground. Factories closed, leading to the emergence of "rust belts"—formerly industrialized areas that were now ghost lands, with vacant lots, rusting machinery, and empty inner cities where prosperous workers once lived. The highly industrialized Ruhr district in northwest West Germany and the factory belts around Detroit, Michigan, were classic examples.

One telling measure of the troubled economy was the misery index, which combined rates of inflation and unemployment in a single, powerfully emotional number. Misery increased on both sides of the Atlantic, but the increase was substantially greater in western Europe, where the hard times were often referred to simply as "the crisis" and unemployment numbers rose dramatically. By 1985 the unemployment rate in western Europe had risen to its highest level since the Great Depression. Nineteen million people were without work.

Ordinary people were hard hit by the crisis, and there were heartbreaking human tragedies—lost jobs, bankruptcies, homelessness, and mental breakdowns. Punk rock songs of the late 1970s captured the mood of

OPEC The Arab-led Organization of Petroleum Exporting Countries.

stagflation Term coined in the early 1980s to describe the combination of low growth and high inflation that led to a worldwide recession.

postindustrial society Society that relies on high-tech and service-oriented jobs for economic growth rather than on heavy industry and manufacturing jobs.

hostility and cynicism among young people. Yet on the whole, the welfare system fashioned in the postwar era prevented mass suffering and degradation. The responsive, socially concerned national state undoubtedly contributed to the preservation of political stability and democracy in the face of economic difficulties that might have brought revolution and dictatorship in earlier times.

The energetic response of governments to support social needs helps explain why total government spending in most European countries continued to rise sharply during the 1970s and early 1980s. In 1982 western European governments spent an average of more than 50 percent of all national income on social programs, as compared to only 37 percent fifteen years earlier. In all countries, people were willing to see their governments increase spending, but they resisted higher taxes. This imbalance contributed to the rapid growth of budget deficits, national debts, and inflation. By the late 1970s a powerful reaction against government's ever-increasing role had set in.

The Conservative Backlash

The transition to a postindustrial society was led by a new generation of conservative political leaders who were willing to make the difficult reforms necessary to restructure the economy, even though this typically led to social dislocation and growing inequality. During the thirty years following World War II, both Social Democrats and the more conservative Christian Democrats had agreed that economic growth and social stability were best achieved through full employment and high wages, some government regulation, and generous welfare provisions. In the late 1970s, however, with a weakened economy and increased global competition, this consensus began to unravel. Whether politics turned to the right, as in Great Britain, the United States, and West Germany, or to the left, as in France and Spain, leaders moved to cut government spending and regulation in attempts to improve economic performance.

The new conservatives of the 1980s followed a philosophy that came to be known as **neoliberalism** because of its distant roots in the laissez-faire policies favored by nineteenth-century liberals such as Adam Smith (see Chapter 22). Neoliberal theorists like U.S. economist Milton Friedman argued that government should cut support of social services such as housing, education, and health insurance; limit business subsidies; and retreat from regulation of all kinds. (Neoliberalism should thus be distinguished from modern American liberalism, which supports welfare programs and some state regulation of the

neoliberalism Philosophy of 1980s conservatives who argued for decreased government spending on social services and privatization of state-run industries.

economy.) Neoliberals also called for privatization — the sale of state-managed industries to private owners. Placing government-owned industries such as transportation and communication networks in private hands, they argued, would both tighten government spending and lead to greater workplace efficiency. The main goal was to increase private profits, which neoliberals believed were the real engine of economic growth.

The effects of neoliberal policies are best illustrated by events in Great Britain. The broad shift toward greater conservatism, coupled with growing voter dissatisfaction with high taxes and runaway state budgets, helped elect Margaret Thatcher (b. 1925) prime minister in 1979. A member of the Conservative Party and a convinced neoliberal, Thatcher was determined to scale back the role of government, and in the 1980s — the "Thatcher years" — she pushed through a series of controversial free-market policies that transformed postwar Britain. Thatcher's Conservative Party government cut spending on health care, education, and public housing. The Conservatives reduced taxes and privatized or sold off government-run enterprises. In one of the most popular actions, Thatcher encouraged low- and moderate-income renters in state-owned housing projects to buy their apartments at rock-bottom prices. This initiative, part of Thatcher's broader privatization campaign, created a whole new class of property owners, thereby eroding the electoral base of Britain's socialist Labour Party. (See "Individuals in Society: Margaret Thatcher," page 973.)

Though she never eliminated all social programs, Thatcher's policies helped replace the interventionist ethos of the welfare state with a greater reliance on private enterprise and the free market. There were significant human costs involved in this transition. In the first three years of her first term, heavy industries such as steel, coal mining, and textiles shut down, and unemployment rates in Britain doubled to over 12 percent. The gap between rich and poor widened, and increasing poverty led to discontent and crime. Working-class strikes and protests sometimes led to violent riots. Street violence often had unfortunate racial overtones: immigrants from former British colonies in Africa, India, and the Caribbean, dismayed with poor jobs and racial prejudice, clashed repeatedly with police. For a while, the "iron lady" successfully rallied support around British victory over Argentina in the brief Falklands War (1982), but over time her position weakened. By 1990 Thatcher's popularity had fallen to record lows, and she was replaced by Conservative Party leader John Major.

In the United States, two-term president Ronald Reagan (r. 1981–1989) followed a similar path, though his success in cutting government was more limited. A leader of the U.S. neoconservative movement, Reagan's campaign slogan — "government is not the solution to

INDIVIDUALS IN SOCIETY

MARGARET THATCHER, THE FIRST WOMAN ELECTED TO LEAD a major European state, was one of the late twentieth century's most significant leaders. The controversial "iron lady" attacked socialism, promoted capitalism, and changed the face of modern Britain.

Raised in a lower-middle-class family in a small city in southeastern England, Thatcher entered Oxford in 1943 to study chemistry. She soon discovered a passion for politics. Elected president of student Conservatives, she ran for Parliament in 1950 in a solidly Labour district to gain experience. Articulate and attractive, she gained the attention of Denis Thatcher, a wealthy businessman who drove her to campaign appearances in his Jaguar. Married a year later, the new Mrs. Thatcher abandoned chemistry, went to law school, gave birth to twins, and became a tax attorney. In 1959 she returned to politics and won a seat in the Conservative triumph.

For the next fifteen years Thatcher served in Parliament and held various ministerial posts when the Conservatives governed. In 1974, as the economy soured and the Conservatives lost two close elections, a rebellious Margaret Thatcher adroitly ran for the leadership position of the Conservative Party and won. In the 1979 election, as the Labour government faced rampant inflation and crippling strikes, Thatcher promised to reduce union power, lower taxes, and promote free markets. Attracting swing votes from skilled workers, she was elected prime minister.

A self-described "conviction politician," Thatcher rejected postwar Keynesian efforts to manage the economy, arguing that governments had created inflation by printing too much money. Thus her government reduced the supply of money and credit, and it refused to retreat as interest rates and unemployment soared. Her popularity plummeted. But Thatcher maintained her position, in part through an aggressive pursuit of foreign policy. In 1982 the generals ruling Argentina suddenly seized the Falkland Islands off the Argentine coast, the home of 1,800 British citizens. Ever a staunch nationalist, Thatcher detached a naval armada that recaptured the Falklands without a hitch. Britain admired Thatcher's determination and patriotism, and she was re-elected in 1983.

Thatcher's second term was the high point of her influence. Her whole-hearted commitment to privatization transformed British industry. More than fifty state-owned companies, ranging from the state telephone monopoly to the nationalized steel trust, were sold to private investors. Small investors were offered shares at bargain prices to promote "people's capitalism." Thatcher also curbed the power of British labor unions with various laws and actions. Most spectacularly, when in 1984 the once-mighty coal miners rejected more mine closings and doggedly struck for a year, Thatcher stood firm and beat them. This outcome had a profound psychological impact on the public, who blamed her for growing unemployment. Thatcher was also accused of mishandling a series of protest hunger strikes undertaken by the Irish Republican Army—in 1981 ten IRA members starved themselves to death in British prisons—but she held her ground, refusing to compromise with those she labeled criminals. As a result, the revolt in Northern Ireland entered one of its bloodiest phases.

Margaret Thatcher as prime minister. (AP Images/Staff-Caulkin)

Elected to a third term in 1987, Thatcher became increasingly stubborn, overconfident, and uncaring. Working with her neoliberal ideological soul mate, U.S. president Ronald Reagan, she opposed greater political and economic unity within the European Community. This, coupled with rising inflation, stubborn unemployment, and an unpopular effort to assert financial control over city governments, proved her undoing. In 1990, as in 1974, party stalwarts suddenly revolted and elected a new Conservative leader. The transformational changes of the Thatcher years nonetheless endured, consolidated by her Conservative successor and largely accepted by the New Labour prime minister, the moderate Tony Blair.

QUESTIONS FOR ANALYSIS

1. Why did Margaret Thatcher want to change Britain, and how did she do it?
2. How do Thatcher's policies reflect the conservative backlash of the 1970s and 1980s?

our problem, government is the problem"—summed up the movement's neoliberal philosophy. With widespread popular support and the agreement of most congressional Democrats as well as Republicans, Reagan in 1981 pushed through major across-the-board cuts in income taxes. But Reagan and Congress failed to limit government spending, which increased as a percentage of national income in the course of his presidency. A massive military buildup was partly responsible, but spending on social programs also grew rapidly. The harsh recession of the early 1980s required the government to spend more on unemployment benefits, welfare benefits, and medical treatment for the poor. Moreover, Reagan's antiwelfare rhetoric mobilized the liberal opposition and eventually turned many moderates against him. The budget deficit soared, and the U.S. government debt tripled in a decade.

The Social Consequences of Thatcherism As police watch in the background, picketers outside the largest coal mine in Britain hold up a poster reading "Save the Pits" during the miners' strike of 1984–1985. Prime Minister Margaret Thatcher broke the strike, weakening the power of Britain's trade unions and easing the turn to free-market economic reforms. Thatcher's neoliberal policies revived economic growth but cut state subsidies for welfare benefits and heavy industries, leading to lower living standards for many working-class Britons and, as this image attests, to popular protest. (Bride Lane Library/Pepperfoto/Getty Images)

West Germany also turned to the right. After more than a decade in power, the Social Democrats were foundering, and in 1982 Christian Democrat Helmut Kohl (b. 1930) became the new chancellor. Like Thatcher, Kohl cut taxes and government spending. His policies led to increasing unemployment in heavy industry but also to solid economic growth. By the mid-1980s West Germany was one of the most prosperous countries in the world. In foreign policy, Kohl drew close to President Reagan. The chancellor agreed to deploy U.S. Pershing II and cruise missiles on West German territory, and so contributed to renewed superpower tensions. In power for sixteen years, Kohl and the Christian Democrats presided over the dismantling of the Berlin Wall in 1989, the reunification of East and West Germany in 1990, and the end of the Cold War (see pages 988–989).

The most striking temporary exception to the general drift to the right in European politics was François Mitterrand (1916–1996) of France. After his election as president in 1981, Mitterrand and his Socialist Party led France on a lurch to the left. This marked a significant change in French politics, which had been dominated by center-right parties for some twenty-five years. Working at first in a coalition that included the French Communist Party, Mitterrand launched a vast program of nationalization and public investment designed to spend the country out of economic stagnation. By 1983 this attempt had clearly failed, and Mitterrand's Socialist government made a dramatic about-face. The Socialists were compelled to reprivatize industries nationalized during the first term. They imposed a wide variety of austerity measures and maintained those policies for the rest of the decade.

Despite persistent economic crises and high social costs, by 1990 the developed nations of western Europe and North America were far more productive than they had been in the early 1970s. Western Europe was at the center of the emerging global economy, and its citizens were far richer than those in Soviet bloc countries (see pages 962–963). Yet the collapse of the postwar consensus and the remaking of Europe in the transitional decades of the 1970s and 1980s generated new forms of protest and dissent across the political spectrum.

Challenges and Victories for Women

The 1970s marked the arrival of a broad-based feminist movement devoted to securing genuine gender equality and promoting the general interests of women. Three basic reasons accounted for this major development. First, ongoing changes in underlying patterns of motherhood and paid work created novel conditions and new demands (see Chapter 29). Second, a vanguard of feminist intellectuals articulated a powerful critique of gender relations, which stimulated many women to rethink

Kohl and Reagan View the Berlin Wall Protected by a sheet of bulletproof glass, West German chancellor Helmut Kohl (right) and U.S. president Ronald Reagan look over the Berlin Wall into East Germany from the balcony of the West German Parliament building during Reagan's state visit in June 1987. In a famous speech made during the trip, Reagan challenged Soviet leader Mikhail Gorbachev to "tear down this wall!" and liberalize the East Bloc. (Dick Halstead/Time Life Pictures/Getty Images)

their assumptions and challenge the status quo. Third, taking a lesson from the civil rights movement in the United States and worldwide student protest against the Vietnam War, dissatisfied women recognized that they had to band together if they were to influence politics and secure fundamental reforms.

Feminists could draw on a long heritage of protest, stretching back to the French Revolution and the women's movements of the late nineteenth century (see Chapters 20 and 23). They were also inspired by more recent works, such as the foundational book *The Second Sex* (1949) by the French writer and philosopher Simone de Beauvoir (1908–1986). Beauvoir, who worked closely with the existentialist philosopher Jean-Paul Sartre (see Chapter 28), analyzed the position of women within the framework of existential thought. Drawing on history, philosophy, psychology, biology, and literature, Beauvoir argued that women had almost always been trapped by particularly inflexible and limiting conditions. Only through courageous action and self-assertive creativity could a woman become a completely free person and escape the role of the inferior "other" that men had constructed for her gender. (See "Listening to the Past: Simone de Beauvoir, a Feminist Critique of Marriage," page 976.)

The Second Sex inspired a generation of women intellectuals, and by the late 1960s and the 1970s a broad-based feminist movement had spread through the United States and Europe. In the United States, American writer and organizer Betty Friedan's (1921–2006) pathbreaking study *The Feminine Mystique* (1963) pointed the way. Friedan called attention to the stifling aspects of women's domestic life, devoted to the service of husbands and children. Housewives lived in a "gilded cage," she concluded, because they were usually not allowed to hold professional jobs or become mature adults and genuine human beings. In 1966 Friedan helped found the National Organization for Women (NOW) to press for women's rights. NOW flourished, growing from seven hundred members in 1967 to forty thousand in 1974.

Many other women's organizations rose to follow NOW in Europe and the United States. The new feminists attacked patriarchy, the domination of society by men, and sexism, the inequalities faced by women simply because they were female. Throughout the 1970s a proliferation of publications, conferences, and institutions devoted to women's issues reinforced the emerging international movement. Advocates of women's rights pushed for new statutes in the workplace: laws against discrimination, equal pay for equal work, and

Simone de Beauvoir, a Feminist Critique of Marriage

LISTENING TO THE PAST

Having grown up in Paris in a middle-class family and become a teacher, novelist, and intellectual, Simone de Beauvoir (1908–1986) turned increasingly to feminist concerns after World War II. Her most influential work was The Second Sex *(1949), a massive declaration of independence for contemporary women.*

As an existentialist, Beauvoir believed that all individuals must accept responsibility for their lives and strive to overcome the tragic dilemmas they face. Studying the experience of women since antiquity, Beauvoir argued that men had generally used education and social conditioning to create a dependent "other," a negative nonman who was not permitted to grow and strive for freedom. Marriage—on men's terms—was part of this unjust and undesirable process. Beauvoir's conclusion that some couples could establish free and equal unions was based in part on her experience with philosopher Jean-Paul Sartre, Beauvoir's encouraging companion and sometime lover.

❝ All human existence is transcendence and immanence at the same time; to go beyond itself, it must maintain itself; to thrust itself toward the future, it must integrate the past into itself; and while relating to others, it must confirm itself in itself. These two moments are implied in every living movement: for *man*, marriage provides the perfect synthesis of them; in his work and political life, he finds change and progress, he experiences his dispersion through time and the universe; and when he tires of this wandering, he establishes a home, he settles down, he anchors himself in the world; in the evening he restores himself in the house, where his wife cares for the furniture and children and safeguards the past she keeps in store. But the wife has no other task save the one of maintaining and caring for life in its pure and identical generality; she perpetuates the immutable species, she ensures the even rhythm of the days and the permanence of the home she guards with locked doors; she is given no direct grasp on the future, nor on the universe; she goes beyond herself toward the group only through her husband as mouthpiece.

Marriage today still retains this traditional form. . . . The male's vocation is action; he needs to produce, fight, create, progress, go beyond himself toward the totality of the universe and the infinity of the future; but traditional marriage does not invite woman to transcend herself with him; it confines her in immanence. She has no choice but to build a stable life where the present, prolonging the past, escapes the threats of tomorrow, that is, precisely to create a happiness. . . .

It is through housework that the wife comes to make her "nest" her own; this is why, even if she has "help," she insists on doing things herself; at least by watching over, controlling, and criticizing, she endeavors to make her servants' results her own. By administrating her home, she achieves her social justification; her job is also to oversee the food, clothing, and care of the familial society in general. Thus she too realizes herself as an activity. But, as we will see, it is an activity that brings her no escape from her immanence and allows her no individual affirmation of herself. . . .

Simone de Beauvoir as a teacher in 1947, when she was writing *The Second Sex.* (Hulton-Deutsch Collection/Corbis)

Few tasks are more similar to the torment of Sisyphus than those of the housewife; day after day, one must wash dishes, dust furniture, mend clothes that will be dirty, dusty, and torn again. The housewife wears herself out running on the spot; she does nothing; she only perpetuates the present; she never gains the sense that she is conquering a positive Good, but struggles indefinitely against Evil. . . .

Washing, ironing, sweeping, routing out tufts of dust in the dark places behind the wardrobe, this is holding away death but also refusing life: for in one movement time is created and destroyed; the housewife only grasps the negative aspect of it. . . .

So the wife's work within the home does not grant her autonomy; it is not directly useful to the group, it does not open onto the future, it does not produce anything. It becomes meaningful and dignified only if it is integrated into existences that go beyond themselves, toward the society in production or action: far from enfranchising the matron, it makes her dependent on her husband and children; she justifies her existence through them: she is no more than an inessential mediation in their lives. . . .

The drama of marriage is not that it does not guarantee the wife the promised happiness — there is no guarantee of happiness — it is that it mutilates her; it dooms her to repetition and routine. The first twenty years of a woman's life are extraordinarily rich; she experiences menstruation, sexuality, marriage, and motherhood; she discovers the world and her destiny. She is mistress of a home at twenty, linked from then on to one man, a child in her arms, now her life is finished forever. Real activity, real work, are the privilege of man: her only occupations are sometimes exhausting but never fulfill her. . . .

Marriage must combine two autonomous existences, not be a withdrawal, an annexation, an escape, a remedy. . . . The couple should not consider itself a community, a closed cell: instead, the individual as individual has to be integrated into a society in which he can thrive without assistance; he will then be able to create links in pure generosity with another individual equally adapted to the group, links founded on the recognition of two freedoms.

This balanced couple is not a utopia; such couples exist sometimes even within marriage, more often outside of it; some are united by a great sexual love that leaves them free in their friendships and occupations; others are linked by a friendship that does not hamper their sexual freedom; more rarely there are still others who are both lovers and friends but without seeking in each other their exclusive reason for living. Many nuances are possible in the relations of a man and a woman: in companionship, pleasure, confidence, tenderness, complicity, and love, they can be for each other the most fruitful source of joy, richness, and strength offered to a human being. 〞

Source: Simone de Beauvoir, *The Second Sex*, trans. Constance Borde and Sheila Malovany-Chevallier. Copyright © 1949 by Editions Gallimard, Paris. Translation copyright © 2009 by Constance Borde and Sheila Malovany-Chevallier. Used by permission of Alfred A. Knopf, a division of Random House, Inc.

QUESTIONS FOR ANALYSIS

1. How did Beauvoir analyze marriage and marriage partners in terms of existential philosophy?

2. To what extent does a married woman benefit from a "traditional" marriage, according to Beauvoir? Why?

3. What was Beauvoir's solution to the situation she described? Was her solution desirable? Realistic?

4. What have you learned about the history of women that supports or challenges Beauvoir's analysis? Include developments since World War II and your own reflections.

measures such as maternal leave and affordable day care designed to help women combine careers and family responsibilities.

The movement further concentrated on gender and family questions, including the right to divorce (in some Catholic countries), legalized abortion, the needs of single mothers, and protection from rape and physical violence. In almost every country, the effort to decriminalize abortion served as a catalyst in mobilizing an effective, self-conscious women's movement (and in creating opposition to it, as in the United States).

In countries that had long placed women in a subordinate position, the legal changes were little less than revolutionary. In Italy, for example, new laws abolished restrictions on divorce and abortion, which had been strengthened by Mussolini and defended energetically by the Catholic Church in the postwar era. By 1988 divorce and abortion were common in Italy, which had the lowest birthrate in Europe. More generally, the sharply focused women's movement of the 1970s won new rights for women. Subsequently, the movement became more diffuse, a victim of both its successes and the resurgence of an antifeminist opposition.

In addition to the feminist movement, many newly empowered women were active in the antinuclear peace movement, which had its roots in the anti-Vietnam

Italian Feminists These women demonstrate in Rome in 1977 for the passage of legislation legalizing abortion, which the pope and the Catholic Church have steadfastly opposed. The demonstrators raise their hands in a feminist salute during the peaceful march. (Bettmann/Corbis)

protests of the 1960s and took on new life as the Cold War heated up in the late 1970s. Appalled by the Soviet invasion of Afghanistan in 1979, the United States and NATO took a number of countermeasures, including an agreement to station limited-range nuclear missiles in Britain, West Germany, Italy, Belgium, and the Netherlands (see pages 983–984). Concerned citizens quickly realized that if a low-level tactical nuclear war broke out between the superpowers, western Europe and particularly West Germany would suffer the consequences. In 1981 hundreds of thousands of demonstrators marched in protest in major cities across western Europe, carrying signs that read "We are not America's guinea pigs" and "Reagan's peace is our death."[3] Western European leaders went ahead with the missile deployment, but determined citizens' groups continued to call attention to the brutal costs of modern war.

The Rise of the Environmental Movement

Like feminist activists and peace advocates, newly formed environmental groups had roots in the 1960s counterculture. Early environmentalists drew inspiration from writers like biologist Rachel Carson, whose book *Silent Spring*, published in the United States in 1962, was quickly translated into twelve European languages. Carson's chilling title referred to a future spring when people in developed society would wake up and hear no birds singing because the birds had all been killed by the rampant overuse of pesticides. The book had a striking impact on the growth of environmental movements in Europe.

By the 1970s the destructive environmental costs of industrial development were everywhere apparent.

Picturing the Past

Green Party Representatives Enter Parliament In 1983 members of the environmentally conscious West German Green Party won enough votes to send several representatives to the parliament for the first time, an important victory for the protest movements that emerged in the 1970s and 1980s. (Bildarchiv Preussischer Kulturbesitz/Art Resource, NY)

ANALYZING THE IMAGE How do the Green Party representatives (center) use visual presentation and symbolism to portray their political beliefs? How would you describe the reaction of the more traditionally dressed members of parliament?

CONNECTIONS What does the Green Party victory in 1983 tell us about political debate in a postindustrial society? Are there continuities with the social activism of the 1960s counterculture, or is this something new?

To complete this activity online, go to the Online Study Guide at bedfordstmartins.com/mckaywest.

The mighty Rhine River, which flows from Switzerland, past France, and through Germany and the Netherlands, was an industrial sewer. The forests of southwestern Germany were dying from acid rain, a result of smokestack effluents. The pristine coasts of Brittany, in northwest France, were fouled by oil spills from massive tanker ships. Nuclear power plants across western Europe were generating toxic waste that would last for centuries (Map 30.1). These are just some examples of the environmental degradation that inspired a growing ecology movement to challenge government and industry to clean up their acts.

The new ecologists had two main agendas. First, they worked to lessen the effects of unbridled industrial development on the natural environment. Second, they linked local environmental issues to poverty, inequality, and violence on a global scale. Environmental groups pursued these goals in many ways. Some used the mass media to reach potential supporters; some worked closely with politicians and public officials to change state policies. Others took a more activist stance. In Denmark in March 1969, in a dramatic example, student protesters at the University of Copenhagen took over a scientific conference on natural history. They locked the conference hall doors, sprayed the professors in attendance with polluted lake water, and held up an oil-doused duck, shouting, "Come and save it . . . you talk about pollution, why don't you do anything about it!"[4]

Environmental protest also took on institutional forms. In 1971 Canadian activists established Greenpeace, a nongovernmental organization dedicated to environmental conservation and protection. Greenpeace quickly grew into an international organization, with strong support in Europe and the United States. In West Germany in 1979 environmentalists founded the Green Party, a political party intended to fight for environmental causes. The West German Greens met with astounding success when they elected members to parliament in the 1983 elections, the first time in sixty years that a new political party had been seated in Germany. Their success was a model for like-minded activists across Europe and the United States, and Green Party members have been elected to parliaments in Belgium, Italy, and Sweden.

Separatism and Right-Wing Extremism

The 1970s also saw the rise of determined separatist movements across Europe. In Ireland, Spain, Belgium, and Switzerland—and in Yugoslavia and Czechoslovakia in the East Bloc—regional ethnic groups struggled for special rights, political autonomy, and even national independence from ruling governments. This new separatist nationalism was most violent in Spain and Northern Ireland, where well-established insurgent groups used

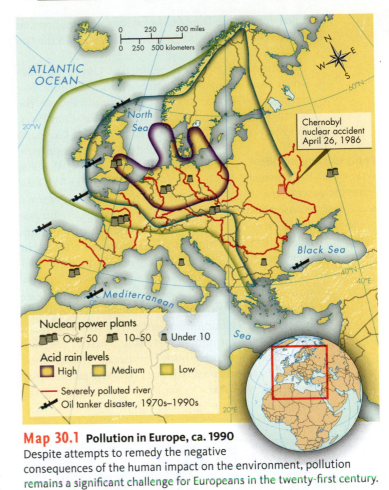

Map 30.1 **Pollution in Europe, ca. 1990** Despite attempts to remedy the negative consequences of the human impact on the environment, pollution remains a significant challenge for Europeans in the twenty-first century.

Map legend:
Nuclear power plants: Over 50, 10–50, Under 10
Acid rain levels: High, Medium, Low
Severely polluted river
Oil tanker disaster, 1970s–1990s

Chernobyl nuclear accident April 26, 1986

terrorist attacks to win government concessions. In the ethnic Basque region of northern Spain, the ETA (short for Basque Homeland and Freedom) tried to use bombings and assassinations to force the government to grant territorial independence. After the death in 1975 of the Spanish fascist dictator Francisco Franco, who had ruled Spain for almost forty years, a new constitution granted the Basque region special autonomy, but it was not enough. The ETA stepped up its terrorist campaigns, killing over four hundred people in the 1980s.

The Provisional Irish Republican Army (IRA), a paramilitary organization in Northern Ireland, used similar tactics. Though Ireland had won autonomy in 1922, Great Britain retained control of six primarily Protestant counties in the north of the country (see Chapter 27). In the late 1960s violence re-emerged as the IRA attacked British security forces its members saw as occupying the district. On Bloody Sunday in January 1972, British soldiers shot and killed thirteen demonstrators, who had been protesting anti-Catholic discrimination, in the town of Derry, and the violence escalated. For the next thirty years the IRA attacked soldiers and civilians in Northern Ireland and in Britain itself. Over two thousand British soldiers, civilians, and IRA members were killed during "the Troubles" before negotiations between the IRA and the British government opened in the late 1990s.

Mainstream European politicians also faced challenges from new political forces on the far right. New right groups such as the National Front in France, the Northern League in Italy, the Austrian Freedom Party, and the National Democratic Party in West Germany

really existing socialism
A term used by Communist leaders to describe the socialist accomplishments of their societies, such as nationalized industry and collective agriculture.

were founded or gained popularity in the 1970s and 1980s. Populist leaders like Jean-Marie Le Pen, the founder of the French National Front, opposed European integration and promised a return to traditional national customs, often at the expense of the non-European immigrants who were a growing proportion of the continent's working-class population (see Chapter 29). New right politicians promoted themselves as the champions of ordinary (white) workers, complaining that immigrants swelled welfare rolls and stole jobs from native-born Europeans. Though their programs at times veered close to open racism, they began to win seats in national parliaments in the 1980s.

The Decline of "Really Existing Socialism"

What internal and external factors weakened communist power in the East Bloc, and how did Soviet leader Mikhail Gorbachev try to reform the system from above? ■

In the postwar decades, the communist states of the East Bloc had achieved a shaky social consensus based on a rising standard of living, an extensive welfare system, and the inevitable political repression. When the Marxist utopia still had not arrived in the 1970s, propagandists told citizens that their totally egalitarian society would be realized sometime in the future. In the meantime, they would have to accept the system as it was; in the long run, leaders claimed, socialism would prove that it was better than capitalism. Such claims were an attempt to paper over serious tensions in socialist society. Everyday life could be difficult; limits on personal and political freedoms encouraged the growth of determined reform movements; and a revival of Cold War tensions accompanied the turn to the right in the United States and western Europe in the 1980s.

When Mikhail Gorbachev burst on the scene in 1985, the new Soviet leader opened an era of reform that was as sweeping as it was unexpected. Although many believed that Gorbachev would soon fall from power, his

reforms rapidly transformed Soviet culture and politics, and drastically reduced Cold War tensions. But communism, which Gorbachev wanted so desperately to revitalize, continued to decline.

State and Society in the East Bloc

By the 1970s many of the professed goals of communism had been achieved. Communist leaders in eastern Europe and the Soviet Union adopted the term **really existing socialism** to describe the accomplishments of their societies. Agriculture had been successfully collectivized, and though Poland was an exception, 80 to 90 percent of Soviet and East Bloc farmers worked on huge collective farms. Industry and business had been nationalized, and only a small percentage of the economy remained in private hands in most East Bloc countries. The state had also gone some way to level class differences. Though some people—particularly party members—clearly had greater access to better opportunities and resources, the gap between rich and poor was far smaller than in the West. An extensive system of government-supported welfare benefits included free medical care, guaranteed employment, inexpensive public transportation, and large subsidies for rent and food.

Everyday life under really existing socialism was defined by an uneasy mixture of outward conformity and private disengagement—or apathy. The Communist Party dominated public life. Mass organizations for youth, women, workers, and sports groups instituted huge rallies, colorful festivals, and new holidays that exposed citizens to the values of the socialist state. East Bloc citizens might grudgingly participate in party-sponsored public events, but at home, and in private, they grumbled about and often sidestepped Communist authority.

East Bloc living standards were well above those in the developing world, but well below living standards in the West. Centralized economic planning continued to lead to shortages of the most basic goods, and people complained about poor quality and lack of choice. Family ties were especially valuable in the bureaucratic one-party state. Informal networks of family and friends helped people find hard-to-get goods and offered support beyond party organizations. Though the secret police persecuted those who openly challenged the system and generated mountains of files on ordinary people, those who put up and shut up had little to fear.

Women in particular experienced the contradictions of the socialist system. On the one hand, the state advocated equal rights for women and encouraged them to join the workforce in positions formerly reserved for men, such as medicine, in numbers greater than those in the West. In addition, an extensive system of state-supported child care freed women to take outside employment and eased the work of parenting. On the other

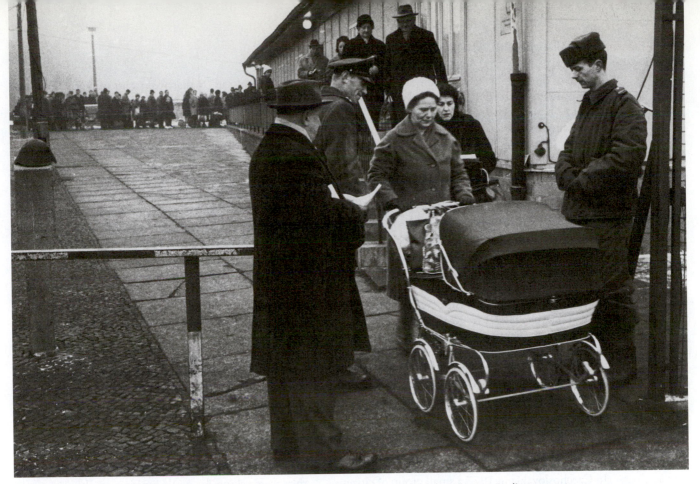

Crossing the Border Between East and West Berlin During the Christmas season of 1965, West Berliners were given special permission to visit relatives in the walled-off eastern part of the city. The limits on travel in the East Bloc were one of the most hated aspects of life under Communist rule. (Bundesarchiv, Berlin)

hand, women rarely made it into the upper ranks of business or politics. And East Bloc women faced the same double burden as those in the West—on top of their full-time jobs, they were expected to do the shopping, the cooking, and the cleaning at home.

The countries of eastern Europe—like those in the West—were hit hard by the energy crisis and stagflation of the 1970s. For a time, access to inexpensive oil from the Soviet Union, which had huge resources, provided a buffer, but this cushion began to fall apart in the 1980s. For a number of reasons, East Bloc leaders refused to make the economic reforms that might have made the socialist system more effective.

First, the transformation to Western-style postindustrial societies would have required fundamental changes in the Communist system. As in the West, it would have hurt the already tenuous living standard of industrial workers. But the workers' states of the East Bloc were dedicated to the working class: coal miners, shipbuilders, factory and construction workers. To pursue the sorts of reforms required to develop a postindustrial economy would have undermined the livelihoods and support of these basic constituencies, which were already showing signs of wear.

East Bloc regimes also refused to cut spending on the welfare state, which was, after all, one of the proudest achievements of socialism. In addition, socialist governments continued to provide subsidies to heavy industries such as steel and mining. High-tech industries failed to take off in eastern Europe, in part because the West maintained embargos on technology exports. The industrial goods produced in the East Bloc became increasingly uncompetitive in the new global system. To stave off total collapse, governments borrowed massive amounts of hard currency from Western banks and governments, helping to convince ordinary people that communism was bankrupt, and setting up a cycle of indebtedness that helped bring down the East Bloc in 1989.

Economic decline was not the only reason people increasingly questioned the socialist system. The best career and educational opportunities were reserved for party members or handed out as political favors, leaving many talented people underemployed and resentful. Tight controls on travel continually called attention to the burdens of daily life in a repressive society. The one-party state had repeatedly quashed popular reform movements and retreated from economic liberalization, even when presented in a nonthreatening way. The liberal freedoms and consumer prosperity of the West were evident for all to see in the television broadcasts that streamed across the iron curtain every evening. Many East Bloc citizens came to doubt the legitimacy of communism altogether:

the dream of distributing goods "from each according to his means, to each according to his needs" (as Marx had once put it) hardly made up for the great weaknesses of really existing socialism.

Reform Movements in Czechoslovakia and Poland

Economic and social stagnation in the East Bloc encouraged small numbers of dedicated people to try to change society from within. Developments in Czechoslovakia and Poland were the most striking and significant, and determined reform movements emerged in both countries in the mid-1970s. Remembering a history of violent repression and Soviet invasion, reformists carefully avoided direct challenges to government leaders. Nor did they try to reform the Communist Party itself, as Dubček and his followers had attempted in the Prague spring of 1968. Instead, they worked to build a civil society from below—to create a realm of freedom beyond formal politics where civil liberties and human rights could be exercised within the Communist system.

Solidarity Outlawed Polish trade union that worked for workers' rights and political reform throughout the 1980s.

In Czechoslovakia in 1977 a small group of citizens, including future Czechoslovak president Václav Havel (see page 988), signed a manifesto that came to be known as Charter 77. The group criticized the government for ignoring the human rights provision of the Helsinki Accords and called on Communist leaders to respect civil and human rights. They also criticized censorship and argued for improved environmental policies. Despite government retaliation, Czech leaders challenged passive acceptance of Communist authority and contributed to growing public dissatisfaction with really existing socialism.

In Poland, which had been an unruly satellite from the beginning, the Communists had failed to monopolize society. Most agricultural land remained in private hands, and the Catholic Church thrived. The Communists also failed to manage the economy effectively. The 1960s saw little economic improvement, and in 1970 Poland's working class rose again in angry protest. A new Communist leader came to power, and he wagered that massive inflows of Western capital and technology, especially from rich and now-friendly West Germany, could produce a Polish economic miracle. Instead, bureaucratic incompetence and the first oil shock in 1973 put the economy into a nosedive. Workers, intellectuals, and the church became increasingly restive. Then the real Polish miracle occurred: Cardinal Karol Wojtyla (KAH-rohl voy-TIH-lah), archbishop of Kraków, was elected pope in 1978 as John Paul II. In June 1979 he returned to Poland from Rome, preaching love of Christ and country and the "inalienable rights of man." The pope drew enormous crowds and electrified the Polish nation.

In August 1980 the sixteen thousand workers at the gigantic Lenin Shipyards in Gdansk (formerly known as Danzig) laid down their tools and occupied the plant. As other workers joined "in solidarity," the strikers advanced the ideals of civil society, including the right to form free-trade unions, freedom of speech, release of political prisoners, and economic reforms. After eighteen days of shipyard occupation, the government gave in and accepted the workers' demands in the Gdansk Agreement. In a state in which the Communist Party claimed to rule on behalf of the proletariat, a working-class revolt had won an unprecedented, even revolutionary, victory.

Led by feisty Lenin Shipyards electrician and devout Catholic Lech Walesa (lehk vah-LEHN-suh) (b. 1943), the workers proceeded to organize a free and democratic trade union called **Solidarity**. As had been the case in Czechoslovakia, Solidarity worked cautiously to shape an active civil society. Joined by intellectuals and supported by the Catholic Church, it became a national union with a full-time staff of 40,000 linking 9.5 million union members. Cultural and intellectual freedom blossomed in Poland, and Solidarity enjoyed tremendous public support. But Solidarity's leaders insisted that they were asking for a self-limiting revolution, meant only to defend the cultural and trade-union freedoms won in the Gdansk Agreement. Solidarity thus practiced moderation, refusing to challenge directly the Communist monopoly on political power. Yet the ever-present threat of calling a nationwide strike gave them real power in ongoing negotiations with the Communist bosses.

Solidarity's combination of strength and moderation postponed a showdown, as the Soviet Union played a waiting game of threats and pressure. After a confrontation in March 1981 Walesa settled for minor government concessions, and Solidarity dropped plans for a massive general strike. Criticism of Walesa's moderate leadership gradually grew, and Solidarity lost its cohesiveness. The worsening economic crisis also encouraged radical actions among disgruntled Solidarity members, and the Polish Communist leadership shrewdly denounced Solidarity for promoting economic collapse and provoking a possible Soviet invasion. In December 1981 Communist leader General Wojciech Jaruzelski (VOY-chek yahr-oo-ZEL-skee) suddenly proclaimed martial law and arrested Solidarity's leaders.

Outlawed and driven underground, Solidarity survived in part because of the government's unwillingness (and probably its inability) to impose full-scale terror. Moreover, millions of Poles decided to continue acting as if they were free—the hallmark of civil society—even though they were not. Cultural and intellectual life remained extremely vigorous as the faltering Polish economy continued to deteriorate. Thus popular sup-

Lech Walesa and Solidarity
An inspiration for fellow workers at the Lenin Shipyards in the dramatic and successful strike against the Communist bosses in August 1980, Walesa played a key role in Solidarity before and after it was outlawed. Speaking here to old comrades at the Lenin Shipyards after Solidarity was again legalized in 1988, Walesa personified an enduring opposition to Communist rule in eastern Europe. (Georges Merillon/Gamma)

port for outlawed Solidarity remained strong under martial law in the 1980s, preparing the way for the union's political rebirth toward the end of the decade.

The rise and survival of Solidarity showed the desire of millions of eastern Europeans for greater political liberty and the enduring appeal of cultural freedom, trade-union rights, patriotic nationalism, and religious feeling. Not least, Solidarity's challenge encouraged fresh thinking in the Soviet Union, ever the key to lasting change in the Eastern bloc.

From Détente Back to Cold War

The Soviets and the leaders of the Soviet satellite states also faced challenges from abroad as optimistic hopes for détente in international relations gradually faded in the late 1970s. Brezhnev's Soviet Union ignored the human rights provisions of the Helsinki agreement, and East-West political competition remained very much alive outside Europe. Many Americans became convinced that the Soviet Union was taking advantage of détente, steadily building up its military might and pushing for political gains and revolutions in Africa, Asia, and Latin America. The Soviet invasion of Afghanistan in December 1979, which was designed to save an increasingly unpopular Marxist regime, was especially alarming to the West. Many Americans feared that the oil-rich states of the Persian Gulf would be next, and once again they looked to the NATO alliance and military might to thwart communist expansion.

President Jimmy Carter (r. 1977–1981) tried to lead NATO beyond verbal condemnation and urged economic sanctions against the Soviet Union, but only Great Britain among the European allies supported the American initiative. The alliance showed the same lack of concerted action when the Solidarity movement rose in Poland. Some observers concluded that NATO had lost the will to act decisively in dealing with the Soviet bloc.

The Atlantic alliance endured, however, and the U.S. military buildup launched by Carter in his last years in office was greatly accelerated by President Reagan, who was swept into office in 1980 by a wave of patriotism and economic discontent. The new American leadership acted as if the military balance had tipped in favor of the Soviet Union, which Reagan anathematized as the "evil empire." Increasing defense spending enormously, the Reagan administration deployed short-range nuclear missiles in western Europe and built up the navy to preserve American power in

The Soviet War in Afghanistan, 1979–1989

- Afghanistan
- Soviet Union
- Soviet invasion
- Controlled by Soviet forces

the post-Vietnam age. The broad shift toward greater conservatism in the 1980s gave Reagan invaluable allies in western Europe. Margaret Thatcher worked well with Reagan and was a forceful advocate for a revitalized Atlantic alliance, and under Helmut Kohl West Germany and the United States once again coordinated military and political policy toward the Soviet bloc.

Gorbachev's Reforms in the Soviet Union

Cold War tensions aside, the Soviet Union's Communist Party elite seemed secure in the early 1980s as far as any challenge from below was concerned. The long-established system of administrative controls continued to stretch downward from the central ministries and state committees to provincial cities, and from there to factories, neighborhoods, and villages. At each level of this massive state bureaucracy, the overlapping hierarchy of the 17.5-million-member Communist Party continued to watch over all decisions and manipulate every aspect of national life. Organized opposition was impossible, and average people left politics to the bosses.

Although the massive state and party bureaucracy safeguarded the elite, it promoted apathy in the masses. When the ailing Brezhnev finally died in 1982, his successor, the long-time chief of the secret police, Yuri Andropov (1914–1984), tried to invigorate the system. Relatively little came of his efforts, but they combined with a sharply worsening economic situation to set the stage for the emergence in 1985 of Mikhail Gorbachev (b. 1931), the most vigorous Soviet leader in a generation.

Trained as a lawyer and having worked his way up as a Communist Party official in the northern Caucasus, Gorbachev was smart, charming, and tough. Gorbachev believed in communism, but he realized it was failing to keep up with Western capitalism and technological developments, and that the Soviet Union's status as a superpower was eroding. Thus Gorbachev (and his intelligent, influential wife, Raisa, a dedicated professor of Marxist-Leninist thought) wanted to save the Soviet system by revitalizing it with fundamental reforms. Gorbachev was also an idealist who wanted to improve conditions for ordinary citizens. Understanding that the endless waste and expense of the Cold War arms race had had a disastrous impact on living conditions in the Soviet Union, he realized that improvement at home required better relations with the West.

In his first year in office, Gorbachev attacked corruption and incompetence in the bureaucracy, and he consolidated his power. He condemned alcoholism and drunkenness, which were deadly scourges of Soviet society, and elaborated his ambitious reform program.

perestroika Economic restructuring and reform implemented by Soviet premier Gorbachev in 1985.

glasnost Soviet premier Gorbachev's popular campaign for openness in government and the media.

Mikhail Gorbachev In his acceptance speech before the Supreme Soviet (the U.S.S.R.'s parliament), newly elected president Mikhail Gorbachev vowed to assume "all responsibility" for the success or failure of perestroika. Previous Soviet parliaments were little more than tools of the Communist Party, but this one actively debated and even opposed government programs. (Boris Yurchenko/AP Images)

The first set of reform policies was designed to transform and restructure the economy in order to provide for the real needs of the Soviet population. To accomplish this economic restructuring, or **perestroika** (pehr-uh-STROY-kuh), Gorbachev and his supporters permitted an easing of government price controls on some goods, more independence for state enterprises, and the setting up of profit-seeking private cooperatives to provide personal services for consumers. These timid economic reforms initially produced a few improvements, but shortages grew as the economy stalled at an intermediate point between central planning and free-market mechanisms. By late 1988 widespread consumer dissatisfaction posed a serious threat to Gorbachev's leadership and the entire reform program.

Gorbachev's bold and far-reaching campaign "to tell it like it is" was much more successful. Very popular in a country where censorship, dull uniformity, and outright lies had long characterized public discourse, the newfound openness, or **glasnost** (GLAZ-nohst), of the government and the media marked an astonishing break with the past. Long-banned and -vilified émigré writers sold millions of copies of their works in new editions, while denunciations of Stalin and his terror became standard fare in plays and movies. Thus initial openness in government pronouncements quickly went much further than Gorbachev intended and led to something approaching free speech and free expression, a veritable cultural revolution.

Democratization was the third element of reform. Beginning as an attack on corruption in the Communist Party, it led to the first free elections in the Soviet Union since 1917. Gorbachev and the party remained in control, but a minority of critical independents was elected in April 1989 to a revitalized Congress of People's Deputies. Millions of Soviets then watched the new congress for hours on television as Gorbachev and his ministers saw their proposals debated and even rejected. Thus millions of Soviet citizens took practical lessons in open discussion, critical thinking, and representative government. An active civil society was emerging—a new political culture at odds with the Communist Party's monopoly of power and control. Democratization ignited demands for greater autonomy and even for national independence by non-Russian minorities, especially in the Baltic region and in the Caucasus.

Finally, Gorbachev brought new political thinking to the field of foreign affairs and acted on it. He withdrew Soviet troops from Afghanistan in February 1989 and sought to reduce East-West tensions. Of enormous importance, the Soviet leader sought to halt the arms race with the United States and convinced President Reagan of his sincerity. In a Washington summit in December 1987, the two leaders agreed to eliminate all land-based intermediate-range missiles in Europe, setting the stage for more arms reductions. Gorbachev also encouraged reform movements in Poland and Hungary and pledged to respect the political choices of the peoples of eastern Europe, repudiating the Brezhnev Doctrine. By early 1989 it seemed that if Gorbachev held to his word, the tragic Soviet occupation of eastern Europe might wither away, taking the long Cold War with it once and for all.

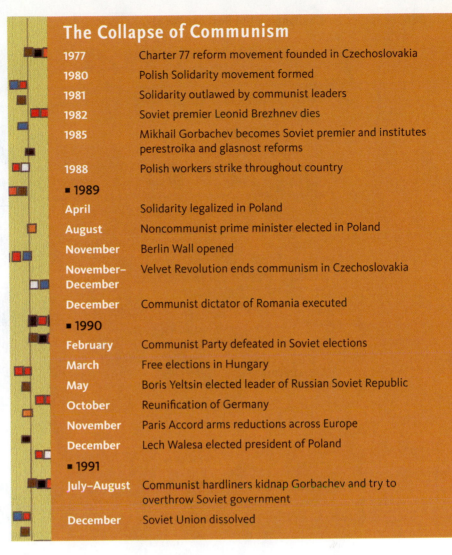

The Collapse of Communism

1977	Charter 77 reform movement founded in Czechoslovakia
1980	Polish Solidarity movement formed
1981	Solidarity outlawed by communist leaders
1982	Soviet premier Leonid Brezhnev dies
1985	Mikhail Gorbachev becomes Soviet premier and institutes perestroika and glasnost reforms
1988	Polish workers strike throughout country
■ 1989	
April	Solidarity legalized in Poland
August	Noncommunist prime minister elected in Poland
November	Berlin Wall opened
November–December	Velvet Revolution ends communism in Czechoslovakia
December	Communist dictator of Romania executed
■ 1990	
February	Communist Party defeated in Soviet elections
March	Free elections in Hungary
May	Boris Yeltsin elected leader of Russian Soviet Republic
October	Reunification of Germany
November	Paris Accord arms reductions across Europe
December	Lech Walesa elected president of Poland
■ 1991	
July–August	Communist hardliners kidnap Gorbachev and try to overthrow Soviet government
December	Soviet Union dissolved

culture after having been conquered and brutalized by Nazis and communists for almost sixty years. Second, West Germany quickly absorbed its East German rival and emerged as the most influential country in Europe. Third, Gorbachev's reforms boomeranged, and a complicated anticommunist revolution swept through the Soviet Union as the multinational empire broke into a large Russia and fourteen other independent states. The long Cold War came to an abrupt end, and the United States suddenly stood as the world's only superpower.

The Revolutions of 1989

Why did anticommunist revolutions sweep through eastern Europe in 1989, and what were the immediate consequences? ■

In 1989 Gorbachev's plan to reform communism in order to save it snowballed out of control. A series of largely peaceful revolutions swept across eastern Europe (Map 30.2), overturning existing communist regimes. The revolutions of 1989 had momentous consequences. First, the peoples of eastern Europe joyfully re-entered the mainstream of contemporary European life and

The Collapse of Communism in Eastern Europe

Solidarity and the Polish people led the way to revolution in eastern Europe. In 1988 widespread labor unrest and strikes, raging inflation, and the outlawed Solidarity's refusal to cooperate with the military government had brought Poland to the brink of economic collapse. Thus Solidarity skillfully pressured Poland's frustrated Communist leaders into another round of negotiations that might work out a sharing of power to resolve the political stalemate and the economic crisis. The subsequent agreement in early 1989 legalized Solidarity and declared

Mapping the Past

Map 30.2 Democratic Movements in Eastern Europe, 1989 Countries that had been satellites in the orbit of the Soviet Union began to set themselves free in 1989.

ANALYZING THE MAP Which countries experienced the largest number of demonstrations? Which countries and/or states within the Soviet Union experienced the fewest?

CONNECTIONS How did Gorbachev's reforms in the Soviet Union contribute to the spread of democratic movements in eastern Europe, and which specific action of his hastened the end of the Cold War?

To complete this activity online, go to the Online Study Guide at bedfordstmartins.com/mckaywest.

that a large minority of representatives to the Polish parliament would be chosen by free elections that June. Still guaranteed a parliamentary majority and expecting to win many of the contested seats, the Communists believed that their rule was guaranteed for four years and that Solidarity would keep the workers in line.

Lacking access to the state-run media, Solidarity succeeded nonetheless in mobilizing the country and winning most of the contested seats in an overwhelming victory. Moreover, many angry voters crossed off the names of unopposed party candidates, so that the Com-

munist Party failed to win the majority its leaders had anticipated. Solidarity members jubilantly entered the Polish parliament, and a dangerous stalemate quickly developed. But Solidarity leader Lech Walesa, a gifted politician who always repudiated violence, adroitly obtained a majority by securing the allegiance of two minor pro-communist parties that had been part of the coalition government after World War II. In August 1989 Tadeusz Mazowiecki (b. 1927), the editor of Solidarity's weekly newspaper, was sworn in as Poland's new non-communist prime minister.

The Fall of the Berlin Wall The sudden and unanticipated opening of the Berlin Wall in 1989 dramatized the spectacular fall of communism throughout east-central Europe. Built on the orders of the Soviet leader Nikita Khrushchev in 1961, the hated barrier had stopped the flow of refugees from East Germany to West Germany. Over the twenty-eight years of its existence, the Wall came to symbolize the limits on personal freedom enforced by Communist dictatorships. (Patrick Piel/Gamma)

In its first year and a half, the new Solidarity government cautiously introduced revolutionary political changes. It eliminated the hated secret police, the Communist ministers in the government, and finally Communist Party leader Jaruzelski himself, but it did so step-by-step in order to avoid confrontation with the army or the Soviet Union. However, in economic affairs, the Solidarity-led government was radical from the beginning. It applied economic **shock therapy**, an intense dose of neoliberal policy designed to make a clean break with state planning and move quickly to market mechanisms and private property. Thus the Solidarity government abolished controls on many prices on January 1, 1990, and reformed the monetary system with a big bang.

Hungary followed Poland. Hungary's Communist Party boss János Kádár (KAH-dahr) had permitted liberalization of the rigid planned economy after the 1956 uprising in exchange for political obedience and continued Communist control. In May 1988, in an effort to retain power by granting modest political concessions, the party replaced Kádár with a reform communist. But opposition groups rejected piecemeal progress, and in the summer of 1989 the Hungarian Communist Party agreed to hold free elections in March 1990. Welcoming Western investment and moving rapidly toward multiparty democracy, Hungary's Communists now enjoyed considerable popular support, and they believed, quite mistakenly it turned out, that they could defeat the opposition in the upcoming elections.

In an effort to strengthen their support at home and also put pressure on East Germany's hard-line Communist regime, the Hungarians opened their border to East Germans and tore down the barbed-wire iron curtain with Austria. Then tens of thousands of dissatisfied East German "vacationers" poured into Hungary, crossed into Austria as refugees, and continued on to immediate resettlement in thriving West Germany. The flight of East Germans led to the rapid growth of a homegrown protest movement in

> **shock therapy** The Solidarity-led government's radical take on economic affairs that abruptly ended state planning and moved to market mechanisms and private property.

Demonstrators During the Velvet Revolution Hundreds of thousands of Czechoslovakian citizens flooded the streets of Prague daily in peaceful protests after the police savagely beat student demonstrators in mid-November 1989. On the night of November 24 three hundred thousand people roared "Dubček-Havel" when Alexander Dubček, the aging reformer ousted in 1968 by the Soviets, stood on a balcony with Václav Havel, the leading opponent of communism. That night the Communists agreed to share power, and a few days later they resigned from the government. (Corbis)

East Germany. Intellectuals, environmentalists, and Protestant ministers took the lead, organizing huge candlelight demonstrations and arguing that a democratic but still socialist East Germany was both possible and desirable. These "stayers" failed to convince the "leavers," however, who continued to flee the country en masse. In a desperate but ad hoc attempt to stabilize the situation, the East German government opened the Berlin Wall in November 1989, and people danced for joy atop that grim symbol of the prison state. East Germany's aging Communist leaders were swept aside, and a reform government took power and scheduled free elections.

In Czechoslovakia, communism died quickly in November–December 1989 in an almost good-humored ousting of Communist bosses. This so-called Velvet Revolution grew out of popular demonstrations led by students, intellectuals, and a dissident playwright-turned-moral-revolutionary named Václav Havel (VAH-slahf HAH-vuhl) (b. 1936). The protesters practically took control of the streets and forced the Communists into a power-sharing arrangement, which quickly resulted in the resignation of the Communist government. As 1989 ended, the Czechoslovakian assembly elected Havel president.

Only in Romania was revolution violent and bloody. There ironfisted Communist dictator Nicolae Ceauşescu (chow-SHES-kou) (1918–1989) had long combined Stalinist brutality with stubborn independence from Moscow. Faced with mass protests in December 1989, Ceauşescu, alone among eastern European bosses, ordered his ruthless security forces to slaughter thousands, thereby sparking a classic armed uprising. After Ceauşescu's forces were defeated, the tyrant and his wife were captured and executed by a military court. A coalition government emerged from the fighting, although the legacy of Ceauşescu's oppression left a very troubled country.

German Unification and the End of the Cold War

The sudden death of communism in East Germany in 1989 reopened the "German question" and raised the threat of renewed Cold War conflict over Germany. Taking power in October 1989, East German reform communists, enthusiastically supported by leading East German intellectuals and former dissidents, wanted to preserve socialism by making it genuinely democratic and responsive to the needs of the people. They argued for a "third way" that would go beyond the failed Stalinism they had experienced and the ruthless capitalism they saw in the West. These reformers supported closer ties with West Germany, but they feared unification and wanted to preserve a distinct East German identity.

Their efforts failed, and over the next year, East Germany was absorbed into an enlarged West Germany, much like a faltering company is merged into a stronger rival and ceases to exist. Three factors were particularly important in this sudden absorption. First, in the first week after the Berlin Wall was opened, almost 9 million East Germans—roughly half of the total population—poured across the border into West Germany. Almost all returned to their homes in the East, but the joy of warm welcomes from long-lost friends and loved ones and the exhilarating experience of shopping in the well-stocked stores of the much wealthier West aroused long-dormant hopes of unity among ordinary citizens.

Second, West German chancellor Helmut Kohl and his closest advisers skillfully exploited the historic opportunity on their doorstep. Sure of support from the United States, whose leadership he had steadfastly followed, in November 1989 Kohl presented a ten-point plan for a step-by-step unification in cooperation with both East Germany and the international community. Kohl then promised the struggling citizens of East Germany an immediate economic bonanza—a one-for-one exchange of all East German marks in savings accounts and pensions into much more valuable West German marks. This generous offer helped a well-financed conservative-liberal Alliance for Germany, which was set up in East Germany and was closely tied to Kohl's West German Christian Democrats, to overwhelm those who argued for the preservation of some kind of independent socialist society in East Germany. In March 1990 the Alliance outdistanced the Socialist Party and won almost 50 percent of the votes in an East German parliamentary election. (The Communists ignominiously fell to fringe-party status.) The Alliance for Germany quickly negotiated an economic union on favorable terms with Chancellor Kohl.

Finally, in the summer of 1990 the crucial international aspect of German unification was successfully resolved. Unification would once again make Germany the strongest state in central Europe and would directly affect the security of the Soviet Union. But Gorbachev swallowed hard—Western cartoonists showed Stalin turning over in his grave—and negotiated the best deal he could. In a historic agreement signed by Gorbachev and Kohl in July 1990, a uniting Germany solemnly affirmed its peaceful intentions and pledged never to develop nuclear, biological, or chemical weapons. Germany also sweetened the deal by promising to make enormous loans to the hard-pressed Soviet Union. In October 1990 East Germany merged into West Germany, forming henceforth a single nation under the West German laws and constitution.

The peaceful reunification of Germany accelerated the pace of agreements to liquidate the Cold War. In November 1990 delegates from twenty-two European countries joined those from the United States and the Soviet Union in Paris and agreed to a scaling down of all their armed forces. The delegates also solemnly affirmed that all existing borders in Europe—from unified Germany to the newly independent Baltic republics—were legal and valid. The Paris Accord was for all practical purposes a general peace treaty, bringing an end to World War II and the Cold War that followed.

Peace in Europe encouraged the United States and the Soviet Union to scrap a significant portion of their nuclear weapons in a series of agreements. In September 1991 a confident President George H. W. Bush canceled the around-the-clock alert status for American bombers outfitted with atomic bombs, and a floundering Gorbachev quickly followed suit. For the first time in four decades, Soviet and American nuclear weapons were not standing ready to destroy capitalism, communism, and life itself.

The Reunification of Germany, 1990

Former boundary between East and West Germany

The Disintegration of the Soviet Union

As 1990 began, revolutionary changes had triumphed in all but two eastern European states—tiny Albania and the vast Soviet Union. The great question now became whether the Soviet Union would follow its former satellites and whether reform communism would give way to a popular anticommunist revolution.

In February 1990, as competing Russian politicians noisily presented their programs and nationalists in the non-Russian republics demanded autonomy or independence from the Soviet Union, the Communist Party suffered a stunning defeat in local elections throughout the country. As in the eastern European satellites, democrats and anticommunists won clear majorities in the leading cities of the Russian Soviet Republic (SFSR), the largest republic in the Soviet Union. Moreover, in Lithuania the people elected an uncompromising nationalist as president, and the newly chosen parliament declared Lithuania an independent state.

Gorbachev responded by placing an economic embargo on Lithuania, but he refused to use the army to crush the separatist government. The result was a tense political stalemate that undermined popular support for Gorbachev. Separating himself further from Communist hardliners, Gorbachev asked Soviet citizens to ratify a new constitution that formally abolished the Communist Party's monopoly of political power and expanded the power of the Congress of People's Deputies. Retaining his post as party secretary, Gorbachev convinced a majority of deputies to elect him president of the Soviet Union.

Gorbachev's eroding power and his unwillingness to risk a universal suffrage election for the presidency strengthened his great rival, Boris Yeltsin (1931–2007). A radical reform communist who had been purged by party conservatives in 1987, Yeltsin embraced the democratic movement, and in May 1990 he was elected parliamentary leader of the Russian Soviet Republic. He boldly announced that Russia itself would put its interests first, and declare its independence from the Soviet Union, thereby broadening the base of the anticommunist movement as he joined the patriotism of ordinary Russians with the democratic aspirations of big-city intellectuals. Gorbachev tried to save the Soviet Union with a new treaty that would link the member republics in a looser, freely accepted confederation, but six of the fifteen Soviet republics rejected Gorbachev's pleas.

Opposed by democrats and nationalists, Gorbachev was also challenged again by the Communist old guard. After Gorbachev was defeated at the Communist Party congress in July 1990, a gang of hardliners kidnapped him and his family in the Caucasus and tried to seize the Soviet government in August 1991. The attempted coup collapsed in the face of massive popular resistance that rallied around Yeltsin, who had recently been elected president of the Russian Soviet Republic by universal

Yeltsin Resists a Coup by Russian Communist Hardliners Standing atop a tank in Moscow in August 1991, the president of the Russian Soviet Republic, Boris Yeltsin (left), reads a statement denouncing the conspirators who were attempting to halt Gorbachev's reforms and hold the Soviet empire together. Yeltsin's brave public demonstration helped foil the coup and paved the way for the dissolution of the Soviet Union. (AP Images)

suffrage. As the spellbound world watched on television, Yeltsin defiantly denounced the rebels from atop a stalled tank in central Moscow and declared the "rebirth of Russia." The army supported Yeltsin, and Gorbachev was rescued and returned to power as head of the Soviet Union.

The leaders of the coup wanted to preserve Communist power, state ownership, and the multinational Soviet Union, but they succeeded only in destroying all three. An anticommunist revolution swept the Russian Soviet Republic as Yeltsin and his supporters outlawed the Communist Party and confiscated its property. Locked in a personal and political duel with Gorbachev, Yeltsin and his democratic allies declared Russia independent, withdrew from the Soviet Union, and renamed the Russian Soviet Republic the Russian Federation. All the other Soviet republics also left. The Soviet Union—and Gorbachev's job—ceased to exist on December 25, 1991. The independent republics of the old Soviet Union then established a loose confederation, the Commonwealth of Independent States, which played only a minor role in the 1990s.

LOOKING BACK LOOKING AHEAD

THE UNEXPECTED AND RAPID collapse of communism in Europe capped three decades of turbulent historical change. In the 1960s powerful challenges to the status quo steered western Europe to the left and attempted (but failed) to wrest power from the communists in the East. In the 1970s a global recession had devastating effects for everyday people in the West and East Blocs alike. And in the 1980s conservative Western leaders made the hard choices necessary to face economic decline and new global competition.

With the world economy on the road to recovery and new free-market systems in place across the former East Bloc, all of Europe would now have the opportunity to enter the information age. After forty years of Cold War division, the continent regained an underlying unity as faith in democratic government and market economics became the common European creed. In 1991 hopes for peaceful democratic progress were almost universal. According to philosopher Francis Fukuyama, the world had reached "the end of history" in that the end of the Cold War would lead to peaceful development based on growing tolerance, free-market economics, and liberal democracy.

The post–Cold War years saw the realization of some of these hopes, but the new era brought its own problems and tragedies. New ethnic and nationalist tensions flared, leading to a disastrous civil war in the former Yugoslavia. The struggle to rebuild the shattered societies of the former East Bloc countries was far more difficult than observers had hoped. Poor economic growth continued to complicate attempts to deal with the wide-open global economy. New conflicts with Islamic nations in the Middle East involved some European nations in open war. The European Union expanded, but political disagreements, environmental issues, increased anxiety about non-Western immigrants, and a host of other problems undermined moves toward true European unity. History was far from over: the realities of a post–Cold War world continued to produce difficult challenges as Europe entered the twenty-first century.

CHAPTER REVIEW

■ How did social and political changes in the 1960s contribute to growing criticism of the postwar consensus that had emerged in the 1950s? (p. 960)

In the early 1960s the prosperous western European society remained relatively stable, and East Bloc governments, bolstered by modest economic growth and committed to generous welfare benefits for their citizens, also generally maintained stability. As the 1960s progressed, however, politics in the West began shifting noticeably to the left, and Social Democratic governments promoted policies of détente designed to normalize East-West relations. Amid this more liberalized society, a youthful counterculture emerged among the children of affluence to critique the status quo. In the East, Khrushchev's limited reforms also inspired rebellions. Activists around the world rose in protest against the perceived inequalities of both capitalism and socialism, leading to dramatic events in 1968, exemplified in Paris and Prague. The actual political results of 1960s-era protests were mixed, but they did create more tolerance for a broad range of lifestyle activities.

■ How did economic decline in the 1970s contribute to fundamental social and political change in the 1980s in western Europe and North America? (p. 970)

In the early 1970s economic crises in Europe and North America shook the hard-won consensus of the postwar decades. The oil shocks of the 1970s created economic turmoil and brought real hardship to millions of people. Governments struggled to maintain welfare programs for their citizens as the global recession slowed growth and the boom years came to an end. By the late 1970s a post-industrial society had begun to emerge, causing even higher rates of unemployment in industrial sectors, but leading to growth in new high-tech and service industries. Even so, frustration with the policies and the perceived ineptitudes of governments set in, ushering in a new era of conservative politics. Leaders like Margaret Thatcher in Great Britain, Helmut Kohl in West Germany, and Ronald Reagan in the United States embraced neoliberal economic philosophies, championing private initiative, lowering taxes, and cutting government spending. At the same time, liberal groups such as feminists and environmentalists gained momentum and promoted their own interests to offset conservative rhetoric and government cutbacks. At the opposite end of the political spectrum, emboldened separatists and right-wing extremists sought political victories with sometimes violent tactics.

■ What internal and external factors weakened communist power in the East Bloc, and how did Soviet leader Mikhail Gorbachev try to reform the system from above? (p. 980)

Though the East Bloc achieved modest economic growth and some social stability during the 1960s, a number of factors weakened Communist rule. Failure to engage in significant internal reforms led to political and economic stagnation, and the global recession further hampered economic growth. Ordinary people chafed under party favoritism and limits on political and social freedom, and they complained about the relative lack of consumer prosperity. Reformists and dissident groups, such as Charter 77 in Czechoslovakia and Solidarity in Poland, worked to establish an active civil society that would expand civil rights within the system, and the revival of Cold War pressures under conservative Western governments further challenged East Bloc leaders. Gorbachev's attempts to use economic restructuring (perestroika) and civil openness (glasnost) to reform the system addressed some of these problems, but they were too little and too late to prevent communism's collapse.

■ Why did anticommunist revolutions sweep through eastern Europe in 1989, and what were the immediate consequences? (p. 985)

By the 1980s the socialist governments of the East Bloc lacked any true popular legitimacy. Moreover, the economies of eastern European countries, already strained by the global crisis, were being pushed to the brink of disaster by striking workers and other protesters, most notably the Solidarity movement in Poland. In 1988 the Polish government finally agreed to negotiate with the leaders of the outlawed Solidarity movement in order to prevent economic collapse. Solidarity's political demands led to a new non-communist government, which proceeded cautiously in order to avoid Soviet military intervention. Soon all the East Bloc countries followed suit, with anticommunist groups demanding — and finally winning — a voice in their government, and Communist leaders were largely ousted. In part because the reformist Soviet leader Mikhail Gorbachev refused to use force, the revolutions of 1989 were almost all nonviolent, celebratory occasions. In a dramatic finale, the two Germanys joined in a single democratic state, and the democratic movement triumphed in the Soviet Union. The Soviet empire fell apart, the Cold War ended, and the United States remained the only superpower.

Suggested Reading

Ash, Timothy Garten. *The Magic Lantern: The Revolution of '89 Witnessed in Warsaw, Budapest, Berlin, and Prague*. 1993. An exciting firsthand narrative of the collapse of the East Bloc in 1989 and 1990.

Bell, Daniel. *The Coming of Post-Industrial Society*. 1976. An early and prophetic forecast of the way the arrival of the information age would transform Western society.

Bernstein, Serge. *The Republic of de Gaulle, 1958–1969*. 2006. An outstanding work on France.

Caute, David. *The Year of the Barricades: A Journey Through 1968*. 1990. A high-energy examination that brings the up-heavals of 1968 to life.

Cioc, Mark. *The Rhine: An Eco-Biography, 1815–2000*. 2002. A pace-setting environmental history of one of Europe's great rivers.

de Grazia, Victoria. *Irresistible Empire: America's Advance Through Twentieth-Century Europe*. 2005. Lively, provocative account of Europe's Americanization.

Guha, Ramachandra. *Environmentalism: A Global History*. 2000. A powerful and readable overview of environmentalism that puts Europe in world context.

Kurlansky, Mark. *1968: The Year That Rocked the World*. 2003. Popular history at its best, a gripping account of the 1960s generation and 1968 across the globe.

McLeod, Hugh. *The Religious Crisis of the 1960s*. 2007. A comparative study of Western religion in decline.

Port, Andrew I. *Conflict and Stability in the German Democratic Republic*. 2007. A penetrating analysis of popular support for communism in this major East Bloc country.

Reitan, Earl. *Tory Radicalism: Margaret Thatcher, John Major, and the Transformation of Modern Britain, 1979–1997*. 1997. Clear, concise, and very useful.

Ross, Kirsten. *May 1968 and Its Afterlives*. 2004. An important book on the way contested memories continue to shape our understanding of France's May events.

Rothschild, Joseph, and Nancy M. Wingfield. *Return to Diversity: A Political History of East Central Europe Since World War II*. 1999. A general overview of politics in the Soviet Bloc.

Scott, Joan W. *Only Paradoxes to Offer: French Feminists and the Rights of Man*. 1997. An important study of French feminism.

Slater, Don. *Consumer Culture and Modernity*. 1997. An overview of consumer society that includes an in-depth look at the consumer revolution of the 1960s.

Smith, Bonnie G. *Global Feminisms Since 1945*. 2000. A broadly cast and accessible overview of feminism after World War II that puts European and American movements in global context.

Stokes, Gale. *The Walls Came Tumbling Down: The Collapse of Communism in Eastern Europe*. 1993. A concise overview of the struggle for liberation from communist domination in the East Bloc.

Notes

1. Quoted in Kessing's Research Report, *Germany and East Europe Since 1945: From the Potsdam Agreement to Chancellor Brandt's "Ostpolitik"* (New York: Charles Scribner's Sons, 1973), pp. 284–285.
2. M. Mitterauer, *The History of Youth* (Oxford: Basil Blackwell, 1992), p. 40.
3. Quoted in F. Gilbert and D. C. Large, *The End of the European Era: 1890 to the Present* (New York: Norton, 2009), p. 498.
4. See R. Guha, *Environmentalism: A Global History* (New York: Longman, 2000), p. 79.

Key Terms

détente (p. 960)
New Left (p. 963)
Brezhnev Doctrine (p. 970)
OPEC (p. 971)
stagflation (p. 971)
postindustrial society (p. 971)
neoliberalism (p. 972)
really existing socialism (p. 980)
Solidarity (p. 982)
perestroika (p. 984)
glasnost (p. 984)
shock therapy (p. 987)

For practice quizzes and other study tools, visit the Online Study Guide at **bedfordstmartins.com/mckaywest**.

For primary sources from this period, see *Sources of Western Society*, **Second Edition**.

For Web sites, images, and documents related to topics in this chapter, visit Make History at **bedfordstmartins.com/mckaywest**.

31

Europe in an Age of Globalization

1990 to the Present

On November 9, 2009, the twentieth anniversary of the fall of the Berlin Wall, jubilant crowds filled the streets around the Brandenburg Gate at the former border between East and West Berlin. International leaders and tens of thousands of onlookers applauded as former Polish president Lech Walesa pushed over a line of one thousand eight-foot-tall foam dominos, symbolizing communism's collapse.

The crowd had reason to celebrate. The end of the Cold War had opened a new chapter in European and world history. Capitalism spread across the former East Bloc and the Soviet Union (now the Russian Federation), bringing potential for democratic reform. Some of these hopes were realized, but the new era also brought its own problems and tragedies. In eastern Europe, the process of rebuilding shattered societies was more difficult than optimists had envisioned in 1991. Across the West and around the world, individuals experienced the benefits and disadvantages of globalization and the digital revolution. The ongoing influx of immigrants into western Europe brought ethnic diversity to formerly homogeneous societies, which sometimes led to fear and conflict.

As Europe faced serious tensions and complex changes at the turn of the century, it also came together to form a strong new European Union that would prove a formidable economic competitor to the United States. Though old ties between Europe and the United States began to loosen, the nations of the West — and the world — could not ignore the common challenges they now faced. Finding solutions to ever-present problems regarding security, energy, the environment, and human rights would require not only innovation, but also cooperation. ∎

AFP/Getty Images

Life in an Age of Globalization. Established in 1895, the Venice Biennale is a major international contemporary art exhibition held every other year in Venice, Italy. Housed at a park where art is displayed at thirty permanent national pavilions, the show draws visitors from around the world and suggests the effect of globalization on the arts. Here a woman takes in a work by the Italian artist Gian Marco Montesano commissioned for the Italian pavilion at the 53rd Biennale in 2009.

CHAPTER PREVIEW

Rebuilding Russia and Eastern Europe
■ How did Russia and the former East Bloc countries meet the challenges of postcommunist reconstruction and political and economic reform?

The New Global System
■ What are the defining features of globalization, and how did changing international structures transform European societies?

Toward a Multicultural Continent
■ How did population decline and large-scale immigration lead to demographic changes in contemporary Europe, and what were the main results of growing ethnic diversity?

Confronting Twenty-First-Century Challenges
■ What key problems faced European societies in the twenty-first century, and how did European states and peoples deal with these critical issues?

Rebuilding Russia and Eastern Europe

How did Russia and the former East Bloc countries meet the challenges of postcommunist reconstruction and political and economic reform? ■

Establishing liberal democratic governments in the former East Bloc countries and the Soviet Union, now renamed Russia, would not prove an easy task. While Russia initially moved toward economic reform and political openness, the nation returned to its authoritarian traditions in the early 2000s.

The transition to democracy in the former communist countries of East-Central Europe was also difficult. After a period of tense reform, some countries, such as Poland, the Czech Republic, Hungary, and the Baltic states, established relatively prosperous democracies and joined NATO and then the European Union. Others, such as Romania and Bulgaria, lagged behind. In multiethnic Yugoslavia, the collapse of communism led to a disastrous civil war and the violent dissolution of the country. Russia and eastern Europe struggled to catch up to and integrate with the West, with mixed results.

Economic Shock Therapy in Russia

Politics and economics were closely intertwined in Russia after the attempted communist coup in 1991 and the dissolution of the Soviet Union (see Chapter 30). President Boris Yeltsin, his democratic supporters, and his economic ministers wanted to create conditions that would prevent a return to communism and would also right the faltering economy. Following the example of some postcommunist governments in eastern Europe, and agreeing with neoliberal Western advisers who argued that a quick turn to free markets and private economies would speed economic growth, the Russian reformers opted for breakneck liberalization in January 1992. Applying the type of economic shock therapy used by Poland (see Chapter 30), the Russians moved quickly to privatize the market, freeing prices on 90 percent of all Russian goods, with the exception of bread, vodka, oil, and public transportation. The government also launched a rapid privatization of industry and

Rich and Poor in Today's Russia A woman sells knitted scarves in front of a department store window in Moscow in September 2005. The collapse of the Soviet Union and the use of shock therapy to reform the Russian economy created new poverty as well as new wealth. (TASS/Sovfoto)

turned thousands of factories and mines over to new private companies. Each citizen received a voucher worth 10,000 rubles (about $22) to buy stock in private companies, but ownership of the privatized companies usually remained in the hands of the old bosses, the managers and government officials from the communist era.

President Yeltsin and his economic reformers believed that shock therapy would revive production and bring widespread prosperity after a brief period of hardship. The results of the reforms were in fact quite different. Prices increased 250 percent on the very first day, and they kept on soaring, increasing twenty-six times in the course of 1992. At the same time, Russian production fell a staggering 20 percent. Nor did the situation stabilize quickly. After 1995, rapid but gradually slowing inflation raged, and output continued to fall. According to most estimates, in 1996 the Russian economy produced at least one-third and possibly as much as one-half less than in 1991. The Russian economy crashed again in 1998 in the wake of Asia's financial crisis.

Rapid economic liberalization worked poorly in Russia for several reasons. Soviet industry had been highly monopolized and strongly tilted toward military goods. Production of many items had been concentrated in one or two gigantic factories or in interconnected combines that supplied the entire economy. With privatization these powerful state monopolies became powerful private monopolies that cut production and raised prices in order to maximize their financial returns. Moreover, powerful corporate managers and bureaucrats forced Yeltsin's government to hand out enormous subsidies to reinforce the positions of big firms and to avoid bankruptcies. New corporate leaders included criminals who intimidated would-be rivals in attempts to prevent the formation of new businesses. In the end, as enterprise directors and politicians converted large portions of previously state-owned industry into their own private property, they undermined the ideal goal of worker ownership.

Runaway inflation and poorly executed privatization brought a profound social revolution to Russia. The new capitalist elite acquired great wealth and power, while large numbers of people fell into abject poverty, and the majority struggled to make ends meet. Managers, former Communist officials, and financiers who came out

1980s–1990s	Emergence of globalization
1990s–2000s	New waves of legal and illegal immigration to Europe
1990–1991	Persian Gulf War
1991	Maastricht Treaty
1991–2001	Civil war in Yugoslavia
1992–1997	Decline of Russian economy
1993	Creation of the European Union
1997–1998	Global economic downturn
1999	Protests against World Trade Organization in Seattle
2000–2008	Resurgence of Russian economy under Putin
2001	September 11 terrorist attack on the United States; war in Afghanistan begins
2002	Euro introduced in European Union
2003	Iraq War begins
2004	Train bombings in Madrid by Islamic extremists
2005	Young Muslims riot in France; subway bombing in London by Islamic extremists
2006	Sectarian conflict in Iraq increases
2008	Worldwide financial crisis
2009	Ratification of Treaty of Lisbon; young Muslims riot in France; Copenhagen summit on climate change

of the privatization process with large shares of the old state monopolies stood at the top of the reorganized society. The richest plums were found in Russia's huge oil and natural resources industries, where unscrupulous enterprise directors pocketed enormous dishonest gains.

The new elite was more highly concentrated than ever before, and maintained control with corrupt business practices and rampant cronyism. By 1996 Moscow, with 5 percent of Russia's population, controlled 80 percent of its capital resources. At the other extreme, the vast majority of people saw their savings become practically worthless. Pensions lost much of their value, and whole markets were devoted to people selling off their personal goods to survive. Perhaps the most telling statistic, which reflected the hardship caused by the collapse of the Soviet welfare state and growing poverty, was the catastrophic decline in the life expectancy of the average Russian male from sixty-nine years in 1991 to only fifty-eight years in 1996. Under these conditions, effective representative government failed to develop, and many Russians came to equate democracy with the corruption, poverty, and national decline they experienced throughout the 1990s.

Russian Revival Under Vladimir Putin

The widespread disillusionment in the first decade of postcommunist Russia set the stage for the "managed democracy" of Vladimir Putin (VLAH-duh-mihr POO-tihn) (b. 1952). First elected president as Yeltsin's chosen successor in 2000, Putin won in a landslide in March 2004. An officer in the secret police in the Communist era, Putin and his United Russia Party maintained relatively free markets in the economic sphere but re-established semi-authoritarian political rule. Proponents of liberal democracy were in retreat, while conservative Russian intellectuals were on the offensive, arguing that free markets and capitalism required strong political rule to control corruption and prevent chaos.

The combination of Putin's autocratic politics and the turn to market economics—aided greatly by high prices for oil and natural gas, Russia's most important exports—led to a decade of strong economic growth. Russia became one of western Europe's main energy sup-

Vladimir Putin on Vacation in 2009 After serving two terms as Russian president (2000–2008), Putin was appointed prime minister and continues to be a powerful Russian leader. Putin's high approval ratings were due in part to his carefully crafted image of strength and manliness. (AFP/Getty Images)

pliers. In 2008 the Russian economy had been expanding for over nine years, encouraging the growth of a new middle class. That same year, the global financial crisis and a rapid drop in the price of oil reversed these trends. Economic growth ground to a halt. The Russian stock market collapsed; although the government initiated a $200 billion rescue plan, the economy continued to falter in 2010.

During his term as president, Putin championed a return to an assertive anti-Western Russian nationalism. He took a forceful stand against the expansion of NATO in the former East Bloc and increasingly challenged the United States in world affairs. Putin expressed pride in the accomplishments of the Soviet Union and downplayed the abuses of the Stalinist system. In addition, the Russian president centralized power in the Kremlin, increased military spending, and expanded the secret police. Putin's carefully crafted manly image and his forceful interaction in international diplomacy soothed the country's injured pride and symbolized its national revival.

Putin's government moved decisively to limit political opposition. The arrest and imprisonment for tax evasion of the corrupt billionaire oil tycoon Mikhail Khodorkovsky, who had openly supported opposition parties, showed that Putin and the United Russia Party would use state powers to stifle dissent. Though freedom of the press is guaranteed by the constitution, the Russian government also cracked down on the independent media. Using a variety of tactics, officials and pro-government businessmen worked to influence news reports and intimidate critical journalists. The suspicious murder in 2006 of journalist Anna Politkovskaya, a prominent critic of Russian human rights abuses and Russia's war in Chechnya, reinforced Western worries that the country was returning to Soviet-style press censorship.

Putin also took an aggressive and at times interventionist stance toward the Commonwealth of Independent States, a loose confederation of the newly independent states on the borders of the former Soviet Union, including Ukraine, Georgia, and the Republic of Belarus (Map 31.1). Conflict has been particularly intense in the oil-rich Caucasus region to the south, where an unstable combination of nationalist separatism and ethnic and religious tensions challenges Russian dominance. Since the breakup of the Soviet Union, Russian troops have repeatedly invaded Chechnya (CHECH-nyuh), a tiny republic of 1 million Muslims on Russia's southern border that in 1991 had declared its independence from the Russian Federation.

Despite nominal Russian control over Chechnya, the cost of the conflict has been high. Thousands on both sides have lost their lives, and both sides have committed serious human rights abuses. Russian security forces have tortured and summarily executed insur-

Map 31.1 Russia and the Successor States, 1991–2010 After the failure of an attempt in August 1991 to depose Gorbachev, an anticommunist revolution swept the Soviet Union. Led by Russia and Boris Yeltsin, the republics that formed the Soviet Union declared their sovereignty and independence. Eleven of the fifteen republics then formed a loose confederation called the Commonwealth of Independent States, but the integrated economy of the Soviet Union dissolved into separate national economies, each with its own goals and policies. Conflict continues to simmer over these goals and policies, as evidenced by the ongoing civil war in Chechnya and the recent conflict between Russia and Georgia over South Ossetia.

gents they had captured. Chechen terrorists, for their part, occupied a crowded theater in Moscow in 2002 and took some twelve hundred hostages in a Russian school in 2004. In both cases government efforts to free the hostages killed not only the terrorists but also hundreds of innocent Russian civilians.

Moscow declared an end to military operations in Chechnya in April 2009, but Chechen insurgents, inspired by separatist nationalism and Islamic radicalism, continued their violent struggle for national independence. The ongoing civil war in Chechnya also contributed to an ongoing crisis in the independent state of Georgia, which won independence from Russia in 1991. Russian troops invaded Georgia in 2008 to sup-

port a separatist movement in South Ossetia (ah-SEE-shuh), which eventually established a breakaway independent republic recognized by Russia, but not by much of the West.

Despite his turn to illiberal domestic politics and heavy-handed foreign intervention, Putin stepped down when his term limits expired in 2008. His handpicked successor, Dimitri Medvedev (mehd-VEHD-yehf) (b. 1965), easily won the Russian presidential elections that year and then appointed Putin prime minister, leading observers to conclude that the former president was still the dominant leader. Medvedev cast himself as a relative liberal compared to the former president, and Russian citizens enjoyed a relatively open cultural life in

> **What we want is for our life to be as easy as it was in the Soviet Union, with the guarantee of a good, stable future and low prices — and at the same time this freedom that did not exist before.**

—**RUSSIAN PENSIONER**

cafés and cultural institutions and on the Internet. Yet by 2010 it seemed clear that Russia had slowed attempts to establish a Western-style democracy and instead reinstituted a system of authoritarian presidential control. Tensions between political centralization and liberal openness continued to define Russia's difficult road away from communism.

Coping with Change in Eastern Europe

Developments in eastern Europe were similar to those in Russia in important ways. The postcommunist former satellites worked to replace state planning and socialism with market mechanisms and private property. Western-style electoral politics also took hold; as in Russia, this politics was marked by intense battles between presidents and parliaments and by weak political parties.

Economic growth in the former communist countries was varied, but most observers agreed that Poland, the Czech Republic, and Hungary were the most successful. Each met the critical challenge of economic reconstruction more successfully than did Russia, and each could claim to be the economic leader in eastern Europe, depending on the criteria selected. The reasons for these successes included considerable experience with limited market reforms before 1989, flexibility and lack of dogmatism in government policy, and an enthusiastic embrace of capitalism by a new entrepreneurial class. In the first five years of reform, Poland created twice as many new businesses as did Russia, with a total population only one-fourth as large.

Ostalgie German term referring to nostalgia for the lifestyles and culture of the vanished East Bloc.

Poland, the Czech Republic, and Hungary also did far better than Russia in creating new civic institutions, legal systems, and independent media outlets that reinforced political freedom and national revival. Lech Walesa in Poland and Václav Havel in Czechoslovakia were elected presidents of their countries and proved as remarkable in power as in opposition (see Chapter 30). After Czechoslovakia's Velvet Revolution in 1989, Havel and the Czech parliament accepted a "velvet divorce" in 1993 when Slovakian nationalists wanted to break

off and form their own state. Above all, and in sharp contrast to Russia, the popular goal of adopting the liberal democratic values of western Europe reinforced political moderation and compromise. In 1997 Poland, Hungary, and the Czech Republic were accepted into the NATO alliance, and in 2004 these countries plus Slovakia gained admission to the European Union (EU) (see page 1005).

Romania and Bulgaria were the eastern European laggards in the postcommunist transition. Western traditions were much weaker there, and both countries were much poorer than their neighbors to the north. Romania and Bulgaria did make progress after 2000, however, and joined NATO in 2004 and the EU in 2007.

The social consequences of reconstruction in the former East Bloc were similar to those in Russia. Ordinary citizens and the elderly were once again the big losers, while the young and former Communists were the big winners. Inequalities between richer and poorer regions also increased. Capital cities such as Warsaw, Prague, and Budapest concentrated wealth, power, and opportunity as never before, while provincial centers stagnated and old industrial areas declined. Crime and gangsterism increased in both the streets and the executive suites.

Though few former East Bloc residents wanted to return to communism, they nonetheless expressed some longings for the stability of the old system. Some missed the guaranteed jobs and generous social benefits provided by the Communist state, and they found the individualism and competitiveness of capitalist democracy cold and difficult. One Russian woman living on a pension of $448 a month in 2003 summed up the dilemma: "What we want is for our life to be as easy as it was in the Soviet Union, with the guarantee of a good, stable future and low prices — and at the same time this freedom that did not exist before."[1] Even the shoddy consumer goods so bemoaned during the communist years became objects of affection. Germans coined the term **Ostalgie** — a combination of the German words for "East" and "nostalgia" — to label this fondness for the lifestyles and culture of the vanished East Bloc.

At the same time, many East Bloc citizens had never fully accepted communism, primarily because they equated it with Russian imperialism and the loss of national independence. The joyous crowds that toppled communist regimes in 1989 believed that they were liberating the nation as well as the individual. Thus, when communism died, nationalism was reborn. Reflecting this new sense of popular nationalism, conservative politicians in the mold of Russia's president Putin found success in Poland, the Czech Republic, and other former East Bloc countries.

The question of whether or how to punish former Communist leaders who had committed political crimes or abused human rights emerged as a pressing question in the former East Bloc. Germany tried major offenders and opened the records of the East German secret police (the Stasi) to the public, and by 1996 more than a million former residents had asked to see their files.[2] Other countries designed various means to deal with former elites who might have committed crimes, with conservative leaders generally taking a more punitive stand against the old Communist bosses. Finding fair solutions proceeded slowly and with much controversy, an ongoing reminder of the troubling legacies of communism and the Cold War.

Tragedy in Yugoslavia

The great postcommunist tragedy was Yugoslavia, which under Josip Tito had been a federation of republics and regions under centralized Communist rule (see Chapter 29). After Tito's death in 1980, power passed increasingly to the sister republics, which encouraged a revival of regional and ethnic conflicts that were exacerbated by charges of ethnically inspired massacres during World War II and a dramatic economic decline in the mid-1980s.

The revolutions of 1989 accelerated the breakup of Yugoslavia. Serbian president Slobodan Milosevic (SLOH-buh-dayn muh-LOH-suh-vihch) (1941–2006), a former Communist bureaucrat, intended to grab land from other republics and unite all Serbs, regardless of where they lived, in a "greater Serbia." In 1989 Milosevic arbitrarily abolished self-rule in the Serbian province of Kosovo, where Albanian-speaking, primarily Islamic peoples constituted the overwhelming majority. Milosevic's moves strengthened the cause of national separatism in the Serbian-controlled federation, and in June 1991 relatively wealthy Slovenia and Croatia declared their independence from Yugoslavia. Milosevic's armies invaded to reassert Serbian control. The Serbs were quickly repulsed in Slovenia, but managed to take about 30 percent of Croatia.

In 1992 the civil war spread to Bosnia-Herzegovina, which had also declared its independence. Serbs—about 30 percent of that region's population—refused to live under the more numerous Bosnian Muslims (Map 31.2). Yugoslavia had once been a tolerant and largely successful multiethnic state with different groups living side by side and often intermarrying. The new goal of both sides in the Bosnian civil war was **ethnic cleansing**: the attempt to establish

ethnic cleansing The attempt to establish ethnically homogeneous territories by intimidation, forced deportation, and killing.

Map 31.2 The Breakup of Yugoslavia, 1991–2006 Yugoslavia had the most ethnically diverse population in eastern Europe. The republic of Croatia had substantial Serbian and Muslim minorities. Bosnia-Herzegovina had large Muslim, Serbian, and Croatian populations, none of which had a majority. In June 1991 Serbia's brutal effort to seize territory and unite all Serbs in a single state brought a tragic civil war.

ethnically homogeneous territories by intimidation, forced deportation, and killing. Serbian armies and irregular militias attempted to "cleanse" the territory of its non-Serb residents, unleashing ruthless brutality, with murder, rape, destruction, and the herding of refugees into concentration camps. Before the fighting in Bosnia ended, some three hundred thousand people were dead, and millions had been forced to flee their homes.

While appalling scenes of horror shocked the world, the Western nations had difficulty formulating an effective and unified response. The turning point came in July 1995 when Bosnian Serbs overran Srebrenica—a Muslim city previously declared a United Nations safe area. Pursuing their violent ethnic cleansing campaign, Serb forces killed 7,400 of the city's Muslim civilians, primarily men and boys. Europe had not seen such atrocities since the horrors of the Nazi Holocaust in World War II (see Chapter 28). Public outrage prompted NATO to bomb Bosnian Serb military targets intensively, and the Croatian army drove all the Serbs from Croatia. In November 1995 President Bill Clinton helped the warring sides hammer out a complicated accord that gave the Bosnian Serbs about 49 percent of Bosnia and the Muslim-Croatian peoples the rest. Troops from NATO countries patrolled Bosnia to try to keep the peace.

The Albanian Muslims of Kosovo had been hoping for a restoration of self-rule, but they gained nothing from the Bosnian agreement. In early 1998 frustrated Kosovar militants formed the **Kosovo Liberation Army (KLA)** and began to fight for independence. Serbian repression of the Kosovars

Kosovo Liberation Army (KLA) Military organization formed in 1998 by Kosovar militants who sought independence from Serbia.

increased, and in 1998 Serbian forces attacked both KLA guerrillas and unarmed villagers, displacing 250,000 people within Kosovo.

By January 1999 the Western Powers, led by the United States, were threatening Milosevic with heavy air raids if he did not withdraw Serbian armies from Kosovo and accept self-government (but not independence) for Kosovo. Milosevic refused, and in March 1999 NATO began bombing Yugoslavia. Serbian paramilitary forces responded by driving about 865,000 Albanian Kosovars into exile. NATO redoubled its highly destructive bombing campaign, which eventually forced Milosevic to withdraw and allowed the Kosovars to regain their homeland. A UN–NATO peacekeeping force occupied the territory, bringing the ten-year cycle of Yugoslavian civil wars to a close. Although U.S.-led NATO intervention finally brought an end to the conflict, the failure to take a stronger stand in the early years led to widespread and unnecessary suffering in the former Yugoslavia.

The war-weary and impoverished Serbs eventually voted the still-defiant Milosevic out of office, and in July 2001 a new pro-Western Serbian government turned him over to the war crimes tribunal in the Netherlands to stand trial for crimes against humanity. After blustering his way through the initial stages of his trial, Milosevic died in 2006 before the proceedings were complete. In 2008, after eight years of administration by the United Nations and NATO peacekeeping forces, the Republic of Kosovo declared its total independence from Serbia. The United States and many western European nations recognized the declaration. Serbia and Russia did not, and the long-term status of this troubled emerging state remained uncertain.

Escape from Srebrenica
A Bosnian Muslim refugee arrives at the United Nations base in Tuzla and with anguished screams tells the world of the Serbian atrocities. Several thousand civilians were murdered at Srebrenica, and Western public opinion finally demanded decisive action. Efforts continue to arrest the Serbs believed responsible and to try them for crimes against humanity. (J. Jones/Corbis)

The New Global System

What are the defining features of globalization, and how did changing international structures transform European societies? ■

Contemporary observers often assert that the world has entered a new era of **globalization**. Though the term is difficult to define, such assertions do not mean that there were never international connections before. Europe has long had close—sometimes productive, sometimes destructive—ties to other parts of the world. Yet new global relationships did emerge in the last decades of the twentieth century.

First, the expansion and ready availability of highly efficient computer and media technologies led to ever-faster exchanges of information and entertainment around the world. Second, the growth of multinational corporations restructured national economies on a global scale. Third, an array of international governing bodies, such as the European Union, the United Nations, the World Bank, and the World Trade Organization, increasingly set policies that challenged the authority of traditional nation-states. Taken together, these global transformations had a remarkable impact—both positive and negative—on many aspects of Western society.

The Digital Age and the Changing Economy

The development of sophisticated personal computer technologies and the Internet at the end of the twentieth century, coupled with the deregulation of national and international financial systems, had a revolutionary impact on international trade. The ability to rapidly exchange information and capital meant that economic activity was no longer centered on national banks or stock exchanges, but rather flowed quickly across international borders. Large cities like London, Moscow, New York, and Hong Kong became global centers of banking, trade, and financial services. The influence of stock markets and insurance companies, as well as of communications conglomerates and energy and legal firms headquartered in these new global cities, extended far beyond the borders of the traditional nation-state.

Multinational corporations flourished in the new global climate. Conglomerates such as Siemens and Vivendi exemplified the new business model. Siemens, with international headquarters in Berlin and Munich and offices around the globe, is one of the world's largest engineering companies, with vast holdings in energy, construction, health care, financial services, and industrial production. Vivendi, an extensive media and telecommunications company headquartered in Paris, controls a vast international network of products, including

music and film, publishing, television broadcasting, pay-TV, Internet services, and video games.

The growing global reach of multinational corporations and the development of sophisticated information technologies have had astonishing effects on everyday life. Cable television, DVDs, and online video streaming greatly diversified home entertainment. Europe's once stodgy public broadcasting systems now competed with a variety of commercial private providers. Compact discs and downloadable audio files replaced vinyl records and cassettes, and digital cameras eliminated the need for film. E-mail and text messaging changed the way friends and families exchanged news, and letter writing with pen and paper became a quaint relic of the past. Many people now relied on the Internet to access consumer goods, entertainment, and information from around the globe. The smart phone, with its multimedia telecommunications features, combined all these activities and more in one small hand-held device.

> **globalization** The emergence of a freer, more technologically connected global economy, accompanied by a worldwide exchange of cultural, political, and religious ideas.

Though globalization in some ways fueled the booming economy and helped create a flashy new world of instant entertainment and communication, the close connections between national economies also made the entire world vulnerable to economic panics and downturns. In 1997 a banking crisis in Thailand spread to Indonesia, South Korea, and Japan, and then echoed around the world. The resulting decline in prices for raw materials such as petroleum and natural gas hit Russia especially hard, leading to high inflation, bank failures, and the collapse of the Russian stock market. The crisis then spread to Latin America, where most countries entered a severe economic downturn in 1998.

A decade later, in 2008, the global recession, triggered by a crisis in the U.S. housing market and financial system, created the worst worldwide economic crisis since the Great Depression of the 1930s. The U.S. government spent massive sums in attempts to recharge the economy. Banks, insurance agencies, auto companies, and financial service conglomerates received billions of federal dollars, but unemployment, a weak housing market, and stagnant production continued.

The recession quickly swept through Europe. One of the worst hit was Iceland, where in October 2008 the currency and banking system collapsed outright. Other countries across Europe were also rocked by the crisis. Ireland and Latvia were forced to make deep and painful cuts in government spending to balance national budgets. By 2010 Britain was deeply in debt, and Spain, Portugal, and especially Greece were close to bankruptcy. In May 2010 Greece promised to raise consumption taxes and drastically reduce spending on public pensions and other popular social benefits in order to accept a 110 billion euro bailout package from the

Financial Meltdown in Iceland
These protesters are on their way to the parliament in Reykjavik, the capital of Iceland, in March 2010 to protest the government's proposed debt repayment policies after the collapse of the Icelandic banking system. One protester carries a sign reading "Stop the Financial Casino." Iceland's financial meltdown, sparked by a major recession in the United States, underscored the close links between national economies in the new era of globalization. (S. Olads/EPA/Corbis)

International Monetary Fund and the European Union. National governments used a variety of initiatives to recharge their flagging economies, even as experts worried about the long-term effects of the recession on European stability and demonstrators took to the streets to protest against cuts in popular social programs.

The Human Side of Globalization

In addition to the financial vulnerabilities inherent in a global economy, the varied forces of globalization encouraged far-reaching social change tied closely to the technological advances of the postindustrial society (see Chapter 30). Low labor costs in the industrializing world—including the former East Bloc, South America, and East Asia—encouraged corporations to outsource labor-intensive manufacturing jobs to these regions. Neoliberal free-trade policies and lowered tariffs made it less expensive to manufacture goods such as steel, automotive parts, computer components, and all manner of consumer goods in developing countries, and then import them for sale in the West. In these new conditions, a car made by Volkswagen could still be sold as a product of high-quality German engineering, but be assembled in Volkswagen's new plant in Chattanooga, Tennessee, with steel imported from South Korea and computer chips made in Taiwan.

Globalization dramatically changed the nature of work in western Europe. In France in 1973, for example, some 40 percent of the employed population worked in industry—in mining, construction, manufacturing, and utilities. About 49 percent worked in services, including retail, the hotel and restaurant trades, transpor-

tation, communications, financial and business services, and social and personal services. In 2004 only 24 percent of the French worked in industry, and a whopping 72 percent worked in services. The numbers varied country by country, yet across Europe the trend was clear: by 2005 only about one in three workers was still employed in the once-booming manufacturing sector.[3]

The deindustrialization of Europe established a multitiered society with real winners and losers. In the top tier was a small, affluent group of highly paid experts, executives, and professionals—about one-quarter of the total population—who managed the new information industries. In the second, larger tier, a struggling middle class experienced stagnating incomes and a declining standard of living. Workers from the formerly well-paid industrial sector faced stubborn unemployment and cuts in both welfare and workplace benefits. Many were forced to take low-paying jobs in the retail service sector.

In the bottom tier—in some areas as much as a quarter of the population—a poorly paid underclass performed the unskilled jobs of a postindustrial economy. In Europe and the United States inclusion in this lowest segment of society was often predicated on race and ethnicity. Recently arrived immigrants had trouble finding jobs and often lived in unpleasant, hastily built suburban apartment blocks, where they teetered on the edge of poverty. In London, unemployment rates among young black men soared above those of their white compatriots, and the connections between race and poverty were similar in other urban areas.

Geographic contrasts further revealed the unequal aspects of globalization. Regions in Europe that had successfully made the move to a postindustrial economy, such as northern Italy and southern Germany and Austria, were centers of affluence and prosperity. Regions that had depended on heavy industry or were historically underdeveloped, including the former East Bloc countries, the factory districts north of London, and the largely rural areas of southern Italy and Spain, lagged behind. In addition, a global north-south divide increasingly separated the relatively affluent countries of Europe and North America from the industrializing nations of Africa and South America. Though India, China, and other East Asian nations experienced solid growth, other industrializing nations struggled to overcome decades of underdevelopment.

The New European Union

Global economic pressures encouraged the expansion and consolidation of the European Community (EC), which in 1993 proudly rechristened itself the **European Union (EU)** (Map 31.3). With its roots in Europe's Common Market (see Chapter 29), the EU worked to add the free movement of European labor, capital, and services to the existing free trade in goods. In addition, member states sought to create a monetary union in which all EU countries would share a single currency. Membership in the monetary union required states to meet the strict financial criteria defined in the 1991 **Maastricht Treaty**, which also set legal standards and anticipated the development of common policies on defense and foreign affairs.

Western European elites and opinion makers generally supported the decisive step toward economic integration embodied in the Maastricht Treaty. They felt that membership requirements, which imposed financial discipline on national governments, would combat Europe's ongoing economic problems, and they viewed the establishment of a single European currency as an irreversible historic step toward basic political unity. This unity would allow western Europe as a whole to regain its place in world politics and to deal with the United States as an equal.

Support for the Maastricht Treaty was not universal. Ordinary people, leftist political parties, and populist nationalists expressed widespread skepticism and considerable opposition to the new rules. Many people resented the EU's ever-growing bureaucracy in Brussels, which sought to impose common standards on everything from cheese to day care and undermined national practices and local traditions. Moreover, increased unity meant yielding still more power to distant "Eurocrats" and political insiders, thereby undermining popular sovereignty and democratic control.

Above all, many ordinary citizens feared that the new Europe was being created at their expense. Joining the monetary union required national governments to meet stringent fiscal standards, impose budget cuts, and contribute to the EU operating budget. The resulting reductions in health care and social benefits hit ordinary citizens and did little to reduce western Europe's high unemployment rate. When put to the public for a vote, ratification of the Maastricht Treaty was usually very close. In France, for example, the treaty passed with just 50.1 percent of the vote.

Even after the Maastricht Treaty was ratified, battles over budgets and high unemployment throughout the EU in the 1990s raised profound questions about the meaning of European unity and identity. Would the EU expand as promised to include the postcommunist nations of eastern Europe, and if it did, how could Muslim Turkey's long-standing application be ignored? How could a European Union of twenty-five to thirty countries have any real cohesion and common identity? Conversely, would a large, cohesive Europe remain closely linked with the United States in the NATO alliance? Would—or could—the EU develop an independent military defense policy? In the face of these questions, western Europeans proceeded cautiously in considering new requests for EU membership, even though former communist states pressed for admission.

European Union (EU)
The economic, cultural, and political alliance of twenty-seven European nations.

Maastricht Treaty The basis for the formation of the European Union, which set financial and cultural standards for potential member states and defined criteria for membership in the monetary union.

Turkey's Struggle for EU Membership Turkey's leaders and the general population seek to join the European Union, but the road to membership is proving difficult. The EU has required Turkey to make many constitutional reforms and to give greater autonomy to Turkish Kurds. Yet even as the other nations standing in line gain admission, the Turks face ever more demands, leading to accusations that the real roadblock is Europe's anti-Muslim feeling. (CartoonStock Limited)

The European Union

- ⬛ Original members, 1951
- ⬛ New members, 1973
- ⬛ New members, 1981
- ⬛ New members, 1986
- ⬛ German reunification, 1990
- ⬛ New members, 1995
- ⬛ New members, 2004
- ⬛ New members, 2007
- ⬛ Candidate countries, 2010
- € Euro Zone countries, 2010

Mapping the Past

Map 31.3 The European Union, 2010 No longer divided by ideological competition and the Cold War, much of today's Europe has banded together in a European Union that facilitates the open movement of people, jobs, and currency across borders.

ANALYZING THE MAP Trace the expansion of membership from its initial founding as the European Economic Union to today. How would you characterize the members who joined during 2004–2007? Whose membership is still pending?

CONNECTIONS Which countries are and are not part of the Euro Zone, and what does this suggest about how successful the European Union has been in adopting the euro?

To complete this activity online, go to the Online Study Guide at **bedfordstmartins.com/mckaywest.**

Then on January 1, 2002, brand-new euros finally replaced the national currencies of all Euro Zone residents. (See "Living in the Past: The Euro," page 1008). The establishment of the European monetary union built confidence and increased willingness to accept new members. On May 1, 2004, the European Union finally began admitting its former East Bloc neighbors, and by 2007 the EU was home to 493 million citizens in twenty-seven different countries. It included most of the former East Bloc and, with the Baltic republics, several territories that had once been inside the Soviet Union.

This rapid expansion underscored the need to reform the EU's unwieldy governing structure. In June 2004 a special commission presented a new EU constitution that created a president, a foreign minister, and a voting system weighted to reflect the populations of the different states. The proposed constitution moved toward a more centralized federal system, but each state retained veto power over taxation, social policy, foreign affairs, and other sensitive areas. After many noisy and contentious referendum campaigns across the continent, the constitution failed to win the unanimous support that it needed to take effect. Ultimately, nationalist fears about losing sovereignty and cultural identity outweighed the perceived benefits of a more unified Europe. Fears that an unwieldy European Union would grow to include Ukraine, Georgia, and Muslim Turkey—countries with cultures and histories that were very different from those of western Europe—were particularly telling.

Though the constitution would not go into effect as written, the long postwar march toward greater European unity did not stop. In 2007 the rejected constitution was replaced with the Treaty of Lisbon. The new treaty kept many sections of the constitution, but further streamlined the EU bureaucracy and reformed its political structure. By November 2009 it had been ratified by all the EU states. When the Treaty of Lisbon went into effect on December 1, 2009, it capped a remarkable fifty-year effort to unify what had been a deeply divided and war-torn continent.

Supranational Organizations

Beyond the European Union, the trend toward globalization empowered a variety of other supranational organizations whose interests and activities crossed the borders of the world's nation-states. National governments still played the leading role in defining and implementing policy, but they increasingly had to take the interests of institutions such as the United Nations and the World Trade Organization into consideration.

The United Nations (UN), established in 1945 after World War II, remains one of the most important players on the world stage. Representatives from all independent countries meet in the UN General Assembly in New York City to manage international agreements and crises. The UN's many offices deal with issues such as world hunger and poverty, and the International Court of Justice in The Hague, Netherlands, hears cases that violate international law. The UN also sends troops to police crisis situations in attempts to preserve peace between warring parties—as in Yugoslavia in the 1990s.

The UN's governing Security Council, which includes the United States, Russia, France, Great Britain, and China, has the power to veto resolutions passed by the General Assembly. The predominance of the United States and western European powers on the Security Council has led some critics to accuse the UN of being a forum for the expression of neocolonial interests (see Chapter 29). Others argue that UN policies should never take precedent over national needs, and UN resolutions are at times ignored or downplayed. The organization nonetheless retains enormous international prestige.

A number of nonprofit international financial institutions, including the World Bank, the International Monetary Fund (IMF), and the **World Trade Organization (WTO)** have also gained power in a globalizing

world. Like the United Nations, the World Bank and the IMF were established in the years following World War II. Initially founded to help rebuild war-torn Europe, the IMF and the World Bank now provide loans to the developing world. Their funding comes primarily from donations from the United States and western Europe, and they often extend loans on the condition that recipient countries adopt free trade, deregulation, and other neoliberal economic policies. After the 1990s the World Bank and the IMF played active roles in shaping economic and social policy in the former East Bloc.

With headquarters in Geneva, Switzerland, the WTO is one of the most powerful supranational financial institutions. It sets trade and tariff agreements for over 150 member countries and so helps manage a large percentage of the world's import-export policies. Like the IMF and the World Bank, the WTO promotes neoliberal policies around the world.

The rise of these institutions, which typically represent the interests of combined national governments in international forums, was paralleled by the emergence of

World Trade Organization (WTO)
A powerful supranational financial institution that sets trade and tariff agreements for over 150 member countries and so helps manage a large percentage of the world's import-export policies. Like the IMF and the World Bank, the WTO promotes neoliberal policies around the world.

Antiglobalization Activism French protesters carry the figure of Ronald McDonald through the streets to protest the trial of José Bové, a prominent leader in campaigns against the human and environmental costs associated with globalization. Bové was accused of demolishing a McDonald's franchise in a small town in southern France. With its worldwide fast-food restaurants that pay little attention to local traditions, McDonald's has often been the target of antiglobalization protests. (Witt/Haley/Sipa)

LIVING IN THE PAST

ON JANUARY 1, 2002, THE RESIDENTS OF MANY EUROPEAN UNION COUNTRIES exchanged their familiar national currencies for the euro, the newly approved coins and banknotes that signaled the arrival of the EU monetary union. The German deutschmark, the French franc, the Italian lira, and many others were now part of history, collectibles, perhaps, but on the way out as legal tender.

The move to the euro was one of the most controversial aspects of the Maastricht Treaty of 1991 that reshaped the EU and laid out a timetable for monetary union. While some countries signed up, Britain, Denmark, and Sweden accepted the main terms of the treaty but refused to join the currency union (or Euro Zone, the group of countries that used the new money). Citizens there rejected the euro, fearing its economic impact and its effects on national autonomy.

To join the Euro Zone, a country was required to maintain stringent economic conditions — low inflation, tight budgets, and small deficits. In 2010 only sixteen of the EU's twenty-seven member states used the euro as their official currency. The former East Bloc nations, such as Poland and Hungary, that joined the EU in 2004 and 2007 were excluded from the Euro Zone, and so remained something of second-class members.

The euro raised basic questions about a common European identity. What images could be portrayed on the new coins and bills that would do justice to both membership in a larger European community and the variety of national states that made up what was in fact a very diverse continent? The solution was ingenious. The front of the coins would show the denomination and a map of Europe, but the reverse would portray national images chosen by individual EU members. Thus the two-euro coin minted in Ireland features a traditional Celtic harp, while that made in France portrays the liberty tree. Banknotes, by contrast, would feature generic architectural images on both sides that looked real but were not, in order to prevent any national prejudice. Thus the arches on the five-euro note resemble a Roman viaduct; the bridge on the ten-euro note resembles a Renaissance bridge; and the glass and steel façade on the five-hundred-euro note resembles a modern urban office building. All are imaginary structures that look "European" but do not actually exist.

The president of Cyprus withdraws the country's first euros on January 1, 2008, after the country formally adopted the euro as its official currency. (Petros Karadjilas/AP Images)

A colorfully dressed anti-euro protester stands outside the British Houses of Parliament in June 2003. (Scott Barbour/Getty Images)

Five-euro, ten-euro, and twenty-euro bills (above). The back of the French (top) and Greek (below) euro coins. (bills: Thinkstock Images/Getty Images; coins: Courtesy, Eurocoins.co.uk)

QUESTIONS FOR ANALYSIS

1. Why did the leaders of the European Union push for a common currency?

2. How do the images portrayed on euro coins and banknotes reflect the dilemmas of establishing a workable European identity?

a variety of so-called **nongovernmental organizations (NGOs)**. Some NGOs act as lobbyists for specific issues; others conduct international programs and activities. Exemplary NGOs include Doctors Without Borders, a charitable organization of physicians headquartered in France; Greenpeace, an international environmental group; and Oxfam, a British-based group dedicated to alleviating famine, disease, and poverty in the developing world. Though NGOs generally rely on donations from governments and private citizens for financial support, their annual budgets can total hundreds of millions of dollars and their work can be quite extensive. Oxfam, for example, in 2008 employed about six thousand staff members across the globe, had over twenty thousand volunteers and thousands of other contributors, and managed an annual budget of about £300 million (about $500 million U.S.).[4]

The rise of globalization has also encouraged the growth of new forms of global protest, often aimed at the leaders and economic structures of globalization itself. Such protest is typically aimed at global corporations and financial groups, which have done little to resolve the world's serious inequalities and problems, such as environmental pollution, unfair labor practices, and poor health and human rights policies. The Slow Food movement that began in Italy, for example, criticized American-style fast-food chains that proliferated in Europe and the world in the 1990s. Cooking with local products and traditional methods, followers argued, was healthier and kept jobs and profits in local neighborhoods. The fast-food giant McDonald's was often targeted as an example of the ills of corporate globalization. José Bové, a French farmer and antiglobalization activist, made world headlines when he drove his truck through the windows of a McDonald's in a small French village to protest the use of hormone-fed beef and genetically modified foods, and the reach of corporate capital.

The general tone of antiglobalization protest was captured in 1999 at the meeting of the World Trade Organization in Seattle, Washington. Tens of thousands of grassroots protesters from around the world, including environmentalists, consumer and antipoverty activists, and labor-rights groups, marched in the streets and disrupted the meeting. As one activist put it, "The WTO seems to be on a crusade to increase private profit at the expense of all other considerations, including the well-being and quality of life of the mass of the world's people. . . . It seems to have a relentless drive to extend its power."[5] Similar protests took place at later meetings of the WTO, the World Bank, and other supranational groups, as activists struggled with powerful public officials to influence the course of world development.

Toward a Multicultural Continent

How did population decline and large-scale immigration lead to demographic changes in contemporary Europe, and what were the main results of growing ethnic diversity? ■

As the twenty-first century opened and globalization began to affect European society and politics, Europeans also saw changes in the ethnic makeup of their nations. On the one hand, Europe experienced a remarkable decline in birthrates that seemed to predict a shrinking and aging population in the future. On the other hand, the peaceful, wealthy European Union attracted rapidly growing numbers of refugees and legal and illegal immigrants from the former Soviet Union, the Middle East, Africa, and Asia. The unexpected arrival of so many newcomers raised perplexing questions about ethnic diversity and the costs and benefits of multiculturalism.

The Prospect of Population Decline

Population is still growing rapidly in many poor countries, but not in the world's industrialized nations. In 2000, families in developed countries had only 1.6 children on average; only in the United States did families have, almost exactly, the 2.1 children necessary to maintain a stable population. In European countries, where birthrates had been falling since the 1950s, national fertility rates ranged from 1.2 to 1.8 children per woman of childbearing age. Italy, once renowned for large Catholic families, had achieved the world's lowest birthrate—a mere 1.2 babies per woman. By 2006 the average European fertility rate was about 1.4 children per woman.

If the current baby bust continues, the long-term consequences could be dramatic, though hardly predictable. At the least, Europe's population would decline and age. Projections for Germany are illustrative. Total German population, barring much greater immigration, would gradually decline from 82 million in 2001 to only 62 million around 2050. The number of people of working age would drop by a third, and almost half of the population would be over sixty. Social security taxes paid by the shrinking labor force would need to soar to meet the skyrocketing costs of pensions and health care for seniors—a recipe for generational tension and conflict. As the premier of Bavaria, Germany's biggest state, has warned, the prospect of demographic decline is a "ticking time bomb under our social welfare system and entire economy."[6]

Why, in times of peace, were Europeans failing to reproduce? The uneven, uninspiring European economic conditions of the 1980s and much of the 1990s played a role. High unemployment fell heavily on young people and often frustrated their plans to settle down and have children. Some observers have also argued that a partial rejection of motherhood and parenting was critical, noting that many Europeans chose to have no children or only one child.

The ongoing impact of careers for married women and the related drive for gender equality were decisive factors in the long-term decline of postwar birthrates. After World War II, Western women married early, had their children early, and then turned increasingly to full-time employment, where they suffered from the discrimination that drove the women's movement. As the twenty-first century opened, women had attained many (but not all) of their objectives. They did as well as or better than men in school, and educated young women earned almost as much as their male counterparts.

Research has shown that European women and men in their twenties, thirties, and early forties still wanted two or even three children—about the same number as their parents had wanted. But unlike their parents, young couples did not realize their ideal family size. Many women postponed the birth of their first child into their thirties in order to finish their education and establish themselves in their careers. Then, finding that balancing a child and a career was more difficult and time-consuming than anticipated, new mothers tended to postpone and eventually forgo the second child. The better educated and the more economically successful a woman was, the more likely she was to stop with a single child or to have no children at all.

By 2005 some population experts believed that European women were no longer postponing having children. At the least, birthrates appeared to have stabilized. Moreover, the frightening implications of dramatic population decline had emerged as a major public issue. Opinion leaders, politicians, and the media started to press for more babies and more support for families with children. Europeans may yet respond with enough vigor to limit the extent of their population decline and avoid societal disaster.

Changing Immigration Flows

As European demographic vitality waned in the 1990s, a surge of migrants from Africa, Asia, and eastern Europe headed for western Europe. Some migrants entered the European Union legally, but increasing numbers were smuggled in past beefed-up border patrols. Large-scale immigration, both legal and illegal, emerged as a critical and controversial issue.

Historically a source rather than a destination of immigrants, booming western Europe drew heavily on North Africa and Turkey for manual laborers from about 1960 until about 1973, when unemployment started to rise and governments abruptly stopped the inflow. Many foreign workers stayed on, however, eventually bringing

Illegal Immigrants from Eritrea Italian police have just rescued these young immigrants from an overloaded boat off the coast of Italy. Fleeing civil war and desperate for work, the immigrants are weary because of the long and dangerous voyage from Libya. Every year, thousands of illegal immigrants try to reach Italy and Spain from North Africa. Many are found dead on the shoreline. (Mimi Mollica/Corbis)

their families and establishing permanent immigrant communities. The postcolonial immigration that began in the 1950s also continued apace (see Chapter 29).

A new and different surge of migration into western Europe began in the 1990s. The collapse of communism in the east and savage civil wars in Yugoslavia sent hundreds of thousands of refugees fleeing westward. Equally brutal conflicts in Afghanistan, Iraq, Somalia, and Rwanda—to name only four countries—brought thousands more from Central Asia and Africa. Illegal immigration into the European Union also exploded, rising from an estimated 50,000 people in 1993 to perhaps 500,000 a decade later, far exceeding the estimated 300,000 unauthorized foreigners entering the United States each year. In 1998 the European Union abolished all border controls between member states, meaning that illegal entrance into one country allowed for unimpeded travel in almost any direction.

Though many migrants in the early twenty-first century continued to apply for political asylum and refugee status, most were eventually rejected and classified as illegal job seekers. Economic opportunity undoubtedly was a major attraction for illegal immigrants. Germans, for example, earned on average five times more than neighboring Poles, who in turn earned much more than people farther east and in North Africa.

Illegal immigration was aided by powerful criminal gangs that turned to people smuggling for big, low-risk profits. Gangs also contributed to the large number of young female illegal immigrants from eastern Europe, especially Russia and Ukraine. Often lured by criminals promising jobs as maids or waitresses, and sometimes simply kidnapped and sold from hand to hand for a few thousand dollars, these women were smuggled into the most prosperous parts of Europe and forced into prostitution.

Ethnic Diversity in Contemporary Europe

By 2010 immigration to Europe had worked profound changes on the ethnic makeup of the continent, though the effects were unevenly distributed. In 2005 immigrants composed about 10 percent of most western European nations, while the former East Bloc nations had far fewer foreign residents. One way to measure the effect of these new immigrants is to consider the rapid rise of their numbers. Since the 1960s the foreign population of western European nations has grown by five to ten times. In the Netherlands in 1960 only 1 percent of the population was foreign born. In 2006 the foreign-born made up 10 percent. Over the same time period the proportion of immigrants grew from 1.2 to 12.3 percent in Germany and from 4.7 to almost 11 percent in France.[7] For centuries the number of foreign residents living in Europe had been relatively small. Now, permanently displaced ethnic groups or **diasporas** brought ethnic diversity to the continent.

The new immigrants were divided into two main groups. A small percentage of the recent arrivals were highly trained specialists who could find work in the upper ranks of education, business, and the high-tech industry. Engineers from English-speaking India, for example, took positions in international computer companies. Many immigrants, however, did not have access to high-quality education or language training, which limited their employment

diasporas Enclaves of ethnic groups settled outside of their homelands.

opportunities and made integration more difficult. They often lived in separate city districts marked by poor housing and crowded conditions, which set them apart from more established residents. In large German cities like Berlin and Hamburg, migrants from Turkey built vast communities with Turkish grocery stores, restaurants, civic organizations, and mosques. Parts of London were home to tens of thousands of immigrants from the former colonies, and in Paris North Africans dominated some working-class *banlieues* (suburbs).

A variety of new cultural forms, ranging from sports and cuisine to music, the fine arts, and film, brought together native and foreign traditions and transformed European lifestyles. The makeup of the teams who play European football (soccer), the continent's favorite sport, clearly reflected the new diversity. In the 1950s and 1960s regional football teams were made almost entirely of local players. By 2005 a single football club in North London included players from across Europe as well as from the Ivory Coast, Brazil, and the United States.[8]

Food is another important case in point. Recipes and cooks from former colonies in North Africa enlivened French cooking, while the döner kebab—the Turkish version of a gyros sandwich—became Germany's "native" fast food. Indian restaurants proliferated across Britain, and controversy raged when the British foreign minister announced in 2001 that chicken tikka masala—a spicy Indian stew—was Great Britain's new national dish. In fact, tikka masala is a hybrid, a remarkable example of the way that peoples, recipes, and ingredients from Central Asia, Persia, and Europe had interacted for over four centuries, changing eating habits in Europe and on the Indian subcontinent alike.[9]

The new ethnic diversity associated with globalization has inspired numerous works in literature and the fine arts. The string of bestselling short stories and novels by Jhumpa Lahiri, an ethnic Bengali born in London, includes *Interpreter of Maladies* (1999) and *The Namesake* (2003), which explore the clash between immigrant and host cultures and the conflict between first- and second-generation immigrants. The bestselling novel *White Teeth* (2000), by British author Zadie Smith, likewise uses family settings to describe the at times painful contact between Bangladeshi Muslims and British Jews and Christians. Museums and annual art exhibitions regularly feature the works of non-Western artists who further explore the conflicts and new forms generated by cultural interaction.

This **multiculturalism** has also had a profound affect on popular music and film. Rai, a folk music that

multiculturalism The mixing of ethnic styles in daily life and in cultural works such as film, music, art, and literature.

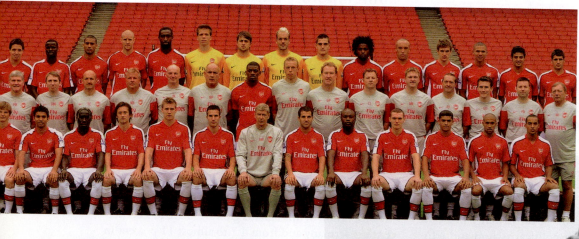

The Changing Face of London's Arsenal Football Club Growing ethnic diversity is transforming many aspects of everyday life in contemporary Europe, including the ethnic makeup of European football (soccer) teams. In 1950 the Arsenal Football Club of northern London was composed entirely of white ethnic Britons (right). Today, its diverse roster includes players from around the globe (above). (1950 team: J. A. Hampton/Hulton Archive/Getty Images; 2010 team: Stuart MacFarlane/Arsenal Football Club)

originated in the Bedouin culture of North Africa, exemplifies the new forms that emerge from cultural mixing. In the 1920s rai traveled with Algerian immigrants to France. In its current form, it blends Arab and North African folk music, U.S. rap, and French and Spanish pop styles. Lyrics range from sentimental love stories to blunt and sometimes bawdy descriptions of daily life. The Algerian Cheb Khaled, the unofficial "king of rai," has become an international superstar. Lyrics of his song "To Flee, but Where?" capture Khaled's dismay with collapsing Islamic traditions in Algeria and the burdens of life in the Algerian diaspora in France:

> *Where has youth gone?*
> *Where are the brave ones?*
> *The rich gorge themselves,*
> *The poor work themselves to death,*
> *The Islamic charlatans show their true face . . .*
> *You can always cry or complain*
> *Or escape . . . but where?*[10]

Feature films have also been an important venue for dramatizing the experience of cross-cultural contact, and they reach large audiences. Older movies typically pictured Europeans and non-Europeans as distinct social groups with radically different social customs. Now the emphasis is on cultural mixing and the surprising new combinations that emerge in a globalized society. In *Bend It Like Beckham* (2002), by Indian-Anglo direc-

tor Gurinder Chada, a teenage girl from Pakistan becomes an accomplished high school soccer player and falls in love with her Irish coach, challenging the traditional values of her family, first-generation Punjabi-Sikhs from northern India. The French film *The Class* (2008), set in a high school in a working-class banlieue in Paris, portrays a bold teacher's attempts to understand and inspire his students, who come from France, North and sub-Saharan Africa, and East Asia. These films and many others reflect both the new openness of cinematic production companies to non-Western directors and stories, and a growing public interest in cross-cultural interaction.

The growth of immigration and ethnic diversity has created rich hybrid social and cultural interactions, but it has also generated intense controversy and conflict in western Europe. Under the citizenship policies of most EU nations, immigrants can become citizens with full rights if they meet certain legal qualifications, even though they might not adopt the culture of the host country. This legal process has raised questions about who, exactly, could or should be European, and about the way these new citizens might change European society. Some commentators have accused the newcomers of taking jobs from the unemployed and undermining national unity. The idea that cultural and ethnic diversity could be a force for vitality and creativity has run counter to deep-seated beliefs about national homogeneity.

Picturing the Past

National Front Campaign Poster This 2009 campaign poster calls on viewers to vote for the far-right French National Front in elections to the European Parliament. It portrays the familiar French image of Lady Liberty (see the image on page 629) with European Union stars circling her head. (Handout/Reuters)

ANALYZING THE IMAGE How is Lady Liberty depicted? What type of mood is the creator trying to elicit in voters via this image?

CONNECTIONS According to the National Front, which issue facing Europe today is a key contributor to Lady Liberty's distress? How effective do you think emotional appeals like this one are in garnering support for far-right parties across Europe?

To complete this activity online, go to the Online Study Guide at bedfordstmartins.com/mckaywest.

Government welfare programs intended to support struggling immigrants have been seen as a misuse of money, especially in times of economic downturn.

Immigration is a highly charged political issue. By the 1990s in France, some 70 percent of the population believed that there were "too many Arabs," and 30 percent supported right-wing politician Jean Marie Le Pen's calls to rid France of its immigrants altogether. Even then-future president Jacques Chirac could claim in 1991 that he understood that good French workers could be driven "understandably crazy" by the "noise and smell" of foreigners in the country.[11] Le Pen's National Front and other far-right political parties, such as the Danish People's Party and Austria's Freedom Party, successfully exploited popular prejudice about what they called "foreign rabble" to make impressive gains in national elections.

Europe and Its Muslim Citizens

General concerns with migration have often fused with fears of Muslim migrants and Muslim residents who have grown up in Europe. Islam is now the largest minority religion in Europe. The EU's 15 to 20 million Muslims outnumber Catholics in Europe's mainly Protestant north, and they outnumber Protestants in Europe's Catholic south. Major cities have substantial Muslim minorities. Muslim residents make up about 25 percent of the population in Marseilles and Rotterdam, 15 percent in Brussels, and about 10 percent in Paris, Copenhagen, and London.[12]

The worries increased after the September 11, 2001, al-Qaeda attack on New York's World Trade Center (see page 1017) and the subsequent war in Iraq. Terrorist attacks in Europe organized by Islamic extremists heightened anxieties. On a morning in March 2004 radical Moroccan Muslims living in Spain exploded bombs planted on trains bound for Madrid, killing 191 commuters and wounding 1,800 more. A year later an attack on the London transit system carried out by British citizens of Pakistani descent killed over 50 innocent people.

The vast majority of Europe's Muslims clearly support democracy and reject radical extremism, but these spectacular attacks and lesser actions by Islamic militants nonetheless sharpened the European debate on immigration. A shrill chorus warned that, in addition to the security danger, Europe's rapidly growing Muslim population posed a dire threat to the West's entire Enlightenment tradition, which embraced freedom of thought, representative government, toleration, separation of church and state, and, more recently, equal rights for women and gays. Conservative critics proclaimed that Islamic extremists and radical clerics settled in Europe rejected these fundamental Western values and preached the supremacy of Islamic laws for Muslims living in Europe.

Some secular Europeans have had a hard time understanding Muslim spirituality. As busy mosques came to outnumber dying churches in parts of some European cities, nationalist-minded politicians tried to exploit widespread doubts that immigrant populations

Terrorist Attack in Madrid In March 2004 radical Islamic terrorists set bombs on commuter trains in Madrid, killing almost two hundred people. The motivation of the perpetrators remains unclear, but the bombings were probably a response to Spanish involvement in the Iraq War. A similar bombing occurred in London the next year, exacerbating anti-Muslim feeling in Europe. (Pablo Torres/Guerrero/El Pais/Reuters)

from Muslim countries would ever assimilate to the different national cultures. A Danish-Muslim imam (spiritual leader) captured the dilemma: "The Danish shelves for faith and spirituality are empty," he said. "They fill them instead with fear of the 'strong foreigner.'"[13] Moreover, conservative critics claimed, many so-called moderate Islamic teachers were really anti-Western radicals playing for time. (See "Individuals in Society: Tariq Ramadan," page 1016.) Time was on the side of Euro-Islam, the critics warned. Europe's Muslim population, estimated at some 20 million in 2010, appeared likely to grow to 30 million by 2025 and to increase rapidly thereafter.

Admitting that Islamic extremism could pose a serious challenge, more mainstream observers have focused instead on the problem of integration. Whereas the first generation of Muslim migrants — predominately Turks in Germany, Algerians in France, Pakistanis in Britain, and Moroccans in the Netherlands — had found jobs as unskilled workers in Europe's great postwar boom, they and their children had been hard hit after 1973 by the general economic downturn. Immigrants also suffered from the ongoing decline of European manufacturing due to globalization. Provided for modestly by the welfare state and housed minimally in dilapidated housing projects, many Muslims of the second and third generations were finding themselves outcasts in their adopted countries. In short, observers suggested, economics, inadequate job training, and discrimination had more influence on immigrant attitudes about their host communities than did religion and extremist teachings.

This argument was strengthened by widespread rioting in France in 2005 and again in 2009 that saw hundreds of young second- and third-generation Muslim immigrants go on a rampage. Almost always French by birth, language, and education, marauding groups labeled "Arabs" in press reports torched hundreds of automobiles night after night in Paris suburbs and large cities. (See "Listening to the Past: William Pfaff, Will the French Riots Change Anything?" page 1018.) The rioters complained bitterly of very high unemployment, systematic discrimination, and exclusion, and studies sparked by the rioting showed that religious ideology had almost no effect on their thinking.

An articulate minority used such arguments to challenge anti-migrant, anti-Muslim discrimination and its racist overtones. They argued that Europe badly needed newcomers — preferably talented newcomers — to limit the impending population decline and provide valuable technical skills. Some scholars conclude that Europe must recognize that Islam is now a European religion and a vital part of European life. This recognition might open the way to eventual political and cultural acceptance of European Muslims and head off the resentment that can drive Europe's Muslim believers to separatism and acts of terror.

Confronting Twenty-First-Century Challenges

What key problems faced European societies in the twenty-first century, and how did European states and peoples deal with these critical issues? ■

As the first decade of the twenty-first century drew to a close, European societies were faced with a number of critical challenges. Growing distance between the United States and Europe revealed differences in international policies and values. Though they had security issues of their own, Washington's traditional western European allies criticized the U.S.-led war on terror. Climate change and water pollution revealed the dangers of heavy dependence on fossil fuels for energy consumption. At the same time, the relative wealth of European societies prompted serious thinking about European identity, Europe's humanitarian mission, and Europe's place in the larger community of nations. These problems underscored Europe's close ties to the rest of the world, and leaders sought global as well as national solutions.

Growing Strains in U.S.-European Relations

In the fifty years after World War II, the United States and western Europe generally maintained close diplomatic relations. Though they were never in total agreement, they usually worked together to promote international consensus under U.S. guidance, as represented by the NATO alliance. For example, a U.S.-led coalition attacked Iraqi forces in Kuwait in the 1990–1991 Persian Gulf War, freeing the small nation from attempted annexation by Iraqi dictator Saddam Hussein. The need for allied force was rare in the post–Cold War world, however. Over time, the growing power of the European Union and the new unilateral thrust of Washington's foreign policy created strains in familiar transatlantic relations.

There were many reasons for the growing gap between the United States and Europe. For one, the European Union was now the world's largest trading block, challenging the predominance of the United States. Prosperous European businesses invested heavily in the United States, reversing a decades-long economic relationship in which investment dollars had flowed the other way. For another, under President George W. Bush (r. 2001–2009), the United States was often willing to ignore international opinion in pursuit of its own interests. Citing the economic impact, Washington refused to ratify the Kyoto Treaty of 1997, which was intended to limit global warming. Nor did the United States join

Tariq Ramadan

INDIVIDUALS IN SOCIETY

RELIGIOUS TEACHER, ACTIVIST PROFESSOR, AND MEDIA STAR, Tariq Ramadan (b. 1962) is Europe's most famous Muslim intellectual. He is also a controversial figure, praised by many as a moderate bridge-builder and denounced by others as an Islamic militant in clever disguise. Born in Switzerland of Egyptian ancestry, Ramadan is the grandson of Hassan al-Banna, the charismatic founder of the powerful Muslim Brother-

hood. Al-Banna, who was assassinated in 1949, fought to reshape Arab nationalism within a framework of Islamic religious orthodoxy and anti-British terrorism. Tariq grew up in Geneva, where his father had sought refuge in 1954 after Nasser's anti-Islamic crackdown in Egypt. He attended mainstream public schools, played soccer, and absorbed a wide-ranging Islamic heritage. For example, growing up fluent in French and Arabic, he learned English mainly from listening to Pakistani Muslims discuss issues with his father, who represented the Muslim Brotherhood and its ideology in Europe.

Ramadan studied philosophy and French literature as an undergraduate at the University of Geneva, and then earned a doctorate in Arabic and Islamic studies. Marrying a Swiss woman who converted to Islam, Ramadan moved his family to Cairo in 1991 to study Islamic law and philosophy. It proved to be a pivotal experience. Eagerly anticipating the return to his Muslim roots, Ramadan gradually realized that only in Europe did he feel truly at home. In this personal experience he found the message that Western Muslims should participate fully as active citizens and feel "at home" in their adopted countries. In developing this message, Ramadan left the classroom and became a publicly prominent intellectual, writing nonscholarly books and making audio cassettes that sell in the tens of thousands.

Slim and elegant in well-tailored suits and open collars, Ramadan is a brilliant speaker. His public lectures in French and English draw hundreds of Muslims and curious non-Muslims. Ramadan argues that Western Muslims basically live in security, have fundamental legal rights, and can freely practice their religion. He notes that Muslims in the West are often more secure than are believers in the Muslim world, where governments are frequently repressive and arbitrary. According to Ramadan, Islamic teaching requires Western Muslims to obey Western laws, although in rare cases they may need to plead conscientious objection and disobey on religious grounds. Becoming full citizens and refusing to live in parallel as the foreign Other, Muslims should work with non-Muslims on matters of common concern, such as mutual respect, better schools, and economic justice.*

Ramadan is most effective with second- and third-generation college graduates. He urges them to think for themselves and to distinguish the sacred revelation of Islam from the nonessential cultural aspects that their parents brought from African and Asian villages.

With growing fame has come growing controversy. In 2004, preparing to take up a professorship in the United States, he was denied an entry visa on the grounds that he had contributed to a Palestinian charity with ties to terrorists. Defenders disputed the facts and charged

Tariq Ramadan. (Salvatore Di Nolfi/Keystone)

that his criticism of Israeli policies and the invasion of Iraq were the real reasons for the denial. Ramadan's critics also claim that he says different things to different groups: hard-edged criticism of the West found on tapes for Muslims belies the reasoned moderation of his books. Some critics also argue that his recent condemnation of Western capitalism and globalization is an opportunistic attempt to win favor with European leftists and does not reflect his self-proclaimed Islamic passion for justice. Yet in 2010 the U.S. State Department lifted the ban that prevented Ramadan from entering the United States, and the scholar's reputation remains intact.† An innovative bridge-builder, he symbolizes the growing importance of Europe's Muslim citizens.

QUESTIONS FOR ANALYSIS

1. What is Ramadan's message to Western Muslims? How did he reach his conclusions?

2. Do you think Ramadan's ideas are realistic? Why?

*See, especially, Tariq Ramadan, *Western Muslims and the Future of Islam* (Oxford: Oxford University Press, 2004).

†See Ian Buruma, "Tariq Ramadan Has an Identity Issue," *The New York Times Magazine*, February 4, 2007.

the International Criminal Court, a global tribunal meant to prosecute individuals accused of crimes against humanity. These unilateral positions troubled EU leaders, as did unflagging U.S. support for Israel in the ongoing Arab-Israeli crisis.

Hard-nosed geopolitical issues relating to NATO widened the gap further. The dissolution of the communist Warsaw Pact left NATO without its traditional Cold War adversaries. Yet NATO continued to expand, primarily in the territories in the former East Bloc. In 1999 Poland, Hungary, and the Czech Republic joined the alliance. By 2010 France had returned to full membership, and the addition of new countries from eastern Europe and the Balkans, including the Baltic republics, Romania, Croatia, and Albania, had swelled the total number of member states to twenty-eight.

With so many members, it could prove difficult for NATO to win unanimous support for its actions. France, for example, did not support NATO's engagement in Bosnia in 1995 (see page 1002) because the alliance failed to get UN approval for the action. NATO allies only reluctantly supported U.S. president Barack Obama's 2010 push for increased troop levels in Afghanistan (see page 1020). As the EU expanded, some argued that Europe should establish its own independent military and defense policy. Meanwhile, Russian leaders were angered by NATO's expansion into former East Bloc countries adjacent to Russia—the defensive belt between the West and the Soviet Union established after World War II—particularly when President Bush moved to deploy missile defense systems in Poland and the Czech Republic in 2008.

The Iraq War, which began in 2003 (see page 1020), likewise placed heavy strains on U.S.-European relations. Some of America's traditional allies, including France and Germany, bitterly opposed the war. The only substantial support for the war came from Great Britain, under Prime Minister Tony Blair. Even there, the majority of the population was opposed, and Blair's popular approval eroded rapidly. The French foreign minister openly questioned the need for war, and in Germany in 2004 Chancellor Gerhard Schröder eked out a paper-thin re-election victory by refusing to support the United States. Hostility increased when U.S. Secretary of Defense Donald Rumsfeld suggested that France and Germany now represented "old Europe," in contrast to the "new" European countries, including Poland, Spain, and Italy, which supported U.S. actions. By 2006 even these supporters had withdrawn their small troop contingents from Iraq.

There was also a values gap. Ever more secular Europeans had a hard time understanding the religiosity of many Americans and of the openly Christian President Bush. Relatively lax gun control laws and the frequent execution of criminals in the United States were viewed with dismay; most European countries had outlawed the private use of handguns and had abolished the death penalty. U.S. reluctance to reform its health-care system shocked Europeans, who took their extensive state-financed medical benefits for granted. Though many Europeans continued to enjoy American films and popular music, critics nonetheless expressed disdain for what they saw as the overcommercialization of U.S. society. Public opinion polls showed that the depth of anti-American sentiment among ordinary European citizens was worse in 2008 than it had been during the war in Vietnam.

The election of Barack Obama, America's first African American president, in 2008 brought some improvement to U.S.-European relations. Though Obama's policies proved divisive at home, the new president was wildly popular among ordinary Europeans. When Obama visited Germany during his 2008 presidential campaign, over two hundred thousand Berliners cheered as he called for a new approach to diplomatic relations and international justice and, in an implicit critique of Bush administration policies, for a renewal of the U.S.-European alliance:

> The walls between old allies on either side of the Atlantic cannot stand. The walls between the countries with the most and those with the least cannot stand. The walls between races and tribes, natives and immigrants, Christian and Muslim and Jew cannot stand. These now are the walls we must tear down.[14]

After his election, Obama made a number of changes in foreign policy that set his administration apart from that of George W. Bush. His attempts to open diplomatic negotiations with countries hostile to U.S. interests, such as North Korea and Iran, and his willingness to advocate climate change control measures won support in European capitals. Obama announced that he would not deploy missiles in central Europe and agreed to reductions in nuclear arms, easing tensions with Russia. When Obama traveled to Oslo, Norway, in December 2009 to accept the Nobel Peace Prize, Europeans hoped that this symbolic recognition, rarely bestowed upon sitting heads of state, would encourage the president to bring a more cooperative face to U.S. foreign policy. Despite these changes, President Obama and the United States continued to fight two unpopular wars in the Middle East, making it difficult to resolve divisions in U.S.-European interests.

The War on Terror and European Security

On the morning of September 11, 2001, two hijacked passenger planes from Boston crashed into and destroyed the World Trade Center towers in New York City. Shortly thereafter a third plane crashed into the Pentagon, and a fourth, believed to be headed for the White House or

LISTENING TO THE PAST

In late November 2005 young Muslim males rioted for several nights in the suburbs of Paris and other French cities. Receiving saturation coverage from the media, their explosion of car-burning and arson ignited controversy and debate throughout France and across Europe. Similar outbreaks occurred in 2007 and 2009. What caused the riots, and why did they persist? Anti-immigrant conservatives interpret the events as an example of the inevitable conflict between Christians and Muslims. More liberal observers have argued that dismal living conditions and failures of assimilation were to blame.

One penetrating commentary, written after the unrest in 2005 and aimed at an American audience, came from William Pfaff, a noted author and political columnist with many years of European experience. As you read Pfaff's analysis, note in particular the portrait he draws of daily life in France's immigrant ghettos and the role of religion in French Muslim society.

❝ The rioting in France's ghetto suburbs is a phenomenon of futility — but a revelation nonetheless. It has no ideology and no purpose other than to make a statement of distress and anger. It is beyond politics. It broke out spontaneously and spread in the same way, communicated by televised example, ratified by the huge attention it won from the press and television and the politicians, none of whom had any idea what to do.

It has been an immensely pathetic spectacle, whose primary meaning has been that it happened. It has been the most important popular social phenomenon in France since the student uprisings of 1968. But those uprisings . . . had consequences for power. The new riots have nothing to do with power.

They started with the accidental electrocutions of two boys hiding from the police, who they thought were after them. The police say there was no pursuit and they had no interest in the boys. However, under the policies of the minister of interior — the presidential candidate Nicolas Sarkozy — there had been a general police crackdown in these ugly suburban clusters of deteriorating high-rise apartments built years ago to house immigrant workers. They were meant to be machines for living. The police attention meant random identity checks, police suspicion, and harassment of young men hanging about — maybe dealing in drugs, maybe simply doing nothing because there is nothing for them to do. (In the past, they at least had to do national military service, which was a strong integrative force, but now France has a professional army.)

Their grandfathers came to France, mostly from North Africa, to do the hard labor in France's industrial reconstruction after the Second World War. Their fathers saw the work gradually dry up as Europe's economies slowed, following the first oil shock in the early 1970s. After that came unemployment. The unemployment rate in the zones where there has been the most violence is nearly 40 percent and among young people it is higher. Many of the young men in these places have never been offered a job. When they applied, their names often excluded them.

Their grandfathers were hard-working men. Their fathers saw their manhood undermined by unemployment. These young men are doomed to be boys. They often take their frustration out on their sisters and girlfriends, who are more likely to have done well in school and found jobs — and frequently a new life — outside the ghetto. . . .

The Muslim mothers and wives of the French ghetto are often confined in the home. Drugs are big business in the American ghetto; they are not that big in France. The crimes of the French ghetto are robbery and shoplifting, stealing mobile phones, stealing cars for joyrides, burning them afterward to eliminate fingerprints, or burning cars just for the hell of it, as well as robbing middle-class students in the city and making trouble on suburban trains, looking for excitement.

Religion is important . . . in the French ghetto, it provides the carapace that protects against the France that excludes Muslims. To the European Muslim, it seems that all of the powerful in the world are in collusion to exclude Muslims — or are at war with them. The war in Iraq, on television, is the constant backdrop to Muslim life in Europe. There are itinerant imams

war on terror American policy under President Bush to fight global terrorism in all its forms.

the U.S. Capitol, crashed into a field in rural Pennsylvania. These terrorist attacks, perpetrated by the radical Islamic group al-Qaeda, took the lives of more than three thousand people from many countries and put the personal safety of ordinary citizens at the top of the West's agenda.

At first, the terrorist attacks seemed to bridge the growing gap between the United States and its European allies. Stunned and horrified, the peoples and governments of Europe and the world joined Americans in heartfelt solidarity. Over time, however, tensions between Europe and the United States re-emerged and deepened markedly, particularly after President Bush declared a unilat-

who can put the young ghetto Muslim on the road to danger and adventure in Afghanistan, Pakistan, Iraq — or elsewhere. There are plenty more who preach a still deeper ghettoization: a retreat inside Islamic fundamentalism, totally shutting out a diabolized secular world.

One would think there would be a revolutionary potential in these ghettos, vulnerability to a mobilizing ideology. This seems not to be so. We may be living in a religious age, but it is not one of political ideology. In any case, it is difficult to imagine how the marginalized, thirteen- to twenty-three-year-old children of the Muslim immigration could change France other than by what they are doing, which is to demonstrate that the French model of assimilating immigrants as citizens, and not as members of religious or ethnic groups, has failed for them. It has failed because it has not seriously been tried.

The ghettoization of immigrant youth in France is the consequence of negligence. It has been as bad as the ghettoization through political correctness of Muslims in Britain and the Netherlands, where many people who thought of themselves as enlightened said that assimilation efforts were acts of cultural aggression. The immigrant in France is told that he or she is a citizen just like everyone else, with all the rights and privileges of citizenship — including the right to be unemployed.

Nicolas Sarkozy's zero tolerance of crime and of the petty mafias in the ghetto contributed to touching off these riots, but until recently he was the only French politician to say there has to be affirmative action to get an immigrant elite out of the ghettos and into important roles in French life, where they can pull their communities after them. Some affirmative action has been attempted in recruiting candidates for the elite *grandes écoles* [state schools] that train the French administrative and political class, where the cultural hurdles are immense for candidates. Virtually no children of the Muslim immigration are prominent in mainstream electoral politics; the political parties have yet to make a serious effort to include them. The present government has one junior minister of Algerian origin. I am not aware of any Muslims of immigrant origin in French diplomacy or the top ranks of police and military.

President Jacques Chirac has announced a civilian national service agency to give training and employ-

Angry youths set vehicles on fire in October 2005 as riots erupt on the streets around Clichy-Sous-Bois, a Paris suburb in which foreign-born residents make up over 35 percent of the population. The riots began after two teenage boys were electrocuted and died while hiding from police in a local power substation. (Jean-Michel Turpin/Corbis)

ment to 50,000 young people from the troubled zones by 2007. The age of apprenticeship has been lowered to fourteen, with a corresponding drop in the age of compulsory academic schooling and new measures to support apprenticeships. There will be more money for schools, local associations, and housing construction and renovation. This is change. Whether it is enough, and in time, is another matter. **"**

Source: William Pfaff, "The French Riots: Will They Change Anything?" *The New York Review of Books*, vol. 52, no. 20, December 15, 2005, pp. 88–89. Reprinted with permission from The New York Review of Books. Copyright © 2005 NYREV, Inc.

QUESTIONS FOR ANALYSIS

1. Describe the situation of young Muslims in France. What elements of their situation strike you most forcefully? How might these contribute to ongoing outbreaks of civic unrest?
2. France has maintained that, since all citizens are equal, they should all be treated the same way. Why has this policy failed for French Muslims? What alternatives would you suggest? Why?

eral U.S. **war on terror** — a determined effort to fight terrorism in all its forms, around the world.

Shortly after the September 11 attacks, the United States announced it would invade Afghanistan to destroy the perpetrators of the crime — Saudi-born millionaire Osama bin Laden's al-Qaeda network of terrorists and Afghanistan's reactionary Muslim government, the Taliban. Drawing on the world's sympathy and building a broad international coalition that included western Europe, Russia, and Pakistan, the United States joined its tremendous air power with local anti-Taliban resistance fighters. In mid-November the Taliban government collapsed. The war in Afghanistan, however, was not over. U.S. and European NATO troops failed to find bin

Dutch Troops in Afghanistan
The commander of a Dutch army platoon serving with NATO forces in the war in Afghanistan speaks with an Afghan village elder during a routine patrol in January 2010. Sending European troops to support U.S. and NATO efforts to end the Taliban insurgency in this central Asian country was unpopular with ordinary Europeans and contributed to growing strains in U.S.-European foreign relations. (Deshakalyan Chowdhury/AFP/ Getty Images)

Laden, and the Taliban insurgents retreated into the mountainous southern regions of the country, where they continued to engage in determined guerrilla warfare. By 2010, as President Obama deployed thirty thousand additional U.S. troops to quell the insurgency, Germany, Italy, the Netherlands, and other NATO contributors were facing growing popular discontent with the war.

Although fighting continued in Afghanistan, in late 2001 the Bush administration turned its attention to Saddam Hussein's Iraq, arguing that it was necessary to expand the war on terror to other hostile regimes in the Middle East. Many in the administration believed that the United States could create a democratic, pro-American Iraq. A remade Iraq, they believed, would transform the Middle East, make peace with Israel, provide easy access to the world's second largest oil reserves, and show small countries the folly of opposing the United States. The most effective prowar argument, however, played on American fears of renewed terrorism and charged that Saddam Hussein was still developing weapons of mass destruction in flagrant disregard of his 1991 promise to end all such programs.

Many Americans shared the widespread doubts held by Europeans about the legality — and wisdom — of an American attack on Iraq. Protesters and some politicians in the United States and Europe argued for a peaceful settlement of the Iraqi crisis, especially after UN inspectors found no weapons of mass destruction in the country. Though the UN failed to approve an invasion, in March 2003 the United States and Britain, with token support from a handful of other European states, invaded Iraq from bases in Kuwait. They quickly overwhelmed the Iraqi army, and Saddam's dictatorship collapsed.

America's subsequent efforts to establish a stable pro-American Iraq proved difficult, if not impossible. Poor postwar planning and management by President Bush and his top aides was one factor, but there were others. Modern Iraq, a creation of Western imperialism after World War I (see Chapter 26), is a fragile state with three distinct groups: non-Arab Kurds, Arab Sunni Muslims, and Arab Shi'ite Muslims. The two groups of Muslims had been divided by a great schism in the seventh century. Ethnic and religious tensions among these groups directly contributed to instability in occupied Iraq, and by 2006 a deadly sectarian conflict had taken hold in Baghdad. American soldiers, continuing loyally to do their duty, were increasingly caught in the crossfire between Sunni and Shi'ite militias.

The fighting had reached a high point in 2006–2007, when President Bush announced that he would initiate new counterinsurgency policies and send additional troops to bolster U.S. forces. By the time President Obama took office in 2009, this troop surge had successfully reduced violence across the country. Though insurgents continued to mount attacks, the number of casualties had declined dramatically, and the Obama administration moved forward with agreements negotiated by President Bush to withdraw all U.S. troops by the end of 2011. The Iraqi government continued to struggle with ethnic divisiveness and security concerns.

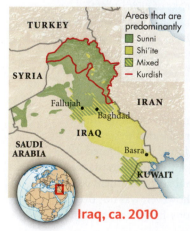

Iraq, ca. 2010

TURKEY

SYRIA

Areas that are predominantly
Sunni
Shi'ite
Mixed
Kurdish

Fallujah
Baghdad
IRAN

IRAQ
Basra

SAUDI ARABIA

KUWAIT

Finding the best way to share power among Iraq's main ethnic groups and divide the country's rich oil resources, particularly with Kurdish groups in the north, proved particularly difficult.

The U.S. invasion of Iraq caused some European leaders, notably in France and Germany, to question Washington's general rationale for the war on terror. Europeans shared U.S. worries about stability in the Middle East, and they faced their own problems with Islamic terrorism, especially after the Madrid and London subway bombings of 2004 and 2005. But European leaders worried that the tactics used in the war, exemplified by Washington's readiness to use its military without international agreements or UN backing, violated international law. Moreover, the U.S.-led war raised serious human rights concerns. The revelation of the harsh interrogation techniques used on prisoners held by American forces in the Iraqi prison Abu Ghraib shocked European public opinion. U.S. willingness to engage in "extraordinary rendition"—secretly moving terrorism suspects to countries that allow coercive interrogation techniques—further disturbed European observers.

Indeed, some leaders in Europe questioned the very idea of a war on terror. Because terrorism is a stateless phenomenon, European security experts asked whether war was the best approach. Terrorism, they maintained, was better fought through police and intelligence measures than through military action. Military victory in a single state, they argued, would hardly end terrorism. Rather, militant groups would simply move to other areas. European states preferred a more controlled but nonetheless determined approach to terrorism. Their security services focused on tighter EU borders, stepped-up airport security, increased public surveillance, and additional support for antiterrorist police investigations. Acknowledging their common goal of preventing future attacks, security forces in Europe also coordinated counterterrorism efforts with experts in the United States to investigate international terrorist cells.

The Dependence on Fossil Fuels

One of the most significant challenges facing Europe and indeed the world in the twenty-first century is the search for adequate energy resources. Maintaining standards of living in industrialized countries requires extremely high levels of energy, and current supplies are heavily dependent on fossil fuels, including oil, coal, and natural gas.

Global conflicts over access to limited energy resources have become an increasingly familiar aspect of life in the twenty-first century. In 2008 Europe and Russia combined had 12 percent of the world's population but consumed about 40 percent of the world's annual natural gas production, 25 percent of the world's oil, and 16 percent of the world's coal. Scholars argue that such high

levels of usage are unsustainable over the long run, that fossil fuel supplies will run out, especially when the nations of the developing world increase their own rates of consumption.[15]

Struggles to control and profit from these shrinking resources often cut across ethnic, religious, and national lines, leading to intractable conflicts and tense new geopolitical arrangements. The need to preserve access to oil has led to a great transformation in military power in the post–Cold War world. Between 1945 and 1990 the largest areas of military buildup were in central Europe, along the iron curtain that separated western Europe from the East Bloc, and in East Asia, where U.S. forces formed a bulwark against the spread of communism. Today military power is increasingly concentrated in oil-producing areas such as the Middle East, which holds about 65 percent of the world's oil reserves. According to some scholars, the Persian Gulf War and the ongoing Iraq War were "resource wars" fought, in large part, to preserve the West's access to the region's oil.[16]

Russian territory has massive quantities of oil and natural gas, and the global struggle for ample energy has placed Russia in a powerful but strained position. The Russian invasions of Chechnya and Georgia were attempts to maintain political influence in these formerly Soviet borderlands, and also to preserve control of the region's rich energy resources.

Beyond military invasions, Russian leaders readily use their control over energy to assert political influence. The Russian corporation Gazprom, one of the world's largest producers of natural gas, sells Europe 28 percent of its natural gas, and the EU treads softly in order to maintain this supply. Russia is willing to play hardball: there have been over fifty politically motivated disruptions of natural gas supply in the former Soviet republics, including one in January 2009 when Russia shut off supplies to Ukraine for three weeks, closing factories and leaving hundreds of thousands without heat. "Yesterday tanks, today oil," a Polish politician remarked about Russia's willingness to use energy to exert influence in central Europe.[17]

Environmental Problems and Progress

Even if the supply of fossil fuels were not of concern, the use of these energy sources has led to serious environmental problems. Burning oil and coal releases

Primary Oil and Gas Pipelines to Europe, ca. 2005

- Oil pipeline
- Gas pipeline
- Supplied by Russia

global warming The increase of average temperatures around the world, caused primarily by carbon dioxide emissions from the burning of fossil fuels.

massive amounts of carbon dioxide (CO_2), the leading cause of **global warming**, into the atmosphere. Thus, fossil fuel usage directly contributes to climate change and the degradation of the world's oceans. While the future effects of climate change are difficult to predict, climatologists meeting in March 2009 in Copenhagen concluded that climate change was proceeding dramatically faster than previously predicted and that some climatic disruption is now unavoidable. Rising average temperatures were melting glaciers and leading to the retreat of glacial ice packs, resulting in the drying up of freshwater sources across the world. Moreover, in the next fifty years rising sea levels will threaten low-lying coastal areas with flooding and inundation.

Since the 1990s the EU has spearheaded efforts to control energy consumption and contain climate change. EU leaders have imposed tight restrictions on emissions, and Germany, the Netherlands, and Denmark have become world leaders in harnessing alternate energy sources such as solar and wind power. Some countries have also taken preemptive measures in an effort to combat the future effects of global warming. The Dutch government, for example, has spent billions of dollars on the construction of new dykes, levees, and floodgates in an attempt to manage the potential crisis.

In addition to the problems presented by climate change, the world's oceans and freshwater lakes, which once seemed to be inexhaustible sources of food and drinking water, have been threatened by overuse and pollution. Usable water resources have been jeopardized by a number of toxins, including chemicals and heavy metals dumped by industry, oil spills, acid rain, and the disposal of nonbiodegradable solid waste, such as plastic packaging, which threatens marine life. Runoff of nitrate-based fertilizers, necessary to feed the growing world population, encourages rapid algae growth that leads to dead zones where marine life cannot survive. The environmental disaster that resulted when an offshore oil rig exploded in the Gulf of Mexico in April 2010, spewing millions of gallons of oil into the gulf waters, underscored the close connections between energy needs and water pollution.

In a revealing example of the international reach of the new global institutions, the EU has issued stringent policies in an effort to limit the human impact on water resources. In 2003, after an extensive review of existing agreements, the EU implemented a new Common Fisheries Policy. The new regulations were designed to halt the dumping of hazardous pollutants into rivers and oceans and preserve noncommercial species such as whales, birds, and sea turtles from harm during fishing. They also addressed public health issues by requiring the strict labeling of seafood for poisonous contaminants

such as PCBs and dioxins. To maintain stocks of commercially valuable fish, the EU placed caps on total allowable catch, limited the number of fishing boats in specific regions, and regulated fishing technology.

Though EU efforts to regulate energy use and control pollution showed some success, the overall effort to control energy consumption has been an uphill battle, underscoring the interconnectedness of the contemporary world. Developing nations such as India have had a difficult time balancing environmental concerns and economic growth. China, however, which surpassed the United States as the largest emitter of CO_2 in 2008, began encouraging "green" energy and moving away from coal. In December 2009 the representatives of 192 nations met in Copenhagen, Denmark, and agreed to reduce CO_2 emissions responsibly and extend financial support to developing countries to help them deal with the effects of global warming. Whether leaders have the political will to carry out this and other plans to limit the human impact on the environment, however, remains uncertain.

Promoting Human Rights

Though regional differences persisted in the twenty-seven EU member states, European residents entering the twenty-first century enjoyed some of the highest living standards in the world, the sweet fruit of more than fifty years of peace, security, and overall economic growth. The agonies of barbarism and war in the former Yugoslavia vividly recalled the horrors of World War II and cast in bold relief the ever-present reality of collective violence in today's world. For some Europeans, the realization of this contrast—that they had so much and so many others had so little—kindled a desire to help. As a result, European intellectuals and opinion makers began to envision a new historic mission for Europe: the promotion of domestic peace and human rights in lands plagued by instability, violence, and oppression.

European leaders and humanitarians believed that more global agreements and new international institutions were needed to set moral standards and to regulate countries, political leaders, armies, corporations, and individuals. In practice, this meant more curbs on the sovereign rights of the world's states, just as the states of the European Union had imposed increasingly strict standards of behavior on themselves in order to secure the rights and welfare of EU citizens. As one EU official concluded, the European Union has a "historical responsibility" to make morality "a basis of policy," because "human rights are more important than states' rights."[18]

In practical terms, western Europe's evolving human rights mission would require, first of all, military intervention to stop civil wars and to prevent tyrannical governments from slaughtering their own people. Thus the

Demonstrating for Peace
Holding torches, some 3,500 people form the peace sign in Heroes Square in central Budapest, the capital of Hungary, in 2006. The rally marked the third anniversary of the U.S.-led invasion of Iraq. Millions long for peace, but history and current events suggest that bloody conflicts will continue. Yet Europeans have cause for cautious optimism: despite episodes of intense violence and suffering, since 1945 wars have been localized, cataclysmic catastrophes like World Wars I and II have been averted, and Europe has become a world leader in the push for global human rights.
(Peter Kollanyi/epa/Corbis)

European Union joined with the United States to intervene militarily to stop the killing in Bosnia, Croatia, and Kosovo and to protect the rights of embattled minorities. The states of the EU also vigorously supported UN initiatives to verify the compliance of anti–germ warfare conventions, outlaw the use of land mines, and establish a new international court to prosecute war criminals.

Europeans also pushed for broader definitions of individual rights. Abolishing the death penalty in the European Union, for example, they condemned its continued use in China, the United States, Saudi Arabia, and some other countries as inhumane and uncivilized. Rights for Europeans in their personal relations also continued to expand. In the pacesetting Netherlands, for example, a growing network of laws gave pensions and full worker's rights to prostitutes (legally recognized income-earners since 1917) and legalized gay and lesbian marriages, the smoking of marijuana in licensed coffee shops, and assisted suicide (euthanasia) for the terminally ill.

As the first decade of the twenty-first century drew to a close, western Europeans also pushed to extend their broad-based concept of social and economic rights to the world's poor countries. These efforts were often related to sharp criticism of globalization and unrestrained neoliberal capitalism. Quite typically, Europe's moderate Social Democrats joined human rights campaigners in 2001 to secure drastic price cuts from international pharmaceutical corporations selling drugs to combat Africa's AIDS crisis. Strong advocates of greater social equality and state-funded health care, European socialists embraced morality as a basis for action and the global expansion of human rights as a primary goal.

LOOKING BACK LOOKING AHEAD

THE TWENTY-FIRST CENTURY opened with changes and new challenges for the Western world. The collapse of the East Bloc brought democracy to central and eastern Europe, but left millions struggling to adapt to a radically different way of life. High-tech information systems that quickened the pace of communications and the global reach of new supranational institutions made the world a smaller place, but globalization left some struggling to maintain their livelihoods. New contacts between peoples, made possible by increased migration, revitalized European society, but raised concerns about cultural difference and sometimes led to violent confrontations.

One thing is sure: despite the success of European democracy and liberalism, and despite the high living standards enjoyed by most of those on the European subcontinent, the challenges won't go away. The search for solutions to environmental degradation and conflicts between ethnic and religious groups and the promotion of human rights across the globe will clearly occupy European and world leaders for some time to come.

However these issues play out, the study of the past puts the present and the future in perspective. Others before us have trodden the paths of uncertainty and crisis, and the historian's ability to analyze and explain the choices they made helps us understand our current situation and helps save us from exaggerated self-pity in the face of our own predicaments. Perhaps our Western heritage may rightly inspire us with measured pride and self-confidence. We stand, momentarily, at the head of the long procession of Western civilization. Sometimes the procession has wandered, or backtracked, or done terrible things. But it has also carried the efforts and sacrifices of generations of toiling, struggling ancestors. Through no effort of our own, we are the beneficiaries of those sacrifices and achievements. Now that it is our turn to carry the torch onward, we may remember these ties with our forebears.

To change the metaphor, we in the West are like card players who have been dealt many good cards. Some of them are obvious, such as our technical and scientific heritage, our environmental resources, and our commitment to human rights and individual freedoms. Others are not so obvious, sometimes half-forgotten or even hidden up the sleeve. Think, for example, of the almost miraculous victory of peaceful revolution in eastern Europe in 1989 — in what Czech playwright-turned-president Václav Havel called "the power of the powerless." Here we again see the regenerative strength of the Western ideals of individual rights and representative government in the European homeland. We hold a good hand.

Our study of history, of mighty struggles and fearsome challenges, of shining achievements and tragic failures, gives a sense of the essence of life itself: the process of change over time. Again and again we have seen how peoples and societies evolve, influenced by ideas, human passions, and material conditions. This process of change will continue as the future becomes the present and then the past. Students of history are better prepared to make sense of this unfolding process because they have already observed it. They understand that change is rooted in existing historical forces, and they have tools to explore the intricate web of change that propels life forward. Students of history are prepared for the new and unexpected in human development, for they have already seen great breakthroughs and revolutions. They have an understanding of how things really happen.

CHAPTER REVIEW

■ **How did Russia and the former East Bloc countries meet the challenges of postcommunist reconstruction and political and economic reform? (p. 996)**

Russia and the former East Bloc countries had mixed success as they worked to remake their political, economic, and social systems after forty-five years of communism. In part, economic problems limited the speed of reform. Russia's experimentation with shock therapy and rapid privatization under President Yeltsin led to runaway inflation, corruption, and a host of social problems. Later, President Putin returned the country to a more managed democracy with some success, but his hard-line anti-Western approach meant fewer freedoms for ordinary people, more human rights abuses, and violent confrontations with Russian provinces and neighboring countries. The newly independent countries of eastern Europe, especially Poland, Hungary, and the Czech Republic, fared somewhat better than Russia, though they generally followed a similar pattern. The former Yugoslavia,

tragically destroyed by resurgent ethnic nationalism and civil war, was a glaring exception to the relative success in the former Soviet bloc.

■ **What are the defining features of globalization, and how did changing international structures transform European societies? (p. 1003)**

Under globalization, neoliberal economic policies, along with the computer and communications revolutions, transformed economic, business, and personal relations around the world. Multinational corporations expanded with great success, but the vulnerabilities of a global economy were revealed in 1997 and 2008 when national crises triggered worldwide recessions. Moreover, globalization, coupled with the effects of the postindustrial society, left many people without the skills to compete and widened the gap between rich and poor. Meanwhile, the European Union, along with other supranational organizations such as the United Nations and the World Trade Organization, grew more powerful under globalization, challenging the traditional prerogatives of the nation-state. Thus, although some corporations, nations, and entities prospered under globalization and many individuals enjoyed the conveniences of new technologies, globalization also had a negative impact on a sizable number of people, not to mention on worldwide financial stability.

■ How did population decline and large-scale immigration lead to demographic changes in contemporary Europe, and what were the main results of growing ethnic diversity? (p. 1010)

After 1990 birthrates across Europe continued to decline, even as ever-larger numbers of legal and illegal immigrants moved to the continent in search of economic opportunity and political asylum. These demographic changes helped make formerly homogeneous societies more ethnically diverse, and by 2010 foreign-born residents made up between 10 and 15 percent of the total population in most western European countries. Growing ethnic diversity had profound effects on European art, culture, and lifestyles, all of which revealed the benefits and challenges of multiculturalism. The social impact of the new immigrants was controversial. Right-wing politicians used anti-immigrant sentiment to make gains in national elections. The growing number of Muslims living in Europe generated intense debate, particularly after the terrorist attacks of September 11, 2001, in the United States and the subway bombings in London and Madrid. War in the Middle East encouraged shrill cries about an ominous Muslim threat from immigrants living in western Europe, but thoughtful consideration by more tolerant observers suggested that these fears were greatly exaggerated.

■ What key problems faced European societies in the twenty-first century, and how did European states and peoples deal with these critical issues? (p. 1015)

As the twenty-first century began, European societies faced a number of different problems, many of which underscored the challenges of an increasingly interconnected world. While the European Union expanded and gained power, the United States increasingly pursued a unilateral foreign policy. Over time, different international interests undermined the close transatlantic ties that the United States and Europe had established after World War II. Though European states had supported U.S. efforts to deal with international terrorism immediately following September 11, 2001, many disagreed with the American war on terror, which led to further distance between Europe and the United States. The West's dependence on a dwindling supply of fossil fuels led to political crises and grave environmental problems, including climate change and the degradation of water supplies. The European Union led global efforts to address important energy and environmental concerns, and by 2010 it had made some progress. The relatively wealthy European countries also played leading roles in promoting human rights around the world, agreeing to intervene in civil wars, promoting international courts of justice, and offering support to poor countries struggling in the face of neoliberal globalization.

Suggested Reading

Caldwell, Christopher. *Reflections on the Revolution in Europe: Immigration, Islam, and the West.* 2009. A controversial and thought-provoking book that emphasizes the problems associated with growing numbers of Muslim immigrants in Europe.

Gillingham, John. *European Integration, 1950–2003: Superstate or New Market Economy?* 2003. A brilliant interpretive history.

Johnson, Lonnie R. *Central Europe: Enemies, Neighbors, Friends.* 2001. A book that ably interprets developments in eastern Europe before and after the revolutions of 1989.

Jordan, Andrew. *Environmental Policy in the European Union: Actors, Institutions and Processes.* 2005. A critical look at the European Union's response to major environmental problems.

Klausen, Jyette. *The Islamic Challenge: Politics and Religion in Western Europe.* 2006. Reviews the goals of Europe's Islamic leaders and takes a positive view of future Muslim integration in western Europe.

Koopmans, Ruud, et al. *Contested Citizenship: Immigration and Cultural Diversity in Europe.* 2005. Explores issues of ethnic diversity, cultural identity, and citizenship in five European countries.

Lampe, John R. *Yugoslavia as History: Twice There Was a Country,* 2d ed. 2003. An excellent, judicious work on the tragedy in Yugoslavia.

Lucassen, Leo. *The Immigrant Threat: The Integration of Old and New Immigrants in Western Europe Since 1850.* 2005. Argues effectively that Muslims are assimilating as rapidly as previous immigrants.

Pinder, John, and Simon Usherwood. *The European Union: A Very Short Introduction.* 2008. Readable overview of the history, institutions, and policies of the European Union.

Reid, T. R. *The United States of Europe: The New Superpower and the End of American Supremacy.* 2005. A lively, informative examination by a perceptive American.

Sakwa, Richard. *Putin: Russia's Choice.* 2003. Puts the Russian leader in social and historical context.

Stiglitz, Joseph E. *Making Globalization Work.* 2006. An excellent overview of the successes and failures of globalization by a distinguished economist.

Key Terms

Ostalgie (p. 1000)
ethnic cleansing (p. 1001)
Kosovo Liberation Army (KLA) (p. 1002)
globalization (p. 1003)
European Union (EU) (p. 1005)
Maastricht Treaty (p. 1005)
World Trade Organization (WTO) (p. 1007)
nongovernmental organizations (NGOs) (p. 1009)
diasporas (p. 1011)
multiculturalism (p. 1012)
war on terror (p. 1019)
global warming (p. 1022)

Suny, Ronald Grigor. *The Soviet Experiment: Russia, the USSR, and the Successor States*. 1998. An outstanding history of Russia in the 1990s.

Tarrow, Sidney. *The New Transnational Activism*. 2005. A sympathetic account of the transnational activism opposed to corporate globalization.

Notes

1. Quoted in T. Judt, *Postwar: A History of Europe Since 1945* (New York: Penguin, 2005), p. 691.
2. Ibid., pp. 698–699.
3. *Quarterly Labor Force Statistics, Volume 2004/4* (Paris: OECD Publications, 2004), p. 64.
4. Oxfam, *Annual Report and Accounts 07/08* (Oxford, U.K.: Oxfam House, 2008), pp. 17, 43.
5. Quoted in Geoffrey Lean, "Trade Wars — The Hidden Tentacles of the World's Most Secret Body," *The Independent*, July 18, 1999.
6. Quoted in *The Economist*, January 6, 2001, p. 6.
7. Mark Mazower, *Dark Continent: Europe's Twentieth Century* (New York: Vintage, 2000), p. 415; *United Nations International Migration Report 2006* (UN Department of Economic and Social Affairs), http://www.un.org/esa/populationpublica tions/2006_MigrationRep/report.htm.
8. Judt, *Postwar*, p. 783.
9. L. Collingham, *Curry: A Tale of Cooks and Conquerors* (London: Oxford University Press, 2006), pp. 2, 9.
10. J. Gross, D. McMurray, and T. Swedenborg, "Rai, Rap, and Ramadan Nights: Franco-Maghribi Cultural Identities," in *Political Islam: Essays from Middle East Report*, ed. Joel Beinin and Joe Stork (London: I. B. Tauris, 1997), p. 265.
11. Ibid., p. 258.
12. J. Klausen, *The Islamic Challenge: Politics and Religion in Western Europe* (New York: Oxford University Press, 2006), p. 16; Malise Ruthven, "The Big Muslim Problem!" *New York Review*, December 17, 2009, p. 62.
13. Quoted in Klausen, *The Islamic Challenge*, p. 16.
14. J. Zeleny and N. Kulish, "Obama, in Berlin, Calls for Renewal of Ties with Allies," *New York Times*, July 25, 2008, p. 1.
15. Statistics in *BP Statistical Review of World Energy June 2009*, www.bp.com/statisticalreview.
16. M. T. Klare, *Resource Wars: The New Landscape of Global Conflict* (New York: Henry Holt, 2001), pp. 25–40.
17. A. E. Kramer, "Eastern Europe Fears New Era of Russian Sway," *New York Times*, October 13, 2009, p. A1.
18. Quoted in Flora Lewis, *International Herald Tribune*, June 15, 2001, p. 6.

Glossary

Afrikaners Descendants of the Dutch settlers in the Cape Colony in southern Africa. (p. 795)

appeasement The British policy toward Germany prior to World War II that aimed at granting Hitler whatever he wanted, including western Czechoslovakia, in order to avoid war. (p. 907)

Balfour Declaration A 1917 British statement that declared British support of a National Home for the Jewish People in Palestine. (p. 844)

Battle of Peterloo A protest that took place at Saint Peter's Fields in Manchester in reaction to the revision of the Corn Laws in 1819; it was broken up by armed cavalry. (p. 702)

Bauhaus A German interdisciplinary school of fine and applied arts that brought together many leading modern architects, designers, and theatrical innovators. (p. 861)

Berlin conference A meeting of European leaders held in 1884 and 1885 in order to lay down some basic rules for imperialist competition in sub-Saharan Africa. (p. 797)

Black Shirts Mussolini's private militia that destroyed socialist newspapers, union halls, and Socialist Party headquarters, eventually pushing Socialists out of the city governments of northern Italy. (p. 898)

Bloody Sunday A massacre of peaceful protesters at the Winter Palace in St. Petersburg in 1905 that triggered a revolution that overturned absolute tsarist rule and made Russia into a conservative constitutional monarchy. (p. 761)

Bolsheviks Lenin's radical, revolutionary arm of the Russian party of Marxian socialism, which successfully installed a dictatorial socialist regime in Russia. (p. 835)

bourgeoisie The middle-class minority who owned the means of production and, according to Marx, exploited the working-class proletariat. (p. 696)

Brezhnev Doctrine Doctrine created by Leonid Brezhnev that held that the Soviet Union had the right to intervene in any socialist country whenever it saw the need. (p. 970)

Carlsbad Decrees Issued in 1819, these decrees were designed to uphold Metternich's conservatism, requiring the German states to root out subversive ideas and squelch any liberal organizations. (p. 689)

Christian Democrats Center-right political parties that rose to power in western Europe after the Second World War. (p. 933)

class-consciousness An individual's sense of class differentiation. (p. 672)

collectivization of agriculture The forcible consolidation of individual peasant farms into large state-controlled enterprises in the Soviet Union under Stalin. (p. 893)

Combination Acts English laws passed in 1799 that outlawed unions and strikes, favoring capitalist business people over skilled artisans. Bitterly resented and widely disregarded by many craft guilds, the acts were repealed by Parliament in 1824. (p. 680)

Common Market The European Economic Community, created by six western European nations in 1957 as part of a larger search for European unity. (p. 935)

Congress of Vienna A meeting of the Quadruple Alliance—Russia, Prussia, Austria, and Great Britain—and restoration France to fashion a general peace settlement that began after the defeat of Napoleon's France in 1814. (p. 686)

constitutional monarchy A form of government in which the king retains his position as head of state, while the authority to tax and make new laws resides in an elected body. (p. 630)

Continental System A blockade imposed by Napoleon to halt all trade between continental Europe and Britain, thereby weakening the British economy and military. (p. 649)

Corn Laws British laws, revised in 1815, that prohibited the importation of foreign grain unless the price at home rose to improbable levels, thus benefiting the aristocracy but making food prices high for working people. (p. 702)

Council for Mutual Economic Assistance (COMECON) An economic organization of communist states meant to help rebuild eastern Europe under Soviet auspices. (p. 930)

Crystal Palace The location of the Great Exhibition in 1851 in London, an architectural masterpiece made entirely of glass and iron. (p. 664)

Dadaism An artistic movement of the 1920s and 1930s that attacked all accepted standards of art and behavior and delighted in outrageous conduct. (p. 864)

Dawes Plan War reparations agreement that reduced Germany's yearly payments, made payment dependent on economic prosperity, and granted large U.S. loans to promote recovery. (p. 873)

dechristianization Campaign to eliminate Christian faith and practice in France undertaken by the revolutionary government. (p. 638)

decolonization The postwar reversal of Europe's overseas expansion caused by the rising demand of the colonized peoples themselves, the declining power of European nations, and the freedoms promised by U.S. and Soviet ideals. (p. 944)

de-Stalinization The liberalization of the post-Stalin Soviet Union led by reformer Nikita Khrushchev. (p. 940)

détente The progressive relaxation of Cold War tensions. (p. 960)

diasporas Enclaves of ethnic groups settled outside of their homelands. (p. 1011)

displaced persons Postwar refugees, including 13 million Germans, former Nazi prisoners and forced laborers, and orphaned children. (p. 925)

Dreyfus affair A divisive case in which Alfred Dreyfus, a Jewish captain in the French army, was falsely accused and convicted of treason in 1894. The Catholic Church sided with the anti-Semites against Dreyfus; after Dreyfus was declared innocent, the French government severed all ties between the state and the church. (p. 769)

dual revolution A term that historian Eric Hobsbawm used for the economic and political changes that tended to fuse and reinforce each other after 1815. (p. 687)

Duma The Russian parliament that opened in 1906, elected indirectly by universal male suffrage but controlled after 1907 by the tsar and the conservative classes. (p. 764)

economic nationalism Policies aimed at protecting and developing a country's economy. (p. 672)

Enabling Act An act pushed through the Reichstag by the Nazis that gave Hitler absolute dictatorial power for four years. (p. 903)

estates The three legal categories, or orders, of France's inhabitants: the clergy, the nobility, and everyone else. (p. 620)

Estates General A legislative body in prerevolutionary France made up of representatives of each of the three classes, or estates; it was called into session in 1789 for the first time since 1614. (p. 625)

ethnic cleansing The attempt to establish ethnically homogeneous territories by intimidation, forced deportation, and killing. (p. 1001)

eugenics A pseudoscientific doctrine that maintains that the selective breeding of human beings can improve the general characteristics of a national population, which helped inspire Nazi ideas about "race and space" and ultimately contributed to the Holocaust. (p. 889)

European Union (EU) The economic, cultural, and political alliance of twenty-seven European nations. (p. 1005)

evolution The idea, applied by thinkers in many fields, that stresses gradual change and continuous adjustment. (p. 744)

existentialism A philosophy that stresses the meaninglessness of existence and the importance of the individual in searching for moral values in an uncertain world. (p. 856)

Factory Act of 1833 English law that led to a sharp decline in the employment of children by limiting the hours that children over age nine could work and requiring younger children to attend factory-run elementary schools. (p. 678)

fascism A movement characterized by extreme, often expansionist nationalism, antisocialism, a dynamic and violent leader, and glorification of war and the military. (p. 889)

February Revolution Unplanned uprisings accompanied by violent street demonstrations begun in March 1917 (old calendar February) in Petrograd, Russia, and that led to the abdication of the tsar and the establishment of a provisional government. (p. 833)

five-year plan A plan launched by Stalin in 1928, and termed the "revolution from above," aimed at modernizing the Soviet Union and creating a new communist society with new attitudes, new loyalties, and a new socialist humanity. (p. 891)

Fourteen Points Wilson's 1918 peace proposal calling for open diplomacy, a reduction in armaments, freedom of commerce and trade, the establishment of the League of Nations, and national self-determination. (p. 842)

functionalism The principle that buildings, like industrial products, should serve as well as possible the purpose for which they were made. (p. 861)

germ theory The idea that disease was caused by the spread of living organisms that could be controlled. (p. 721)

Girondists A moderate group that fought for control of the French National Convention in 1793. (p. 635)

glasnost Soviet premier Gorbachev's popular campaign for openness in government and the media. (p. 984)

globalization The emergence of a freer, more technologically connected global economy, accompanied by a worldwide exchange of cultural, political, and religious ideas. (p. 1003)

global warming The increase of average temperatures around the world, caused primarily by carbon dioxide emissions from the burning of fossil fuels. (p. 1022)

Grand Empire The empire over which Napoleon and his allies ruled, encompassing virtually all of Europe except Great Britain and Russia. (p. 649)

Great Depression A worldwide economic depression from 1929 through 1939, unique in its severity and duration and with slow and uneven recovery. (p. 874)

Great Famine The result of four years of potato crop failure in Ireland, a country that had grown dependent on potatoes as a dietary staple. (p. 705)

Great Fear The fear of noble reprisals against peasant uprisings that seized the French countryside and led to further revolt. (p. 629)

great migration The mass movement of people from Europe in the nineteenth century; one reason that the West's impact on the world was so powerful and many-sided. (p. 788)

Great Rebellion The 1857 and 1858 insurrection by Muslim and Hindu mercenaries in the British army that spread throughout northern and central India before finally being crushed. (p. 804)

great white walls Laws designed by Americans and Australians in the 1880s to keep Asians from settling in their countries. (p. 794)

guest worker programs Government-run programs in western Europe designed to recruit labor for the booming postwar economy. (p. 951)

gunboat diplomacy The use or threat of military force to coerce a government into economic or political agreements. (p. 786)

Holocaust The systematic effort of the Nazi state to exterminate all European Jews and other groups deemed racially inferior during the Second World War. (p. 912)

Holy Alliance An alliance formed by the conservative rulers of Austria, Russia, and Prussia in September 1815 that became a symbol of the repression of liberal and revolutionary movements all over Europe. (p. 687)

Homestead Act A result of the American Civil War that gave western land to settlers, reinforcing the concept of free labor in a market economy. (p. 758)

hundred days of reform A series of Western-style reforms launched in 1898 by the Chinese government in an attempt to meet the foreign challenge. (p. 807)

id, ego, and superego Freudian terms to describe the three parts of the self and the basis of human behavior, which Freud saw as basically irrational. (p. 859)

Industrial Revolution A term first coined in the 1830s to describe the burst of major inventions and economic expansion that took place in certain industries, such as cotton textiles and iron. (p. 656)

iron law of wages Theory proposed by English economist David Ricardo suggesting that the pressure of population growth prevents wages from rising above the subsistence level. (p. 665)

Jacobin club A political club in revolutionary France whose members were well-educated radical republicans. (p. 634)

Kosovo Liberation Army (KLA) Military organization formed in 1998 by Kosovar militants who sought independence from Serbia. (p. 1002)

kulaks The better-off peasants who were stripped of land and livestock under Stalin and were generally not permitted to join collective farms; many of them starved or were deported to forced-labor camps for "re-education." (p. 893)

Kulturkampf Bismarck's attack on the Catholic Church within Germany from 1870 to 1878, resulting from Pius IX's declaration of papal infallibility. (p. 767)

labor aristocracy The highly skilled workers, such as factory foremen and construction bosses, who made up about 15 percent of the working classes from about 1850 to 1914. (p. 727)

laissez faire A doctrine of economic liberalism that believes in unrestricted private enterprise and no government interference in the economy. (p. 691)

Lateran Agreement A 1929 agreement that recognized the Vatican as an independent state, with Mussolini agreeing to give the church heavy financial support in return for public support from the pope. (p. 900)

League of Nations A permanent international organization, established during the 1919 Paris peace conference, designed to protect member states from aggression and avert future wars. (p. 842)

liberalism The principal ideas of this movement were equality and liberty; liberals demanded representative government and equality before the law as well as individual freedoms such as freedom of the press, freedom of speech, freedom of assembly, and freedom from arbitrary arrest. (p. 691)

logical positivism A philosophy that sees meaning in only those beliefs that can be empirically proven, and that therefore rejects most of the concerns of traditional philosophy, from the existence of God to the meaning of happiness, as nonsense. (p. 855)

Luddites Group of handicraft workers who attacked whole factories in northern England in 1812 and after, smashing the new machines that they believed were putting them out of work. (p. 674)

Maastricht Treaty The basis for the formation of the European Union, which set financial and cultural standards for potential member states and defined criteria for membership in the monetary union. (p. 1005)

Marshall Plan American plan for providing economic aid to western Europe to help it rebuild after WWII. (p. 930)

Meiji Restoration The restoration of the Japanese emperor to power in 1867, leading to the subsequent modernization of Japan. (p. 806)

Mines Act of 1842 English law prohibiting underground work for all women and girls as well as for boys under ten. (p. 680)

modernism A label given to the artistic and cultural movements of the late nineteenth and early twentieth centuries, which were typified by radical experimentation that challenged traditional forms of artistic expression. (p. 861)

modernization The changes that enable a country to compete effectively with the leading countries at a given time. (p. 759)

Mountain, the Led by Robespierre, the French National Convention's radical faction, which seized legislative power in 1793. (p. 635)

multiculturalism The mixing of ethnic styles in daily life and in cultural works such as film, music, art, and literature. (p. 1012)

Napoleonic Code French civil code promulgated in 1804 that reasserted the 1789 principles of the equality of all male citizens before the law and the absolute security of wealth and private property as well as restricting rights accorded to women by previous revolutionary laws. (p. 644)

National Assembly The first French revolutionary legislature, made up primarily of representatives of the third estate and a few from the nobility and clergy, in session from 1789 to 1791. (p. 627)

nationalism The idea that each people had its own genius and its own specific unity, which manifested itself especially in a common language and history, and often led to the desire for an independent political state. (p. 691)

national self-determination The notion that people should be able to live free from outside interference in nations with clearly defined borders, and should be able to choose their own national governments through democratic majority-rule elections. (p. 842)

National Socialism   A movement born of extreme national-ism and racism, led by Adolf Hitler, that ruled Germany from 1933 to 1945 and forced Europe into the Second World War. (p. 901)

NATO   The North Atlantic Treaty Organization, an anti-Soviet military alliance of Western governments. (p. 930)

neoliberalism   Philosophy of 1980s conservatives who argued for decreased government spending on social services and privatization of state-run industries. (p. 972)

New Economic Policy (NEP)   Lenin's 1921 policy to re-establish limited economic freedom in an attempt to rebuild agricul-ture and industry in the face of economic disintegration. (p. 891)

new imperialism   The late-nineteenth-century drive by Eu-ropean countries to create vast political empires abroad. (p. 794)

New Left   A movement of students in the West who advocated simpler, purer societies based on an updated, romanticized version of Marxism. (p. 963)

New Order   Hitler's program based on racial imperialism, which gave preferential treatment to the Nordic peoples; the French, an "inferior" Latin people, occupied a middle position, and Slavs and Jews were treated harshly as "subhu-mans." (p. 910)

"new woman"   Somewhat stereotypical image of the modern and independent working woman popular in the 1920s. (p. 867)

nonalignment   Policy of postcolonial governments to remain neutral in the Cold War and play both the United States and the Soviet Union for what they could get. (p. 945)

nongovernmental organizations (NGOs)   Independent or-ganizations with specific agendas, such as humanitarian aid or environmental protection, that conduct international programs and activities. (p. 1009)

October Manifesto   The result of a great general strike in Oc-tober 1905, it granted full civil rights and promised a popu-larly elected Duma (parliament) with real legislative power. (p. 764)

OPEC   The Arab-led Organization of Petroleum Exporting Countries. (p. 971)

opium trade   The sale of opium—grown legally in British-occupied India—by British merchants in China, where the drug was illegal; it became a destructive and ensnaring vice of the Chinese. (p. 785)

Ostalgie   German term referring to nostalgia for the lifestyles and culture of the vanished East Bloc. (p. 1000)

People's Budget   A bill proposed after the Liberal Party came to power in England in 1906, it was designed to increase spending on social welfare services, but was initially vetoed in the House of Lords. (p. 769)

perestroika   Economic restructuring and reform implemented by Soviet premier Gorbachev in 1985. (p. 984)

Petrograd Soviet   A huge, fluctuating mass meeting of two to three thousand workers, soldiers, and socialist intellectuals modeled on the revolutionary soviets of 1905. (p. 834)

Popular Front   A short-lived New Deal–inspired alliance in France led by Léon Blum that encouraged the union move-ment and launched a far-reaching program of social reform. (p. 882)

postcolonial migration   The postwar movement of people from former colonies and the developing world into Eu-rope. (p. 953)

postindustrial society   Society that relies on high-tech and service-oriented jobs for economic growth rather than on heavy industry and manufacturing jobs. (p. 971)

proletariat   The industrial working class who, according to Marx, were unfairly exploited by the profit-seeking bour-geoisie. (p. 696)

realism   A literary movement that stressed the depiction of life as it actually was. (p. 744)

really existing socialism   A term used by Communist leaders to describe the socialist accomplishments of their societies, such as nationalized industry and collective agriculture. (p. 980)

Red Shirts   The guerrilla army of Giuseppe Garibaldi, who in-vaded Sicily in 1860 in an attempt to liberate it, winning the hearts of the Sicilian peasantry. (p. 754)

Reform Bill of 1832   A major British political reform that in-creased the number of male voters by about 50 percent and gave political representation to new industrial areas. (p. 702)

Reichstag   The popularly elected lower house of government of the new German Empire after 1871. (p. 767)

Reign of Terror   The period from 1793 to 1794 during which Robespierre's Committee of Public Safety tried and executed thousands suspected of treason and a new revolutionary cul-ture was imposed. (p. 637)

revisionism   An effort by moderate socialists to update Marx-ian doctrines to reflect the realities of the twentieth century. (p. 775)

Rocket   The name given to George Stephenson's effective loco-motive that was first tested in 1830 on the Liverpool and Manchester Railway at 16 miles per hour. (p. 663)

romanticism   A movement at its height from about 1790 to the 1840s that was in part a revolt against classicism and the Enlightenment, characterized by a belief in emotional exu-berance, unrestrained imagination, and spontaneity in both art and personal life. (p. 697)

sans-culottes   The laboring poor of Paris, so called because the men wore trousers instead of the knee breeches of the aristocracy and middle class; the word came to refer to the militant radicals of the city. (p. 636)

Schlieffen Plan   Failed German plan calling for a lightning at-tack through neutral Belgium and a quick defeat of France before turning on Russia. (p. 821)

second industrial revolution   The burst of industrial creativ-ity and technological innovation that promoted strong economic growth toward the end of the nineteenth century. (p. 741)

second revolution From 1792 to 1795, the second phase of the French Revolution, during which the fall of the French monarchy introduced a rapid radicalization of politics. (p. 635)

separate spheres A gender division of labor with the wife at home as mother and homemaker and the husband as wage earner. (p. 679)

shock therapy The Solidarity-led government's radical take on economic affairs that abruptly ended state planning and moved to market mechanisms and private property. (p. 987)

Social Darwinists A group of thinkers who applied the theory of biological evolution to human affairs and saw the human race as driven by an unending economic struggle that would determine the survival of the fittest. (p. 744)

socialism A backlash against the emergence of individualism and the fragmentation of society, and a move toward cooperation and a sense of community; the key ideas were economic planning, greater economic equality, and state regulation of property. (p. 693)

Solidarity Outlawed Polish trade union that worked for workers' rights and political reform throughout the 1980s. (p. 982)

spinning jenny A simple, inexpensive, hand-powered spinning machine created by James Hargreaves in 1765. (p. 657)

stagflation Term coined in the early 1980s to describe the combination of low growth and high inflation that led to a worldwide recession. (p. 971)

steam engines A breakthrough invention by Thomas Savery in 1698 and Thomas Newcomen in 1705 that burned coal to produce steam, which was then used to operate a pump; the early models were superseded by James Watt's more efficient steam engine, patented in 1769. (p. 660)

stream-of-consciousness technique A literary technique, found in works by Virginia Woolf, James Joyce, and others, that uses interior monologue—a character's thoughts and feelings as they occur—to explore the human psyche. (p. 860)

sweated industries Poorly paid handicraft production, often by married women paid by the piece and working at home. (p. 730)

Tanzimat A set of reforms designed to remake the Ottoman Empire on a western European model. (p. 764)

tariff protection A government's way of supporting and aiding its own economy by laying high taxes on imported goods from other countries, as when the French responded to cheaper British goods flooding their country by imposing high tariffs on some imported products. (p. 670)

theory of special relativity Albert Einstein's theory that time and space are relative to the observer, and that only the speed of light remains constant. (p. 857)

Thermidorian reaction A reaction to the violence of the Reign of Terror in 1794, resulting in the execution of Robespierre and the loosening of economic controls. (p. 643)

thermodynamics A branch of physics built on Newton's laws of mechanics that investigated the relationship between heat and mechanical energy. (p. 741)

Third World A term that refers to the nonindustrialized nations of Africa, Asia, and Latin America as a single unit. (p. 782)

totalitarianism A radical dictatorship that exercises "total claims" over the beliefs and behavior of its citizens by taking control of the economic, social, intellectual, and cultural aspects of society. (p. 888)

total war A war in which distinctions between the soldiers on the battlefield and civilians at home are blurred, and where the government plans and controls economic social life in order to supply the armies at the front with supplies and weapons. (p. 821)

Treaty of Brest-Litovsk Peace treaty signed in March 1918 between the Central Powers and Russia that ceded Russian territories containing a third of the Russian empire's population to the Central Powers. (p. 837)

Treaty of Versailles The 1919 peace settlement that ended war between Germany and the Allied powers. (p. 841)

trench warfare A type of fighting behind rows of trenches, mines, and barbed wire used in WWI; the cost in lives was staggering and the gains in territory minimal. (p. 823)

Triple Alliance The alliance of Austria, Germany, and Italy. Italy left the alliance when war broke out in 1914 on the grounds that Austria had launched a war of aggression. (p. 817)

Triple Entente The alliance of Great Britain, France, and Russia in the First World War. (p. 817)

Truman Doctrine America's policy geared to containing communism to those countries already under Soviet control. (p. 929)

utilitarianism The idea of Jeremy Bentham that social policies should promote the "greatest good for the greatest number." (p. 719)

war communism The application of centralized state control during the Russian civil war, in which the Bolsheviks seized grain from peasants, introduced rationing, nationalized all banks and industry, and required everyone to work. (p. 838)

war guilt clause An article in the Treaty of Versailles that declared that Germany (with Austria) was solely responsible for the war and had to pay reparations equal to all civilian damages caused by the fighting. (p. 843)

war on terror American policy under President Bush to fight global terrorism in all its forms. (p. 1019)

Warsaw Pact Soviet-backed military alliance of eastern European nations. (p. 930)

water frame A spinning machine created by Richard Arkwright that had a capacity of several hundred spindles and used waterpower; it therefore required a larger and more specialized mill—a factory. (p. 657)

white man's burden The idea that Europeans could and should civilize more primitive nonwhite peoples and that imperialism would eventually provide nonwhites with modern achievements and higher standards of living. (p. 802)

World Trade Organization (WTO) A powerful supranational financial institution that sets trade and tariff agreements for over 150 member countries and so helps manage a large percentage of the world's import-export policies. Like the IMF and the World Bank, the WTO promotes neoliberal policies around the world. (p. 1007)

Young Turks Fervent patriots who seized power in the revolution of 1908 in the Ottoman Empire, forcing the conservative sultan to implement reforms. (p. 765)

Zionism A movement toward Jewish political nationhood started by Theodor Herzl. (p. 771)

■ Index

	Government	Society and Economy
3000 B.C.E.	Emergence of first cities in Mesopotamia, ca. 3000 Unification of Egypt; Archaic Period, ca. 3100–2600 Old Kingdom of Egypt, ca. 2660–2180 Dominance of Akkadian empire in Mesopotamia, ca. 2331–2200 Middle Kingdom in Egypt, ca. 2080–1640	Neolithic peoples rely on settled agriculture, while others pursue nomadic life, ca. 7000–3000 Expansion of Mesopotamian trade and culture into the modern Middle East and Turkey, ca. 2600
2000 B.C.E.	Babylonian empire, ca. 2000–1595 Code of Hammurabi, ca. 1790 Hyksos invade Egypt, ca. 1640–1570 Hittite Empire, ca. 1600–1200 New Kingdom in Egypt, ca. 1570–1075	First wave of Indo-European migrants, by ca. 2000 Extended commerce in Egypt, by ca. 2000 Horses introduced into western Asia, by ca. 2000
1500 B.C.E.	Third Intermediate Period in Egypt, ca. 1100–653 Unified Hebrew kingdom under Saul, David, and Solomon, ca. 1025–925	Use of iron increases in western Asia, by ca. 1300–1100 Second wave of Indo-European migrants, by ca. 1200 "Dark Age" in Greece, ca. 1100–800
1000 B.C.E.	Hebrew kingdom divided into Israel and Judah, 925 Assyrian Empire, ca. 900–612 Phoenicians found Carthage, 813 Kingdom of Kush conquers and reunifies Egypt, ca. 800–700 Roman monarchy, ca. 753–509 Medes conquers Persia, 710 Babylon wins independence from Assyria, 626 Dracon issues law code at Athens, 621 Solon's reforms at Athens, ca. 594 Cyrus the Great conquers Medes, founds Persian Empire, 550 Persians complete conquest of ancient Near East, 521–464 Reforms of Cleisthenes in Athens, 508	Phoenician seafaring and trading in the Mediterranean, ca. 900–550 First Olympic games, 776 Concentration of landed wealth in Greece, ca. 750–600 Greek overseas expansion, ca. 750–550 Beginning of coinage in western Asia, ca. 640
500 B.C.E.	Persian wars, 499–479 Struggle of the Orders in Rome, ca. 494–287 Growth of the Athenian Empire, 478–431 Peloponnesian War, 431–404 Rome captures Veii, 396 Gauls sack Rome, 390 Roman expansion in Italy, 390–290 Phillip II of Macedonia conquers Greece, 338 Conquests of Alexander the Great, 334–323 Punic Wars, 264–133 Reforms of the Gracchi, 133–121	Growth of Hellenistic trade and cities, ca. 330–100 Beginning of Roman silver coinage, 269 Growth of slavery, decline of small farmers in Rome, ca. 250–100 Agrarian reforms of the Gracchi, 133–121

Religion and Philosophy	Science and Technology	Arts and Letters
Growth of anthropomorphic religion in Mesopotamia, ca. 3000–2000	Development of wheeled transport in Mesopotamia, by ca. 3000	Egyptian hieroglyphic writing, ca. 3100
Emergence of Egyptian polytheism and belief in personal immortality, ca. 2660	Use of widespread irrigation in Mesopotamia and Egypt, ca. 3000	Sumerian cuneiform writing, ca. 3000
Spread of Mesopotamian and Egyptian religious ideas as far north as modern Turkey and as far south as central Africa, ca. 2600	Construction of Stonehenge monument in England, ca. 3000–1600	
	Construction of first pyramid in Egypt, ca. 2600	
Emergence of Hebrew monotheism, ca. 1700	Construction of first ziggurats in Mesopotamia, ca. 2000	*Epic of Gilgamesh*, ca. 1900
Mixture of Hittite and Near Eastern religious beliefs, ca. 1595	Widespread use of bronze in ancient Near East, ca. 1900	
	Babylonian mathematical advances, ca. 1800	
Exodus of the Hebrews from Egypt into Palestine, ca. 1300–1200	Hittites introduce iron technology, ca. 1400	Phoenicians develop alphabet, ca. 1400
Akhenaten imposes monotheism in Egypt, 1367–1350		Naturalistic art in Egypt under Akhenaten, 1367–1350
		Egyptian *Book of the Dead*, ca. 1300
Era of the prophets in Israel, ca. 1100–500	Babylonian astronomical advances, ca. 750–400	Homer, traditional author of *Iliad* and *Odyssey*, ca. 800
Beginning of the Hebrew Bible, ca. 950–800	Construction of Parthenon in Athens begins, 447	Hesiod, author of *Theogony* and *Works and Days*, ca. 800
Intermixture of Etruscan and Roman religious cults, ca. 753–509		Aeschylus, first significant Athenian tragedian, ca. 525–456
Growing popularity of local Greek religious cults, ca. 700 B.C.E.–337 C.E.		
Introduction of Zoroastrianism, ca. 600		
Babylonian Captivity of the Hebrews, 587–538		
Pre-Socratic philosophers, ca. 500–400	Hippocrates, formal founder of medicine, ca. 430	Sophocles, tragedian whose plays explore moral and political problems, ca. 496–406
Socrates executed, 399	Building of the Via Appia begins, 312	Herodotus, "father of history," ca. 485–425
Plato, student of Socrates, 427–347	Aristarchos of Samos, advances in astronomy, ca. 310–230	Euripides, most personal of the Athenian tragedians, ca. 480–406
Diogenes, leading proponent of cynicism, ca. 412–323	Euclid codifies geometry, ca. 300	Thucydides, historian of Peloponnesian War, ca. 460–440
Aristotle, student of Plato, 384–322	Herophilus, discoveries in medicine, ca. 300–250	Aristophanes, greatest Athenian comic playwright, ca. 445–386
Epicurus, founder of Epicurean philosophy, 340–270	Archimedes, works on physics and hydrologics, ca. 287–212	
Zeno, founder of Stoic philosophy, 335–262		
Emergence of Mithraism, ca. 300		
Greek cults brought to Rome, ca. 200		
Spread of Hellenistic mystery religions, ca. 200–100		

	Government	Society and Economy
100 B.C.E.	Dictatorship of Sulla, 88–79 B.C.E. Civil war in Rome, 88–31 B.C.E. Dictatorship of Caesar, 45–44 B.C.E. Principate of Augustus, 31 B.C.E.–14 C.E. "Five Good Emperors" of Rome, 96–180 C.E. "Barracks Emperors'" civil war, 235–284 C.E.	Reform of the Roman calendar, 46 B.C.E. "Golden age" of Roman prosperity and vast increase in trade, 96–180 C.E. Growth of serfdom in Roman Empire, ca. 200–500 C.E. Economic contraction in Roman Empire, ca. 235–284 C.E.
300 C.E.	Constantine removes capital of Roman Empire to Constantinople, ca. 315 Visigoths defeat Roman army at Adrianople, 378 Bishop Ambrose asserts church's independence from the state, 380 Odoacer deposes last Roman emperor in the West, 476 Clovis issues Salic law of the Franks, ca. 490	Barbarian migrations throughout western and northern Europe, ca. 378–600
500	Law code of Justinian, 529 Spread of Islam across Arabia, the Mediterranean region, Spain, North Africa, and Asia as far as India, ca. 630–733	Gallo-Roman aristocracy intermarries with Germanic chieftains, ca. 500–700 Decline of towns and trade in the West; agrarian economy predominates, ca. 500–1800
700	Charles Martel defeats Muslims at Tours, 732 Pippin III anointed king of the Franks, 754 Charlemagne secures Frankish crown, r. 768–814	Height of Muslim commercial activity with western Europe, ca. 700–1300
800	Imperial coronation of Charlemagne, Christmas 800 Treaty of Verdun divides Carolingian kingdom, 843 Viking, Magyar, and Muslim invasions, ca. 850–1000 Establishment of Kievan Rus, ca. 900	Invasions and unstable conditions lead to increase of serfdom in western Europe, ca. 800–900 Height of Byzantine commerce and industry, ca. 800–1000
1000	Seljuk Turks conquer Muslim Baghdad, 1055 Norman conquest of England, 1066 Penance of Henry IV at Canossa, 1077	Decline of Byzantine free peasantry, ca. 1025–1100 Growth of towns and trade in the West, ca. 1050–1300 *Domesday Book* in England, 1086
1100	Henry I of England, r. 1100–1135 Louis VI of France, r. 1108–1137 Frederick I of Germany, r. 1152–1190 Henry II of England, r. 1154–1189	Henry I of England establishes the Exchequer, 1130 Beginnings of the Hanseatic League, 1159

Religion and Philosophy	Science and Technology	Arts and Letters
Mithraism spreads to Rome, 27 B.C.E.–270 C.E. Life of Jesus, ca. 3 B.C.E.–29 C.E.	Engineering advances in Rome, ca. 100 B.C.E.–180 C.E.	Flowering of Latin literature: Virgil, 70–19 B.C.E.; Livy, ca. 59 B.C.E.–17 C.E.; Ovid, 43 B.C.E.–17 C.E.
Constantine legalizes Christianity, 312 Theodosius declares Christianity the official state religion, 380 Donatist heretical movement at its height, ca. 400 St. Augustine, *Confessions*, ca. 390; *The City of God*, ca. 425 Clovis adopts Roman Christianity, 496	Construction of Arch of Constantine, ca. 315	St. Jerome publishes Latin *Vulgate*, late 4th c. Byzantines preserve Greco-Roman culture, ca. 400–1000
Rule of St. Benedict, 529 Life of the Prophet Muhammad, ca. 571–632 Pope Gregory the Great publishes *Dialogues, Pastoral Care, Moralia*, 590–604 Monasteries established in Anglo-Saxon England, ca. 600–700 Publication of the Qur'an, 651 Synod of Whitby, 664	Using watermills, Benedictine monks exploit energy of fast-flowing rivers and streams, by 600 Heavy plow and improved harness facilitate use of multiple-ox teams; harrow widely used in northern Europe, by 600 Byzantines successfully use "Greek fire" in naval combat against Arab fleets attacking Constantinople, 673, 717	Boethius, *The Consolation of Philosophy*, ca. 520 Justinian constructs church of Santa Sophia, 532–537
Bede, *Ecclesiastical History of the English Nation*, ca. 700 Missionary work of St. Boniface in Germany, ca. 710–750 Iconoclastic controversy in Byzantine Empire, 726–843 Pippin III donates Papal States to the papacy, 756		Lindisfarne Gospel Book, ca. 700 *Beowulf*, ca. 700 Carolingian Renaissance, ca. 780–850
Foundation of abbey of Cluny, 909 Byzantine conversion of Russia, late 10th c.	Stirrup and nailed horseshoes become widespread in combat, 900–1000 Paper (invented in China, ca. 150) enters Europe through Muslim Spain, ca. 900–1000	Byzantines develop Cyrillic script, late 10th c.
Schism between Roman and Greek Orthodox churches, 1054 Lateran Council restricts election of pope to College of Cardinals, 1059 Pope Gregory VII, 1073–1085 Theologian Peter Abelard, 1079–1142 First Crusade, 1095–1099 Founding of Cistercian order, 1098	Arab conquests bring new irrigation methods, cotton cultivation, and manufacture to Spain, Sicily, southern Italy, by 1000 Avicenna, Arab scientist, d. 1037	Muslim musicians introduce lute, rebec (stringed instruments, ancestors of violin), ca. 1000 Romanesque style in architecture and art, ca. 1000–1200 *Song of Roland*, ca. 1095
Universities begin, ca. 1100–1300 Concordat of Worms ends investiture controversy, 1122 Height of Cistercian monasticism, 1125–1175	Europeans, copying Muslim and Byzantine models, construct castles with rounded towers and crenellated walls, by 1100	Troubadour poetry, especially of Chrétien de Troyes, circulates widely, ca. 1100–1200 *Rubaiyat of Umar Khayyam*, ca. 1120 Dedication of abbey church of Saint-Denis launches Gothic style, 1144

Government	Society and Economy
1100 (cont.) Thomas Becket, archbishop of Canterbury, murdered 1170 Philip Augustus of France, r. 1180–1223	
1200 Spanish victory over Muslims at Las Navas de Tolosa, 1212 Frederick II of Germany and Sicily, r. 1212–1250 Magna Carta, charter of English political and civil liberties, 1215 Louis IX of France, r. 1226–1270 Mongols end Abbasid caliphate, 1258 Edward I of England, r. 1272–1307 Philip IV (the Fair) of France, r. 1285–1314	European revival, growth of towns; agricultural expansion leads to population growth, ca. 1200–1300 Crusaders capture Constantinople (Fourth Crusade) and spur Venetian economy, 1204
1300 Philip IV orders arrest of Pope Boniface at Anagni, 1303 Hundred Years' War between England and France, 1337–1453 Political disorder in Germany, ca. 1350–1450 Merchant oligarchies or despots rule Italian city-states, ca. 1350–1550	"Little ice age," European economic depression, ca. 1300–1450 Black Death appears ca. 1347; returns intermittently until ca. 1720 Height of the Hanseatic League, 1350–1450 Peasant and working-class revolts: Flanders, 1328; France, 1358; Florence, 1378; England, 1381
1400 Joan of Arc rallies French monarchy, 1429–1431 Medici domination of Florence begins, 1434 Princes in Germany consolidate power, ca. 1450–1500 Ottoman Turks under Mahomet II capture Constantinople, May 1453 War of the Roses in England, 1455–1471 Establishment of the Inquisition in Spain, 1478 Ferdinand and Isabella complete reconquista in Spain, 1492 French invasion of Italy, 1494	Population decline, peasants' revolts, high labor costs contribute to decline of serfdom in western Europe, ca. 1400–1650 Flow of Balkan slaves into eastern Mediterranean, of African slaves into Iberia and Italy, ca. 1400–1500 Christopher Columbus reaches the Americas, 1492 Portuguese gain control of East Indian spice trade, 1498–1511
1500 Charles V, Holy Roman emperor, 1519–1556 Habsburg-Valois Wars, 1521–1559 Philip II of Spain, r. 1556–1598 Revolt of the Netherlands, 1566–1598 St. Bartholomew's Day massacre in France, 1572 English defeat of the Spanish Armada, 1588 Henry IV of France issues Edict of Nantes, 1598	Consolidation of serfdom in eastern Europe, ca. 1500–1650 Balboa discovers the Pacific, 1513 Magellan's crew circumnavigates the earth, 1519–1522 Spain and Portugal gain control of regions of Central and South America, ca. 1520–1550 Peasants' Revolt in Germany, 1524–1525 "Time of Troubles" in Russia, 1598–1613

Religion and Philosophy	Science and Technology	Arts and Letters

Aristotle's works translated into Latin, ca. 1140–1260

Third Crusade, 1189–1192

Pope Innocent III, height of the medieval papacy, 1198–1216

Underground pipes with running water and indoor latrines installed in some monasteries, such as Clairvaux and Canterbury Cathedral Priory, by 1100; elsewhere rare until 1800

Windmill invented, ca. 1180

Founding of the Franciscan order, 1210

Fourth Lateran Council accepts seven sacraments, 1215

Founding of Dominican order, 1216

Thomas Aquinas, height of scholasticism, 1225–1274

Notebooks of architect Villard de Honnecourt, a major source for Gothic engineering, ca. 1250

Development of double-entry bookkeeping in Florence and Genoa, ca. 1250–1340

Venetians purchase secrets of glass manufacture from Syria, 1277

Mechanical clock invented, ca. 1290

Parzifal, Roman de la rose, King Arthur and the Round Table celebrate virtues of knighthood and chivalry, ca. 1200–1300

Height of Gothic style, ca. 1225–1300

Pope Boniface VIII declares all Christians subject to the pope in *Unam Sanctam*, 1302

Babylonian Captivity of the papacy, 1309–1376

Theologian John Wyclif, ca. 1330–1384

Great Schism in the papacy, 1378–1417

Edward III of England uses cannon in siege of Calais, 1346

Clocks in general use throughout Europe, by 1400

Paintings of Giotto mark emergence of Renaissance movement in the arts, ca. 1305–1337

Dante, *Divine Comedy*, ca. 1310

Petrarch develops ideas of humanism, ca. 1350

Boccaccio, *The Decameron*, ca. 1350

Jan van Eyck, Flemish painter, 1366–1441

Brunelleschi, Florentine architect, 1377–1446

Chaucer, *Canterbury Tales*, ca. 1387–1400

Council of Constance ends the schism in the papacy, 1414–1418

Pragmatic Sanction of Bourges affirms special rights of French crown over French church, 1438

Expulsion of Jews from Spain, 1492

Water-powered blast furnaces operative in Sweden, Austria, the Rhine Valley, Liège, ca. 1400

Leonardo Fibonacci's *Liber Abaci* popularizes use of Hindu-Arabic numerals, important in rise of Western science, 1402

Paris and largest Italian cities pave streets, making street cleaning possible, ca. 1450

European printing and movable type, ca. 1450

Height of Renaissance movement: Masaccio, 1401–1428; Botticelli, 1444–1510; Leonardo da Vinci, 1452–1519; Albrecht Dürer, 1471–1528; Michelangelo, 1475–1564; Raphael, 1483–1520

Machiavelli, *The Prince*, 1513

More, *Utopia*, 1516

Luther, *Ninety-five Theses*, 1517

Henry VIII of England breaks with Rome, 1532–1534

Merici establishes Ursuline order for education of women, 1535

Loyola establishes Society of Jesus, 1540

Calvin establishes theocracy in Geneva, 1541

Council of Trent shapes essential character of Catholicism until the 1960s, 1545–1563

Peace of Augsburg, official recognition of Lutheranism, 1555

Scientific revolution in western Europe, ca. 1540–1690: Copernicus, *On the Revolutions of the Heavenly Bodies*, 1543; Galileo, 1564–1642; Kepler, 1571–1630; Harvey, 1578–1657

Erasmus, *The Praise of Folly*, 1509

Castiglione, *The Courtier*, 1528

Baroque movement in arts, ca. 1550–1725: Rubens, 1577–1640; Velasquez, 1599–1660

Shakespeare, West's most enduring and influential playwright, 1564–1616

Montaigne, *Essays*, 1598

Government	Society and Economy
1600	
Thirty Years' War begins, 1618	Chartering of British East India Company, 1600
Richelieu dominates French government, 1624–1643	English Poor Law, 1601
Frederick William, Elector of Brandenburg, r. 1640–1688	Chartering of Dutch East India Company, 1602
English Civil War, 1642–1649	Height of Dutch commercial activity, ca. 1630–1665
Louis XIV, r. 1643–1715	
Peace of Westphalia ends the Thirty Years' War, 1648	
The Fronde in France, 1648–1660	
1650	
Anglo-Dutch wars, 1652–1674	Height of mercantilism in Europe, ca. 1650–1750
Protectorate in England, 1653–1658	Agricultural revolution in Europe, ca. 1650–1850
Leopold I, Habsburg emperor, r. 1658–1705	Principle of peasants' hereditary subjugation to their lords affirmed in Prussia, 1653
English monarchy restored, 1660	Colbert's economic reforms in France, ca. 1663–1683
Ottoman siege of Vienna, 1683	Cossack revolt in Russia, 1670–1671
Glorious Revolution in England, 1688–1689	
Peter the Great of Russia, r. 1689–1725	
1700	
War of the Spanish Succession, 1701–1713	Foundation of St. Petersburg, 1701
Peace of Utrecht redraws political boundaries of Europe, 1713	Last appearance of bubonic plague in western Europe, ca. 1720
Frederick William I of Prussia, r. 1713–1740	Growth of European population, ca. 1720–1789
Louis XV of France, r. 1715–1774	Enclosure movement in England, ca. 1730–1830
Maria Theresa of Austria, r. 1740–1780	
Frederick the Great of Prussia, r. 1740–1786	
1750	
Seven Years' War, 1756–1763	Growth of illegitimate births in Europe, ca. 1750–1850
Catherine the Great of Russia, r. 1762–1796	Industrial Revolution in western Europe, ca. 1780–1850
Partition of Poland, 1772–1795	Serfdom abolished in France, 1789
Louis XVI of France, r. 1774–1792	
American Revolution, 1775–1783	
French Revolution, 1789–1799	
Slave insurrection in Saint-Domingue, 1791	
1800	
Napoleonic era, 1799–1815	British takeover of India complete, 1805
Haitian republic declares independence, 1804	British slave trade abolished, 1807
Congress of Vienna re-establishes political power after defeat of Napoleon, 1814–1815	German Zollverein founded, 1834
Greece wins independence from Ottoman Empire, 1830	European capitalists begin large-scale foreign investment, 1840s
French conquest of Algeria, 1830	Great Famine in Ireland, 1845–1851
Revolution in France, 1830	First public health law in Britain, 1848
Great Britain: Reform Bill of 1832; Poor Law reform, 1834; Chartists, repeal of Corn Laws, 1838–1848	
Revolutions in Europe, 1848	

Religion and Philosophy	Science and Technology	Arts and Letters
Huguenot revolt in France, 1625	Further development of scientific method: Bacon, *The Advancement of Learning*, 1605; Descartes, *Discourse on Method*, 1637	Cervantes, *Don Quixote*, 1605, 1615 Flourishing of French theater: Molière, 1622–1673; Racine, 1639–1699 Golden age of Dutch culture, ca. 1625–1675: Rembrandt van Rijn, 1606–1669; Vermeer, 1632–1675
Social contract theory: Hobbes, *Leviathan*, 1651; Locke, *Second Treatise on Civil Government*, 1690 Patriarch Nikon's reforms split Russian Orthodox Church, 1652 Test Act in England excludes Roman Catholics from public office, 1673 Revocation of Edict of Nantes, 1685 James II tries to restore Catholicism as state religion, 1685–1688	Tull (1674–1741) encourages innovation in English agriculture Newton, *Principia Mathematica*, 1687	Construction of baroque palaces and remodeling of capital cities, central and eastern Europe, ca. 1650–1725 Bach, great late baroque German composer, 1685–1750 Enlightenment begins, ca. 1690: Fontenelle, *Conversations on the Plurality of Worlds*, 1686; Voltaire, French philosopher and writer whose work epitomizes Enlightenment, 1694–1778 Pierre Bayle, *Historical and Critical Dictionary*, 1697
Wesley, founder of Methodism, 1703–1791 Montesquieu, *The Spirit of Laws*, 1748	Newcomen develops steam engine, 1705 Charles Townsend introduces four-year crop rotation, 1730	
Hume, *The Natural History of Religion*, 1755 Rousseau, *The Social Contract* and *Emile*, 1762 Fourier, French utopian socialist, 1772–1837 Papacy dissolves Jesuits, 1773 Smith, *The Wealth of Nations*, 1776 Church reforms of Joseph II in Austria, 1780s Kant, *What Is Enlightenment?*, 1784 Reorganization of church in France, 1790s Wollstonecraft, *A Vindication of the Rights of Women*, 1792 Malthus, *Essay on the Principle of Population*, 1798	Hargreaves's spinning jenny, ca. 1765 Arkwright's water frame, ca. 1765 Watt's steam engine promotes industrial breakthroughs, 1780s Jenner's smallpox vaccine, 1796	*Encyclopedia*, edited by Diderot and d'Alembert, published 1751–1765 Classical style in music, ca. 1770–1830: Mozart, 1756–1791; Beethoven, 1770–1827 Wordsworth, English romantic poet, 1770–1850 Romanticism in art and literature, ca. 1790–1850
Napoleon signs Concordat with Pope Pius VII regulating Catholic Church in France, 1801 Spencer, Social Darwinist, 1820–1903 Comte, *System of Positive Philosophy*, 1830–1842 Height of French utopian socialism, 1830s–1840s List, *National System of Political Economy*, 1841 Nietzsche, radical and highly influential German philosopher, 1844–1900 Marx, *Communist Manifesto*, 1848	First railroad, Great Britain, 1825 Faraday studies electromagnetism, 1830–1840s	Staël, *On Germany*, 1810 Balzac, *The Human Comedy*, 1829–1841 Delacroix, *Liberty Leading the People*, 1830 Hugo, *The Hunchback of Notre Dame*, 1831

Government	Society and Economy
1850 Second Empire in France, 1852–1870	Crédit Mobilier founded in France, 1852
Crimean War, 1853–1856	Japan opened to European influence, 1853
Britain crushes Great Rebellion in India, 1857–1858	Russian serfs emancipated, 1861
Unification of Italy, 1859–1870	First Socialist International, 1864–1871
U.S. Civil War, 1861–1865	
Bismarck leads Germany, 1862–1890	
Unification of Germany, 1864–1871	
Britain's Second Reform Bill, 1867	
Third Republic in France, 1870–1940	
1875 Congress of Berlin, 1878	Full property rights for women in Great Britain, 1882
European "scramble for Africa," 1880–1900	Second Industrial Revolution; birthrate steadily declines in Europe, ca. 1880–1913
Britain's Third Reform Bill, 1884	Social welfare legislation, Germany, 1883–1889
Dreyfus affair in France, 1894–1899	Second Socialist International, 1889–1914
Spanish-American War, 1898	Witte directs modernization of Russian economy, 1892–1899
South African War, 1899–1902	
1900 Russo-Japanese War, 1904–1905	Women's suffrage movement, England, ca. 1900–1914
Revolution in Russia, 1905	Social welfare legislation, France, 1904, 1910; Great Britain, 1906–1914
Balkan wars, 1912–1913	Agrarian reforms in Russia, 1907–1912
1914 World War I, 1914–1918	Planned economics in Europe, 1914
Armenian genocide, 1915	Auxiliary Service Law in Germany, 1916
Easter Rebellion, 1916	Bread riots in Russia, March 1917
U.S. declares war on Germany, 1917	
Bolshevik Revolution, 1917–1918	
Treaty of Versailles, World War I peace settlement, 1919	
1920 Mussolini seizes power in Italy, 1922	New Economic Policy in U.S.S.R., 1921
Stalin comes to power in U.S.S.R., 1927	Dawes Plan for reparations and recovery, 1924
Hitler gains power in Germany, 1933	Great Depression, 1929–1939
Rome-Berlin Axis, 1936	Rapid industrialization in U.S.S.R., 1930s
Nazi-Soviet Non-Aggression Pact, 1939	Start of Roosevelt's New Deal in U.S., 1933
World War II, 1939–1945	
1940 United Nations founded, 1945	Holocaust, 1941–1945
Decolonization of Asia and Africa, 1945–1960s	Marshall Plan enacted, 1947
Cold War begins, 1947	European economic progress, ca. 1950–1970
Founding of Israel, 1948	European Coal and Steel Community founded, 1952
Communist government in China, 1949	European Economic Community founded, 1957
Korean War, 1950–1953	
De-Stalinization of Soviet Union under Khrushchev, 1953–1964	
1960 Building of Berlin Wall, 1961	Civil rights movement in U.S., 1960s
U.S. involvement in Vietnam War, 1964–1973	Stagflation, 1970s
Student rebellion in France, 1968	Feminist movement, 1970s

Religion and Philosophy	Science and Technology	Arts and Letters
Decline in church attendance among working classes, ca. 1850–1914	Modernization of Paris, ca. 1850–1870	Realism in art and literature, ca. 1850–1870
Mill, *On Liberty*, 1859	Great Exhibition in London, 1851	Flaubert, *Madame Bovary*, 1857
Pope Pius IX, *Syllabus of Errors*, denounces modern thoughts, 1864	Freud, founder of psychoanalysis, 1856–1939	Tolstoy, *War and Peace*, 1869
Marx, *Das Capital*, 1867	Darwin, *On the Origin of Species*, 1859	Impressionism in art, ca. 1870–1900
Doctrine of papal infallibility, 1870	Pasteur develops germ theory of disease, 1860s	Eliot (Mary Ann Evans), *Middlemarch*, 1872
	Suez Canal opened, 1869	
	Mendeleev develops periodic table, 1869	
Growth of public education in France, ca. 1880–1900	Emergence of modern immunology, ca. 1875–1900	Zola, *Germinal*, 1885
Growth of mission schools in Africa, 1890–1914	Electrical industry: lighting and streetcars, ca. 1880–1900	Kipling, "The White Man's Burden," 1899
	Trans-Siberian Railroad, 1890s	
	Marie Curie, discovery of radium, 1898	
Separation of church and state in France, 1901–1905	Planck develops quantum theory, ca. 1900	Modernism in art and literature, ca. 1900–1929
Hobson, *Imperialism*, 1902	First airplane flight, 1903	Conrad, *Heart of Darkness*, 1902
Schweitzer, *Quest of the Historical Jesus*, 1906	Einstein develops theory of special relativity, 1905–1910	Cubism in art, ca. 1905–1930
		Proust, *Remembrance of Things Past*, 1913–1927
Keynes, *Economic Consequences of the Peace*, 1919	Submarine warfare introduced, 1915	Spengler, *The Decline of the West*, 1918
	Ernest Rutherford splits atom, 1919	
Emergence of modern existentialism, 1920s	"Heroic age of physics," 1920s	Gropius, Bauhaus, 1920s
Revival of Christianity, 1920s–1930s	First major public radio broadcasts in Great Britain and U.S., 1920	Dadaism and surrealism, 1920s
Wittgenstein, *Essay on Logical Philosophy*, 1922	First talking movies, 1930	Woolf, *Jacob's Room*, 1922
Heisenberg's principle of uncertainty, 1927	Radar system in England, 1939	Joyce, *Ulysses*, 1922
		Eliot, *The Waste Land*, 1922
		Remarque, *All Quiet on the Western Front*, 1929
		Picasso, *Guernica*, 1937
De Beauvoir, *The Second Sex*, 1949	U.S. drops atomic bombs on Japan, 1945	Cultural purge in Soviet Union, 1946–1952
Communists fail to break Catholic Church in Poland, 1950s	Big Science in U.S., ca. 1945–1965	Van der Rohe, Lake Shore Apartments, 1948–1951
	Watson and Crick discover structure of DNA molecule, 1953	Orwell, *1984*, 1949
	Russian satellite in orbit, 1957	Pasternak, *Doctor Zhivago*, 1956
		"Beat" movement in U.S., late 1950s
Second Vatican Council announces sweeping Catholic reforms, 1962–1965	European Council for Nuclear Research founded, 1960	The Beatles, 1960s
Pope John II, 1978–2005	Space race, 1960s	Solzhenitsyn, *One Day in the Life of Ivan Denisovich*, 1962

	Government	**Society and Economy**
1960 (cont.)	Soviet tanks end Prague Spring, 1968 Détente between U.S. and U.S.S.R., 1970s Soviet occupation of Afghanistan, 1979–1989	Collapse of postwar monetary system, 1971 OPEC oil price increases, 1973, 1979
1980	U.S. military buildup, 1980s Solidarity in Poland, 1980 Unification of Germany, 1989 Revolutions in eastern Germany, 1989–1990 Persian Gulf War, 1990–1991 Dissolution of Soviet Union, 1991 Civil war in Yugoslavia, 1991–2001 Separatist war breaks out in Chechnya, 1991	Growth of debt in the West, 1980s Economic crisis in Poland, 1988 Maastricht Treaty proposes monetary union, 1990 European Community becomes European Union, 1993 Migration to western Europe increases, 1990s
2000	Terrorist attacks on U.S., Sept. 11, 2001 War in Afghanistan begins, 2001 War in Iraq begins, 2003	Euro enters circulation, 2002 Voters reject new European Union constitution, 2005 Immigrant riots in France, 2005, 2009 Worldwide financial crisis begins, 2008

Religion and Philosophy	Science and Technology	Arts and Letters
	Russian cosmonaut first to orbit globe, 1961 American astronaut first person on moon, 1969	Carson, *Silent Spring*, 1962 Friedan, *The Feminine Mystique*, 1963 Servan-Schreiber, *The American Challenge*, 1967
Revival of religion in Soviet Union, 1985– Growth of Islam in Europe, 1990s Fukuyama proclaims "end of history," 1991	Reduced spending on Big Science, 1980s Computer revolution continues, 1980s–1990s U.S. Genome Project begins, 1990 First World Wide Web server and browser, 1991 Pentium processor invented, 1993 First genetically cloned sheep, 1996	Solzhenitsyn returns to Russia, 1994; dies 2008 Author Salman Rushdie exiled from Iran, 1989 Gehry, Guggenheim Museum, Bilbao, 1997
Ramadan, *Western Muslims and the Future of Islam*, 2004 Conservative elected as Pope Benedict XVI, 2005	Growing concern about global warming, 2000s First hybrid car, 2003 Copenhagen Summit on climate change, 2009	Movies and books exploring clash between immigrants and host cultures popular: *Bend It Like Beckham*, 2002; *The Namesake*, 2003; *White Teeth*, 2003; *The Class*, 2008

About the Authors

John P. McKay (Ph.D., University of California, Berkeley) is professor emeritus at the University of Illinois. He has written or edited numerous works, including the Herbert Baxter Adams Prize–winning book *Pioneers for Profit: Foreign Entrepreneurship and Russian Industrialization, 1885–1913* (1970) and *Tramways and Trolleys: The Rise of Urban Mass Transport in Europe* (1976). He most recently contributed to *Imagining the Twentieth Century* (1997).

Bennett D. Hill (Ph.D., Princeton University), late of the University of Illinois, was the history department chair from 1978 to 1981. He published *English Cistercian Monasteries and Their Patrons in the Twelfth Century* (1968), *Church and State in the Middle Ages* (1970), and numerous articles and reviews, and was one of the contributing editors to *The Encyclopedia of World History* (2001). A Benedictine monk of St. Anselm's Abbey in Washington, D.C., he was also a visiting professor at Georgetown University.

John Buckler (Ph.D., Harvard University) taught history at the University of Illinois. Published books include *Theban Hegemony, 371–362 B.C.* (1980), *Philip II and the Sacred War* (1989), and *Aegean Greece in the Fourth Century B.C.* (2003). With Hans Beck, he most recently published *Central Greece and the Politics of Power in the Fourth Century* (2007).

Clare Haru Crowston (Ph.D., Cornell University) teaches at the University of Illinois, where she is currently associate professor of history. She is the author of *Fabricating Women: The Seamstresses of Old Regime France, 1675–1791* (2001), which won the Berkshire and Hagley Prizes. She edited two special issues of the *Journal of Women's History* (vol. 18, nos. 3 and 4), has published numerous journal articles and reviews, and is a past president of the Society for French Historical Studies and a former chair of the Pinkney Prize Committee.

Merry E. Wiesner-Hanks (Ph.D., University of Wisconsin–Madison) taught first at Augustana College in Illinois, and since 1985 at the University of Wisconsin–Milwaukee, where she is currently UWM Distinguished Professor in the department of history. She is the coeditor of the *Sixteenth Century Journal* and the author or editor of more than twenty books, most recently *The Marvelous Hairy Girls: The Gonzales Sisters and Their Worlds* (2009) and *Gender in History* (2nd ed., 2010). She currently serves as the Chief Reader for Advanced Placement World History.

Joe Perry (Ph.D., University of Illinois at Urbana-Champaign) is associate professor of modern German and European history at Georgia State University. He has published numerous articles and is author of the recently published book *Christmas in Germany: A Cultural History* (2010). His current research interests include issues of consumption, gender, and television in East and West Germany after World War II.